Along These Lines

Writing Paragraphs and Essays

with Writing from Reading Strategies

Seventh Edition

John Sheridan Biays, professor emeritus of English
Broward College

Carol Wershoven, professor emerita of English
Palm Beach State College

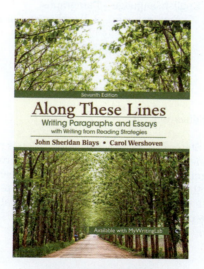

PEARSON

Boston   Columbus   Hoboken   Indianapolis   New York   San Francisco
Amsterdam   Cape Town   Dubai   London   Madrid   Milan   Munich   Paris   Montreal   Toronto
Delhi   Mexico City   São Paulo   Sydney   Hong Kong   Seoul   Singapore   Taipei   Tokyo

Executive Editor: Matthew Wright
Senior Development Editor: Anne Brunell Ehrenworth
Marketing Manager: Jennifer Edwards
Executive Digital Producer: Stefanie Snajder
Content Specialist: Erin E. Reilly
Program Manager: Eric Jorgensen
Project Manager: Denise Phillip Grant
Project Coordination, Text Design, and Electronic
   Page Makeup: Laserwords Private Ltd.
Design Lead: Barbara Atkinson
Cover Designer: Kristina Mose-Libon/ Lumina Datamatics, Inc.
Cover Photo: superoke/Shutterstock
Senior Manufacturing Buyer: Roy L. Pickering Jr.
Printer/Binder: Courier/Kendallville
Cover Printer: Courier/Kendallville

Acknowledgments of third-party content appear on page 635, which constitute an extension of this copyright page.

Library of Congress Cataloging-in-Publication Data

Biays, John Sheridan.
    Along these lines : writing paragraphs and essays with, writing from reading strategies /
      John Sheridan Biays, Broward College; Carol Wershoven, Palm Beach
      State College.—Seventh Edition.
        pages cm
    ISBN 978-0-321-98400-5
    ISBN 0-321-98400-5
      1. English language—Sentences.   2. English language—Paragraphs.
      3. English language—Rhetoric.   4. College readers.   I. Wershoven, Carol, author.
      II. Title.
    PE1441.B53 2014
    808'.042—dc23

                                  2014036624

10 9 8 7 6 5 4 3 2 1—CRK—18 17 16 15

www.pearsonhighered.com

Student Edition
ISBN 10:   0-321-98400-5
ISBN 13: 978-0-321-98400-5

A la Carte
ISBN 10:   0-321-99137-0
ISBN 13: 978-0-321-99137-9

Contents

Grammar for Writers   365

Appendix: Readings for Writers 581

Preface for Instructors

As you know all too well, developmental education has been under intense scrutiny nationwide, and severe budget cuts have taken their toll on many college campuses. Whether your department has been actively involved in curriculum reform/course redesign, or your state legislature has mandated that developmental courses become strictly optional, one fact remains constant: *Today's students need more help than ever in becoming proficient writers and effective communicators.* We applaud your ongoing commitment to helping developing writers become confident learners, and we remain extremely grateful for your ongoing trust in our work.

Along These Lines: Writing Paragraphs and Essays with Writing from Reading Strategies, 7/e, retains the intensive coverage of the writing process that adopters have praised, and the self-contained chapters provide a flexible framework that can accommodate myriad learning styles and instructional preferences. A host of caring reviewers offered insightful, practical, and creative revision suggestions; thanks to their collective wisdom, this edition is the most visually appealing and engaging text to date. We hope you'll agree.

NEW FEATURES AND ENHANCEMENTS IN THE SEVENTH EDITION

- **New instruction and in-text exercises reinforce the key roles of revision, editing, and proofreading during the writing process**; differences between basic revision strategies and in-text editing are clearly distinguished.

- **New critical-thinking tips and emphasis on critical thinking's connection to effective writing and reading** are now interspersed throughout the text.

- **New "Writing from Reading" chapter** includes instruction on prereading/marking a selection, taking notes, summarizing, and reacting to an author's premise.

- **New and engaging teaching tips, including ones tailored for English language learners (ELLs) in your classroom**, are provided in the *Annotated Instructor's Edition.*

- **New and comprehensive section on APA-style documentation** supplements the existing instruction on MLA rules.

- **New and expanded exercises on fragments, run-ons, coordination and subordination, verb tense consistency, and slang avoidance** have been incorporated based on reviewer feedback.

- **New high-interest readings** include thought-provoking selections on workplace bullies, Internet gambling, and one coach's journey from arrogant tyrant to caring mentor; vocabulary, comprehension checks, and writing topics accompany selections.

A SAMPLING OF PRAISE FROM *ALONG THESE LINES* ADOPTERS

"Along These Lines is easy to follow for my students, and the Annotated Instructor's Edition provides copious suggestions for student engagement and integration of essay writing. The sample essays and the strike-through examples of 'too broad' versus 'a narrower, better topic sentence' are straightforward, quick, and useful resources for students who need to be reassured they are on the right track."

Johnnerlyn M. Johnson, Sandhills Community College

"I highly recommend Along These Lines and sing its praises to my students. It is well organized and thorough, and there are more than enough practice exercises for students. I tell my students that if they steadfastly . . . studied the book, they could teach themselves and not even need me."

Ann M. Moore, Florence-Darlington Technical College

"I have used Along These Lines for quite some time through several editions. I find the textbook to be reader-friendly. The sample essays take the reader through all stages of the writing process . . . and they are especially helpful for my students. As an instructor, I find this textbook to be easy to use and easy to understand."

Iris Chao, Saddleback College

POPULAR FEATURES RETAINED

Based on positive feedback from current users and new reviewers, the following popular and distinctive features have been retained:

The Writing Chapters

- Web-based writing topics and activities are ideal for group work and peer interaction.
- Visually appealing checklists, charts, and colorful "Info Boxes" provide quick reference and reinforcement of key terms and ideas.
- A "Walk-Through" assignment in each chapter guides students, step-by-step, through the stages of the writing process.

The Grammar Chapters

- Three types of grammar exercises: **Practice** (simple reinforcement), **Collaborate** (partner or group work), and **Connect** ("in context" identification of grammatical errors to strengthen editing skills)
- Grammar concepts taught step-by-step, as in "Two Steps to Check for Fragments"
- A Chapter Test at the end of chapters, ideal for class review or quick quizzes

Reading Instruction and Selections

- Easily applied prereading procedures and quick summarizing techniques
- Carefully selected readings reflecting a broad range of timely, high-interest themes
- Numerous writing options, including critical-thinking topics, sparked by a selection's content and designed to encourage careful analysis and independent thought

WRITING RESOURCES AND SUPPLEMENTS

Annotated Instructor's Edition for Along These Lines: Writing Paragraphs and Essays with Writing from Reading Strategies
ISBN 0321992202 / 9780321992208

Instructor's Resource Manual for Along These Lines: Writing Paragraphs and Essays with Writing from Reading Strategies
ISBN 0321991303 / 9780321991300

Test Bank for Along These Lines: Writing Paragraphs and Essays with Writing from Reading Strategies
ISBN 0133928640 / 9780133928648

PowerPoint Presentation for Along These Lines: Writing Paragraphs and Essays with Writing from Reading Strategies
ISBN 0321991389 / 9780321991386

Answer Key for Along These Lines: Writing Paragraphs and Essays with Writing from Reading Strategies
ISBN 0321991346 / 9780321991348

MyWritingLab™

Where Practice, Application, and Demonstration Meet to Improve Writing

MyWritingLab, a complete online learning program, provides additional resources and effective practice exercises for developing writers. *MyWritingLab* accelerates learning through layered assessment and a personalized learning path utilizing the Knewton Adaptive Learning Platform™ which customizes educational content to piece together the perfect personalized content for each student. With over eight thousand exercises and immediate feedback to answers, the integrated learning aids of *MyWritingLab* reinforce learning throughout the semester.

What Makes *MyWritingLab* More Effective?

Diagnostic Testing: *MyWritingLab*'s diagnostic Path Builder test comprehensively assesses students' skills in grammar. Students are provided with an individualized learning path based on the diagnostic's results, identifying the areas where they most need help.

Progressive Learning: The heart of *MyWritingLab* is the progressive learning that students experience as they complete the Overview, Animation,

Recall, Apply, and Write exercises along with the Post-test within each topic. Students move from preparation (Overview, Animation) to literal comprehension (Recall) to critical understanding (Apply) to the ability to demonstrate a skill in their own writing (Write) to total mastery (Post-test). This progression of critical thinking enables students to master the skills and concepts they need to become successful writers.

Online Gradebook: All student work in *MyWritingLab* is captured in the Online Gradebook. Instructors can see what and how many topics their students have mastered. They can also view students' individual scores on all assignments throughout *MyWritingLab*, as well as overviews by student, and class performance by module. Students can monitor their progress in new Completed Work pages, which show their totals, scores, time on task, and date and time of work by module.

A Deeper Connection between Print and Media: The *MyWritingLab* logo (show logo) is used throughout the book to indicate exercises and writing activities that can be completed and submitted through *MyWritingLab* (appropriate results flow directly to the Instructor Gradebook).

ACKNOWLEDGMENTS

We are indebted to the following professionals for their comprehensive reviews, practical advice, and creative suggestions regarding the *Along These Lines* series:

Stephanie Alexander	Mountwest Community and Technical College
Elizabeth Andrews	South Florida State College
Elizabeth Barnes	Daytona State College
Iris Chao	Saddleback College
Patty Crockett	Bishop State Community College
Mellisa Dalton	Lanier Technical College
Linda Hasty	Motlow State Community College
Gregg Heitschmidt	Surry Community College
Johnnerlyn Johnson	Sandhills Community College
Therese Jones	Lewis University
Cassi Lapp	Northwest Arkansas Community College
Ann Moore	Florence-Darlington Technical College
Deana Pendley	Copiah-Lincoln Community College
Sandra Valerio	Del Mar College

The success of any new edition relies on a wealth of expertise from talented individuals. We are very grateful to Matt Wright, senior acquisitions editor, for his ongoing support and enthusiasm for our series. Additionally, we are indebted to Anne Brunell Ehrenworth, senior development editor, for mapping out revision plans so expertly and efficiently. Anne made judicious suggestions, streamlined every chapter, guided two new contributors, reviewed every page with us, and kept a keen eye on the permissions status of our preferred readings. With welcome humor and enviable tenacity, Anne kept everything on track and on budget. A million thanks, Anne!

We also extend our deepest gratitude to Christina Cavage and Paula Bonilla for taking on the lion's share of revision duties and deadlines. Christina provided key exercise updating and instructional refinements, including creative ELL teaching tips and effective critical-thinking strategies.

Paula updated many of our chapter openers, reshaped or devised new writing topics and exercises, provided new reading-selection activities, and wrote the Instructor's Manuals for the *ATL* series. Additionally, Paula provided the new material on APA-style documentation, which several reviewers had requested. We can't thank Christina and Paula enough for their valuable contributions.

Rebecca Lazure, full service production manager at SPi Global (Maine), once again worked miracles and calmly reassured everyone that all would be fine. We know our series couldn't have been in better or more caring hands. Additionally, many thanks and kudos to the charter members of "Team ATL," including Laura Marenghi, editorial assistant, for expertly coordinating reviews and corresponding with us regularly; Laura Specht Patchkofsky, copy editor; the entire design team at SPi Global; Joe Croscup, permissions project manager; Jennifer Edwards, marketing manager; and Megan Zuccarini, marketing assistant extraordinaire, whose professionalism and good cheer keep us sane and in good spirits even during selling-season chaos.

We also want to pay tribute to all of the unsung heroes in the classroom who help struggling students overcome adversity, find their voice, and reach their potential. We are humbled by your dedication and tenacity, and you exemplify effective teaching at its best.

Finally, and most importantly, we send heartfelt thanks to the thousands of students who have intrigued, impressed, and inspired us over the years. You have taught us far more than you can ever imagine, and you have made our journey extraordinary along *all* lines.

John Sheridan Biays
Carol Wershoven

Writing in Stages:
The Process Approach

INTRODUCTION

MyWritingLab™
Access the "Writing in Stages" videos in *MyWritingLab*.

Learning by Doing

Writing is a skill, and like any skill, writing improves with practice. This book provides you with ample practice to improve your writing through a variety of individual and group activities. Whether you complete assignments at home or in the classroom, just remember that *good writing takes practice:* you can learn to write well by writing.

Steps Make Writing Easier

Writing is easier if you *do not try to do too much at once*. To make the task of writing easier, *Along These Lines* breaks the process into stages:

PREWRITING

In this stage, you think about your topic, and you *gather ideas*. You *react* to your own ideas and add even more thoughts. You can also react to other people's ideas as a way of expanding your own.

PLANNING

In this stage, you *examine your ideas* and begin to *focus* them around one main idea. Planning involves combining, dividing, and even eliminating some ideas. Placing your specific details in a logical order often involves *outlining*.

DRAFTING AND REVISING

In this stage, the thinking and planning begin to take shape as a piece of writing. You complete a draft of your work, a *rough version* of the finished product. Then you examine the draft and consider ways to *revise* it, a process that may require writing and reworking several versions of your original draft.

EDITING AND PROOFREADING

In this stage, you give your latest revised draft one last, careful *review* when you are rested and alert. You concentrate on refining your style and identifying and correcting any mistakes in sentence structure, word choice, spelling, or punctuation you may have overlooked. This stage is the *final check* of your work to make your writing the best it can be.

These four stages in the writing process—*prewriting, planning, drafting and revising*, and *editing and proofreading*—may overlap. You may be changing your plan even as you work on the draft of your paper. Throughout this book, you will have many opportunities to become familiar with the stages of effective writing. Working individually and with your classmates, you can become a better writer along *all* lines.

CHAPTER 1

Writing a Paragraph

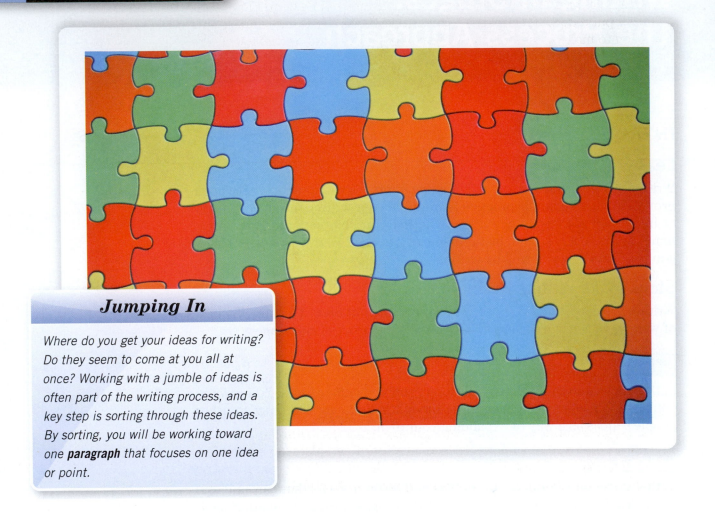

Jumping In

Where do you get your ideas for writing? Do they seem to come at you all at once? Working with a jumble of ideas is often part of the writing process, and a key step is sorting through these ideas. By sorting, you will be working toward one **paragraph** *that focuses on one idea or point.*

Learning Objectives

In this chapter, you will learn how to:

1 Prewrite to generate a paragraph topic.

2 Recognize and write clear topic sentences.

3 Write a paragraph reflecting effective unity, support, and coherence.

WHAT IS THE ROLE OF A PARAGRAPH?

Usually, students write because they have a writing assignment requiring them to write on some topic or choice of topics, and the writing is due by a certain day. So assume that you get such an assignment and it calls for one paragraph. You might wonder, "Why a paragraph? Why not something large, like a two- or three-page paper? After all, many classes will ask for papers, not just paragraphs."

For one thing, all essays are a series of paragraphs. If you can write one good paragraph, you can write more than one. The **paragraph** is the basic building block of any essay. It is a group of sentences focusing on *one idea* or one point. Keep this concept in mind: *one idea to a paragraph*. Focusing on one idea or one point gives a paragraph **unity**. If you have a new point, start a new paragraph.

You may ask, "Doesn't this mean a paragraph will be short? How long should a paragraph be, anyway?" To convince a reader of one main point, you need to make it, support it, develop it, explain it, and describe it. There will be shorter and longer paragraphs, but for now, you can assume your paragraph will be somewhere between seven and twelve sentences long.

This chapter guides you through each stage of the writing process:

- **Prewriting**—how to generate and develop ideas for your paragraph
- **Planning**—how to organize your ideas
- **Drafting and Revising**—how to create and revise
- **Editing and Proofreading**—how to review and make one final check

We give extra emphasis to the prewriting stage in this chapter to give you some extra help in getting started.

PREWRITING   A PARAGRAPH

1 Prewrite to generate a topic.

Suppose your instructor asks you to write a paragraph about your favorite city or town. Writing about your favorite city or town is your general **topic**, but you must choose one city or town to make the topic more specific. With this topic, you already know your **purpose**—to write a paragraph that makes some point about the city or town. You have an **audience** since you are writing this paragraph for your instructor and classmates. Often, your purpose is to write a specific kind of paper for a class. Occasionally, you may have to write with a different purpose or audience, such as writing instructions for a new employee at your workplace, a letter of complaint to a manufacturer, or a short biographical essay for a scholarship application. Knowing your audience and purpose is important in writing effectively.

Freewriting, Brainstorming, and Keeping a Journal

Once you have identified your purpose and audience, you can begin by finding some way to *think on paper*. You can use the techniques of freewriting, brainstorming, or keeping a journal to gather ideas and potential details.

Freewriting   Give yourself fifteen minutes to write whatever comes into your mind on your subject. If your mind is a blank, write, "My mind's a blank. My mind's a blank," over and over until you think of something else. The main goal here is to *write without stopping*. Do not stop to tell yourself, "This is stupid," or "I can't use any of this in a paper." Do not stop to correct your spelling or punctuation. Just write. Let your ideas flow. Write *freely*. Here is an example:

> **Freewriting About a Favorite City or Town**
>
> Favorite city or town. City? I like New York. It's so big and exciting. Haven't been there much, though. Only once. My hometown. I like it. It's just another town but comfortable and friendly. Maybe St. Augustine. Lots of fun visits there. Grandparents there. Hard to pick a favorite. Different places are good for different reasons.

Brainstorming   This technique is like freewriting because you write whatever comes into your head, but it is a little different because you can pause *to ask yourself questions* that will lead to new ideas. When you brainstorm

---

Brainstorming About a Favorite City or Town

Favorite place

City or town

What's the difference between a city and a town?

Doesn't matter. Just pick one. Cities are bigger.

How is city life different from town life?

Cities are bigger. More crowded, like Atlanta.

Which do you like better, a city or a town?

Sometimes I like cities.

Why?

There is more to do.

So, what city do you like?

I like New York and St. Augustine.

Is St. Augustine a city?

Yes. A small one.

Do you like towns?

I loved this little town in Mexico.

---

alone, you "interview" yourself about a subject. You can also brainstorm and ask questions within a group.

If you feel like you are running out of ideas in brainstorming, try to form a question out of what you've just written. *Go where your questions and answers lead you.* For example, if you write, "There is more to do in cities," you could form these questions:

What is there to do? Sports? Entertainment? Outdoor exercise? Meeting people?

You could also make a list of your brainstorming ideas, but remember to *do only one step at a time.*

Keeping a Journal A **journal** is a notebook of your personal writing, a notebook in which you write *regularly and often. It is not a diary, but it is a place to record your experiences, reactions, and observations.* In it, you can write about what you have done, heard, seen, read, or remembered. You can include sayings that you would like to remember, news clippings, snapshots— anything that you would like to recall or consider. A journal provides an enjoyable way to practice your writing, and it is a great source of ideas for writing.

Journal Entry About a Favorite City or Town

I'm not going south to see my grandparents this winter. They're coming here instead of me going to St. Augustine. I'd really like to go there. I like the warm weather. It's better than months of snow, ice, and rain here in Easthampton. I'll miss going there. I've been so many times that it's like a second home. St. Augustine is great around Christmastime.

Finding Specific Ideas

Whether you freewrite, brainstorm, or consult your journal, you end up with something on paper. Follow those first ideas; see where they can take you. You are looking for specific ideas, each of which can focus on the general topic you started with. At this point, you do not have to decide which specific idea you want to write about. You just want to *narrow your range* of ideas.

You might think, "Why should I narrow my ideas? Won't I have more to say if I keep my topic big?" But remember that a paragraph has one idea; you want to state it clearly and with convincing details for support. If you try to write one paragraph on city life versus town life, for example, you will probably make so many general statements that you will say very little, or you will bore your reader with big, sweeping statements. General ideas are big, broad ones. Specific ideas are smaller, narrower ones. If you scanned the freewriting example on a favorite city or town, you might underline many specific ideas as possible topics:

> Favorite city or town. City? I like <u>New York</u>. It's so big and exciting. Haven't been there much, though. Only once. <u>My hometown</u>. I like it. It's just another town but comfortable and friendly. Maybe <u>St. Augustine</u>. Lots of fun visits there. Grandparents there. Hard to pick a favorite. Different places are good for different reasons.

Consider the underlined terms. They are specific places. You could write a paragraph about any one of these places. Or you could underline specific places in your brainstorming questions and answers:

> Favorite place
> City or town
>
> **What's the difference between a city and a town?**
> Doesn't matter. Just pick one. Cities are bigger.
>
> **How is city life different from town life?**
> Cities are bigger. More crowded, like <u>Atlanta</u>.
>
> **Which do you like better, a city or a town?**
> Sometimes I like cities.
>
> **Why?**
> There is more to do.
>
> **So, what city do you like?**
> I like <u>New York</u> and <u>St. Augustine</u>.
>
> **Is St. Augustine a city?**
> Yes. A small one.
>
> **Do you like towns?**
> I loved this <u>little town in Mexico</u>.

Each of these specific places could be a topic for your paragraph.

If you reviewed the journal entry on a favorite city or town, you would also be able to underline specific places:

> I'm not going south to see my grandparents this winter. They're coming here instead of me going to <u>St. Augustine</u>. I'd really like to go there. I like the warm weather. It's better than months of snow, ice, and rain here in <u>Easthampton</u>. I'll miss going there. I've been so many times that it's like a second home. St. Augustine is great around Christmastime.

Remember: Following the steps can lead you to specific ideas.

Critical Thinking and the Writing Process

As you know by now, one of the popular methods of prewriting is called *brainstorming*, the practice of asking yourself key questions that can lead you to new ideas and directions related to your writing topic. During your college career, you will find that such questioning can enable you to engage in **critical thinking**, a type of reasoning that has several meanings and practical uses. For now, just remember that any time you evaluate the relevance of supporting details, determine their order of importance, and attempt to justify their inclusion, you are making judgments that are considered *critical*. Making such judgments will become more common for you as you tackle college writing assignments.

You will soon appreciate the crucial role critical thinking plays in effective writing, whether you are comparing and contrasting ideas, identifying a trend's causes and effects, arguing rationally for or against a proposal, or questioning what you read. Additionally, whenever you evaluate a piece of writing based on such criteria as unity, support, coherence, and intended audience, you will be sharpening your critical thinking skills.

Critical thinking and writing options can be found at the end of each writing chapter and at the end of each reading selection in this book. These topics may require you to take a stand, defend a choice, imagine a certain scenario, or examine a trend. Whether you discuss these topics with peers or decide to write about them, keeping an open mind will help you become a better writer and a stronger critical thinker.

Selecting One Topic

Once you have a list of specific ideas that can lead you to a specific topic, you can pick one topic. Let's say you decided to work with the list of places you gathered through brainstorming:

> Atlanta
> New York
> St. Augustine
> a little town in Mexico
> Shanghai

Looking at this list, you decide you want to write about St. Augustine as your favorite city.

MyWritingLab™ | **Exercise 1** **Practice: Creating Questions for Brainstorming**

Following are several topics. For each one, brainstorm by writing at least four questions related to the topic that could lead you to further ideas. The first topic is done for you.

1. topic: music videos

Question 1: Why are music videos so popular?

Question 2: What kind of music videos are most popular?

Question 3: Who watches music videos most?

Question 4: Do people watch videos online or on TV?

2. topic: driving

Question 1: _____

Question 2: _____

Question 3: _____

Question 4: _____

3. topic: smartphones

Question 1: _____

Question 2: _____

Question 3: _____

Question 4: _____

Exercise 2 **Practice: Finding Specific Details in Freewriting**   My**Writing**Lab™

Below are two samples of freewriting. Each is a written response to a different topic. Read each sample, and then underline any words and phrases that could become the focus of a paragraph.

Freewriting Reaction to the Topic of Summer

Summer used to be summer vacation. Now I have to work in the summer, just like I work the rest of the year. At least the days are longer in summer. Can get outdoors after work. Can go for a walk. Jog. Do yard work or sit on the porch. Summer holidays, too. July 4th. Labor Day. Warm weather means summer food and barbecues.

Freewriting Reaction to the Topic of Online Gaming

I love online gaming. It's a fun way to connect with my friends as well as make new friends. Multiplayer games are the most fun. I tell my friends when to log on. We always meet up in a room to start. Some people say online gaming is addictive. I don't believe it. I think it's a way to play without leaving the house. Online games are always available—and they are cheap!

Exercise 3 **Practice: Finding Specific Details in a List**   My**Writing**Lab™

Below are several lists of words or phrases. In each list, one item is a general term; the others are more specific. Underline the words or phrases that are more specific. The first list is done for you.

1. <u>apple pie</u>
   <u>ice cream</u>
   desserts
   <u>butterscotch pudding</u>
   <u>jello</u>
   <u>chocolate brownies</u>

2. instant messaging
   e-mail
   chat
   social networking
   Internet

3. English
   biology
   academics
   business management
   computer science
   algebra

4. health care
   prescription medicine
   health insurance
   emergency room
   surgery
   checkups

Collaborate

Exercise 4 **Collaborate: Finding Topics Through Freewriting**

The following exercise must be completed with a partner or a group. Below are several topics. Pick one and freewrite on it for ten minutes. Then read your freewriting to your partner or group. Ask your listener(s) to jot down any words or phrases from your writing that could lead to a specific topic for a paragraph.

Your listener(s) should read the jotted-down words or phrases to you. You will be hearing a collection of specific ideas that came from *your* writing. As you listen, underline the words in your freewriting.

Freewriting topics (pick one):

1. A career goal
2. A disappointment
3. A childhood memory

Freewriting on (name of topic chosen): _____

_____

_____

_____

_____

_____

CRITICAL THINKING

When adding more detail to your topic, create *wh*-questions. Ask . . .

What?	*When?*
Who?	*Why?*
Where?	*How?*

Adding Details to a Specific Topic

You can develop the specific topic you picked in a number of ways:

1. *Check your list* for other ideas that seem to fit with the specific topic you've picked.
2. *Brainstorm*—ask yourself more questions about your topic, and use the answers as details.
3. *List* any new ideas you have that may be connected to your topic.

One way to add details is to go back and check your brainstorming for other ideas about St. Augustine:

I like St. Augustine.
a small city

Now you can **brainstorm** some questions that will lead you to more details. The questions do not have to be connected to each other; they are just questions that could lead you to ideas and details:

What's so great about St. Augustine?

People can go to the beach nearby.

Is it a clean, big beach?

Sure. And the water is a clear blue.

What else can people do in St. Augustine?

There's lots of history.

Like what?

A fort. The oldest schoolhouse. Old houses.

Another way to add details is to list any ideas that may be connected to your topic. The list might give you more specific details:

grandparents live there
warm in winter
grandparents feed me
I use their car

If you had tried all three ways of adding detail, you would end up with this list of details connected to the topic of a favorite city or town:

a small city	clear blue water
no freeways	lots of history
no skyscrapers	a fort
not millions of people	oldest schoolhouse
thousands of visitors every day	grandparents live there
can always visit family for free	warm in winter
beach nearby	grandparents feed me
clean, big beach	I use their car

INFO BOX   Beginning the Prewriting: A Summary

The prewriting stage of writing a paragraph enables you to gather ideas. This process begins with several steps:

1. **Think on paper and write down any ideas that you have about a topic.** You can do this by freewriting, by brainstorming, or by keeping a journal.

2. **Scan your writing for specific ideas that have come from your first efforts.** List these specific ideas.

3. **Pick one specific idea.** Then, by reviewing your early writing, by questioning, and by thinking further, you can add details to the one specific idea.

This process may seem long, but once you have worked through it several times, it will become nearly automatic. When you think about ideas before you try to shape them into a paragraph, you are off to a good start. Confidence comes from having something to say, and once you have a specific idea, you will be ready to begin shaping and developing details that support your idea.

MyWritingLab™ Exercise 5 **Practice: Adding Details to a Topic by Brainstorming**

Below are two topics. Each is followed by two or three details. Brainstorm more questions, based on the existing details, that can lead to more details.

1. topic: advantages of bringing a lunch to work or school
details: saves money
healthier

Question 1: _____

Question 2: _____

Question 3: _____

Question 4: _____

2. topic: earning a lower grade than expected
details: causes stress
requires extra time for studying
can be upsetting

Question 1: _____

Question 2: _____

Question 3: _____

Question 4: _____

MyWritingLab™ Exercise 6 **Practice: Adding Details By Listing**

Following are three topics for paragraphs. For each topic, list details that seem to fit the topic.

1. topic: online shopping
details: a. _____   c. _____
b. _____   d. _____

2. topic: an ideal day off
details: a. _____   c. _____
b. _____   d. _____

3. topic: nosy neighbors
details: a. _____   c. _____
b. _____   d. _____

Focusing the Prewriting

The next step of writing is to *focus your ideas around some point*. Your ideas will begin to take a focus if you reexamine them, looking for *related ideas*. Here are two techniques that you can use:

- marking a list of related ideas
- mapping related ideas

Listing Related Ideas

To develop a marked list, take another look at the list we developed under the topic of a favorite city or town. The same list is shown below, but you will notice some of the items have been marked with symbols that show related ideas:

N marks ideas about St. Augustine's natural good points
H marks ideas about St. Augustine's history
F marks ideas about family in St. Augustine

Here is the marked list of ideas related to the topic of a favorite city or town:

a small city	**N** clear blue water
no freeways	**H** lots of history
no skyscrapers	**H** a fort
not millions of people	**H** oldest schoolhouse
thousands of visitors every day	**F** grandparents live there
F can always visit family for free	**N** warm in winter
N beach nearby	**F** grandparents feed me
N clean, big beach	**F** I use their car

You have probably noticed that some items are not marked: a small city, no freeways, no skyscrapers, not millions of people, thousands of visitors every day. Perhaps you can come back to them later, or you may decide you do not need them in your paragraph.

To make it easier to see what ideas you have, and how they are related, try *grouping related ideas*, giving each list a title, like this:

Natural Good Points of St. Augustine

beach nearby	clear blue water
clean, big beach	warm in winter

History in St. Augustine

lots of history	oldest schoolhouse
a fort	

Family in St. Augustine

can always visit family for free	grandparents live there
grandparents feed me	I use their car

Mapping

Another way to focus your ideas is to mark your first list of ideas, and then cluster the related ideas into separate lists. You can **map** your ideas, like this:

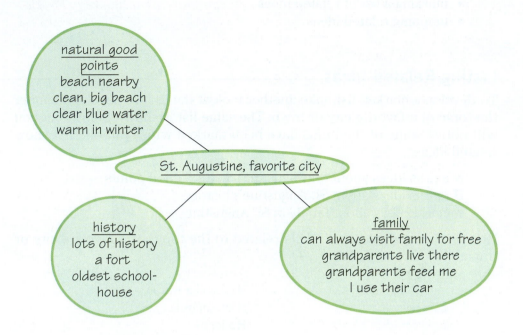

Whatever way you choose to examine and group your details, you are working toward *a focus, a point*. You are asking and beginning to answer the question, "Where do the details lead?" The answer will be the **topic sentence** of your paragraph. It will be the *main idea* of your paragraph.

② Recognize and write a clear topic sentence.

Forming a Topic Sentence

To form a topic sentence, you can do the following:

1. Review your details and see if you can form some general idea that can summarize the details.

2. Write that general idea as one sentence.

Your sentence that summarizes the details is the **topic sentence**. It makes a general point, and the more specific details you have gathered will support this point.

To form a topic sentence about your favorite city, St. Augustine, review the many details you have listed about the city. It is time to ask questions about those details. You could ask yourself, "What kind of details do I have? Can I summarize them?" You might then write the summary as the topic sentence:

I love St. Augustine because it has sun and sea, history, and family.

Check the sentence against your details. Does it cover the natural good points of St. Augustine? Yes. The topic sentence sums them up as *sun and sea*.

Does it cover history and family? Yes. The topic sentence says the place has *history and family*.

Writing Good Topic Sentences

Be careful. *Topics are not the same as topic sentences. Topics are the subjects you will write about.* A topic sentence states the *main idea* you have developed on a topic. Consider the differences between the topics and the topic sentences below:

> **topic:** Why courtesy is important
> **topic sentence:** Courtesy takes the conflict out of unpleasant
>   encounters.
>
> **topic:** Dogs and their owners
> **topic sentence:** Many dog owners begin to look like their pets.

Topic sentences *do not announce; they make a point.* Look at the sentences below, and notice the differences between the sentences that announce and the topic sentences.

> **announcement:** I will discuss the process of changing a tire.
> **topic sentence:** Changing a tire is easy if you have the right tools
>   and follow a simple process.
>
> **announcement:** An analysis of why recycling paper is important will
>   be the subject of this paper.
> **topic sentence:** Recycling paper is important because it saves trees,
>   money, and even certain animals.

Topic sentences can be too big to develop in one paragraph. A topic sentence that is *too broad* may take many paragraphs, even pages of writing, to develop. Look at the very broad sentences below, and then notice how they can be narrowed.

> **too broad:** Athletes get paid too much money. (This sentence is too
>   broad because "athletes" could mean anything from professional
>   boxers to neighborhood softball teams; "too much money" could
>   mean any fee or bonus.)
> **a narrower, better topic sentence:** Last year, several professional
>   baseball players negotiated high but fair salaries.
>
> **too broad:** I changed a great deal in my last year of high school.
>   (The phrase "changed a great deal" could refer to physical changes,
>   intellectual changes, emotional changes, or just about any other
>   change you can think of.)
> **a narrower, better topic sentence:** In my last year of high school,
>   I overcame my shyness.

Topic sentences can be too small to develop in one paragraph. A topic sentence that is *too narrow* cannot be supported by detail. It may be a fact, which cannot be developed. A topic sentence that is too narrow leaves you with nothing more to say.

> **too narrow:** Broccoli is healthy.
> **an expanded topic sentence:** Broccoli is healthy for two reasons.

too narrow: It takes twenty minutes to get out of the airport parking lot.

an expanded topic sentence: Congestion at the airport parking lot is causing problems for travelers.

The prewriting stage begins with free, unstructured thinking and writing. As you work through the prewriting process, your thinking and writing will become more focused.

Focusing the Prewriting: A Summary

The prewriting stage of writing a paragraph enables you to develop an idea into a topic sentence and related details. You can focus your thinking by working in steps.

1. Try marking a list of related detail, or try mapping to group your ideas.

2. Write a topic sentence that summarizes your details.

3. Check that your topic sentence is a sentence, not a topic. Make sure that it is not too broad or too narrow and that it is not an announcement. Check that it makes a point and focuses the details you have developed.

MyWritingLab™ **Exercise 7** **Practice: Grouping Related Items in Lists of Details**

Below are lists of details. In each list, circle the items that seem to fit into one group; then underline the items that seem to belong to a second group. Some items may not belong in either group. The first list is done for you.

1. **topic:** online learning

lack of connection   freedom from school

convenient   saves time

feel isolated   no parking problem

no child care issues   need self-discipline

self-paced   procrastination anytime, anyplace

2. **topic:** clothes

jeans   shirts

evening gown   silk tie

high heels   sneakers

underwear   tuxedo

sweatpants   flip-flops

3. **topic:** fame

public admiration   media interviews

sudden riches   loss of privacy

false friends   photographers

nasty Internet rumors   personal power

famous athletes   stalkers

MyWritingLab™ **Exercise 8** **Practice: Writing Topic Sentences for Lists of Details**

Below are lists of details that have no topic sentence. Write an appropriate topic sentence for each one.

1. topic sentence: _____

_____

Latino families celebrate *quinceañera*, the fifteenth birthday of their daughters.

Jewish families celebrate the *bar mitzvah*, or coming of age of thirteen-year-old Jewish boys.

Jewish girls have their own similar ceremony, the *bat mitzvah*.

For many young American women, a Sweet Sixteen party is a tradition to mark a teen's growth into adulthood.

Every year, thousands of twenty-year-old Japanese men and women come together on one day.

They participate in a traditional ceremony, similar to a graduation ceremony, with speeches and celebrations.

In Korea, a coming-of-age party is held for young women at age fifteen and young men at age twenty. During the young man's celebration, he must lift a heavy rock over his head. Once he does, he is declared a man.

2. topic sentence: _____

_____

Emily Dominguez was the prettiest girl in my first-grade class.

She had long hair and wide eyes.

I used to watch her in class, admiring the way she held her pencil or raised her hand.

One day she caught me looking at her.

Emily smiled and turned her head.

Now I was truly in love because I believed Emily liked me.

For a few days, I lived in a dream in which Emily, the princess, chose me as her hero.

Then I saw her at recess, giggling with Tommy Malone on the playground.

I knew my dream would not come true.

3. topic sentence: _____

_____

My roommate Etienne is Haitian, so at first, I had a hard time understanding his English.

He also seemed very shy.

I didn't see him much, so I figured he was socializing with his own friends and didn't like me.

Then one night I had an important algebra test to study for. I went to the tutoring center to get some help with my math.

Etienne was there, wrapped up in books.

Later, I learned he was there every night, studying English, but also tutoring other people in math.

Etienne and I are good friends now; I help him with English, and he teaches me algebra.

Exercise 9 **Practice: Turning Topics into Topic Sentences**

Below is a list. Some of the items in the list are topic sentences, but some are topics. Put an *X* by the items that are topics. In the lines below the list, rewrite the topics into topic sentences.

1. _____ Two simple ways to lose weight without following a strict diet or taking diet pills.

2. _____ The happiest day in my life started out as a bad day.

3. _____ Having poor study habits and facing the consequences.

4. _____ Worrying about the future can become an obsession.

5. _____ How I chose my major.

6. _____ Why procrastinating is a destructive habit.

7. _____ One strong family can survive many tragedies.

8. _____ College classes are not what I expected.

9. _____ Volunteering at a nature preserve gives me a break from my worries.

10. _____ My ten-year-old niece is obsessed with makeup.

Rewrite the topics. Make each one into a topic sentence.

_____

_____

_____

_____

_____

_____

_____

_____

Exercise 10 **Practice: Revising Topic Sentences That Are Too Broad**

Below is a list of topic sentences. Some of them are too broad to support in one paragraph. Put an *X* by the ones that are too broad. Then, on the lines below the list, rewrite those sentences, focusing on a limited idea, a topic sentence that could be supported in one paragraph.

1. _____ Childhood is a time of innocence.

2. _____ The best part of studying in the library is that I must turn my smartphone off and focus completely on my work.

3. _____ Trust is the most important factor in negotiations.

4. _____ Omar needs to be more realistic about his goals.

5. _____ Colin has two jobs so that he can afford to go to college next year.

6. _____ American teenagers are deeply troubled.

7. _____ Jie always loved drawing; she knew she wanted to enter a major that included art and that is why she is majoring in graphic design.

8. _____ When I finish my education, I want to do some meaningful work.

9. _____ My mother would have liked to be a stay-at-home mother.

10. _____ My life as a thirty-year-old student is nothing like the lives of college students in most movies.

Rewrite the broad sentences. Make each one more limited.

_____

_____

_____

_____

_____

_____

_____

_____

_____

_____

_____

Exercise 11   **Practice: Making Announcements into Topic Sentences**   MyWritingLab™

Below is a list of sentences. Some are topic sentences. Some are announcements. Put an *X* by the announcements. Then, on the lines below the list, rewrite the announcements, making them into topic sentences.

1. _____ Sticking to a budget can be difficult for a college student.

2. _____ This paper will be about the loss of green space in our town.

3. _____ I want to become a nurse for many reasons.

4. _____ Flowers are a convenient, all-purpose gift, but they can be expensive.

5. _____ Why my brother is in prison is the subject of this essay.

6. _____ The need for more and better campus lighting is the area to be discussed.

7. _____ The smartest change I made all year was to put down my smartphone when I study.

8. _____ The topic of this paper will be the recent carjacking on Patriot Road.

9. _____ I will discuss the reasons for taking the bus to work.

10. _____ Arthur O'Malley deserves a reward for heroism.

Rewrite the announcements. Make each one a topic sentence.

_____

_____

_____

_____

_____

_____

_____

_____

MyWritingLab™   **Exercise 12**   **Practice: Revising Topic Sentences That Are Too Narrow**

Below is a list of topic sentences. Some of them are topics that are too narrow; they cannot be developed with details. Put an *X* by the ones that are too narrow. Then, on the lines below, rewrite those sentences as broader topic sentences that could be developed in one paragraph.

1. _____ My father has to sell my grandmother's house.

2. _____ Every night, I cook dinner for my children.

3. _____ Adrian Levine's people skills made him a good psychologist.

4. _____ Armando has a commercial pilot's license.

5. _____ The movie theater is across the street from the mall.

6. _____ Once classes got out for break, the campus was like a ghost town.

7. _____ Heavy flooding drove hundreds of people from their Kansas homes.

8. _____ There was a fire at the abandoned bowling alley on Dowling Road.

9. _____ Our first day of English class was full of surprises.

10. _____ Ted and I played basketball all Saturday afternoon and most of Sunday morning.

Rewrite the narrow sentences. Make each one broader.

_____

_____

_____

_____

_____

_____

_____

_____

_____

_____

_____

PLANNING   A PARAGRAPH

Checking Your Details

Once you have a topic sentence, you can begin working on an **outline** for your paragraph. The outline is a plan that helps you stay focused in your writing. The outline begins to form when you write your topic sentence and write your list of details beneath the topic sentence. You can now look at your list and ask yourself an important question: "Do I have **enough details** to **support** my topic sentence?" Remember, your goal is to write a paragraph of seven to twelve sentences.

Consider this topic sentence and list of details:

topic sentence:	People can be very rude when they shop in supermarkets.
details:	talk on phone
	express lane
	too many items

Does the list contain enough details for a paragraph of seven to twelve sentences? Probably not.

Adding Details When There Are Not Enough

To add details, try brainstorming. Ask yourself some questions like these:

Where else in supermarkets are people rude?
Are they rude in other lanes besides the express lane?
Are they rude in the aisles? How?
Is there crowding anywhere? Where?

By brainstorming, you might come up with this detail:

topic sentence:	People can be very rude when they shop in supermarkets.
details:	talk on phone
	too many items
	hit my cart with theirs in aisles
	block aisles while they decide
	push ahead in deli area
	argue with cashier over prices

Keep brainstorming until you feel you have enough details for a seven- to twelve-sentence paragraph. Remember that it is better to have too many details than too few, for you can always edit the extra details later.

If you try brainstorming and still do not have many details, you can refer to your original ideas—your freewriting or journal—for other details.

Eliminating Details That Do Not Relate to the Topic Sentence

Sometimes, what you thought were good details do not relate to the topic sentence because they do not fit or support your point. Eliminate details that do not relate to the topic sentence. For example, the following list contains details that really do not relate to the topic sentence. Those details are crossed out.

topic sentence:	Waiters have to be very patient in dealing with their customers.
details:	customers take a long time ordering
	~~waiter's salary is low~~
	waiters have to explain specials twice
	customers send orders back
	customers blame waiters for any delays
	waiters can't get angry if customer gets angry
	~~waiters work long shifts~~
	customers change their mind after ordering

From List to Outline

Take another look at the topic sentence and list of details on a favorite city or town:

topic sentence:	I love St. Augustine because it has sun and sea, history, and family.

details:		
	a small city	clear blue water
	no freeways	lots of history
	no skyscrapers	a fort
	not millions of people	oldest schoolhouse
	thousands of visitors every day	grandparents live there
	can always visit family for free	warm in winter
	beach nearby	grandparents feed me
	clean, big beach	I use their car

After you scan that list, you are ready to develop the outline of the paragraph.

An outline is a plan for writing, and it can be a type of draft in list form. It sketches what you want to write and the order in which you want to present it. *An organized, logical list will make your writing unified since each item on the list will relate to your topic sentence.*

When you plan, keep your topic sentence in mind:

I love St. Augustine because it has <u>sun</u> and <u>sea</u>, <u>history</u>, and <u>family</u>.

Notice the underlined key words, which lead to three key parts of your outline:

> sun and sea
> history
> family

You can put the details on your list together so that they connect to one of these parts:

sun and sea

> beach nearby, clean, big beach, clear blue water, warm in winter

history

> lots of history, a fort, oldest schoolhouse

family

> can always visit family for free, grandparents live there, grandparents feed me, I drive their car

With this kind of grouping, you have a clearer idea of how to organize a paragraph.

Now that you have grouped your ideas with key words and details, you can write an outline.

An Outline for a Paragraph

topic sentence	I love St. Augustine because it has sun and sea, history, and family.
details	
sun and sea	It is warm in the winter. There is a beach nearby. It is big and clean. The water is clear blue.
history	It has lots of history. There is a fort. The oldest schoolhouse is there.
family	My grandparents live in St. Augustine. I stay at their house. They feed me. I use their car.

As you can see, the outline combined some of the details from the list. Even with these combinations, the details are very rough in style. As you reread the list, you will notice items that could be combined and ideas that need more explanation. Keep in mind that an outline is merely a very rough organization of your paragraph. You can review the following checklist as you work through the steps of devising an outline.

Checklist for an Outline

✓ **Unity:** Are all of the details relate to the topic sentence? If they do, the paragraph will be unified.

✓ **Support:** Do you have enough supporting ideas? Can you add to these ideas with even more specific details?

✓ **Coherence:** Are the details listed in the right order? If the order of points is logical, the paragraph will be coherent.

Coherence: Putting Your Details in Proper Order

Check the sample outline again, and you will notice that the details are grouped in the same order as the topic sentence: first, details about sun and sea; next, details about history; last, details about family in St. Augustine. Putting the details in an order that matches the topic sentence is a logical order for this paragraph.

Putting the details in logical order makes the ideas in your paragraph easy to follow. The most logical order for a paragraph depends on the subject of the paragraph. If you are writing about an event, you might use **time order** (such as telling what happened first, second, and so forth); if you are arguing some point, you might use **emphatic order** (such as saving your most convincing idea for last); if you are describing a room, you might use **space order** (such as from left to right, or from top to bottom).

The format of the outline helps to organize your ideas. The topic sentence is written above the list of details. This position helps you to remember that the topic sentence is the *main idea*, and the details that support it are written under it. The topic sentence is the most important sentence of the paragraph. You can easily check the items on your list, one by one, against your main idea. You can also develop the *unity* (relevance) and *coherence* (logical order) of your details.

When you actually write a paragraph, the topic sentence does not necessarily have to be the first sentence in the paragraph. Read the paragraphs below, and notice where each topic sentence is placed.

Topic Sentence at the Beginning of the Paragraph

<u>Watching a horror movie on the late show can keep me up all night</u>. The movie itself scares me to death, especially if it involves a creepy character sneaking up on someone in the dark. After the movie, I'm afraid to turn out all the lights and be alone in the dark. Then every little noise seems like the sound of a sinister intruder. Strange shapes seem to appear in the shadows. My closet becomes a place where someone could be hiding. There might even be a creature under the bed! And if I go to sleep, these strange invaders might appear from under the bed or in the closet.

Topic Sentence in the Middle of the Paragraph

The kitchen counters gleamed. In the spice rack, every jar was organized neatly. The sink was polished, and not one spot marred its surface. The stove burners were surrounded by dazzling stainless steel rings. <u>The chef kept an immaculate kitchen</u>. There were no finger marks on the refrigerator door. No sticky spots dirtied the floor. No crumbs hid behind the toaster.

Topic Sentence at the End of the Paragraph

On long summer evenings, we would play softball in the street. Sometimes we'd play until it was so dark we could barely see the ball. Then our mothers would come to the front steps of the row houses and call us in, telling us to stop our play. But we'd pretend we couldn't hear them. If they insisted, we'd beg for a few minutes more or for just one more game. It was so good to be outdoors with our friends. It was warm, and we knew we had weeks of summer vacation ahead. There was no school in the morning; there would be more games to play. <u>We loved those street games on summer nights</u>.

Note: Many of your paragraph assignments will require a clear topic sentence, so be sure you follow your own instructor's directions about placement of the topic sentence.

Exercise 13   **Practice: Adding Details to Support a Topic Sentence**   MyWritingLab™

The topic sentences below have some—but not enough—details. Write sentences to add details to the list below each topic sentence.

1. topic sentence: A bad cold can be a miserable experience.

   a. No one wants to be around a person with a cold.

   b. My head hurts because of congestion.

   c. A constantly dripping nose makes it hard to do any work.

   d. _____

   e. _____

   f. _____

   g. _____

2. topic sentence: Unexpected time off can be a great gift.

   a. I used to love snow days when I was in elementary school.

   b. I could stay home, play in the snow, or watch television.

   c. _____

   d. _____

   e. _____

   f. _____

   g. _____

3. **topic sentence:** Anyone who has moved to a new place knows what loneliness means.

   a. There is no old friend to visit nearby.

   b. At work, everyone seems to have a closed group of friends.

   c. Those groups don't need a new person at the workplace.

   d. _____

   e. _____

   f. _____

   g. _____

MyWritingLab™   Exercise 14   **Practice: Eliminating Details That Do Not Fit**

Below are topic sentences and lists of supporting details. Cross out the details that do not fit the topic sentence.

1. **topic sentence:** A gray and rainy day has a special kind of appeal for me.

   details: When I wake up on a dark, rainy morning, I appreciate my bed.
   It is warm and comfortable.
   I like to stay in bed for a few minutes and savor the sound of the rain.
   Unfortunately, I can't stay in bed forever.
   Drinking a hot cup of coffee and seeing the dripping trees outside, I feel safe and protected.
   Even when I have to drive to work in the rain, I enjoy the glistening streets and misty air.
   Everywhere I look, I see drivers racing through puddles and splashing the poor pedestrians on the sidewalks.

2. **topic sentence:** A new seatbelt law has made me angry and upset.
   details: The old law allowed the police to check for a seatbelt violation only if they spotted another violation first.
   The new law says police can now randomly check for seatbelt violations.
   Last week, police offers stopped me and about forty other students just as we pulled out of the parking lot at our college.
   I was so busy trying to pull out of my parking space and slip into the long line of cars that I forgot to buckle up.
   Between classes, the parking lot is jammed with people coming and going.
   Instead of giving me a warning, an officer issued a ticket that costs more than a hundred dollars.
   I am furious about this unfair treatment.
   My mother says that the officer was trying to protect me, but she's just being silly.

Exercise 15   **Practice: Coherence: Putting Details in the Right Order**   MyWritingLab™

These outlines have details that are in the wrong order. In the space provided, number the sentences in the right order: 1 would be the number for the first sentence, and so on.

1. topic sentence: Finding emergency day care for my son was difficult.

_____   Ryan, my four-year-old son, was a little grumpy at breakfast on Friday morning.

_____   Michelle said my son had a slight fever and a runny nose.

_____   By 8:00 a.m., when I dropped him off at his regular day care facility, he seemed better.

_____   My second was to call my sister, but I reached her at my aunt's house, two hours away.

_____   Michelle wanted me to pick up Ryan immediately so that the other children would not be infected.

_____   My first option was to leave work and risk being fired.

_____   At noon, while I was at work, I got a call from Michelle, the owner of the day care facility.

_____   As I listened to Michelle, I examined my options.

_____   Finally, my brother, who works at night, brought Ryan home and stayed with him until I finished work.

2. topic sentence: My argument with Patrick was a silly quarrel between two stubborn people.

_____   Our quarrel ended when the theater ran out of tickets before we reached the ticket window.

_____   It started over a movie that we both wanted to see.

_____   We arranged to go to a nine o'clock showing.

_____   When we got to the theater, a huge line snaked around the building.

_____   At 9:20, we were still in line, and I wanted to leave.

_____   "You won't miss any of the movie," Patrick answered, "just the advertisements and the coming attractions."

_____   "I hate to miss any of the movie," I said," so let's go and come back another time."

_____   Patrick's words irritated me, so I replied, "You go to the movie if you want to. I'll just wait in the car."

_____   "Fine," Patrick snarled, "you sit in the car for two hours."

DRAFTING AND REVISING   A PARAGRAPH

③ Write a paragraph that is unified, supported with detail, and coherent.

Drafting a Paragraph

The outline is a draft in list form. You are now ready to write the list in paragraph form, to "rough out" a draft of your assignment. This stage of writing is the time to draft, revise, and draft again. You may write several drafts in this stage, but don't think of this as an unnecessary chore or a punishment. It is a way of taking the pressure off yourself. By revising in steps, you are reminding yourself that the first try does not have to be perfect.

Review the outline on a favorite city or town on page 21. You can create a first draft of this outline in the form of a paragraph. (Remember that the first line of each paragraph is indented.) In the draft of the following paragraph, the first sentence of the paragraph is the topic sentence.

First Draft of a Paragraph

I love St. Augustine because it has sun and sea, history, and family. St. Augustine is warm in the winter. There is a beach nearby. It is clean and big. The water is clear blue. St. Augustine has lots of history. There is an old stone fort. The oldest schoolhouse is there. I can always visit my family for free. My grandparents live in St. Augustine. They feed me. I use their car.

Revising

Once you have a first draft, you can begin to think about **revising** it. Revising involves reviewing and changing your paper's organization, structure, and content. This often requires moving sentences around or reordering sentences, as well as adding more information, including examples and details.

One way to begin revising is to read your work aloud to yourself. Listen to your words, and consider the questions in the following checklists.

Checklist for Revising Your Draft of a Paragraph

✓ Are all the sentences on topic and staying on my point? (No)

✓ Should I take out any ideas that do not relate? (Yes)

✓ Do I have enough to say about my point? (No)

✓ Should I add any details? (Yes. I could add more details about the schoolhouse or the beach.)

✓ Should I change the order of my sentences? (Maybe)

If your instructor agrees, you can work with your classmates. You can read your draft to a partner or a group. Your listener(s) can react to your draft by applying the questions on the checklist and by making notes about your draft as you read. When you are finished reading aloud, your partner(s) can discuss the notes about your work. **Remember that writing and revising several drafts may be necessary before you are satisfied with your paragraph content.**

Revised Draft of a Paragraph

(Note: Editing still needed to correct errors and improve style.)

added *Florida* to be more specific	I love St. Augustine <u>Florida</u> because it has sun and sea, history and family. St. Augustine is warm in the winter. There is a beach near-by. It is clean and big. The water is clear blue. St. Augustine has lots of history. There is an old stone fort. <u>It looks out over the ocean.</u> The old-est schoolhouse <u>in America</u> is there; <u>it is made of wood.</u> <u>My favorite part of St. Augustine is my family.</u> ~~I can always visit my family for free.~~ My grandparents live in St. Augustine. <u>They are my favorite relatives. They always make me feel welcome and take good care of me.</u> ~~They feed me. I use their car.~~ <u>When I visited them, my grandmother cooks wonderful meals, and my grandfather lets me use his car to see the sights.</u>

added detail about the stone fort

added detail about the schoolhouse

connected my family to why I like St. Augustine

added more detail to why I love visiting my family

deleted sentences that appeared disconnected to topic

Exercise 16 **Collaborate: Adding Details to a Draft**

Collaborate

Complete this exercise with a partner or a group. The paragraph below lacks the kind of details that would make it more interesting. Working with a partner or a group, add the details to the blank spaces provided. When you are finished with the additions, read the revised paragraph to the class.

Paragraph to be revised:

Students are busy and often broke. As a result, their meals are not always healthy and are often eaten on the run. Instead of eating a nutritional breakfast, many students grab _____, _____, or _____ and gobble it on their way to class. Lunch is likely to come from a vending machine and be filled with sugar or fat. Every day, students drink soft drinks such as _____ or _____ when they have a break between classes; they munch on bags of _____ or little plastic packets of _____. Of course, every student appreciates the student activities that include free food; these include fairs sponsored by various clubs, multicultural celebrations, and _____. Some students who sign up for an evening class fortify themselves by grabbing fast food from popular restaurants like _____, _____, and _____ so that they will have the energy for a two- or three-hour class.

EDITING AND PROOFREADING A PARAGRAPH

After you are satisfied with the latest revised draft of your paragraph, you are ready to edit. **Editing** often involves making improvements or correcting errors you may have overlooked during the revision process. Examining sentence patterns and length, checking appropriate word choice, and ensuring that specific details are lined smoothly are all natural refinements during editing.

Checklist for Editing Your Revised Draft

✓ Is my choice of words appropriate? (Some wording is too informal.)

✓ Is my choice of words repetitive? (No)

✓ Are my sentences too long? Too short? (Some are too short.)

✓ Should I combine any sentences? (Yes)

✓ Am I running sentences together? (No)

✓ Am I writing in complete sentences? (Yes)

✓ Are my verb choices appropriate? (No)

✓ Can I link my ideas more smoothly? (Maybe)

Review the following edited version of the paragraph on a favorite city and compare it with the revised draft on page 27. Changes are labeled for easy reference.

Edited Version of a Revised Draft

added a comma before *because*

combined sentences that were too short

rewrote description of schoolhouse

corrected verb mistake of *visited*

I love St. Augustine, Florida, because it has sun and sea, history, and family. St. Augustine is warm in the winter, and has a big, clean beach with clear blue water. St. Augustine has a lot of history, including an old stone fort that looks out over the ocean. It also has the oldest schoolhouse in America, a tiny wooden building. My favorite part of St. Augustine is my family. My grandparents live in St. Augustine, and they are my favorite relatives. They always make me feel welcome and take good care of me. When I visit them, my grandmother cooks wonderful meals, and my grandfather lets me use his car to see the sights.

A side-by-side comparison of the first draft and the edited version reveals significant improvement in style and content thus far:

First Draft	Revised and Edited Paragraph
I love St. Augustine because it has sun and sea, history, and family. St. Augustine is warm in the winter. There is a beach nearby. It is clean and big. The water is clear blue. St. Augustine has lots of history. There is an old stone fort. The oldest schoolhouse is there. I can always visit my family for free. My grandparents live in St. Augustine. They feed me. I use their car.	I love St. Augustine, Florida, because it has sun and sea, history, and family. St. Augustine is warm in the winter, and has a big, clean beach with clear blue water. St. Augustine has a lot of history, including an old stone fort that looks out over the ocean. It also has the oldest schoolhouse in America, a tiny wooden building. My favorite part of St. Augustine is my family. My grandparents live in St. Augustine, and they are my favorite relatives. They always make me feel welcome and take good care of me. When I visit them, my grandmother cooks wonderful meals, and my grandfather lets me use his car to see the sights.

Exercise 17 **Practice: Editing a Draft by Combining Sentences**

MyWritingLab™

The paragraph below has many short, choppy sentences, which are underlined. Wherever you see two or more underlined sentences clustered next to each other, combine the clustered sentences into one clear, smooth sentence. Write your revised version of the paragraph in the spaces above the lines.

Paragraph to be revised:

I have often claimed that I would love a rainy holiday. I swore that it would be a perfect time for me. It would be a time for me to relax. It would be a time for me to enjoy my solitude. I was wrong. Last week, because of the Memorial Day holiday, I had a free three-day weekend. The rain began on Saturday morning. I watched the water splatter the windows. It gushed from the gutters. "Fine," I thought. I planned to enjoy every minute of my freedom. I started with a leisurely cup of coffee. I spent some time calling all my friends. How wonderful it is to have all this time, I thought. By late afternoon, it was raining hard. I was bored. I did a few chores. I took a nap. I woke up to darkness and pouring rain. The rain continued on Sunday. Now I was feeling cheated of my great weekend. I could not play softball. I could not sunbathe in the park. I could not have a picnic or go for a walk. My friends did not want to get together in the nasty weather. By Monday, as the rain continued, I had to admit that rainy holidays do not put me in a holiday mood.

Proofreading

Once you have edited your latest draft to check for precise word choice, accurate spelling, coherent sentence structure, and appropriate punctuation, you are ready to **proofread** it. When you proofread, you make a clean copy of your work, and then check it for any careless errors in format, spelling, punctuation, and typing. You can then submit a clean, final version to your instructor for evaluation.

Giving Your Paragraph a Title

When you prepare the final version of your paragraph, you may be asked to give it a title. The title should be short and should fit the subject of the paragraph. For example, an appropriate title for the paragraph on a favorite city or town could be "My Favorite City" or "The City I Love." Check with your instructor to see if your paragraph needs a title. In this book, the paragraphs do not have titles.

The Final Version of a Paragraph

Even though the writer carefully revised and edited his paragraph, he found a few more ways to improve it as he prepared his final version. Notice that he added two specific details, refined some wording, and devised a concluding sentence to re-emphasize the paragraph's main point.

Final Version of a Paragraph

(Note: Changes from the edited draft are underlined.)

I love St. Augustine, Florida, because it has sun and sea, history, and family. St. Augustine is warm in the winter, and a <u>wide</u>, clean beach with clear blue water is <u>ten minutes away</u>. In addition, St. Augustine is <u>filled with</u> history, including an old stone fort that looks out on the water. It also has the oldest schoolhouse in America, a tiny wooden building <u>smaller than a two-car garage</u>. Best of all, my grandparents live in St. Augustine. They are my favorite relatives, and they make me feel very welcome. When I am in St. Augustine, I stay with them, enjoy their <u>delicious</u> <u>Spanish</u> food, and use their car. St. Augustine has the natural advantages, history, and family connections to make it my favorite city.

Reviewing the Writing Process

This chapter has taken you through four important stages in writing. As you become more comfortable with them, you will be able to work through them more quickly. For now, try to remember the four stages.

INFO BOX **The Stages of the Writing Process**

Prewriting: gathering and developing ideas, thinking on paper through freewriting, brainstorming, mapping, or keeping a journal

Planning: planning the paragraph by combining and dividing details, focusing the details with a topic sentence, listing the supporting details in proper order, and devising an outline

Drafting and Revising: writing and revising several drafts of the paragraph

Editing and Proofreading: reviewing the latest revised draft of the paragraph to improve style and then checking for any careless errors in grammar, punctuation, spelling, and format

Exercise 18 **Practice: Proofreading to Prepare the Final Version** MyWritingLab™

Following are two paragraphs with the kind of errors it is easy to overlook when you prepare the final version of an assignment. Correct the errors by writing above the lines. There are eleven errors in the first paragraph and nine errors in the second paragraph.

1. Andrew is working hard, but is having a hard time coping with the pressures of his first semester in college. Andrew was not a very good student in High School because he had other intrests. He was friends with some ruff people and even got arrested 2 times. Andrew managed to get a high school diploma but really didn't know what to do next? After two years of working at jobs such as delivering pizza and washing cars, Andrew faced the reality. He knew he needed a better education so he could find more satisfying work. The decision was a huge first step in Andrew's journey to a better life. How ever, Andrew is not use to taking the small and difficult steps toward success in college. Concentrating in class is difficult for a man who never paid much attention in his high school classes. Homework seems to pile up and threatens to overwhelm him. Fortunately, he has an advisor who encourages him to be patience and take one small step, at a time.

2. Because I dont have a car, I depend on half a dozen people to get me to my job, my classes, the supermarket, and my mother's house. My cousin and I work in the same mall so I ride with him. Since our schedules are nearly identicle, this plan works fairly well, especially because, I split the cost of gas with my cousin. Of course, if he misses a day of work, I have to find someone to get me to my job. Then I beg one of my coworkers to take me home. Fortunately, I have a room mate who attends college, owns a car, and has several classes at times when I am also in class. My roommate also drive me to visit my mother because my mother cooks us fabulous dinners. Grocery shopping, visiting a pharmacy, or taking advantage of bargains at a big discount store, present problems. sometimes my sister takes me to a supermarket. I wish that I could afford a car or lived near a bus line, but I'm lucky to have a kind and generous support system of friends and families.

Lines of Detail: A Walk-Through Assignment

This assignment involves working within a group to write a paragraph.

Step 1: Read the three sentences below. Pick the one sentence you prefer as a possible topic sentence for a paragraph. Fill in the blank for the sentence you chose.

Pick one sentence and fill in the blank:

a. The most frightening movie I've ever seen was

_____ (fill in the title).

b. If money were no problem, the best car to buy is

_____ (fill in the name of the car).

c. People who are watching their weight should avoid

_____ (fill in the name of the food).

Collaborate

Step 2: Join a group composed of other students who picked the same topic sentence you picked. In your class, you'll have "movie" people, "car" people, and "food" people. Brainstorm in a group. Discuss questions that could be used to get ideas for your paragraph.

For the movie topic, sample questions could include "What was the most frightening part of the movie?" or "What kind of movie was it—a ghost story, a horror movie, or some other kind?" For the car topic, sample questions could include, "Have you ever driven this kind of car?" or "Do you know anyone who has one?" For the food topic, sample questions could include, "Did you eat this food when you were a child?" or "When are you tempted to eat this food?"

As you discuss, write the questions, not the answers, below. Keep the questions flowing. Do not stop to say, "That's silly" or "I can't answer that." Try to devise **at least five questions**.

Five Brainstorming Questions:

1. _____

2. _____

3. _____

4. _____

5. _____

Step 3: Split up. Alone, begin to think on paper. Answer as many questions as you can, or add more questions and answers, or freewrite.

Step 4: Draft an outline of the paragraph. You will probably have to change the topic sentence to fit the details you have gathered. For example, your new topic sentence might be something like:

_____ was the most frightening movie

I have ever seen; it creates fear by using _____

_____, _____, and

_____.

or

If money were no problem, the best car to buy is a

_____ because of its performance,

_____, and _____.

or

People who are watching their weight should avoid

eating _____ because _____

_____.

Remember to look at your details to see where they lead you. The details will help you to refine your topic sentence.

Step 5: Prepare the first draft of the paragraph.

Step 6: Read the draft aloud to your writing group, the same people who met to brainstorm. Ask each member of your group to make at least one positive comment and one suggestion for revision.

Step 7: Revise your draft extensively, considering the group's ideas and your own ideas for improvement.

Step 8: Edit your draft to improve style and correct any serious errors or omissions.

Step 9: Prepare a final version and proofread it carefully to spot and correct any careless spelling, punctuation, format, or typing errors.

Topics for Writing a Paragraph

When you write on any of these topics, follow the four basic stages of the writing process in preparing your paragraph.

1. Begin this assignment with a partner. The assignment requires an interview. Your final goal is to write a paragraph that will introduce a class member, your partner, to the rest of the class. In the final paragraph, you may design your own topic sentence or use one of the topic sentences below, filling in the blanks with the material you have discovered:

Collaborate

There are several details you should know about

_____ (fill in your partner's name).

or

Three unusual events have happened to _____

(fill in your partner's name).

Before you write the paragraph, follow these steps:

Step 1: Prepare to interview a classmate. Make a list of five questions you might want to ask. They can be questions like, "Where are you from?" or "Have you ever done anything unusual?" List the questions on the following interview form, leaving room to fill in short answers later.

Interview Form

Question 1: _____

Answer: _____

Question 2: _____

Answer: _____

Question 3: _____

Answer: _____

Question 4: _____

Answer: _____

Question 5: _____

Answer: _____

Step 2: Meet and interview your partner. Ask the questions on your list. Jot down brief answers. Ask *any other questions* you think of as you are talking; write down the answers.

Step 3: Change places. Let your partner interview you.

Step 4: Split up. Use the list of questions and answers about your partner as the prewriting part of your assignment. Work on the planning and drafting stages.

Step 5: Ask your partner to read the draft version of your paragraph, to write any comments or suggestions for improvement below the paragraph, and to mark any spelling or grammar errors in the paragraph itself.

Step 6: After you are satisfied with your latest draft, edit it to improve style.

Step 7: Prepare a final version and proofread carefully to correct any careless errors. Then read your paragraph to the class.

2. Below are some topic sentences. Select one and use it to write a paragraph.

MyWritingLab™

A student's experience with college registration can be

_____.

My secret dream is to become a _____.

Most college students tend to be _____.

3. Write a paragraph on one of the topics below. Create your own topic sentence; explain and support it with specific details.

MyWritingLab™

a favorite activity   a challenging class   an interactive game

4. Examine the photograph of the celebration. After you have looked at it carefully, write a paragraph with this topic sentence:

MyWritingLab™

Celebrations are an important part of culture.

The photograph can provide you with some details, but come up with others on your own.

Topics for Critical Thinking and Writing

Note: College writing assignments will often require you to engage in *critical thinking*. Evaluating and questioning your own views and assumptions is a natural part of critical thinking and the writing process. The following topics will involve a careful analysis of some of your basic attitudes and opinions.

1. Do you make major decisions quickly, or do you take considerable time evaluating your options? Write about a major decision, perhaps a life-changing one, you have made. Include the factors that led to this decision and how pleased or dissatisfied you are with it.

2. Imagine that someone has given you an acre of land in your town to use any way you desire. What, if anything, would you do with this land? Include the specific reasons for your choice.

> **Note:** Additional writing options can be found in the "Readings for Writers" appendix of this book.

Illustration

CHAPTER 2

Jumping In

*Have you ever volunteered to help out in your community? Often, people who volunteer their time, resources, or companionship find that everyone benefits. People who are hungry are fed, sick people and their families are comforted, and homeless animals receive care. In addition, the volunteers gain a feeling of satisfaction from helping out. When you discuss the ways that everyone wins when people volunteer in the community, you are developing a topic by **illustration**.*

Learning Objectives

In this chapter, you will learn how to:

1. Distinguish between general statements and specific details.

2. Prewrite to generate an illustration paragraph topic.

3. Write a clear topic sentence.

4. Write an illustration paragraph that uses transitions and details effectively.

WHAT IS ILLUSTRATION?

Illustration uses specific examples to support a general point. In your writing, you often use illustration because you frequently want to support a point by providing a specific example.

1 Distinguish between general statements and specific details.

Hints for Writing an Illustration Paragraph

Knowing what is specific and what is general.

A *general* statement is a broad point. The following statements are general:

Traffic can be bad on Hamilton Boulevard.
Revising an essay is easier on a computer.
It is difficult to meet people at my college.

You can support a general statement with specific examples:

general statement: Traffic can be bad on Hamilton Boulevard.

specific examples: During the morning rush hour, the exit to First Avenue is jammed.

If there is an accident, cars can be backed up for a mile.

general statement: Revising an essay is easier on a computer.

specific examples: Last week I wrote an essay in class, and it took me one hour to rewrite it by hand.

Professor Smith makes us write an essay every week, but we can write it on a computer, so that helps save time.

general statement: It can be difficult to meet people at college.

specific examples: After class, most students rush to their jobs.

There are often few places to sit and talk between classes.

When you write an illustration paragraph, be careful to support a general statement with specific examples, not with more general statements.

not this—general statement: College is harder than I thought it would be.

~~**more general statements:**~~ ~~It is tough to be a college student.~~
~~Studying takes a lot of my time.~~

but this—general statement: College is harder than I thought it would be.

specific examples: I cannot afford to miss any classes.

I have to study at least two hours a day.

If you remember to illustrate a broad statement with specific examples, you will have the key to this kind of paragraph.

MyWritingLab™   **Exercise 1** **Practice: Recognizing Broad Statements**

Each list below contains one broad statement and three specific examples. Underline the broad statement.

1. Students who come to class early often start conversations.

Some students get to know each other in study groups formed in class.

As a class ends, students tend to share their reactions to the latest quiz or assignment.

Classes are a good place to start new friendships.

2. One of my roommates always borrows my tablet without asking me.

Borrowing even small items can become a nasty habit.

A man in my business class relies on me for a pencil and never returns one.

I used to infuriate my father by scooping up all his spare change from the hall table each day.

3. Choosing a major is often a long process.

I know many business majors.

Computer science majors can work in the health care industry.

Everyone tells me I should major in nursing.

4. People fill the movie theaters when rain spoils their plans for a holiday outdoors.

Malls are popular places on a wet, hot, or snowy holiday.

Bad weather on a holiday can mean big profits for certain businesses.

When the weather gets too nasty, many people call a pizza delivery service.

Exercise 2   **Practice: Distinguishing the General Statement From the Specific Example**   MyWritingLab™

Each general statement below is supported by three items of support. Two of these items are specific examples; one is too general to be effective. Underline the one that is too general.

1. **general statement:**   Adolescent boys are very choosy about their footwear.

   support: They know that some shoes will make them outcasts at school.

   Shoes chosen by their parents make teenage boys cringe.

   They select their sneakers and other footwear according to strict standards.

2. **general statement:**   Vegan food choices are more popular than ever.

   support: More and more people are turning to vegan dishes.

   Today, veggie burgers are sold in almost every supermarket.

   Major restaurant chains have vegan meals on their menus.

3. **general statement:**   Many preteen girls adore the color pink.

   support: Many young girls dream of an all-pink bedroom.

   Pink handbags, shoes, and clothing dominate the aisles in the preteen sections of department stores.

   Many girls between the ages of two and twelve love pink.

Collaborate

| **Exercise 3** | **Collaborate: Adding Specific Examples to a General Statement** |

With a partner or group, add four specific examples to each general statement below.

1. general statement: Mother's Day is associated with several popular gifts.

examples: _____

_____

_____

_____

2. general statement: The sense of being ignored is a painful feeling.

examples: _____

_____

_____

_____

3. general statement: People caught in a sudden rainstorm have creative ways to stay dry.

examples: _____

_____

_____

_____

② Prewrite to generate an illustration paragraph topic.

WRITING THE ILLUSTRATION PARAGRAPH IN STEPS

PREWRITING ILLUSTRATION

Suppose your instructor asks you to write a paragraph about some aspect of **serving the community.** You can begin by thinking about your subject to gather ideas and to find a focus for your paragraph. Looking through entries in your journal might lead you to the following underlined entry:

Journal Entry About Serving the Community

Tomorrow I'm going to <u>help my father</u>. He's <u>giving out Thanksgiving baskets</u>. We'll go to the <u>Harvest Center Food Bank</u>. It <u>sounds sad</u>. I did it last year. It was <u>a happy experience</u> for me. The <u>families</u> who got baskets <u>were pleased</u>. Everybody waited in line. They were <u>patient</u>. <u>Volunteering put me in a good mood</u>. Now <u>I volunteer at the food bank on weekends</u>. We are a <u>father-and-son team</u>.

The underlined terms can lead you to a list:

help my father
giving out Thanksgiving baskets
Harvest Center Food Bank
sounds sad
a happy experience

families were pleased
patient
Volunteering put me in a good mood
I volunteer at the food bank on weekends
father-and-son team

Consider the underlined terms. Many of them are specific ideas about serving the community. You could write a paragraph about one item or about several related items on the list.

Adding Details to an Idea

Looking at the list of ideas on page 40, you might decide you want to write something about this topic: family volunteering. To add details, you decide to brainstorm:

Who else in your family volunteers?

My mother does. So does my sister.

What do they do?

My mother helps visitors. My sister walks dogs.

Where do they volunteer?

My mother goes to the hospital. My sister goes to the animal shelter.

Who benefits from the volunteering?

Hungry people, worried people, animals.

Why do your family members volunteer?

To help people or pets in trouble. To give to the community. To feel good.

How stressful is volunteering?

Seeing suffering is tough.

You now have this list of ideas connected to the topic of family volunteering:

help my father	mother and sister volunteer
giving out Thanksgiving baskets	mother helps visitors at the hospital
Harvest Center Food Bank	sister walks dogs at the animal shelter
sounds sad	people and animals benefit
I did it last year	family wants to help people or pets in trouble
a happy experience	
families pleased	family wants to give to the community
put me in a good mood	family wants to feel good
father-and-son team	seeing suffering is tough

Creating a Topic Sentence

③ Write a clear topic sentence.

If you examine this list, looking for *related ideas*, you can create a topic sentence. The ideas on the list include (1) details on who volunteers, (2) details about why they volunteer, and (3) details about who benefits from the volunteering. Not all of the details fit into these three categories, but many do.

Grouping the related ideas into the three categories can help you focus your ideas into a topic sentence.

Who Volunteers

Father and son volunteer at Harvest Center Food Bank
Mother helps visitors at the hospital
Sister volunteers at the animal shelter

Why They Volunteer

Help people or pets in trouble
Family wants to give to the community
Family wants to feel good

Who Benefits

Hungry adults and children
Animals at the shelter
The volunteers

You can summarize these related ideas in a topic sentence:

In my family, volunteering is a way to give to the community and to share our good fortune.

Check the topic sentence against your details. Does it explain who volunteers? Yes. It says that the writer's family volunteers. Does it explain why they volunteer? Yes. It says that the family members want "to give to the community and to share our good fortune." Does it cover the people who get rewarded? Yes. It talks about the community that receives the benefits of others' volunteering, and it mentions that the volunteers themselves are rewarded. The topic sentence has given you a focus for your illustration paragraph.

MyWritingLab™ **Exercise 4** **Practice: Finding Specific Ideas in Freewriting**

Following are two samples of freewriting. Each is a response to a broad topic. Read each sample, and then underline any words that could become a more specific topic for a paragraph.

Freewriting Reaction to the Topic of Gambling

I never gamble. Well, I have bought a lottery ticket or two. Of course, I've never won anything. Lottery tickets are just a form of wishful thinking. Would I like to go to Las Vegas? Just to see it once. Afraid to lose a lot of money there. Maybe I'd play the slot machines just once. I guess I do have a gambling streak in me.

Freewriting Reaction to the Topic of Physical Exercise

I don't get enough exercise. Running. Basketball. Going to a gym regularly. Regular exercise takes time out of a person's schedule. Only a super-organized person schedules exercise. Or a fanatic like my brother. He works out every morning at 6:00 a.m. I can't imagine sweating in a gym at dawn. So, how can I get easy exercise? Walk. Jog. Take the stairs. Just burn a few calories when I can. Exercise videos. Why are they popular?

MyWritingLab™ **Exercise 5** **Practice: Finding Specific Ideas in Lists**

Following are two lists. Each is a response to a broad topic. Read each list, and then underline any words that could become a more specific topic for a paragraph.

1. **topic:** the environment

   environmental issues
   water pollution
   recycling at my workplace
   cloth shopping bags
   Environmental Protection Agency

   a community garden
   dangers of greenhouse gases
   saving rainwater in your yard
   endangered species
   wasting paper at home

2. topic: apps

games	share with friends
use apps for productivity	connect with people from all
learn a language	over the world
free vs. paid	using apps for entertainment
better on particular smartphone	run smoothly on tablet
protect identity theft	

Exercise 6   **Practice: Grouping Related Ideas in Lists of Details**   MyWritingLab™

Following are lists of details. In each list, circle the items that seem to fit into one group; then underline the items that seem to fit into a second group. Some items may not fit into either group.

1. topic: courage

seeking treatment for depression	attending patriotic events
volunteering for military service	bullying a child
recovering from addiction	reading books about heroes
accepting one's mistakes	confronting a gang member
rescuing a drowning person	admitting an addiction

2. topic: living with a roommate

less loneliness	too little privacy
male or female	different concepts of neatness
risk of clashing personalities	international students
can share a social life	split the cost of rent
possible lifelong friendship	unauthorized borrowing

Exercise 7   **Practice: Writing Topic Sentences for Lists of Details**   MyWritingLab™

Following are lists of details that have no topic sentences. Write an appropriate topic sentence for each one.

1. topic sentence: _____

_____

A salesperson who made a big sale may rush home to share the news with a loved one.

A worker who gets a promotion could celebrate with friends at a local restaurant.

A man who just became a father could react by telling everyone he knows.

A lottery winner may keep staring at the winning ticket, safely stashed away.

2. topic sentence: _____

_____

Posting negative comments about coworkers can cause problems.

Posting inappropriate pictures can send the wrong message.

Human Resources departments often look through social media sites to ensure employees are representing the company positively.

Not using proper security settings can give strangers access to private information.

3. topic sentence: _____

_____

> Alexander Depree was born in Haiti in the same month that his father died.
>
> Alexander and his mother struggled against the constant threat of starvation in their village.
>
> When Alexander was ten, he and his mother were admitted to the United States as refugees.
>
> Alexander and his mother knew only a few words of English.
>
> Alexander struggled to survive in a school where almost all the students spoke English or Spanish.
>
> After high school, he found a night job as a janitor in a large business complex; in the daytime, he attended the police academy.
>
> Now a police officer, Alexander is respected by his fellow officers and a mentor to boys in the growing Haitian community.

MyWritingLab™   Exercise 8   **Practice: Choosing the Better Topic Sentence**

Following are lists of details. Each list has two possible topic sentences. Underline the better topic sentence for each list.

1. possible topic sentence:

a. High school can be a source of exciting memories.

b. Reunions can be disappointing when one friend has grown up but the other hasn't.

> Michael had the same best friend for all four years of high school.
>
> He and Brian, his friend, were known for their carefree attitudes and crazy pranks.
>
> After they finished high school, Michael joined the U.S. Navy.
>
> Brian left their hometown in Virginia to look for work in California.
>
> Michael lost touch with Brian but liked to remember their wild times.
>
> Five years after their high school graduation, the two friends reunited.
>
> Michael was home on leave from his Army base in Germany.
>
> Brian was visiting his family and having another wild time.
>
> Although Michael had looked forward to the reunion, he was saddened by the meeting.
>
> Michael shared the adventures and struggles he had experienced in the military.

Brian had worked at a series of jobs, but none of the jobs had worked out, he said.

All Brian wanted to do was to relive their glory days in high school.

2. possible topic sentence:

a. Being popular sometimes means not being yourself.

b. Friendship can be strange and confusing.

My sister Tanya feels sorry for me because I'm not as popular as she is.

Her phone is always ringing, and she has hundreds of friends online and locally.

On the other hand, I have just a few friends.

Many of Tanya's friends are interested in parties and drinking.

I like sports, hiking, and nature.

I have tried to fit in with Tanya's friends.

However, I realized that, in order to fit in, I would have to pretend I liked socializing all night and getting drunk.

My group of friends doesn't go to huge parties or drink much.

They understand me.

I decided to be myself and enjoy my small circle of friends.

PLANNING   ILLUSTRATION

When you plan your outline, keep your topic sentence in mind:

In <u>my family</u>, volunteering is a way to <u>give to the community</u> and to <u>share our good fortune</u>.

Notice the three key phrases:

> my family
> give to the community
> share our good fortune

Assign each detail to **one** of the key phrases:

my family

> my father and I volunteer at the food bank
> my mother helps visitors at the local hospital
> my sister volunteers at the animal shelter

give to the community

> help hungry people
> help other people or pets in trouble

share our good fortune

> a happy experience
> needy families pleased
> animals at the shelter
> family members feel good

With this kind of grouping, you have a clearer idea of how to organize a paragraph.

Outline for an Illustration Paragraph

topic sentence   In my family, volunteering is a way to give to the community and to share our good fortune.

details

who volunteers —
My father and I volunteer every weekend at a local food bank.
My mother helps visitors at the hospital.
My sister volunteers at the animal shelter.

why they volunteer –
My father and I want to help hungry people.
Some family members want to help other people or pets in trouble.
Family members want to feel good.

who shares our good fortune —
Hungry adults and children are fed.
Visitors to the hospital are comforted.
Homeless pets receive love.
Family members get to give back to the community.
Family members gain a good feeling.

As you can see, the outline combined some of the details from the list. You can combine other details, avoid repetition, and add more details as you draft your essay.

Collaborate

Exercise 9   **Collaborate: Adding Details to an Outline**

Below are three partial outlines. Each has a topic sentence and some details. Working with a partner or group, add more details that support the topic sentence.

1. **topic sentence:** Sleeping habits vary a great deal.

   a. Some people like to sleep without a pillow.

   b. Others like to sleep with a pillow covering their face.

   c. Some people like to sleep with a window open, even in winter.

   d. _____

   e. _____

   f. _____

   g. _____

2. **topic sentence:** Choosing either a tablet for viewing an e-book or reading a paper book is a personal choice.

   a. Holding a book is important for many people.

   b. Many students often prefer carrying one tablet over five heavy textbooks.

   c. Reading with a tablet can be hard on your eyes after a while.

   d. _____

e. _____

f. _____

g. _____

Exercise 10 **Eliminating Details That Are Repetitive**   MyWritingLab™

In the following outlines, some details use different words to repeat an example given earlier in the list. Cross out the repetitive details.

1. **topic sentence:** Lying may help a person in the short term, but it can be self-destructive in the long term.

   Lying as an excuse for lateness or for broken promises can work for a while.

   Eventually the excuses aren't believable and make a bad habit more obvious.

   People who lie about their money or background to impress others may gain admiration at first.

   Sooner or later, people will spot the lying braggart and become resentful or contemptuous.

   Telling too many elaborate stories about car problems, family emergencies, or illness does not work forever.

   Lies of infidelity may get a husband or wife out of a difficult situation.

   However, a cheating spouse can become entangled in too many lies.

   Someone who creates a phony image of wealth is bound to be exposed and mocked.

2. **topic sentence:** Nosy neighbors can be helpful people, even lifesavers.

   They may appear to be gossipy, nasty people.

   However, they may be lonely and just want something to fill their time.

   They will collect your mail when you are away.

   If you are away for a few days, you can ask them to keep an eye on your house.

   The neighbors who are not minding their own business could spot a crime such as a burglary in progress.

   You can ask them to check your mailbox if you are going to be out of town.

   People who observe the comings and goings of their neighbors can spot a change in someone's routine.

   That change could involve someone who hasn't left the house for days.

   A person who slipped or fell at home, can't walk, and can't crawl to a phone would welcome a rescue by a nosy neighbor.

   A nosy neighbor acts like your own Neighborhood Crime Watcher.

   He or she can be almost as good as a paramedic.

4 Write an illustration paragraph that uses transitions and details effectively.

DRAFTING AND REVISING   **ILLUSTRATION**

Review the outline on family volunteering on page 46. You can create a first draft of this outline in the form of a paragraph. Then as you begin to revise your drafts, you can add details and transitions to link your ideas. You can use the following checklist.

Checklist for Revising an Illustration Paragraph

✓ Do I need more or better transitions?

✓ Should I add more details to support my points?

✓ Should some of the details be more specific?

Transitions

As you revise your illustration paragraph, you may find places where one idea ends and another begins abruptly. This problem occurs when you forget to add **transitions**, which are words, phrases, or sentences that connect one idea to another. Using transitions effectively will make your writing clear and smooth. When you write an illustration paragraph, you will need some transitions that link one example to another and other transitions to link one section of your paragraph to another section. Here are some transitions you may want to use in writing an illustration paragraph.

INFO BOX   Transitions for an Illustration Paragraph

another example	in the case of	other kinds
a second example	like	such as
for example	one example	the first instance
for instance	one instance	another instance
in addition	other examples	to illustrate

Look carefully at the following draft of the paragraph on family volunteering, and note how it combines sentences, adds details, and uses transitions to transform the outline into a clear and developed paragraph. You can assume that the writer worked through several rough drafts to get to this point.

Revised Draft of an Illustration Paragraph

(Note: Editing and proofreading is still necessary to refine style and correct errors.)

topic sentence —————————— In my family, volunteering is a way to give to the community and to share our good fortune. <u>One</u>

transition ————————————— <u>example</u> of this volunteering is the weekend work

detail added ————————————— my father and I do at the <u>Harvest Center Food Bank</u>.

transition added ———————————— <u>A second example</u> is the work of my mother, who

detail added ————————————— <u>spend her Thursdays</u> helping visitors at the

transition added ———————————— local hospital. <u>Another example of a volunteer</u>

detail added ————————————— is my sister, who <u>devote a part of each weekend</u> to

detail added ———— working at the animal shelter. She <u>comforts</u>
<u>homeless dogs by walking and playing with them.</u>
detail added ———— Every member of the family wants to give something
to the community. <u>The comunity has been good</u>
<u>to us.</u> Most of all, we enjoy the good feeling that
comes with sharing time, food, or love. <u>In our volun-</u>
transition ———— <u>teering</u>, everyone benefits. <u>For instance</u>, hungry
adults and children receive food. Friends and family
of the sick receive comfort. Homeless animals
transition ———— receive love. <u>In addition</u>, everyone in my family gets
the great reward that comes from sharing.

Exercise 11   **Adding Details to a Draft**

Collaborate

The paragraph below lacks the kind of details that would make it more interesting. Working with a partner or group, add details to the blank spaces provided. When you are finished, read the revised paragraph to the class.

　　People who need to cut back on their spending handle the challenge in different ways. One of the first cuts involves nonessential clothing purchases. Teens may buy fewer _____, _____, and _____. Their parents may decide not to buy any more of the _____, _____, and _____ they regularly wear to work. Some people decide to cut their spending on fuel. To save money on gasoline, they may limit their driving and avoid trips to _____ and _____. To save on gas or electric heating and cooling at home, residents will turn up the thermostat on their air conditioning, and _____.

　　Finally, food shopping changes when people are short of money. In good times, a food budget may leave room for a few luxuries such as _____, _____, and _____. In more challenging times, shoppers are likely to replace pricey goodies with cheaper treats such as _____, _____, and _____.

MyWritingLab™ **Exercise 12** **Practice: Revising a Draft by Adding Transitions**

The paragraph below needs some transitions. Add appropriate transitions (words or phrases) to the blanks.

Meeting people is difficult for me. I never know what to say after shaking hands or mumbling "Hi." Should I say "Nice to meet you"? Should I ask "How are you doing?"? Then there is the problem of eye contact. This problem has many facets. _____ making eye contact is supposed to indicate openness and good character. _____, eye contact shows that a person is confident. However, I am afraid to hold the eye contact for too long or too short a time. _____ I can remember a time when I felt myself looking down at the floor too soon. I must have looked as if I were ashamed of something. Other examples involve holding eye contact for too long.

_____ I felt as if I were invading the other person's space.

_____ I felt uncomfortable because my lengthy eye contact made me look too needy. To cope with my fears about meeting people, I pay close attention to television and movie scenes where people meet. The actors always seem confident and suave. Actors _____ Will Smith and Denzel Washington never seem nervous or tongue-tied. Maybe I can learn to act confident even when I feel nervous.

EDITING AND PROOFREADING **ILLUSTRATION**

After you are satisfied with your latest revised draft, you are ready to edit. As you begin to edit your paragraph, look for the correct verb forms, redundant words, ways to combine sentences, and any spelling mistakes. You can use the following checklist.

Checklist for Editing Illustration Paragraph

✓ Are all the verb forms correct and consistent?

✓ Are any words redundant?

✓ Should some of the sentences be combined?

✓ Is everything spelled correctly?

Finally, proofread your writing. Read every word carefully to be sure that what you've written makes sense and is error free.

Final Version of an Illustration Paragraph

(Note: Changes from previous draft are underlined.)

verb form corrected: *spends*	In my family, volunteering is a way to give to the community and to share our good fortune. One example of this volunteering is the weekend work my father and I do at the Harvest Center Food Bank. A second example is the work of my mother, who <u>spends</u> her Thursdays helping visitors at the local hospital. Another volunteer
verb form corrected: *devotes*	is my sister, who <u>devotes</u> a part of each weekend to working at the animal shelter. She comforts homeless dogs by walking and playing with them. Every member
sentences combined and spelling of *community* corrected	of the family wants to give something to the <u>community</u> that has been good to us. Most of all, we enjoy the good feeling that comes with sharing time, food, or love. In our volunteering, everyone benefits. <u>For instance, hungry adults and children receive food; friends and family of the sick receive comfort; and homeless animals receive love.</u> In addition, everyone in my family <u>gains</u>
sentences combined	
wording improved	the <u>emotional</u> reward that comes from sharing.

For your information: A sample illustration essay based on the same topic and following the same writing steps can be found in Chapter 12.

Exercise 13 Editing a Draft by Combining Sentences

MyWritingLab™

The paragraph below has many short, choppy sentences, which are underlined. Wherever you see two or more underlined sentences clustered next to each other, combine them into one clear, smooth sentence. Write your revised version of the paragraph in the spaces above the lines.

My sister Patrice loves the color red. <u>She has red shoes. She has six pairs of</u>

<u>them. They include bright red sneakers, tomato-colored platform heels, and scarlet boots.</u> Her love of red does not end with clothing. <u>Her hair is dyed crimson. It</u>

<u>is not a natural shade.</u>

Of course, her nails are always painted bright red, and she never appears in public without a shiny red coating of lipstick. Patrice collects red purses and bags, too.

She haunts thrift shops in search of vintage bags in red. She hits the sales at the mall. She looks for designer handbags in red. All this searching makes Patrice happy because she can survey her collection and know that she will never run out of red accessories. The greatest and most beloved item in her collection is not an item at all. It is her dog Pepper. He is a red Irish setter.

MyWritingLab™   Exercise 14   **Practice: Editing and Proofreading to Prepare the Final Version**

The following is an illustration paragraph that has the kinds of errors that are easy to overlook when you prepare the final version of an assignment. Correct the errors by writing above the lines. There are ten errors in the paragraph.

Sleep is a precious gift, but not all sleep are equal. People with deep anxieties or sorrows can suffer thru a broken sleep that leaves them exhausted and trouble. Passengers in a car, bus, train, or plane often fall into a long doze interrupted by periods of semi-consciousness. They incorporate the sound of engines, the talk of other passenger, and the jolts of travel into their sleep. They wake up feeling, grimy, disoriented, and cramped. A person who has worked for too many hours without sleeping may finally fall into a exhausted sleep. However, that sleep is'nt alway's refreshing. The best sleep is a soft, gentle fall into peace and silence. Its' rare and valuable, and the people who enjoy it regularly should be greatful.

Lines of Detail: A Walk-Through Assignment

Your assignment is to write an illustration paragraph about music.

Step 1: Freewrite or brainstorm on this broad topic for ten minutes.

Step 2: Review your freewriting or brainstorming. Underline any parts that are a specific idea related to the broad topic of music.

Step 3: List all the specific ideas. Choose one as the narrowed topic for your paragraph.

Step 4: Add related ideas to your chosen, narrowed topic. Do this by reviewing your list for related ideas and by brainstorming for more related ideas.

Step 5: List all your related ideas and review their connection to your narrowed topic. Then write a topic sentence for your paragraph.

Step 6: Write a first draft of your paragraph.

Step 7: Revise your first draft. Be sure it has enough details and clear transitions, and work through several drafts if necessary. Combine any choppy sentences.

Step 8: Edit your latest draft to refine word choice, combine sentences, and correct serious errors.

Step 9: Prepare a final version and proofread it to catch any spelling, punctuation, format, or typing errors.

Topics for Writing an Illustration Paragraph

When you write on any of these topics, follow the four basic stages of the writing process in preparing your illustration paragraph.

1. Begin this assignment with a partner or group. Together, write down as many old sayings as you can. (Old sayings include statements like, "It's not whether you win or lose; it's how you play the game that's important," or "Money can't buy happiness.") To review quotations categorized by topics, visit *quoteland.com*.

    Collaborate

    Once you have a long list of sayings, split up. Pick one saying; then write a paragraph on that saying. Your paragraph should give several examples that illustrate the truth of the saying.

2. Below are two topic sentences. Select one and use it to write a paragraph in which you use examples to support (illustrate) the topic sentence.

    MyWritingLab™

    _____ makes me nervous.

    A rainy day is a good day to _____.

3. Select one of the topics listed below. Write an illustration paragraph on some narrowed part of the topic. If you choose the topic of jobs, for example, you might narrow the topic to illustrate the benefits or drawbacks of your job.

    MyWritingLab™

jobs	money	food	mistakes
smartphones	children	sleep	surprises
fashion	challenges	anger	kindness

4. Examine the image of the angry driver. After you have looked at it carefully, write a paragraph with this topic sentence:

    MyWritingLab™

    Whenever a driver is delayed by a traffic jam on a major highway, that person can react in several ways.

Topics for Critical Thinking and Writing

MyWritingLab™

1. Everyone has made general statements such as "This town has nothing to make young people want to stay here" or "People who don't have children have no idea how stressful life can be." Think of a similar generalization and use specific examples to illustrate the degree of truth in that statement. Be careful to avoid further generalizations in your supporting details.

MyWritingLab™

2. Assume that you are a member of a student advisory board at your college, and you have been charged with identifying several potential safety hazards. After reviewing your list of potential dangers, choose the most severe hazard and illustrate why it poses such a serious threat to students and/or campus life in general. (You may want to share your initial list with your peers to elicit their feedback.)

> **Note:** Additional writing options suitable for illustration-related assignments can be found in the "Readings for Writers" appendix at the end of this book.

Jumping In

*What is your strongest impression of this scene? Does the scene evoke feelings of power? Excitement? Anxiety? Examining the scene carefully, along with your reactions, will help you **describe** it effectively.*

Learning Objectives

In this chapter you will learn how to:

1 Use specific words and phrases, including sense words.

2 Prewrite to generate a descriptive paragraph topic that supports a dominant impression.

3 Write a descriptive paragraph that uses specific details and transitions effectively.

WHAT IS DESCRIPTION?

Description shows a reader what a person, place, thing, or situation is like. When you write description, you try to *show, not tell about,* something. You want to make the reader see that person, place, or situation, and then, perhaps, to make the reader think about or act on what you have shown.

HINTS FOR WRITING A DESCRIPTIVE PARAGRAPH

Using Specific Words and Phrases

Using specific words and phrases will help the reader "see" what you are describing. If a word or phrase is *specific,* it is *exact and precise.* The opposite of specific language is language that is vague, general, or fuzzy. Think of the difference between specific and general in this way:

Imagine that you are browsing through a used-car lot. A salesman approaches you.

1 Use specific words and phrases, including sense words.

"Can I help you?" the salesman asks.

"I'm looking for a good, reliable car," you say.

"Well, what kind of car did you have in mind?" asks the salesman.

"Not too old," you say.

"A sports car?" asks the salesman.

"Maybe," you say.

The conversation could go on and on. You are being very general in saying that you want a "good, reliable" car. The salesman is looking for specific details: How old a car do you want? What model of car?

In writing, if you use words like *good* or *nice* or *bad* or *interesting*, you will not have a specific description or a very effective piece of writing. Whenever you can, try to use a more precise word instead of a general term. To find a more explicit term, ask yourself such questions as, "What type?" or "How?" The examples below show how a general term can be replaced by a more specific one.

general word: hat (Ask "What type?")
more specific words: beret, fishing hat, baseball cap

general word: textbook (Ask "What type?")
more specific words: biology, English, algebra

general word: ran (Ask "How?")
more specific words: raced, sprinted, loped

general word: nice (Ask "How?")
more specific words: friendly, outgoing, courteous

MyWritingLab™   **Exercise 1**   **Practice: Identifying General and Specific Words**

Below are lists of words. Put an *X* by the one term in each list that is a more general term than the others. The first one is done for you.

List 1	List 2	List 3
__X__ science	_____ physical exercise	_____ blog
_____ botany	_____ lifting weights	_____ Internet
_____ biology	_____ running	_____ wiki
_____ astronomy	_____ swimming	_____ e-mail
_____ geology	_____ rock climbing	_____ social networking

MyWritingLab™   **Exercise 2**   **Practice: Ranking General and Specific Items**

Below are lists of items. In each list, rank the items, from the most general (1) to the most specific (4).

List 1	List 2	List 3
_____ car interiors	_____ advising	_____ money
_____ seats in cars	_____ major advising	_____ coins
_____ cars	_____ course advising	_____ quarters
_____ leather seats in cars	_____ academic advising	_____ silver-colored coins

Exercise 3   **Collaborate: Interviewing for Specific Answers**

Collaborate

To practice being specific, interview a partner. Ask your partner to answer the questions below. Write his or her answers in the spaces provided. When you have finished, change places. In both interviews, your goal is to find specific answers, so you should both be as explicit as you can in your answers.

Interview Questions

1. What is your favorite class or subject?

   _____

   _____

2. What did you eat and drink for breakfast this morning?

   _____

   _____

3. What is your favorite professional sports team?

   _____

   _____

4. If you could buy any car in the world, what car would you choose?

   _____

   _____

5. What type of homework do you prefer (online, reading, writing, problem solving)?

   _____

   _____

6. When you think of a brave person, who comes to mind?

   _____

   _____

7. What smell reminds you of a family holiday?

   _____

   _____

8. What is the most enjoyable city or town you have visited?

   _____

   _____

Exercise 4 **Practice: Finding Specific Words or Phrases**

List four specific words or phrases beneath the (underlined) general one in each list. The first word on List 1 is done for you.

List 1

general word: After dinner, we ate some <u>dessert</u>.

specific word or phrase: _coconut cake_____

_banana pudding_____

_chocolate chip cookies_____

_brownies_____

List 2

general word: Kenny was my <u>buddy</u>.

specific word or phrase: _____

_____

_____

_____

List 3

general word: I need some <u>rest</u>.

specific word or phrase: _____

_____

_____

_____

Exercise 5 **Practice: Identifying Sentences That Are Too General**

Below are lists of sentences. Put an *X* by one sentence in each group that is general and vague.

1. a. _____ I thrive on excitement.

 b. _____ I like violent movies.

 c. _____ I can't stay home alone on the weekends.

2. a. _____ Jen's algebra teacher is helpful.

 b. _____ Jen's algebra teacher meets with students individually after class to clarify assignments.

 c. _____ Jen's algebra teacher continually updates a class Web site where students can find explanations and extra practice.

3. a. _____ At the free concert, the crowd cried for an encore.

 b. _____ Everyone had a nice time at the free concert.

 c. _____ Everyone clapped their hands and danced at the free concert.

Using Sense Words in Your Descriptions

One way to make your description specific and vivid is to *use sense words.* As you plan a description, ask yourself,

What does it **look** like?
What does it **sound** like?
What does it **smell** like?
What does it **taste** like?
What does it **feel** like?

The sense details can make the description vivid. Try to include details about the five senses in your descriptions. Often you can brainstorm sense details more easily if you focus on specific details that relate to each sense.

Exercise 6   **Collaborate: Brainstorming Sense Details for a Descriptive Paragraph**

Collaborate

Review the Info Box. Then, with a partner or a group, brainstorm the topic ideas for a paragraph by listing at least six questions and answers that could help you find sense details. Be prepared to read your completed exercise to another group or to the class.

INFO BOX   Devising Sense Details

For the sense of	think about
sight	colors, light and dark, shadows, or brightness
hearing	noise, silence, or the kinds of sounds you hear
smell	fragrance, odors, scents, aromas, or perfume
taste	bitter, sour, sweet, or compare the taste of one thing to another
touch	the feel of things: texture, hardness, softness, roughness, smoothness

1. topic: The closet was a mess.
Brainstorm questions and answers:

Q: _____

Q: _____

Q: _____

Q: _____

Q: _____

Q: _____

2. topic: The energy drink was disgusting.
Brainstorm questions and answers:

Q: _____

Q: _____

Q: _____

Q: _____

Q: _____

Q: _____

MyWritingLab™ **Exercise 7** **Practice: Writing Sense Words**

Write sense descriptions for the items below.

1. Write four words or phrases to describe the texture of sand on a beach:

_____

_____

2. Write four words or phrases to describe what a kitten looks like:

_____

_____

3. Write four words or phrases to describe the sounds of a garbage truck collecting your garbage:

_____

_____

WRITING THE DESCRIPTIVE PARAGRAPH IN STEPS

② Prewrite to generate a descriptive paragraph topic that supports a dominant impression.

PREWRITING **DESCRIPTION**

Writing a descriptive paragraph begins with thinking on paper, looking for specific details and sense descriptions. You can think by brainstorming, freewriting, or writing in a journal. For example, you might decide to write about the contents of someone's garage. Brainstorming might lead you to something like the following list of ideas.

Brainstorming a List for a Descriptive Paragraph

- my husband
- Bradley's motorcycle
- cycle always in pieces
- his tools for the cycle, yard work, home repairs
- paint cans
- bulletin board with photos
- his little plastic containers of nails, screws
- dusty shelves on walls
- oil stains and smells on the floor
- Bradley's work bench
- musty smell of Bradley's boxes of junk on the floor
- noise of engine running
- bags of fertilizer
- garbage can smells
- gasoline smells
- Bradley's camping gear, a tent
- my collection of hand-painted ceramic bowls doesn't fit

The Dominant Impression

When you think you have enough details, you can begin to think about focusing them. Look over these details and consider where they are taking you.

If you were to look at the list above, you might identify ideas that keep appearing in the details:

- my husband
- Bradley's motorcycle
- cycle always in pieces
- his tools for the cycle, yard work, and home repairs
- bulletin board with photos
- little plastic containers of nails, screws
- dusty shelves on walls
- oil stains and smells on the floor
- Bradley's work bench
- musty smell of Bradley's boxes of junk on the floor
- noise of engine running
- bags of fertilizer
- garbage can smells
- gasoline smells
- Bradley's camping gear, a tent

Reading over this list, you realize that all the items and details connect to Bradley. The cycle, work bench, tools, and camping gear reflect his hobbies and interests. The garbage can and tools may relate to his chores. Therefore, the garage seems to be Bradley's territory. This idea is the **dominant impression**, or the main point of the description. In a descriptive paragraph, the dominant impression is the topic sentence. For example, the topic sentence could be:

The garage is my husband's territory.

Once you have a dominant impression, you are ready to add more ideas to explain and support it. You should try to make the added details specific by using sense description where appropriate.

| Exercise 8 | **Practice: Adding Details to a Dominant Impression** |

MyWritingLab™

Following are sentences that could be used as a dominant impression in a descriptive paragraph. Some details to explain and support the dominant impression are already given. Add more details.

1. **dominant impression:**   The bodyguard looked intimidating.

    details: a. He was over six feet tall. _____

    b. He weighed about 250 pounds. _____

    c. _____

    d. _____

    e. _____

2. **dominant impression:**   My toddler enjoyed the wrapping paper more than the gift inside it.

    details: a. _____

    b. _____

    c. He concentrated on the bright paper. _____

    d. _____

    e. _____

MyWritingLab™   Exercise 9   **Practice: Creating a Dominant Impression from a List of Details**

Following are lists of details. For each list, write one sentence that could be used as the dominant impression created by the details.

1. **dominant impression:** _____

         _____

    details: Clarice's hair was tangled. The hair on the back of her head was flat.

               She was wearing rumpled pajamas.

               Her eyes were half-closed.

               She was barefoot.

               She walked hesitantly.

2. **dominant impression:** _____

         _____

    details: The salespeople stared from behind the counters.

               They did not make eye contact with each other.

               They avoided looking at the shoppers browsing through the departments.

               When they made a sale, the clerks spoke without any emotion.

               After they completed the transaction, they stared into space again.

3. **dominant impression:** _____

         _____

    details: My five-year-old son David begins to jump when he sees an ice cream cone in my hand.

               He grabs it from me, crying, "Yum!"

               First, he licks it from the top, pushing the soft ice cream out of the sides of the cone.

               To get the last drops of ice cream out of the cone, he turns the cone upside down.

               He licks the inside of the cone with gusto.

               Finally, he crushes the cone, eats it, and grins.

Collaborate

PLANNING   **DESCRIPTION**

The sentence you created as the dominant impression can be the topic sentence for your outline. Beneath the topic sentence, list the details you have collected. Once you have this rough list, check the details by asking:

Do all the details relate to the topic sentence?
Are the details in logical order?

Following are the topic sentence and list of details for the paragraph describing the contents of the garage. The details that are crossed out don't "fit" the topic sentence.

topic sentence: The garage is my husband's territory.

- my husband
- Bradley's motorcycle
- cycle always in pieces
- his tools for the cycle, yard work, home repairs
- paint cans
- bulletin board with photos
- his little plastic containers of nails, screws
- dusty shelves on walls
- oil stains and smells on the floor
- Bradley's work bench
- musty smell of Bradley's boxes of junk on the floor
- ~~noise of engine running~~
- bags of fertilizer
- garbage can smells
- gasoline smells
- Bradley's camping gear, a tent
- ~~my collection of hand-painted ceramic bowls doesn't fit~~

Notice what is crossed out. The detail about the noise of the engine running doesn't fit because the paragraph is about the contents of the garage, not what happens in the garage. In addition, the detail about the wife's collection of ceramic bowls is not related to the topic sentence because the topic sentence focuses on the garage as Bradley's place. It is about his interests and responsibilities.

Remember that as you write and revise, you may decide to eliminate other ideas, to reinsert ideas you once rejected, or even to add new ideas. Changing your mind is a natural part of revising.

Once you have decided upon your best list of details, check their order. Remember, when you write a description, you are trying to make the reader *see*. It will be easier for the reader to imagine what you see if you put your description in a simple, logical order. You might want to put descriptions in order by **time sequence** (first to last), by **spatial position** (top to bottom, or right to left), or by **similar types** (for example, all about the flowers, then all about the trees in a park).

If you are describing a house, for instance, you may want to start with the outside of the house and then describe the inside. You do not want the details to shift back and forth, from outside to inside and back to outside. If you are describing a person, you might want to group all the details about his face before you describe his body. You might describe a meal from first course to dessert.

Look again at the details describing the garage. It is logical to use these categories: from the bare floor, to the covered floor, and to the walls. Now look at the following outline and notice how this order works.

Outline for a Descriptive Paragraph

topic sentence	The garage is my husband's territory.
details	The area of bare floor is covered in oil stains.
bare floor	It smells like gasoline.
	This area is very small.
	Most of the garage floor is filled.
	Boxes of Bradley's junk give off a musty odor.
	Bradley's work bench is pushed into one corner.
covered floor	Bradley's camping gear and a tent fill another corner.
	His motorcycle, usually in pieces, fills one third of the space.
	The garbage can smells of rotting food.
	The back and side walls are covered with dusty metal shelves.
	They contain tools for cycle repair, yard work, and home repair.
walls	Old, crusty paint cans are on the shelves.
	Bags of fertilizer are on the shelves.
	Dozens of small plastic containers of nails and screws are there.
	One wall has a bulletin board with photos.

You probably noticed that the outline has more details than the original list. These details help to make the descriptions more specific. You can add them to the outline and to the drafts of your paragraph.

Once you have a list of details focused on a topic sentence and arranged in some logical order, you can begin writing a draft of your descriptive paragraph.

MyWritingLab™   **Exercise 10**   **Practice: Finding Details That Do Not Relate**

Survey the following lists. Each includes a topic sentence and several details. In each list, cross out the details that do not relate to the topic sentence.

1. **topic sentence:** At my apartment building, the laundry facilities are inadequate and unreliable.

   details: Twenty apartments share one washer and one dryer.

   Whenever I try to do laundry, the machines are full of someone else's clothes.

   The washer is medium-sized, so I have to pay for two loads instead of one.

   The washer breaks down at least once a week.

   The dryer is inefficient.

   The dryer tends to spin my sheets or clothes into a long, rope-like tangle.

   I never remember to bring enough money to the laundry room.

   The laundry room shares a little hut with the mail boxes.

2. topic sentence: My academic advisor is a good listener.

  details: He is genuinely interested in what I have to say.

              He likes to sit in a quiet place.

              He never interrupts me with his opinions or criticism.

              He maintains eye contact.

              After I finish talking, he asks questions that show he has been listening carefully.

              He can keep a secret.

3. topic sentence: The Bread Basket is a great restaurant for college students.

  details: It has a wide choice of soups, salads, sandwiches, fresh bread, and bagels.

              A big menu is posted on one wall.

              It also offers the cookies, muffins, and brownies that students love.

              For those who need to wake up or stay awake, the coffee is excellent.

              The prices are reasonable.

              The parking lot is usually overcrowded.

              Many students come to eat and socialize indoors or on the patio.

              Others place their laptops on the wide tables and booths indoors, do their homework, and study in peace.

              No one pushes out the students who linger over their homework or conversation.

Exercise 11   **Practice: Putting Details in Order**   MyWritingLab™

Following are lists that start with a topic sentence. The details under each topic sentence are not in the right order. Put the details in logical order by labeling them, with 1 being the first detail, 2 the second, and so forth.

1. topic sentence: My job interview at a local restaurant confused me. (Arrange the details in time order.)

  details: _____ After fifteen minutes of waiting, the manager led me to a small table near the kitchen.

          _____ When I came in, a hostess told me to wait because the manager was busy.

          _____ Waiting, I felt lost in a crowd of customers in line for tables.

          _____ At the table, I struggled to hear the manager's words over the noise from the kitchen.

          _____ I did my best to answer the manager's questions, but I couldn't hear half of what she was saying.

2. topic sentence: The exterior of the candy store was designed to bring out the love of candy in all children and adults. (Arrange the details from the top of the store to the bottom.)

details: _____ Hanging from the bottom of the sign, a line of brightly lighted gingerbread men danced.

_____ On either side of the store's entrance, huge windows displayed enormous piles of dark chocolate, milk chocolate, and white chocolate bonbons.

_____ The strangest part of the store was the roof, topped by a giant candy cane.

_____ Directly below the roof, huge pink gumdrops spelled out the words "Candy Haven" on a brightly colored sign.

_____ Even the welcome mat at the store's entrance looked like a line of red and black licorice sticks.

3. topic sentence: As soon as Michelle and Liam saw the house, they dreamed of owning it. (Arrange the details from outside to inside.)

details: _____ A stone walkway began at the front gate.

_____ The walkway, bordered by brightly colored flowers, led to the front door.

_____ The small brick home was set back from the street.

_____ Inside the front door, a small tiled hall contained a framed mirror, an antique wooden table, and a dark green coat rack.

_____ The living room, which followed the hall, had a brick fireplace, soft carpet, and large windows facing the sun.

MyWritingLab™ **Exercise 12** **Practice: Creating Details Using a Logical Order**

The following lists include a topic sentence and indicate a required order for the details. Write five sentences of details in the required order.

1. topic sentence: The first class meeting with my math instructor was a little frightening. (Describe the meeting from beginning to end.)

a. _____

b. _____

c. _____

d. _____

e. _____

2. topic sentence: The Student Center was noisy and bright.
(Describe the noise; then describe the lighting.)

a. _____

b. _____

c. _____

d. _____

e. _____

3. topic sentence: As my sister ran her first marathon, her expression changed.
(Describe the changes from beginning to end.)

a. _____

b. _____

c. _____

d. _____

e. _____

DRAFTING AND REVISING   DESCRIPTION

③ Write a descriptive paragraph that uses specific details and transitions effectively.

After you have an outline, the next step is creating a first rough draft of the paragraph. Your goal is simply to put your ideas in paragraph form so that you can see how they look and you can check them to see what needs to be improved.

The first draft of a paragraph will not be perfect. If it were perfect, it wouldn't be a first draft. Once you have the first draft, check it using the following list.

Checklist for Revising a Descriptive Paragraph

✓   Are there enough details?

✓   Are the details specific?

✓   Do the details use sense words?

✓   Are the details in order?

✓   Is there a dominant impression?

✓   Do the details connect to the dominant impression?

✓   Have I made my point?

A common problem in writing description is creating a fuzzy, vague description. Take a look at the following fuzzy description:

The soccer fans were rowdy and excited. They shouted when their team scored. Some people jumped up. The fans showed their support by cheering and stomping. They were enjoying every minute of the game.

The description could be revised so that it is more specific and vivid:

> The soccer fans were rowdy and excited. When their team scored, they yelled, "Way to go!" or "Stomp 'em! Crush 'em!" until they were hoarse. Three fans, wearing the team colors of blue and white on their shirts, shorts, and socks, jumped up, spilling their drinks on the teenagers seated below them. During timeouts, the fans chanted rhythmically, and throughout the game they stomped their feet in a steady beat against the wooden bleachers. As people chanted, whooped, and woofed, they turned to grin at each other and thrust their clenched fists into the air.

The vivid description meets the requirements of the checklist. It has sufficient specific details. The details use sense words to describe what the fans looked and sounded like. The details also support a dominant impression of rowdy, excited fans. The vivid, specific details make the point.

As you revise the drafts of your essay, you will notice how the right details, sense words, and a focus on the dominant impression (the topic sentence) improve your description.

MyWritingLab™   Exercise 13   **Practice: Revising a Paragraph, Finding Irrelevant Sentences**

Following are two descriptive paragraphs. In each, there are sentences that are irrelevant, meaning they do not have anything to do with the first sentence, the topic sentence. Cross out the irrelevant sentences in the paragraphs below.

1. The heavy rain made driving difficult. The downpour was so strong that drivers could barely see. It was a typical autumn storm. The huge drops, falling fast and hard, covered the cars' windshields. Drivers could barely make out the shapes of the cars and trucks around them. Surrounded by a curtain of water, the drivers inched their way down the road. A few impatient drivers created a hazard by racing past the cautious ones, causing dangerous waves of water. Anyone trying to get out of a parked car would be soaked in seconds. Within minutes, the pounding rain had left four or five inches of water on the road. Now the sound of drivers testing their brakes joined the noise of the downpour.

2. My six-month-old nephew has the face of an angel. His soft, fuzzy hair barely covers his scalp, but it looks like a halo. I like to touch the strands of his hair because it is so different from mine. Benjamin's eyes are large and round; they radiate innocence and joy. They always seem to show his surprise at the wonderful world he has entered. He has a perfect little snub nose. Finally, his

small mouth is exactly like the mouths of the angels shown on valentines and

Christmas cards. When he smiles, Benjamin looks a little more mischievous than

an angel.

Exercise 14   **Practice: Revising a Paragraph for More Specific Details**   MyWritingLab™

In the following paragraphs, the details that are underlined are not specific.
Change the underlined sentences to more specific descriptions. Write the
changes in the lines below each paragraph.

1. The eccentric millionaire dressed in an odd combination of clothing. <u>On

his head was a weird hat</u>. He wore an expensive silk tie around his neck, but his

shirt was made of faded cotton with a flower print. The sleeves were rolled up,

and the ragged shirttails hung over a pair of expensive, neatly pressed khakis. He

wore white socks with a dark blue band around the top. <u>His shoes, however, did

not match the socks</u>.

revisions: _____

_____

2. The plane taking us to Hayden Springs represented air travel at its worst.

The roof of the aircraft was low, threatening each entering passenger with decapi-

tation. After one step inside, passengers wanted to leave. <u>The interior of the plane

smelled awful</u>. The storage bins held only tiny bags or boxes, and the doors on the

bins would not close. The hard, narrow seats imprisoned the passengers. <u>There

was hardly any leg room</u>. In addition, those with window seats could barely see

through the filthy window.

revisions: _____

_____

Transitions

As you revise your descriptive paragraph, you may notice places in the paragraph that seem choppy or abrupt. That is, one sentence may end, and
another may start, but the two sentences don't seem to be connected.
Reading your paragraph aloud, you may sense that it is not very smooth.

You can make the writing smoother and make the content clearer by
using **transitions**, which are words or phrases that link one idea to another
idea. They tell the reader what he or she has just read and what is coming next.
Below are some transitions you may want to use in writing a description.

> **INFO BOX** Transitions for a Descriptive Paragraph
>
> **To show ideas brought together:**
>
> | | | |
> |---|---|---|
> | and also | in addition | next |
>
> **To show a contrast:**
>
> | | | | |
> |---|---|---|---|
> | although | however | on the contrary | unlike |
> | but | in contrast | on the other hand | yet |
>
> **To show a similarity:**
>
> | | | | |
> |---|---|---|---|
> | all | each | like | similarly |
> | both | | | |
>
> **To show a time sequence:**
>
> | | | | |
> |---|---|---|---|
> | after | first | next | then |
> | always | second (etc.) | often | when |
> | before | meanwhile | soon | while |
>
> **To show a position in space:**
>
> | | | | |
> |---|---|---|---|
> | above | between | in front of | over |
> | ahead of | beneath | inside | there |
> | alongside | beyond | near | toward |
> | among | by | nearby | under |
> | around | close | next to | up |
> | away | down | on | underneath |
> | below | far | on top of | where |
> | beside | here | outside | |

There are many other transitions you can use, depending on what you need to link your ideas. Take a look at a draft of the description paragraph of a garage. Compare it to the outline on page 64. A sentence of details has been added to the end of the paragraph; it gives specific details about another of Bradley's interests. You will also notice that more sense details have been added. Transitions have been added, too. Pay particular attention to the transitions in this draft.

Revised Draft of a Descriptive Paragraph

(Note: Editing and proofreading are still necessary.)

transition added	The garage is my husband Bradley's territory. <u>Near</u> the
added details	entrance to the garage is small <u>area of bare floor</u>. This area is covered in oil stains and smells like gasoline. <u>Next to</u> this patch
transition added	of open floor is the <u>long, cluttered part of the floor</u>. <u>On one side</u>,
details, transition added	boxes of Bradley's sweatshirts, rags, boots, and a motorcycle manual give off a musty odor. Bradley's work bench is pushed
transition added	into one corner. <u>In front of</u> it is Bradley's motorcycle. It is usually in pieces. The cycle fills one third of the space in the garage.
transition added	Pushed <u>close to</u> the bench and the cycle, the garbage can smells of roting food. Dusty metal shelves cover the back and side walls. The
transition added	shelves <u>next to</u> the motorcycle contain tools for motorcycle repair and

details	<u>a few items</u> for home repair and yard work. <u>On the opposite wall</u>,
transition added	old, crusty paint cans <u>share space with</u> dozens of small plastic
details added	container of nails and screws. <u>Heavy</u> bags of <u>lawn</u> fertilizer <u>cause</u> <u>the shelves of the back wall</u> to sag. Sitting on the <u>top shelf</u> of this
details	wall, a <u>cork</u> board is covered with photographs. <u>Bradley's camping</u>
sentence of detail added	<u>gear and a small tent are stuffed in to the lower shelves of the back</u> <u>wall</u>. This garage gives a portrait of my husband as a man who maintains the house and the yard and who loves the out doors.

Exercise 15   **Practice: Recognizing Transitions**   MyWritingLab™

Underline the transitions in the paragraph below.

My college roommate and I found an apartment in a perfect location. Nearby was

a bus stop where we could catch the regularly scheduled buses to campus. A huge

supermarket a block away from our apartment met our needs for groceries and

snacks; next to it were a pizza shop, a drug store, and an Asian restaurant. About a

mile beyond our apartment, a huge public park attracted us. It offered jogging trails, a

bike path, a small lake, and acres of huge green trees. Here we could exercise, study,

and relax. In addition, we could meet new people who might soon become friends.

EDITING AND PROOFREADING   DESCRIPTION

After you have revised your description, the next step is editing. At this point, you can check grammatical structures, sentence length and structure, word forms, punctuation, and spelling. Once you have revised your draft, you can check it using the following list.

Checklist for Editing a Descriptive Paragraph

✓ Are the verb forms correct and consistent?

✓ Are other grammatical structures correct?

✓ Can any sentences be combined?

✓ Did you correctly punctuate?

✓ Is everything spelled correctly?

Exercise 16   **Practice: Combining Sentences and Using Transitions**   MyWritingLab™

The following description has some choppy sentences that could be combined to create a smoother paragraph. Combine each pair of underlined sentences by revising them in the space above each pair and using appropriate transitions.

At Thanksgiving, my Uncle Chris, the worst cook in the world, insists on cooking dinner for victims who cannot say "no." His entire family gathers for a meal that always begins with a fruit cocktail. He serves tiny glass bowls with chunks of pears and peaches, red grapes, and one or two red cherries. <u>All the fruit has come straight out of a can. It is swimming in the sugary sweet liquid that also came from the can</u>. Next is the main course. The side dishes are always the same. We guests have a choice of vegetables. <u>We can eat tough green beans. They come from a can</u>. Corn is another choice. <u>It is not on the cob</u>. It is corn kernels from a freezer bag. Uncle Chris also serves sweet potatoes. <u>These potatoes have been baked. They have not been baked long enough</u>. Nothing is worse than trying to put a fork into a potato that is hard in the middle. The turkey arrives last. Unfortunately, Uncle Chris tends to burn the bird. <u>The turkey may not be perfect. It is edible</u>. All that is left is dessert, and even Uncle Chris can't spoil an apple pie from the local bakery. My uncle is pleased that the pie is a hit. Yet he can't understand why, after a large holiday meal, all his guests have such a huge appetite for dessert.

MyWritingLab™ | Exercise 17 | **Proofreading to Prepare the Final Version**

The following descriptive paragraph has the kinds of errors it is easy to overlook when you write the final version of an assignment. Correct the errors, writing above the lines. There are twelve errors in the paragraph.

At one shop in the mall, I feel like an intruder. The store is a clothing store, and it offers clothes for people in my age group. However, I do not feel comftable in the store. The windows draw me in with glimpses of attractive jeans, shirts, sweater, and jackets. Unfortunately, when I take a few steps inside the store, I sense that I do not belong. The store is unnaturaly quiet; no one seems to be shopping. In addition, The racks of clothing are in perfect order. Not a hanger is out of place. The color-coded shirts and sweaters on the shelves are stacked in immaculate piles. On look at the price of a sweater tells me I cant afford the style, and fashion in this place. I leave before 1 of the salespeople approach me and reconizes me as to broke, two sloppy, or too unfashionable for this establishment.

Finally, proofread your writing. Read every word carefully to be sure that what you've written makes sense and is error free.

Final Version of a Descriptive Paragraph

(Note: Changes from the previous draft are underlined.)

the article *a* is added ——————

verb consistency—present time ——

comma added ——————————

spelling corrected: *rotting* ——

need plural for *containers* ——

into one word ——————————

wording improved ——————————

The garage is my husband Bradley's territory. Near the entrance to the garage is <u>a</u> small area of bare floor. This area is covered in oil stains and smells like gasoline. Next to this patch of open floor <u>is</u> the long, cluttered part of the floor. On one side, boxes of Bradley's sweatshirts, rags, boots, and motorcycle manuals give off a musty odor. Bradley's work bench is pushed into one corner. In front of it is Bradley's motorcycle<u>,</u> which is usually in pieces. The cycle fills one third of the space in the garage. Pushed close to the bench and the cycle, the garbage can smells of <u>rotting</u> food. Dusty metal shelves cover the back and side walls. The shelves next to the motorcycle contain tools for motorcycle repair and a few items for home repair and yard work. On the opposite wall, old crusty paint cans share space with dozens of small plastic <u>containers</u> of nails and screws. Heavy bags of lawn fertilizer cause the shelves of the back wall to sag. Sitting on the top shelf of this wall, a cork board is covered with photographs. Bradley's camping gear and a small tent are stuffed <u>into</u> the lower shelves of the back wall. This garage <u>is a true reflection</u> gives a portrait of my husband, a man who maintains the house and the yard and who loves the outdoors.

For your information: A sample descriptive essay based on the same topic and following the same writing steps can be found in Chapter 12.

Lines of Detail: A Walk-Through Assignment

Your assignment is to write a paragraph describing a popular place for socializing. Follow these steps:

Step 1: To begin, freewrite about a place where people socialize online. For example, you could write about a place where people share stories, exchange pictures, or video chat.

Step 2: Read your freewriting. Underline all the words, phrases, and sentences of description.

Step 3: List everything you underlined, grouping the ideas in some order. Maybe the details can be listed from what the site looks like, or maybe they can be put into categories such as, profile, photos, friends, and comments.

Step 4: After you've surveyed the list, write a sentence about the dominant impression of the details.

Step 5: Using the dominant impression as your topic sentence, write an outline. Add specific details where you need them. Concentrate on details that appeal to the senses.

Step 6: Write a first draft of your paragraph. Be sure to check the order of your details. Combine short sentences and add transitions.

Step 7: Revise your first draft version to be sure you have sufficient sensory details arranged in a logical sequence.

Step 8: Edit your latest draft to improve style and check for serious errors or omissions.

Step 9: Prepare a final version and proofread carefully to spot and correct any careless errors in spelling, punctuation, format, and typing.

Topics for Writing a Descriptive Paragraph

When you write on any of the following topics, work through the stages of the writing process in preparing your descriptive paragraph. Be sure that your paragraph is based on a dominant impression, and put the dominant impression into your topic sentence.

MyWritingLab™

1. Write a paragraph that describes one of the items below:

your college library	a professor or instructor
your favorite meal	an eccentric friend
a tranquil retreat	a messy car
the bookstore	an irritating relative
a vacation spot	a person who changed your life
your favorite classroom	an activity that energizes you

MyWritingLab™

2. Describe a place that creates one of these impressions:

peace	tension	warmth
cheerfulness	danger	safety

MyWritingLab™

3. Describe a person who conveys one of these impressions:

confidence	style	shyness
intelligence	nervousness	strength

MyWritingLab™

4. Visit the Web site of your local newspaper and find a photograph of a local event involving two or more individuals. Describe where the people are, what the event is, what the people are doing, what their facial expressions suggest, and anything you find unique about the setting. You may have to look through the archives of the Web site until you find a photograph that prompts such details. Be sure your details relate to a dominant impression of the scene, and be sure to select a photograph that you find interesting or unique. Attach the photograph to the completed paragraph.

Collaborate

5. Interview a partner so that you and your partner can gather details and then write a description paragraph with the title, "My Ideal Room."

First, prepare a list of at least six questions to ask your partner. Write down the answers your partner gives and use those answers to form more questions. For example, if your partner says her ideal room would be a game room, ask her what games she'd like to have in it. If your partner says his ideal room would be a workshop, ask him what kind of workshop.

When you've finished the interview, switch roles. Let your partner interview you. Feel free to add more questions or to follow up on previous ones.

Give your partner his or her interview responses. Take your own responses and use them as the basis for gathering as many details as you can on your perfect room. Then go on to the outline, draft, and final version of your paragraph. Be prepared to read your completed paragraph to your partner.

6. Study the photograph below. Then write a paragraph that describes and explains the dominant impression of this scene.

MyWritingLab™

Topics for Critical Thinking and Writing

1. Have you ever heard the old saying, "First impressions are lasting ones"? Do you agree with that statement? If so, describe a person or place that, on further acquaintance, proved to be very similar to your first impressions. If you do not accept the truth of the saying, describe a person or place that proved to be very different from your first assessment.

MyWritingLab™

2. Imagine that one of your relatives from another state or country planned to visit you for the first time and wanted to see a little bit of your town. Make a list of some of your town's more memorable natural attractions, buildings, or landmarks. If your visitor had time to see only one place, which one would you choose? Describe your choice by using as many sense details as possible.

MyWritingLab™

Note: Additional writing options suitable for description-related assignments can be found in the "Readings for Writers" appendix of this book.

Jumping In

*What do you think happened just before this dramatic scene? Can you imagine what led to the tense atmosphere? There must be a story behind this picture, and if you write the story, you will be writing a **narrative** paragraph.*

Learning Objectives

In this chapter, you will learn how to:

1. Recognize that a narrative paragraph needs a point.
2. Prewrite to generate a narrative paragraph topic.
3. Write a narrative paragraph that uses details and transitions effectively.

WHAT IS NARRATION?

Narration means telling a story. Everybody tells stories; some people are better storytellers than others. When you write a **narrative** paragraph, you can tell a story about something that happened to you or to someone else, or about something that you saw or read.

A narrative, like a description, relies on specific details, but it is also different from a description because it covers events in a time sequence. While a description can be about a person, a place, or an object, a narrative is always about happenings: events, actions, incidents.

Interesting narratives do more than just tell what happened. They help the reader become involved in the story by providing vivid details. These details come from your memory, your observation, or your reading. Using good details, you don't just tell the story; you *show* it.

Give the Narrative a Point

1 Recognize that a narrative paragraph needs a point.

We all know people who tell long stories that seem to lead nowhere. These people talk on and on; they recite an endless list of activities and soon become boring. Their narratives have no point.

The difficult part of writing a narrative is making sure that it has a point. That point will be included in the topic sentence. The point of a narrative is the meaning of the incident or incidents you are writing about. To get to the point of your narrative, ask yourself questions like these:

What did I learn?
What is the meaning of this story?
What is my attitude toward what happened?
Did it change me?
What emotion did it make me feel?
Was the experience a good example of something (such as unfairness, kindness, generosity, or some other quality)?

The answers to such questions can lead you to a point. An effective topic sentence for a narrative is

not this: I'm going to tell you about the time I flunked my driving test. (This is an announcement; it does not make a point.)

but this: When I failed my driving test, I learned not to be overconfident.

not this: Yesterday I was late for my favorite class. (This identifies the incident but does not make a point. It is also too narrow to be a good topic sentence.)

but this: When I walked into my favorite class twenty minutes late, I was distraught and embarrassed.

The topic sentence, stating the point of your narrative paragraph, can be placed in the beginning, middle, or end of the paragraph. You may want to start your story with the point so that the reader knows exactly where your story is headed, or you may want to conclude your story by leaving the point until last. Sometimes the point can even fit smoothly into the middle of your paragraph.

Consider the narrative paragraphs below. The topic sentences are in various places.

Topic Sentence at the Beginning

When I was five, I learned how serious it is to tell a lie. One afternoon, my seven-year-old friend Tina asked me if I wanted to walk down the block to play ball in an empty lot. When I asked my mother, she said I couldn't go because it was too near dinner time. I don't know why I lied, but when Tina asked me if my mother had said yes, I nodded my head in a lie. I wanted to go play, and I did. Yet as I played in the dusty lot, a dull buzz of guilt or fear distracted me. As soon as I got home, my mother confronted me. She asked me whether I had gone to the sandlot and whether I had lied to Tina about getting permission. This time, I told the truth. Something about my mother's tone of voice made me feel ashamed. I had let her down.

Topic Sentence in the Middle

When I was little, I was afraid of diving into water. I thought I would go down and never come back up. Then one day, my father took me to a pool where we swam and fooled around, but he never forced me to try a dive. After about an hour of playing, I walked round and round the edge of the pool, trying to get the courage to dive in. Finally, I did it. <u>When I made that first dive, I felt blissful because I had done something I had been afraid to do.</u> As I came to the surface, I wiped the water from my eyes and looked around. The sun seemed more dazzling, and the water sparkled. Best of all, I saw my father looking at me with a smile. "You did it," he said. "Good for you! I'm proud of you."

Topic Sentence at the End

It seemed like I'd been in love with Reeza for years. Unfortunately, Reeza was always in love with someone else. Finally, she broke up with her boyfriend Nelson. I saw my chance. I asked Reeza out. After dinner, we talked and talked. Reeza told me all about her hopes and dreams. She told me about her family and her job, and I felt very close to her. We talked late into the night. When she left, Reeza kissed me. "Thanks for listening," she said. "You're like a brother to me." <u>Reeza meant to be kind, but she shattered my hopes and dreams.</u>

MyWritingLab™   **Exercise 1**   **Practice: Finding the Topic Sentence in a Narrative Paragraph**

Underline the topic sentence in each narrative paragraph below.

Paragraph 1

After I finished high school, I wanted to have some fun. I was sick of studying and worrying about test scores. I spent the summer going to the beach, surfing, and socializing with my friends. I kept my part-time job at a discount store and lived at my parents' house so that I could afford to live a carefree life. Summer was great, and the days went by quickly. Soon it was fall, and my friends became too busy for fun. They found full-time work, started college, or combined work and school. On a rainy day in October, I sat alone on a sand dune. I realized that it was time for me to grow up. My friends had moved on, and here I was, feeling anxious about my future. I did not want to become known as the oldest surfer in town. Soon after, I started looking for a full-time job. Then I spoke with a counselor at a local community college. She told me about early registration for the next term. We also discussed careers.

Paragraph 2

Hurting my knees gave me a small hint of what it means to be disabled or elderly. In a silly accident, I slipped on the wet pavement near my house. I went flying onto my hands and knees. My knees were bloody, but I picked myself up and kept walking. At first, all that concerned me was the blood on my knees. People might see me and wonder if I had been mugged, I thought. Later, I felt an ache in my shoulders. Then my knees began to hurt whenever I sat or bent down. When I got out of bed the next morning, the pain was worse. I avoided bending over or picking up heavy bags. Walking was unpleasant. The discomfort was not great, but it was there. I had never had to think about whether a simple physical movement like kneeling or bending over was worth the effort or pain it might bring. I felt overcautious, constricted, and conscious of my weakness.

Exercise 2   **Practice: Writing the Missing Topic Sentences in Narrative Paragraphs**   MyWritingLab™

Following are two paragraphs. If the paragraph already has a topic sentence, write it in the lines provided. If it does not have a topic sentence, create one. (Two of the paragraphs have no topic sentence.)

Paragraph 1

I have never felt as much shame as the shame I felt after my one involvement in cheating. At eighteen, I was facing pressures I had never faced before. I was taking a few college courses, working, and helping my mom out at home. I really wanted to succeed, but felt so pressured at work and at home, I didn't put the time and energy I needed to at school. One day my English instructor told me that my grades were quite low and if I didn't score high on my last essay, I would have to repeat the course. I was furious. So, I went to the library and started writing away. However, nothing sounded A-like. I found a book on the topic and copied a few sentences from the book. I typed up the paper, and handed it in. The next class period Ms. Hubbs asked to see me after class. I knew I was in trouble. She asked if I had written everything in my paper. I panicked and told her that I did. She asked me again. I told her I did write everything in my paper. Then, she showed me the exact book I had used in the library. She told me that copying from a book is plagiarism. Next, she told me I would fail the paper and the course. I was so upset with myself.

If the paragraph already has a topic sentence, write it here. If it does not have a

topic sentence, create one. _____

_____

_____

Paragraph 2

My seventh birthday was here, and I was sure that I wouldn't celebrate it much. My father was living in a distant state, and he had stopped sending child support checks for me and my sisters several months earlier. At school, I thought of better birthdays when my folks had been together and money had not been such a problem. As I walked slowly home from school, I told myself, "A cake will be fine." However, I kept hoping that at least one small gift would be waiting for me. My little sisters, smiling, opened the door. My mother, trying to smile, stood by the kitchen table. On it were six chocolate cupcakes, each with a blue candle in the chocolate icing. "So this is it," I thought. I loved my mother and sisters, and they loved me. However, this wasn't much of a birthday celebration for a seven-year-old. Suddenly my four-year-old sister Rosalee began to jump up. "Look under the table!" she cried. There was a big box beneath the table. I picked it up, and it felt heavy, with the weight in it shifting from side to side. Inside the box was the most beautiful orange and white kitten I had ever seen.

If the paragraph already has a topic sentence, write it here. if it does not have a

topic sentence, create one. _____

_____

_____

Hints for Writing a Narrative Paragraph

Everyone tells stories, but some people tell stories better than others. When you write a story, be sure to

- Be clear.
- Be interesting.
- Stay in order.
- Pick a topic that is not too big.

1. Be clear. Put in all the information the reader needs in order to follow your story. Sometimes you need to explain the time or place or the relationships of the people in your story in order to make the story clear. Sometimes you need to explain how much time has elapsed between one action and another. This paragraph is not clear:

> I've never felt so stupid as I did on my first day of work. I was stocking the shelves when Mr. Cimino came up to me and said, "You're doing it wrong." Then he showed me how to do it. An hour later, he told me to call the produce supplier and check on the order for grapefruit. Well, I didn't know how to tell Mr. Cimino that I didn't know what phone to use or how to get an outside line. I also didn't know how to get the phone number of the produce supplier, or what the order for the grapefruit was supposed to be and when it was supposed to arrive. I felt really stupid asking these questions.

The narrative lacks some key information. Who is Mr. Cimino? Is he the boss? Is he a produce supervisor? And, more importantly, what kind of place is the writer's workplace? The reader knows the place has something to do with food, but is it a supermarket, a fruit market, or a warehouse?

2. Be interesting. A general narrative that does not give specific details can make even the greatest adventure sound a bit dull:

> I had a wonderful time on prom night. First, we went out to dinner. The meal was excellent. Then we went to the dance and saw all our friends. Everyone was dressed up great. We stayed until late. Then we went out to breakfast. After breakfast we watched the sun come up.

Good specific details are the difference between an interesting story and a dull one.

3. Stay in order. Put the details in a clear order so that the reader can follow your story. Usually, time order is the order you follow in narration. This narrative has a confusing order:

> My impatience cost me twenty dollars last week. There was an expensive pair of shoes I really wanted. I had wanted them for weeks. So, when payday came around, I went to the mall and checked the price on the shoes. I had been checking the price for weeks before. The shoes were expensive, but I really wanted them. On payday, a friend who works at the shoe store told me the shoes were about to go on sale. But I was impatient. I bought them at full price, and three days later, the shoes were marked down twenty dollars.

There's a better approach. Tell the story in the order it happened: first, I saw the expensive shoes and wanted them; second, I checked the price for several weeks; third, I got paid; fourth, on the same day, I checked the price again; fifth, my friend at the store told me the shoes were about to go on sale; sixth, I paid full price right away; seventh, three days later the shoes went on sale. A clear time sequence helps the reader follow your narrative.

4. **Pick a topic that is not too big.** If you try to write about too many events in a short space, you run the risk of being superficial. You cannot describe anything well if you cover too much. This paragraph covers too much:

> Starting my sophomore year at a new high school was a difficult experience. Because my family had just moved to town, I didn't know anybody at school. On the first day of school, I sat by myself at lunch. Finally, two students at another table started a conversation with me. I thought they were just feeling sorry for me. At the end of the first week, it seemed like the whole school was talking about exciting plans for the weekend. I spent Friday and Saturday night at home, doing all kinds of things to keep my mind off my loneliness. On Monday, people casually asked, "Have a good weekend?" I lied and said, "Of course."

This paragraph would be better if it discussed one shorter time period in greater depth and detail. It could cover the first day at school, or the first lunch at school, or the first Saturday night at home alone, when the writer was doing "all kinds of things" to keep from feeling lonely.

Using a Speaker's Exact Words in a Narrative

Some of the examples of narratives that you have already seen have included the exact words someone said. You may want to include part of a conversation in your narrative. To do so, you need to know how to punctuate speech.

A person's exact words get quotation marks around them. If you change the words, you do not use quotation marks.

exact words: "You're being silly," he told me.
not exact words: He told me that I was being silly.

exact words: My sister said, "I'd love to go to the party."
not exact words: My sister said she would love to go to the party.

There are a few other points to remember about punctuating a person's exact words. Once you've started quoting a person's exact words, periods and commas generally go inside the quotation marks. Here are two examples:

Richard said, "Nothing can be done."
"Be careful," my mother warned us.

When you introduce a person's exact words with phrases like *She said* or *The teacher told us*, put a comma before the quotation marks. Here are two examples:

She said, "You'd better watch out."
The teacher told us, "This will be a challenging class."

> If you are using a person's exact words and have other questions about punctuation, read about the use of quotation marks in Chapter 28 in the grammar section of this book.

② Prewrite to generate a narrative paragraph topic.

WRITING THE NARRATIVE PARAGRAPH IN STEPS

PREWRITING **NARRATION**

Finding something to write about can be the hardest part of writing a narrative paragraph because it is usually difficult to think of anything interesting or significant that you have experienced. By answering the following questions you can gather topics for your paragraph.

Collaborate

Exercise 3 **Collaborate: Questionnaire for Gathering Narrative Topics**

Answer the questions below and list details in the spaces provided. Then read your answers to a group. The members of the group should then ask you follow-up questions. Write your answers on the lines provided; the answers will add details to your list.

Finally, ask each member of your group to circle one topic or detail on your questionnaire that could be developed into a narrative paragraph. Discuss the suggestions. Repeat this process for each member of the group.

Narrative Questionnaire

1. Have you ever gotten lost (in a new town, on strange streets, in a mall, at a college, or elsewhere)? When? Write three details you remember about the occasion:

    a. _____

    b. _____

    c. _____

    Additional details, to be added after working with the group:

    _____

    _____

2. Have you ever had a pleasant surprise? Write three details about what happened before, during, and after:

    a. _____

    b. _____

    c. _____

    Additional details, to be added after working with the group:

    _____

    _____

3. Have you ever won anything (a game, a contest, a raffle, some other prize or competition?) Write three details about the experience:

    a. _____

    b. _____

    c. _____

Additional details, to be added after working with the group:

_____

_____

Freewriting for a Narrative Topic

One good way to discover something to write about is to freewrite. For example, if your instructor asks you to write a narrative paragraph about something that changed you, you might begin by freewriting.

Freewriting for a Narrative Paragraph

Topic: Something That Changed Me

Something that changed me. I don't know. What changed me? Lots of things happened to me, but I can't find one that changed me. Graduating from high school? Everybody will write about that, how boring, and anyway, what was the big deal? I haven't gotten married. No big change there. Divorce. My parents' divorce really changed the whole family. A big shock to me. I couldn't believe it was happening. I was really scared. Who would I live with? They were really calm when they told me. I've never been so scared. I was too young to understand. Kept thinking they'd just get back together. They didn't. Then I got a stepmother. The year of the divorce was a hard time for me. Kids suffer in divorce.

Narrowing and Selecting a Suitable Narrative Topic

After you freewrite, you can assess your writing, looking for words, phrases, or sentences that you could expand into a paragraph. The sample writing has several ideas for a narrative:

> high school graduation
> learning about my parents' divorce
> adjusting to a stepmother
> the year of my parents' divorce

Looking for a topic that is not too big, you could use:

> high school graduation
> learning about my parents' divorce

Since the freewriting has already called graduation a boring topic, the divorce seems to be a more attractive subject. In the freewriting, you already have some details related to the divorce; add to these details by brainstorming. Follow-up questions and answers might include the following:

How old were you when your parents got divorced?

I was seven years old when my mom and dad divorced.

Are you an only child?

My sister was ten.

Where did your parents tell you? Did they both tell you at the same time?

They told us at breakfast, in the kitchen. Both my folks were there. I was eating toast. I remember I couldn't eat it when they both started talking. I remember a piece of toast with one bite out of it.

What reasons did they give?

They said they loved us, but they couldn't get along. They said they would always love us kids.

If you didn't understand, what did you think was happening?

At first I just thought they were having another fight.

Did you cry? Did they cry?

I didn't cry. My sister cried. Then I knew it was serious. I kept thinking I would have to choose which parent to live with. Then I knew I'd really hurt the one I didn't choose. I felt so much guilt about hurting one of them.

What were you feeling?

I felt ripped apart.

Questions can help you form the point of your narrative. After brainstorming, you can go back and survey all the details. Do they lead you to a point? Try asking yourself the questions listed earlier in this chapter: What did I learn? What is the meaning of this story? What is my attitude toward what happened? Did it change me? What emotion did it make me feel? Was the experience a good example of something (like unfairness, or kindness, or generosity)?

For the topic of the divorce, the details mention a number of emotions: confusion, pain, shock, disbelief, fear, guilt. The *point* of the paragraph cannot list all these emotions, but it could be started this way:

When my parents announced they were divorcing, I felt confused by all my emotions.

Now that you have a point and several details, you can move on to the planning stage of writing a narrative paragraph.

MyWritingLab™   Exercise 4   **Practice: Distinguishing Good Topic Sentences from Bad Ones in Narration**

Below are sentences. Some would make good topic sentences for a narrative paragraph. Others would not: they are too big to develop in a single paragraph, or they are so narrow they can't be developed, or they make no point about an incident or incidents. Put an *X* by the sentences that would not make good topic sentences.

1. _____ At a ceremony at the courthouse, I became a U.S. citizen.

2. _____ Nothing has pleased me more than my mother's words to me at my high school graduation.

3. _____ My sister's obsession with video games is causing problems for our entire family.

4. _____ When I passed my driving test, I felt an enormous sense of freedom.

5. _____ Last Tuesday night, I spent five hours waiting in a local hospital's emergency room.

6. _____ One hour in the writing lab taught me a lot about how to plan and organize an essay.

7. _____ I come from a small Midwestern town where everybody knows everyone else.

8. _____ Years of working at a bakery made me hate the smell of baking bread.

9. _____ I blamed myself when I saw what vandals had done to my car.

10. _____ After my last experience at Crescent Beach, I will never again swim in rough seas.

Exercise 5   **Practice: Developing a Topic Sentence from a List of Details**   MyWritingLab™

Following is a list of details with an incomplete topic sentence. Read the details carefully; then complete the topic sentence.

topic sentence: Failing my final paper caused me to feel _____

_____

details: I waited until the night before my paper was due to begin working on it.

I couldn't think of anything to write.

To help me get some ideas, I went to the library.

I found a great book that had some great ideas I could include in my paper.

The author stated everything so clearly, I didn't want to change a thing.

I used several sentences from the book without quotations.

Our professor said we didn't need sources, so I didn't include any information about the book I used.

The next day, I handed in the paper.

The following class period the teacher handed everyone's essay back but mine.

Next, she asked if she could see me after class.

After class, she asked if the paper was all my own work.

I was embarrassed; I didn't know what to say.

I told her it was all my own work.

Next, she pulled out the exact book I used to help write my paper and asked if it looked familiar.

I was ashamed again. It was the book.

I apologized to my professor. She stated that I failed this paper for plagiarism.

PLANNING   **NARRATION**

The topic of how an experience changed you has led you to a point and a list of details. You can now write a rough outline, with the point as the topic sentence. Once you have the rough outline, check it for these qualities:

Relevance: Do all the details connect to the topic sentence?
Order: Are the details in a clear order?
Development: Does the outline need more details? Are the details specific enough?

Your revised outline might look like the following:

Outline for a Narrative Paragraph

topic sentence   When my parents announced that they were divorcing, I felt confused by all my emotions.

details   I was seven when my mom and dad divorced.
My sister was ten.
Both my folks were there.
They told us at breakfast, in the kitchen.

background of the narrative ———   I was eating toast.
I remember I couldn't eat anything when they started talking.
I remember a piece of toast with one bite out of it.

story of the divorce announcement ———   My parents were very calm when they told us.
They said they loved us but couldn't get along.
They said they would always love us kids.
It was a big shock to me.
I couldn't believe it was happening.
At first I just thought they were having another fight.
I was too young to understand.
I didn't cry.
My sister cried.

my reactions at each stage ———   Then I knew it was serious.
I kept thinking I would have to choose which parent to live with.
I knew I'd really hurt the one I didn't choose.
I felt so much guilt about hurting one of them.
I felt ripped apart.

Once you have a revised outline, you're ready to write a draft of the narrative paragraph.

MyWritingLab™

Exercise 6   **Practice: Finding Details That Are Out of Order in a Narrative Outline**

The following outline has details that are out of order. Put the details in correct time order by numbering them 1, 2, and so forth.

1. topic sentence: A small surprise changed my attitude on Sunday.

details: _____   Sunday started as a rainy day.

_____   The rain matched my mood.

_____   Even if it had been sunny, I couldn't have gone outdoors because I had responsibilities.

_____   After two hours with my chemistry textbook, my head was exploding.

_____   I began by dealing with the worst part of the day: studying for a chemistry test.

_____   Working through the chapters I had never read, I felt doomed to fail.

_____   I decided to give my head a break, but it was not an enjoyable break.

_____   During this break, I began to sort the dirty laundry piled in my closet.

_____   Frustrated and irritated, I tossed the dirty clothes back into the closet.

_____   As I sorted, I realized that I was too broke to do my laundry.

_____   As a pair of jeans hit the closet floor, I heard a clink.

_____   I looked in the direction of the clink and saw a quarter.

_____   After retrieving the coin, I checked the pockets of the jeans.

_____   I didn't find any more coins, but I did find a ten-dollar bill.

_____   Life no longer seemed so bleak, for I could skip the laundry and get a pizza.

Exercise 7   **Practice: Recognizing Irrelevant Details in a Narrative Outline**   MyWritingLab™

The following outline has details that are not relevant to the topic sentence. Cross out the details that do not fit.

topic sentence: Meeting my uncle led me to an important decision.

details: My Uncle Benjamin lives far away from us, so I first met him when I was twelve years old.

He is a cook in a famous restaurant in California, and he visited us to cook for my sister's engagement party.

My sister is the kind of person who enjoys elaborate parties.

Bored by the fancy celebration, I watched my uncle in the kitchen.

He prepared the kitchen efficiently, assembling bowls, utensils, pots, pans, and spices.

Working quickly, he chopped vegetables, sautéed garlic, onions, and capers, and sliced meat into thin strips.

It's not a big kitchen, but Uncle Benjamin was able to work efficiently in a small space.

When he began to cook, he expertly managed all four burners on the stove at once.

My uncle concentrated intently on managing complicated tasks.

The guests in the living room were drinking toasts to my sister and her fiancé.

My uncle sautéed, he blended, he mixed sauces, and he added spices with precision.

His work was like an art.

Uncle Benjamin's talent and skill made me want to learn what he knew: the culinary art.

③ Write a narrative paragraph that uses details and transitions effectively.

DRAFTING AND REVISING **NARRATION**

After you have a revised outline for your narration paragraph, you can begin working on a rough draft of the paragraph. As you write your first draft, you can combine some of the short sentences of the outline. Once you have a draft, you can check it for places you would like to improve. Remember that revising largely involves improving your structure and content as you organize your details as clearly and logically as possible. (Later, you can improve your style and correct mistakes during the editing and proofreading stage of the writing process.) The following checklist will help you as you revise your narrative:

Checklist for Revising Your Draft of a Narrative Paragraph

✓ Is my narrative vivid?

✓ Are the details clear and specific?

✓ Does the topic sentence relate to all of the details?

✓ Are the details written in a clear order?

✓ Do the transitions make the narrative easy to follow?

✓ Have I made my point?

Revising for Sharper Details

A good idea for a narrative can be made better if you revise for sharper details. In the paragraph below, the underlined words and phrases could be revised to create better details. In the following example, see how the second draft has more vivid details than the first draft.

First Draft: Details Are Dull

A woman at the movies showed me just how rude and selfish people can be. It all started when I was in line with <u>a lot</u> of other people. We had been waiting <u>a long time</u> to buy our tickets. We were outside, and it <u>wasn't pleasant</u>. We were impatient because time was running out and the movie was about to start. Some people were <u>making remarks</u>, and <u>others were pushing</u>. Then <u>a woman cut to</u> the front of the line. The cashier at the ticket window <u>told</u> the woman there was a line and she would have to go to the end of it. The woman <u>said she didn't want to wait because her son didn't want to miss the beginning of the movie.</u>

Second Draft: Better Details

A woman at the movies showed me just how rude and selfish people can be. It all started when I was in line with <u>forty or fifty other people</u>. We had been waiting to buy our tickets for <u>twenty minutes</u>. We were outside, <u>where the temperature was about 90 degrees and it looked like rain</u>. We were all getting impatient because time was running out and the movie was about to start. <u>I heard two people mutter about how ridiculous the wait was, and someone else kept saying, "Let's go!" The man directly behind me kept pushing me, and each new person at the end of the line pushed the whole line forward against the ticket window</u>. Then a woman <u>with a loud voice and a large purse thrust her purse and her body in front of the ticket window</u>. The cashier <u>politely</u> told the woman there was a line and she had to go to the end of it. But the woman answered <u>indignantly. "Oh no," she said. "I'm with my son Mickey. And Mickey really wants to see this martial arts movie. And he hates to miss the first part of any movie. So I can't wait. I've got to have those tickets now."</u>

Checking the Topic Sentence

Sometimes you think you have a good idea, a good topic sentence, and specific details, but when you write the draft of the paragraph, you realize the topic sentence does not quite relate to all of the details. When that happens, you can either revise the details or *rewrite the topic sentence.*

In the paragraph below, the topic sentence (underlined) does not quite fit all the details, so the topic sentence should be rewritten.

<u>I didn't know what to do when a crime occurred in front of my house</u>. At 9:00 p.m., I was sitting in my living room, watching television, when I heard what sounded like a crash outside. At first, I thought it was a garbage can that had fallen over. Then I heard another crash and a

shout. I ran to the window and I looked out into the dark. I couldn't see anything because the street light in front of my house was broken. I heard at least two voices, and they sounded angry and threatening. I heard another voice, and it sounded like someone moaning. I was afraid. I ran to the telephone. I was going to call 911, but then I froze in fear. What if the police came, and people got arrested? Would the suspects find out I was the one who had called the police? Would they come after *me*? Would I be a witness at a trial? I didn't want to get involved. So I just stood behind the curtain, peeking out and listening. Pretty soon the shouting stopped, but I still heard sounds like hitting. I couldn't stand it anymore. I called the police. When they came, they found a young teenager, badly beaten, in the street. They said my call may have saved his life.

The paragraph above has good details, but the story has more of a point than "I didn't know what to do." The person telling the story did, finally, do something. Following is a better topic sentence that covers the whole story.

> **topic sentence rewritten:** I finally found the courage to take the proper action when a crime occurred in front of my house.

MyWritingLab™ **Exercise 8** **Practice: Adding Better Details to a Draft of a Narrative**

The following paragraph has some details that could be more vivid. Rewrite the paragraph in the lines below, replacing the underlined details with more vivid words, phrases, or sentences.

Even the most stubborn people have to admit they are sometimes wrong. My father is extremely <u>bad</u> when he drives to a new destination. He insists that he knows how to get to the place. He refuses to look at a map or at a tracking system before we all pile into the car. Then we watch him drive happily in the wrong direction, but we hesitate to correct him. If we try to steer my father to the right route, he reacts <u>badly</u>. He says that he knows exactly where he is going. <u>Things</u> deteriorate when we passengers begin to notice certain landmarks appearing three or four times as my father blindly circles and recircles the wrong streets. Meanwhile, my father is getting <u>mad</u>, and we are getting <u>madder</u>. Eventually, my father does acknowledge that he is lost. We feel <u>good</u> now that my father is ready to take directions.

rewrite: _____

_____

_____

_____

_____

_____

_____

_____

_____

_____

_____

_____

_____

_____

_____

Exercise 9 **Practice: Writing a Better Topic Sentence for a Narrative**   MyWritingLab™

The paragraphs below could use better topic sentences. (In each paragraph, the current topic sentence is underlined.) Read each paragraph carefully, then write a new topic sentence for it in the lines below.

1. <u>Last week my brother told me a terrible story</u>. It started when he left his workplace. His boss had just promised to give him some extra hours of work, and my brother was happy to hear of the opportunity. As my brother drove out of the parking lot, he wanted to share the good news with Nicole, his girlfriend. Merging slowly into traffic, my brother began texting Nicole. Soon after, he was absorbed in writing her his news. Suddenly, he heard horns honking and metal crunching. My brother, intent on text-messaging, had run a red light. A woman had been injured when my brother, preoccupied, had driven into the driver's side of her car. If only he had waited to contact his girlfriend and had concentrated on driving, an innocent woman would not be suffering from bruises and broken bones. In addition, my brother would still be celebrating his good news.

new topic sentence: _____

_____

2. <u>Janelle and I saw a beautiful red fox recently</u>. We live in a typical suburban neighborhood, and the most exotic animals we see are the squirrels and mice that appear near the dumpsters at our apartment. However, we do have a few wooded areas between the houses and apartment buildings that make up our town. One day, Janelle and I were walking through our neighborhood when she grabbed my arm. "Look," she said, nodding her head toward an undeveloped area of trees and bushes. I saw a blur of fur, about the size of a large cat. It was standing at the edge of the property as if it were waiting to cross the street. "It's a fox," Janelle whispered. When we stood still, we were able to focus on its long legs, its red and white body, and its black nose. Then the animal seemed to sense our presence and loped gracefully back into the bush. Janelle and I looked at each other, stunned by the sight of a wild animal hiding and surviving in the middle of our civilized, regulated environment.

new topic sentence: _____

_____

Using Transitions Effectively in Narration

When you tell a story, you have to be sure that your reader can follow you as you move through the steps of your story. One way to make your story easier to follow is to use transitions. Most of the transitions in narration relate to time. Below is a list of transitions writers often use in writing narration.

INFO BOX **Transitions for a Narrative Paragraph**

after	before	in the meantime	soon after
again	during	later	still
always	finally	later on	suddenly
at first	first	meanwhile	then
at last	second (etc.)	next	until
at once	frequently	now	when
at the same time	immediately	soon	while

A Revised Draft

Following is a revised draft of the paragraph on divorce. As you read it, you will notice some changes that are typical of narrative writing. Because telling a story (narrative) involves events in time order, a first draft tends to focus on simply putting those events in the correct sequence. However, once the time order is correct, a writer has to focus on two important issues: (1) making sure that the narrative is more than a list of the details, in time sequence, and (2) avoiding short, choppy writing. When you study this revised draft, you will notice the many **transitions** that help create a seamless shift from one stage of the divorce announcement to another. You will also notice several places where **sentences** from the outline have been **combined** for smoother, more logical connections. Finally, using the exact words of **dialogue** in part of the story adds realistic detail. (You can assume the writer worked through several drafts prior to the current revised draft.)

Revised Draft of a Narrative Paragraph

(Note: Changes from the outline are underlined; editing and proofreading are still necessary to refine style and correct errors.)

transition	When my parents announced that they divorcing, I felt confusing by all my emotions. <u>At the time</u> of their
sentences combined	announcement, <u>I was seven and my sister was ten</u>. Both my parents parents were there to tell us. They told us at breakfast in the kitchen. <u>I was eating toast,</u>
sentences combined and transition	<u>but I remember I couldn't eat anything when they</u> <u>started talking. In fact</u>, I remember staring

at a piece of toast with one bite taken out of it. My parents were very calm when they told us. <u>"We love both of you very much," my dad said "but your mother and I aren't get along."</u> They said they would always love us. <u>The announcement was such a shock to me that I couldn't believe it was happening.</u> At first I just thought they were having another fight. <u>Because I was too young to understand I didn't cry. Suddenly, my sister started to cry, and then I knew it was serious.</u> I kept thinking I would have to chose which parent to live with. <u>I knew I'd really hurt the one I didn't choose, so I felt terrible guilt about hurting one of them.</u> I felt riped apart.

dialogue added

sentences combined

sentences combined

transition added

sentences combined and transition added

Exercise 10 **Practice: Recognizing Transitions in a Narrative Paragraph**   MyWritingLab™

Underline the transitions in the following paragraph.

A little work in my mother's garden provided a tough lesson for me. My mother has always loved her plants and flowers, and I had always thought of her yard work as a sweet little hobby. Frequently, she would ask me to come outside, enjoy the fresh air, and join her in a little pruning, trimming, and weeding. Finally, I agreed. At once she handed me a pair of heavy gardening gloves and a bucket. Then she led me to a patch of lawn covered in feathery green stalks. "Pull out the weeds," she said, pointing to the feathery stalks, "and put them in the bucket." It couldn't be much work to pull out a clump of these little green things, I told myself. When I began my work, I discovered that the weeds could not be pulled in clumps, and even a single feathery weed did not come out without a fight. Soon I realized that squatting on the ground is hard on the knees. After what seemed like hours, I had to get up and stretch. Looking at my watch, I saw that I had been working for fifteen minutes. Meanwhile, my mother had filled a huge bucket with the ornery weeds.

Exercise 11 **Practice: Adding the Right Transitions to a Narrative Paragraph**

In the following paragraph, circle the correct transition in each of the pairs.

When / After I was ten, I had my first infatuation, which was a blend of elation and pain. My beloved was a singer on the Disney Channel, and I watched his performances faithfully. Now / Soon I could repeat every word of his dialogue on his show and every lyric in his songs. Until / Then I discovered his Web site, and my heart beat faster. Frequently / During I created elaborate fantasies in which my loved one met me and was immediately / still stricken with a burning love. These dreams sustained me through months of the ordinary days of a ten-year-old at school and home. Suddenly / Before my fantasies became nightmares. Pictures of my hero with a beautiful teenage girl began to appear on the Web. The two seemed to be in love. At first / Always I was overcome by a sense of loss. Immediately / Later my grief began to subside. However, I can finally / still remember the strong and often terrible emotions of my fantasy romance.

EDITING AND PROOFREADING NARRATION

After you have revised your narration, the next step is editing. At this point, you can look at grammatical structure, sentence length and structure, word forms, punctuation, and spelling. Once you have revised your draft, you can check it using the following list.

Checklist for Editing a Narrative Paragraph

✓ Are the verb forms correct and consistent?

✓ Are other grammatical structures correct?

✓ Can any sentences be combined?

✓ Did you correctly punctuate?

✓ Is everything spelled correctly?

For your information: A sample narrative essay based on this topic and following the same writing steps can be found in Chapter 12, "Different Essay Patterns: Part One."

Exercise 12 **Practice: Combining Sentences in a Draft of a Narrative**   MyWritingLab™

The following paragraph contains some short, choppy sentences, which are underlined. Wherever you see two or more underlined sentences clustered next to each other, combine them into one clear, smooth sentence. Write your revised version of the paragraph in the spaces above the lines.

Mother Nature pulled me out of a dark mood this morning. Caught in a rainstorm, I was driving to work in rush hour traffic and checking my watch every two minutes. I began making a mental list of all my worries. In addition to being afraid of getting to work late, I was worried about being broke. My last credit card bill had been astronomical. <u>I couldn't afford to get caught in a cycle. The cycle would be dangerous. The cycle would involve high interest rates and increasing debt.</u> School was another worry. <u>I had a quiz coming up in my accounting class. I was nervous about it. I was afraid that I wouldn't pass the quiz.</u> All these fears and the frustration of a slow ride in heavy traffic made me feel that I was drowning in misery. Then I looked up. <u>Beyond the rain was a beautiful sight. I saw a bright, clear rainbow.</u> It curved across the horizon like an arch of glowing colors. <u>I felt that the rainbow was a sign. The sign told me to be cheerful.</u> Almost against my will, I began to feel better.

Final Version of Your Narrative Paragraph

The final version of your narrative paragraph should reflect your best writing efforts. In the sample below, notice the crucial role final proofreading plays in correcting errors.

Final Version of a Narrative Paragraph

(Note: Corrections from the previous draft are underlined.)

verb added: were — When my parents announced that they <u>were</u> divorcing, I

spelling corrected: confused — felt <u>confused</u> by all my emotions. At the time of their announcement, I was seven and my sister was ten. Both my parents were there to tell us. They told us at breakfast<u>,</u>

comma added — in the kitchen. I was eating toast, but I remember I couldn't eat anything when they started talking. In fact, I remember staring at a piece of toast with one bite taken out of it. My parents were very calm when they told us. "We love both

comma after *said* — of you very much," my dad said, "<u>b</u>ut your mother and I aren't getting along." They said they would always love us. The announcement was such a shock to me that I

comma added — couldn't believe it was happening. At first<u>,</u> I just thought they were having another fight. Because I was too young

comma added ——————— to understand, I didn't cry. Suddenly, my sister started to cry, and then I knew it was serious. I kept thinking I would have to choose which parent to live with. I knew I'd really hurt the one I didn't choose, so I felt terrible guilt about

spelling corrected: *ripped* —— hurting one of them. I felt <u>ripped</u> apart.

MyWritingLab™   **Exercise 13** **Proofreading to Prepare the Final Version**

The following narrative paragraph has the kinds of errors that are easy to overlook when you prepare the final version of an assignment. Correct the errors, writing above the lines. There are eleven errors.

   I discovered a new world when a friend dragged me, to a lecture on the star's. I had no thing to do last Tuesday nite and my best friend encouraged me to accompany him to a lecture at the college planetarium. He had to go so that he could earn some extra credit in his astronomy class. I had never cared much about the stars or the planets; but I didn't want to spend the evening sitting in my room. Consequently, I followed my freind into the planetarium. First, I noticed that the building was impressive. We passed a giant telescope as we made our way to a Theater with stadium seating. When the lecture began, the lights dimmed, the speaker pressed a button, an the ceiling disappeared. A glass dome took it's place. Beyond it, we could see the stars. Soon, the lecture became a sound and light show with thrilling music spectacular close-ups, and dramatic language. After the presentation, my friend and me left the building and immediately looked up at the night sky.

Lines of Detail: A Walk-Through Assignment

Write a paragraph about an incident in your life that embarrassed, amused, frightened, saddened, or angered you. In writing the paragraph, follow these steps:

Step 1: Begin by freewriting. Then read your freewriting, looking for both the details and focus of your paragraph.

Step 2: Brainstorm for more details. Then write all the freewriting and brainstorming as a list.

Step 3: Survey your list. Write a topic sentence that makes a point about the details.

Step 4: Write an outline. As you write the outline, check that your details fit the topic sentence and are in clear order. As you revise your outline, add details where they are needed.

Step 5: Write and revise a draft of your paragraph. Revise until your details are specific and in a clear order and your transitions are smooth.

Step 6: Edit your latest draft for better style by combining choppy sentences and adding a speaker's exact words to be even more specific.

Step 7: Prepare a clean copy and proofread it carefully to spot and correct any careless errors in spelling, punctuation, format, or typing.

Topics for Writing a Narrative Paragraph

When you write on any of the following topics, be sure to work through the stages of the writing process in preparing your narrative paragraph.

1. Write about some surprising or shocking event you saw that you will never forget. Begin by freewriting. Then read your freewriting, looking for both the details and the focus of your paragraph.

   Collaborate

   If your instructor agrees, ask a writing partner or group to (a) listen to you read your freewriting, (b) help you focus it, and (c) help you add details by asking questions.

2. Write a narrative paragraph about a mistake you made at school. Include how that mistake proved to be a valuable lesson.

   MyWritingLab™

3. Interview an older family member or friend. Ask him or her to tell you an interesting story about his or her past. Ask questions as the person speaks. Take notes. If you have a recorder, you can record the interview, but take notes as well.

   MyWritingLab™

   When you've finished the interview, review the information with the person you've interviewed. Ask the person if he or she would like to add anything. If you wish, ask follow-up questions.

   Next, on your own, find a point to the story. Work through the stages of the writing process to turn the interview into a narrative paragraph.

4. Visit the Web site of your local newspaper and find a news article about a crime that involved a sequence of events leading to a confrontation, arrest, or escape. Write the details of the story in time order, and be sure to use effective transitions. Your topic sentence should state what type of crime occurred as well as the outcome of it. (As you take notes from the article, be aware that newspaper accounts are not written in time order, so you will have to do some reordering of events.) Include a copy of the article with your paragraph.

   MyWritingLab™

5. Write a narrative about the disaster in the photograph on the next page. You can include events you imagine happened before, during, and after the dramatic scene in the photograph.

   MyWritingLab™

Topics for Critical Thinking and Writing

MyWritingLab™

1. Have you ever been involved in a car accident, a serious dispute with a friend or family member, a sudden ending to a relationship, or some other emotionally difficult event? Write a narrative paragraph about this moment, but write it from the perspective of another person involved in the event. For example, how would the other driver involved in an accident tell his story? How would a friend tell the story of his or her unpleasant encounter with you?

MyWritingLab™

2. If your job involves dealing with the public, write a narrative about one of your best or worst experiences with a customer or client. Afterwards, imagine that you are the customer, and write a narrative from his or her perspective. Use the same verb tense and sequence of events for both versions. Share your narratives with your classmates to see which version they prefer.

> **Note:** Additional writing options suitable for narration-related assignments can be found in the "Readings for Writers" appendix at the end of this book.

Jumping In

*Finding the right apartment takes planning and careful investigation. What should you do before, during, and after the process to ensure a successful move? How would you share what you've learned about finding a great apartment? Understanding the steps in a **process** helps us share our experiences with others who face similar challenges.*

Learning Objectives

In this chapter, you will learn to:

1. Recognize the difference between directional and informational processes.
2. Prewrite to generate a process paragraph topic.
3. Write a process paragraph that uses transitions and correct grammatical person.

WHAT IS PROCESS?

Process writing explains how to do something or describes how something happens or is done. When you tell the reader how to do something (a **directional process**), you speak directly to the reader, giving clear, specific instructions about performing some activity. Your purpose is to explain an activity so that a reader can do it. For example, you may have to leave instructions telling a new employee how to log in to a system or use the copier. A directional process uses "you," or in the way it gives directions, the word "you" is understood.

When you describe how something happens or is done (an **informational process**), your purpose is to explain an activity without telling a reader how to do it. For example, you can explain how a boxer trains for a fight or how a special effect for a movie was created. Instead of speaking

> 1 Recognize the difference between directional and informational processes.

directly to the reader, an informational process speaks about "I," "he," "she," "we," "they," or about a person by his or her name.

A Process Involves Steps in Time Order

Whether a process is directional or informational, it describes something that is done in steps, and these steps are in a specific order: a **time order**. The process can involve steps that are followed in minutes, hours, days, weeks, months, or even years. For example, the steps in changing a tire may take minutes, whereas the steps taken to lose ten pounds may take months.

You should keep in mind that a process involves steps that *must follow a certain order*, not just a range of activities that can be placed in any order. This sentence *signals a process:*

> Learning to search the Internet is easy if you follow a few simple directions. (Using the Internet involves following steps in order; that is, you cannot search before you turn on the computer.)

This sentence *does not signal a process:*

> There are several ways to get a person to like you. (Each way is separate; there is no time sequence here.)

Telling a person, in a conversation, how to do something or how something is done gives you the opportunity to add important points you may have overlooked or to throw in details you may have skipped at first. Your listener can ask questions if he or she does not understand you. Writing a process, however, is more difficult. Your reader is not there to stop you, to ask you to explain further, or to question you. In writing a process, you must be organized and clear.

Hints for Writing a Process Paragraph

1. **In choosing a topic, find an activity you know well.** If you write about something familiar to you, you will have a clearer paragraph.

2. **Choose a topic that includes steps that must be done in a specific time sequence.**

> **not this:** I find lots of things to do on a rainy day.
> **but this:** I have a plan for cleaning the garage.

3. **Choose a topic that is fairly small.** A complicated process cannot be covered well in one paragraph. If your topic is too big, the paragraph can become vague, incomplete, or boring.

> **too big:** There are many stages in the process of a bill becoming a law.
> **smaller and manageable:** Will power and support were the most important elements in my struggle to quit smoking.

4. **Write a topic sentence that makes a point.** Your topic sentence should do more than announce. Like the topic sentence for any paragraph, it should have a point. As you plan the steps of your process and gather details, ask yourself some questions: What point do I want to make about this process? Is the process hard? Is it easy? Does the process require certain tools? Does the process require certain skills, like organization, patience, endurance?

> **an announcement:** This paragraph is about how to change the oil in your car.
> **a topic sentence:** You do not have to be a mechanic to change the oil in your car, but you do have to take a few simple precautions.

5. Include all of the steps. If you are explaining a process, you are writing for someone who does not know the process as well as you do. Keep in mind that what seems clear or simple to you may not be clear or simple to the reader, and be sure to tell what is needed before the process starts. For instance, what ingredients are needed to cook the dish? Or what tools are needed to assemble the toy?

6. Put the steps in the right order. Nothing is more irritating to a reader than trying to follow directions that skip back and forth. Careful planning, drafting, and revising can help you get the time sequence right.

7. Be specific in the details and steps. To be sure you have sufficient details and clear steps, keep your reader in mind. Put yourself in the reader's place. Could you follow your own directions or understand your steps?

If you remember that a process explains how to do something or how something is done, you will focus on being clear. Now that you know the purpose and strategies of writing a process, you can begin the prewriting stage.

Exercise 1   **Practice: Recognizing Good Topic Sentences for Process Paragraphs**   MyWritingLab™

If a sentence is a good topic sentence for a process paragraph, put *OK* on the line provided. If a sentence has a problem, label that sentence with one of these letters:

    A This is an announcement; it makes no point.

    B This sentence covers a topic that is too big for one paragraph.

    S This sentence describes a topic that does not require steps.

1. _____ You can use a simple procedure to remove stains from a carpet.

2. _____ When I became a babysitter, I discovered a simple way of getting and holding a child's attention.

3. _____ This essay is about the way to wash a car so that it gleams in the sunshine.

4. _____ Many things contribute to giving a dynamic speech in front of a business organization.

5. _____ Selling items on e-Bay is a business that grew over several years.

6. _____ Finding the right Valentine's Day gift for a loved one demands some creative thinking and strategic shopping.

7. _____ Several tips can help you to get a good deal on a laptop.

8. _____ The process of training for a career in nursing is not for those without a true commitment to quality, compassionate care.

9. _____ How a security system in a twenty-four-hour food mart works is the subject of this paper.

10. _____ If you know how to bargain, you can get a good deal on used furniture at a garage sale.

Collaborate

Exercise 2 **Collaborate: Including Necessary Materials in a Process**

Below are two possible topics for a process paragraph. For each topic, work with a partner or a group and list the items (materials, ingredients, tools, utensils, supplies) the reader would have to gather before he or she began the process. When you've finished the exercise, compare your lists with another group's list to see if you've missed any items.

1. **topic:** cutting a person's hair

needed items: _____

_____

2. **topic:** gift wrapping an object

needed items: _____

2 Prewrite to generate a process paragraph topic.

WRITING THE PROCESS PARAGRAPH IN STEPS

PREWRITING   PROCESS

The easiest way to start writing a process paragraph is to pick a small topic, one that you can cover well in one paragraph. Then you can gather ideas by listing or freewriting or both.

If you decide to write about how to find the right apartment, you might begin by freewriting.

Then you might check your freewriting, looking for details that have to do with the process of finding an apartment. You can underline those details, as in the example that follows.

Freewriting for a Process Paragraph

Topic: Finding the right apartment

You have to <u>look around. Don't pick the first apartment you see</u>. Sean did that, and he ended up with a dump. <u>Look at a bunch</u>. But <u>not too many</u>, or you'll get confused. <u>The lease</u>, too. <u>Check it carefully. How much is the security deposit? How many bedrooms do you want? Friends can help</u> if they know of any nice apartments. I found my place that way. Maybe somebody you know lives in <u>a good neighborhood</u>. A <u>convenient location can be more expensive</u>. But <u>can save you money on transportation</u>.

Next, you can put what you've underlined into a list, in correct time sequence:

before the search

How many bedrooms do I want?
Friends can help.
a good neighborhood
a convenient location can be more expensive
can save you money on transportation

during the search

look around
Don't pick the first apartment you see.
Look at a bunch.
not too many

after the search

Check the lease carefully.
How much is the security deposit?

Check the list. Are some details missing? Yes. A reader might ask, "What other ways (besides asking friends) can help you find apartments? What else should you do before you search? When you're looking at apartments, what should you be looking for? What questions should you ask? After the search, how do you decide which apartment is best? And what, besides the security deposit, should you check on the lease?" Answers to questions like these can give you the details needed to write a clear and interesting directional process.

Writing a Topic Sentence for a Process Paragraph

Freewriting and a list can now help you focus your paragraph by identifying the point of your process. You already know what the subject of your paragraph is: finding the right apartment. But what's the point? Is it easy to find the right apartment? Is it difficult? What does it take to find the right apartment?

Maybe a topic sentence could be

Finding the right apartment takes planning and careful investigation.

Once you have a topic sentence, you can think about adding details that explain your topic sentence and you can begin the planning stage of writing.

Exercise 3 **Practice: Finding the Steps of a Process in Freewriting**   MyWritingLab™

Read the following freewriting, then reread it, looking for all the words, phrases, or sentences that relate to steps. Underline all those items. Then once you've underlined the freewriting, put what you've underlined into a list of specific steps.

How To Cut Back on Complaining: Freewriting

Cut back? Wouldn't it be better just to stop complaining? Everybody complains. Maybe it's impossible to stop complaining. After you've started counting complaints, notice what you complain about. Decide that you will make a conscious effort to reduce the number of times you complain. Start by noticing how often you complain. Next, focus on changing your conversations. As soon as you hear yourself starting to complain, change the subject or cut off your whining. Try to shift your dark mood to a lighter one. It's tough to shift from a negative attitude to a positive one; you may feel a little bit phony. However, if you focus on the positive, you'll eventually feel better and make others feel better, too.

Your List of Steps in Time Sequence

1. _____

   _____

2. _____

   _____

3. _____

   _____

4. _____

   _____

5. _____

   _____

6. _____
   _____
   _____

7. _____
   _____

PLANNING **PROCESS**

Using the freewriting and topic sentence on finding an apartment, you can make an outline. Then you can revise it, checking the topic sentence and the list of details, improving them where you think they could be better. A revised outline on finding the right apartment is shown below.

CRITICAL THINKING

Process paragraphs need to include *what* and *how* for each *when*. Example:

The *when*: Before the search
The *what*: Decide what you want.
The *how*: Check the advertisements.

Outline for a Process Paragraph

topic sentence	Finding the apartment you want takes planning and careful investigation.
details	Decide what you want.
	Ask yourself, "Do I want a one-bedroom?" "What can I afford?"
	A convenient location can be expensive.
before the search	It can also save you money on transportation.
	Friends can help you with names of nice apartments.
	Maybe somebody you know lives in a good neighborhood.
	Check the advertisements in the newspapers and online.
	Look around.
	Don't pick the first apartment you see.
	Look at several.
	But don't look at too many.
during the search	Check the cleanliness, safety, plumbing, and appliances of each one.
	Ask the manager about the laundry room, additional storage, parking facilities, and maintenance policies.
	Compare the two best places you saw.
	Consider the price, location, and condition of the apartments.
after the search	Check the leases carefully.
	Check the requirements for first and last month's rent deposits.

The following checklist may help you revise an outline for your own process paragraph:

Checklist for Revising a Process Outline

✓ Is my topic sentence focused on some point about the process?

✓ Does it cover the whole process?

✓ Do I have all of the steps?

✓ Are they in the right order?

✓ Have I explained the steps clearly?

✓ Do I need better details?

Exercise 4   **Practice: Revising the Topic Sentence in a Process Outline**   MyWritingLab™

The topic sentence below doesn't cover all the steps of the process. Read the outline several times; then write a topic sentence that covers all the steps of the process and has a point.

topic sentence: You can make a bathroom sink shine if you take your time.

details: First, assemble a few tools and products.

You need a small bucket of warm, soapy water.

You need an old washcloth or other clean, absorbent cloth.

You need a cleaning product that will remove soap scum and grit but is not too abrasive.

You need an old toothbrush.

Begin the cleaning by using the old toothbrush.

Use it to scrub the grimy dirt that collects around the bottom of the faucets and the opening of the drain.

This part of the cleaning takes time and determination because the dirt is hard to reach.

Once this dirt has fallen into the sink, rinse the dirt down the drain.

Rinse the old toothbrush clean.

Now, use a little bit of the cleaner and a wet cloth to scrub away the soap scum in the sink.

Scrub all over the sink, not just at the bottom of it.

Finally, rinse off the scum, rinse out the cloth, and enjoy the sight of a shiny sink.

revised topic sentence: _____

_____

_____

MyWritingLab™   Exercise 5   **Practice: Revising the Order of Steps in a Process Outline**

The steps in each outline are out of order. Put numbers in the spaces provided, indicating what step should be first, second, and so on.

1. **topic sentence:** Whenever my brother sits down to study, he gets sidetracked in a process that defeats him.

   details: _____ As he places his books, a notebook, pencils, and his laptop on the table, he seems focused and serious.

   _____ Mike starts the process with good intentions.

   _____ His first mistake is to turn on his computer before he looks at his textbooks or checks his assignments.

   _____ Once his laptop is on, Mike does a quick check of his e-mail.

   _____ The quick check of the e-mail takes time because Mike is popular.

   _____ Checking the e-mail leads Mike to deleting some of the e-mail and replying to most of it.

   _____ Once Mike has finished dealing with his e-mail, he makes his second big mistake.

   _____ By the time he has checked his favorite blogs and sites, an hour has passed.

   _____ The second mistake is his decision to check a few sites and blogs, just to see what is new.

   _____ After an hour of focusing on his laptop, Mike feels a slight headache coming on.

   _____ He decides to treat his headache by taking a break before he deals with his homework.

   _____ Most of the time, Mike's break lasts until the next day, and he never gets around to studying.

2. **topic sentence:** Sal's Sports Center has survived for twenty years because Sal, the owner, has a perfect system for making his customers feel free to roam but never ignored.

   details: _____ A bell rings as soon as a customer enters Sal's Sports Center.

   _____ Most customers say, "No thanks; I'm just looking around."

   _____ Once he hears the bell, Sal approaches and says, "Can I help you with anything?"

   _____ Sal knows how to respond to "No thanks"; he just goes back to the counter and leaves the customer to roam the aisles.

_____ Usually, Sal's customers, grateful for his relaxed
attitude, leave with a purchase.

_____ Every ten or fifteen minutes, Sal walks through the
store, stocking or straightening the shelves.

_____ "Have a great day!" Sal says, as another satisfied
customer leaves with a purchase.

_____ On these periodic trips, Sal is available to answer
questions or give help, but he never pushes himself
on a shopper.

Exercise 6   **Practice: Listing All of the Steps in an Outline**   MyWritingLab™

Following are two topic sentences for process paragraphs. Write all the steps
needed to complete an outline for each sentence. After you've listed all the
steps, number them in the correct time order.

1. **topic sentence:** You can make restaurant-quality garlic bread at
home with a few simple ingredients, some basic
kitchen supplies, and very little skill.

steps: _____

_____

_____

_____

_____

_____

_____

_____

_____

_____

_____

_____

_____

_____

_____

_____

_____

_____

_____

_____

_____

2. **topic sentence:** A few simple steps will help you to make the most
of a free outdoor concert.

steps: _____

_____

_____

_____

_____

_____

_____

_____

_____

_____

_____

③ Write a process paragraph that uses transitions and correct grammatical person.

PROCESS

You can take the outline and write it in paragraph form, and you'll have a first draft of the process paragraph. As you write the first draft, you can combine some of the short sentences from the outline. Then you can review your draft and revise it for organization, details, and clarity.

Using Transitions Effectively

As you revise your draft, you can add transitions. Transitions are particularly important in a process paragraph because you are trying to show the steps in a _specific sequence_, and you are trying to show the _connections_ between steps. Effective transitions will also keep your paragraph from sounding like a choppy, boring list.

Following is a list of some of the time transitions you can use in writing a process paragraph. Be sure that you use transitional words and phrases only when it is logical to do so, and try not to overuse the same transitions in a paragraph.

INFO BOX **Transitions for a Process Paragraph**

after	during	last	the second step, etc.
afterward	eventually	later	then
as	finally	meanwhile	to begin
as he/she is	first	next	to start
as soon as	second, etc.	now	until
as you are	first of all	quickly	when
at last	gradually	sometimes	whenever
at the same time	in the beginning	soon	while
before	immediately	suddenly	while I am . . .
begin by	initially	the first step	

When you write a process paragraph, you must pay particular attention to clarity. As you revise, keep thinking about your audience to be sure your steps are easy to follow. The following checklist can help you revise your draft:

Checklist for Revising a Process Paragraph

✓ Does the topic sentence cover the whole paragraph?

✓ Does the topic sentence make a point about the process?

✓ Is any important step left out?

✓ Should any step be explained further?

✓ Are the steps in the right order?

✓ Have I used transitions effectively?

Exercise 7   **Revising Transitions in a Process Paragraph**   MyWritingLab™

The transitions in this paragraph could be better. Rewrite the underlined transitions directly above each one so that the transitions are smoother.

Walking on wet or muddy pavement can be treacherous if you're not prepared and vigilant. <u>First</u>, wear sensible footwear. "Sensible" means shoes or boots with some traction on the soles, not flip-flops or high heels. <u>Second</u>, as you walk, concentrate on walking. That is, don't think about your plans, your worries, or your fantasies. Focus on the process of walking on slippery terrain. <u>Third</u>, be careful about hazards such as steps, curbs, or cracks in the pavement. <u>Fourth</u>, look ahead for deep puddles or oily pavement that can lead you into a sudden slide onto your knees or back. <u>Fifth</u>, do not let down your guard until you are safely indoors in a dry, not slippery, hallway or room. <u>Six</u>, you can relax and take off your muddy shoes.

A Revised Draft

The following is a revised draft of the process paragraph on finding an apartment. This draft has more details than the outline on page 104, and you can assume that the writer has worked through several drafts already. You may see that new transitions and additional details make this directional process authoritative and complete. (You may also notice that this revised draft still has a few spelling and grammatical errors which can be corrected during the editing and proofreading stage.)

Revised Draft of a Process Paragraph

(Note: Changes from the outline are underlined; editing and proofreading are still necessary.)

transition added ——————— Finding the apartment you want takes planning and investigation. <u>First of all</u>, you must decide what you want. Ask yourself, "Do I want a one-bedroom apartment?" or "<u>Do I want a studio apartment?</u>"

added detail and transition ——————— <u>Most important</u>, ask yourself, "What can I afford?"

(Continued)

added detail and transition	<u>A convenent location can be expensive. On the other hand, that location can save you money on transportation.</u> <u>Before</u> I start looking for a place, do some research. Freinds can help you with the names of nice apartments. Be sure to check the ad-
transition added	vertisements in the newspaper and online. <u>Once</u> you begin your search, don't pick the first place you see. You should look at several places But <u>looking</u>
detail added	<u>at too many can make your search confusing</u>. Just remember to check each apartment's clean, safety,
transition added	plumbing, and appliances. <u>Then</u> ask the manager about the laundry room, additional storage, park- ing facility, and maintenance policies. <u>After</u> you've
transition added	completed your search, compare the two best plac- es you saw. Consider each one's price, location, and condition. Carefully checking each lease, <u>studying</u>
detail added	<u>the amount of the security</u> deposit, the deposit for first and last months' rent, <u>and the rules for tenants</u>.
detail added	When you've completed your comparison, you're ready to chose the apartment you want.

Using the Same Grammatical Person

Remember that the *directional* process speaks directly to the reader, calling him or her "you." Sentences in a directional process use the word "you," or they imply "you."

> **directional:** *You* need a good paintbrush to get started. Begin by making a list. ("You" is implied.)

Remember that the *informational* process involves somebody doing the process. Sentences in an informational process use words like "I," "we," "he," "she," or "they" or a person's name.

> **informational:** *Chip* needed a good paintbrush to get started. First, *I* can make a list.

One common error found in process papers is shifting from describing how someone did something to telling someone how to do an activity. You must decide whether your process paragraph will be directional or informational.

In grammar, the words "I" and "we" are considered to be in the *first person*. "You" is in the *second person* and "he," "she," "it," and "they" are in the *third person*. If these words refer to one, they are *singular*, if they refer to more than one, they are *plural*. The following list may help you remember singular and plural subject pronouns:

INFO BOX A List of Subject Pronouns

First person singular:	I
Second person singular:	you
Third person singular:	he, she, it, or a person's name
First person plural:	we
Second person plural:	you
Third person plural:	they, or the names of more than one person

---

Below are two examples of a **shift in person**; study how each shift is corrected.

shift in person: After *I* preheat the oven to 350 degrees, *I* mix the egg whites and sugar with an electric mixer set at high speed. *Mix* until stiff peaks form. Then *I* put the mixture in small mounds on an ungreased cookie sheet. ("Mix until stiff peaks form" is a shift to the "you" person.)

shift corrected: After *I* preheat the oven to 350 degrees, *I* mix the egg whites and sugar with an electric mixer set at high speed. *I* mix until stiff peaks form. Then *I* put the mixture in small mounds on an ungreased cookie sheet.

shift in person: *A salesperson* has to be very careful when a customer tries on clothes. *The clerk* can't hint that a suit may be a size too small. *You* can insult a customer with a hint like that. (The sentences shifted from "salesperson" and "clerk" to "you.")

shift corrected: *A salesperson* has to be very careful when customers try on clothes. *The clerk* can't hint that a suit may be a size too small. *He or she* can insult a customer with a hint like that.

EDITING AND PROOFREADING PROCESS

After you have revised your process paragraph, the next step is editing.

At this point, you can check grammatical structure, sentence length, word form, punctuation, and spelling. Once you have edited your draft, you can double-check it using the following list:

Checklist for Editing a Process Paragraph

✓ Are the verb forms correct and consistent?

✓ Have you used the same person throughout the paragraph to describe the process?

✓ Should any sentences be combined?

✓ Did you punctuate correctly?

✓ Is everything spelled correctly?

Exercise 8   **Practice: Correcting Shifts in Person in a Process Paragraph**

Below is a paragraph that shifts from being an informational to a directional process in several places. Those places are underlined. Rewrite the underlined parts directly above the original ones so that the whole paragraph is an informational process.

My sister Colleen has a system for getting the most out of a bottle of shampoo. As soon as she stands in the shower and opens a new bottle of shampoo, she is careful to pour only a tiny portion of the liquid into the palm of her hand. She knows the temptation to slap a huge glop of shampoo right onto <u>your</u> head. Pouring on the shampoo is wasteful, and it also saturates her hair with too many soapy suds. Colleen carefully takes the liquid from the palm of her hand and smears it onto the top of her head. Then she carefully adds a little water to the shampoo on her head. Now <u>you</u> can massage the mixture into her hair and scalp. She doesn't waste shampoo or water on a rinse followed by a second shampooing. Instead, she simply rinses her hair thoroughly once. Then <u>you cap</u> the shampoo so that it will not drip or collect dripping water. Next, <u>you</u> must place the shampoo bottle in a safe part of the shower so that the bottle will not fall, pop open, and leak. When she is near the end of her bottle of shampoo, <u>add</u> a little water to the bottle and <u>you</u> can get enough shampoo to last a week or more.

Exercise 9   **Practice: Combining Sentences in a Process Paragraph**

The paragraph following has many short, choppy sentences, which are underlined. Wherever you see two or more underlined sentences clustered next to each other, combine them into one clear, smooth sentence. Write your revised versions of those sentences in the space above the original.

My dog has a clever way of telling me that she needs a bedtime visit outdoors. First, her bedtime is not my bedtime. If it were, my dog's system for getting outside would not be necessary. However, my dog gets restless about half an hour before I want to turn off the television and go to bed. <u>Her routine always begins at the same time. I am watching a contest or a drama. It is about to reach its peak.</u> Just as the winner is about to be announced or the criminal exposed, my dog begins to stir. <u>She wakes up from her nap. She has been dozing on the couch. She begins to look around.</u> This is

my first clue that my dog is nearly ready to travel outdoors. <u>Soon, she begins licking my</u>
<u>hand. She also licks my face</u>. When these forms of persuasion do not work, she resorts
to her final tactic. <u>She jumps onto the floor. Then she starts to moan</u>. Now I begin to
think that she needs to go outside immediately. When I open the door to the backyard,
my dog runs out happily. <u>She sniffs the bushes. She explores the area beneath the trees.</u>
<u>She checks for any animal intruders</u>. Finally, she relieves herself and runs inside
for her nighttime dog biscuit. While I have been waiting at the open door and have
missed the climax of the television show, my dog has gotten just what she wanted.

Preparing Your Final Version

After you have edited your latest draft, prepare a clean copy and proofread
it carefully. Reading your paragraph aloud can help you identify and correct
any careless errors in punctuation and spelling, and you may even catch
some missing words or typos. Your goal is to make your work error-free. As
you review the sample final version, compare these editing and proofreading
changes to the draft on page 109–110:

- *Convenient* is now spelled correctly.
- Sentences are now combined in two places.
- Subject pronoun *I* is replaced by *you* for pronoun consistency.
- *Friends* is now spelled correctly.
- *Cleanliness* now appears instead of the incorrect *clean*.
- *Facilities* is now in the plural form.
- *Check* is now in the correct verb form.
- *Choose* is now spelled correctly.

Final Version of a Process Paragraph

(Note: Changes from editing and proofreading are underlined.)

Finding the apartment you want takes planning and investigation. First of all,
you must decide what you want. Ask yourself, "Do I want a one-bedroom apartment?"
or "Do I want a studio apartment?" Most important, ask yourself, "What can I afford?"
A <u>convenient location can be expensive; on the other hand, that location can save</u>
<u>you money on transportation</u>. Before <u>you</u> start looking for a place, do some research.
<u>Friends</u> can help you with the names of apartments. Be sure to check the advertise-
ments in the newspaper and online. Once you begin your search, don't pick the first
place you see. <u>You should look at several places, but looking at too many can make</u>
<u>your search confusing</u>. Just remember to check each apartment's <u>cleanliness</u>, safety,
plumbing, and appliances. Then ask the manager about the laundry room, additional storage, parking <u>facilities</u>, and maintenance policies. After you've completed
your search, compare the two best places you saw. Consider each one's price, location, and condition. Carefully <u>check</u> each lease, studying the amount of the security
deposit, the deposit for first and last months' rent, and the rules for tenants. When
you've completed your comparison, you're ready to <u>choose</u> the apartment you want.

> **For your information:** A sample process essay based on this topic and following the same writing steps can be found in Chapter 12, "Different Essay Patterns: Part One."

My**Writing**Lab™   **Exercise 10**   **Practice: Proofreading to Prepare the Final Paragraph**

The following process paragraph has the kind of errors it is easy to overlook when you prepare the final version of an assignment. Correct the errors, writing above the lines. There are ten errors in the paragraph

Sooner or later, every one gets a cold, so I dealing with a cold by preparing for it, and accepting it. To prepare for a cold, I stock up on supplies. I make sure that I have tea, honey, and chicken noodle soup in my kitchen When I feel a cold begining, I decide to give in to it. Instead of trying to endure my stuffy head, sneezing, and general misery at work and school; I stay home. I can sleep as long as I need to, and I can sneeze without spreading my germs at work or in class. Once I get out of bed, I do not force myself to eat when I feel sick. Instead, I do what I can to make myself feel comftable. I lay on the couch, and cover my self with a blanket. I watch videos or television Until I fall asleep again. If I am feeling energetic, I get up to make myself some soothing tea with honey or a bowl of soup.

Lines of Detail: A Walk-Through Assignment

Your assignment is to write a paragraph on how to plan a special day. Follow these steps:

Step 1: Focus on one special day. If you want to, you can begin by using your own experience. Ask yourself such questions as, Have I ever planned a birthday party? A baby or wedding shower? A surprise party? A picnic? A reunion? A barbecue? A celebration of a religious holiday? Have I ever seen anyone else plan such a day? If so, how would you teach a reader about planning for such a day?

Step 2: Once you have picked the day, freewrite. Write anything you can remember about the day and how you or someone else planned it.

Step 3: When you've completed the freewriting, read it. Underline all the details that refer to steps in planning that event. List the underlined details in time order.

Step 4: Add to the list by brainstorming. Ask yourself questions that can lead to more details. For example, if an item on your list is "Send out invitations early," ask questions like "How early?" and "How do you decide whom to invite?"

Step 5: Survey your expanded list. Then write a topic sentence that makes some point about your planning for this special day. To reach a point, think of questions like these: "What makes a plan successful?" or "If you are planning for a special day (birthday, barbecue, surprise party, and so forth), what must you remember?"

Step 6: Use the topic sentence to prepare an outline. Be sure that the steps in the outline are in the correct time order.

Step 7: Write a draft of the paragraph and revise it extensively, adding and reordering details as necessary. Work through several drafts if necessary.

Step 8: Edit your draft for better style by combining sentences and using effective transitions.

Step 9: Prepare a clean copy and proofread carefully; correct any careless errors in spelling, punctuation, typing, or format.

Topics for Writing a Process Paragraph

When you write on one of these topics, be sure to work through the stages of the writing process in preparing your process paragraph. Also, be sure to write from your own experience.

1. Write a **directional** or **informational process** about one of these topics:

   MyWritingLab™

preparing for a test	getting to work on time
participating in a cultural ritual	setting up a social network account
painting a room	performing a family ritual
video chatting online	breaking a specific habit
preparing your favorite meal	gaining weight
pinning on a board	giving a pet a bath
coping with rejection	preparing for a job interview

2. Write about the worst way to do something, or the worst way you (or someone else) did it. You can use any of the topics in the list above, or you can choose your own topic.

   MyWritingLab™

3. Interview one of the counselors at your college. Ask the counselor to tell you the steps for applying for financial aid. Take notes or record the interview, get copies of any forms that are included in the application process, and ask questions about these forms.

   MyWritingLab™

   After the interview, write a paragraph explaining the process of applying for financial aid. Your explanation is directed at a high school senior who has never applied for aid.

4. Interview someone whose cooking you admire. Ask that person to tell you the steps involved in making a certain dish. Take notes or tape the interview. After the interview, write a paragraph, *not* a recipe, explaining how to prepare the dish. Your paragraph will explain the process to someone who is a beginner at cooking.

   Collaborate

MyWritingLab™

5. Visit your college's Web site and follow any links that are associated with your campus bookstore. After reviewing the information about shopping for books and supplies, and based on your own experience, write a paragraph that explains the most efficient way to avoid long lines and waiting periods. If your college bookstore offers online purchasing, be sure to include the steps involved in this option.

MyWritingLab™

6. Examine the photograph of the basketball player, and then write a paragraph on how an athlete can focus his or her concentration for maximum benefit.

Topics for Critical Thinking and Writing

MyWritingLab™

1. What steps do you follow when you are faced with a major decision? Do you consult others to help you make a choice? Do you seek information that will clarify your choices and help you weigh the pros and cons of your options? If you can identify the steps involved in your decision making, write a process paragraph about a major decision you have made as an adult. Be sure to provide specific details for each of the steps you cover, including why or how you undertook each step.

MyWritingLab™

2. Many students have to work either part time or full time to afford college tuition and fees. Learning to manage time efficiently can be a difficult process. In a process paragraph, describe the steps you undertook to manage work and school responsibilities. You can consider how you worked out a schedule that recognizes the commitment of time and effort involved in meeting school and work demands.

> **Note:** Additional writing options suitable for process-related assignments can be found in the "Readings for Writers" appendix at the end of this book.

Comparison and Contrast

CHAPTER 6

Jumping In

Clearly, there are differences between riding a bike and riding a motorcycle. Can you think of several differences? Are there any similarities? Examining similarities and differences is a way of comparing and contrasting.

Learning Objectives

In this chapter, you will learn to:

1 Recognize the difference between comparing and contrasting.

2 Organize your comparison or contrast paragraph subject-by-subject or point-by-point.

3 Prewrite to generate a comparison or contrast paragraph topic.

4 Write a comparison or contrast paragraph using either a point-by-point or subject-by-subject pattern.

WHAT IS COMPARISON? WHAT IS CONTRAST?

1 Recognize the difference between comparing and contrasting.

To **compare** means to point out *similarities*. To **contrast** means to point out *differences*. **When you compare or contrast, you need to come to some conclusion**. It's not enough to say, "These two things are similar" or "They are different." Your reader will be asking, "So what? What's your point?" You may be showing the differences between two restaurants to explain which is the better buy:

> If you like Mexican food, you can go to either Café Mexicana or Juanita's, but Juanita's has lower prices.

Or you may be explaining the similarities between two family members to explain how people with similar personalities can clash.

> My cousin Bill and my brother Karram are both so stubborn they can't get along.

117

Hints for Writing a Comparison or Contrast Paragraph

1. Limit your topic. When you write a comparison or contrast paragraph, you might think that the easiest topics to write about are broad ones with many similarities or differences. However, if you make your topic too large, you will not be able to cover it well, and your paragraph will be full of very large, boring statements.

Here are some topics that are too large for a comparison or contrast paragraph: two countries, two periods in history, two kinds of addiction, two wars, two economic or political systems, two presidents.

2. Avoid the obvious topic. Some people think it is easier to write about two items if the similarities or differences between them are obvious, but with an obvious topic, you will have nothing new to say, and you will risk writing a boring paragraph.

Here are some obvious topics: the differences between high school and college, the similarities between *Hunger Games* and *Catching Fire*. If you are drawn to an obvious topic, *try a new angle* on the topic. Write about the unexpected, using the same topic. Write about the similarities between high school and college, or the differences between *Hunger Games* and *Catching Fire*. You may have to do more thinking before you come up with ideas, but your ideas may be more interesting to write about and to read.

CRITICAL THINKING

Comparing and contrasting often involves evaluating the positive and negative features of two different but similar items or concepts. When evaluating, be sure to make word choices that carry strong meanings, such as *reliable*, *loyal*, *committed*, and *passionate*.

---

3. Make your point in the topic sentence of your comparison or contrast paragraph. Indicate whether the paragraph is about similarities or differences in a topic sentence like this:

> Because he is so reliable and loyal, Michael is a much better friend to me than Stefan. (The phrase "much better" indicates differences.)

> My two biology teachers share a love of the environment and a passion for protecting it. (The word "share" indicates similarities.)

4. Do not announce in the topic sentence. The sentences below are announcements, not topic sentences:

> This paper will explain the similarities between my two biology teachers.

> Let me tell you how Michael is a different kind of friend than Stefan.

5. Make sure your topic sentence has a focus. It should indicate similarities or differences; it should focus on the specific kind of comparison or contrast you will make:

> **not focused:** My old house and my new one are different.

> **focused:** My new home is bigger, brighter, and more comfortable than my old one.

6. In the topic sentence, cover both subjects to be compared or contrasted.

> **covers only one subject:** The beach at Santa Lucia was dirty and crowded.
>
> **covers both subjects:** The beach at Santa Lucia was dirty and crowded, but the beach at Fisher Bay was clean and private.

Be careful. It is easy to get so carried away by the details of your paragraph that you forget to put both subjects into one sentence.

Exercise 1 Practice: Identifying Suitable Topic Sentences for a Comparison or Contrast Paragraph

MyWritingLab™

Following is a list of possible topic sentences for a comparison or contrast paragraph. Some would make good topic sentences. The ones that wouldn't make good topic sentences have one or more of these problems: they are announcements, they don't indicate whether the paragraph will be about similarities or differences, they don't focus on the specific kind of comparison or contrast to be made, they cover subjects that are too big to write about in one paragraph, or they don't cover both subjects.

Mark the problem sentences with an *X*. If a sentence would make a good topic sentence for a comparison or contrast paragraph, mark it *OK*.

1. _____ Both expensive jeans and bargain-priced jeans appeal to a wide range of ages, offer a variety of styles, and can be worn almost anywhere.

2. _____ Driving in heavy rain and driving in heavy snow require similar precautions.

3. _____ On the one hand, there are Hollywood movies; on the other, there are Bollywood movies.

4. _____ Child actors and child singers can become rich, famous, and loved by audiences.

5. _____ Ricci's Restaurant has a more extensive menu, a better location, and friendlier service.

6. _____ Forest Park High School and Richmond Academy have demanding academic programs, caring teachers, and various extracurricular activities.

7. _____ This essay will discuss the similarities between my first summer job and my first summer at band camp.

8. _____ Bollywood and Hollywood movies are dramatic, entertaining, and extremely popular around the world.

9. _____ On the one hand, there are expensive jeans; on the other hand, there are bargain-priced jeans.

10. _____ Texting is more convenient, saves more time, and is less of an interruption than phoning.

2 Organize your comparison or contrast paragraph subject-by-subject or point-by-point.

Organizing Your Comparison or Contrast Paragraph

Whether you decide to write about similarities (to compare) or differences (to contrast), you will have to decide how to organize your paragraph. You can choose between two patterns of organization: subject-by-subject or point-by-point.

Subject-by-Subject Organization In the subject-by-subject pattern, you support and explain your topic sentence by first writing all your details on one subject and then writing all your details on the other subject. If you choose a subject-by-subject pattern, be sure to discuss the points for your second subject *in the same order* as you did for the first subject. For example, if your first subject is an amusement park, and you cover (1) the price of admission, (2) the long lines at rides, and (3) the quality of the rides, when you discuss the second subject, another amusement park, you should write about its prices, lines, and quality of rides *in the same order*.

Look carefully at the outline and comparison paragraph below for a subject-by-subject pattern.

Comparison Outline: Subject-by Subject Pattern

topic sentence

Once I realized that my brother and my mother are very much alike in temperament, I realized why they don't get along.

details

subject 1, James—temper — My brother James is a hot-tempered person.
It is easy for him to lose control of his temper.

unkind words — When he does, he often says things he later regrets.

stubbornness — James is also very stubborn.
In an argument, he will never admit he is wrong.
Once we were arguing about baseball scores.
Even when I showed him the right score printed in the paper, he wouldn't admit he was wrong.
He said the newspaper had made a mistake.
James's stubbornness overtakes his common sense.

subject 2, mother—temper — James has inherited many of his character traits from our mother.
She has a quick temper, and anything can provoke it.
Once, she got angry because she had to wait too long at a traffic light.

unkind words — She also has a tendency to use unkind words when she's mad.

stubbornness — She never backs down from a disagreement or concedes she was wrong.
My mother even quit a job because she refused to admit she'd made a mistake in taking inventory.
Her pride can lead her into foolish acts.
After I realized how similar my brother and mother are, I understood how such inflexible people are likely to clash.

A Comparison Paragraph: Subject-by-Subject Pattern

subject 1,
James—temper

unkind words

stubbornness

subject 2,
mother—temper

unkind words

stubbornness

Once I realized that my brother and my mother are very much alike in temperament, I realized why they don't get along. My brother James is a hot-tempered person. It is easy for him to lose control of his temper, and when he does, he often says things he regrets. James is also very stubborn. In an argument, he will never admit he is wrong. I remember one time when we were arguing about baseball scores. Even when I showed him the right scores printed in the newspaper, he wouldn't admit he was wrong. James insisted that the newspaper must have made a mistake in printing the score. As this example shows, sometimes James's stubbornness overtakes his common sense. It took me a while to realize that my stubborn brother James has inherited many of his traits from our mother. Like James, she has a quick temper, and almost anything can provoke it. She once got angry because she had to wait too long at a traffic light. She also shares James's habit of saying unkind things when she's angry. And just as James refuses to back down when he's wrong, my mother will never back down from a disagreement or concede she's wrong. In fact, my mother once quit a job because she refused to admit she'd made a mistake in taking inventory. Her pride is as powerful as James's pride, and it can be just as foolish. After I realized how similar my mother and brother are, I understood how such inflexible people are likely to clash.

Look carefully at the paragraph in the subject-by-subject pattern, and you'll notice the following:

- It begins with a topic sentence about both subjects—James and his mother.
- It gives all the details about one subject—James.
- It then gives all the details about the second subject—his mother, in the same order.

Point-by-Point Organization In the point-by-point pattern, you support and explain your topic sentence by discussing each point of comparison or contrast, switching back and forth between your subjects. You explain one point for each subject, then explain another point for each subject, and so on.

Look carefully at the outline and the comparison paragraph below for the point-by-point pattern.

Comparison Outline: Point-by-Point Pattern

topic sentence

details

point 1,
temper
James and
mother

Once I realized that my brother and my mother are very much alike in temperament, I realized why they don't get along.

My brother James is a hot-tempered person.
It is easy for him to lose control of his temper.
My mother has a quick temper, and anything can provoke it.
Once she got angry because she had to wait too long at a traffic light.

(Continued)

point 2,
unkind words
James and mother

When my brother gets mad, he often says things he regrets. My mother has a tendency to use unkind words when she's mad.

James is very stubborn.

In an argument, he will never admit he is wrong.

Once we were arguing about baseball scores.

Even when I showed him the right score printed in the newspaper, he wouldn't admit he was wrong.

He said the newspaper had made a mistake.

point 3,
stubbornness
James and mother

James's stubbornness overtakes his common sense.

My mother will never back down from a disagreement or admit she is wrong.

She even quit a job because she refused to admit she'd made a mistake in taking inventory.

She was foolish in her stubbornness.

After I realized how similar my mother and brother are, I understood how such inflexible people are likely to clash.

Comparison Paragraph: Point-by-Point Pattern

point 1,
temper
James and mother

point 2,
unkind words
James and mother

point 3,
stubbornness
James and mother

Once I realized that my brother and my mother are very much alike in temperament, I realized why they don't get along. My brother is a hot-tempered person, and it is easy for him to lose control of his temper. My mother shares James's quick temper, and anything can provoke her anger. Once, she got angry because she had to wait too long at a traffic light. When my brother gets mad, he often says things he regrets. Similarly, my mother is known for the unkind things she's said in anger. James is a very stubborn person. In an argument, he will never admit he's wrong. I can remember one argument we were having over baseball scores. Even when I showed him the right score printed in the newspaper, he wouldn't admit he had been wrong. He simply insisted the paper had made a mistake. At times like that, James's stubbornness overtakes his common sense. Like her son, my mother will never back down from an argument or admit she was wrong. She even quit a job because she refused to admit she'd made a mistake in taking inventory. In that case, her stubbornness was as foolish as James's. It took me a while to see the similarities between my brother and mother. Yet after I realized how similar these two people are, I understood how two inflexible people are likely to clash.

Look carefully at the paragraph in the point-by-point pattern, and you'll note that it

- begins with a topic sentence about both subjects—James and his mother;
- discusses how both James and his mother are alike in these points: their quick tempers, the unkind remarks they make when they are angry, and their often foolish stubbornness;
- switches back and forth between the two subjects.

The subject-by-subject and point-by-point patterns can be used for either a comparison or contrast paragraph. But whatever pattern you choose, remember these hints:

1. Be sure to use the same points to compare or contrast two subjects. If you are contrasting two cars, you can't discuss the price and safety features of one, then the styling and speed of the other. You must discuss the price of both, or the safety features, styling, or speed of both.

You don't have to list the points in your topic sentence, but you can include them, like this: "My old Ford turned out to be a cheaper, safer, and faster car than my boyfriend's new Mazda."

2. Be sure to give roughly equal space to both subjects. This rule doesn't mean you must write the same number of words—or even sentences—on both subjects. It does mean you should be giving fairly equal attention to the details of both subjects.

Since you will be writing about two subjects, this type of paragraph can involve more details than other paragraph formats. Thus, a comparison or contrast paragraph may be longer than twelve sentences.

Using Transitions Effectively for Comparison or Contrast

How and when you use transitions in a comparison or contrast paragraph depend on the answers to two questions:

1. Are you writing a comparison or contrast paragraph?

- When you choose to write a *comparison* paragraph, you use transitional words, phrases, or sentences that point out *similarities*.

- When you choose to write a *contrast* paragraph, you use transitional words, phrases, or sentences that point out *differences*.

2. Are you organizing your paragraph in the point-by-point or subject-by-subject pattern?

- When you choose to organize your paragraph in the *point-by-point* pattern, you need transitions *within* each point *and between points*.

- When you choose to organize in the *subject-by-subject pattern*, you need *most of your transitions* in the *second half* of the paragraph, to remind the reader of the points you made in the first half.

Here are some transitions you can use in writing comparison or contrast. Many others you may think of will also be appropriate for your ideas.

INFO BOX **Transitions for a Comparison or Contrast Paragraph**

To show similarities:

additionally	both	in the same way	similar to
again	each of	just like	similarly
also	equally	like	so
and	furthermore	likewise	too
as well as	in addition		

To show differences:

although	even though	instead of	though
but	except	nevertheless	unlike
conversely	however	on the other hand	whereas
despite	in contrast to	otherwise	while
different from	in spite of	still	yet

Writing a comparison or contrast paragraph challenges you to make decisions: Will I compare or contrast? Will I use a point-by-point or a subject-by-subject pattern? Those decisions will determine what kind of transitions you will use and where you will use them.

MyWritingLab™ | **Exercise 2** | **Practice: Writing Appropriate Transitions for a Comparison or Contrast Paragraph**

Below are pairs of sentences. First, decide whether each pair shows a comparison or contrast. Then combine the two sentences into one, using an appropriate transition (either a word or a phrase). You may have to rewrite parts of the original sentences to create one smooth sentence. The first pair is done for you.

1. My mother loves to go out dancing.
   My father has danced only once: at his wedding.

   combined: _My mother loves to go out dancing, yet my father has_

   danced only once: at his wedding.

2. Young children should go to bed at the same time each night.
   Young children should have regularly scheduled meal times.

   combined: _____

   _____

3. A steady job can be tiring and stressful.
   Unemployment can be painful and terrifying.

   combined: _____

   _____

4. Playing chess with my uncle taught me to think deeply and plan my next move.
   When I was a member of a high school football team, I learned about the importance of strategy.

   combined: _____

   _____

WRITING THE COMPARISON OR CONTRAST PARAGRAPH IN STEPS

3 Prewrite to generate a comparison or contrast paragraph topic.

PREWRITING **COMPARISON OR CONTRAST**

One way to get started on a comparison or contrast paragraph is to list as many differences or similarities as you can on one topic. Then you can see whether you have more similarities (comparisons) or differences (contrasts), and decide which approach to use. For example, if you are asked to compare or contrast two restaurants, you could begin with a list like the one that follows.

List for Two Restaurants: Victor's and The Garden

similarities
both offer lunch and dinner
very popular
nearby

differences

Victor's	The Garden
formal dress	informal dress
tablecloths	placemats
food is bland	spicy food
expensive	moderate
statues, fountains, fresh flowers	dark wood, hanging plants

Getting Points of Comparison or Contrast

Whether you compare or contrast, you are looking for points of comparison or contrast, items you can discuss about both subjects.

If you surveyed the list on the two restaurants and decided you wanted to contrast the two restaurants, you'd see that you already have these points of contrast:

dress   food
decor   prices

To write your paragraph, start with several points of comparison or contrast. As you work through the stages of writing, you may decide you don't need all the points you've jotted down, but it is better to start with too many points than with too few.

Exercise 3 **Collaborate: Developing Points of Comparison or Contrast**

Collaborate

Do this exercise with a partner or a group. Below are some topics that could be used for a comparison or contrast paragraph. Underneath each topic, write three points of comparison or contrast. Be ready to share your answers with another group or with the class. The first topic is done for you.

1. **topic:** Compare or contrast two rooms.
   points of comparison or contrast:

   a. their size

   b. their furniture

   c. their color scheme

2. **topic:** Compare or contrast two smartphones.
   points of comparison or contrast:

   a. _____

   b. _____

   c. _____

3. topic: Compare or contrast two annual holidays.
points of comparison or contrast:

a. _____

b. _____

c. _____

MyWritingLab™　　Exercise 4　**Practice: Finding Differences in Subjects That Look Similar**

Following are pairs of subjects that seem very similar but that do have differences. List three differences for each pair.

1. subjects: pens and pencils

differences: a. _____

b. _____

c. _____

2. subjects: regular coffee and decaffeinated coffee

differences: a. _____

b. _____

c. _____

3. subjects: school library and online library

differences: a. _____

b. _____

c. _____

MyWritingLab™　　Exercise 5　**Practice: Finding Similarities in Subjects That Look Different**

Following are pairs of subjects that are different but have some similarities. List three similarities for each pair.

1. subjects: getting fired and getting hired

similarities: a. _____

b. _____

c. _____

2. subjects: becoming an older adult and becoming a teenager

similarities: a. _____

b. _____

c. _____

3. subjects: spending money and saving money

similarities: a. _____

b. _____

c. _____

Adding Details to Your Points

Once you have some points, you can begin adding details to them. The details may lead you to more points. If they do not, they will still help you develop the ideas of your paragraph. If you were to write about the differences in restaurants, for example, your new list with added details might look like this:

List for a Contrast of Restaurants

Victor's	The Garden
dress—formal	informal dress
men in jackets, women in dresses	everyone in jeans
decor—pretty, elegant	placemats, on table is a card
statues, fountains	listing specials, lots of dark wood
fresh flowers on tables	and brass, green hanging plants
tablecloths	
food—bland tasting	spicy and adventurous
traditional, broiled fish or	pasta in tomato sauces, garlic
chicken, steaks,	in everything, curry,
appetizers like shrimp cocktail,	appetizers like tiny tortillas,
onion soup	ribs in honey-mustard sauce
price—expensive	moderate
everything costs extra,	price of dinner includes
like appetizer, salad	appetizer and salad

Reading the list about restaurants, you might conclude that some people may prefer The Garden to Victor's. Why? There are several hints in your list. The Garden has cheaper food, better food, and a more casual atmosphere. Now that you have a point, you can put it into a topic sentence. A topic sentence contrasting the restaurants could be

> Some people would rather eat at The Garden than at Victor's because The Garden offers better, cheaper food in a more casual environment.

Once you have a possible topic sentence, you can begin working on the outlines stage of your paragraph.

Exercise 6   **Practice: Writing Topic Sentences for Comparison or Contrast**   MyWritingLab™

Below are lists of details. Some lists are for comparison paragraphs; some are for contrast paragraphs. Read each list carefully; then write a topic sentence for each list.

   1. topic sentence: _____

   _____

List of Details

cat training	**dog training**
litter box training	housebreaking
using a scratching post	walking on a leash
jumping on kitchen counters	behaving around people or pets
	obeying commands

benefits of personality	**benefits of personality**
affectionate	loving
mysterious	unpredictable
amusing	always entertaining
intuitive	sympathetic

great moments	**great moments**
curling up in bed	sneaking into bed
greeting owner	joyfully jumping on owner
playing with a cat toy	playing fetch

2. topic sentence: _____

_____

List of Details

red	**blue**
emotion	**emotion**
hearts are red	people feel blue, or sad
Valentine's Day decorations are red	blue paint is used to create a calm environment
in some countries red is worn at a wedding	blue skies refer to happy times

jewelry	**jewelry**
rubies are expensive gems	turquoise jewelry is popular and stylish
garnets are less expensive	a blue topaz is a lower-cost gem for rings
red beads are common in multistrand necklaces	dark blue stones appear on bangle bracelets

transportation	**transportation**
red sports cars are a popular image of money and daring	many airlines paint their planes blue and white (or blue and silver)
a red convertible is another image of adventure	police cars are often blue and white

PLANNING   **COMPARISON OR CONTRAST**

With a topic sentence, you can begin to draft an outline. Before you can write an outline, however, you have to make a decision: What pattern do you want to use in organizing your paragraph? Do you want to use the subject-by-subject or the point-by-point pattern?

The following is an outline of a contrast paragraph in point-by-point form. (A sample subject-by-subject outline appears later in this chapter.)

Outline of a Contrast Paragraph: Point-by-Point Pattern

topic sentence

Some people would rather eat at The Garden than at Victor's because The Garden offers better, cheaper food in a more casual environment.

details

Food at Victor's is bland-tasting and traditional.

The menu has broiled fish, chicken, traditional steaks.

The spices used are mostly parsley and salt.

The food is the usual American food with a little French food on the list.

point 1, food

Appetizers are the usual things like shrimp cocktail or onion soup.

Food at The Garden is more spicy and adventurous.

There are many pasta dishes in tomato sauce.

There is garlic in just about everything.

The Garden serves four different curry dishes.

It has all kinds of ethnic food.

Appetizers include items like tiny tortillas and hot, honey-mustard ribs.

point 2, prices

The prices of the two restaurants differ.

Victor's is expensive.

Everything you order costs extra.

An appetizer and a salad costs extra.

Food at The Garden is more moderately priced.

The price of a dinner includes an appetizer and a salad.

point 3, environment

Certain diners may feel uncomfortable in Victor's, which has a formal environment.

Everyone is dressed up, the men in jackets and ties and the women in dresses.

Less formal diners would rather eat in a more casual place.

People don't dress up to go to The Garden; they wear jeans.

conclusion

Many people prefer a place where they can relax, with reasonable prices and unusual food, to a place that's a little stuffy, with a traditional and expensive menu.

Once you've drafted an outline, check it. Use the following checklist to help you review and revise your outline.

Checklist for an Outline of a Comparison or Contrast Paragraph

✓ Do I have enough details?

✓ Are all of my details relevant?

✓ Have I covered all the points on both sides?

✓ If I'm using a subject-by-subject pattern, have I covered the points in the same order for both subjects.

✓ Have I tried to cover too many points?

✓ Have I made my main idea clear?

Using this checklist as your guide, compare the outline with the prewriting list on page 125. You may notice several changes:

- Some details on decor in the list have been omitted because there were too many points.

- A concluding sentence has been added to reinforce the main idea.

MyWritingLab™   Exercise 7   **Practice: Adding a Point and Details to a Comparison or Contrast Outline**

The following outline is too short. Develop it by adding a point of comparison and details to both subjects to develop the comparison.

topic sentence: People who wear caps and those who wear hats often choose them for similar reasons.

details: Caps and hats both make a statement.

Caps are often marked with the name of a tractor company, a football team, or a college, so they indicate an affiliation or interest.

Hats often indicate a person's interests, hobbies, or employment.

Fishing hats are worn by people who fish for fun or profit.

Cowboy hats appear on the heads of working ranchers and people on vacation.

Caps and hats can be a way for people to fit in.

Most people at a football or basketball game want to be seen with their team's insignia on their caps.

New students at a college like to wear the college's name on a cap.

In some places of worship, women like to wear elaborate hats on special occasions.

People who attend country music concerts like to come in cowboy hats.

Add a new point of comparison, and details, about caps and hats:

_____

_____

_____

_____

_____

_____

_____

| Exercise 8 | **Practice: Finding Irrelevant Details in a Comparison or Contrast Outline** | MyWritingLab™ |

The following outline contains some irrelevant details. Cross out the details that don't fit.

topic sentence: Fibs and lies are quite different in intention, consequences, and in the nature of fibbers and liars.

details: Fibs tend to be small distortions of the truth.

When people have to choose between hurting another person's feelings by telling the truth and sparing that person some pain, they tell a fib.

"Your haircut looks great," a fibber will say.

Hair is a very sensitive subject with some people.

Lies are larger falsehoods.

Some people lie about being faithful to a partner.

So that they will not get caught cheating, they may say they were working late.

Many people are unemployed these days.

The consequences of telling a fib are not likely to be as serious as the consequences of lying.

Because a fib is about a small matter, it has a fairly small impact.

A fib told to avoid hurting another person may not be kind in the long run, but it isn't cruel.

It would be difficult for an average person to count all the fibs he or she has told.

Lies, on the other hand, can create great harm.

Lies about infidelity can poison a marriage.

The unsuspecting partner can sense a painful distance growing between the spouses.

The cheater is caught in a web of guilt.

Cheating is often portrayed on television as funny, but it is not.

Essentially, fibbers and liars are different types of people.

Young children may sense that fibbing is wrong, but their fibs are meant to save themselves, not to hurt others.

In the same way, adults who fib usually mean to avoid an awkward situation, but the fibs are not intentionally cruel.

Liars are most often adults, and their lies can be toxic.

Although unfaithful partners tell themselves they are not hurting anyone, they know better.

Their lies are both selfish and dangerous.

Everyone is human and therefore flawed, but fibbers are far less dangerous than liars.

MyWritingLab™   Exercise 9   **Practice: Revising the Order in a Comparison or Contrast Outline**

Following is an outline written in the subject-by-subject pattern. Rewrite the part of the outline that is in italics so that the points in the second half follow the order of the first half. You do not have to change any sentences; just rearrange them.

topic sentence: Carl and Sean could not have been more different, yet they were college roommates who became best friends.

details: Carl was a country boy.

Carl's family lived on a ten-acre property fifteen miles from the nearest mall.

Carl had two horses, which he cared for himself.

He was used to seeing foxes, snakes, and possum in his back yard.

Carl loved football.

He had been a star player at his high school.

He drove two hours to attend every football game at the nearest university.

On his satellite television, he watched every professional game he could find.

Carl also loved country music.

When he wasn't watching football on television, he turned to country music channels.

The only concerts he attended featured country music superstars.

Sean loved hip-hop.

Hip-hop blasted from his MP3 player.

Clubs that offered hip-hop entertainment were Sean's favorite hangouts.

Sean was a typical suburban teen.

He and his family lived in a three-bedroom house with a two-car garage and a small back yard.

Sean had never had a pet, but his mother had a Yorkshire terrier.

The creatures that lived in his yard were likely to be crows, squirrels, and worms.

He lived within a ten-minute drive to two huge malls, ten restaurants, and a multiplex movie theater.

A major part of Sean's life was basketball.

He had played basketball in high school.

He attended all the games at the nearby college.

He regularly drove half an hour to a nearby sports center where he watched nationally known teams play.

rewritten order: _____

_____

_____

_____

_____

_____

_____

_____

_____

_____

_____

_____

_____

_____

_____

_____

_____

DRAFTING AND REVISING   COMPARISON OR CONTRAST

When you've revised your outline, you can write the first draft of the restaurant paragraph. As you work through several drafts, you may decide to rearrange your points or refine your topic sentence. Adding vivid details and linking them

④ Write a comparison or contrast paragraph using either a point-by-point or subject-by-subject pattern.

effectively can make your paragraph more than a mere list of comparisons or contrasts. Remember that some sentences can serve as transitional links from one point of contrast (or comparison) to another.

A Sample Revised Draft

When you study the sample revised draft below, you'll notice changes from the outline on page 129. The order of some details in the outline has been changed, and a few transitions have been added. Additional refinements and corrections are still necessary during the editing and proofreading stage, but you will still see considerable improvement. You can assume the writer worked through prior drafts to get to this point.

Revised Draft of a Contrast Paragraph, Point-by-Point Pattern

(Note: Changes from the outline are underlined; editing and proofreading are still necessary.)

Some people would rather eat at The Garden than at Victor's because The Garden offers better, cheap food in a more casual environment. The food at Victor's is bland-tasting and traditional. The menu has broiled fish, chicken, and steaks. The food is the usual American food with a little French food on the list. Appetizers are the usual things like shrimp cocktail and onion soup. The spices used are mainly parsly and salt.

transition — Food at The Garden, <u>however</u>, is more spicy and adventurous.

sentence order changed — <u>The restaurant has all kinds of ethnic food</u>. There are many pasta dishes with tomato sauce. The menu has five kinds of curry on it. The appetizers include items like tiny tortillas and hot, honey-mustard ribs.

transitional phrase — <u>And if parsley is the spice of choice at Victor's</u>, garlic is the favorite spice at The Garden. The prices at the restaurants differ, <u>too</u>. Victor's is expensive because everything you order costs extra. An appetizer or a salad costs extra.

transition — Food at The Garden, <u>in contrast</u>, is more moderately priced of a dinner includes an appetizer and a salad.

transitional sentences — <u>Price and menu are important, but the most important difference between the restaurants has to do with environment</u>. Certain diners may feel uncomfortable at Victor's, which has a formal kind of atmosphere. Everyone is dressed up, the men in jackets and ties and the women in dresses. Less formal dinners would rather eat in a more casual place. People don't dress up for The Garden; they wear jeans. Many people prefer a place where they can relax, with reasonable prices and unusual food, to a place that is a little stuffy, with a traditional and expensive menu.

The following checklist may help you revise your own draft:

Checklist for Revising Your Draft of a Comparison or Contrast Paragraph

✓ Did I include a topic sentence that covers both subjects?

✓ Are the paragraph's details arranged in a clear order?

✓ Does it stick to one pattern, either subject-by-subject or point-by-point?

✓ Are both subjects given roughly the same amount of space?

✓   Do all the details relate to the topic sentence?

✓   Are the details specific and vivid?

✓   Are transitions (and transitional sentences) used effectively?

✓   Have I made my point?

Exercise 10   **Practice: Revising the Draft of a Comparison or Contrast Paragraph by Adding Vivid Details**   MyWritingLab™

You can do this exercise alone, with a writing partner, or with a group. The following contrast paragraph lacks the vivid details that could make it interesting. Read it; then rewrite the underlined parts in the space above them. Replace the original words with more vivid details.

   I had always planned on getting a dog, but when I finally got one, the experience was not at all what I had expected. First of all, I had always imagined myself visiting the local animal shelter where I would find the largest dog in the place. He would be a great watchdog and know how to <u>do a lot of things</u>. After I selected him, I would take him back to <u>my place</u>, and he would <u>fit right in</u>. I felt sure that the dog would soon <u>learn the rules and be cool</u>. Finally, I dreamed of a dog that would love to <u>have all kinds of fun</u>. However, the reality of getting a dog was nothing like my fantasy. First, I didn't find my dog; she found me. I saw her on campus, and her tongue was hanging out. After I gave her some water, she followed me all day. She even tried to follow me into <u>some places at college</u>. When I had to leave at the end of the day, I picked her up and put her in my car. She was easy to pick up because, unlike the dog of my dreams, she <u>was not big</u>. When I took her to my apartment, she didn't exactly conform to my fantasies of a pet. Instead of fitting in, she took over my territory. Within the first ten minutes of her arrival, she had jumped on the sofa, chewed one of my old sneakers, and eaten part of a roll of toilet paper. Finally, I discovered that my idea of fun is not hers. She does not want to catch a ball, and she does not want to learn any tricks. However, she is fearless and loves to <u>do some wild stuff</u>. My dog is not the fantasy pet I expected to own, but she is a real dog with a courage and a joy for living that is all her own.

EDITING AND PROOFREADING   **COMPARISON OR CONTRAST**

Contrast Paragraph: Point-by-Point Pattern

When you edit your latest draft of your comparison or contrast paragraph, you can check whether any short sentences should be combined for smoother style. You can also determine if any word choices need improvement. When you are ready to proofread a clean copy of your paragraph, you can check for any careless errors in spelling, punctuation, or format. The following checklist will help you edit effectively:

Checklist for Editing a Compare or Contrast Paragraph

✓   Do all sentences have a subject and a verb?

✓   Are verb forms consistent?

✓   Can short sentences be combined?

✓   Are punctuation marks used correctly?

✓   Does each sentence begin with a capital letter?

✓   Is everything spelled correctly?

- *Cheap* has been corrected to *cheaper*.
- The repetitive use of *usual* has been replaced by the synonym *typical and standard*.
- *Onion soup* has been changed to *French* onion soup.
- The spelling of *parsley* has been corrected.
- "Everything *you* order" has been corrected to "everything *a person* orders."
- A *formal kind of atmosphere* has been changed to a *formal environment*.
- Two sentences have been combined, referring to some diners' preference for a less formal restaurant and casual attire.

In the following final version of a contrast paragraph in a point-by-point pattern, you may notice the following changes and corrections from the sample draft on page 134:

Final Version of a Contrast Paragraph: Point-by-Point Pattern

(Note: Changes from the draft are underlined.)

Some people would rather eat at The Garden than at Victor's because The Garden offers better and <u>cheaper</u> food in a more casual environment. The food at Victor's is bland-tasting and traditional. The menu has broiled fish, chicken, and steaks. The food is <u>typical</u> American food with a little French food on the list. Appetizers are <u>standard</u> things like shrimp cocktail and <u>French</u> onion soup. The spices are mostly <u>parsley</u> and salt. Food at The Garden, however, is more spicy and adventurous. The restaurant has all kinds of ethnic food. There are many pasta dishes with tomato sauce. The menu has four kinds of curry on it. The appetizers include items like tiny tortillas and hot, honey-mustard ribs. And if parsley is the spice of choice at Victor's, garlic is the favorite spice at The Garden. The prices at the restaurants differ, too. Victor's is expensive because everything <u>a person orders</u> costs extra. An appetizer or a salad costs extra. Food at The Garden, in contrast, is more moderately priced because the price of a dinner includes an appetizer and a salad. Price and menu are important, but the most important difference between the two restaurants has to do with environment. Certain diners may feel uncomfortable at Victor's, which has a <u>formal environment</u>. Everyone is dressed up, the men in jackets and ties and the women in dresses. <u>Less formal diners would rather eat in a more casual place like The Garden, where everyone wears jeans</u>. Many people prefer a place where they can relax, with reasonable prices and unusual food, to a place that is a little stuffy, with a traditional and expensive menu.

For your information: A sample point-by-point contrast essay based on this topic and following the same writing steps can be found in Chapter 12, "Different Essay Patterns: Part One."

Exercise 11 **Practice: Editing a Draft by Combining Sentences**　　　MyWritingLab™

The paragraph below has many short, choppy sentences, which are underlined. Whenever you see two or more underlined sentences clustered next to each other, combine them into one smooth, clear sentence.

Whenever I visit a doctor, I feel as if I were going to prison. First, there is the weird atmosphere of the doctor's waiting room. The room is unusually quiet. It is full of people. <u>They are sitting. They are staring ahead. They are awaiting their doom</u>. The staff behind the glass partition reminds me of a group of prison guards who keep the latest prisoners in order until the big door opens and incarceration begins. At long intervals, each patient's name is called. Each time, I look up. I hope the name is mine so that, like a prisoner, I can begin my ordeal and soon end it. On the other hand, I dread entering the space behind the big door. <u>That space contains another kind of waiting room. This is the solitary waiting area. Here I generally sit on a chair or on the edge of an examination table. Here I can dwell on what is wrong with me</u>. In a similar way, prisoners are supposed to use their incarceration to think about what they have done wrong. <u>I sit alone in the small, cell-like room. I fear the arrival of the doctor</u>. I have gone to the doctor to find out what is wrong. <u>However, I feel that I have committed some crime. Maybe I have eaten too much fatty food. Maybe I have skimped on exercise</u>. As I wait for the doctor to examine me, I feel as if a warden were about to enter, study me critically, and frown. Like a prisoner, I am unable to escape.

The Same Contrast Paragraph: Subject-by-Subject Pattern

To show you what the same paragraph contrasting restaurants would look like in a subject-by-subject pattern, an outline, sample draft, and final version follow.

Outline: Subject-by-Subject Pattern

topic sentence   Some people would rather eat at The Garden than at Victor's because The Garden offers better, cheaper food in a more casual environment.

details   Food at Victor's is bland-tasting and traditional.
The menu has broiled fish, chicken, and steaks.
The spices used are mostly parsley and salt.
The food is the usual American food with a little French food on the list.

subject 1, Victor's: food, prices, atmosphere   Appetizers are the usual things like shrimp cocktail and onion soup.
Victor's is expensive.
Everything you order costs extra.
An appetizer or salad costs extra.
Certain diners may feel uncomfortable at Victor's, which has a formal environment.
Everyone is dressed up, the men in jackets and ties and the women in dresses.

Food at The Garden is more spicy and adventurous.
There are many pasta dishes in tomato sauce.
There is garlic in just about everything.
The Garden serves four different curry dishes.
It has all kinds of ethnic food.

subject 2, The Garden: food, prices, atmosphere   Appetizers include items like tiny tortillas and hot, honey-mustard ribs.
Food at The Garden is moderately priced.
The price of a dinner includes an appetizer and a salad.
The Garden is casual.
People don't dress up to go there; they wear jeans.

conclusion   Many people prefer a place where they can relax, with reasonable prices and unusual food, to a place that's a little stuffy, with a traditional and expensive menu.

Draft: Subject-by-Subject Pattern

(Note: Changes from the outline are underlined; editing and proofreading are still necessary.)

Some people would rather eat at The Garden than at Victor's because The Garden offers better, cheaper food in a more casual environment. The food at Victor's is bland-tasting and traditional. The menu has broiled fish, chicken, and steaks on it. The food is the usual American food with a little French food on the list. Appetizers are the usual things like shrimp

sentence order changed, sentences combined — cocktail and onion soup. <u>At Victor's, the spices are mostly parsley and salt. Eating traditional food at Victor's is expensive, since everything you order costs extra.</u> An appetizer or a salad, <u>for instance</u>,

transition —

transitional sentence — costs extra. <u>Victor's prices make some people nervous, and the restaurant's formal environment makes them uncomfortable.</u> At Victor's, everyone is dressed up, the men in jackets and ties and the women in dresses. <u>The formal atmosphere, the food,</u>

transitional sentence — <u>and the prices attract some diners, but others would rather go to The Garden for a meal.</u> The food at The Garden is more spicy and adventurous <u>than the offerings at Victor's.</u> The place has all kinds of ethnic food. <u>There are many pasta dishes in tomato sauce,</u>

sentences combined — <u>and The Garden serves four different curry dishes.</u> Appetizers include items like tiny tortillas and hot, honey-mustard ribs. <u>If Victor's relies on parsley and</u>

transitional phrase — <u>salt to flavor its food,</u> The Garden sticks to garlic, which is in just about everything. Prices are lower

transition — at The Garden <u>than they are at Victor's.</u> The Garden's meals are more moderately priced because,

transition — <u>unlike Victor's,</u> The Garden includes an appetizer and a salad in the price of a dinner. <u>And in contrast</u>

transition — <u>to Victor's,</u> The Garden is a casual restaurant. People don't dress up to go to The Garden; everyone wears jeans. Many people prefer a place where they can relax, with unusual food at reasonable prices, to a place that's a little stuffy, with a traditional and expensive menu.

Final Version: Subject-by-Subject Pattern

(Note: Minor editing changes from the draft are underlined.)

    Some people would rather eat at The Garden than at Victor's because The Garden offers better, cheaper food in a more casual environment. The food at Victor's is bland-tasting and traditional. The menu has broiled fish, chicken, and steaks on it. The food is typical American food, with a little French food on the list. Appetizers are the <u>standard</u> things like shrimp cocktail and <u>French</u> onion soup. At Victor's, the spices are mostly parsley and salt. Eating traditional food at Victor's is expensive, since everything <u>a person</u> orders costs extra. An appetizer or a salad, for instance, costs extra. Victor's prices make some people nervous, and the restaurant's formal environment makes them uncomfortable. At Victor's, everyone is dressed up, the men in jackets and ties and the women in dresses. The formal <u>environment</u> and the prices attract some diners, but others would rather go to The Garden for a meal. The food at The Garden is more spicy and adventurous than the offerings at Victor's. The place has all kinds of ethnic food. There are many pasta dishes in tomato sauce, and The Garden serves four different curry dishes. Appetizers include items like tiny tortillas and hot, honey-mustard ribs. If Victor's relies on parsley and salt to flavor its food, The Garden sticks to garlic, which is in just about everything. Prices are lower at The Garden than they are at Victor's. The Garden's meals are moderately priced because, unlike Victor's, The Garden

(Continued)

includes an appetizer and a salad in the price of a dinner. And in contrast to Victor's, The Garden is a casual restaurant. People don't dress up to go to The Garden; everyone wears jeans. Many people prefer a place where they can relax, with unusual food at reasonable prices, to a place that's a little stuffy, with a traditional and expensive menu.

> **For your information:** A sample contrast essay based on this topic and following the same writing steps can be found in Chapter 12, "Different Essay Patterns: Part One."

MyWritingLab™ **Exercise 12** **Proofreading to Prepare the Final Version**

The following paragraph has the kinds of errors that are easy to overlook in a final copy of an assignment. Correct the errors, writing your corrections above the lines. There are fourteen errors in the paragraph.

My car is an old Toyota Camry that used to belong to my Mother, and I was

thrilled when I get the chance to drive my uncle's newer BMW for a few weeks

while he was out of town. However, I was surprised that my life did not change

very much when I get the newer, sportier car. First, I axpected to attract more

attention when I drove the BMW. No one looks twice at an old Camry in need of a

paint job, so I always felt invisible when I drove it. People did look more closely at

the BMW, but they didnt look at me. Another disappointment was related to the

excessories and upgrades in my uncles car. At first, the BMW was like a great toy

for me, with every automotive option, every entertainment choice, and every com-

fort I could imagine. It took me several days to learn what I could do, and how I

could do it in this luxury car. It was wonderful to try out the satellite radio, the

temperature controls, and all the other options in the car. Unfortunately, learning

how to play with these gadgets and remembering how to use the upgrades

becomes irritating after a while, especially when I couldn't get them to work. My

greatest disappointment related to the car as a driving machine. At first, I enjoy

the power of the BMW. I could weave in and out of Traffic, turn corners easily, and

feel the car respond instantly when I stepped on the gas. But once I had been driv-

ing the car for a week, I felt less of a sense of adventure. After all, driving fast on

the highway and burning to much gas is thrilling for only a short time. I loved my uncle's car, and I'm glad I got to drive it. However, I'm quite satisfied to be back in my old Camry. I'v learned that a car with a glamorous image, great accessories, and a terrific engine are fun, but the car doesn't make a new person out of the driver.

Lines of Detail: A Walk-Through Assignment

Write a paragraph that compares or contrasts any experience you've heard about with the same experience as you lived it. For example, you could compare or contrast what you heard about starting college with your actual experience of starting college. You could compare or contrast what you heard about falling in love with your experience of falling in love, or what you heard about playing a sport with your own experience playing that sport. To write your paragraph, follow these steps:

Step 1: Choose the experience you will write about; then list all the similarities and differences between the experience as you heard about it and the experience as you lived it.

Step 2: To decide whether to write a comparison or contrast paragraph, survey your list to see which has more details, the similarities or the differences.

Step 3: Add details to your comparison or contrast list. Survey your list again, and group the details into points of comparison or contrast.

Step 4: Write a topic sentence that includes both subjects, focuses on comparison or contrast, and makes a point.

Step 5: Decide whether your paragraph will be in the subject-by-subject or point-by-point pattern. Write your outline in the pattern you choose.

Step 6: Write a draft of your paragraph and revise it extensively by checking the order of the points, the number of details, and the relevance and vividness of the details.

Step 7: Edit your draft for better style by combining short, choppy sentences and using effective transitions.

Step 8: Prepare a clean copy of your paragraph and proofread carefully to spot and correct any careless errors in spelling, punctuation, typing, or format.

Topics for Writing a Comparison or a Contrast Paragraph

When you write on one of these topics, be sure to follow the stages of the writing process in preparing your comparison or contrast paragraph.

1. Compare or contrast what is most important in your life now to what was most important to you as a child. You may want to brainstorm about your values then and now before narrowing your focus to specific similarities or differences.   MyWritingLab™

2. Compare or contrast any of the following: MyWritingLab™

two gifts	two jobs	two college classes
two professors	two TV shows	two apartment complexes
two relatives	two athletic teams	two friends' Facebook pages

If your instructor agrees, you may want to brainstorm points of comparison or contrast with a writing partner or a group.

MyWritingLab™

3. Compare or contrast your taste in music, or dress, or ways of spending leisure time with that of a close friend or family member.

Collaborate

4. Interview a person of your age group who comes from a different part of the country. (Note: There may be quite a few people from different parts of the country in your class.) Ask him or her about similarities or differences between his or her former home and this part of the country. You could ask about similarities or differences in dress, music, dating, nightlife, ways to spend leisure time, favorite entertainers, or anything else that you like.

   After the interview, write a paragraph that either shows how people of the same age group but from different parts of the country have different tastes in something like music or dress or share the same tastes in music, dress, etc. Whichever approach you use, include details you collected in the interview.

MyWritingLab™

5. Look carefully at the photograph of the children and their surroundings. Write a paragraph contrasting the mood of the children with the atmosphere of the background.

Topics for Critical Thinking and Writing

MyWritingLab™

1. When you were five or ten years younger, what did you expect to be doing and how did you expect to be living at the age you are now? Have you reached certain goals? If so, write about how closely your life today reflects those goals. If you haven't reached

those goals yet, contrast the ways your present life is better or less satisfying than you once anticipated.

2. As a child, you probably admired several individuals whom you considered heroes or role models. Today, you may have different individuals you admire. Write a paragraph about the ways a hero or role model from your childhood is similar to or different from one you currently admire. To develop your details, you may need to examine the values you held as a child and the ones you deem important today.

MyWritingLab™

Note: Additional writing options suitable for comparison or contrast–related assignments can be in the "Readings for Writers" appendix at the end of this book.

CHAPTER 7

Classification

Jumping In

*Electronic devices, from smartphones and tablets to laptops and desktops, come with apps (short for "applications")— software programs that help you tap into a variety of activities. You can customize your devices by downloading apps for the activities you like to do most. When you search through the thousands of apps, you'll see they are grouped in categories: games, weather, reference, finance, news, social networking, and other types. Similarly, when you write about the different subgroups of a larger topic, you are **classifying**, or breaking your topic down into clear-cut categories.*

Learning Objectives

In this chapter, you will learn to:

1. Organize details into appropriate categories.
2. Prewrite to generate a classification paragraph topic.
3. Write a classification paragraph using transitions effectively.

WHAT IS CLASSIFICATION?

When you **classify**, you divide something into different categories, and you do it according to some basis. For example, you may classify the people in your neighborhood into three types: those you know well, those you know slightly, and those you don't know at all. Although you may not be aware of it, you have chosen a basis for this classification. You are classifying the people in your neighborhood according to *how well you know them.*

Hints for Writing a Classification Paragraph

1 Organize details into appropriate categories.

1. Divide your subject into three or more categories or types. If you are thinking about classifying Blu-ray players, for instance, you might think about dividing them into cheap players and expensive players. Your basis for classification would be the price of Blu-ray players. But you would need at least one more type—moderately priced players. Using at least three types helps you to be reasonably complete in your classification.

2. Pick one basis for classification and stick with it. If you are classifying Blu-ray players by price, you cannot divide them into cheap, expensive, and Chinese. Two of the categories relate to price, but "Chinese" does not.

In the following examples, notice how one item does not fit its classification and has been crossed out.

fishermen

fishermen who fish every day
weekend fishermen
~~fishermen who own their own boat~~

(If you are classifying fishermen on the basis of how often they fish, "fishermen who own their own boat" does not fit.)

tests

essay tests
objective tests
~~math tests~~
combination essay and objective tests

(If you are classifying tests on the basis of the type of questions they ask, "math tests" does not fit because it describes the subject being tested.)

CRITICAL THINKING

Classifying involves evaluation. Evaluate potential topics for a common thread, or characteristic.

3. Be creative in your classification. While it is easy to classify drivers according to their age, your paragraph will be more interesting if you choose another basis for comparison, such as how drivers react to a very slow driver in front of them.

4. Have a reason for your classification. You may be classifying to help a reader understand a topic or choose something, or you may be trying to attack, criticize, or prove a point.

A classification paragraph must have a unifying reason behind it, and the detail for each type should be as descriptive and specific as possible. Determining your audience and deciding why you are classifying can help you stay focused and make your paragraph more interesting.

Exercise 1 **Practice: Finding a Basis for Classifying**

Write three bases for classifying each of the following topics. The first topic is done for you.

1. **topic to classify:** famous vacation locations
   You can classify on the basis of

   a. location

   b. weather

   c. activities

2. **topic to classify:** bicycles
   You can classify bicycles on the basis of

   a. _____

   b. _____

   c. _____

3. **topic to classify:** greeting cards
   You can classify greeting cards on the basis of

   a. _____

   b. _____

   c. _____

Exercise 2 **Practice: Identifying What Does Not Fit the Classification**

In each list below, one item does not fit because it is not classified on the same basis as the others on the list. First, determine the basis for the classification. Then cross out the one item on each list that does not fit.

1. **topic:** pizza

   basis for classification: _____

   list: pepperoni pizza

   medium pizza

   mushroom pizza

   peppers and onions pizza

2. **topic:** scary movies

   basis for classification: _____

   list: special effects movies

   alien invasion movies

   slasher movies

   ghost movies

3. **topic:** teachers

   basis for classification: _____

   list: psychology teachers

   kindergarten teachers

   high school teachers

   college teachers

Exercise 3 **Practice: Finding Categories That Fit One Basis for Classification** MyWritingLab™

In the lines under each topic, write three categories that fit the basis of classification that is given. The first one is done for you.

1. **topic:** cartoons on television

   basis for classification: when they are shown

   categories:

   a. *Saturday morning cartoons*

   b. *weekly cartoon series shown in the evening*

   c. *cartoons that are holiday specials*

2. **topic:** football players

   basis for classification: at what level they play

   categories:

   a. _____

   b. _____

   c. _____

3. **topic:** business people

   basis for classification: how frequently they interact with the public

   categories:

   a. _____

   b. _____

   c. _____

WRITING THE CLASSIFICATION PARAGRAPH IN STEPS

PREWRITING **CLASSIFICATION**

2 Prewrite to generate a classification paragraph topic.

First, pick a topic for your classification. The next step is to choose some basis for your classification.

Brainstorming a Basis for Classification

Sometimes the easiest way to choose one basis is to brainstorm about different types related to your topic and to see where your brainstorming leads you. For example, if you were to write a paragraph classifying phone calls, you could begin by listing anything about phone calls that occurs to you.

Phone Calls

sales calls at dinner time	people who talk too long
short calls	calls I hate getting
calls in the middle of the night	wrong numbers
calling plans	waiting for a call

The next step is to survey your list. See where it is leading you. The list on phone calls seems to have a few items about *unpleasant phone calls*:

> sales calls at dinner time
> wrong numbers
> calls in middle of night

Maybe you can label these "Calls I Do Not Want," and that will lead you toward a basis for classification. You might think about calls you *do not* want and calls you *do* want. You think further and realize that you want or do not want certain calls because of their effect on you.

You decide to use the effect of the calls on you as the basis for classification. Remember, however, that you need at least three categories. If you stick with this basis for classification, you can come up with three categories:

> calls that please me
> calls that irritate me
> calls that frighten me

By brainstorming, you can then gather details about your three categories.

Added Details for Three Categories

calls that please me
from boyfriend
good friends
catch-up calls—someone I haven't talked to for a while
make me feel close

calls that irritate me
sales calls at dinner time
wrong numbers
calls that interrupt
invade privacy

calls that frighten me
emergency call in middle of night
break-up call from boyfriend
change my life, indicate some bad change

Matching the Points Within the Categories

As you begin thinking about details for each of your categories, try to write about the same points in each type. For instance, in the list on phone calls, each category includes some details about who made the call:

> calls that please me—from good friends, my boyfriend
> calls that irritate me—from salespeople, unknown callers
> calls that frighten me—from the emergency room, my boyfriend

Each category also includes some details about why you react to them in a specific way:

> *calls that please me—make me feel close*
> *calls that irritate me—invade privacy*
> *calls that frighten me—indicate some bad change*

You achieve unity by covering the same points for each category.

Writing a Topic Sentence for a Classification Paragraph

The topic sentence for a classification paragraph should do two things:

1. It should mention what you are classifying,

2. It should indicate the basis for your classification by stating the basis or by listing your categories, or both.

Consider the details on phone calls. To write a topic sentence about the details, you should do the following:

1. Mention what you are classifying: phone calls.

2. Indicate the basis for classifying by (a) stating the basis (their effect on me) or (b) listing the categories (calls that please me, calls that irritate me, and calls that frighten me). You may also state both the basis and the categories in the topic sentence.

Following these guidelines, you can write a topic sentence like this:

> *I can classify phone calls according to their effect on me.*

or

> *Phone calls can be grouped into the ones that please me, the ones that irritate me, and the ones that frighten me.*

Both of these topic sentences state what you're classifying and give some indication of the basis for the classification. Once you have a topic sentence, you are ready to begin the planning stage of writing the classification paragraph.

Exercise 4   **Collaborate: Creating Questions to Get Details for a Classification Paragraph**

Collaborate

Do this exercise with a partner or group. Each list below includes a topic, the basis for classifying that topic, and three categories. For each list, think of three questions that you could ask to get more details about the types. The first list is done for you.

1. **topic:** sports fans expressing support for a team

   basis for classification: how supportive they are

   categories: loyal fans, extremely loyal fans, fanatic fans

   questions you can ask:

   a. How will team support be expressed on each type's car?

   b. How much team-related clothing will each type wear to a game?

   c. How will each type's support be reflected in body decoration?

2. **topic:** college students waiting in line to register for classes

   basis for classification: how stressed they are

   categories: the calm, the mildly stressed, and the overstressed

   questions you can ask:

   a. _____

   b. _____

   c. _____

3. **topic:** apps

   basis for classification: how helpful they are

   categories: productivity, educational, entertainment

   questions you can ask:

   a. _____

   b. _____

   c. _____

MyWritingLab™   **Exercise 5**   **Practice: Writing Topic Sentences for a Classification Paragraph**

Review the topics, bases for classification, and categories in Exercise 4. Then, using that material, write a good topic sentence for each topic.

Topic Sentences

for topic 1: _____

_____

for topic 2: _____

_____

for topic 3: _____

_____

PLANNING **CLASSIFICATION**

Effective Order in Classifying

After you have a topic sentence and a list of details, you can create an outline. Think about which category you want to write about first, second, and so on. The order of your categories will depend on what you're writing about. If you're classifying ways to meet people, you can save the best for last. If you're classifying three habits that are bad for your health, you can save the worst one for last.

If you list your categories in the topic sentence, list them in the same order you will use to explain them in the paragraph.

Following is an outline for a paragraph classifying phone calls. The details have been put into categories. The underlined sentences have been added to clearly define each category before the details are given.

CRITICAL THINKING

To determine the best order of categories, you will need to evaluate each category's importance.

Outline for a Classification Paragraph

topic sentence

Phone calls can be grouped into the ones that please me, the ones that irritate me, and the ones that frighten me.
<u>There are some calls that please me.</u>
They make me feel close to someone.

category 1, details

I like calls from my boyfriend, especially when he calls just to say he is thinking of me.
I like to hear from good friends.
I like catch-up calls.
These are calls from people I haven't talked to in a while.
<u>There are some calls that irritate me.</u>
These calls invade my privacy.
Sales calls always come at dinner time.

category 2, details

Most are recorded and offer me help with my credit card bills.
I get at least four wrong-number calls each week.
All these calls irritate me, and I have to interrupt what I'm doing to answer them.
<u>There are some calls that frighten me.</u>
They are the calls that tell me about some bad change in my life.

category 3, details

I once got a call in the middle of the night.
It was from a hospital emergency room.
The nurse said my brother had been in an accident.
I once got a call from a boyfriend.
He said he wanted to break up.

You can use the following checklist to help you revise your own classification outline.

Checklist for Revising the Classification Outline

✓ Do I have a consistent basis for classifying?

✓ Does my topic sentence mention what I am classifying and indicate the basis for classification?

✓ Do I have enough to say about each category in my classification?

✓ Are the categories presented in the most effective order?

✓ Am I using clear and specific details?

With a revised outline, you can begin writing your draft.

Exercise 6   **Practice: Recognizing the Basis for Classification Within the Topic Sentence**

The topic sentences below do not state a basis for classification, but you can recognize the basis nevertheless. After you've read each topic sentence, write the basis for classification on the lines provided. The first one is done for you.

1. **topic sentence:** People at the supermarket can be classified into those who qualify for the express lane, those who push a moderately filled cart, and those who drag overloaded carts.

    basis for classification: <u>how much they have in their carts</u>

2. **topic sentence:** Singers fall into three categories: the ones preteens adore, the ones college students enjoy, and the ones grandparents remember.

    basis for classification: _____

3. **topic sentence:** There are three types of traffic police: the kind, the reasonable, and the rigid.

    basis for classification: _____

Collaborate

Exercise 7   **Collaborate: Adding Details to a Classification Outline**

Do this exercise with a partner or group. In this outline, add details where the blank lines indicate. Match the points covered in the other categories.

topic sentence: Talkers in my family can be classified into the non-stop conversationalists, the moderately talkative, and the silent minority.

details: My little brother is a nonstop conversationalist.

He has just started kindergarten.

He comes home full of excitement.

He wants to tell me about his day.

He is full of stories about his activities, his class-mates, and even the pet turtle in his classroom.

My mother is less talkative.

She works in a dentist's office.

She is tired when she comes home.

_____

_____

My father, unlike my little brother and my mother, rarely talks unless he must.

_____

He doesn't want to talk about his job, where he is under constant stress.

He will answer "yes" and "no" if I ask him a direct question.

I know the members of my family well, and I understand the reasons behind each one's level of communication.

DRAFTING AND REVISING CLASSIFICATION

You can transform your outline into a first draft of a paragraph by writing the topic sentence and the details in paragraph form. As you write, you can begin adding details and inserting transitions.

③ Write a classification paragraph using transitions effectively.

Transitions in Classification

Various transitions can be used in a classification paragraph. The transitions you select will depend on what you are classifying and the basis you choose for classifying. For example, if you are classifying roses according to how pretty they are, you can use transitions like, "*one lovely kind* of rose," and "*another, more beautiful kind*," and "*the most beautiful kind*." In other classifications you can use transitions like, "the first type," "another type," or "the final type." In revising your classification paragraph, use the transitions that most clearly connect your ideas.

As you write your own paragraph, you may want to refer to a "kind" or a "type." For variety, try such other words as "class," "group," "species," "form," or "version" if it is logical to do so.

After you have a draft of your paragraph, you can revise it. The following checklist may help you with your revisions.

Checklist for Revising the Draft of a Classification Paragraph

✓ Does my topic sentence state what I am classifying?

✓ Does it indicate the basis of my classification?

✓ Do my transitions clearly connect my ideas?

✓ Should I add more details to any of the categories?

✓ Are the categories presented in the most effective order?

Following is a draft of the classification paragraph on phone calls. Compare these changes to the outline on page 151:

- An introduction has been added, in front of the topic sentence, to make the paragraph smoother.
- Some details have been added.
- Transitions have been added.
- A final sentence has been added so that the paragraph makes a stronger point.

Draft of a Classification Paragraph

(Note: Changes from the outline are underlined; editing and proofreading are still necessary.)

introduction added ———— <u>I get many phone calls, but most of them fit into three types</u>. Phone calls can be grouped into the ones that please me, the ones that irritate me, and the ones that frighten me. There are some calls that please me. They make me feel close to someone. I like calls from my boyfriend, especially when he called just to say he is thinking of me. I like to hear from my good friends. I like catch up calls. The calls from people I haven't talked to in a while.

added detail ———— <u>They fill me in on what they have been doing.</u>

transition ———— There are <u>also</u> calls that irritate me because they invade my privacy. Sales calls that feature recorded voices offer me help with my credit card bills always come at dinner

transition ———— time. <u>In addition</u>, I get at least four wrong-number calls each week. All these calls iritate me, and I have to interrupt what I'm doing to answer them. <u>The more serious</u>

added detail ———— <u>calls</u> are the ones that frighten me. They are the calls that tell me about some bad change in my life. I once got a midnight call from a hospital emergency room. It

transition ———— informed me my brother had been in an accident. <u>Another</u> time, a boyfriend called to tell me he wanted to break up.

final sentence added ———— When I get bad news by phone, I realize that the telephone can bring frightened calls as well as friendly or irritating ones.

MyWritingLab™   Exercise 8   **Practice: Identifying Transitions in a Classification Paragraph**

Underline all the transitions in the paragraph below. The transitions may be words or groups of words.

Insects that sneak into my house can be classified into the ones I expect to find, the ones that startle me, and the ones that horrify me. The first type, the ones I expect to find, are mainly ants. I am used to seeing trails of ants in my kitchen. These ants make their way across the floor when I have spilled a few drops of a sugary drink or a few crumbs of a cookie. It is easy to get rid of these insects. I simply spray a bit of insect spray or wipe up the ants with a wet paper towel. There is another kind of insect that appears in my house frequently but still makes me cringe. This group of bugs includes all species of roaches, especially the ones that fly. Roaches are sly, and they can be large. When they fly, I feel as if they are trying to bomb me. I hate to kill a roach by stepping on it or swatting it with a newspaper because the roach may not die, or worse, it may die and leave a gooey mess. As a result, I waste about half of a can of insecticide on one roach. The final kind of intruder insect is rare. However, I am now on the lookout for it. This species showed up just outside my back door recently. It was a three-inch, fat, brown, and shiny centipede. The idea that this form of garden pest was waiting to enter my house sent me into shock. In this case, I called on my friend to deal with the scary creature. However, I continue to think about the possibility that, barefoot, I could have stepped out the back door and onto this latest version of an insect intruder.

EDITING AND PROOFREADING   CLASSIFICATION

Once you are satisfied with your latest draft, it is time to edit. You can begin by combining short sentences, and refining word choice. Then you can check for any grammar, spelling, and punctuation errors. The following checklist may help you with your editing.

Checklist for Editing the Draft of the Classification Paragraph

✓ Should any of the sentences be combined?

✓ Are the verb forms consistent in tense?

✓ Are the word choices appropriate?

✓ Is the spelling correct?

✓ Is the punctuation correct?

If you compare the draft of the paragraph on page 154 to the final version, you'll notice these improvements:

- Two sentences have been combined into *There are some calls that please me because they make me feel close to a person I care about.*

- Three sentences have been combined into *I like catch-up calls, the calls from people I haven't talked to in a while that fill me in on what friends have been doing.*

- The verb form *offer* has been corrected to *offering.*

- Two sentences have been combined into *I once got a midnight call from a hospital emergency room informing me that my brother had been in an accident.*

- *Frightened* has been corrected to *frightening.*

- *My* has been added to the second sentence to be more specific.

- The word choice has been refined: *someone* has been changed to *a person I care about* to make the detail more precise, and a reference to *irritate* has been changed to *annoy* to avoid repetition. The phrase *bad change in my life* has been replaced by *some crisis in my life,* a more precise description.

Final Version of a Classification Paragraph

(Note: Changes from the draft are underlined.)

I get many phone calls, but most of them fall into one of three types. <u>My</u> phone calls can be grouped into the ones that please me, the ones that <u>irritate</u> me, and the ones that frighten me. <u>There are some calls I want to receive because they make me feel close to a person I care about.</u> I like <u>calls</u> from my boyfriend, especially when he calls just to say he is thinking of me. I like to hear from my good friends. I <u>like catch-up calls, the calls from people I haven't talked to in a while that fill me in on what friends are doing.</u> There are also calls I don't want because they invade my privacy. Sales calls that feature recorded voices <u>offering</u> me help with my credit card bills always come at dinner time. In addition, I get at least four wrong-number calls each week. All these calls <u>annoy</u> me, and I have to interrupt what I'm doing to answer them. The more serious calls are the ones I really don't want to receive. They are the calls that tell me about <u>some crisis in my life.</u> <u>I once got a midnight call from a hospital emergency room informing me that my brother had been in an accident.</u> Another time, a boyfriend called to tell me he wanted to break up. When I get bad news by phone, I realize that the telephone can bring <u>frightening</u> calls as well as friendly or irritating ones.

For your information: A sample classification essay based on this topic and following the same writing steps can be found in Chapter 13, "Different Essay Patterns: Part Two."

MyWritingLab™   **Exercise 9**   **Editing: Combining Sentences for a Better Classification Paragraph**

The paragraph below has some short sentences that would be more effective if they were combined. Combine each pair of underlined sentences into one sentence. Write the new sentence in the space above the old ones.

The three types of worries in my life are brief worries, nagging little worries, and deep, serious worries. <u>Brief worries are frequent. They don't bother me for long.</u> A brief worry may occur when I notice that I need air in my left front tire. <u>For a moment, I have a vision. I see myself stranded on the highway. I am stranded because my left front tire is completely flat.</u> As soon as I make a mental note to put air in the tire the next time I use the car, the worry goes away. Nagging little worries are different. <u>They are minor concerns. They keep returning.</u> For instance, I know that I need to lose some weight. <u>I can push this concern to the back of my mind. I can even keep this worry out of my awareness for days. It still comes back.</u> Until I make a real effort to get more exercise, I will continue to worry about my weight. The worst kind of worry is the dark and serious kind. <u>For example, I lost a cousin last year. He was an inno-</u><u>cent bystander. He happened to be near a drive-by shooting</u>. Now I fear for the safety of all the people I love. <u>However, I am working hard. I want to accept</u> <u>the loss of my cousin. I would also like to live my life as fully as I can in spite</u> <u>of my fear</u>.

Exercise 10	**Practice: Proofreading to Prepare the Final Version**	MyWritingLab™

The following classification paragraph has the kind of errors it is easy to overlook when you prepare the final version of an assignment. Correct the errors, writing above the lines. The paragraph has twelve errors.

People who do not own a car have several options for getting from one place to another; and these options include taking a bus, riding a bicycle, and walking. Each of the options have its advantages. For example riding a bus keeps a person out of rain, snow, and other, bad weather. In addition, riding a bus is generally a safe and reliable way to get around. Another advantage is that passengers on a bus have time to read, study, call their friends, or make new friends with other passengers. For other reasons, ridding a bike is attractive. One great reason is the healthy exercise that bike riding provides. Also, a person who owns a bike owns transportation that is always available as long as they takes minimal care of the bike. Best of all, bikeriders can weave their way around traffic jams and often reach their destination faster than car's and buses can. Walkers enjoy unique benefits, to. They don't have to pay bus fair, so they can save money. They don't have to maintain a bicycle find a place to put it, or worry about someone stealing it. Walkers rely souly on their bodies to get them where they want to go. Walking is an uncomplicated way to travel.

Lines of Detail: A Walk-Through Assignment

Write a paragraph that classifies bosses on the basis of how they treat their employees. To write the paragraph, follow these steps:

Step 1: List all the details you can remember about bosses you have worked for or known.

Step 2: Survey your list. Then list three categories of bosses, based on how they treat their employees.

Step 3: Now that you have three categories, study your list again, looking for matching points for all three categories. For example, all three categories could be described by this matching point: where the boss works.

Step 4: Write a topic sentence that (a) names what you are classifying and (b) states the basis for classification or names all three categories.

Step 5: Write an outline. Check that your outline defines each category, uses matching points for each category, and puts the categories in an effective order.

Step 6: Write a draft of the classification paragraph. Revise it until it has sufficient details linked logically within each category.

Step 7: Edit your paragraph to improve style by using effective sentence combining and checking for precise word choice.

Step 8: Prepare a clean copy of your paragraph and proofread it carefully to identify and correct any careless errors in punctuation, spelling, word choice, or format.

Topics for Writing a Classification Paragraph

When you write on any of these topics, be sure to work through the stages of the writing process in preparing your classification paragraph.

Collaborate

1. Write a classification paragraph on any of the topics listed below. As a first step, you will need to narrow the topic. For example, instead of classifying all cars, you can narrow the topic to *sports* cars, or food to *food at a barbecue*. If your instructor agrees, brainstorm with a partner or a group to come up with (1) a basis for your classification, (2) categories related to the basis, and (3) points you can make to give details about each of the categories.

cartoon heroes	food	haircuts
horror movies	apps	dreams
romantic movies	cars	social networks
parents	smartphone options	dancers
students	e-mail	weddings
professors	rumors	apologies
coaches	shoes	hobbies

Collaborate

2. Below are some topics. Each one already has a basis for classification. Write a classification paragraph on one of these choices. If your instructor agrees, work with a partner or group to brainstorm categories, matching points and details for the categories.

Classify the Following:

a. Exams on the basis of how *difficult they are*
b. Weekends on the basis of how *busy they are*
c. Valentines on the basis of how *romantic they are*
d. Breakfasts on the basis of how *healthy they are*
e. Holidays on the basis of *how pleasant they are for you*
f. Relatives on the basis of *how close they are to you*
g. Urban legends on the basis of *how illogical they are*

3. Look carefully at the photograph that follows. Then use its details to write a classification paragraph with this topic sentence:

MyWritingLab™

   College students can be classified according to the way they react to a professor's explanation of a concept.

Topics for Critical Thinking and Writing

1. Make a list or freewrite about your major goals and then see if you can classify them according to a single basis. For example, you might group them according to how long it will take to fulfill them (immediate, mid-range, and long-term), or you might group them according to quality-of-life goals (such as career, relationship, and humanitarian goals). You may even have several secret goals that you do not share with many people. After you have determined the basis for classifying these goals, be sure your details about each goal relate to your basis of classification.

MyWritingLab™

2. Music is an integral part of many people's lives, and some individuals believe that it plays a crucial role in coping with or celebrating life itself. Consider how important music is to people you know and classify them on the basis of how much they depend on music in their lives.

MyWritingLab™

Note: Additional writing options suitable for classification-related assignments can be found in the "Readings for Writers" appendix at the end of this book.

Jumping In

Can you define the expression on this child's face in one word? Why did you use that word? What does that word mean to you? By exploring such questions, you are now working toward a personal **definition**.

Learning Objectives

In this chapter, you will learn how to:

1. Identify a word or phrase that has a personal meaning.
2. Prewrite to generate a definition paragraph topic.
3. Write a definition paragraph that uses transitions effectively.

1 Identify a word or phrase that has a personal meaning.

WHAT IS DEFINITION?

A **definition** paragraph is one that explains *what a term means to you.* You can begin thinking about what a term means by consulting the dictionary, but your paragraph will include much more than a dictionary definition. It will communicate a personal definition.

You can select several ways to explain the meaning of a term. You can give examples, you can tell a story, or you can contrast your term with another term. If you were writing a definition of perseverance, for example, you could do one or more of the following: You could give examples of people you know who have persevered, you could tell a story about someone who persevered, or you could contrast *perseverance* with another quality, like impatience. You could also write about times when perseverance is most needed or about the rewards of perseverance.

Hints for Writing a Definition Paragraph

1. Pick a word or phrase that has a personal meaning for you and that allows you room to develop your idea. Remember that you will be writing a full paragraph on this term. Therefore, a term that can be defined quickly, in only one way, is not a good choice. For example, you would not have much to say about terms like "cauliflower" or "dental floss" unless you have strong personal feelings about cauliflower or dental floss. If you don't have such feelings, your paragraph will be very short.

When you think about a term to define, you might think about some personal quality you admire or dislike. If some quality provokes a strong reaction in you, you will probably have something to write about that term.

2. The topic sentence should have three parts. Include these items:

- the *term* you are defining
- the broad *class* or *category* into which your term fits
- the specific *distinguishing characteristics* that make the term different from all the others in the class or category

Each of the following topic sentences could be a topic sentence for a definition paragraph because it has the three parts.

     term   **category**   **distinguishing characteristics**
Resentment is the *feeling* that *life* has been unfair.

     term   **category**   **distinguishing characteristics**
A *clock watcher* is a *worker* who *is just putting in time, not effort.*

3. Select an appropriate class or category when you write your topic sentence.

> **not this:** Resentment is a thing that makes you feel life has been unfair. (Resentment is a feeling or an attitude. Say so.)

> **not this:** Resentment is when you feel life has been unfair. (*When* is a word that refers to a time, like noon or 7:00 p.m. *Resentment* is a feeling, not a time.)

> **not this:** Resentment is where a person feels life has been unfair. (*Where* is a word that refers to a place, like a kitchen or a beach. *Resentment* is not a place; it is a feeling.)

> **but this:** Resentment is the feeling that life has been unfair.

4. Express your attitude toward the term you are defining in the "distinguishing characteristics" part of the topic sentence. Make that attitude clear and specific.

> **not this:** Resentment is the feeling that can be bad for a person. (Many feelings can be bad for a person. Hate, envy, anger, and impatience, for instance, can all be bad. What is special about resentment?)

> **not this:** Resentment is an attitude of resenting another person or a circumstance. (Do not define a word with another form of the word.)

> **but this:** Resentment is the feeling that life has been unfair.

5. Use specific and concrete examples to explain your definition. *Concrete* terms refer to things you can see, touch, taste, smell, or hear. Using concrete terms and specific examples will make your definition interesting and clear.

You may be asked to define an *abstract* idea like happiness. Even though an abstract idea cannot be seen, touched, tasted, smelled, or heard directly, you can give a personal definition of it by using concrete terms and specific examples.

> **not this:** Happiness takes place when you feel the joy of reaching a special goal. ("Joy" and "special goal" are abstract terms. Avoid defining one abstract term by using other abstract terms.)

> **but this:** I felt happiness when I saw my name at the top of the list of athletes picked for the team. Three months of daily, six-hour practices had paid off, and I had achieved more than I had set out to do. (The abstract idea of happiness is linked to a specific, concrete example of feeling happiness.)

If you remember to show, not tell, your reader what your term means, you'll have a better definition. Be especially careful not to define a term with another form of that term.

MyWritingLab™   **Exercise 1**   **Practice: Recognizing Abstract and Concrete Words**

In the list below, put an *A* by the abstract words and a *C* by the concrete words.

1. _____ respect	9. _____ webmaster
2. _____ trust	10. _____ patriotism
3. _____ propeller	11. _____ beauty
4. _____ traitor	12. _____ song
5. _____ sorrow	13. _____ suspicion
6. _____ island	14. _____ bracelet
7. _____ Internet	15. _____ rainbow
8. _____ courtesy	16. _____ dignity

MyWritingLab™   **Exercise 2**   **Practice: Completing a Topic Sentence for a Definition Paragraph**

Following are unfinished topic sentences for definition paragraphs. Finish each sentence so that the sentence expresses a personal definition of the term and has the three requirements for a definition's topic sentence.

1. A penny pincher is a person who _____

    _____

2. A game plan is a strategy for _____

    _____

3. Tailgating is the traffic offense of _____

    _____

4. A selfie _____

_____

5. A sore loser is a competitor who _____

_____

6. Nitpicking is the habit of _____

_____

7. A lemon is a car that _____

_____

8. Cyber crime is a term for illegal activity that _____

_____

| Exercise 3 | **Practice: Recognizing Problems in Topic Sentences for Definition Paragraphs** |

MyWritingLab™

Review the three components that should be included in the topic sentence for a definition paragraph. Then read the topic sentences below, put an *X* next to each sentence that has a problem, and underline the part of the sentence that is faulty.

1. _____ A sense of fun is a gift for enjoying the humor in everyday situations.

2. _____ An amusement park is a place where people go to amuse themselves.

3. _____ Rage is when a person feels uncontrollable anger at another person or about a situation.

4. _____ Emotional stability is where someone feels in control of his or her emotions.

5. _____ Doubt is the inability to trust another person or oneself.

6. _____ Adolescence is the thing that all teenagers struggle to endure.

7. _____ A crisis is a sudden situation that creates fear and extreme stress.

8. _____ A temper tantrum is a loud and juvenile expression of anger.

| Exercise 4 | **Collaborate: Writing Examples for Definition Paragraphs** |

Collaborate

Below are incomplete statements from definition paragraphs. Complete them in the spaces below by writing specific examples. When you have completed the statements, share your work with a group. After each group member has read his or her examples aloud, discuss the examples. Which examples did you like best? Which are the clearest and most specific? Do some examples lead to a different definition of a term than other examples do?

The first part of each sentence has been started for you.

1. I first experienced bullying when _____

_____

_____

Another example of bullying took place at _____ and the

victim was _____

_____

_____

2. One person who was extremely generous to me was my older

brother. He gave me _____

when _____

_____

Some people are generous to family members; others perform acts

of generosity to total strangers. For example, _____

_____

_____

3. A time when a person must learn to forgive is when _____

_____

_____

I saw forgiveness in action when _____

_____

_____

2 Prewrite to generate a definition paragraph topic.

WRITING THE DEFINITION PARAGRAPH IN STEPS

PREWRITING **DEFINITION**

To pick a topic for your definition paragraph, begin with some personality trait or type of person. For instance, you might define "the insecure person." If you listed your first thoughts, your list might look like this:

the insecure person
someone who is not emotionally secure
wants (needs?) other people to make him or her feel good
lacks self-esteem

CRITICAL THINKING

Selecting a topic involves differentiating meaning. Words often have different meanings for different cultural or social groups. Analyze and evaluate your topic based on one group's meaning.

Using Questions to Get Details

Often, when you look for ideas to define a term, you get stuck with big, general statements or abstract words, or you simply cannot come up with enough to say. If you are having trouble getting ideas, think of questions about your term. Jot these questions down without stopping to answer them.

One question can lead you to another question. Once you have five or more questions, you can answer them, and the answers will provide details for your definition paragraph.

If you were writing about the insecure person, for example, you could begin with questions like these:

What are insecure people like?
What behavior shows a person is insecure?
How do insecure people dress or talk?
What makes a person insecure?
How do insecure people relate to others?
Does insecurity hurt the insecure person? If so, how?
Does the insecure person hurt others? If so, how?

By scanning the questions and answering as many as you can, you can add details to your list. Once you have a longer list, you can review it and begin to group the items on the list. Following is a list of grouped details on the insecure person.

Grouped Details on the Insecure Person

wants (needs?) other people to make him or her feel important

lacks self-esteem

insecure people have to brag about everything

a friend who brags about his car

they tell you the price of everything

they put others down

saying bad things about other people makes insecure people feel better

insecure people can never relax inside

can never enjoy being with other people

other people are always their competitors

must always worry about what others think of them

The Topic Sentence

Grouping the details can help you arrive at several main ideas. Can they be combined and revised to create a topic sentence? Following is a topic sentence on the insecure person that meets the requirements of naming the term, placing it in a category, and distinguishing the term from others in the category:

>   **term**   **category**   **distinguishing characteristics**
> The *insecure person* is *someone* who *needs other people to make him or her feel respected and important.*

Once you have a topic sentence, you can begin working on the planning stage of the paragraph.

Exercise 5 **Practice: Designing Questions to Gather Details**   MyWritingLab™

Following are terms that could be defined in a paragraph. For each term, write five questions that could lead you to details for the definition. The first one has been done for you as an example.

1. **term:** arrogance

   questions: a. <u>Do I know anyone who displays arrogance?</u>

   b. <u>Is there any celebrity I think is arrogant?</u>

   c. <u>What is an arrogant action?</u>

   d. <u>What kind of remark is an example of arrogance?</u>

   e. <u>Why are people arrogant?</u>

2. **term:** a nagger

   questions: a. _____

   b. _____

   c. _____

   d. _____

   e. _____

3. **term:** flexibility

   questions: a. _____

   b. _____

   c. _____

   d. _____

   e. _____

MyWritingLab™   **Exercise 6**   **Practice: Grouping Related Ideas for a Definition Paragraph**

Following is a list of ideas for a definition paragraph. Read the list several times; then group all the ideas on the list into one of the three categories below. Put the letter of the category next to each idea.

Categories:

   G = how secrecy can be **good**

   B = how secrecy can be **bad**

   D = **dealing** with secrecy

List

1. _____ Too much secrecy can poison a marriage or other close relationship.

2. _____ A surprise birthday party can be a wonderful secret.

3. _____ To protect national security, some countries have to keep certain weapons programs a secret.

4. _____ A shameful family secret can poison generations who try to hide the truth.

5. _____ Trusting a friend or sibling can mean allowing that person the privacy of small secrets such as the content of his or her e-mail.

6. _____ Spying to discover a secret is rarely a good idea unless life-or-death matters are involved.

7. _____ Secret codes or ID numbers protect consumers' credit.

8. _____ Children should be allowed the privacy of having a secret, imaginary friend.

9. _____ In most cases, if a friend confides a secret pain or sorrow to another friend, the listener should keep the secret.

10. _____ A bank that hides the reality of its failing investments puts the well-being of thousands in jeopardy.

PLANNING   DEFINITION

To make an outline for a definition paragraph, start with the topic sentence and list the grouped details. Often, a first outline does not have many examples or concrete, specific details. A good way to be sure you put specific details and concrete examples into your paragraph is to include shortened versions of them in your revised outline. If you compare the following outline to the grouped list of details on page 165, you will see how specific details and concrete examples have been added.

Outline for a Definition Paragraph

topic sentence The insecure person is someone who needs other people to make him or her feel respected and important.

details Insecure people have to brag about everything.
An insecure friend may brag about his car.

added detail — Insecure people wear expensive jewelry and tell you what it costs.

added detail — They brag about their expensive clothes.

added detail — They make sure they wear clothes with trendy labels, another kind of bragging.

added example — When some friends were talking about Susan's great new job, Jill had to make mean remarks about Susan. Jill hated having Susan look like a winner.
Insecure people can never relax inside.
They can never enjoy being with other people.
Other people are always their competitors.

added example — Luke can't enjoy any game of basketball unless he is the star.

concluding sentence — Insecure people must always worry about what others think of them.

When you prepare your own definition outline, use the following checklist to help you revise.

Checklist for Revising a Definition Outline

✓ Does my topic sentence include a category and the characteristics that show how my term is different from others in the category?

✓ Have I defined my term so that it is different from any other term?

✓ Am I being concrete and specific in the details?

✓ Do I have enough examples?

✓ Do my examples relate to the topic sentence?

✓ Are my details in the most effective order?

With a revised outline, you are ready to begin writing a rough draft of your definition paragraph.

MyWritingLab™   **Exercise 7**   **Practice: Rewriting a Topic Sentence for a Definition Paragraph**

Below is an outline in which the topic sentence does not make the same point as the rest of the outline. Rewrite the topic sentence so that it relates to the details.

topic sentence: A sixth sense is a strange sense.

details: My grandmother believes that her sixth sense changed the course of her life.

At seventeen, my grandmother was engaged to be married to a man she had known all her life.

He was kind, handsome, and hardworking.

A month before the wedding, she met a new man, Daniel, at a cousin's party.

Daniel was a tall, skinny man with few social skills.

Although my grandmother thought Daniel was quite unattractive and irritating, she could not stop thinking about him.

A week later, she cancelled her wedding to her fiancé.

Daniel and my grandmother soon married and have been happy together for forty-five years.

I never believed in a sixth sense until recently.

I have taken the same route to work for years.

It involves crossing an old bridge.

One day last month, I was approaching the bridge when I had a sick feeling.

I decided to turn around and take a different way to work.

Later that day, a portion of the old bridge collapsed into the water.

Two drivers were seriously hurt.

Even animals seem to have a sixth sense.

I recently read the story of a mutt and his family.

At 4:00 a.m., the dog began whining, trying to wake up the mother and father.

Then the dog began running to the baby in her crib.

The father got up to push the dog outside.

Outside, the dog began to cry.

At last, the father opened the door and the dog ran inside, still crying.

Finally, both parents looked inside the crib.

The baby was unconscious and had a dangerously high fever.

In the emergency room, a doctor said the dog had saved the baby's life.

Rewrite the topic sentence: _____

_____

Exercise 8   **Practice: Revising an Example to Make It More Concrete and Specific**   MyWritingLab™

The following outline contains one example that is too abstract. In the lines provided, rewrite the example that is too abstract, using more specific, concrete details.

topic sentence:	Culture shock is an extreme reaction to a new way of living.
details: **example 1**	I first experienced culture shock when I was sent away to summer camp.

At first I was horrified by the living conditions at the camp.

I and five other boys had to sleep in a rustic cabin with rickety bunk beds.

The bathrooms were primitive.

We went to bed early and were awakened even earlier.

I hated the food, but there was no place to buy snacks.

It took me a week of misery before I adjusted to the campers' lifestyle.

example 2   A weekend visit to New York City was my next experience of culture shock.

I could not believe the thousands of people cramming the sidewalks.

I tried hard to keep up with the pace of the New Yorkers as they confidently and aggressively made their way.

The crush of travelers on the subway made me nervous.

In my grandfather's New York apartment, I couldn't see how the man could live in such a small, dark, dirty place surrounded by constant noise.

example 3   Culture shock also struck on my first days on a college campus.

Students looked different than they did in high school.

Classes were different, too.

My schedule seemed so easy.

I felt a little confused because the rules seemed looser than those in high school.

On the other hand, I was nervous about messing up.

revised example: _____

_____

_____

_____

_____

_____

_____

_____

_____

_____

_____

_____

_____

_____

_____

3 Write a definition paragraph that uses transitions effectively.

DRAFTING AND REVISING   **DEFINITION**

To write the first draft of your definition paragraph, you can rewrite the outline in paragraph form, combining some of the short sentences and adding more details. Remember that your purpose in this definition paragraph is to explain your personal understanding of a term. Therefore, you want to be sure that your topic sentence is clear and that your explanation connects your details to the topic sentence. Careful use of transitions will link your details to your topic sentence.

Transitions

Since you can define a term in many ways, you can also use many transitions. If you are listing several examples in your paragraph, you can use transitions like "first," "second," and "finally." If you are contrasting your term with another, you can use transitions like "on the other hand" or "in contrast." You may want to alert or remind the reader that you are writing a definition paragraph by using phrases like "can be defined as," "can be considered as," "means that," or "implies that."

Because many definitions rely on examples, the transitions below are ones you may want to use.

INFO BOX Transitions for a Definition Paragraph

a classic case of ____ is ____	in fact	another time
another case	in one case	sometimes
for example	in one instance	specifically
for instance	one time	

Sample Draft

Following is a draft of the definition paragraph on the insecure person. When you read it, you'll notice several changes from the outline on page 167.

- Transitions have been added in several places. Some transitions let the reader know an example is coming, some transitions link one point about the topic to another point, and other transitions connect an example to the topic sentence.
- Examples have been made concrete and specific.

You may also spot some careless errors that can be corrected during the editing and proofreading stage.

Draft of a Definition Paragraph

(Note: Changes from the outline are underlined; editing and proofreading are still necessary.)

The insecure person is someone who needs other people to make him or her feel respected and important. The insecure person loves to brag about everything. <u>For instance</u>, a friend may brag about his car. <u>He tells everyone he meets that he drives a Mercedes.</u> An insecure person tells you the price of everything. He wears expensive jewelry and tells you what it costs, <u>like</u> the person who always flashes his <u>Rolex</u> watch. <u>Another</u> insecure person will brag about her expensive cloth or make sure she always wears clothes with trendy labels, <u>another kind</u> of bragging. <u>Bragging is not the only way an insecure person tries to look good;</u> he or she may put other people down. Saying bad things about other people can put the insecure person on top. <u>For instance</u>, some friends were recently talking about another friend, Susan, who had just started a great new job. Jill had to

(Continued)

Labels (left column): transition; specific details; transition; added detail, transition; transition; transitional sentence; transition

added details ⎯⎯⎯ ⎧ add some mean remarks <u>about how lucky Susan had been</u>
<u>to get the job since Susan really wasn't qualified for it</u>. Jill hated
to have Susan look like a winner. The insecure person can hurt

transition ⎯⎯⎯⎯⎯⎯ others <u>but also</u> suffers inside. <u>Such a person</u> can never relax
because he or she always sees other people as competitors. <u>An</u>
<u>example of this attitude is</u> seen in Luke, <u>a college acquaintance</u>

added details ⎯⎯⎯ ⎩ <u>who always plays pickup basketball games. Even though the</u>
<u>games are just for fun</u> Luke can't enjoy any game unless he is
the star. Luke is a typically insecure person, for he must always
worry about what others think of him.

The following checklist may help you revise the draft of your own definition
paragraph:

Checklist for Revising the Draft of a Definition Paragraph

✓   Is my topic sentence clear?

✓   Have I written enough to define my term clearly?

✓   Is my definition interesting?

✓   Could it use another example?

✓   Could it use more details?

✓   Do I need any words, phrases, or sentences to link the examples or details
to the topic sentence?

✓   Do I need any words, phrases, or sentences to reinforce the topic
sentence?

MyWritingLab™   Exercise 9   **Practice: Adding Examples to a Draft of a Definition**
Paragraph

Two of the following paragraphs need examples with concrete, specific
details to explain their points. Where the lines indicate, write an example
with concrete, specific details. Each example should be at least two sentences long. The first paragraph is done for you.

1. Listlessness is the feeling that nothing is worth starting. After a hectic

week, I often wake up on Saturday morning feeling listless. I just do not have the

energy to do the things I intended to do. <u>I may have planned to wash my car, for</u>

<u>example, but I cannot bring myself to get going. I cannot put together the bucket,</u>

<u>detergent, brushes, and window cleaner I need to start the process. I tell myself,</u>

<u>"Why wash the car? It will probably rain anyway."</u> Another time I feel listless is when

I am faced with a big assignment. <u>For instance, I hate to start a term paper because there is so much to do. I have to think of a topic, do research, read, take notes, plan, write, and revise. When I am faced with so many things to do, I don't do anything. I tell myself it is not worth starting because I will probably get a bad grade on the paper anyway.</u> I put off getting started. I let listlessness get the better of me.

2. Tact is the ability to express oneself without needlessly hurting another person's feelings. My boss at the clothing store where I work is a very tactful person. Customers often ask my boss how they look in an item they are trying on. My boss must be tactful in her answer. _____

_____

_____

_____ I have tried to be tactful in declining an invitation.

_____

_____

_____

_____

Of course, there are times when there is no way to be both tactful and honest.

_____

_____

_____

Although tact cannot always prevent others from feeling embarrassment or pain, tact is a great tool in many situations.

3. A clock watcher is a person who always wants to leave a place early. Clock watchers are commonly seen in the workplace. _____

_____

_____

_____

_____ Clock

watchers have a hard time sitting still in a classroom. _____

_____

_____

_____

Clock watchers sometimes obsess about leaving a large sports or social event

early. _____

_____

_____

_____ Clock watchers cannot really experience

the present moment because they are preoccupied with getting away from it.

MyWritingLab™   **Exercise 10** **Practice: Identifying the Words That Need Revision in a Definition Paragraph**

The following paragraph has too many vague, abstract words. Underline the words that you think should be replaced with more specific or concrete words or examples.

Chronic complainers are people who rarely appreciate what they have or where they are and who like to share their dissatisfaction. A chronic complainer might have a nice car, but he will always note its flaws. For example, he will remind others that his car doesn't get the best gas mileage or doesn't have other stuff. Chronic complainers are also likely to be unhappy with their jobs or financial situation. A chronic complainer who works in a bank, for example, may whine that she is only a teller when she should be higher up by now. Another chronic complainer will spend hours moaning that he cannot afford anything because his boss is unfair. Eventually, friends and relatives tend to spend less time with a chronic complainer. It is not fun to be around someone who can poison any social event, even a conversation over a cup of coffee, with bitterness, anger, and whatnot. Sooner or later, a chronic complainer will be unhappy about losing friends.

Exercise 11 **Practice: Adding the Right Transitions to a Definition Paragraph**   MyWritingLab™

In the following paragraph, circle the correct transition in each of the pairs.

Calm is a state of mind in which a person can think clearly. Words such as "agitated," "upset," "elated," or "thrilled" describe the opposite of calm. Neither emotional lows nor highs are a good background for making a major decision. For instance / In one case, people making choices about getting a job, leaving college, or starting a relationship must be able to weigh the positive and negative aspects of their choice. In one instance / Specifically, when they reach a decision, people need to rely on their ability to reason rather than on a momentary high or low mood. That is, they must reach a level of calm. One way that people can recognize a calm state of mind is to be sure that they do not feel rushed into making a decision. Sometimes / In another case, people refer to "calm seas," and the term refers to a good time to sail. In calm seas, ships may not sail as fast, but they are not tossed about by rough waves. In the same way, calm people are not tossing up and down emotionally. One time / In fact, calm people are slowly but confidently moving to a choice.

EDITING AND PROOFREADING   DEFINITION

Once you are satisfied with your latest draft, it is time to edit. You can begin by combining short sentences and refining word choice. Then you can review your draft for grammar, spelling, and punctuation errors. The checklist below may help you edit effectively:

Checklist for Editing the Draft of the Definition Paragraph

✓ Should any of the sentences be combined?

✓ Are the verb forms correct and consistent?

✓ Are the word choices appropriate?

✓ Is the spelling correct?

✓ Is the punctuation correct?

If you compare the draft on page 171 to the following final version of the paragraph on the insecure person, you will see these changes:

- To keep the paragraph consistent in person, the word *you* has been dropped.
- *Cloth* has been corrected to *clothes*.
- *Criticize* replaced *put other people down*, and *criticizing* replaced *saying bad things*.
- A comma has been added after the subordinating clause *Even though the games are just for fun*.
- The wording has been improved so that it is more precise.

Final Version of a Definition Paragraph

(Note: Changes from the draft are underlined.)

The insecure person is someone who needs other people to make him or her feel respected and important. <u>To get respect</u>, the insecure person loves to brag about everything. For instance, a friend may brag about his car. He tells everyone he meets that he drives a Mercedes. An insecure person tells <u>people</u> the price of everything. He wears expensive <u>jewelry</u> and tells <u>people</u> what it costs, like the man who always flashes his Rolex watch. Another insecure person will brag about her expensive <u>clothes</u> or make sure she wears clothes with trendy labels, another kind of bragging. Bragging isn't the only way an insecure person tries to look good; he or she may also <u>criticize</u> other people. <u>Criticizing</u> others can put the insecure person on top. For instance, some friends were recently talking about another friend, Susan, who had just started a great new job. Jill had to add some mean remarks about how lucky Susan had been to get the job since Susan really wasn't qualified for it. Jill couldn't stand to have Susan look like a winner. The insecure person <u>like Jill</u> can hurt others but also suffers inside. Such a person can never relax because he or she always sees other people as competitors. An example of this attitude can be seen in Luke, a college acquaintance who always plays pick-up basketball games. <u>Even though the games are just for fun,</u> Luke can't enjoy any game unless he is the star. Luke is a typically insecure person, for he must always worry about what others think of him.

> **For your information:** A sample definition essay based on this topic and following the same writing steps can be found in Chapter 13, "Different Essay Patterns: Part Two."

MyWritingLab™   **Exercise 12   Practice: Combining Sentences in a Definition Paragraph**

The following definition paragraph has some short, choppy sentences that could be combined. These pairs or clusters of sentences are underlined. Combine each pair or cluster into one smooth sentence, and write the new sentence in the space above the original ones.

A peacemaker is a socially gifted person who knows how to resolve con-

flicts. My mother is a peacemaker. <u>She has a natural skill. Her skill enables her to</u>

<u>detect a family conflict. It is a family conflict that is about to begin. She can</u>

resolve it. <u>She can resolve it quickly</u>. She coaxes the unhappy family members into

conversing honestly and calmly. Soon, what could have been a hot argument has

cooled down. My high school hockey coach was a peacemaker, too. <u>However, he</u>

<u>was different from my mother. He was a tough, often physically involved settler of</u>

<u>arguments</u>. Hockey can be a brutal game. My coach could sense anger brewing

between players. <u>Before it started and spread, he did something. He grabbed the</u>

<u>unhappy players. He scolded, shouted, and threatened them</u>. His talent was his

ability to push the players face to face before they created a chaotic situation. In a

less physical way, some diplomats can bring nations together. <u>A diplomat can do</u>

<u>this by convincing hostile countries to send their representatives. Each country's</u>

<u>representatives meet at a neutral location</u>. There the representatives and the dip-

lomats talk calmly. <u>In the neutral atmosphere, things can happen. Treaties can be</u>

<u>written. Trade agreements can be reached</u>. Peacemaking can be global, or it can

be personal. Either way, a special person has to initiate it.

Exercise 13   **Practice: Correcting Errors in the Final Version of a**
                  Definition Paragraph   MyWritingLab™

The following definition paragraph has the kinds of errors that are easy to
overlook in a final version. Correct the errors by writing above the lines.
There are eleven errors in the paragraph.

    A luxury is a pleasant experience that a person does not usally have a

chance to enjoy. For example, to a person who works 8 or ten hours a day at a

demanding job, getting out of work two hrs. early is, a luxury. It gives that person

time to do anything he or she choses, from catching up on chores to spending time

with a friend. A millionaire whose schedule allows his more freedom may think a

luxury is a trip to the Seychelles Islands for sun and scuba diving. On the other

hand, a child who doesn't spend much time with his busy parents' will feel that a

whole day spent with his mother or father is a luxury. One Strange aspect of lux-

ury is that something that was once a luxury may lose it's appeal if it is experience

regularly. For example, the worker who becomes accustomed to leaving work

early may gradually take the new schedule for granted. Similarly, a rich woman who can travel anywhere may become bored by cruises and sightseeing. However, lonely children who gets to spend more time with a parent may no longer consider that time a luxury, but they will never become sick of the attention.

Lines of Detail: A Walk-Through Assignment

Write a paragraph that gives a personal definition of the secure person. To write the paragraph, follow these steps:

Step 1: List all your ideas about a secure person.

Step 2: Write at least five questions that can add details about a secure person. Answer the questions as a way of adding details to your list.

Step 3: Group your details; then survey your groups.

Step 4: Write a topic sentence that includes the term you are defining, puts the term into a category, and distinguishes the term from others in the category.

Step 5: Write an outline. Begin by writing the topic sentence and the groups of details. Then add more details and specific examples.

Step 6: Write a draft of your paragraph. To revise, check that you have enough examples, that your examples fit your definition, and that the examples are in an effective order and linked logically. Remember that careful revision may involve writing several rough drafts before you are satisfied.

Step 7: Edit your latest draft by focusing on improving your sentence structure, word choices, and transitions. Also, correct any serious spelling or grammatical errors.

Step 8: Proofread a clean copy of your work to check for missing words and any careless errors in spelling, punctuation, format, or typing.

Topics for Writing a Definition Paragraph

When you write on any of these topics, be sure to work through the stages of the writing process in preparing your definition paragraph.

Collaborate

1. Define an abstract term using concrete, specific details. Choose from the following list. You can begin by looking up the term in a dictionary to be sure you understand the dictionary meaning. Then write a personal definition.

   You can begin by freewriting. If your instructor agrees, you can read your freewriting to a group for reactions and suggestions. If you prefer, you can begin by brainstorming a list of questions to help you define the term. Again, if your instructor agrees, you can work with a group to develop brainstorming questions. Here is the list of abstract terms:

loyalty	loneliness	success
superstition	generosity	bliss
boredom	style	persistence
initiative	charisma	envy
ambition	charity	independence
suspicion	selfishness	self-discipline

2. Write a definition of a type of person. Develop your personal definition with specific, concrete details. You can choose one of the following types or choose your own type.

Collaborate

Freewriting on the topic is one way to begin. If your instructor agrees, you can read your freewriting to a group for reactions and suggestions. You can also begin by brainstorming a list of questions to help you define your term. If your instructor agrees, you can work with a group to develop brainstorming questions. Following is the list of types.

the procrastinator	the bully	the old reliable friend
the braggart	the bodybuilder	the jock
the organizer	the neatness fanatic	the joker
the optimist	the dieter	the dreamer
the workaholic	the manipulator	the fan
the compulsive liar	the whiner	the achiever

3. Think of one word that best defines you. In a paragraph, define that word, using yourself as a source of examples and details. To begin, you may want to freewrite about several words that define you; then you can select the most appropriate one.

MyWritingLab™

4. Using Google or a similar search engine, type in the words "Web log" and "blog." Investigate as many definitions as you can of the term "blog." Based on this information, write a definition of this term and assume your audience is a group of adults who have never read or written a blog. Your definition may include examples of blogs from the fields of politics, entertainment, news, business, and education.

MyWritingLab™

5. Study the photograph of the soldiers in battle. Then write a paragraph that defines (1) combat stress or (2) courage under fire.

MyWritingLab™

Topics for Critical Thinking and Writing

MyWritingLab™ 1. Think of a word or phrase that has different meanings to different groups (age groups, political groups, people in different levels of socioeconomic status, and so on). For example, "freedom" means something different to a person in prison than it means to a teen who has a curfew. Choose an abstract word and write at least three meanings of it. Be sure to assign each meaning to a specific group or type of individual.

MyWritingLab™ 2. Too often, people resort to using stereotypes when they describe a group or even a type of person. For example, the word "politician" is a derogatory term when it is spoken with a condescending tone of voice in certain circumstances, but not all those who choose a career in public service are the same. As another example, "a free spirit" can be described as someone who is either highly creative and independent or unpredictable and erratic. Consider three terms that are commonly used today as quick, stereotypical definitions for complicated issues. In addition, explain how each term has alternate meanings.

> **Note:** Additional writing options suitable for definition-related assignments can be found in the "Readings for Writers" appendix at the end of this book.

MyWritingLab™ Visit Chapter 8, "Definition," in *MyWritingLab* to test your understanding of the chapter objectives.

Cause and Effect

CHAPTER 9

Jumping In

*What do you think may have helped this individual get this far in college? How can her college experience help her face new challenges? The answers to these questions focus on the **causes** and **effects** of her college success.*

Learning Objectives

In this chapter, you will learn how to:

1 Identify immediate and long-range cause and effect.

2 Prewrite to generate a cause or effect paragraph topic, deciding on the best order in which to present details.

3 Write a cause or effect paragraph that incorporates transitions and details effectively.

WHAT IS CAUSE AND EFFECT?

Almost every day, you consider the causes or effects of events so that you can make choices and take action. In writing a paragraph, when you explain the **reasons** for something, you are writing about **causes**. When you write about the **results** of something, you are writing about **effects**. Often in writing, you consider both the causes and effects of a decision, an event, a change in your life, or a change in society, but in this chapter, you will be asked to *concentrate on either causes (reasons) or effects (results)*.

1 Identify immediate and long-range cause and effect.

Hints for Writing a Cause or Effect Paragraph

1. Pick a topic you can handle in one paragraph. A topic you can handle in one paragraph is one that (a) is not too big and (b) doesn't require research.

Some topics are so large that you probably can't cover them in one paragraph. Topics that are too big include ones such as:

Why People Get Angry
Effects of Unemployment on My Family

Other topics require you to research the facts and to include the opinions of experts. They would be good topics for a research paper, but not for a one-paragraph assignment. Topics that require research include ones such as:

The Causes of Divorce
The Effects of Television Viewing on Children

When you write a cause or effect paragraph, choose a topic you can write about by using what you already know. That is, make your topic smaller and more personal. Topics that use what you already know are ones such as:

Why Children Love Animal Cartoon Characters
The Causes of My Divorce
What Enlistment in the Navy Did for My Brother
How Alcoholics Anonymous Changed My Life

2. Try to have at least three causes or effects in your paragraph. Be sure you consider immediate and remote causes or immediate and remote effects. Think about your topic and gather as many causes or effects as you can *before* you start drafting your paragraph.

An event usually has more than one cause. Think beyond the obvious, the **immediate cause**, to more **remote causes**. Although the immediate cause of your car accident might be the other driver who hit the rear end of your car, the more remote causes might include the weather conditions or the condition of the road.

Situations can have more than one effect, too. If you take Algebra I for the second time and you pass the course with a "C," an **immediate effect** (result) is that you fulfill the requirements for graduation. But there may be **long-range effects** (also called **remote results**). Your success in Algebra I may help to change your attitude toward mathematics courses, may build your confidence in your ability to handle college work, or may lead you to sign up for another course taught by the same teacher.

3. Make your causes and effects clear and specific. If you are writing about why short haircuts are popular, don't write, "Short haircuts are popular because everybody is getting one," or "Short haircuts are popular because they are a trend." If you write either of those statements, you have really said, "Short haircuts are popular because they are popular."

Think further. Have any celebrities been seen with this haircut? Write the names of actors, athletes, or musicians who have the haircut, or the name of the movie and the actor that started the trend. By giving specific details that explain, illustrate, or describe a cause or effect, you help the reader understand your point.

 4. Write a topic sentence that indicates whether your paragraph is about causes or effects. You should not announce, but you can *indicate*.

> **not this:** The effects of my winning the scholarship are going to be discussed. (an announcement)

> **but this:** Winning the scholarship changed my plans for college. (indicates effects will be discussed)

You can *list* a short version of all your causes or effects in your topic sentence, like this:

> The high price of concert tickets has enriched a few performers and promoters, excluded many fans, and threatened the future of live entertainment.

You can just *hint* at your points by summarizing them, like this:

> The high price of concert tickets has brought riches to a few but hurt many others.

Or you can use words that *signal* causes or effects.

> **words that signal causes:** reasons, why, because, motives, intentions

> **words that signal effects:** results, impact, consequences, changed, threatened, improved

---

Exercise 1   **Practice: Selecting a Suitable Topic for a Cause or Effect Paragraph**   MyWritingLab™

Below is a list of topics. Some are suitable for a cause or effect paragraph. Some are too large to handle in one paragraph, some would require research, and some are both too large and would require research. Put an *X* next to any topic that is not suitable.

 1. _____ The Effects of Alcoholism on the Children of Alcoholics

 2. _____ The Impact of Unemployment on College Students

 3. _____ The Reasons I Was Accused of Burglary

 4. _____ My Father's Motives for Leaving His Family

 5. _____ How a Stranger's Kindness Changed One Baby's Fate

 6. _____ The Worldwide Consequences of Texting While Driving

 7. _____ The Causes of Online Gaming Addiction

 8. _____ How Gambling Changes Personalities

CRITICAL THINKING

When devising a topic and developing a paragraph, think carefully about immediate causes and effects as well as remote causes and long-range effects. Think of a row of dominoes. Touching the first one affects the last one as well.

MyWritingLab™ **Exercise 2** **Practice: Recognizing Cause and Effect in Topic Sentences**

In the list below, if the topic sentence is for a cause paragraph, put *C* next to it. If the sentence is for an effect paragraph, put *E* next to it.

1. _____ Once my brother left home, he developed more mature attitudes toward earning, spending, and saving money.

2. _____ Chloe's trip to Brazil had a surprising impact on her career plans.

3. _____ I broke up with my boyfriend to escape his constant criticism, make my own friends, and reconnect with my family.

4. _____ Dr. Menendez has three reasons for opening a free clinic near the farm workers' camp.

5. _____ One successful semester at college changed my mother's hopes, ambitions, and self-esteem.

6. _____ When adult children leave home, their parents may feel lonely, unfocused, and even unloved.

7. _____ Failing an advanced biology class affected my career choice.

8. _____ One way to explain the impact of social networking on our lives is to examine how people regularly use it.

WRITING THE CAUSE OR EFFECT PARAGRAPH IN STEPS

2 Prewrite to generate a cause or effect paragraph topic, deciding on the best order in which to present details.

PREWRITING **CAUSE OR EFFECT**

Once you've picked a topic, the next—and very important—step is getting ideas. Because this paragraph will contain only causes *or* effects and details about them, you must be sure you have enough causes or effects to write a developed paragraph.

Freewriting on a Topic

One way to get ideas is to freewrite on your topic. Since causes and effects are so clearly connected, you can begin by freewriting about both and then choose one, causes or effects, later.

If you were thinking about writing a cause or effect paragraph on owning a car, you could begin by freewriting something such as:

Freewriting on Owning a Car

A car of my own. Why? I needed it. Couldn't get a part-time job without one. Because I couldn't get to work. Needed it to get to school. Of course I could have taken the bus to school. But I didn't want to. Feel like a grown-up when you have a car of your own. Freedom to come and go. I was the last of my friends to have a car. Couldn't wait. An old Ford. But I fixed it up nicely. Costs a lot to maintain. Car payments, car loan. Car insurance.

Now you can review the freewriting and make separate lists of the causes and effects you wrote down:

causes (reasons)

needed to get a part-time job
needed to get to school
my friends had cars

effects (results)

feel like a grown-up
freedom to come and go
costs a lot to maintain
car payments
car loan
car insurance

Because you have more details on the effects of owning a car, you decide to write an effects paragraph.

Your list of effects can be used several ways. You can add to it if you think of ideas as you are reviewing your list. You can begin to group ideas in your list and then add to it. Following is a grouping of the list of effects; grouping helps you see how many effects and details you have.

effects of getting my own car

effect 1: I had to pay for the car and related expenses.
details: costs a lot to maintain
           car payments
           car loan
           car insurance
effect 2: I had the freedom to come and go.
details: none
effect 3: I felt like a grown-up.
details: none

Will these effects work in a paragraph? One way to decide is to try to add details to the ones that have no details. Ask questions to get those details.

effect 2: I had the freedom to come and go.

What do you mean?

Well, I didn't have to beg my father for his truck anymore. I didn't have to get rides from friends. I could go to the city when I wanted. I could ride around just for fun.

effect 3: I felt like a grown-up.

What do you mean, "like a grown-up"?

Adults can go where they want, when they want. They drive themselves.

If you look carefully at the answers to the questions above, you'll find that the two effects are really *the same*. By adding details to both effects, you'll find that both are saying that owning a car gives you the adult freedom to come and go.

So the list needs another effect of owning a car. What else happened, how else did things change when you got your car? You might answer:

I worried about someone hitting my car.
I worried about bad drivers.
I wanted to avoid the scratches you get in parking lots.

With answers like these, your third effect could be:

I became a more careful driver.

Now that you have three effects and some details, you can rewrite your list. You can add details as you rewrite.

List of Effects of Getting My Own Car

effect 1:	*I had to pay for the car and related expenses.*
details:	*costs a lot to maintain*
	car loans
	car insurance
effect 2:	*I had the adult freedom to come and go.*
details:	*didn't have to beg my father for his truck*
	didn't have to get rides from friends
	could go to the city when I wanted
	could ride around for fun
effect 3:	*I became a more careful driver.*
details:	*worried about someone hitting the car*
	worried about bad drivers
	wanted to avoid the scratches cars get in parking lots

Devising a Topic Sentence

With at least three effects and some details for each effect, you can create a topic sentence. The topic sentence for this paragraph should indicate that the subject is the *effects* of getting a car. You can summarize all three effects in your topic sentence, or you can just hint at them. A possible topic sentence for the paragraph can be:

Owning my own car cost me money, gave me freedom, and made me more careful about how I drive.

or

Once I got a car of my own, I realized the good and bad sides of ownership.

With a topic sentence and a fairly extensive list of details, you are ready to begin the planning stage in preparing your paragraph.

Collaborate

Exercise 3   **Collaborate: Devising Questions for a Cause or Effect Paragraph**

Below are four topics for cause or effect paragraphs. For each topic below, write five questions that could lead you to ideas on the topic. (The first one is completed for you.) After you've written five questions for each topic, give your list to a member of your writing group. Ask him or her to add one question to each topic and then to pass the exercise on to the next member of the group. Repeat the process so that each group member adds to the lists of all the other members.

Later, if your instructor agrees, you can answer the questions (and add more questions and answers) as a way to begin writing a cause or effect paragraph.

1. **topic:** the effects of cell-phone cameras on crime

   questions that can lead to ideas and details:

   a. <u>Are unsuspecting people photographed and blackmailed?</u>

   b. <u>Can the cameras be used to photograph confidential documents?</u>

   c. <u>Are the cameras being used by Peeping Toms?</u>

   d. <u>Can criminals use the camera-phones to photograph banks?</u>

   e. <u>Can citizens photograph a crime in progress?</u>

   additional questions: <u>Can citizens photograph a suspect or perpetrator?</u>
   <u>Can police use the cameras in surveillance?</u>

2. **topic:** the effects of a regularly scheduled, widely available bus service to campus

   questions that can lead to ideas and details:

   a. _____

   b. _____

   c. _____

   d. _____

   e. _____

   additional questions: _____

   _____

3. **topic:** why many adults drink beverages full of sugar

   questions that could lead to ideas and details:

   a. _____

   b. _____

   c. _____

   d. _____

   e. _____

   additional questions: _____

   _____

Exercise 4   **Practice: Creating Causes or Effects for Topic Sentences**   MyWritingLab™

For each of the following topic sentences, create three causes or effects, depending on what the topic sentence requires. The first one is completed for you.

1. **topic sentence:** Sticking to an exercise routine has both improved and complicated my life.

   a. <u>I am in better physical shape than I have been in years.</u>

   _____

    b. The physical exercise also gives me a mental boost. _____

    _____

    c. I now have to find time to fit my routine into my busy schedule. _____

    _____

2. **topic sentence:** Studying with a friend can be a useful way to pre-pare for a test.

    a. _____

    _____

    b. _____

    _____

    c. _____

    _____

3. **topic sentence:** There are several reasons why people gain weight in the winter.

    a. _____

    _____

    b. _____

    _____

    c. _____

    _____

PLANNING   **CAUSE OR EFFECT**

With a topic sentence and a list of causes (or effects) and details, you can draft an outline of your paragraph. Once you have a rough outline, you can work on revising it. You may want to add to it, to take out certain ideas, to rewrite the topic sentence, or to change the order of the ideas. The following checklist may help you revise your outline:

Checklist for Revising the Outline of a Cause or Effect Paragraph

✓   Does my topic sentence make my point?

✓   Does it indicate whether my paragraph is about causes or effects?

✓   Does the topic sentence relate to the rest of the outline?

✓   Have I included enough causes or effects to make my point?

✓   Have I included enough details?

✓   Should I eliminate any ideas?

✓   Is the order of my causes or effects clear and logical?

The Order of Causes or Effects

Looking at a draft outline can help you decide on the best order for your causes or effects. There is no single rule for organizing causes or effects. Instead, you should think about the ideas you are presenting and decide on the most logical and effective order. For example, if you are writing about some immediate and some long-range effects, you might want to discuss the effects in a **time order**. You might begin with the immediate effect, then discuss what happens later, and end with what happens last of all. If you are discussing three or four effects that are not in any particular time order, you might save the most important effect for last, for an **emphatic order**. If one cause leads to another, then use the **logical order** of discussing the causes.

Compare the following outline on owning a car to the list of effects on page 186. Notice that, in the outline, the carefree side of owning a car comes first, and the cares of owning a car, the expense and the worry, come later. The topic sentence follows the same order.

Outline for an Effects Paragraph

revised topic sentence

Owning my own car gave me freedom, cost me money, and made me careful about how I drive.

effect 1 details
I had the adult freedom to come and go.
I didn't have to beg my father for his truck.
I didn't have to get rides from my friends.
I could go to the city when I wanted.
I could ride around for fun.

effect 2 details
I had to pay for the car and related expenses.
A car costs a lot to maintain.
I had a car loan to pay.
I had car insurance.

effect 3 details
I became a more careful driver.
I worried about someone hitting the car.
I worried about bad drivers.
I wanted to avoid the scratches cars can get in a parking lot.

Once you have a revised outline of your cause or effect paragraph, you are ready to begin writing your draft.

Exercise 5 **Practice: Writing Topic Sentences for Cause or Effect Outlines**   MyWritingLab™

The following outline has no topic sentence. Read the outline carefully several times. Then write a topic sentence.

topic sentence: _____

_____

details: Many of my high school friends were planning to attend Coolidge Technical College.

As a result, I would have people to socialize with at the college.

I wouldn't feel as lonely as I would at a college full of strangers.

Coolidge Technical College offered two-year degrees in Culinary Science, and I was thinking of becoming a chef.

I like the idea of learning a marketable skill in two years.

Location was my main reason for choosing to attend Coolidge Technical College.

The college was only fifteen minutes away from my parents' house.

I could save money on rent and food by continuing to live at home.

I could save on transportation costs, too.

MyWritingLab™   **Exercise 6**   **Practice: Revising the Order of Causes or Effects**

Following are topic sentences and lists of causes or effects. Reorder each list according to the directions given at the end of the list. Put "1" by the item that would come first, and so forth.

1. **topic sentence:** Going on a diet changed my father's life.

   _____ He learned the difference between healthy and unhealthy food.

   _____ After eating right for a year, my father was better able to control his diabetes.

   _____ Once my father began to choose more healthy foods such as fruits, vegetables, and fish, he began to have more energy.

   Use this order: Time order

2. **topic sentence:** Reducing my work hours so that I could attend college has had negative and positive effects on me.

   _____ I am constantly short of money.

   _____ I can see the career possibilities that education can offer.

   _____ I enjoy the challenge of college.

   Use this order: The order indicated by the topic sentence, from bad to good.

CRITICAL THINKING

When determining the most effective ordering of items, you will need to evaluate the time sequence and importance of each item.

Exercise 7 **Practice: Developing an Outline** MyWritingLab™

The following outline needs one more cause or effect and details for that cause or effect. Fill in the missing parts.

topic sentence: People give many reasons for ending a relationship.

cause 1: Some say they are not ready for a commitment.

details: They say they need time to find themselves.
They swear that they value their freedom.
They feel that the relationship has developed too quickly.

cause 2: Others tend to blame the partner in the relationship.

details: Some say the partner is too possessive.
Others claim the partner is too demanding.
Others complain that they do not want to argue anymore.

cause 3: _____

_____

details (at least two sentences): _____

_____

_____

_____

_____

DRAFTING AND REVISING CAUSE OR EFFECT

Once you have an outline in good order, with a sufficient number of causes or effects and a fair amount of detail, you can write a first draft of the paragraph. When the first draft is complete, you can read and reread it, deciding how you'd like to improve it. The checklist below may help you revise.

3 Write a cause or effect paragraph that incorporates transitions and details effectively.

Checklist for Revising the Draft of a Cause or Effect Paragraph

✓ Does my topic sentence indicate cause or effect?

✓ Does it relate to the rest of the paragraph?

✓ Do I have enough causes or effects to make my point?

✓ Do I have enough details for each cause or effect?

✓ Are my causes or effects explained clearly?

✓ Is there a clear connection between my ideas?

✓ Have I shown the links between my ideas?

✓ Do I need an opening or closing sentence?

Linking Ideas in Cause or Effect

When you write about how one event or situation causes another, or about how one result leads to another, you have to be very clear in showing the connections between events, situations, or effects.

One way to be clear is to rely on transitions. Some transitions are particularly helpful in writing cause and effect paragraphs.

INFO BOX Transitions for a Cause or Effect Paragraph

For cause paragraphs:

because	for	for this reason	since
due to			

For effect paragraphs:

as a result	hence	so	therefore
consequently	in consequence	then	thus

Making the Links Clear

Using the right transition is not always enough to make your point. Sometimes you have to write the missing link in your line of thinking so that the reader can understand your point. To write the missing link means writing phrases, clauses, or sentences that help the reader follow your point.

> **not this:** Many mothers are working outside the home. Consequently, microwave ovens are popular.

> **but this:** Many mothers are working outside the home and have less time to cook. Consequently, microwave ovens, which can cook food in minutes, are popular.

The hard part of making clear links between ideas is that you have to put yourself in your reader's place. Remember that your reader cannot read your mind, only your paper. Connections between ideas may be very clear in your mind, but you must spell them out on paper.

Revising the Draft

Assume that the following paragraph is a revised draft of the paragraph on owning a car. When you read it, you'll notice many changes from the outline on page 189.

- The details on "car payments" and "a car loan" said the same thing, so the repetition has been cut.
- Some details about the costs of maintaining a car and about parking have been added.
- The order of the details about the costs of a car has been changed. Now, paying for a car comes first; maintaining it comes after.
- Sentences have been combined.
- Transitions have been added.

You may spot some careless errors that can be corrected during the editing and proofreading stage.

Draft of an Effects Paragraph

(Note: Changes from the outline are underlined; editing and proofreading are still necessary.)

transition

transition

order of details changed

added details

transitional phrase

transition

Owning my own car gave me freedom, cost me money, and made me more careful about how I drive. <u>First of all</u>, my car gives me the adult freedom to come and go. I didn't have to beg my father for his truck. I didn't have to ask for rides from my friends anymore. I could go to the city or even ride around for fun when I wanted. <u>On the negative side</u>, I had to pay for the car and related expenses. I had to pay for the car loan. I also had to pay for the car insurance. <u>A car costs a lot to maintain, too. I paid for oil changes, tune-ups, tires, belts and filters. With so much of my money put into my car</u>, I became a more careful driver. I worried about someone hitting the car and watched out for bad drivers. <u>In addition</u>, I wanted to avoid the scratchs a car can get in a parking lot, so I always parked far away from other cars.

Exercise 8 **Practice: Making the Links Clear**

MyWritingLab™

Following are ideas that are linked, but their connection is not clearly explained. Rewrite each pair of ideas, making the connection clear.

1. It's been raining all week. As a result, I've been taking an allergy pill every day.

   rewritten: _____

   _____

   _____

   _____

   (**Hint:** What is the connection between your allergies and rain?)

2. Alex wanted a real Cuban dish of beans and rice. Therefore, he went home for the weekend.

   rewritten: _____

   _____

   _____

   _____

   (**Hint:** Can someone at home make Alex a real Cuban dish of beans and rice?)

3. The first dog I saw at the animal shelter had a long, thick coat of red hair. Consequently, I chose a brown dog with shorter hair.

   rewritten: _____

   _____

   _____

   _____

   (**Hint:** Were you worried about the amount of hair the first dog would shed?)

Exercise 9   **Practice: Revising a Paragraph by Adding Details**

The following paragraph is missing details. Add at least two details as you extend the paragraph by two additional sentences.

Being diagnosed with diabetes had a tremendous impact on me. When the doctor told me the news, I was horrified. My first thoughts focused on losing a limb or dying young. In addition, the misery of constantly monitoring my blood sugar levels, giving myself frequent injections, and rigidly following a limited diet scared me. Once I became more informed and rational about the challenges I faced, I was angry. I could not understand why I had the bad luck of developing diabetes. I cursed my situation and wallowed in self-pity. Learning to eat healthy foods, to control my blood sugar, and to avoid infections seemed like punishments I did not deserve. When I finally accepted my situation, I understood that the doctor's diagnosis had been a gift of life. _____

_____

_____

_____

_____

_____

Once I let go of misery, fear, and anger, I found a new gratitude for being alive.

EDITING AND PROOFREADING   **CAUSE OR EFFECT**

Once you are satisfied with your latest draft, it is time to edit. As you strive to improve your style and check for mistakes, the following checklist will help you edit effectively:

Checklist for Editing a Draft of a Cause or Effect Paragraph

✓ Should any sentences be combined?

✓ Are the verb forms correct and consistent?

✓ Are the word choices appropriate?

✓ Is the spelling correct?

✓ Is the punctuation correct?

As you check your latest draft for errors in sentence length, grammar, spelling, or preparation, you can also look out for small improvements in the style and continuity of the paragraph. When you contrast the final version with the draft on page 193, you'll notice several changes:

- An introductory sentence has been added.
- The transitional phrase *to avoid dangers in the parking lot as well as on the road* has been added for better style.
- The verb form *gives* has been corrected to *gave*.
- The sentence *I didn't have to beg my father for his truck* has been combined with *I didn't have to get rides from my friends anymore.*
- The sentence *I had to pay for the car loan* has been combined with *I had to pay for car insurance.*
- A comma has been added after *belts*.
- The spelling of *scratches* has been corrected.
- Some words have been changed so that the language is more precise.

Changes in style, word choice, and transitions can all be made before you decide on the final version of your paragraph. You may also want to add an opening or closing sentence to your paragraph.

Final Version of an Effects Paragraph

(Note: Changes from the draft are underlined.)

When I bought my first car, I wasn't prepared for all the changes it made in my life. Owning my own car gave me freedom, cost me money, and made me careful about how I drive. First of all, my car gave me the adult freedom to come and go. I didn't have to beg my father for his truck or get rides from my friends anymore. I could go to the city or even ride around for fun when I wanted. On the negative side, I had to pay for the car and related expenses. I had to pay for both the car loan and car insurance. A car costs money to maintain, too. I paid for oil changes, tune-ups, tires, belts, and filters. With so much of my money put into my car, I became a more careful driver. I worried about someone hitting the car and watched out for bad drivers. To avoid dangers in the parking lot as well as on the road, I always parked my car far away from other cars, keeping my car safe from scratches.

For your information: A sample effects essay based on this topic and following the same writing steps can be found in Chapter 13, "Different Essay Patterns: Part Two."

Exercise 10   **Practice: Editing a Draft by Combining Sentences**   MyWritingLab™

Combine the underlined sentences in the following paragraph. Write your combinations in the space above the original sentences.

Quitting smoking changed me in some unexpected ways. First, it gave me a

real sense of power. I had been sure that quitting would be impossible for me.

I was smoking a pack a day. At that time, I decided to try cutting back. My initial goal was to cut my smoking in half. <u>I was able to do this. It did not take much effort. It took me about three months</u>. When I had achieved this goal, I aimed to push ahead. I tried hard to cut my cigarette habit to five cigarettes per day. <u>Eventually I succeeded in limiting myself to five a day. Then I tried four a day. Next I cut my limit to three</u>. The hardest part was giving them up entirely, but I did it. Once I quit, I changed in another way. I developed a new understanding of the reasons that nonsmokers avoid smokers. <u>I realized that rooms do absorb the smell of cigarettes. The clothes that smokers wear smell, too. Smokers also have bad breath</u>. Suddenly I became someone who avoided smoke-filled people and rooms. Finally, breaking the smoking habit led me to make another big change. I stopped drinking. During the time when I was cutting back on cigarettes, I became aware that nothing made me crave a cigarette more than drinking a beer or mixed drink. In my final days as a smoker, I avoided any temptation to smoke. As a result, I stopped drinking. Now I am determined to stay nicotine-free. <u>I am alcohol-free as well. I have broken two habits. I am twice as healthy as I expected to be</u>.

MyWritingLab™ | **Exercise 11** | **Practice: Correcting a Final Copy of a Cause or Effect Paragraph**

Following are one cause and one effects paragraph with the kind of errors it is easy to overlook when you prepare the final version of an assignment. Correct the errors, writing above the lines. There are thirteen errors in the first (cause) paragraph; there are twelve errors in the second (effects) paragraph.

Paragraph 1

I got my job at a Discount Appliance store for three reason's. First, I used my imagination and asked myself, "Who would want to hire me"? I didn't have much experience because I had spent the last three years at one job. That job was unpacking merchandise at my uncle's dollar store. When he had to close his store, I started thinking about my skills. I was able to carry heavy loads, I was careful not to break the merchandise, and I knowed how to make the best use of storage space. When, I realized that I did have some skills, I kept looking for a place that needed them.

After any employer turned me down, I checked with him or her several more times. Soon I became a familiar, face. I smiled, and learned the names of the boss and the staff at each place of work. However, I also learned not to a nuisance. The last reason that I eventually found work was the more important. I swore that I was willing to work for a low wage. I was not to proud to accept any offer. I now have a job at the delivery entrance to a large household appliance store. I unload and fit large boxes of Refrigerators, stoves, washers, and dryers into tight storeage areas. By selling my skills, persevering, and accepting a minimum wage, I found employment.

Paragraph 2

When I was younger, I had a mania for clothes shopping and the crazyness hurt me in several way. First, I shopped in a state of elation, and I lost my common sense. The first item that caught my eye became irresistible. I felt that bying it would, change my life. I knew that I had to have it. After I bought it, some shoes or jeans or a jacket seemed to be calling me. I craved them, too. In such an irrational state, I bought some hideous clothes. Second, I never truely enjoyed the experience of buying the items because the endless shopping was a compulsion. In every store, I acted like a robot. Hours after I returned home, I look at my purchases and felt disappointed. The new clothes hadn't changed much about my life. In fact; all the new purchases have done was to change my bank balance. The worse affect of my mania was the constant worry about paying for my shopping spree's. This fear became overwhelming as the bills kepped coming. My mania brought me three emotions: a rush of elation, inevitable disappointment, and endless fear.

Lines of Detail: A Walk-Through Assignment

Write a paragraph on this topic: Why Many Adults Drink Beverages Full of Sugar. To write your paragraph, follow these steps:

Step 1: Go back to Exercise 3 starting on page 186. Topic 3 is the same topic as this assignment. If you have already done that exercise, you have 5 or more questions that can lead you to ideas and details. If you haven't completed the exercise, try topic 2 on page 187.

Step 2: Use the answers to your questions to prepare a list of ideas and details. Put the items on your list into groups of causes and related details. Add to the groups until you have at least three causes (and related details) for the similarity in many college students' wardrobes.

Step 3: Write a topic sentence that fits your causes.

Step 4: Write an outline. Check that your outline has sufficient details and that you have put the causes in the best order.

Step 5: Write a rough draft of your paragraph and revise it until you have enough specific details to explain each cause. Your details should be logical, clearly stated, and ordered effectively. You may have to work through several drafts until you are satisfied.

Step 6: Edit your work extensively to improve style and correct any serious mistakes. Decide if your paragraph needs an opening sentence and/or a concluding sentence for better structure.

Step 7: Prepare a clean copy of your paragraph and proofread it carefully to spot and correct any careless spelling, punctuation, typing, or format errors.

Topics for Writing a Cause or Effect Paragraph

When you write on any of the following topics, be sure to work through the stages of the writing process in preparing your cause or effect paragraph.

MyWritingLab™

1. Write a cause paragraph on one of the following topics. You create the topic by filling in the blanks.

   Why People Choose _____

   Why People Stop _____

   Why People Enjoy _____

   Why People Start _____

Collaborate

2. Write a one-paragraph letter of complaint to the manufacturers of a product you bought or to the company that owns a hotel, a restaurant, an airline, or some other service you used. In your letter, write at least three reasons why you (1) want your money refunded or (2) want the product replaced. Be clear and specific about your reasons. Be sure your letter has a topic sentence.

   If your instructor agrees, read a draft of your letter to a writing partner while your partner pretends to be the manufacturer or the head of the company. Afterwards, ask your partner to point out where your ideas are not clear or convincing and where you make your point effectively.

Collaborate

3. Think of a current fad or trend. The fad can be a popular style of clothing, type of movie, style of music, a sport, a pastime, a kind of food or drink, an athlete, a gadget, an invention, an appliance, and so on. Write a paragraph on the causes of this fad or trend or the effects of it.

   If your instructor agrees, begin by brainstorming with a group. Create a list of three or four fads or trends. Then create a list of questions to ask (and answer) about each fad or trend. If you are going to write about **causes**, for example, you might ask questions like these:

What changes in society have encouraged this trend?
Have changes in the economy helped to make it popular?
Does it appeal to a specific age group? Why?
Does it meet any hidden emotional needs? For instance, is it a way to gain status, to feel safe, or to feel powerful?

If you are going to write about **effects**, you might ask questions like these:

Will this trend last?
Has it affected competitors?
Is it spreading?
Is the fad changing business, education, or the family?
Has it improved daily life?

4. Write a paragraph that summarizes the effects of relying on a computer for composing most, if not all, of your writing assignments. Remember that the effects may be both positive and negative, so you will need to brainstorm or freewrite first. Be sure your final version of the paragraph reflects logical organization of details and appropriate transitions.

   MyWritingLab™

5. After looking at the photograph, write a paragraph on why joining an exercise group can have social benefits.

   MyWritingLab™

Topics for Critical Thinking and Writing

1. Why do you think so many Americans do not register or even bother to vote? Pose this question to some of your peers and friends to gather as many reasons as you can for so much voter apathy. Determine three main causes and use emphatic order (least to most significant) as you explain each cause.

   MyWritingLab™

2. Applying the same techniques suggested in topic 1, ask friends, peers, and family members who are registered voters why they feel voting is so important. Determine three main causes and use emphatic order as you explain each cause.

3. Police often have difficulty finding witnesses to a crime such as a violent street assault or a neighborhood robbery. Why are some eyewitnesses reluctant or afraid to cooperate with authorities? As you brainstorm or freewrite about this topic, consider both rational and irrational reasons people give for not helping with an investigation. Discuss the three most common reasons and include the degree of rationality in each reason.

> **Note:** Additional writing options suitable for cause- or effect-related assignments can be found in the "Readings for Writers" appendix at the end of this book.

Jumping In

Is competition good or bad? Does participation in sports keep teens out of trouble? Should athletes who are found guilty of using banned substances be admitted to the Hall of Fame? When you use reasons and details to persuade readers to agree with your opinion on such issues, you are writing an **argument**.

Learning Objectives

In this chapter, you will learn how to:

1 Recognize the argument's targeted audience.

2 Prewrite to generate an argument paragraph topic, grouping ideas and ordering reasons.

3 Write a convincing argument paragraph that incorporates transitions effectively.

WHAT IS ARGUMENT?

A written **argument** is an attempt to *persuade* a reader to think or act in a certain way. When you write an argument paragraph, your goal is to get people to see your point so that they are persuaded to accept it and perhaps to act on it.

In an argument paragraph, you take a stand. Then you support your stand with reasons. In addition, you give details for each reason. Your goal is to persuade your reader by making a point that has convincing reasons and details.

① Recognize the argument's targeted audience.

Hints for Writing an Argument Paragraph

1. Pick a topic you can handle. Your topic should be small enough to be covered in one paragraph. For instance, you can't argue effectively for world peace in just one paragraph.

2. Pick a topic you can handle based on your own experience and observation. Topics like legalizing drugs, gun control, capital punishment, or air pollution require research into facts, figures, and expert opinions to make a complete argument. They are topics you can write about convincingly in a longer research paper, but for a one-paragraph argument, pick a topic based on what you've experienced yourself.

> **not this topic:** Organized Crime
> **but this topic:** Starting a Crime Watch Program in My Neighborhood

3. Do two things in your topic sentence: name the subject of your argument and take a stand. The following topic sentences do both.

> **subject**   **takes a stand**
> The college cafeteria should serve more healthy snacks.

> **subject**   **takes a stand**
> High school athletes who fail a course should not be allowed to play on a school team.

You should take a stand, but *don't* announce it:

> **not this:** This paragraph will explain why Springfield needs a teen center.
> **but this:** Springfield should open a teen center. (This is a topic sentence with a subject and a stand.)

4. Consider your audience. Consider why these people should support your points. How will they be likely to object? How will you get around these objections? For instance, you might want to argue to the residents of your community that the intersection of Hawthorne Road and Sheridan Street needs a traffic light. Would anyone object?

At first, you might think, "No. Why would anyone object? The intersection is dangerous. There's too much traffic there. People risk major accidents getting across the intersection." However, if you think further about your audience, which is the people in your community, you might identify these objections: (1) Some town residents may not want to pay for a traffic signal, and (2) some drivers may not want to spend extra time waiting for a light to change.

There are several ways to handle objections:

> You can *refute* an objection. To refute it means to prove that it isn't valid, that it isn't true. For instance, if someone says that a light wouldn't do any good, you might say that a new light has already worked in a nearby neighborhood.

> Sometimes it's best to admit the other side has a point. You have to *concede* that point. For instance, traffic lights do cost money, and waiting for a light to change does take time.

> Sometimes you can *turn an objection into an advantage*. When you acknowledge the objection and yet use it to make your own point, you show that you've considered both sides of the argument. For instance,

you might say that the price of a traffic signal at the intersection is well worth the expense because that light will buy safety for all the drivers who try to cross Hawthorne Road and Sheridan Street. As an alternative, you might say that waiting a few moments for the light to change is better than waiting many minutes for an opening in the heavy traffic of the intersection.

5. Be specific, clear, and logical in your reasons. As always, think before you write. Think about your point and your audience. Try to come up with at least three reasons for your position.

Be careful that your reasons do not overlap. For instance, you might write the following:

topic sentence:	College students should get discounts on movie tickets.
audience:	Owners of movie theaters
reasons:	1. Many college students can't afford current ticket prices.
	2. The cost of tickets is high for most students.
	3. More people in the theater means more popcorn and candy sold at the concession stand.

But reasons 1 and 2 overlap; they are really part of the same reason.

Be careful not to argue in a circle. For instance, if you say, "One reason for having an after-school program at Riverside Elementary School is that we need one there," you've just said, "We need an after-school program because we need an after-school program."

Finally, be specific in stating your reasons.

not this: One reason to start a bus service to and from the college is to help people.

but this: A bus service to and from the college would encourage students to leave their cars at home and use travel time to study.

Exercise 1 **Practice: Recognizing Good Topic Sentences for an Argument Paragraph**   MyWritingLab™

Some of the topic sentences below are appropriate for an argument paragraph. Some are for topics that are too large for one paragraph, and some are for topics that would require research. Some are announcements. Some do not take a stand. Put *OK* next to the sentences that would work well in an argument paragraph.

1. _____ Residents of the Whispering Pines neighborhood must not let their dogs run loose.

2. _____ We must learn to protect our national forests and green spaces if we wish to save our planet.

3. _____ Our community needs a local noise ordinance forbidding excessively loud sound systems in cars and trucks.

4. _____ Something must be done about the growing problem of identity theft.

5. _____ Why flu shots should be free to children is the topic to be discussed.

6. _____ More online courses should be available to juniors and seniors at Emerson High School.

7. _____ The mini-mart outside of our town should provide better security for its night clerks.

8. _____ Quality First, the largest employer in the county, needs an on-site child care center for the children of its employees.

Collaborate

| Exercise 2 | **Collaborate: Recognizing and Handling Objections** |

Below are the topic sentences of arguments. Working with a group, list two possible objections to each argument that might come from the specific audience identified. Then think of ways to handle each objection, by refuting it, conceding it, or trying to turn it to your advantage. On the lines provided, write the actual sentence(s) you would use in a paragraph.

1. **topic sentence:** The downtown area of Carsonville needs a network of bike paths.

   audience: The residents of Carsonville

   possible objections from this audience:

   a. _____

   _____

   b. _____

   _____

   answering objections:

   a. _____

   _____

   b. _____

   _____

2. **topic sentence:** Large commercial moving vans should not be allowed to park on the streets of Bayside overnight.

   audience: residents of Bayside who are planning to move and need to use a van

   possible objections from this audience:

   a. _____

   _____

   b. _____

   _____

   answering objections:

   a. _____

   _____

   b. _____

   _____

WRITING THE ARGUMENT PARAGRAPH IN STEPS

`PREWRITING` **ARGUMENT**

Imagine that your instructor has given you this assignment:

> Write a one-paragraph letter to the editor of your local newspaper. Argue for something in your town that needs to be changed.

CRITICAL THINKING

Remember that your argument involves persuading, so be sure you have valid information and convincing details to present a compelling case.

One way to begin is to **brainstorm** for some specific thing that you can write about.

> Is there a part of town that needs to be cleaned up?
> Should something be changed at a school?
> What do I notice on my way to work or school that needs improvement?
> What could be improved in my neighborhood?

By answering these questions, you may come up with one topic, and then you can list ideas on it.

topic
Cleaning Up Roberts Park

ideas
dirty and overgrown
benches are all cracked and broken
full of trash
could be fixed up
people work nearby
they would use it

You can consider your audience and possible objections:

audience
people of all ages who read the local paper

possible objections from this audience
would cost money
more important things to spend money on

answering objections
Money would be well spent to beautify the downtown.
City children could play there in the fresh air and in nature; workers could eat lunch there.

Grouping Your Ideas

Once you have a list, you can start grouping the ideas on your list. Some of the objections you wrote down may actually lead you to reasons that support your argument. That is, by answering objections, you may come up with reasons that support your point. Following is a list with a point to argue, three supporting reasons, and some details about cleaning up Roberts Park.

List for an Argument Paragraph

point:	We should fix up Roberts Park.
reason:	Improving the park would make the downtown area more attractive to shoppers.
details:	Shoppers could stroll in the park or rest from their shopping.
	Friends could meet in the park for a day of shopping and lunch.
reason:	City children could play in the park.
details:	They could get fresh air.
	They could play in a natural setting.
reason:	Workers could eat lunch outdoors.
details:	Several office complexes are nearby.
	Workers would take a break outdoors.

With three reasons and some details for each, you can draft a topic sentence. Remember that your topic sentence for an argument should (1) name your subject and (2) take a stand. Below is a topic sentence about Roberts Park that does both.

> subject   takes a stand
> Roberts Park should be cleaned up and improved.

With a topic sentence, you are ready to move on to the planning stage of preparing an argument paragraph.

MyWritingLab™   Exercise 3   **Practice: Distinguishing Between Reasons and Details**

The following list has three reasons and details for each reason. Put *reason 1*, *reason 2*, and *reason 3* next to the points on the following list. Then put *detail for 1*, *detail for 2*, or *detail for 3* by the items that give details about each reason. There may be more than one sentence of detail connected to one reason.

topic sentence: Crystal Lake needs a weekly farmers' market.

_____ Many people want fresh, locally grown produce, plants, crafts, and baked goods.

_____ Small, local farmers need local outlets for their produce.

_____ Seasonal vegetables and fruits straight from the fields taste better than supermarket produce.

_____ Small family farms can bring their products to a nearby market and save money on shipping costs.

_____ Neighbors meet at the market, talk, and share coffee and homemade muffins.

_____ Fresh produce is healthier than food treated with preservatives and other chemicals.

_____ Farmers' markets bring a community together.

_____ Those who regularly shop at the market become friends with the merchants.

_____ Many supermarket chains deal only with agricultural conglomerates and don't sell local produce.

_____ When a farmer can tell a customer how to prepare a vegetable or how to use a fruit in a salad, the farmer is likely to make a sale.

Exercise 4   **Practice: Finding Reasons to Support an Argument**   MyWritingLab™

Give three reasons that support each point. In each case, the readers of your local newspaper will be the audience for an argument paragraph.

1. **point:** Ridgeview needs regular bus service on the weekends, not just on the weekdays.

   reasons: a. _____

   _____

   b. _____

   _____

   c. _____

   _____

2. **point:**   Backpacks should be banned at elementary schools.

   reasons: a. _____

   _____

   b. _____

   _____

   c. _____

   _____

PLANNING   ARGUMENT

With a topic sentence and a list of reasons and details, you can draft an outline. Then you can review it, making whatever changes you think it needs. The checklist below may help you to review and revise your outline.

Checklist for Revising an Argument Outline

✓ Does my topic sentence make my point? Does it state a subject and take a stand?

✓ Have I considered the objections to my argument so that I am arguing intelligently?

✓ Do I have all of the reasons I need to make my point?

✓ Do any reasons overlap?

✓ Are my reasons specific?

✓ Do I have enough details for each reason?

✓ Are my reasons in the most effective order?

The Order of Reasons in an Argument

When you are giving several reasons, it is a good idea to keep the most convincing or most important reason for last. Saving the best for last is called using **emphatic order**. For example, you might have these three reasons to tear down an abandoned building in your neighborhood: (1) The building is ugly. (2) Drug dealers are using the building. (3) The building is infested with rats. The most important reason, the drug dealing, should be used last, for emphatic order.

Following is an outline on improving Roberts Park. When you look at the outline, you'll notice several changes from the list on page 206:

- Since the safety of children at play is important, it is put as the last reason.

- Some details have been added.

- A sentence has been added to the end of the outline. It explains why improving the park is a good idea even to people who will never use the park themselves. It is a way of answering these people's objections.

Outline for an Argument Paragraph

topic sentence	Roberts Park should be cleaned up and improved.
reason	Improving the park would make the downtown area more attractive to shoppers.
details	Shoppers could stroll through the park or rest there after shopping. Friends could meet at the park for a day of shopping and lunch.
reason	Workers from nearby offices and stores could eat lunch outdoors.
details	Several office complexes are nearby. An hour outdoors is a pleasant break from work.
reason	City children could play there.
details	They would get fresh air. They would play on grass, not on asphalt. They would not have to play near traffic.
concluding sentence: benefit	An attractive park improves the city, and all residents benefit when the community is beautified.

MyWritingLab™   Exercise 5   **Practice: Working with the Order of Reasons in an Argument Outline**

Following are topic sentences and lists of reasons. For each list, put an *X* by the reason that is the most significant, the reason you would save for last in an argument paragraph.

1. topic sentence: Door-to-door sales of candy, raffle tickets, or other fundraising items should be outlawed.

reason 1: _____ The solicitations are annoying.

reason 2: _____ Opening a door to a stranger can lead to a crime.

reason 3: _____ People feel pressured to buy overpriced items.

2. **topic sentence:** Students at the local college need an emergency health center near the campus.

   reason 1: _____ A nearby health center would make a campus epidemic less likely.

   reason 2: _____ Many college students think they are invincible and ignore the symptoms of an illness.

   reason 3: _____ Flu and other highly contagious illnesses spread quickly on college campuses.

Exercise 6   **Practice: Recognizing Reasons That Overlap**   MyWritingLab™

Following are topic sentences and lists of reasons. In each list, two reasons overlap. Put an X by the two reasons that overlap.

1. **topic sentence:** The salad bar at Kiki's Pizza needs improvement.

   a. _____ There is little variety in the offerings.

   b. _____ The lettuce is limp, and the leaves often have a brown edge.

   c. _____ There are mushy chunks of cucumbers.

   d. _____ The salad always contains the same items: lettuce from a bag, soft pieces of tomatoes, and shredded carrots.

2. **topic sentence:** The Student Action Club should hold a coat giveaway each fall.

   a. _____ Cold weather hits hard at the homeless and others who are struggling.

   b. _____ Children are especially vulnerable to illnesses caused by the cold.

   c. _____ Many people have old coats and jackets they would be willing to give away.

   d. _____ Boys and girls need the protection of warm clothing.

Exercise 7   **Practice: Identifying a Reason That Is Not Specific**   MyWritingLab™

For each of the following lists, put an X by the reason that is not specific.

1. **topic sentence:** All cell phones should be turned off in movie theaters.

   a. _____ Movies theaters are filled with strangers who must be considerate of other audience members if they are all to enjoy the film.

   b. _____ Ringing phones or phone conversations distract and annoy many people in the audience.

   c. _____ Being aware of the feelings and rights of others is always a good policy.

   d. _____ When strangers in a theater become irritated by phone conversations, complaints, and insults can escalate into violence.

2. **topic sentence:** Crystal River Mall needs more than two maps of the mall inside the complex.

  a. _____ Shoppers want to have a pleasant experience as they walk through the mall.

  b. _____ Every shop in the mall wants potential customers to be able to locate its store quickly.

  c. _____ With four main entrances to the mall, but only two maps, many shoppers wander around until they become frustrated and leave.

  d. _____ The design of the mall is complicated, with twists, turns, and dead ends.

MyWritingLab™   **Exercise 8**   **Practice: Adding Details to an Outline**

Following is part of an outline. It includes a topic sentence and three reasons. Add at least two sentences of details to each reason. Your details may be examples or descriptions.

 topic sentence: Students in evening classes at Crescent State College deserve the same services that students in day classes enjoy.

 reason: Students in evening classes may have jobs or other responsibilities during the day, but, like all students, they need to see counselors.

 details: _____

_____

 details: _____

_____

 reason: Students in evening classes may be on a tight schedule and may need to grab a quick snack on campus.

 details: _____

_____

 details: _____

_____

 reason: Darkness makes it important for every night student to be as safe as a day student.

 details: _____

_____

 details: _____

_____

DRAFTING AND REVISING   **ARGUMENT**

Once you are satisfied with your outline, you can write the first draft of your paragraph. When you have completed it, you can begin revising the draft so that your argument is as clear, logical, and convincing as it can be. The checklist below may help you with your revisions.

3 Write a convincing argument paragraph that incorporates transitions effectively.

Checklist for Revising a Draft of an Argument Paragraph

✓   Have I left out a serious or obvious reason?

✓   Should I change the order of my reasons?

✓   Do I have enough details?

✓   Are my details specific?

✓   Do I need to explain the problem or issue I am writing about?

✓   Do I need to link my ideas more clearly?

✓   Do I need a concluding sentence that reinforces my point?

Checking Your Reasons

Be sure that your argument has covered all the serious or obvious reasons. Sometimes writers get so caught up in drafting their ideas that they forget to mention something very basic to the argument. For instance, if you were arguing for a leash law for your community, you might state that dogs who run free can hurt people and damage property. But don't forget to mention another serious reason to keep dogs on leashes: Dogs who are not restrained can get hurt or killed by cars.

One way to see if you have left out a serious or obvious reason is to ask a friend or classmate to read your draft and to react to your argument. Another technique is to put your draft aside for an hour or two and then read it as if you were a reader, not the writer.

Explaining the Problem or the Issue

Sometimes your argument discusses a problem so obvious to your audience that you do not need to explain it. On the other hand, sometimes you need to explain a problem or issue so that your audience can understand your point. If you tell readers of your local paper about teenage vandalism at Central High School, you probably need to explain what kind of vandalism has occurred and how often. Sometimes it is wise to describe the seriousness of a situation by providing a few examples so that readers will be more interested in your argument.

Transitions That Emphasize Your Reasons

In writing an argument paragraph, you can use any transition, depending on how you arrange your reasons and details. However, no matter how you present your reasons, you will probably want to *emphasize* one of them. Below are some transitions that can be used for emphasis.

> **INFO BOX** Transitions to Use for Emphasis
>
> | | | | |
> |---|---|---|---|
> | above all | finally | most important | most significant |
> | especially | mainly | most of all | primarily |

For example, by saying, "*Most important*, broken windows at Central High School are a safety problem," you put the emphasis for your audience on this one idea.

Revising a Draft

Following is a draft of the argument paragraph on Roberts Park. When you read it, you'll notice these changes from the outline on page 208:

- A description of the problem has been added.
- Details have been added.
- Transitions, including two sentences of transition, have been added. "Most important" and "Best of all"—transitions that show emphasis—have been included.

You may also notice some careless errors that can be corrected during the editing and proofreading stage.

Draft of an Argument Paragraph

(Note: Changes from the outline are underlined; editing and proofreading are still necessary.)

description of the problem — Roberts Park was once a pretty little park, but today it is overgrown with weeds and cluttered with trash and rusty benches. Roberts Park could be cleaned up and improved. Improving the park would make the downtown area more attractive to shoppers. Shopers could

added detail — stroll through a renovated park or rest there after shop-

transition — ping. Friends could also meet there for a day of shop-

transitional sentence — ping and lunch. Shoppers are not the only ones who could enjoy the park. Workers from nearby offices and stores could eat lunch outdoors. Several office complex is near the park, and workers from these offices could

added details — bring their lunch to work and eat outside in good weather. I think many people would agree that an hour spent outdoors is a pleasant break from work. Most

transition — important, city children could play in an improved Roberts Park. They would get fresh air. They can play on

transition — grass, not asphalt. Best of all, they would not have to play near traffic. Children, shoppers, and workers would

transitional sentence — benefit from a clean-up of Roberts Park, but so would others. An attractive park improves the city and all residents benefit when a community is beautified.

MyWritingLab™   **Exercise 9**   **Practice: Adding an Explanation of the Problem to an Argument Paragraph**

This paragraph could use an explanation of the problem before the thesis. Write a short explanation of the problem in the lines provided.

_____

_____

_____

_____

_____

The local drivers' license bureau needs a larger, better furnished, and electronically updated waiting area. For the applicants who have come to renew, reinstate, or be tested for a license, a large room would help them to feel less stressed. The increased size would reduce the anxiety of being crushed in a crowd of people, all waiting for an item as important as a driver's license. Finally, better furniture in the new area would encourage the applicants to feel welcome and respected rather than unwelcome and annoyed. Adequate seating would allow people to wait in some comfort and a calmer atmosphere. Finally, waiting would be more bearable if a clock or electric sign posted the estimated wait time. Applicants who arrived on a break from work would know whether to wait or return later. Posting the wait time would also eliminate the many questions about time that the staff must handle. These changes to the waiting room could reduce the irritation, misery, and even resentment of a necessary but unpleasant chore.

| Exercise 10 | **Practice: Recognizing Transitions in an Argument Paragraph** | MyWritingLab™ |

Underline all the transitions—words, phrases, or sentences—in the paragraph below. Put a double line under any transitions that emphasize reasons.

On Saturdays, the entrance to many local supermarkets shelters boys or girls accompanied by several caring adults who are the parent sponsors of the children's group. The group can be an athletic team, a school club, or a chapter of a national boys' or girls' club. The children are selling something—cookies, popcorn, chocolate bars—to raise money for their school, team, or charitable organization. Although it is easy to walk past the children, we should support their efforts. First of all, the children are nervous, and they need encouragement. If a child can make a sale while other children and the adults are watching, that child feels proud and empowered. More important, all the children are learning about working hard for a cause. They may be raising money for a club, a school team, or a national organization that helps children. However, each child is collecting money for something bigger than him- or herself. The process brings them pleasure and pride in working for others. Most important, if we buy the item, we become part of something larger than ourselves. By spending a few dollars on chocolate or cookies, we join a circle of giving. The children's parents give their time, support, and protection, the children give their efforts and courage, and the buyers give their money to a needy organization. As a result, each small purchase does a small world of good.

EDITING AND PROOFREADING ARGUMENT

Once you are satisfied with your latest draft, it is time to edit. You can begin by combining short sentences and refining word choice. Then you can check for spelling and punctuation lapses. The following checklist may help you with your revisions:

Checklist for Editing a Draft of an Argument Paragraph

✓ Should any sentences be combined?

✓ Are the verb forms consistent?

✓ Are the word choices appropriate?

✓ Is the spelling correct?

✓ Is the punctuation correct?

Following is the final version of the argument paragraph on Roberts Park. It includes several improvements since preparation of the draft on page 212. As you review this version, you will notice the following refinements:

- The first sentence has been changed so that it is more descriptive and uses a parallel pattern for emphasis.
- *Could* has been changed to *should*.
- *Shoppers* has been correctly spelled.
- *Renovated* has been changed to *restored*, and *a bag* precedes "lunch" for clarity.
- *Several complex is* has been corrected to *Several complexes are*.
- The sentence *They would get fresh air* has been combined with the sentence *They can play on grass, not asphalt*.
- A comma has been added after *city* (in the last line).

Final Version of an Argument Paragraph

(Note: Changes from the draft are underlined.)

Roberts Park was once a pretty little park, but today it is overgrown with weeds, <u>littered with trash, and cluttered with rusty benches</u>. Roberts Park <u>should</u> be cleaned up and improved. Improving the park would make the downtown area more attractive to shoppers. <u>Shoppers</u> could stroll through a <u>restored</u> park or rest there after shopping. Friends could also meet at the park for a day of shopping and lunch. Shoppers are not the only ones who could enjoy the park. Workers from nearby offices and stores could eat lunch outdoors. Several office <u>complexes are</u> near the park, and workers from these offices could bring <u>their</u> lunch to work and eat outside in good weather. I think many people would agree that an hour spent outdoors is a pleasant break from work. Most important, city children could play in an improved Roberts Park. <u>They would get fresh air while they played on grass, not asphalt</u>. Best of all, they would not have to play near traffic. Children, shoppers, and workers would benefit from a clean-up of Roberts Park, but so would others. An attractive park improves the city, and all residents benefit when a community is beautified.

For your information: A sample argument essay based on this topic and following the same writing steps can be found in Chapter 13, "Different Essay Patterns: Part Two."

Exercise 11   **Practice: Editing a Draft by Combining Sentences**   MyWritingLab™

In the following paragraph, combine each cluster of underlined sentences into one clear, smooth sentence. Write your combinations in the space above the original sentences.

Nicholson College has an impressive campus of nine large buildings set in green grass, large trees, and open spaces. <u>It is beautiful. It presents a challenge for most people</u>. These people include current students, new students, and applicants. Nicholson College needs more signs on every building. Current students are likely to become bad-tempered at the beginning of a new term. On the first day of class, they check their printed copies of their class schedules. <u>At that moment, they realize their next class is scheduled for a building. The building is one that is far away. The building is one they have never entered</u>. They rush to find the building, but they are lost. At Nicholson College, each structure has its name in one place, on one wall. <u>The sign is impressive. However, even longtime students may not find it.</u> <u>They may be approaching the building from the wrong direction</u>. As a result, these students wander on the outskirts of one, two, or three buildings that they don't know well. New students suffer near panic as they struggle to find their classes. New students have many worries. <u>They worry about arriving late to class. They worry about looking ridiculous in front of a room full of seated students. They are afraid of irritating a professor.</u> Roaming the halls and sidewalks is not a good way to begin a term. However, the worst impact of insufficient signs hits applicants to the college. <u>Applicants may be visiting the campus for the first time. They may be unsure whether the place is right for them. They may be considering several colleges.</u> Anyone new to the college is likely to become irritated and frustrated as he or she wanders aimlessly. College maps are no help if the visitor cannot find signs on the buildings. A first-time visitor may decide to look somewhere else to start his or her college career or give up on college altogether. Nicholson College has much to offer, but it needs to offer clear directions to old, new, and aspiring students.

MyWritingLab™ **Exercise 12** **Proofreading to Prepare the Final Version**

The following paragraph has the kinds of errors that are easy to overlook when you prepare the final version of an assignment. Correct the errors, writing above the lines. There are fifteen errors in the paragraph.

Not all college students have access to computers at the homes. Most colleges have technology labs where students can use the computers to work on writing assignments or research projects. Unfortunately, the branch campuss where I attend college does not offer much access to technology. Eastside business College need to offer more computers and more hours for students to use them. Today, the college has only 1 computer lab for students' use. Unfortunately, the lab fills up at 7:30 a.m., and most students have to stand in line for access. It is also difficult to concentrate in a glass-walled room while inpatient students line up outside the windows. Meanwhile, the students outside are wasting their time. Another reason that access is poor involves the computer lab's hours. The lab closes at 9:00 p.m. on weekdays, 5:00 p.m. on Saturdays, and is not open on

Sundays. The students who takes evening classes and has a full-time day job rarely gets access to the lab unless they come to the College on Saturday mornings. Saturday afternoons at the lab are especially crowded. Finally, many of the student's who rely on the college's one lab are already struggling to stay focused on college. Most likely, they, cannot afford there own computers. Many of them have very little free time to commute to campus on Saturdays. Eastside Business College must consider it's students' needs, and goals. It must offer wider and better access to basic technology.

Lines of Detail: A Walk-Through Assignment

Write a one-paragraph letter to the editor of your local newspaper. Argue for some change you want for your community. You could argue for a traffic light, turn signal, or stop sign at a specific intersection. Or you could argue for bike paths in certain places, a recycling program, more bus service, or for any other specific change you feel is needed. To write your paragraph, follow these steps:

Step 1: Begin by listing all the reasons and details you can about your topic. Survey your list and consider any possible objections. Answer the objections as well as you can, and see if the objections can lead you to more reasons.

Step 2: Group your reasons, listing the details that fit under each reason. Add details where they are needed and check to see if any reasons overlap.

Step 3: Survey the reasons and details and draft a topic sentence. Make sure that your topic sentence states the subject and takes a stand.

Step 4: Write an outline; then revise it, checking that you have enough reasons to make your point. Also check that your reasons are specific and in an effective order. Make sure that you have sufficient details for each reason. Check that your outline includes answers to any significant objections.

Step 5: Write a draft of your argument. Revise the draft until it includes any necessary explanations of the problem being argued, all serious or obvious reasons, and sufficient specific details. Also check that the most important reason is stated last. Add necessary transitions to link your reasons and details.

Step 6: Edit your latest draft to refine word choice, combine short sentences, and correct serious mistakes. Also, be sure that your transitions are logical and effective.

Step 7: Prepare a clean copy of your paragraph, and decide whether you need a final sentence to reinforce your point. Proofread carefully to spot and correct any careless errors in spelling, punctuation, format, or typing.

Topics for Writing an Argument Paragraph

When you write on any of the topics below, be sure to work through the stages of the writing process in preparing your argument paragraph.

MyWritingLab™

1. Write a paragraph for readers of your local newspaper, arguing for one of the following:
   a. A local ban on all advertising of alcohol
   b. Punishments for cyber-bullying
   c. Mandatory school uniforms for all public elementary and middle schools
   d. A fine for all dog or cat owners who have not had their animals neutered, to be used to support animal shelters

Collaborate

2. In a paragraph, argue one of the following topics to the audience specified. If your instructor agrees, brainstorm your topic with a group before you start writing. Ask the group to "play audience" by reacting to your reasons, raising objections, and asking questions.

   topic a: Early-morning classes should be abolished at your college.
   audience: The dean of academic affairs

   topic b: College students should get discounts at movie theaters.
   audience: The owner of your local movie theater

   topic c: Your college should provide a day-care facility for students with children.
   audience: The president of your college

   topic d: Businesses should hire more student interns.
   audience: The president of a company (name it) you'd like to work for

MyWritingLab™

3. Write a paragraph for or against any of the following topics. The audience for this argument is your classmates and your instructor.

   For or Against

   a. Allowing police to stop drivers solely for a seat-belt check
   b. A city's hidden cameras to catch drivers who run red lights
   c. The elimination of preferred parking (except for the handi-capped) on campus
   d. A higher tax on cigarettes to be used to pay the health costs of smokers with smoking-related illnesses
   e. More minimum-wage student jobs on campus

MyWritingLab™

4. Some educators and parents are very concerned about the poten-tially harmful effects of violent video games on children. Using a search engine such as Google, type in the words "video games" and "action." See if you can find the manufacturer's description of a video game you have played, and find the targeted age range. Using this information, argue for or against this point: (*Name of the video game*) is suitable for children ages _____ to _____.

MyWritingLab™

5. Study the photograph of the traffic jam. One way to relieve such congestion is for employers to offer telecommuting (working from home via a computer connected to a company's main office). Write an argument for more telecommuting jobs and be sure to include specific benefits to the employees and employers.

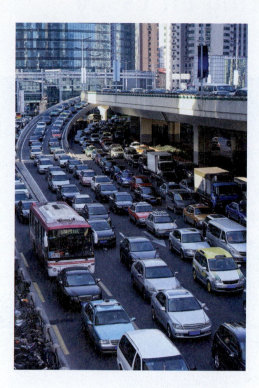

Topics for Critical Thinking and Writing

1. Many drivers often complain about dangerous street conditions and the high rate of accidents and fatalities near their neighborhood. Commonly proposed solutions involve traffic calming, a way of slowing down impatient drivers and reducing the number of deadly collisions. Traffic-calming methods include traffic circles ("roundabouts") and narrower lanes to discourage drivers from passing in a turn lane. Argue for or against a particular traffic-calming method and consider how it would or would not be practical for alleviating dangerous driving conditions on your commute to work or school. You may need to research the principles and practices of traffic calming and imagine how various methods apply to your local roadways.

    MyWritingLab™

2. Assume that a university wants to build a research center in your area of the state. You live in a region that is home for some major corporations but also has thousands of acres of farmland. Argue in favor of establishing either an agricultural-related research center or a business-related research center based on the most pressing needs of your region.

    MyWritingLab™

> **Note:** Additional writing options suitable for argument-related assignments can be found in the "Readings for Writers" appendix at the end of this book.

CHAPTER 11

Writing an Essay

Jumping In

A quality home often reflects logical design, solid foundation and support, and careful attention to finishing touches. Similarly, an effective **essay** stems from careful preliminary work (prewriting and outlining techniques), well-constructed body paragraphs for thesis support (through drafting and revising), and meticulous attention to final details (editing and proofreading).

Learning Objectives

In this chapter, you will learn how to:

1 Identify the basic parts of an essay.

2 Recognize the difference between a topic sentence and a thesis statement.

3 Prewrite to narrow your topic.

4 Write a multi-paragraph essay with sufficient supporting details and effective transitions.

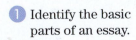 Identify the basic parts of an essay.

WHAT IS AN ESSAY?

You write an essay when you have more to say than can be covered in one paragraph. An **essay** can consist of one paragraph, but in this book, we take it to mean a writing of more than one paragraph. An essay has a main point, called a **thesis statement** (or **thesis**), supported by subpoints. The subpoints are the **topic sentences**. Each paragraph in the **body**, or main part, of the essay has a topic sentence. In fact, each paragraph in the body of the essay is like the paragraphs you've already written because each one makes a point and then supports it.

Comparing the Single Paragraph and the Essay

Read the paragraph and the essay that follow, both about Bob, the writer's brother. You will notice many similarities.

A Single Paragraph

I think I'm lucky to have a brother who is two years older than I am. For one thing, my brother Bob fought all of the typical child–parent battles, and I was the real winner. Bob was the one who made my parents understand that sixteen-year-olds shouldn't have an 11:00 p.m. curfew on weekends. He fought for his rights. By the time I turned sixteen, my parents had accepted the later curfew, and I didn't have to fight for it. Bob also paved the way for me at school. He was such a great athlete that I benefited from his reputation. When I tried out for the basketball team, I had an advantage before I hit the court. I was Bob Cruz's younger brother, so the coach thought I had to be pretty good. At home and at school, my big brother was a big help to me.

An Essay

Some people complain about being the youngest child or the middle child in the family. These people believe older children get all of the attention and grab all the power. I'm the younger brother in my family, and I disagree with the complainers. I think I'm lucky to have a brother who is two years older than I am.

For one thing, my brother Bob fought all the typical child–parent battles, and I was the real winner. Bob was the one who made my parents understand that sixteen-year-olds shouldn't have an 11:00 p.m. curfew on weekends. He fought for his rights, and the fighting wasn't easy. I remember months of arguments between Bob and my parents as Bob tried to explain that not all teens on the street at 11:30 are punks or criminals. Bob was the one who suffered from being grounded or who lost the use of my father's car. By the time I turned sixteen, my parents had accepted the later curfew, and I didn't have to fight for it.

Bob also paved the way for me at school. Because he was so popular with the other students and the teachers, he created a positive image of what the boys in our family were like. When I started school, I walked into a place where people were ready to like me, just as they liked Bob. I remember the first day of class when the teachers read the new class rolls. When they got to my name, they asked, "Are you Bob Cruz's brother?" When I proudly replied, "Yes, I am," they smiled. Bob's success opened doors for me in school sports, too. He was such a great athlete that I benefited from his reputation. When I tried out for the basketball team, I had an advantage before I hit the court. I was Bob Cruz's younger brother, so the coach thought I had to be pretty good.

I had many battles to fight as I grew up. Like all children, I had to struggle to gain independence and respect. In my struggles at home and at school, my big brother was a big help to me.

If you read the two selections carefully, you noticed that they make the same main point, and they support that point with two subpoints.

main point: I think I'm lucky to have a brother who is two years older than I am.

subpoints: 1. My brother Bob fought all the typical child–parent battles, and I was the real winner.
2. Bob also paved the way at school.

You also noticed that the essay is longer because it has more details and examples to support the points. You may have also noticed that each supporting point is its own paragraph.

② Recognize the difference between a topic sentence and a thesis statement.

ORGANIZING AN ESSAY

When you write an essay of more than one paragraph, the **thesis** (also called the **thesis statement**) is the focus of your entire essay; it is the major point of your essay. The other important points that relate to the thesis are within topic sentences.

> **thesis:** Working as a salesperson has changed my character.
> **topic sentence:** I have learned patience.
> **topic sentence:** I have developed the ability to listen.
> **topic sentence:** I have become more tactful.

Notice that the thesis expresses a bigger idea than the topic sentences below it, and it is supported by the topic sentences. The essay has an introduction, a body, and a conclusion.

1. **Introduction:** The first paragraph is usually the introduction. The thesis is included in this paragraph.
2. **Body:** This central part of the essay is the part where you support your main point (the thesis). Each paragraph in the body of the essay has its own topic sentence.
3. **Conclusion:** Usually one paragraph long, the conclusion reminds the reader of the thesis.

Writing the Thesis

There are several characteristics of a thesis:

1. It is expressed in a sentence. A thesis is *not* the same as the topic of the essay or the title of the essay.

> **topic:** quitting smoking
> **title:** Why I Quit Smoking
> **thesis:** I quit smoking because I was concerned for my health, and I wanted to prove to myself that I could break the habit.

2. A thesis *does not announce*; it makes a point about the subject.

> **announcement:** This essay will explain the reasons why young adults should watch what they eat.
> **thesis:** Young adults should watch what they eat so they can live healthy lives today and prevent future health problems.

3. A thesis *is not too broad.* Some ideas are just too big to cover well in an essay. A thesis that tries to cover too much can lead to a superficial or boring essay.

> **too broad:** People all over the world should work on solving their interpersonal communication problems.
> **acceptable thesis:** As a Southerner, I had a hard time understanding that some New Yorkers think slow speech is ignorant speech.

4. A thesis *is not too narrow.* Sometimes, writers start with a thesis that looks good because it seems specific and precise. Later, when they try to support such a thesis, they can't find anything to say.

too narrow: My sister pays forty dollars a week for a special formula for her baby.

acceptable thesis: My sister had no idea what it would cost to care
for a baby.

Hints for Writing a Thesis

1. Your thesis can **mention the specific subpoints** of your essay. For
example, your thesis might be as follows:

I hated *The Chronicles of Narnia* because the film's plot was disorganized, its conflict was unrealistic, and its scenes were overly
dramatic.

With this thesis, you have indicated the three subpoints of your essay: *The
Chronicles of Narnia* had a disorganized plot, it had an unrealistic conflict,
and it had overly dramatic scenes.

2. You can **make a point** without listing your subpoints. For example,
you can write a thesis like this:

I hated *The Chronicles of Narnia* because it was a mess.

With this thesis, you can still use the subpoints stating that the movie had a
disorganized plot, an unrealistic conflict, and overly dramatic scenes. You
just don't have to mention all of your subpoints in the thesis.

Exercise 1   **Practice: Recognizing Good Thesis Sentences**   MyWritingLab™

Following is a list of thesis statements. Some are acceptable, but others are
too broad or too narrow. Some are announcements; others are topics, not
sentences. Put a *G* next to the good thesis sentences.

1. _____ Fighting a speeding ticket involved me in plenty of frustration and drama.

2. _____ My landlord is evicting the family in the apartment next to
mine.

3. _____ Ultraviolent movies are desensitizing viewers to the realities of suffering around the world.

4. _____ Why too much sugar is unhealthy for adults and children.

5. _____ Learning a second language was more difficult than I had
expected.

6. _____ Rising unemployment rates affect every age group and
social class.

7. _____ By the time I got married, I had learned three important
rules about apologizing.

8. _____ School shootings are horrible.

9. _____ Habits that can keep a person from financial success.

10. _____ How the cost of electricity is causing local residents to
change their ways.

MyWritingLab™ **Exercise 2**   **Practice: Selecting a Good Thesis Sentence**

For each of the following pairs of thesis statements, put a *G* next to the good one.

1. a. _____ Global water shortages threaten to change the face of the earth in our lifetime.

   b. _____ Residents in Santa Elisa can adopt three simple ways to save water.

2. a. _____ Excessive sunbathing leads to leathery skin, wrinkles, and skin cancer.

   b. _____ The dangers of excessive sunbathing are the subject to be discussed in this essay.

3. a. _____ I found the perfect roommate through sheer luck.

   b. _____ How I found the perfect roommate is the topic of this essay.

MyWritingLab™   **Exercise 3**   **Practice: Writing a Thesis That Relates to the Subpoints**

Following are lists of subpoints that could be discussed in an essay. Write a thesis for each list. Remember that there are two ways to write a thesis: you can write a thesis that includes the specific subpoints, or you can write one that makes a point without listing the subpoints. As an example, the first one is done for you, using both kinds of topic sentences.

1. **one kind of thesis:** If you want a pet, a cat is easier to care for than a dog.

   _____

   another kind of thesis: Cats make better pets than dogs because cats don't

   need to be walked, don't mind being alone, and don't make any noise.

   subpoints: a. Cats don't have to be walked and exercised like dogs do.

      b. Cats are independent and don't mind being home alone, but a dog gets lonely.

      c. Cats are quieter than dogs.

2. **thesis:** _____

   _____

   subpoints: a. A professional athlete risks permanent damage from injuries such as concussions or broken bones.

      b. The use of steroids is a constant temptation in many professional sports.

      c. A professional athlete who must travel constantly and perform flawlessly endures high stress levels.

      d. Media attention can create a superstar but deprive a professional athlete of a private life.

3. thesis: _____

_____

subpoints: **a.** Many high school graduates will long remember the most popular song of their senior year.

b. Married couples reminisce about the song played for the first dance of their wedding celebration.

c. Parents remember the song they sang to help their baby fall asleep.

WRITING THE ESSAY IN STEPS

In an essay, you follow the same steps you learned in writing a paragraph—prewriting, planning, drafting and revising, and editing and proofreading—but you adapt them to the longer essay form.

PREWRITING AN ESSAY

Often you begin by *narrowing a topic*. Your instructor may give you a large topic so that you can find something smaller, within the broad one, that you would like to write about.

3 Prewrite to narrow your topic.

Some students think that because they have several paragraphs to write, they should pick a big topic, one that will give them enough to say. But big topics can lead to boring, superficial, general essays. A smaller topic can challenge you to find the specific, concrete examples and details that make an essay effective.

If your instructor asked you to write about college, for instance, you might *freewrite* some ideas as you narrow the topic:

narrowing the topic of college

what college means to me—too big, and it could be boring
college versus high school—everyone might choose this topic
college students—too big
college students who have jobs—better!
problems of working and going to college—OK!

In your freewriting, you can consider your *purpose*—to write an essay about some aspect of college—and *audience*—your instructor and classmates. Your narrowed topic will appeal to this audience because many students hold jobs and instructors are familiar with the problems of working students.

Listing Ideas

Once you have a narrow topic, you can use whatever process works for you. You can brainstorm by writing a series of questions and answers about your topic, you can freewrite on the topic, you can list ideas on the topic, or you can do any combination of these processes.

Following is a sample listing of ideas on the topic of the problems of working and going to college:

problems of working and going to college

early classes	weekends only time to study
too tired to pay attention	no social life
tried to study at work	apartment a mess
got caught	missed work for makeup test
got reprimanded	get behind in school
slept in class	need salary for tuition
constantly racing around	impatient with customers
no sleep	girlfriend ready to kill me
little time to do homework	

Clustering the Ideas

By clustering related items on the list, you'll find it easier to see the connections between ideas. The following items have been clustered (grouped), and they have been listed under a subtitle:

Problems of Working and Going to College: Ideas in Clusters

problems at school
early classes
too tired to pay attention
slept in class
little time to do homework
get behind in school

problems at work
tried to study at work
got caught
got reprimanded
missed work for makeup test
rude to customers

problems outside of work and school
weekends only time to study
no social life
apartment a mess
girlfriend ready to kill me

When you surveyed the clusters, you probably noticed that some of the ideas from the original list were left out. These ideas—constantly racing around, not getting enough sleep, and needing tuition money—could fit into more than one place or might not fit anywhere. You might come back to them later.

When you name each cluster by giving it a subtitle, you move toward a focus for each body paragraph of your essay. And by beginning to focus the body paragraphs, you start thinking about the main point, the thesis of the essay. Concentrating on the thesis and on focused paragraphs helps you to *unify* your essay.

Reread the clustered ideas. When you do so, you'll notice that each cluster is about problems at a different place. You can incorporate that concept into a thesis with a sentence like this:

Students who work while they attend college face problems at school, at work, and at home.

Once you have a thesis statement and a list of details, you can begin working on the planning part of your essay.

Exercise 4 **Collaborate: Narrowing Topics**

Collaborate

Working with a partner or a group, narrow these topics so that the new topics are related, but smaller and suitable for short essays between four and six paragraphs long. The first topic is narrowed for you.

1. **topic:** summer vacation
   smaller, related topics:

   a. _a car trip with children_

   b. _finding the cheapest flight to Mexico_

   c. _my vacation job_

2. **topic:** luck
   smaller, related topics:

   a. _____

   b. _____

   c. _____

3. **topic:** music
   smaller, related topics:

   a. _____

   b. _____

   c. _____

4. **topic:** anger
   smaller, related topics:

   a. _____

   b. _____

   c. _____

Exercise 5 **Practice: Clustering Related Ideas**

MyWritingLab™

Below are two topics, each with a list of ideas. Mark all the related items on the list with the same number (1, 2, or 3). Not all items will get a number. When you've finished marking the list, write a title for each number that explains the cluster of ideas.

1. **topic:** my worst birthday celebration

   _____ my girlfriend gave me some smelly cologne

   _____ the birthday cake was chocolate, and I am allergic to chocolate

   _____ celebrated my twenty-second birthday in May

   _____ my best friend showed up an hour late

   _____ I knocked over the chips and salsa

   _____ one friend gave me a set of wooden bowls I had seen in the dollar store

_____ I hate surprise parties

_____ my girlfriend's best friend told an embarrassing story about me

The ideas marked *1* can be titled _____

The ideas marked *2* can be titled _____

The ideas marked *3* can be titled _____

2. topic: when tears are a universal reaction

_____ a loved one dies

_____ the birth of a baby

_____ at a wedding

_____ a comedian tells a string of hilarious jokes

_____ watching a long, funny scene in a movie

_____ your employment is terminated

_____ attending a child's graduation

_____ carrying tissues to wipe away tears

_____ parents announce they are divorcing

The items marked *1* can be titled _____

The items marked *2* can be titled _____

The items marked *3* can be titled _____

CRITICAL THINKING

As you plan the paragraph for your essay, you will need to distinguish between general and specific examples and understand how details support topic sentences.

PLANNING   AN ESSAY

In the next stage of writing your essay, draft an outline. Use the thesis to focus your ideas. There are many kinds of outlines, but all are used to help a writer organize ideas. When you use a **formal outline**, you show the difference between a main idea and its supporting detail by *indenting* the supporting detail. In a formal outline, Roman numerals (numbers I, II, III, and so on) and capital letters are used. Each Roman numeral represents a paragraph, and the letters beneath the numeral represent supporting details.

The Structure of a Formal Outline

first paragraph	I.	Thesis
second paragraph	II.	Topic sentence
		A.
		B.
details		C.
		D.
		E.

third paragraph	III. Topic sentence
details	A. B. C. D. E.
fourth paragraph	IV. Topic sentence
details	A. B. C. D. E.
fifth paragraph	V. Conclusion

Hints for Outlining

Developing a good, clear outline now can save you hours of confused, disorganized writing later. The extra time you spend to make sure your outline has sufficient details and that *each paragraph stays on one point* will pay off in the long run.

1. Check the topic sentences. Keep in mind that each topic sentence in each body paragraph should support the thesis sentence. If a topic sentence is not carefully connected to the thesis, the structure of the essay will be confusing. Here are a thesis and a list of topic sentences; the topic sentence that does not fit is crossed out:

thesis:	I.	A home-cooked dinner can be a rewarding experience for the cook and the guests.
topic sentences:	II.	Preparing a meal is a satisfying activity.
	III.	It is a pleasure for the cook to see guests enjoy the meal.
	IV.	~~Many recipes are handed down through generations~~.
	V.	Dinner guests are flattered that someone cooked for them.
	VI.	Dining at home is a treat for everyone at the table or in the kitchen.

Since the thesis of this outline is about the pleasure of dining at home for the cook and the guests, topic sentence IV doesn't fit: it isn't about the joy of cooking *or* of being a dinner guest. It takes the essay off track. A careful check of the links between the thesis and the topic sentences will help keep your essay focused.

2. Include enough details. Some writers believe that they don't need many details in the outline. They feel they can fill in the details later, when they actually write the essay. Even though some writers do manage to add details later, others who are in a hurry or who run out of ideas will have problems.

For example, imagine that a writer has included very few details in an outline, like this outline for a paragraph:

II. Meeting with a teacher after class can help students improve.

   A. Students can ask for extra help.

   B. Teachers realize that the student is interested in the class.

The paragraph created from that outline might be too short, lack specific details, and look like this:

> Meeting with a teacher after class can help students improve. First of all, students can ask for extra help. Second, students show teachers that they are interested in succeeding.

If you have difficulty thinking of ideas when you write, try to tackle the problem in the outline. The more details you put into your outline, the more detailed and effective your draft essay will be. For example, suppose the same outline on the topic of meeting with teachers after class had more details, like this:

II. Meeting with a teacher after class can help students improve.

more details about
{
A. Students can ask for extra help.
B. They can ask the teacher to go over certain points discussed in class.
C. They can bring a graded test or paper and ask the teacher to go over it.
D. They can ask the teacher for advice about how to improve their grade.
}

more details about
{
E. In addition, students show teachers that they are interested in succeeding.
F. Students can demonstrate that they are serious about learning.
G. Students can discuss how the topics raised in class relate to their own lives and career goals.
}

You will probably agree that the paragraph will be more detailed, too.

3. Stay on one point. It is a good idea to check the outline of each body paragraph to see whether the paragraph stays on one point. Compare each topic sentence, which is at the top of the list for the paragraph, against the details indented under it. Staying on one point gives each paragraph unity.

Below is the outline for a paragraph that has problems staying on one point. See if you can spot the problem areas.

III. Sonya is a generous person.

A. I remember how freely she gave her time when our club had a car wash.
B. She is always willing to share her lecture notes with me.
C. Sonya gives 10 percent of her salary to her church.
D. She is a member of Big Sisters and spends every Saturday with a disadvantaged child.
E. She can read people's minds when they are in trouble.
F. She knows what they are feeling.

The topic sentence of the paragraph is about generosity. However, sentences E and F talk about Sonya's insight, not her generosity.

When you have a problem staying on one point, you can solve the problem two ways:

1. Eliminate details that do not fit your main point.
2. Change the topic sentence to cover all the ideas in the paragraph.

For example, you could cut sentences E and F about Sonya's insight, getting rid of the details that do not fit. As an alternative, you could change the topic sentence in the paragraph so that it relates to all the ideas in the paragraph. A better topic sentence would be "Sonya is a generous and insightful person."

Revisiting the Prewriting Stage

Writing an outline can help you identify undeveloped places in your plan, places where your paragraphs will need more details. You can get these details in two ways:

1. Go back to the writing you did in the prewriting stage. Check whether items on a list or ideas from prewriting can lead you to more details for your outline.

2. Brainstorm for more details by a question-and-answer approach. For example, if the outline includes "My apartment is a mess," you might ask, "Why? How messy?" Or if the outline includes "I have no social life," you might ask, "What do you mean? No friends? No activities? Or what about school organizations?"

The time you spend writing and revising your outline will make it easier for you to write an essay that is well developed, unified, and coherently structured. The checklist below may help you to revise.

Checklist for Revising the Outline of an Essay

✓ **Unity:** Do the thesis and topic sentences all lead to the same point? Does each paragraph make one, and only one, point? Do the details in each paragraph support the topic sentence? Does the conclusion unify the essay?

✓ **Support:** Do the body paragraphs have enough supporting details?

✓ **Coherence:** Are the paragraphs in the most effective order? Are the details in each paragraph arranged in the most effective order?

A sentence outline on the problems of working and going to college follows. It includes the thesis in the first paragraph. The topic sentences have been created from the titles of the ideas clustered earlier. The details have been drawn from ideas in the clusters and from further brainstorming. The conclusion has just one sentence that unifies the essay.

Outline for an Essay

paragraph 1 — I. Thesis: Students who work while going to college face problems at school, at work, and at home.

paragraph 2, topic sentence — II. Trying to juggle job and school responsibilities creates problems at school.

details about problems at school —
A. Early classes are difficult.
B. I am too tired to pay attention.
C. Once I slept in class.
D. I have little time to do homework.
E. I get behind in school assignments.

(Continued)

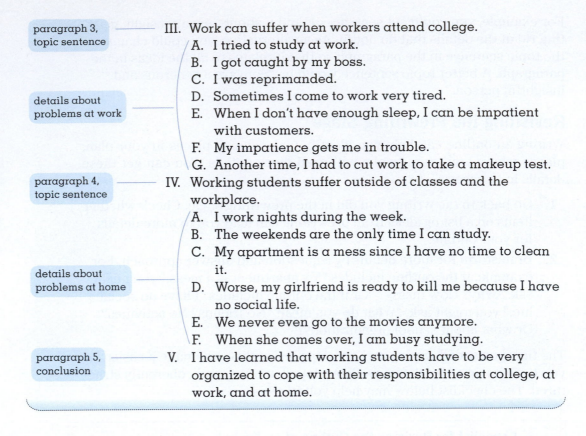

paragraph 3, topic sentence

III. Work can suffer when workers attend college.
   A. I tried to study at work.
   B. I got caught by my boss.
   C. I was reprimanded.

details about problems at work

   D. Sometimes I come to work very tired.
   E. When I don't have enough sleep, I can be impatient with customers.
   F. My impatience gets me in trouble.
   G. Another time, I had to cut work to take a makeup test.

paragraph 4, topic sentence

IV. Working students suffer outside of classes and the workplace.
   A. I work nights during the week.
   B. The weekends are the only time I can study.
   C. My apartment is a mess since I have no time to clean it.

details about problems at home

   D. Worse, my girlfriend is ready to kill me because I have no social life.
   E. We never even go to the movies anymore.
   F. When she comes over, I am busy studying.

paragraph 5, conclusion

V. I have learned that working students have to be very organized to cope with their responsibilities at college, at work, and at home.

MyWritingLab™   Exercise 6   **Practice: Completing an Outline for an Essay**

Following is part of an outline that has a thesis and topic sentences, but no details. Add the details and write in complete sentences. Write one sentence for each capital letter. Be sure that the details are connected to the topic sentence.

   I. Thesis: Many college students who live on their own do very little cooking.

   II. For many students, fast-food restaurants are more popular than supermarkets.

      A. _____

         _____

      B. _____

         _____

      C. _____

         _____

      D. _____

         _____

      E. _____

         _____

III. A microwave or toaster is the only cooking device that students need.

A. _____

_____

B. _____

_____

C. _____

_____

D. _____

_____

E. _____

_____

IV. When hunger strikes college students, they can resort to delivery services.

A. _____

_____

B. _____

_____

C. _____

_____

D. _____

_____

E. _____

_____

V. College students may no longer enjoy home cooking, but they have plenty of choices.

Exercise 7   **Practice: Focusing an Outline for an Essay**   MyWritingLab™

The outline below has a thesis and details, but it has no topic sentences for the body paragraphs. Write the topic sentences.

I. Thesis: Just once in my life, I would love the luxury of a new car.

II. _____

_____

A. No dirt would soil the floor.

B. There would be no scratches or tears on the upholstery.

C. I would own an elaborate car sound system that worked perfectly.

D. The only smell in the automobile would be the distinctive smell of a new car.

E. The interior of the car would be filled with gadgets I had never dreamed of.

III. _____

_____

A. The hubcaps and rims would shine.

B. There would be no scratches on the paint.

C. The paint would not be faded.

D. No dents would appear in the fenders or bumpers.

E. As for the tires, not a bit of wear would be evident.

IV. I have always dreamed of the day when I would drive a brand new car out of the car dealer's lot.

---

4 Write a multi-paragraph essay with sufficient supporting details and effective transitions.

DRAFTING AND REVISING AN ESSAY

When you are satisfied with your outline, you can begin drafting and revising the essay. Start by writing a first draft of the essay, which includes these parts: introduction, body paragraphs, and conclusion.

WRITING THE INTRODUCTION

Where Does the Thesis Go?

The **thesis** should appear in the introduction of the essay, in the first paragraph. But most of the time, it should not be the first sentence. In front of the thesis, write a few (three or more) sentences of introduction. Generally, the thesis is the *last sentence* in the introductory paragraph.

Why put the thesis at the end of the first paragraph? First of all, writing several sentences in front of your main idea gives you a chance to lead into it, gradually and smoothly. This will help you build interest and gain the reader's attention. Also, by placing the thesis after a few sentences of introduction, you will not startle the reader with your main point.

Finally, if your thesis is at the end of the introduction, it states the main point of the essay just before that point is supported in the body paragraphs. Putting the thesis at the end of the introduction is like an arrow pointing to the supporting ideas in the essay.

Hints for Writing the Introduction

There are a number of ways to write an introduction.

1. You can begin with some general statements that gradually lead to your thesis:

general statements   Students face all kinds of problems when they start college. Some students struggle with a lack of basic math skills; others have never learned to write a term paper. Students who were stars in high school have to cope with being just another Social Security number at a large institution. Students with small children have to find a way to be good parents and good students, too. Although all these problems are common, I found an even more typical conflict. **thesis at end** <u>My biggest problem in college was learning to organize my time.</u>

2. You can begin with a quotation that smoothly leads to your thesis. The quotation can be from someone famous, or it can be an old saying. It can be something your mother always told you, or it can be a slogan from an advertisement or the words of a song.

quotation   Everybody has heard the old saying, "Time flies," but I never really thought about that statement until I started college. I expected college to challenge me with demanding coursework. I expected it to excite me with the range of people I would meet. I even thought it might amuse me with the fun and intrigue of dating and romance. But I never expected college to exhaust me. I was surprised to discover that **thesis at end**   <u>my biggest problem in college was learning to organize my time.</u>

3. You can tell a story as a way of leading into your thesis. You can open with the story of something that happened to you or to someone you know, a story you read about or heard on the news.

story   My friend Alexis is two years older than I am, and so she started college before I did. When Alexis came home from college for the Thanksgiving weekend, I called her with plans for fun, but Alexis told me she planned to spend most of the weekend sleeping. I didn't understand her when she told me she was worn out. When I started college myself, I understood her perfectly. Alexis was a victim of that old college ailment: not knowing how to handle time. I developed the same **thesis at end**   disease. <u>My biggest problem in college was learning to organize my time.</u>

4. You can explain why this topic is worth writing about. Explaining could mean giving some background on the topic, or it could mean discussing why the topic is an important one.

explain   I do not remember a word of what was said during my freshman orientation, and I wish I did. I am sure somebody somewhere warned me about the problems I would face in college. I am sure somebody talked about getting organized. Unfortunately, I didn't listen, and I had to learn **thesis at end**   the hard way. <u>My biggest problem in college was learning to organize my time.</u>

5. Use one or more questions to lead into your thesis. You can open with a question or questions that will be answered by your thesis. Or you can open with a question or questions that catch the reader's attention and move toward your thesis.

question	Have you ever stayed up all night to study for an exam, then fallen asleep at dawn and slept right through the time of the exam? If you have, then you were probably the same kind of college student I was. I was the student who always ran into class three minutes late, the one who begged for an extension on the term paper, the one who pleaded with the teacher to postpone the test. I just could not get things done on schedule.
thesis at end	<u>My biggest problem in college was learning to organize my time.</u>

6. You can open with a contradiction of your main point as a way of attracting the reader's interest and leading to your thesis. You can begin with an idea that is the opposite of what you will say in your thesis. The opposition of your opening and your thesis creates interest.

contradiction	People who knew me in my freshman year probably felt really sorry for me. They saw a girl with dark circles under her bloodshot eyes, a girl who was always racing from one place to another. Those people probably thought I was exhausted from overwork. But they were wrong. My problem in college was definitely not too much work; it was the way I handled my work. <u>My biggest problem in college was learning to organize my time.</u>
thesis at end	

MyWritingLab™ | Exercise 8 **Practice: Writing an Introduction**

Following are three thesis sentences. Pick one. Then write an introductory paragraph on the lines provided. Your last sentence should be the thesis sentence. If your instructor agrees, read your introduction to others in the class who wrote an introduction to the same thesis, or read your introduction to the entire class.

Thesis Sentences:

1. Being alone makes some people uncomfortable.

2. Three people have supported me in times when I was under stress.

3. Fame does not always bring happiness.

Write an introduction: _____

_____

_____

_____

_____

WRITING THE BODY OF THE ESSAY

In the body of the essay, the paragraphs *explain, support, and develop* your thesis. In this part of the essay, each paragraph has its own topic sentence. The topic sentence in each paragraph does two things:

1. It focuses the sentences in the paragraph.
2. It makes a point connected to the thesis.

The thesis and the topic sentences are ideas that need to be supported by details, explanations, and examples. You can visualize the connections among the parts of an essay like this:

Introduction with Thesis

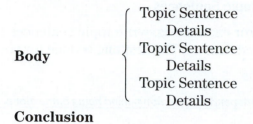

Body
- Topic Sentence
  Details
- Topic Sentence
  Details
- Topic Sentence
  Details

Conclusion

When you write topic sentences, refer to the checklist below to help you organize your essay.

Checklist for Topic Sentences of an Essay

✓ Does the topic sentence give the point of the paragraph?

✓ Does the topic sentence connect to the thesis of the essay?

How Long Are the Body Paragraphs?

Remember that the body paragraphs of an essay are the place where you explain and develop your thesis. Those paragraphs should be long enough to explain your points, not just list them. To do this well, try to make your body paragraphs *at least seven sentences* long. As you develop your writing skills, you may find that you can support your ideas in fewer than seven sentences.

Developing the Body Paragraphs

You can write well-developed body paragraphs by following the same steps you used in writing single paragraphs for the earlier assignments in this book. As you work through the stages of the writing process—whether gathering ideas and planning, drafting and revising, or editing and proofreading—you will gradually create detailed and effective paragraphs.

To focus and develop the body paragraphs, ask the questions below as you revise:

Checklist for Developing Body Paragraphs for an Essay

✓ Does the topic sentence cover everything in the paragraph?

✓ Do I have enough details to support the topic sentence?

✓ Do all of the details in the paragraph explain, develop, or illustrate the topic sentence?

MyWriting**Lab**™   **Exercise 9**   **Practice: Creating Topic Sentences**

Following are thesis sentences. For each thesis, write topic sentences (as many as indicated by the numbered blanks). The first one is done for you.

1. **thesis:** Cats make good pets.

   topic sentence 1: _Cats are independent and don't mind being home alone._

   _____

   topic sentence 2: _Cats are easy to litter-train._

   _____

   topic sentence 3: _Cats are fun to play with._

   _____

2. **thesis:** Most college students live on a tight budget.

   topic sentence 1: _____

   _____

   topic sentence 2: _____

   _____

   topic sentence 3: _____

3. **thesis:** The loss of a job can signal a time of crisis, but it can also be a time of opportunity.

   topic sentence 1: _____

   _____

   topic sentence 2: _____

   _____

   topic sentence 3: _____

   _____

   topic sentence 4: _____

   _____

WRITING THE CONCLUSION

The last paragraph in the essay is the **conclusion**. It does not have to be as long as a body paragraph, but it should be long enough to unify the essay and remind the reader of the thesis. You can use any of these strategies in writing the conclusion.

1. You can restate the thesis in new words. Go back to the first paragraph of your essay and reread it. For example, this could be the first paragraph of an essay:

introduction	Even when I was a child, I did not like being told what to do. I wanted to be my own boss. When I grew up, I figured that the best way to be my own boss was to own my own business. I thought that being in charge would be easy. I
thesis at end	now know how difficult being an independent business person can be. <u>Independent business owners have to be smart, highly motivated, and hard-working</u>.

The thesis, underlined above, is the sentence that you can restate in your conclusion. Your task is to *keep the point but put it in different words*. Then work that restatement into a short paragraph, like this:

restating the thesis	People who own their own business have to be harder on themselves than any employer would ever be. Their success is their own responsibility; they cannot blame company policy or rules because they set the policy and make the rules. <u>If the business is to succeed, their intelligence, drive, and effort are essential</u>.

2. You can make a judgment, valuation, or recommendation. Instead of simply restating your point, you can end by making some comment on the issue you've described or the problem you've illustrated. If you were looking for another way to end the essay on owning one's own business, for example, you could end with a recommendation.

ending with a recommendation	People often dream of owning their own business. Dreaming is easy, but the reality is tough. <u>Those who want to succeed in their own venture should find a role model</u>. Studying a role model would teach them how ambition, know-how, and constant effort lead to success.

3. You can conclude by framing your essay. You can tie your essay together neatly by *using something from your introduction* as a way of concluding. When you take an example, a question, or even a quotation from your first paragraph and refer to it in your last paragraph, you are "framing" the essay. Take another look at the introduction to the essay on owning your own business. The writer talks about not liking to be told what to do, being one's own boss, and believing that being in charge would be easy. The writer also mentions the need to be smart, highly motivated, and hard-working. Now consider how the ideas of the introduction are used in this conclusion:

frame	Children <u>who do not like to take directions</u>
frame	may think that <u>being their own boss will be easy</u>. Adults who try to start a business soon discover that they must be totally self-directed; that is,
frame	they must be strong enough to <u>keep learning</u>, to
frame	<u>keep pushing forward</u>, and to <u>keep working</u>.

MyWritingLab™   **Exercise 10** **Practice: Choosing a Better Way to Restate the Thesis**

Following are three clusters. Each cluster consists of a thesis sentence and two sentences that try to restate the thesis. Each restated sentence could be used as part of the conclusion to an essay. Put *B* next to the sentence in each pair that is a better restatement. Remember that the better choice repeats the same idea as the thesis but does not rely on too many of the same words.

1. **thesis:** Drinking water instead of energy drinks can improve a person's health.

    restatement 1: _____ People can improve their health when they drink water instead of energy drinks.

    restatement 2: _____ Water is a healthy substitute for energy drinks.

2. **thesis:** One act of kindness can lead the way to many other good deeds.

    restatement 1: _____ One kind act can be like a seed that grows and spreads.

    restatement 2: _____ Several other good deeds can result from one act of kindness.

3. **thesis:** Regularly playing a sport or getting another form of exercise helps a person stay sane in a crazy world.

    restatement 1: _____ A person can stay sane in a world of craziness if he or she regularly plays a sport or gets another form of exercise.

    restatement 2: _____ When the world has gone mad, a person who exercises regularly can remain sane.

Revising the Draft

Once you have a rough draft of your essay, you can begin revising it. The following checklist may help you to make the necessary changes in your draft.

Checklist for Revising the Draft of an Essay

✓ Does the essay have a clear, unifying thesis?

✓ Does the thesis make a point?

✓ Does each body paragraph have a topic sentence?

✓   Is each body paragraph focused on its topic sentence?

✓   Are the body paragraphs roughly the same size?

✓   Do any of the words need to be changed?

✓   Are the ideas linked smoothly?

✓   Does the introduction catch the reader's interest?

✓   Is there a definite conclusion?

✓   Does the conclusion remind the reader of the thesis?

Transitions Within Paragraphs

In an essay, you can use two kinds of transitions: those within a paragraph and those between paragraphs.

Transitions that link ideas *within a paragraph* are the same kinds you used earlier. Your choice of words, phrases, or even sentences depends on the kind of connection you want to make. Here is a list of some common transitions and the kinds of connections they express.

INFO BOX   **Common Transitions Within a Paragraph**

To join two ideas:

again	another	in addition	moreover
also	besides	likewise	similarly
and	furthermore		

To show a contrast or a different opinion:

but	instead	on the other hand	still
however	nevertheless	or	yet
in contrast	on the contrary		

To show a cause-and-effect connection:

accordingly	because	for	therefore
as a result	consequently	so	thus

To give an example:

for example	in the case of	such as	to illustrate
for instance	like		

To show time:

after	first	recently	subsequently
at the same time	meanwhile	shortly	then
before	next	soon	until
finally			

Transitions Between Paragraphs

When you write something that is more than one paragraph long, you need transitions that link each paragraph to the others. There are several effective ways to link paragraphs and remind the reader of your main idea and of how the smaller points connect to it. Restatement and repetition are two of these ways:

1. Restate an idea from the preceding paragraph at the start of a new paragraph. Look closely at the two paragraphs below and notice how the second paragraph repeats an idea from the first paragraph and provides a link.

> If people were more patient, driving would be less of an an ordeal. If, for instance, the driver behind me didn't honk his horn as soon as the traffic light turned green, both he and I would probably have lower blood pressure. He wouldn't be irritating himself by pushing so hard. Also, I wouldn't be reacting by slowing down, trying to irritate him even more, and getting angry at him. When I get impatient in heavy traffic, I just make a bad situation worse. My hurry doesn't get me to my destination any faster; it just stresses me out.

transition restating an idea

> <u>The impatient driver doesn't get anywhere; neither does</u> the impatient customer at a restaurant. Impatience at restaurants doesn't pay. I work as a hostess at a restaurant, and I know that the customer who moans and complains about waiting for a table won't get one any faster than the person who makes the best of the wait. In fact, if a customer is too aggressive or obnoxious, the restaurant staff may actually slow down the process of getting that customer a table.

2. Use synonyms and repetition as a way of reminding the reader of an important point. For example, in the two paragraphs below, notice how certain repeated words, phrases, and synonyms all remind the reader of a point about facing fear. The repeated words and synonyms are underlined.

> Some people just <u>avoid</u> whatever they <u>fear</u>. I have an uncle who is <u>afraid</u> to fly. Whenever he has to go on a trip, he does anything he can to <u>avoid</u> getting on an airplane. He will drive for days, travel by train, take a bus trip. Because he is so <u>terrified</u> of flying, he lives with <u>constant anxiety</u> that some day he may have to fly. He is always thinking of the one emergency that could force him to <u>confront what he most dreads</u>. Instead of <u>dealing directly with his fear</u>, he lets it <u>haunt</u> him.
>
> Other people are even worse than my uncle. He won't <u>attack his fear</u> of something external. But there are people who won't <u>deal with their fear</u>. My friend Sam is a good example of this kind of person. Sam has a serious drinking problem. All of Sam's friends

know he is an alcoholic, but Sam <u>will not admit</u> his addiction. I think he is <u>afraid to face</u> that part of himself. So he <u>denies</u> his problem, saying he can stop drinking any time he wants to. Of course, until Sam has the courage to <u>admit what he is most afraid of</u>, his alcoholism, he won't be able to change.

A Draft Essay

Below is a draft of the essay on working and going to college. As you read it, you'll notice many changes from the outline on pages 231–232:

- An introduction has been added, written in the first person, "I," to unify the essay.
- Transitions have been added within and between paragraphs; many transitions are complete sentences.
- General statements have been replaced by more specific ones.
- Many new, specific details and examples develop the body paragraphs.
- Word choice has been improved.
- A conclusion has been added. Some of the ideas added to the conclusion came from the original list of ideas about the topic of work and school. They are ideas that do not belong in the body paragraphs but are useful in the conclusion.

You may also notice some careless errors in punctuation and spelling that can be corrected during the editing and proofreading stage.

Draft of an Essay

(Note: Changes from the outline are underlined; editing and proofreading is still necessary.)

introduction added that tells a story	I work thirty hours a week at the front desk of a motel in Riverside. When I first signed up for college classes I figured college would be fairly easy to fit into my schedule. After all, college students are not in class all day, as high school students are. So I thought the twelve hours a week I'd spent in class wouldn't be too much of a load. But I was in for a big surprise.
thesis statement at the end of the paragraph	<u>My first semester at college showed me that students who work while going to school face problems at school, at work, and at home</u>.
transition, topic sentence	<u>First of all, trying to juggle job and school responbilitys creates problems at school</u>. Early-
transition	morning classes, <u>for example</u>, are particularly diffi-
added sentence of detail	cult for me. <u>Because I work every weeknight from six to midnight, I don't get home until 1:00 a.m., and I can't fall asleep until 2:00 a.m. or later</u>. I am too tired to pay
added detail	attention in <u>my 8:00 a.m.</u> class. Once, I even fell asleep
transitional sentence added	on that class. <u>My work hours create other conflicts</u>.
sentence added	<u>They cut into my study time</u>, so I have little time to do
added detail	<u>all the assigned reading and papers</u>. I get behind in these assignments, and <u>I never seem to have enough
added detail and transition	time to catch up. Consequently, my grades are not good as they could be</u>.

(Continued)

transitional sentences;
topic sentence

added detail

added detail

transition

added example

transition

added detail

transitional sentence
and topic sentence

transitional sentence

repeats focus of body
paragraphs

concluding sentence restates
thesis in new words

Because I both work and go to school, I have problems doing well at school. But work can also suffer when workers attend college. Students can bring school into the workplace. One night I tried to study at work, but my boss caught me reading my biology textbook at the front desk. I was reprimanded, and now my boss doesn't trust me. Sometimes I come to work very tired. When I don't get enough sleep, I can be impatient with motel guests. Then the impatience can get me into trouble. I remember on particular guest. She reported me because I was sarcastic to her. She had spent a half hour complaining about her bill, and I had been too tired to be patient. Once again, my boss reprimanded me. Another time, school interfered with my job when I had to cut work to take a makeup test at school. I know my boss was unhappy with me then, too.

As a working student, I run into trouble on the job and at college. Working students also suffer outside of classes and the workplace. Since I work nights during the week the weekends are the only time I can study. Because I have to use my weekends to do schoolwork, I can't do other things. My apartment is a mess since I have no time to clean it. Worse, my girlfriend is ready to kill me because I have no social life. We never even go to the movies anymore. When she comes over, I am busy studying.

With responsibilities at home, work, and college, I face a cycle of stress. I am constantly racing around, and I can't break the cycle. I want a college education, and I must have a job to pay my tuition. The only way I can manage is to learn to manage my time. I have learned that working students have to be very organized to cope with their responsibilities at college, at work, and at home.

MyWritingLab™   **Exercise 11** **Practice: Identifying the Main Points in the Draft of an Essay**

Below is the draft of a five-paragraph essay. Read it, then reread it and underline the thesis and the topic sentences in each body paragraph and in the conclusion.

Until this year, I had never considered spending my free time helping others in my community. Volunteer work, I thought, was something retired folks and rich people did to fill their days. Just by chance, I became a volunteer for the public library's Classic Connection, a group that arranges read-a-thons and special programs for elementary school children. Although I don't receive a salary, working with some perceptive and entertaining third graders has been very rewarding in other ways.

Currently, I meet with a small group of four girls and three boys each Saturday morning from ten to eleven o'clock, and they have actually taught me more than I ever thought possible. I usually assign the children various passages in an illustrated children's classic like *The Little Prince*, and I help them with the difficult words as they read aloud. When I occasionally read to them, they follow right along, but when it's their turn, they happily go off track. I've learned that each child has a mind of his or her own, and I now have much more respect for day-care workers and elementary school teachers who must teach, entertain, and discipline thirty rowdy children all day long. I'm tired after one hour with just seven children.

I have also learned the value of careful planning. I arrive at each session with a digital voice recorder and have the children record sound effects related to the story we'll be reading. At certain points during the session, we stop to hear the sound effects. They love to hear themselves and seem more focused on reading when I use this method. I feel more relaxed when I am well prepared and the sessions go smoothly.

I have enjoyed making several new friends and contacts through Classic Connection. I've become friendly with the parents of the kids in my reading group, and one of the fathers has offered me a good-paying job at his printing business. He even mentioned he could be flexible about my schedule. I asked him if he could help me put a collection together of the group's most outrageous original stories, and he said he'd be glad to do it in *his* free time. I've thus learned that the spirit of volunteerism is indeed contagious.

I plan to keep volunteering for Classic Connection's programs and look forward to a new group that should be starting soon. I don't know if I'm ready to graduate to an older group. After all, third graders still have much to teach me.

MyWritingLab™ | Exercise 12 | **Practice: Adding Transitions to an Essay**

The following essay needs transitions. Add the transitions where indicated, and add the kind of transition—word, phrase, or sentence—indicated.

I am a fairly good student, but I have to work hard to earn decent grades. Most of that work is the long, sometimes boring time spent studying. Since I need to study as much as I can, I have found three places that offer me at least a little study time.

The first place isn't meant for studying. _____ (add a word) I have managed to slip a few minutes of cramming into the hours I spend there. This place is the supermarket where I work. Of course, work at a supermarket is constant, and I am always under supervision. _____ (add a word or phrase) I have found ways to incorporate a little mental work. When I have a test coming up, I write key terms, rules, or definitions on note cards. On my ten-minute breaks at the store, I sit outside and study my cards. When I return to the store, I try to repeat the information I have just learned. Of course, this repetition is silent _____ (add a word) I don't want to alarm the customers by muttering in the aisles.

The second place is more appropriate for studying. It is the college I attend. I try to find a quiet place like an empty bench where I can sit between classes. If I have a free hour or more, I go somewhere more private _____ (add a word or phrase) the library. Sometimes the library has too many students talking in the aisles or at the computers _____ (add a word or phrase), I find a spot under a tree and sit on the lawn.

_____

_____ (add a sentence). That place is my home. I am lucky to have my own bedroom, and when my family has finished dinner, I retreat to my room. First, I close the door. _____ (add a word) I spread out my books and notes on the bed. Sometimes I sit on the bed to study, but when I feel myself getting sleepy, I move to the floor. On the floor, I am less comfortable but more alert. My room is a quiet place. _____ (add a word or phrase) I do suffer one or two interruptions. Before she goes to bed, my little sister comes in to chat or kiss me goodnight. She can break my train of

thought _____ (add a word or phrase) she is a sweet and affectionate visi-

tor. Most of the time, my room gives me the peace that I need.

Studying for my college classes takes up more of my time than I had ever

expected. _____ (add a word or phrase) it is more difficult than I had

expected. _____ (add a word or phrase) my efforts are carrying me

through the challenges of college. _____ (add a word or phrase) I am

happy to spend the time on the work that will determine my future.

Exercise 13 **Practice: Recognizing Synonyms and Repetition Used
to Link Ideas in an Essay**

MyWritingLab™

In the following essay, underline all the synonyms and repetition (of words
or phrases) that help remind the reader of the thesis sentence. (To help you,
the thesis is underlined.)

We can make many changes in our lives. We can choose to move to a new

town, to attend a certain college, or to train for a specific career. However, some-

times the changes in our lives are not our choices. In such cases, the changes can

signal trouble. <u>Like everyone, I have felt the pain and the loss of control that can

come with change, but I have also learned that loss can lead me to a better life.</u>

The first time that I suffered from a sudden change was when my best friend

left the area. At the time, my friend and I were fourteen, and we spent most of our

free time together. We confided in each other and created our private world of

jokes, adventures, and pranks. When my friend's mother was offered a good job in

a distant city, there was nothing I could do to keep my friend near me. At first, I

was so upset that I became angry at my friend, and I refused to acknowledge that

he was suffering, too. When the day came for him to leave, we were both resigned

to the pain of separating.

My second experience of such misery came years later when my girlfriend

announced that she was leaving me. One day she decided that she wanted to

"move on" in her relationships. I was unprepared for the hurt of her blunt speech.

Nothing that I said could change her mind, and I could not escape the suffering that followed. When the shock wore off, I struggled to cope with the inevitable loneliness. The worst part of this conflict was my fear of getting hurt again. This fear kept me locked in misery.

A year later, my life changed again when the terror began to lose its grip on me. Slowly, I began to move closer to people who could be my friends. Each step was risky, but each step helped me to get stronger. When I began to trust again and feel that I had some value, I started to believe that other people might accept me. I admitted that I would never be able to control all my interactions with other people. I might be hurt again, but I might also find friends and even someone to love.

As I began to let go of my fears, I also gave up the past: I let go of the suffering and self-doubt that had come when I could not hold on to my friend or girlfriend. I made these changes by taking a risk. I stepped back into the real world where I could lose control of events again, but where I could also find fulfillment.

EDITING AND PROOFREADING AN ESSAY

Once you are satisfied with your latest draft, it is time to edit. You can begin by combining short sentences, and refining word choice. Then check for spelling and punctuation errors. The following checklist may help you edit effectively:

Checklist for Editing the Draft of an Essay

✓ Should any of my sentences be combined?

✓ Are the verb forms correct and consistent?

✓ Are the word choices appropriate?

✓ Is the spelling correct?

✓ Is the punctuation correct?

Creating a Title

When you are satisfied with the edited version of your essay, you can begin to think of a short title that is connected to your thesis. Since the title is the reader's first contact with your essay, an imaginative title can create a good first impression. If you can't think of anything clever, try using a key phrase from your essay.

The title is placed at the top of your essay, about an inch above the first paragraph. Always capitalize the first word of the title and all major words such as nouns, pronouns, verbs, adjectives, and adverbs. Minor words such as articles (*the, an, a*), prepositions (*of, in, between*), and coordinating conjunctions (*and, but, so*) are not capitalized unless they are the first or last words of the title. *Do not* underline or put quotation marks around your title.

The Final Version of an Essay

As you know, careful editing and proofreading can lead to an error-free essay reflecting effective organization, refined style, and balanced, detailed paragraphs. When you compare the sample final version of an essay to the draft on page 243, you may notice several improvements and corrections which include the following:

- In the first paragraph, the words *I thought* have been added to make it clear that the statement is the writer's opinion.
- One topic sentence, in paragraph two, has been edited to include the word *students* to make the meaning more precise.
- Words have been changed to sharpen the meaning (e.g., *registered* instead of *signed up*).
- Transitional words, phrases, and sentences have been added to link ideas smoothly.
- A title has been added.
- *Responsibilitys* has been corrected to *responsibilities*.
- The verb error *spent* has been corrected to *spend*.
- Sentences have been combined.

Final Version of an Essay

(Note: Changes from the draft are underlined.)

Problems of the Working College Student

I work thirty hours a week at the front desk of a motel in Riverside. When I first <u>registered</u> for college <u>classes</u>, I figured college would be fairly easy to fit into my schedule. After all, <u>I thought</u>, college students are not in class all day, as high school students are. So I <u>assumed</u> the twelve hours a week I'd <u>spend</u> in class wouldn't be too much of a load. But I was in for a big surprise. My first semester at college showed me that students who work while going to college face problems at school, at work, and at home.

First of all, <u>students who try</u> to juggle job and school <u>responsibilities</u> <u>find trouble at school</u>. Early-morning classes, for example, are particularly difficult for me. Because I work every weeknight from six to midnight, I don't get home until 1:00 a.m., and I can't fall asleep until 2:00 a.m. or later. <u>Consequently</u>, I am too tired to pay attention in my 8:00 a.m class. Once, I even fell asleep <u>in</u> that class. My work hours create other conflicts. They cut into my study time, so I have little time to do all the assigned reading and papers. I get behind in the assignments, and I never seem to have enough time to catch up. <u>As a result</u>, my grades are not as good <u>as</u> they could be.

Because I both work and go to school, I have problems doing well at school. But work can also suffer when workers attend college. Students can bring school

(Continued)

into the workplace. <u>I've been guilty of this practice and have paid the price</u>. One night I tried to study at work, but my boss caught me reading my biology textbook at the front desk. I was reprimanded, and now my boss doesn't trust me. Sometimes I come to work very tired, <u>another problem</u>. When I don't get enough sleep, I can be impatient with <u>motel</u> guests who give me a hard time. Then my impatience can get me into trouble. <u>I remember one particular guest who reported me because I was sarcastic to her</u>. She had spent a half hour complaining about her bill, and I had been too tired to be patient. Once again, my boss reprimanded me. Another time, school interfered with my job when I had to cut work to take a makeup test at school. I know my boss was unhappy with me then, too.

As a working student, I run into trouble on the job and at college. Working students also suffer outside of classes and the workplace. <u>My schedule illustrates the conflicts of trying to juggle too many duties</u>. Since I work nights during the <u>week</u>, the weekends are the only time I can study. Because I have to use my weekends to do schoolwork, I can't do other things. My apartment is a mess since I have no time to clean it. Worse, my girlfriend is ready to kill me because I have no social life. We never even go to the movies anymore. When she comes over, I am busy studying.

With responsibilities at home, at work, and at college, I face a cycle of stress. I am constantly racing around, and I can't break the cycle. I want a college education, and I must have a job to pay my tuition. The only way I can manage is to learn to manage my time. <u>In my first semester at college, I've realized</u> that working students have to be very organized to cope with the responsibilities of college, work, and home.

MyWritingLab™ **Exercise 14** **Practice: Proofreading to Prepare the Final Version**

Following is an essay with the kinds of errors that are easy to overlook when you prepare the final version of an assignment. Correct the errors, writing above the lines. There are nineteen errors in the essay.

A Free Morning

Most morning's begin with responsibilities. A person has to work at a certain time follow a specific routine, and rush to work, school, or to other commitments. A morning without duties, chores, or schedules is rare. When someone has the gift of a free morning, they can consider three of the best ways to spend it.

One of the most luxurious ways to enjoy a morning without chores is to turn off the alarm clock, and go back to sleep. The irritating sound of the alarm makes the freedom to stop the noise a pleasure. If someone turns off the clock the night be fore the free morning, he or she will not enjoy the luxury of hearing the noise, at first assuming that the sound signals another hectic morning, and then realize-ing, that the clock is powerless on this day. Next, the sleeper can enjoy the plea-sure of staying in bed, snuggling into the pillows, and slip into a long nap.

A morning without responsibilities can also be a time to wake up at a reasonable hour but to have nothing planned. A person can linger over a cup of coffee. On a free morning, he or she may have time to eat toast or cereal instead of rushing off, to begin another round of work and worry. The gift of time mean a chance to check phone messages sit calmly at a computer read a book, or listen to music. Without a plan, a person can choose to do nearly anything or nothing at all.

the best way to enjoy a free morning is to spend it out doors. Since their are many way to enjoy nature, a person can do as little or as much as he or she desires. An athlete can run, bike, or power-walk in the neighborhood. Someone less active can sit on a porch or patio, and enjoy the trees, the birds, or the squirrels. Parks, benches, lakes, and mountains may be nearby, and nature can be as calming or invigorating as someone wants it to be.

Most people are constantly short of time. They are behind in their responsibilities at work and at home. A free morning should be a time without responsibilities. Instead of using it to catch up on endless chores and duties, people should think of the morning as a gift with know strings attached.

Lines of Detail: A Walk-Through Assignment

Think of two careers that you believe would be right for you. They do not have to be careers for which you are studying or preparing now but can be the kind of work that you would choose if you had unlimited funds; time to study, train, or otherwise prepare; and the freedom to change your circumstances so that you could begin focusing on one of these two careers.

Step 1: Begin with some investigation. Even if you are extremely familiar with these two careers, do as much of the following as you can: talk to an expert in the college's career center and begin to investigate each career's required training/educational requirements as well as the necessary mental, psychological, and physical ability that this career demands. You can talk to a person who is presently working in this career field or to a student who is preparing for the field. Online research and time spent in the college or local public library will help you to become more informed.

Step 2: As you investigate, take notes. Keep in mind that your purpose is to discover what to expect if you were to work toward earning the qualifications for employment in this field.

Step 3: After your visit, survey your notes. Try to focus on a point that you can make about the two possible careers. Do they both require the same type of personality? What are the rewards of each? What are the drawbacks? What is the job market for those whose education or training prepares them for either of the two careers?

The answers to such questions can help you focus on a thesis.

Step 4: Once you have a thesis, you can begin to cluster the details you gathered in your visits.

Step 5: Once you have a thesis and clustered details, draft an outline. Revise your draft outline until it is unified, expresses the ideas in a clear order, and has enough supporting details.

Step 6: Write a draft of your essay. Revise the draft, checking it for balanced paragraphs, relevant and specific details, and a strong conclusion.

Step 7: Edit your latest draft to refine word choice, combine sentences, strengthen transitions, and correct any serious errors or omissions.

Step 8: Prepare a clean copy of your essay and proofread carefully to identify and correct any careless errors in spelling, punctuation, format, or typing.

Topics for Writing an Essay

When you write on any of these topics, be sure to work through the stages of the writing process in preparing your essay.

Collaborate

1. Take any paragraph you have already written for this class and develop it into an essay of four or five paragraphs. If your instructor agrees, read the paragraph to a partner or group, and ask your listener(s) to suggest points inside the paragraph that could be developed into paragraphs of their own.

MyWritingLab™

2. Write an essay using one of the following thesis statements:

If I did not have to work for a living, I would spend my time doing _____.

Most families waste natural resources every day, simply by going through their daily routines.

I would love to live in _____ because _____.

I believe that in fifty years, the planet will be in better/worse shape than it is today.

Three items that every college student needs are _____, _____, and _____.

Collaborate

3. Write an essay on earliest childhood memories. Interview three classmates to gather detail and to focus your essay. Ask each one to tell you about the earliest memory he or she has of childhood. Before you begin interviewing, make a list of questions like these: What is your earliest memory? How old were you at the time of that recollection? What were you doing? Do you remember other people or events in that scene? If so, what were the others doing? Were you indoors? Outdoors? Is this a pleasant memory? Why do you think this memory has stayed with you? Use the details

collected at the interviews to write a five-paragraph essay with a thesis sentence like one of the following:

Childhood memories vary a great deal from person to person.

The childhood memories of different people are surprisingly similar.

Although some people's first memories are painful, others remember a happy time.

Some people claim to remember events from their infancy, but others can't remember anything before their third (or fourth, fifth, etc.) birthday.

4. Freewrite for ten minutes on the two best days of your life. After you've completed the freewriting, review it. Do the two days have much in common? Or were they very different? Write a four-paragraph essay based on their similarities or differences, with a thesis like one of these: **My**WritingLab™

The two best days of my life were both _____. (Focus on similarities.)

While one of the best days of my life was _____, the other great day was _____. (Fill in with differences.)

5. Write a five-paragraph essay on one of the following topics: **My**WritingLab™

Three Careers for Me	The Three Worst Jobs
Three Workplace Hazards	Three Workplace Friends
Three Hobbies I Love	Three Wishes
Three Family Traditions	Three Decisions for Me

6. Narrow one of the following topics and then write an essay on it. Remember that brainstorming and freewriting can help you narrow your focus.   **My**WritingLab™

nature	family	lies	music	romance
habits	books	money	health	travel
students	teachers	online games	animals	fashion

7. Many people are turning to online dating services as a way to meet people and potential partners. Find an online dating service and investigate its methods, claims, and fees. Based on your research, write an essay that takes a stand on the following statement: **My**WritingLab™

_____, an online dating service, is ethical/unethical (choose one) in its promises.

As an alternative, if you or someone you know has ever used an online dating service, write an essay based on the following statement:

Finding a suitable mate through an online dating service can be a(n) _____ experience.

8. Look closely at the photo that follows of the couple seeking a ride to Anywhere. Write a five-paragraph essay in which you describe a situation that the picture may represent. In one body paragraph, you can write about how these two people met and decided to head for Anywhere; in another paragraph, about what they are hoping for as they stand together hitchhiking; and in another paragraph, about what may happen to them next.   **My**WritingLab™

Topics for Critical Thinking and Writing

MyWritingLab™

1. Everyone has to make compromises. The father of a large family, for example, may have dreamed of buying a big house for his family. However, economic realities may have forced him to compromise by renting a small duplex. Your brother may have dreamed of becoming a professional athlete but settled for spending weekends playing on a city softball team. Write an essay about three compromises you have made, explaining what you dreamed of, what you settled for, and how you accepted these compromises.

MyWritingLab™

2. Social media networks such as Twitter, Facebook, and LinkedIn are popular among a wide spectrum of users for both personal and professional reasons. Freewrite about the ways in which social media improves the quality of life for its users, and then write an essay about the top three benefits of using social media outlets.

or

If you feel that the drawbacks of social media outweigh the benefits, write about the three most significant negative aspects. Be sure to incorporate specific details and examples for each drawback.

Note: Additional writing options suitable for essay assignments can be found in the "Readings for Writers" appendix at the end of this book.

Different Essay Patterns: Part One

CHAPTER 12

Jumping In

Carpenters or mechanics might have access to many different tools, but what makes them experts at their craft is knowing which tool to use and when. Similarly, good writers know how to use tools like **the stages of the writing process** and **the basics of organizing essays** and apply them in a variety of rhetorical (writing) patterns.

Learning Objectives

In this chapter, you will learn to:

1. Write an illustration essay with specific examples that support a general point.
2. Write a descriptive essay with specific details and a clear order.
3. Write a narrative essay that has a point and clear stages.
4. Write a process essay that makes a point and includes logical steps and detail.
5. Write a comparison or contrast essay that makes a statement and is supported by specific points.

You can write essays in a number of patterns, but any pattern will develop more easily if you follow the writing steps in preparing your essay. The examples in this chapter take you through the steps of preparing an essay in several patterns. Each sample essay expands on its related paragraph pattern in an earlier chapter of this book.

① Write an illustration essay with specific examples that support a general point.

ILLUSTRATION

Hints for Writing an Illustration Essay

1. Use specific examples to support a general point. Remember that a *general* statement is a broad point, and a *specific* example is narrow.

> **general statement:** The weather was terrible yesterday.
> **specific example:** It rained for six hours.

> **general statement:** I am having trouble in my math class.
> **specific example:** I can't understand the problems in Chapter 12.

2. Be sure that you support a general statement by using specific examples instead of merely writing another general statement.

> **not this: general statement:** The weather was terrible yesterday.
> **more general statements:** ~~It was awful outside~~.
> ~~Yesterday brought nasty weather~~.

> **but this: general statement:** The weather was terrible yesterday.
> **specific examples:** It rained for six hours.
> Several highways were flooded.

3. Be sure that you have sufficient examples and that you develop them well. If you use one or two examples and do not develop them effectively, you will have a skimpy paragraph. You can use fewer examples and develop each one, or you can use more examples and develop them less extensively.

> **not this: a skimpy paragraph:**
>
> The weather was terrible yesterday. It rained for six hours. Several highways were flooded.

> **but this: a paragraph with a few examples, each one well developed:**
>
> The weather was terrible yesterday. It rained for six hours. The rain was heavy and harsh, accompanied by high winds that lashed the trees and signs on stores and restaurants. The downpour was so heavy that several highways were flooded. Drivers who usually take the Collins Road Expressway were diverted to a narrow city street and crawled home at 30 mph. Additionally, traffic on the interstate highway was at a standstill because drivers slowed to gawk at the numerous accidents caused by the lack of visibility and water-slicked roads.

CRITICAL THINKING

When evaluating topics, keep in mind that the purpose of an illustration essay is to show, explain, or prove a point through examples.

WRITING THE ILLUSTRATION ESSAY IN STEPS

PREWRITING ILLUSTRATION ESSAY

If you were asked to write an illustration essay about some aspect of serving the community, you might first freewrite.

Freewriting for an Illustration Essay

Police serve the community. I'd like a job in law enforcement. What other kinds of people serve the community? Firefighters. Do you have a job serving the community? What about volunteers? Even volunteer firefighters. My mother works at the hospital one day a week. She's been doing it for years. Volunteering on her day off from work. Then there's the food bank. That's my father's place. I volunteer there, too. That's serving the community.

Some additional brainstorming might lead you to recognize that everyone in your family, including your sister, volunteers. You might ask yourself some questions about why each family member volunteers and receives the benefits of the volunteering. Next, you are able to write a thesis sentence:

> In my family, volunteering is a way for all of us to give to the community and to share our good fortune.

This thesis contains three parts: it explains who volunteers (all the family members), it explains why they volunteer ("to give to the community and to share our good fortune"), and who benefits (the community).

With a thesis statement and some of the ideas from your freewriting and brainstorming, you can begin to think about an outline.

PLANNING ILLUSTRATION ESSAY

Following is an outline for an illustration essay on family volunteering. Study the outline carefully and be prepared to respond to the exercise that follows it.

Outline for an Illustration Essay

paragraph 1 —— I. Thesis: In my family, volunteering is a way for all of us to give to the community and to share our good fortune.

paragraph 2, topic sentence —— II. Parents and children all volunteer.

    A. My father and I volunteer at a local food bank every weekend.

    B. We work in the warehouse.

    C. We sort and stack donations of food from several sources.

details about family volunteers and where they volunteer

    D. My mother spends every Thursday helping visitors at the local hospital.

    E. She is a greeter at the information desk directly inside the main entrance.

    F. My sister volunteers at an animal shelter.

    G. She spends her time with homeless dogs.

paragraph 3, topic sentence —— III. Each member of the family has several reasons for volunteering.

(Continued)

A. My father likes the work of organizing the food and stacking each item neatly.

B. I enjoy surveying the amounts and kinds of donations and seeing what is new.

details about different reasons for volunteering —— C. We both like knowing that many hungry people will be able to eat.

D. My mother likes comforting the sick or supporting their loved ones.

E. She is the first person that people see when they enter the hospital.

F. My sister finds her own comfort with homeless animals.

G. They spend almost all their time in cages.

paragraph 4, topic sentence —— IV. All of us want to give back to the community.

A. The town helped us when our house caught fire.

B. We have shelter, food, work, and good educations.

details about family's shared motive for volunteering —— C. The best feelings come when we share our time, food, and love with others.

D. My father and I like to think about a hungry child getting dinner.

E. My mother likes to see people in crisis find some relief.

F. My sister loves to see a dog play or pull at a leash in joy.

paragraph 5, conclusion —— V. When we volunteer, comfort and happiness spreads.

The outline combined some of the ideas from the freewriting and new details devised during the outlining process. As you write and revise your draft, you can continue to add details. Later in the writing process as you edit, you can combine sentences, strengthen transitions, and refine word choices.

MyWritingLab™   Exercise 1   **Practice: Keeping the Examples in Order**

In the outline for the essay on family volunteering, each body paragraph uses the same order in giving the examples of who volunteers, their different reasons for volunteering, and their one shared motive. Survey the three body paragraphs and list that order.

_____

_____

_____

_____

DRAFTING AND REVISING   **ILLUSTRATION ESSAY**

Following is a revised draft of the essay on family volunteering. As you read it, you'll notice many changes from the outline on pages 257–258 (excluding some careless errors that can be corrected by careful editing and proofreading).

- An introduction has been added.
- Transitions have been added within and between paragraphs.
- Details have been added.
- A concluding paragraph has been added.

Study the draft carefully and be prepared to respond to the exercises that follow it.

Draft of an Illustration Essay

(Note: Thesis, topic sentences, and conclusion are underlined; editing and proofreading are still necessary.)

The members of my family do not spend much free time at home. Our home is often empty because each one of us is busy somewhere else. We rarely go to a mall, a fitness club, or a pub. We do have a social life but socializing is not the largest part of our free time. <u>In my family, volunteering is a way to give to the community and to share our good fortune.</u>

<u>Parents and children all volunteer.</u> My father and I volunteer at a local food bank every weekend. We work in the warehouse, sorting and stacking different kinds of food donations from several sources. My mother spends every Thursday, her day off from work, helping visitors at the local hospital. She is a greeter at the information desk directly inside the main entrance. On Saturdays, my sister works at the county animal shelter. She spends her time with homeless dogs.

<u>Each member of the family has several reasons for volunteering.</u> At the food bank, my father likes the work of organizing the food and stacking each item neatly. I like surveying the amounts and kinds of donations and seeing what is new. We both like knowing that many people will be able to eat. My mother likes comforting the sick or supporting their loved ones. She is the first person that people see when they enter the hospital. My sister finds her own comfort in working with homeless dogs. They spend most of their time in cages.

<u>All of us share one motive: we want to give back to the community.</u> We are grateful for the help we receive from our town when a fire damaged our home. Today we have a safe place to live, enough food, steady work, and good educations. Most of all, we know that happiness comes to us when we share our time, food, and love with others. My father and I like to think about a hungry child getting dinner. My mother likes to see people in crisis find some relief. My sister often walks or plays with a shelter dog. She loves to see one jump, run, or pull at a leash in joy. Then she finds pleasure herself.

My parents, sister, and I may not spend much of our free time at home. Pubs, malls, and fitness clubs are not part of our social life. In my family, we have other interests. Because we volunteer, hungry people get food, frightened people find comfort, and homeless animals receive love. In addition, everyone in my family enjoys the great rewards of sharing. <u>When we volunteer, comfort and happiness spreads.</u>

Exercise 2   **Practice: Using Framing to Conclude an Essay**   *My*WritingLab™

Framing, which is discussed in Chapter 11 ("Writing an Essay"), is one way to tie an essay together neatly. It involves using something from the introduction as a way of concluding. You can take an example, a question, or even some general statement from the introduction and use that idea (though not necessarily the same words) in your conclusion. In the essay on volunteering, the conclusion uses the framing device.

Reread the introduction, then reread the conclusion. Notice the repetition of certain ideas. Underline that repetition in the concluding paragraph.

Once you are satisfied with your latest draft, it is time to edit. You can begin by combining short sentences, refining word choice, and checking for serious errors. You may even want to eliminate wordy or awkward phrases for more precise language. Then you can print a clean copy and proofread to catch any careless errors. The following checklist may help you with your refinements:

Checklist for Editing the Draft of an Essay

✓   Should any of my sentences be combined?

✓   Are the verb forms correct and consistent?

✓   Are the word choices appropriate?

✓   Is the spelling correct?

✓   Is the punctuation correct?

When you compare it to the draft on page 259, you will notice some changes:

- A title has been added.
- Punctuation has been corrected.
- Sentences have been combined.
- Verb form of *receive* has been corrected in the final paragraph.
- Spelling of *neatly* has been corrected in Paragraph 3.
- Some of the word choices have been refined to make a description more precise or to eliminate an awkward phrase.
- A transitional sentence has been added to the first paragraph so that the thesis sentence does not come so abruptly.
- New details have been added to Paragraph 2.
- Paragraphs 3 and 4 contain new examples of sentence combining.

Study the final version carefully and be prepared to respond to the exercise that follows it.

Final Version of an Illustration Essay

The Power of Volunteering

The members of my family do not spend much free time at home. Our home is often empty because each one of us is busy somewhere else. We rarely go to a mall, a fitness club, or a pub. We do have a social life, but socializing is not the largest part of our free time. Instead, we spend our time volunteering. In my family, volunteering is a way to give to the community and to share our good fortune.

Parents and children all volunteer. My father and I volunteer at a local food bank every weekend. We work in the warehouse, sorting and stacking different kinds of food donations from several sources such as supermarkets, bakeries, and local farms. My mother spends every Thursday, her day off from work, helping visitors at the local hospital. She is a greeter at the information desk directly inside the main entrance. On Saturdays, my sister works at the county animal shelter where she spends her time with homeless dogs.

Each member of the family has several reasons for volunteering. At the food bank, my father likes the work of organizing the food and stacking each item neatly. I like surveying the amounts and kinds of donations and seeing what is new.

We both like knowing that many people will be able to eat. My mother likes comforting the sick or supporting their loved ones. She is the first person that people see when they enter the hospital. On Saturdays, my sister finds her own comfort in working with homeless dogs who spend most of their time in cages.

All of us share one motive: we want to give back to the community. We are grateful for the help we received from our town when a fire damaged our home. Today we have a safe place to live, enough food, steady work, and good educations. Most of all, we know that happiness comes to us when we share our time, food, and love with others. My father and I like to think about a hungry child getting dinner. My mother likes to see people in crisis find some relief. My sister often walks or plays with a shelter dog. When she sees one jump, run, or pull at a leash in joy, she finds pleasure herself.

My parents, sister, and I may not spend much of our free time at home. Pubs, malls, and fitness clubs are not part of our social life. In my family, we have other interests. Because we volunteer, hungry people receive food, frightened people find comfort, and homeless animals receive love. In addition, everyone in my family enjoys the great rewards of sharing. When we volunteer, comfort and happiness spreads.

Exercise 3   **Practice: Identifying the Changes in a Final Version of an Illustration Essay**   **My**WritingLab™

To become more aware of the kinds of changes that can improve an essay, underline the following changes: (1) the transition sentence in Paragraph 1; (2) the added details in Paragraph 2; (3) the sentences combined in Paragraph 2; (4) the sentences combined in Paragraph 3; (5) the sentences combined in Paragraph 4.

Topics for Writing an Illustration Essay

When you write on any of these topics, work through the stages of the writing process in preparing your essay.

1. Complete one of the following statements and use it as the thesis   **My**WritingLab™
   for an illustration essay.

   Losing a friend can be _____.

   Students under financial pressure are likely to

   _____.

   A close family is _____.

   My most effective study habit is _____.

2. Choose one of the following topics. Narrow it to a more specific   **My**WritingLab™
   topic and then write a thesis statement about it. Use that thesis to
   write an illustration essay.

employment	driving	loneliness
money	fatigue	sports
college cafeteria	safety	popularity
science	legends	ambition

   Collaborate

3. To begin this assignment, brainstorm with a partner or a group.
   Together, write down as many overused slang expressions as you
   can. For example, many people regularly use "awesome" to
   describe anything from a beautiful beach to a good dinner. After
   you have a list of tired slang, work independently on an essay.

Begin by picking three examples of overused slang from the list. In a five-paragraph essay, discuss one expression in each body paragraph. Include examples of the many meanings assigned to the slang expression and suggest other, more specific words or phrases that can replace it.

MyWritingLab™

4. To begin this assignment, look around your classroom. Now, write a general statement about some aspect of the classroom: the furniture, the condition of the room, what the students carry to class, the students' footwear, facial expressions, hairstyles, and so forth. For example, if you observed the size of your classroom and the number of students in it, you might conclude that "Cramming too many students into a small space makes learning difficult." You could write a five-paragraph essay using that general statement as your thesis and support with specific examples and details from your observation.

Topics for Critical Thinking and Writing

MyWritingLab™

1. In conversation, we often use expressions that are meant to hide what we really mean. We may want to conceal our motives, avoid hurting another person's feelings, or avoid taking responsibility. For instance, a statement from a boy- or girlfriend to a significant other may be, "I think it's time we started seeing other people." This may be coded, softer language for such messages as "I've found somebody I like better than you" or "I'm bored and need more excitement in my life." When talking to the parents of a badly behaved child, we may say, "He has a lot of energy" or "She certainly has a mind of her own, doesn't she?"

   Think of three situations in which people are likely to use less than frank expressions for a variety of reasons. For instance, people tend to be tactful at weddings, at dinners where they are guests, when they have to let an employee go, and so forth. Devote one body paragraph to each situation and illustrate your point with specific examples.

MyWritingLab™

2. Various organizations commonly rely on volunteers to improve the quality of life for many individuals. From your observations or knowledge of various volunteer groups in your hometown or school, illustrate the ways volunteers give more than money to the needy in your community. For example, some volunteers staff emergency hotlines for people in distress while others make quilts for the homeless.

2 Write a descriptive essay with specific details and a clear order.

DESCRIPTION

Hints for Writing a Descriptive Essay

1. **Use many specific details.**   Because an essay is usually longer than one paragraph, you will need more details to develop an essay. To ensure that your details create an effective description, make them specific.

2. **Decide on a clear order.**   Without a clear order, a descriptive essay will become a jumble of details spread over several paragraphs. Decide on a clear order (from inside to outside, from top to bottom, and so forth) and stick to it. Each body paragraph can focus on one part of that order.

CRITICAL THINKING

The purpose of a descriptive essay is to describe something or someone vividly. Think of information questions: *Who? What? When? Where? Why?* and *How?* Your goal is to paint a picture that the reader can imagine.

WRITING THE DESCRIPTIVE ESSAY IN STEPS

PREWRITING   DESCRIPTIVE ESSAY

If you were going to write an essay describing the contents of your garage, you might first brainstorm a list.

Brainstorming a List for a Descriptive Essay

Topic: The Contents of Our Garage

- my husband
- Bradley's motorcycle
- his tools for the cycle, yard work, home repairs
- paint cans
- bulletin board with photos
- little plastic containers of nails, screws
- dusty shelves on the walls
- oil stains and smells on the floor
- Bradley's work bench
- musty smell of Bradley's junk on the floor
- noise of engine running
- garbage can smells
- Bradley's camping gear
- my collection of hand-painted pottery doesn't fit

After surveying the list, you want to think about what point it makes. For this list, your thoughts might lead you to the idea that most of the details connect to Bradley. That main point is the *dominant impression*. For this list, the dominant impression could be this sentence:

The garage is my husband's territory.

This sentence could be the thesis statement of the descriptive essay.

PLANNING   DESCRIPTIVE ESSAY

Following is an outline for a descriptive essay on Bradley's garage. Study the outline carefully and be prepared to respond to the exercise that follows it.

Outline for a Descriptive Essay

paragraph 1	I.	Thesis: The garage is my husband's territory.
paragraph 2, topic sentence	II.	The bare floor is a small space.
		A. It is an area by the garage door.
		B. It also includes enough space to enter the door to the house.

(Continued)

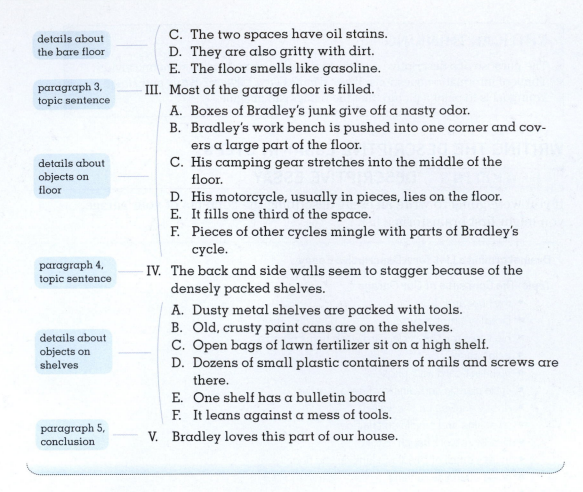

details about the bare floor

C. The two spaces have oil stains.
D. They are also gritty with dirt.
E. The floor smells like gasoline.

paragraph 3, topic sentence

III. Most of the garage floor is filled.

details about objects on floor

A. Boxes of Bradley's junk give off a nasty odor.
B. Bradley's work bench is pushed into one corner and covers a large part of the floor.
C. His camping gear stretches into the middle of the floor.
D. His motorcycle, usually in pieces, lies on the floor.
E. It fills one third of the space.
F. Pieces of other cycles mingle with parts of Bradley's cycle.

paragraph 4, topic sentence

IV. The back and side walls seem to stagger because of the densely packed shelves.

details about objects on shelves

A. Dusty metal shelves are packed with tools.
B. Old, crusty paint cans are on the shelves.
C. Open bags of lawn fertilizer sit on a high shelf.
D. Dozens of small plastic containers of nails and screws are there.
E. One shelf has a bulletin board
F. It leans against a mess of tools.

paragraph 5, conclusion

V. Bradley loves this part of our house.

The outline combined some of the details from the list with new details gathered during the outlining process. As you write and revise your drafts, you can continue to add details. Later, as you edit, you can combine sentences, add transitions, and work on word choice.

MyWritingLab™   **Exercise 4**   **Practice: Recognizing Sense Descriptions**

A good description relies on many words that relate to the five senses of sight, sound, taste, touch (or texture), and smell. In the outline above, underline one example of a word or phrase that refers to each of the following: (1) sight, (2) smell, and (3) touch. Use 1, 2, or 3 to identify the type of sense description.

DRAFTING AND REVISING   **DESCRIPTIVE ESSAY**

Following is a revised draft of the essay on Bradley's garage. As you read it, you'll notice many changes from the outline on pages 263–264.

- An introduction has been added.
- Transitions have been added within and between paragraphs.
- Details have been added.
- A concluding paragraph has been written.

Study the draft carefully and be prepared to respond to the exercises that follow it.

Draft of a Descriptive Essay

(Note: Thesis, topic sentences, and conclusion are underlined; editing and proofreading are still necessary.)

Everyone likes one part of his or her living space better than the other parts. Some people find pleasure in their comfortable living rooms. Others love a bedroom that reflects their tastes. My husband Bradley prefers a different part of our house. <u>The garage is my husband's territory</u>.

<u>The bare floor is a small space</u>. It is an area by the garage door and includes a small space near the door to the house. These two spaces are speckled with oil stains. They are also gritty with dirt. One good aspect of the grit is that it protects people from slipping on the oily patches on the floor. The floor smells like gasoline. Bradley doesn't mind the smell at all.

<u>Most of the garage floor is filled</u>. Boxes of Bradley's junk give off a nasty odor. These boxes contain lots of junk, but Bradley wants to save it all. Although the boxes take up space, Bradley's big work bench fills lots more space. It is pushed into one corner of the garage. In addition, his camping gear stretches into the middle of the floor. Bradley's motorcycle, which is usually in pieces, lies on the floor. Pieces of other cycles also mingle with parts of Bradley's cycle.

<u>The walls of the garage are also heavily loaded</u>. In fact, the back and side walls seem to stagger because of their densely loaded shelves. Some of these dusty metal shelves are packed with tools. Old, crusty paint cans are also on the shelves. Open bags of lawn fertilizer spill their contents on a high shelf. Dozens of small plastic containers of nails and screws are stacked between piles of cleaning rags and towels. One shelf contains a bulletin board that leans against a mess of tools.

The garage is not a showplace in a model home. It doesn't look like the clean, organized garages that appear in commercials for home improvement stores. However, it is a real garage. <u>Although I cannot imagine spending time in it, Bradley loves his garage</u>.

Exercise 5   **Practice: Identifying the Type of Lead-In**   MyWritingLab™

Circle the type of lead-in used in this essay: (1) beginning with some general statements, (2) telling a story, or (3) explaining why this topic is worth writing about.

Exercise 6   **Practice: Noticing How Contrast Is Used in the Conclusion**   MyWritingLab™

In the conclusion, several contrasts are used to lead to a rewording of the thesis. One of these contrasts, "Although I cannot imagine spending time in it," is used as a transition to "Bradley loves his garage." Underline one other use of contrast in the final paragraph (there are several).

EDITING AND PROOFREADING   DESCRIPTIVE ESSAY

Following is a final version of the essay on Bradley's garage. When you compare it to the draft above, you will notice some changes:

- A new transition sentence opens one of the body paragraphs.
- Some repetitive words, such as the word *space*, have been replaced.
- Specific details have been added to all the body paragraphs.

- More sense words have been added.
- Two more sentences have been combined.
- Word choice, such as the replacement of the word *mess* in Paragraph 4 with a more specific word, has been improved.
- A title has been added.

Study the final version carefully and be prepared to respond to the exercise that follows it.

Final Version of a Descriptive Essay

One Person's Preference

Everyone likes one part of his or her living space better than the other parts. Some people find pleasure in their comfortable living rooms. Others love a bedroom that reflects their tastes. My husband Bradley prefers a different part of our house. The garage is my husband's territory.

The least noticeable part of the garage is the open floor. The bare floor is a small space. It is an area by the garage door and includes a small space near the door to the house. These two places are speckled with shiny, smelly oil stains. They are also gritty with dirt. One good aspect of the grit is that it protects people from slipping on the oily patches on the floor. The floor smells like gasoline, but Bradley doesn't mind the smell at all.

Most of the garage floor is filled. It is covered in boxes of Bradley's junk that give off a nasty odor. These boxes contain junk such as rags, cracked plastic flower pots, and rusted garden tools, but Bradley wants to save it all. Although the boxes take up space, Bradley's big work bench fills much more space. It is pushed into one corner of the garage. In addition, his camping gear, including a tent and a sleeping bag, stretches into the middle of the floor. In addition, Bradley's motorcycle, which is usually in pieces, lies on the floor. Pieces of other cycles also mingle with parts of Bradley's cycle.

The walls of the garage are also heavily loaded. In fact, the back and side walls seem to stagger because of their densely loaded shelves. Some of these dusty metal shelves are packed with tools such as wrenches, screwdrivers, and pliers. Old, crusty paint cans, some without any paint, are also on the shelves. Open bags of lawn fertilizer spill their contents on a high shelf. Dozens of small plastic containers of nails and screws are stacked between piles of cleaning rags and towels. One shelf contains a bulletin board that leans against a jumble of tools.

The garage is not a showplace in a model home. It doesn't look like the clean, organized garages that appear in commercials for home improvement stores. However, it is a real garage. Although I cannot imagine spending time in it, Bradley loves his garage.

MyWritingLab™   **Exercise 7**   **Practice: Recognizing the Changes in the Final Version of a Descriptive Essay**

Compare the draft and the final version of the paragraph. Then, in the final version, underline and number these changes from the draft version: (1) an added transitional sentence; (2) a change in word choice to avoid too much repetition of the word *space*; (3) additional sense words; (4) two sentences that have been combined. All of these changes are in Paragraph 2.

Topics for Writing a Descriptive Essay

When you write on any of these topics, work through the stages of the writing process in preparing your essay.

1. Think about a place on your campus and consider what emotions you associate with that place. For example, does a crowded campus parking lot create feelings of frustration or tension? Do you feel a certain comfort when you meet a classmate in the computer lab? Describe the place, the feelings it evokes, and why you react to it in a particular way.

2. Begin this essay with a partner. Describe the car, truck, or motorcycle you would love to own. Ask your partner to (1) jot down the details of your description and (2) help you come up with specific details by asking you follow-up questions each time you run out of ideas. Work together for at least ten minutes. Then change roles. Let your partner describe his or her dream car, truck, or cycle and take notes for your partner. Then split up and use the details you collected to write an essay.

3. If you could choose your own workplace, what would it look like? Would it be a private office? An outdoor space such as a mountain park or a playing field? Would it be a home office? What items would be essential? How would you personalize the space? What would your job be?

MyWritingLab™

Collaborate

MyWritingLab™

Topics for Critical Thinking and Writing

1. How important to you is open space such as woods, lakes, beaches, hills, and desert? Are you more content in an urban space surrounded by people and a rush of activity? Consider why your choice of space appeals to you. As you revise your drafts, try to use as many vivid images as possible.

2. If you have fond memories of a particular place (e.g., park, playground, nature path, neighborhood street, and so forth) that you liked to visit as a child, see if you can remember specific sights, sounds, smells, or emotions associated with it. Freewrite about these memories and then determine the most vivid images you want to include in your essay. For this descriptive essay, your details should focus on more of the atmosphere and/or appearance of the place rather than merely your activities there.

MyWritingLab™

MyWritingLab™

NARRATION

Hints for Writing a Narrative Essay

1. Give the essay a point and stick to it. A narrative essay tells a story. A story without a point becomes a list of moments that lead nowhere. Once you have your point, check that your use of details does not lead you away from the point.

2. Divide your narrative into clear stages. In an essay, you divide your narrative into several paragraphs. Check that each body paragraph has a clear focus (in the topic sentence) and that you have a clear reason for your division. You may decide to divide your body paragraphs into (a) before, during, and after or (b) the first part of the story, the middle part, and the ending.

③ Write a narrative essay that has a point and clear stages.

WRITING THE NARRATIVE ESSAY IN STEPS

PREWRITING NARRATIVE ESSAY

If you were asked to write a narrative essay about something that changed you, you might begin by freewriting.

Freewriting for a Narrative Essay

Topic: Something That Changed Me

Something that changed me. I don't know. What changed me? Lots of things happened to me, but I can't find one that changed me. Graduating from high school? Everybody will write about that, how boring, and anyway, what was the big deal? I haven't gotten married. No big change there. Divorce. My parents' divorce really changed the whole family. A big shock to me. I couldn't believe it was happening. I was really scared. Who would I live with? They were real calm when they told me. I've never been so scared. I was too young to understand. Kept thinking they'd just get back together. They didn't. Then I got a stepmother. The year of the divorce was a hard time for me. Kids suffer in divorce.

Reviewing your freewriting, you decide to write on the topic of your parent's divorce. Once you have this topic, you begin to brainstorm about your topic, asking yourself questions that can lead to further details about the divorce.

   With more details, you can decide that your essay will focus on the announcement of your parents' divorce and the emotions you felt. You devise the following thesis statement:

> When my parents announced that they were divorcing, I felt confused by all of my emotions.

CRITICAL THINKING

A narrative tells a story, and all parts of the story must be present. Think again about the sequence of *who*, *what*, *where*, *when*, *why*, and *how*.

PLANNING NARRATIVE ESSAY

Following is an outline for a narrative essay on the announcement of your parents' divorce and the emotions you felt. As you read it, note how it divides the announcement into three parts: (1) the background of the announcement, (2) the story of the divorce announcement, and (3) the emotions connected to the announcement. Study the outline carefully and be prepared to respond to the exercise that follows it.

Outline for a Narrative Essay

paragraph 1 ——— I. Thesis: When my parents announced that they were divorcing, I felt confused by all my emotions.

paragraph 2, ——— II. I will never forget how one ordinary day suddenly topic sentence became a terrible one.

   A. I was seven when my mom and dad divorced.

   B. My sister was ten.

   C. Both of my parents were there.

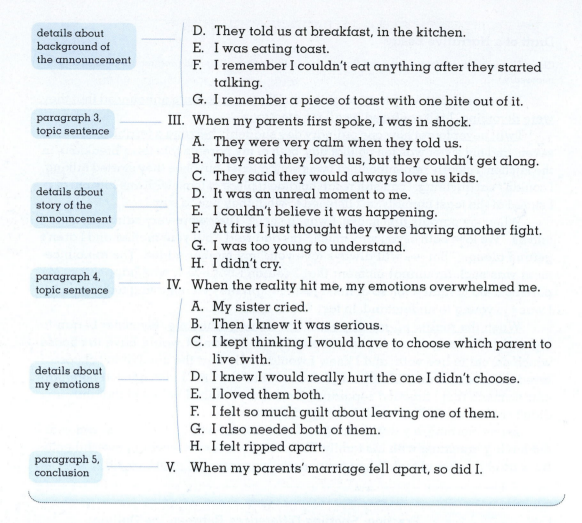

details about background of the announcement

    D. They told us at breakfast, in the kitchen.
    E. I was eating toast.
    F. I remember I couldn't eat anything after they started talking.
    G. I remember a piece of toast with one bite out of it.

paragraph 3, topic sentence

III. When my parents first spoke, I was in shock.

    A. They were very calm when they told us.
    B. They said they loved us, but they couldn't get along.
    C. They said they would always love us kids.

details about story of the announcement

    D. It was an unreal moment to me.
    E. I couldn't believe it was happening.
    F. At first I just thought they were having another fight.
    G. I was too young to understand.
    H. I didn't cry.

paragraph 4, topic sentence

IV. When the reality hit me, my emotions overwhelmed me.

    A. My sister cried.
    B. Then I knew it was serious.
    C. I kept thinking I would have to choose which parent to live with.

details about my emotions

    D. I knew I would really hurt the one I didn't choose.
    E. I loved them both.
    F. I felt so much guilt about leaving one of them.
    G. I also needed both of them.
    H. I felt ripped apart.

paragraph 5, conclusion

V. When my parents' marriage fell apart, so did I.

The outline combined some of the details from the freewriting with new details gathered through brainstorming and during the outlining process. As you write and revise your draft, you can continue to add details. As you edit later in the writing process, you can combine sentences, strengthen transitions, and refine word choices.

Exercise 8   **Practice: Recognizing New Details in the Outline**   MyWritingLab™

Look at the writer's freewriting and note its details on the writer's emotions. Then compare those details to the details about emotions in Paragraph 4 of the outline. Underline the additional details in this section of the outline.

DRAFTING AND REVISING   **NARRATIVE ESSAY**

Following is a revised draft of the essay on an announcement of divorce. As you read it, you'll notice many changes from the outline on pages 268–269.

- An introduction has been added.
- Transitions within the paragraphs have been added.
- Details have been added.
- Some dialogue has been added.
- A concluding paragraph has been added.

Study the draft carefully and be prepared to respond to the exercises that follow it.

Draft of a Narrative Essay

(Note: Thesis, topic sentences, and conclusion are underlined; editing and proofreading are still necessary.)

Divorce can be really hard on children. <u>When my parents announced that they were divorcing, I felt confused by all my emotions.</u>

<u>I will never forget how one ordinary day suddenly became a terrible one.</u> I was seven, and my sister was ten on that day. Both of my parents told us at breakfast, in the kitchen. I clearly remember that I was eating toast, but once they started talking, I couldn't eat anything. I can still recall holding a piece of toast with one bite out of it. I stared at the toast stupidly as I listened to what they had to say.

<u>When my parents first spoke, I was in shock.</u> They were very calm when they told us. "We love both of you very much," my dad said, "but your mother and I aren't getting along." "But we will always love you," my mother added. The announcement was such an unreal moment that I couldn't believe it was happening. My parents used to fight a lot, so at first I just thought they were having another fight. I was too young to understand. In fact, I didn't even cry.

<u>When the reality hit me, my emotions overwhelmed me.</u> My sister began to cry, and I suddenly knew it was serious. I kept thinking I would have to choose which parent to live with, and I knew I would really hurt the one I didn't choose. I loved them both. I was filled with guilt about hurting one. I also needed both parents so much that I dreaded separating from one of them. I believed that the one I didn't choose would hate me. I felt ripped apart.

In one morning, my world changed. One minute, I was an ordinary seven-year-old having breakfast with his family. The next, I was experiencing powerful emotions no child should feel. <u>When my parents' marriage fell apart, so did I.</u>

MyWritingLab™   **Exercise 9**   **Practice: Spotting Differences Between the Outline and the Draft**

Compare paragraph 2 in the outline to the same paragraph in the draft. The draft of the paragraph is better because it (1) combines sentences (twice) and (2) adds a sentence of new details. Underline and number these changes in the draft.

MyWritingLab™   **Exercise 10**   **Practice: Evaluating the Effectiveness of the Introduction and Conclusion**

Compare the introduction to the concluding paragraph. Which do you think is more effective, and why? _____

EDITING AND PROOFREADING   **NARRATIVE ESSAY**

Following is the final version of the essay on an announcement of divorce. When you compare it to the draft, you will notice some changes:

- The introduction has been developed and improved.
- More specific details have been added.
- The word choice has been improved in several places to avoid repetition, to remove an overused phrase (*a lot*), and to change from an informal word for a parent (my *dad*) to a more formal one (my *father*).

- To improve the style in Paragraph 4, some sentences have been combined.
- A title has been added.

Study the final version carefully and be prepared to respond to the exercise that follows it.

Final Version of a Narrative Essay

An Emotional Morning

No childhood is perfect, and part of growing up is facing disappointment, change, and loss. However, there is one loss that can be overwhelming. Divorce can be really hard on children. When my parents announced that they were divorcing, I felt confused by all my emotions.

I will never forget how one ordinary day suddenly became a terrible one. I was seven, and my sister was ten on that day. Both of my parents told us at breakfast, in the kitchen. I clearly remember that I was eating toast, but once they started talking, I couldn't eat anything. I can still recall holding a piece of whole wheat toast with one bite out of it. I stared at the toast stupidly as I listened to what they had to say.

When my parents first spoke, I was in shock. They were very calm when they told us. "We love both of you very much," my father said, "but your mother and I aren't getting along." "But we will always love you," my mother added. The announcement was such an unreal moment that I couldn't believe it was happening. My parents used to fight often, so at first I just thought they were having another argument. I was too young to understand. In fact, I didn't even cry.

Then the reality hit me, and my emotions overwhelmed me. My sister began to cry, and I suddenly knew the situation was serious. I kept thinking I would have to choose which parent to live with, and I knew I would really hurt the one I didn't choose. Because I loved them both, I was filled with guilt about hurting one. I also needed both parents so much that I dreaded separating from one of them. I believed that the one I didn't choose would hate me. I felt ripped apart.

In one morning, my world changed. One minute, I was an ordinary seven-year-old having breakfast with his family. The next, I was experiencing powerful emotions no child should feel. When my parents' marriage fell apart, so did I.

Exercise 11   **Practice: Recognizing Changes in the Final Version**   MyWritingLab™

Compare the draft version of this essay to the final version. Underline these changes in word choice: the word that replaced *a lot*; the word that replaced *fight*, so that *fight* no longer appears twice in one sentence; and the word that replaced *it* in the draft phrase *it was serious*.

Topics for Writing a Narrative Essay

When you write on any of these topics, work through the stages of the writing process in preparing your essay.

1. This assignment begins with an interview. Ask one (or both) of your   MyWritingLab™
   parents to tell you about the day you were born. Be prepared to ask
   questions. (For example, were you expected that day, or did you
   surprise your family? Was there a rush to the hospital?) Get as many
   details as you can. Then write a narrative essay about that day.

MyWritingLab™   2. Write about a time you learned an important lesson. Use the events of the time to explain how you learned the lesson.

MyWritingLab™   3. Write the story of moving to a new place. When was it? How did you feel?

MyWritingLab™   4. Write about an incident in your life that seemed to be fate (that is, meant to happen).

MyWritingLab™   5. Write on any of the following topics:

your first day at work	your first day at college
a dangerous event	your first time in a courtroom
the day you decided on a career	a final goodbye

Topics for Critical Thinking and Writing

MyWritingLab™   1. Write an essay about an incident involving you and a friend or family member. It can be a quarrel, a misunderstanding, a promise, a shared secret, or some other interaction between the two of you. In a five-paragraph essay, write one body paragraph on the way you perceived the incident and how you reacted to it. Then write another body paragraph imagining how the other person must have perceived the same incident based on his or her reactions. In the third body paragraph, include some valuable lessons you learned from these two perspectives.

MyWritingLab™   2. If you have recently enjoyed some success in school, at work, or with others, write a narrative about an event or experience that contributed to your understanding of what it means to be successful.

④ Write a process essay that makes a point and includes logical steps and detail.

PROCESS

Hints for Writing a Process Essay

1. Remember that there are two kinds of process essays: A **directional** process essay tells the reader how to do something; an **informational** process essay explains an activity without telling the reader how to do it. Whether you write a directional or an informational process essay, be sure to make a point. That point is expressed in your thesis.

When you write a process essay, it is easy to confuse a topic with a thesis.

topic: How to change the oil in your car
thesis: You don't have to be an expert to learn how to change the oil in your car.

topic: How gardeners squirrel-proof their backyards
thesis: Gardeners have to think like squirrels to keep the critters away from plants and trees.

2. Find some logical way to divide the steps into paragraphs. If you have seven steps, you probably don't want to put each one into a separate paragraph, especially if they are short steps. You would run the risk of having a list instead of a well-developed essay. To avoid writing a list, try to cluster your steps according to some logical division.

If you are writing about how to prepare for a yard sale, you could divide your steps into groups such as (1) what to do a week before the sale, (2) what to do the day before the sale, and (3) what to do early on the day of the sale. Or if you are writing about how to cope with a bad cold, you could divide the steps into (1) recognizing the first signs of a cold, (2) assembling cold-fighting foods and vitamins, and (3) struggling through the days of misery.

3. Develop your paragraphs by explaining each step thoroughly and by using details.   If you are explaining how to make a cake, you can't simply tell the reader to mix the combined ingredients well. You need to explain how long to mix and whether to mix with a fork, spoon, spatula, or electric mixer. Fortunately, an essay gives you the time and space to be clear, especially if you put yourself in the reader's place and anticipate his or her questions.

CRITICAL THINKING

A process essay provides instruction on how to do something (directional) or explains the steps of a procedure from start to finish, such as how a bill becomes a law (informational). It's important not to omit any steps. What may seem simple and logical to you may not seem as clear to your reader.

WRITING THE PROCESS ESSAY IN STEPS

PREWRITING   PROCESS ESSAY

If you were writing a process essay about finding an apartment, you might first freewrite your ideas on the topic. Brainstorming and listing your ideas might lead you to group your ideas into three categories, organized in time order:

Listing and Grouping Ideas for a Process Essay

Topic: Finding an Apartment

before the search

How many bedrooms?

Friends can help

A good neighborhood

A convenient location can be more expensive

Can save you money on transportation

during the search

Look around

Don't pick the first apartment you see

Look at a bunch

But not too many

after the search

Check the lease carefully

How much is the security deposit?

After some more thinking, you could summarize these ideas in a thesis:

Finding the apartment you want takes planning and careful investigation.

With a thesis sentence and some ideas clustered in categories, you can write an outline for your essay.

PLANNING **PROCESS ESSAY**

Following is an outline for a process essay on finding an apartment. Study the outline carefully and be prepared to respond to the exercise that follows it.

Outline for a Process Essay

paragraph 1
    I. Thesis: Finding the apartment you want takes planning and careful investigation.

paragraph 2, topic sentence
    II. You can save yourself stress by doing some preliminary work.

      A. Decide what you want.
      B. Ask yourself, "How many bedrooms do I want?" and "What can I afford?"

details: what to consider before the search
      C. Weigh the pros and cons of your wishes.
      D. A convenient location can be expensive.
      E. It can also save you money on transportation.
      F. Friends can help you with the names of nice apartments.
      G. Maybe somebody you know lives in a good neighborhood.
      H. Check the classified advertisements in the newspapers.

paragraph 3, topic sentence
    III. On your search, be patient, look carefully, and ask questions.

      A. Look around.
      B. Don't pick the first apartment you see.

details: what to do during the search
      C. Look at several.
      D. But don't look at too many.
      E. Check the cleanliness, safety, plumbing, and appliances of each one.
      F. Ask the manager about the laundry room, additional storage, parking facilities, and maintenance policies.

paragraph 4, topic sentence
    IV. When you've seen enough apartments, take time to examine your options.

      A. Compare the two best places you saw.
      B. Consider the price, locations, and condition of the apartments.
      C. Check the leases carefully.

details: what to do after the search
      D. Are pets allowed?
      E. Are there rules about getting roommates?
      F. Check the amount of the security deposit.
      G. Check the requirements for the first and last months' rent deposit.

paragraph 5, conclusion
    V. With the right strategies and a thorough search, you can get the apartment that suits you.

The outline used each cluster of steps as one body paragraph. A topic sentence for each body paragraph made some point about that group of steps. It also added many new details gathered during the outline process. As you write and revise your draft, you can continue to add details. Later, during editing, you can combine sentences, strengthen transitions, and refine word choices.

Exercise 12 **Practice: Recognizing Added Details in the Outline Stage**   MyWritingLab™

Paragraph 2 of the outline is quite different from the list of ideas grouped for the same category ("Before the Search") on page 273. In the outline, a topic sentence and a number of new details have been added. Underline the added details in Paragraph 2.

DRAFTING AND REVISING   PROCESS ESSAY

Following is a revised draft of the essay on finding an apartment. As you read it, you'll notice many changes from the outline on page 274.

- An introduction has been added.
- Transitions have been added within and between paragraphs.
- Details have been added.
- Direct questions have been turned into sentences.
- A concluding paragraph has been added.

Study the revised draft carefully and be prepared to respond to the exercises that follow it.

Draft of a Process Essay

(Note: Thesis, topic sentences, and conclusion are underlined; editing and proofreading are still necessary.)

Some people drive around a neighborhood until they see an apartment complex with a "Vacancy" sign. They talk to the building manager, visit the apartment, and sign a lease. Soon they are residents of their new apartment, and often they are unhappy with their home. These people went about their search the wrong way. They did not realize that finding the apartment you want takes planning and careful investigation.

You can save yourself stress by doing some preliminary work. First of all, decide what you want. Determine how many bedrooms you want and what you can afford. Weigh the pros and cons of your wishes. You may want a convenient location, but that can be expensive. On the other hand, that location can save you money on transportation. When you've decided what you want, rely on friends to help you with your search. They can help you with the names of nice apartments. Maybe somebody you know lives in a good neighborhood and can help you find an apartment. In addition, check the classified advertisements in the newspapers. They are full of possibilities.

In your search, be patient, look carefully, and ask questions. It's important to look around and not to pick the first apartment you see. Look at several so that you can get a sense of your options. However, don't look at so many apartments that they all become a blur in your memory. As you visit each apartment, check its cleanness, safety, plumbing, and appliances. You don't want an apartment that opens onto a bad area or one with a leaky refrigerator. Be sure to ask the apartment manager whether there are a laundry room, a storage area, and sufficient assigned parking and guest parking. Check to see if a maintenance person lives on the premises.

(Continued)

<u>When you've seen enough apartments, take the time to examine your options</u>. First, compare the two best places you saw. Now that you have narrowed your search, consider the price, location, and condition of each apartment. Check the leases carefully. If you have or are thinking of getting a pet, check to see if pets are allowed. Check the rules about roommates, too. Next, check to see how much money you will have to put up initially. Does the lease specify the amount of the security deposit? Does it require a payment of first and last months' rent? The answers to these questions can help you reach a decision.

Once you have followed the steps of the process, you are ready to make your choice. While these steps take more time than simply picking the first place you see on the street, they are worth it. <u>With the right strategies and a thorough search, you can get the apartment that suits your needs</u>. Finally, you are ready to settle into your new home.

MyWritingLab™   **Exercise 13** **Practice: Recognizing How an Outline Can Be Developed into a Draft**

Study Paragraph 3 in its outline form. Then examine the same paragraph in draft form. The paragraph includes new details about (1) a reason to look at several apartments, (2) the danger of looking at too many apartments, (3) why it is important to check the safety of the apartment and the condition of the appliances, and (4) what to ask about maintenance. Underline these new details.

MyWritingLab™   **Exercise 14** **Practice: Recognizing Effective Transitions**

The concluding paragraph carries the reader into the final step in the process of finding an apartment. Notice how effective time transitions lead the reader from the first part of the paragraph, then past the restatement of the thesis to the final sentence. Underline the time transitions.

EDITING AND PROOFREADING   **PROCESS ESSAY**

Following is the final edited version of the essay on finding an apartment. When you compare it to the draft on pages 275–276, you will notice some changes:

- A transition has been added to the beginning of Paragraph 2 so that there is a smoother link from the thesis at the end of Paragraph 1 and the topic sentence of Paragraph 2.
- The words *nice*, *good*, and *bad* have been changed to more specific descriptions.
- More details have been added to the end of Paragraph 3.
- *Cleanness* has been corrected to *cleanliness* in Paragraph 3.
- A title has been added.

Study the final version carefully and be prepared to respond to the exercise that follows it.

Final Version of a Process Essay

How to Find a Suitable Apartment

Some people drive around a neighborhood until they see an apartment complex with a "Vacancy" sign. They talk to the building manager, visit the apartment, and sign a lease. Soon they are residents of their new apartment, and often they are unhappy with their home. These people went about their search the wrong way. They did not realize that finding the apartment you want takes planning and careful investigation.

When it comes to choosing an apartment, you can save yourself stress by doing some preliminary work. First of all, decide what you want. Determine how many bedrooms you want and what you can afford. Weigh the pros and cons of your wishes. You may want a convenient location, but that can be expensive. On the other hand, that location can save you money on transportation. When you've decided what you want, rely on friends to help you with your search. They can help you with the names of suitable apartments. Maybe somebody you know lives in an attractive neighborhood and can help you find an apartment. In addition, check the classified advertisements in the newspapers. They are full of possibilities.

In your search, be patient, look carefully, and ask questions. It's important to look around and not to pick the first apartment you see. Look at several so that you can get a sense of your options. However, don't look at so many apartments that they all become a blur in your memory. As you visit each apartment, check its cleanness, safety, plumbing, and appliances. You don't want an apartment that opens onto a dark and deserted area or one with a leaky refrigerator. Be sure to ask the apartment manager whether there are a laundry room, storage area, and sufficient assigned parking and guest parking. Check to see if a maintenance person lives on the premises or if a rental agency handles emergencies and repairs.

When you've seen enough apartments, take the time to examine your options. First, compare the two best places you saw. Now that you have narrowed your search, consider the price, location, and condition of each apartment. Check the leases carefully. If you have or are thinking of getting a pet, check to see if pets are allowed. Check the rules about roommates, too. Next, check to see how much money you will have to put up initially. Does the lease specify the amount of the security deposit? Does it require a payment of first and last months' rent? The answers to these questions can help you reach a decision.

Once you have followed the steps of the process, you are ready to make your choice. While these steps take more time than simply picking the first place you see on the street, they are worth it. With the right strategies and a thorough search, you can get the apartment that suits your needs. Finally, you are ready to settle into your new home.

Exercise 15 **Practice: Recognizing Small Improvements in the Final Version of a Process Essay**   MyWritingLab™

Underline (1) the more specific descriptions that have replaced the words *nice*, *good*, and *bad* used in the draft and (2) the new detail added to the end of Paragraph 3.

Topics for Writing a Process Essay

When you write on any of these topics, work through the stages of the writing process in preparing your essay.

MyWritingLab™

1. Write a directional or informational process essay about one of these topics:

trying out for a team	childproofing a room
finding a roommate	teaching someone to drive
selling a car	applying for a loan
getting a good night's sleep	studying for a test

MyWritingLab™

2. You may work through some process at work. For example, you may have to open or close a store, clean a piece of machinery, fill out a report, use a specific computer program, or follow a process in making telemarketing calls. You may have to maintain the appearance of a work area (like aisles in a supermarket), or follow a procedure in dealing with complaints. If you follow a process at work, write an essay that teaches the process to a new employee.

MyWritingLab™

3. Think of a time when you had to make an important decision. Write an essay about how you reached that decision. You can write about the circumstances that led to making a choice and about the steps you followed. For example, what did you consider first? Did you weigh the pros and cons of your options? What was your first choice? Did you stay with that decision or change your mind? Trace the steps of your thought process.

Topics for Critical Thinking and Writing

MyWritingLab™

1. A turning point in one's life can be the result of taking risks, planning carefully, or even both. Write an essay about the series of steps you followed to make a decision that significantly changed your life.

MyWritingLab™

2. Assume that your manager or supervisor has asked you to gather suggestions about ways to improve employee morale, but these suggestions should not involve raises. He or she has said that it would be entirely up to you how you gather as much information and employee feedback as possible. You have agreed to compile suggestions but need to devise a plan to ensure that as many employees as possible are involved. What are the steps you would undertake to ensure optimal employee participation? You may want to consider such steps as forming a committee, recruiting colleagues, devising a survey, and so forth.

⑤ Write a comparison or contrast essay that makes a statement and is supported by specific points.

COMPARISON AND CONTRAST

Hints for Writing a Comparison or Contrast Essay

1. Use the thesis of your comparison or contrast to make a statement. Your essay must do more than explain the similarities or differences between two people, places, or things. It must make some statement about the two. For instance, if you are writing about the differences between your first and second semester of college, your thesis may be that a person can change radically in a short time.

2. Use your points of comparison or contrast as a way to organize your body paragraphs. A comparison or contrast essay needs points; each point focuses on a specific similarity or difference. For example, you might use three points to compare two dogs: their appearance, their temperament, and their abilities. You can write one body paragraph on each of these points of comparison.

3. Use a point-by-point pattern. That is, each body paragraph can explain one point of comparison or contrast. The topic sentence can summarize the point, and the details about the two subjects (people, places, or things you are comparing) can support the topic sentence. These details can be grouped so that you first discuss one subject, and then the other. You might, for example, compare the appearance of two dogs. An outline for one body paragraph might look like the following:

topic sentence	II. My German shepherd and my border collie are similar in appearance.
point: appearance **subject 1:** **my German shepherd**	A. Max, my shepherd, has long, shiny black and brown hair. B. His ears stand up as if he is always alert. C. His eyes are dark and intelligent.
subject 2: my border collie	D. Sheba, my collie, has glossy black and white hair. F. Her pointed ears make it seem as if she is always listening to something. G. Her black eyes are knowing and wise.

WRITING THE COMPARISON OR CONTRAST ESSAY IN STEPS

PREWRITING   **COMPARISON OR CONTRAST ESSAY**

One way to get started on a comparison or contrast paragraph is to list as many differences or similarities as you can on one topic. Then you can see whether you have more similarities (comparisons) or differences (contrasts), and decide which approach to use. For example, if you decide to compare or contrast two restaurants, you could begin with a list like this:

Listing Ideas for a Comparison or Contrast Essay

Topic: Two Restaurants: Victor's and The Garden

similarities
both offer lunch and dinner
very popular
nearby

differences

Victor's	The Garden
formal dress	informal dress
tablecloths	placemats
food is bland	spicy food
expensive	moderate
statues, fountains, fresh flowers	dark wood, hanging plants

Getting Points of Comparison or Contrast

Whether you compare or contrast, you are looking for points of comparison or contrast, items you can discuss about both subjects.

If you surveyed the list on the two restaurants and decided you wanted to contrast the two, you'd see that you already have these points of contrast:

dress   food
decor   prices

To write your essay, start with several points of comparison or contrast. As you work through the stages of writing, you may decide you don't need all the points you've jotted down, but it is better to start with too many points than with too few.

Once you have some points, you can begin adding details to them. The details may lead you to more points. If they do not, they will still help you develop the ideas of your paragraph. If you were to write about the differences in restaurants, for example, your new list with added details might look like this:

Listing Ideas for a Contrast Essay

Topic: Two Restaurants

Victor's	The Garden
dress–formal	informal dress
men in jackets, women in dresses	all in jeans
decor– pretty, elegant	placemats, on table is a card listing specials
statues, fountains, fresh flowers on tables, tablecloths	lots of dark wood, brass, green hanging plants
food– bland tasting, broiled fish or chicken, steaks, appetizers like shrimp cocktail, onion soup	spicy and adventurous pasta in tomato sauces, garlic in everything, curry appetizers like tiny tortillas, ribs in honey-mustard sauce
price– expensive	moderate
everything costs extra, like appetizer, salad	price of dinner includes appetizer and salad

---

Reading the list about restaurants, you might conclude that some people may prefer The Garden to Victor's. Why? There are several hints in your list. The Garden has cheaper food, better food, and a more casual atmosphere. Now that you have a point, you can shape a thesis statement contrasting the restaurants as follows:

> Some people would rather eat at The Garden than at Victor's because The Garden offers better, cheaper food in a more casual environment.

After you are satisfied with your thesis statement, you can begin the planning stage for your essay.

PLANNING **CONTRAST ESSAY**

Following is an outline for a contrast essay on two restaurants. Study the outline carefully and be prepared to respond to the exercise that follows it.

Outline for a Contrast Essay

paragraph 1 — I. Thesis: Some people would rather eat at The Garden than at Victor's because The Garden offers better, cheaper food in a more casual environment.

paragraph 2, topic sentence — II. The menus at the two restaurants reveal significant differences.

details about food: Victor's

    A. Food at Victor's is bland-tasting and traditional.
    B. The menu has broiled fish, chicken, and steaks.
    C. The spices used are mostly parsley and salt.
    D. The food is the usual American food, with a little French food on the list.
    E. Food at The Garden is more spicy and adventurous.
    F. There are many pasta dishes in tomato sauce.

details about food: The Garden

    G. There is garlic in just about everything.
    H. The Garden serves five different curry dishes.
    I. It has all kinds of ethnic food.
    J. Appetizers include items like tiny tortillas and hot honey-mustard ribs.

paragraph 3, topic sentence — III. There is a contrast in prices at the two restaurants.

details about price: Victor's

    A. Victor's is expensive.
    B. Everything you order costs extra.
    C. An appetizer or a salad costs extra.
    D. Even a potato costs extra.
    E. Food at The Garden is more moderately priced.

details about price: The Garden

    F. The price of a dinner includes an appetizer and a salad.
    G. All meals come with a potato, pasta, or rice.

paragraph 4, topic sentence — IV. At Victor's and The Garden, meals are served in opposing environments.

details about environment: Victor's

    A. Certain diners may feel uncomfortable in Victor's, which has a formal atmosphere.
    B. Everyone is dressed up, the men in jackets and ties and the women in dresses.
    C. Even the children in the restaurant are in their best clothes and sit up straight.
    D. Less formal diners would rather eat in a more casual place.

details about environment: The Garden

    E. People don't dress up to go to The Garden; they wear jeans.
    F. Some come in shorts and sandals.
    G. The children often wear sneakers and caps.
    H. They wriggle in their seats and even crawl under the table.

paragraph 5, conclusion — V. Many people prefer a place where they can relax, with reasonable prices and unusual food, to a place that's a little stuffy, with a traditional and expensive menu.

The outline added some new details gathered during the outlining process. The topic sentences of the body paragraphs are based on the points of contrast on the earlier list. One point of contrast, the decor of the restaurants, has been omitted. The details about decor may be useful in the introduction or conclusion of the essay.

As you write and revise your draft, you can continue to add details. During editing, later in the writing process, you can combine sentences, add transitions, and improve word choices.

MyWritingLab™   **Exercise 16** **Practice: Recognizing How an Outline Evolves from a List**

Compare the list of ideas on dress in the two restaurants to the outline section on the topic. Underline the ideas that have been added to the outline.

DRAFTING AND REVISING   CONTRAST ESSAY

Following is a revised draft of the essay on two restaurants. Compare it to the outline on page 281, you may notice the following changes:

- An introduction has been added, and it contains some of the details on decor gathered earlier.
- Transitions have been added within and between paragraphs.
- Details have been added.
- The word choice has been improved.
- A concluding paragraph has been added.

Study the draft carefully and be prepared to respond to the exercises that follow it.

Draft of a Contrast Essay

(Note: Thesis, topic sentences, and conclusion are underlined; editing and proofreading are still necessary.)

There are two well-known restaurants in town. One, Victor's, is an elegant place with white linen tablecloths and fresh flowers on each table. The other, The Garden, has paper placemats on the tables. The only other item on the tables is a small card listing the day's specials. While it might seem that Victor's is a more attractive setting for a meal, The Garden has its advantages. <u>Some people would rather eat at The Garden than at Victor's because The Garden offers better, cheaper food in a more casual environment.</u>

<u>The menus at the two restaurants reveal significant differences.</u> Food at Victor's is bland-tasting and traditional. The menu offers broiled fish, baked chicken, and typical steaks like T-bone and sirloin. The spices used are mostly parsley and salt. Victor's serves standard American food with a little French food on the list; for example, the appetizers include an American favorite, shrimp cocktail, and French onion soup. While food at Victor's relies on old, safe choices, food at The Garden is more spicy and adventurous. There are many pasta dishes in tomato sauce. Garlic appears in just about everything from mashed potatoes to pork roasts. The Garden serves five different curry dishes. In fact, it has all kinds of ethnic food; tiny tortillas and ribs dipped in honey and hot Chinese mustard are the most popular appetizers.

Food choice is not the only difference between Victor's and The Garden; <u>there is also a contrast in prices at the two restaurants</u>. Victor's is expensive. Everything you order, such as an appetizer or a salad, costs extra. Even a baked potato costs extra. An entree like a steak, for example, comes on a platter with a sprig of parsley. If you want a potato or a vegetable, you have to pay extra for it. Food at The Garden is more moderately priced. The price of a dinner includes an appetizer and a salad; in addition, all meals come with a potato, pasta, or rice, so there are few pricey extras to pay for.

The cost of a meal at Victor's is different from one at The Garden, and the atmosphere in which the meal is enjoyed is different, too. <u>At the two places, meals are served in opposing settings.</u> Certain diners may feel uncomfortable in Victor's, which has a formal atmosphere. Everyone is dressed up, the men in jackets and ties, and the women in dresses. Even the children at Victor's are dressed in their best and sit straight up in their chairs. Less formal diners would rather eat in a more casual place, like The Garden. People don't dress up to go to The Garden; they wear jeans or shorts and sandals. The children often wear sneakers and baseball caps. They wriggle in their seats and even explore under the table.

Sometimes adults want to let go, just as children do. They want to sit back, not up, stretch their legs in casual clothes, not jackets and ties or dresses, and explore new food choices, not the same old standards. The Garden appeals to that childlike need for physical comfort and adventurous dining, at a moderate cost. <u>People</u> choose it over Victor's because they <u>prefer a place where they can relax, with reasonable prices and unusual food, to a place that's a little stuffy, with a traditional and expensive menu.</u>

Exercise 17 **Practice: Spotting Synonyms**   MyWritingLab™

In an essay about food, the word "food" can be overused. One way around this repetition is to use synonyms. These synonyms can be general (such as "menu") or specific (such as "potato"). Search the essay and underline as many words or phrases as you can find that refer to specific things to eat or to spices.

Exercise 18 **Practice: Recognizing the Power of Transitions**   MyWritingLab™

An essay that compares or contrasts needs effective transitions to keep the ideas flowing smoothly. Three paragraphs in this essay open with transitional sentences that link a new idea to a previous one. Underline this type of transition.

EDITING AND PROOFREADING **CONTRAST ESSAY**

Following is a final version of the essay on two restaurants. When you compare it to the draft on pages 282–283, you will notice some changes:

- More specific details have been added.
- Two sentences in Paragraph 3 have been revised so that the shift to *you* is eliminated.
- The phrase *explore under the table* in Paragraph 4 has been changed to *explore the spaces under the table* for clarity.
- One sentence in the conclusion has been revised so that it has a stronger parallel structure.
- A title has been added.

Study the final version carefully and be prepared to respond to the exercise that follows it.

Final Version of a Contrast Essay

Victor's and The Garden: Two Contrasting Restaurants

There are two well-known restaurants in town. One, Victor's, is an elegant place with white linen tablecloths and fresh flowers on each table. The other, The Garden, has paper placemats on the tables. The only other item on the tables is a small card listing the day's specials. While it might seem that Victor's is a more attractive setting for a meal, The Garden has its advantages. Some people would rather eat at The Garden than at Victor's because The Garden offers better, cheaper food in a more casual environment.

The menus at the two restaurants reveal significant differences. Food at Victor's is bland-tasting and traditional. The menu offers broiled fish, baked chicken, and typical steaks like T-bone and sirloin. The spices used are mostly parsley and salt; pepper, garlic, and curry are nowhere to be found. Victor's serves standard American food with a little French food on the list; for example, the appetizers include an American favorite, shrimp cocktail, and French onion soup. While food at Victor's relies on old, safe choices, food at The Garden is more spicy and adventurous. There are many pasta dishes, from linguini to lasagna, in a rich tomato sauce. Garlic appears in just about everything from mashed potatoes to pork roasts. The Garden serves five different curry dishes. In fact, it has all kinds of ethnic food; tiny tortillas and ribs dipped in honey and hot Chinese mustard are the most popular appetizers.

Food choice is not the only difference between Victor's and The Garden; there is also a contrast in prices at the two restaurants. Victor's is expensive. Everything a person orders, such as an appetizer or a salad, costs extra. Even a baked potato costs extra. An entree like a steak, for example, comes on a platter with a sprig of parsley. Anyone who wants a potato or a vegetable has to pay extra for it. Food at The Garden is more moderately priced. The price of a dinner includes an appetizer and a salad; in addition, all meals come with a potato, pasta, or rice, so there are few pricey extras to pay for.

The cost of a meal at Victor's is different from one at The Garden, and the atmosphere in which the meal is enjoyed is different, too. At the two places, meals are served in opposing settings. Certain diners may feel uncomfortable in Victor's, which has a formal atmosphere. Everyone is dressed up, the men in jackets and ties, and the women in fancy dresses. Even the children at Victor's are dressed in their best and sit straight up in their chairs. Less formal diners would rather eat in a more casual place, like The Garden. People don't dress up to go to The Garden; they wear jeans or shorts and sandals. The children often wear sneakers and baseball caps. They wriggle in their seats and even explore the spaces under the table.

Sometimes adults want to let go, just as children do. They want to sit back, not up, stretch their legs in casual clothes, not hold their breath in tight ties or fancy dresses, and explore new food choices, not settle for the same old standards. The Garden appeals to that childlike need for physical comfort and adventurous dining, at a moderate cost. People choose it over Victor's because they prefer a place where they can relax, with reasonable prices and unusual food, to a place that's a little stuffy, with a traditional and expensive menu.

MyWritingLab™ **Exercise 19** **Practice: Correcting a Shift in Persons**

A shift in persons is a grammar error that occurs when, for example, the third person (*he, she, it, they,* or *the name of a person, place, or thing*) suddenly shifts to another person such as the second person (*you*). In the draft version of the essay, there was a shift in persons from the third person (*people, food, it*) to the second person (*you*). The shift occurs twice in Paragraph 3. Read the draft version of Paragraph 3; note where the shifts occur, and then check the final version. Underline what replaced *you* and what replaced the verbs that followed *you* in the draft version.

Topics for Writing a Comparison or Contrast Essay

When you write on any of these topics, work through the stages of the writing process in preparing your essay.

1. Compare or contrast any of the following: **MyWritingLab™**

two video games	two surprises
two role models	two employment opportunities
two expensive purchases	two places you've lived in
two clothing styles	two assignments

2. Compare or contrast the person you were two years ago to the person you are today. You might consider such points of comparison as your worries, fears, hopes, goals, or relationships.   **MyWritingLab™**

3. Compare or contrast the way you spend a weekday with the way you spend a day off. You can consider what you do in the morning, afternoon, and evening as points of comparison or contrast.   **MyWritingLab™**

4. Compare or contrast your expectations of some aspect of college life (such as the instructors, the grading policies, the classroom environment, and so forth) with the reality you are now experiencing.   **MyWritingLab™**

Topics for Critical Thinking and Writing

1. Today's consumer has more choices than ever regarding cell phones. Write about the similarities or differences between a basic cell phone and one of the smartphones available today. Assume your audience for this essay is someone unfamiliar with various new features, and be objective in your style (i.e., do not take a stand). Be as specific as possible with your examples and details so your reader can decide which type of phone would be best suited for his or her needs.   **MyWritingLab™**

2. If you have experience working at an independent store (only one of its kind) as well as at a chain or franchised store (multiple locations), write an essay about the stores' similarities or differences in three main areas. Brainstorm about hiring practices, working conditions, opportunities for promotion, sales training, and so forth before you determine the best areas to compare or contrast. Try to incorporate as many details as possible that would be important or surprising to the general public.   **MyWritingLab™**

CHAPTER 13

Different Essay Patterns: Part Two

Jumping In

Artists and designers often use interesting patterns in their work, but patterns can be seen all around us. The distinctive shapes in tile, carpet, or fabric combine and repeat to form patterns arranged to have a particular effect on viewers. Patterns help to organize what we see. In the same way, patterns of development in an essay organize what we write. Determining effective patterns of development can help you maintain the interest of your readers in the same way that patterns in art attract and hold the interest of viewers.

Learning Objectives

In this chapter, you will learn to:

1. Write a classification essay that has a clear basis (reason) for classifying (dividing) a topic into distinct types or categories.

2. Write a definition essay that explains a term, label, or phrase by providing distinguishing characteristics based on personal observations.

3. Write a cause or effect essay with developed body paragraphs that both explain and describe.

4. Write an argument essay that takes a stand, uses reason, and considers its audience.

5. Write a multipattern essay that has a clear topic and thesis, employs the same pattern within a paragraph, and uses transitions effectively.

CLASSIFICATION

Hints for Writing a Classification Essay

1. Be sure to have a point in your classification. Remember that you need to do more than divide something into three or more types, according to some basis, and explain and describe these types. You must have a reason for your classification. For example, if you write about three types of scooters, you may be writing to evaluate them, and your point may state which type is the best buy. If you are classifying weight-loss programs, you may be studying each type so that you can prove that two types are dangerous.

2. A simple way to structure your classification essay is to explain each type in a separate body paragraph. Then use the same kind of details to describe each type. For instance, if you describe the medical principles, food restrictions, and results of one type of weight-loss program, describe the medical principles, food restrictions, and results of the other types of weight-loss programs.

> **1** Write a classification essay that has a clear basis (reason) for classifying (dividing) a topic into distinct types or categories.

WRITING THE CLASSIFICATION ESSAY IN STEPS

PREWRITING   CLASSIFICATION ESSAY

First, pick a topic for your classification. The next step is to choose some basis for your classification. For example, if you were to write a paragraph classifying phone calls, you could write about phone calls on the basis of their effect on you. With this basis for classification, you can come up with three categories:

calls that please me
calls that irritate me
calls that frighten me

By brainstorming, you can then gather details about your three categories as follows:

CRITICAL THINKING

Think of classifying as a way of dividing a topic into groups to help the reader understand it more easily.

Added Details for Three Categories of a Classification Essay

Topic: Phone Calls

calls that please me
from boyfriend
good friends
catch-up calls—someone I haven't talked to for a while
make me feel close

calls that irritate me
sales calls at dinnertime
wrong numbers

(Continued)

calls that interrupt
invade privacy

calls that frighten me
emergency call in middle of night
break-up call from boyfriend
change my life, indicate some bad change

With these categories and details, you can write a thesis that (1) mentions what you are classifying and (2) indicates the basis for your classifying by listing all three categories or by stating the basis, or both. Here is a thesis that follows the guidelines:

> Phone calls can be grouped into the ones that please me, the ones that irritate me, and the ones that frighten me.

This thesis mentions what you are classifying: *phone calls*. It indicates the basis for classification, the effect of the phone calls, by listing the types: *the ones that please me*, *the ones that irritate me*, and *the ones that frighten me*. Here is another thesis that follows the guidelines:

> I can classify phone calls according to their effect on me.

This thesis also mentions what you are classifying, *phone calls*, but it mentions the basis for classification, *their effect on me*, instead of listing the types.

Once you have a thesis sentence and a list of ideas, you are ready to begin the planning stage of writing the classification essay.

PLANNING CLASSIFICATION ESSAY

Following is an outline for a classification essay on phone calls. Study the outline carefully and be prepared to respond to Exercise 1 that follows on the next page.

Outline for a Classification Essay

paragraph 1 ———— I. Thesis: Phone calls can be grouped into the ones that please me, the ones that irritate me, and the ones that frighten me.

paragraph 2, topic sentence ———— II. Calls that please me make me feel close to someone.

A. I like calls from my boyfriend, especially when he calls to say he is thinking of me.

B. I like to hear from good friends.

C. My two best friends call me at least twice a day.

details about pleasing calls ———— D. I like catch-up calls.

E. These are calls from people I haven't talked to in a while.

F. A friend I hadn't seen in a year called me from Ecuador to say "Happy Birthday."

G. We talked for a long time.

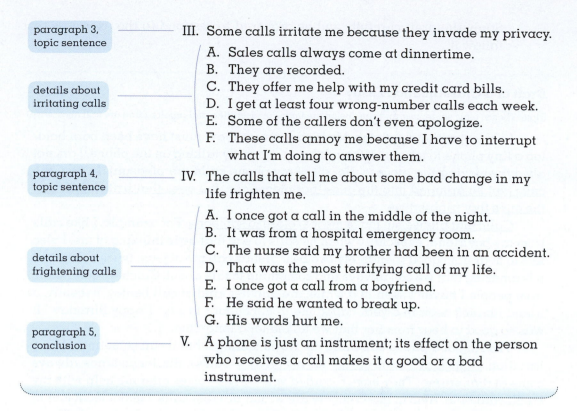

paragraph 3, topic sentence

III. Some calls irritate me because they invade my privacy.

details about irritating calls

A. Sales calls always come at dinnertime.
B. They are recorded.
C. They offer me help with my credit card bills.
D. I get at least four wrong-number calls each week.
E. Some of the callers don't even apologize.
F. These calls annoy me because I have to interrupt what I'm doing to answer them.

paragraph 4, topic sentence

IV. The calls that tell me about some bad change in my life frighten me.

details about frightening calls

A. I once got a call in the middle of the night.
B. It was from a hospital emergency room.
C. The nurse said my brother had been in an accident.
D. That was the most terrifying call of my life.
E. I once got a call from a boyfriend.
F. He said he wanted to break up.
G. His words hurt me.

paragraph 5, conclusion

V. A phone is just an instrument; its effect on the person who receives a call makes it a good or a bad instrument.

The outline combined some of the details from the list with new details gathered during the writing process. It used the three categories as the basis for the topic sentences for the body paragraph. Each topic sentence has two parts: (1) the name of the category, such as pleasing calls, and (2) the effect of calls in this category. For example, here is one topic sentence:

(1) the category   (2) the effect of calls in this category
Calls that please me make me feel close to someone.

Since the point of the essay is to show the effect of different kinds of calls, this topic sentence is effective.

As you write and revise your draft, you can continue to add details and concentrate on your essay's organization. During the editing and proofreading stage, you can combine sentences, add or strengthen transition, refine word choice, and correct errors.

Exercise 1   **Practice: Identifying the Added Details in Paragraph 2 of the Outline**   MyWritingLab™

Compare the list of details (under the heading "Calls That Please Me") in the Prewriting section for the classification essay with the list of details in the outline. Underline the additional details.

DRAFTING AND REVISING   CLASSIFICATION ESSAY

Following is a revised draft of the essay on phone calls. As you read it, you'll notice many changes from the outline on pages 288–289.

- An introduction has been added.
- Transitions have been added within and between paragraphs.
- Details have been added.
- A concluding paragraph has been added.

Study the draft carefully and be prepared to respond to the exercises that follow it.

Draft of a Classification Essay

(Note: Thesis, topic sentences, and conclusion are underlined; editing and proofreading are still necessary.)

I am lost without a phone. My friends swear that I must have been born holding a tiny phone to my ear. Although I am constantly talking on the phone, I am not always enjoying the process. Not all of my phone calls are pleasant. In fact, the calls can be grouped into the ones that please me, the ones that irritate me, and the ones that frighten me.

Calls that please me make me feel close to someone. For example, I like calls from my boyfriend, especially when he calls to say that he is thinking of me. I also like to hear from good friends. My two best friends call me at least twice a day, and it is amazing that we can always find something to talk about. Catch-up calls, calls from people I haven't seen in a while, are another kind of call I enjoy. Recently, a friend I hadn't seen in a year called me from Ecuador to say "Happy Birthday." It was so good to hear from her that we talked for a long time.

The ring of a phone can bring me warm feelings, but it can sometimes bring irritation. Calls that irritate me invade my privacy. Sales calls, for instance, always come at dinnertime. They have recorded voices. The voices offer me help with my credit card bills. Also in this category are wrong-number calls. I get at least four of these a week, and some of the callers don't even apologize for bothering me. These calls annoy me because I have to interrupt what I'm doing to answer them.

Finally, there are the worst calls of all. The calls that frighten me tell me about some bad change in my life. I once got a call in the middle of the night. It was from a hospital emergency room; the nurse told me my brother had been in an accident. That was the most terrifying call of my life. Another time, a boyfriend called to say he wanted to break up. His cold words surprised and hurt me.

I rely on the telephone, but it is not always good to me. Ever since I received the call about my brother's accident, I tremble when the phone rings late at night. However, I have come to realize that a phone is just an instrument; its effect on the person who receives a call makes it a good or a bad instrument.

MyWritingLab™ **Exercise 2** **Practice: Examining the Introduction**

Look carefully at the introduction in the draft above and notice how smoothly it moves from one idea to another. Underline the sentence that introduces the idea that the writer spends a great deal of time on the phone. Then underline the sentence that moves to another idea: that not all calls are pleasant. Finally, underline the transition that introduces the thesis.

EDITING AND PROOFREADING **CLASSIFICATION ESSAY**

Following is the final version of the essay on phone calls. When you compare it to the draft above, you will notice some changes:

- Two sentences have been combined.
- Some of the word choices have been refined to make details more specific, to eliminate repetition, or to eliminate an awkward phrase.

- A final sentence has been added to Paragraph 4 to reinforce the point that both examples in the paragraph are about a life-changing phone call.
- The last sentence in the concluding paragraph has been revised to make a more precise statement about the basis for the classification: the effect of each type of phone call.
- A title has been added.

Study the final version carefully and be prepared to respond to Exercise 3 that follows it.

Final Version of a Classification Essay

Phone Calls: Good, Bad, and Ugly

I am lost without a phone. My friends swear that I must have been born holding a tiny phone to my ear. Although I am constantly talking on the phone, I am not always enjoying the process. Not all of the conversations are pleasant. In fact, the calls can be grouped into the ones that please me, the ones that irritate me, and the ones that frighten me.

Calls that please me make me feel close to someone. For example, I like calls from my boyfriend, especially when he calls to say that he is thinking of me. I also like to hear from good friends. My two best friends call me at least twice a day, and it is amazing that we can always find something to talk about. Catch-up calls, calls from people I haven't seen in a while, are another kind of call I enjoy. Recently, a friend I hadn't seen in a year called me from Ecuador to say "Happy Birthday." It was so good to hear from her that we talked for an hour.

The ring of a phone can bring me warm feelings, but it can sometimes bring irritation. Calls that irritate me invade my privacy. Sales calls that feature recorded voices always come at dinnertime. They offer help with my credit card bills. Also in this category are wrong-number calls. I get at least four of these a week, and some of the callers don't even apologize for bothering me. These calls annoy me because I have to interrupt what I'm doing to answer them.

Finally, there are the worst calls of all. The calls that frighten me tell me about some crisis in my life. I once got a call in the middle of the night. It was from a hospital emergency room; the nurse told me my brother had been in an accident. That was the most terrifying call of my life. Another time, a boyfriend called to say he wanted to break up. His cold words surprised and hurt me. Both of these calls brought me news that changed my life, and the news was totally unexpected.

I rely on the telephone, but it is not always good to me. Ever since I received the call about my brother's accident, I tremble when the phone rings late at night. However, I have come to realize that a phone is just an instrument; it conveys a message. Its effect on the person who receives that message makes it a welcome, annoying, or dreaded instrument.

Exercise 3 **Practice: Evaluating the Concluding Sentence**   MyWritingLab™

Compare the last paragraph of the draft essay to the last paragraph of the final version. (1) Why did the final essay end by describing a phone as a "welcome, annoying, or dreaded instrument"? (2) How is this a more appropriate phrase than "good or bad instrument" in the draft version?

_____

_____

Topics for Writing a Classification Essay

When you write on any of these topics, work through the stages of the writing process in preparing your essay.

Collaborate

1. Write a classification essay on any of the topics below. If your instructor agrees, brainstorm with a partner or group to come up with a basis for your classification and categories related to the basis.

   your classes   your dreams   your mistakes
   military heroes   your job responsibilities your goals
   beloved pets   discount stores   computer applications

MyWritingLab™

2. You may not know it, but you are probably an expert on something. For example, you may work in a jewelry store and know all about diamonds. You may be a paramedic and know about medical emergencies. If you are a veterinarian's assistant, you know about cats and dogs. If you collect Barbie dolls, you are an expert on these toys. Consider what you know best through your work, hobbies, education, or leisure activities, and write a classification essay about a subject in that area. If you know about diamonds, you can classify engagement rings. If you work at a veterinarian's office, you can classify pet owners or poodles.

MyWritingLab™

3. Below are some topics. Each one already has a basis for classification. Write a classification essay on one of the choices.

   Classify
   a. babysitters on the basis of how competent they are
   b. small children on the basis of their sleeping habits
   c. teens on the basis of their favorite sport
   d. roads on the basis of how safe they are
   e. fads on the basis of how long they last
   f. auto repair shops on the basis of their reliability

MyWritingLab™

4. This assignment requires a little research. Write an essay that classifies some product according to price. For example, you can classify laptops or electronic reading devices (or hair dryers, backpacks, hiking boots, motorcycles, and so forth) according to their cost. Assume that you are writing to advise readers who may want to buy this product and want the best deal for their money. Research the details of this product in different price ranges; for example, explain what the most expensive laptop includes and how useful these features are, and then explain what mid-priced and low-priced laptops offer for their price. Use your essay to recommend the best deal for the money.

Topics for Critical Thinking and Writing: Classification Essay

MyWritingLab™

1. Think about the ways in which you may be classified. For example, if you are reading this book, you are probably classified as a college student. But are you classified as a part-time or full-time student?

Your racial or ethnic background may be difficult to categorize. Today there are so many ways each person can be classified—by income level, marital status, spending habits, and so forth—that most people defy simple classifications. In your body paragraphs, write about three ways in which you might be classified incorrectly. For each classification, include examples of how these terms do not truly describe you.

2. Throughout your formal education thus far, you have probably been exposed to various teaching methods and settings that may be considered nontraditional. Brainstorm about nontraditional types of schools or teaching methods you have encountered, and classify them on the basis of how effective they were in teaching you new concepts or subject matter. As you make these judgments and draft your essay, include details about why certain methods or environments worked well or were largely ineffective for you.

MyWritingLab™

DEFINITION

Hints for Writing a Definition Essay

1. Write a personal definition, not a dictionary definition. To develop a definition essay, you need to define a term that can be explained by more than the words in a dictionary. You can develop your essay with concrete terms and specific examples that help define the term.

2️⃣ Write a definition essay that explains a term, label, or phrase by providing distinguishing characteristics based on personal observations.

> **terms that won't work in a personal definition:** photosynthesis, DNA, the Colt Revolver, the Renaissance
>
> **terms that will work in a personal definition:** self-pity, patience, the team player, the pessimist

2. Include in your thesis (1) the term you are defining, (2) the broad class or category into which your term fits, and (3) the specific distinguishing characteristics that make the term different from all others in the class or category. Each of the following sentences could be the thesis for a definition essay.

> **term   category   distinguishing characteristics**
> *Envy* is *the desire for what others have.*

> **term   category   distinguishing characteristics**
> A *nit-picker* is a *person who worries excessively about minor details.*

3. Form your body paragraphs from different aspects of your term. For example, if you defined *patience*, you might write one paragraph on the times when patience is necessary and another on the times when people need to stop being patient and take action. If you write about *temptation*, you might write one paragraph on how to resist temptation and another on when to give in to temptation.

WRITING THE DEFINITION ESSAY IN STEPS

PREWRITING **DEFINITION ESSAY**

To pick a topic for your definition essay, you can begin with some personality trait or type of person. For instance, you might define "the insecure person." If you listed your first thoughts, your list might look like this:

> the insecure person
> someone who is not emotionally secure
> wants (needs?) other people to make him or her feel good
> lack of self-esteem

Often, when you look for ideas to define a term, you get stuck with big, general statements or abstract words, or you simply cannot come up with enough to say. If you are having trouble getting ideas, think of questions about your term. Jot these questions down without stopping to answer them. One question can lead you to another question. Once you have five or more questions, you can answer them, and the answers will provide details for your definition paragraph.

If you were writing about an insecure person, for example, you could begin with questions like these:

> What are insecure people like?
> What behavior shows a person is insecure?
> How do insecure people dress or talk?
> What makes a person insecure?
> Is insecurity a bad trait?
> How do insecure people relate to others?

By scanning the questions and answering as many as you can, you can add details to your list. Once you have a longer list, you can review it and begin to group its items. Following is a list of grouped details on the insecure person.

Grouped Details for a Definition Essay

Topic: The Insecure Person

wants (needs?) other people to make him or her feel important
lack of self-esteem

insecure people have to brag about everything
a friend who brags about his car
they tell you the price of everything

they put others down
saying bad things about other people makes insecure people feel better

insecure people can never relax inside
can never enjoy being with other people
other people are always their competitors
must always worry about what others think of them

Grouping the details can help you arrive at several main ideas. Can they be combined and revised to create a thesis statement? Following is a thesis on the insecure person that meets the requirements of naming the term, placing it in a category, and distinguishing the term from others in the category:

term   category   distinguishing characteristics
The *insecure person* is *someone* who *needs other people to make him or her feel respected and important.*

Once you have a thesis statement, you can begin working on the planning stage of the paragraph.

PLANNING **DEFINITION ESSAY**

Following is an outline for a definition essay on the insecure person. Study the outline carefully and be prepared to respond to Exercise 4 that follows it. The outline combined some of the details from the list with new details and examples gathered during the outlining process. As you write and revise your

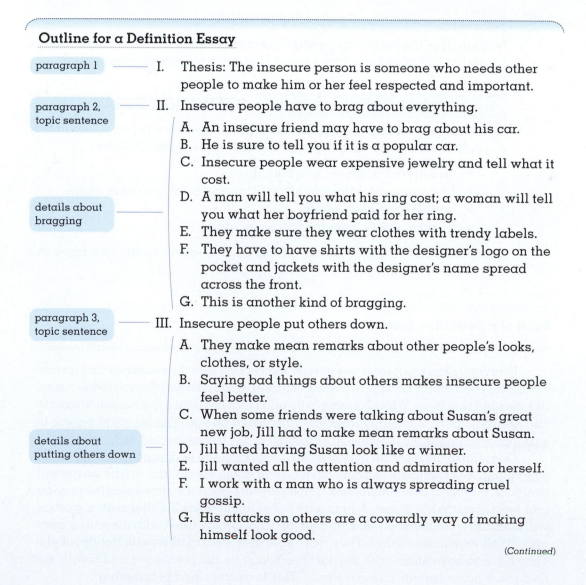

Outline for a Definition Essay

paragraph 1 —— I. Thesis: The insecure person is someone who needs other people to make him or her feel respected and important.

paragraph 2, topic sentence —— II. Insecure people have to brag about everything.

    A. An insecure friend may have to brag about his car.
    B. He is sure to tell you if it is a popular car.
    C. Insecure people wear expensive jewelry and tell what it cost.
    D. A man will tell you what his ring cost; a woman will tell you what her boyfriend paid for her ring. *(details about bragging)*
    E. They make sure they wear clothes with trendy labels.
    F. They have to have shirts with the designer's logo on the pocket and jackets with the designer's name spread across the front.
    G. This is another kind of bragging.

paragraph 3, topic sentence —— III. Insecure people put others down.

    A. They make mean remarks about other people's looks, clothes, or style.
    B. Saying bad things about others makes insecure people feel better.
    C. When some friends were talking about Susan's great new job, Jill had to make mean remarks about Susan.
    D. Jill hated having Susan look like a winner. *(details about putting others down)*
    E. Jill wanted all the attention and admiration for herself.
    F. I work with a man who is always spreading cruel gossip.
    G. His attacks on others are a cowardly way of making himself look good.

(Continued)

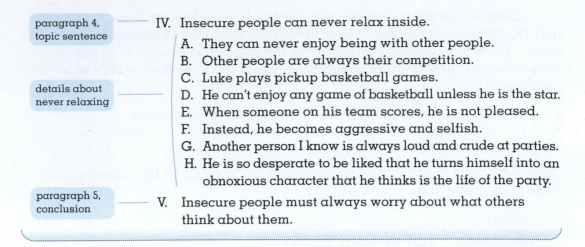

paragraph 4, topic sentence — IV. Insecure people can never relax inside.

A. They can never enjoy being with other people.
B. Other people are always their competition.
C. Luke plays pickup basketball games.

details about never relaxing — D. He can't enjoy any game of basketball unless he is the star.
E. When someone on his team scores, he is not pleased.
F. Instead, he becomes aggressive and selfish.
G. Another person I know is always loud and crude at parties.
H. He is so desperate to be liked that he turns himself into an obnoxious character that he thinks is the life of the party.

paragraph 5, conclusion — V. Insecure people must always worry about what others think about them.

draft, you can continue to add details and work on the essay's organization. Later, during editing, you can combine sentences, add or strengthen transition, and refine word choice. You can also combine sentences, add transitions, and work on word choice.

MyWritingLab™   **Exercise 4**   **Practice: Recognizing Synonyms**

Section III of the outline focuses on insecure people's need to criticize others. Underline the phrases in this section that refer to hurtful comments.

DRAFTING AND REVISING   **DEFINITION ESSAY**

Following is a revised draft of the essay on the insecure person. As you read it, you'll notice many changes from the outline on pages 295–296.

- An introduction has been added.
- Transitions have been added within and between paragraphs.
- Details have been added.
- A concluding paragraph has been added.

Study the draft carefully and be prepared to respond to the exercises that follow it.

Draft of a Definition Essay

(Note: Thesis, topic sentences, and conclusion are underlined; editing and proofreading are still necessary.)

Everybody knows at least one person who seems to feel so superior that no one could ever reach his or her status. Sometimes this person annoys others; at other times, this person hurts them. While it seems to be pride that motivates this person to irritate and belittle others, it is really insecurity disguised as ego. <u>The insecure person is someone who needs other people to make him or her feel respected and important</u>.

One sign of the insecure person is bragging. <u>Insecure people have to brag about everything</u>. An insecure friend may have to brag about his car and will be sure to tell everyone that he drives a Mercedes. Some insecure people wear expensive jewelry and brag about what it cost. A man may boast about what his ring cost; a woman will mention what her boyfriend paid for her ring. Others filled with insecurity brag about their expensive clothes. They make sure they wear clothes with trendy labels. They have to have shirts with the designer's logo on the pocket or jackets with the designer's name spread across the front. This is another kind of bragging.

<u>Insecure people</u> not only like to build themselves up, but they also <u>have to put others down</u>. They make mean remarks about other people's looks, clothes, and style. Saying bad things about others makes insecure people feel better. Recently, some friends were talking about our classmate Susan's great new job. While most of us were happy for Susan, Jill had to add some comments about how lucky Susan had been to get the job since Susan was not qualified for it. Because she wants all the attention and admiration for herself, Jill hated having Susan looking like a winner. Another insecure person is a man I work with who is always spreading cruel gossip. His attacks on others are his cowardly way of making himself look good.

The constant need to shine in other people's opinion means that <u>insecure people can never relax inside</u>. Other people are always their competition for attention or approval. One such person is Luke, a college acquaintance who always plays on our pickup basketball games. Even though the games are just for fun, Luke can't enjoy any game of basketball unless he is the star. When someone on his team scores, he isn't pleased. Instead, he becomes aggressive and selfish. He wants to win every game singlehandedly. Another person who is eager to shine is always loud and crude at parties. He is so desperate to be liked that he turns himself into an obnoxious character that he thinks is the life of the party.

Insecure people can be mean and obnoxious, but they are mainly sad. <u>Insecure people must always worry about what others think of them</u>. Because they care so much about others' opinions, they cannot be spontaneous or open. They must get very tired of hiding their fears behind their bragging and criticizing. They must also be very lonely.

Exercise 5   **Practice: Recognizing Variations in Wording**   MyWritingLab™

In Paragraph 2 of the preceding draft, each example of bragging uses a slightly different word or phrase to describe the insecure bragger. The first example refers to the "insecure person." The next refers to "insecure people." Underline the other synonyms or variations used in the paragraph.

Exercise 6   **Practice: Spotting Added Details**   MyWritingLab™

The story of Susan, whose new job prompted some mean remarks, gets some added details in the draft of the essay. Underline these new details in Paragraph 3.

EDITING AND PROOFREADING   DEFINITION ESSAY

Following is the final version of the essay on the insecure person. When you compare it to the draft on pages 296–297, you will notice some changes:

- Sentences in Paragraph 2 have been combined for a smoother style.
- The word *this* in the last sentence of Paragraph 2 has been replaced with a more specific phrase: *This obsession with designer clothes*.
- Some of the word choices have been improved to avoid repetition or to be more precise.
- A specific example has been added to Paragraph 4.
- A title has been added.

Study the final version carefully and be prepared to respond to Exercise 7 that follows it.

Final Version of a Definition Essay

The Insecure Person

Everybody knows at least one person who seems to feel so superior that no one could ever reach his or her status. Sometimes this person annoys others; at other times, this person hurts them. While it seems to be pride that motivates this person to irritate and belittle others, it is really insecurity disguised as ego. The insecure person is someone who needs other people to make him or her feel respected and important.

One sign of the insecure person is bragging, for insecure people have to brag about everything. An insecure friend may have to brag about his car and will be sure to tell everyone that he drives a Mercedes sports car. Some insecure people wear expensive jewelry and brag about what it cost. A man may boast about what his ring cost; a woman will mention what her boyfriend paid for her ring. Others filled with insecurity show off their expensive clothes. They make sure they wear clothes with trendy labels. They have to have shirts with the designer's logo on the pocket or jackets with the designer's name spread across the front. This obsession with designer clothes is another kind of bragging.

Insecure people not only like to build themselves up, but they also have to put others down. They make mean remarks about other people's looks, clothes, and style. Making nasty comments about others makes insecure people feel better. Recently, some friends were talking about our classmate Susan's great new job. While most of us were happy for Susan, Jill had to add some comments about how lucky Susan had been to get the job since Susan was not qualified for it. Because she wants all of the attention and admiration for herself, Jill hated having Susan looking like a winner. Another insecure person is a man I work with who is always spreading cruel gossip. His attacks on others are his cowardly way of making himself look good.

The constant need to shine in other people's opinion means that insecure people can never relax inside. Other people are always their competition for attention or approval. One such person is Luke, a college acquaintance who always plays on our pickup basketball games. Even though the games are just for fun, Luke can't enjoy any game of basketball unless he is the star. When someone on his team scores, he isn't pleased. Instead, he becomes aggressive and selfish. He wants to win every game singlehandedly. Another person who is eager to shine is my cousin Jamie, a generally good-natured person, who is always loud and crude at parties. He is so desperate to be liked that he turns himself into an obnoxious character that he thinks is the life of the party.

Insecure people can be mean and obnoxious, but they are mainly sad. Insecure people must always worry about what others think of them. Because they care so much about others' opinions, they cannot be spontaneous or open. They must get very tired of hiding their fears behind their bragging and criticizing. They must also be very lonely.

MyWritingLab™   Exercise 7   **Practice: Distinguishing the Changes**

In draft form, Paragraph 4 contains one example that names a specific person. In the final version of the essay, another example now includes a named person. Name the person and consider how a little added description makes him more human.

_____

_____

_____

Topics for Writing a Definition Essay

When you write on any of these topics, work through the stages of the writing process in preparing your essay.

1. What is the one quality you most admire in other people? Is it courage, kindness, drive, or another character trait? Choose a quality and write an essay defining it.   MyWritingLab™

2. Define any of the terms below, using specific details and examples. You can begin by looking up the term in a dictionary to make sure you understand the dictionary meaning. Then write a personal definition.   MyWritingLab™

dedication	satisfaction	shyness
paranoia	trust	will power
boldness	brotherhood	compassion
sympathy	perseverance	generosity

3. Write a personal definition of a specific type of person. Develop your definition by using specific details and examples. Following is a list of types, but you may write about another type of your choosing.   MyWritingLab™

the natural athlete	the rebel	the loner
the big brother/sister	the ideal mate	the planner
the control freak	the technology geek	the nagger
the good sport	the hypochondriac	the critic

4. We often use terms that we understand and that we assume everyone knows. However, these terms may not have clear definitions. Write your definition of such a term. Examples of these terms are listed below, but you can also choose your own term.   MyWritingLab™

street smarts	change agent	fashion sense
people skills	a people person	personal issues
comfort zone	people pleaser	alpha male

Topics for Critical Thinking and Writing: Definition Essay

1. Think of a slang term or phrase that is currently popular and then define it. In your essay, be sure to include several meanings associated with this term or phrase. You may also want to explain its original definition, popularity, the age groups and backgrounds of the people that use the word or phrase, and the duration of its popularity.   MyWritingLab™

2. As you have matured, your views about life and what is important to you have probably changed numerous times. Today, what does the phrase "a satisfying life" mean to you? You may need to examine your aspirations in several areas of your life (family, relationships, career, hobbies, and so forth) in order to write this essay.   MyWritingLab™

CAUSE AND EFFECT

Hints for Writing a Cause or Effect Essay

1. Choose either causes or effects.   If you try to do both in a short essay, you will make your task more difficult. In addition, you need a longer and more complex essay to cover both causes and effects adequately.

③ Write a cause or effect essay with developed body paragraphs that both explain and describe.

2. You can use each cause or effect as the focus of one body paragraph. You can develop the paragraph by explaining and describing that cause or effect.

WRITING THE CAUSE OR EFFECT ESSAY IN STEPS

PREWRITING CAUSE OR EFFECT ESSAY

If you were thinking about writing a cause or effect paragraph on owning a car, you could begin by freewriting something like this:

Freewriting for a Cause or Effect Essay

Topic: Owning a Car
A car of my own. Why? I needed it. Couldn't get a part-time job without one. Because I couldn't get to work. Needed it to get to school. Of course I could have taken the bus to school. But I didn't want to. Feel like a grown-up when you have a car of your own. Freedom to come and go. I was the last of my friends to have a car. Couldn't wait. An old Ford. But I fixed it up nicely. Costs a lot to maintain. Car payments, car loan. Car insurance.

Then you could review the freewriting and write separate lists of causes and effects of owning a car:

causes (reasons)

needed to get a part-time job
needed to get to school
my friends had cars

effects (results)

feel like a grown-up
freedom to come and go
costs a lot to maintain
car payments
car loan
car insurance

If you had compiled more details on the effects of owning a car, you would then decide to write an effects essay.

After brainstorming questions to help you generate more effects and details, you would be ready to create another list:

List of Effects for an Effect Essay

Topic: Owning a Car

effect 1: I had to pay for the car and related expenses.
details: costs a lot to maintain
car payments
car loans
car insurance

---

effect 2: **I had the adult freedom to come and go.**
details: didn't have to beg my father for his truck
didn't have to get rides from friends
could go to the city when I wanted
could ride around for fun

effect 3: **I became a more careful driver.**
details: worried about someone hitting the car
worried about bad drivers
wanted to avoid the scratches cars get in parking lots

With at least three effects and some details for each effect, you could create a thesis. The thesis for this paragraph should indicate that the subject is the *effects* of getting a car. You can summarize all three effects in your thesis, or you can just hint at them. A possible thesis statement for the paragraph might be:

> Owning my own car cost me money, gave me freedom, and made me more careful about how I drive.

The thesis summarizes all three effects. Another possible thesis hints at the effects:

> Once I got a car, I realized the good and bad sides of ownership.

With a thesis statement, three effects, and a list of details, you would be ready to write an outline for your essay.

PLANNING   EFFECTS ESSAY

Following is an outline for an effects essay on owning a car. Study the outline carefully and be prepared to respond to the exercise that follows it.

Outline for an Effects Essay

paragraph 1 ——— I.   Thesis: Owning my own car gave me freedom, cost me money, and made me a more careful driver.

paragraph 2, topic sentence ——— II.   The wonderful part of owning a car was the adult freedom it gave me.

A. I didn't have to beg my father for his truck.
B. Every time I asked him, he seemed reluctant to lend it to me.
C. He was always worried that I would get the interior dirty.

details about effect 1: freedom ———
D. I didn't have to get rides from my friends.
E. I was really tired of begging rides from my buddies, and I am sure they were sick of driving me around.
F. I could go to the city whenever I wanted.
G. I could even ride around for fun.

(Continued)

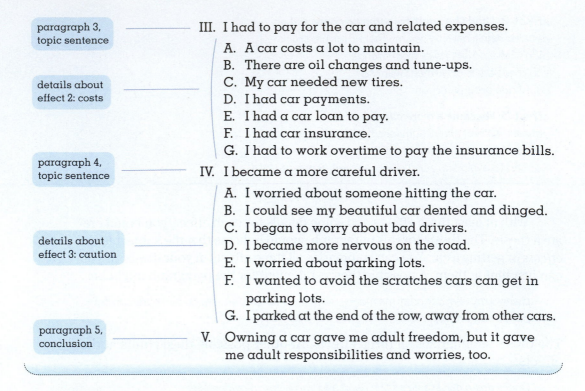

paragraph 3, topic sentence —— III. I had to pay for the car and related expenses.

    A. A car costs a lot to maintain.

details about effect 2: costs ——

    B. There are oil changes and tune-ups.
    C. My car needed new tires.
    D. I had car payments.
    E. I had a car loan to pay.
    F. I had car insurance.
    G. I had to work overtime to pay the insurance bills.

paragraph 4, topic sentence —— IV. I became a more careful driver.

    A. I worried about someone hitting the car.
    B. I could see my beautiful car dented and dinged.
    C. I began to worry about bad drivers.

details about effect 3: caution ——

    D. I became more nervous on the road.
    E. I worried about parking lots.
    F. I wanted to avoid the scratches cars can get in parking lots.
    G. I parked at the end of the row, away from other cars.

paragraph 5, conclusion —— V. Owning a car gave me adult freedom, but it gave me adult responsibilities and worries, too.

CRITICAL THINKING

Notice that the thesis statement specifies the effects or results of owning a car. You will need to determine whether causes or effects will be better to use for your own thesis statement.

The outline categorized each effect as a separate body paragraph. It combined some of the details from the list with details gathered during the outlining process. As you write and revise your draft, you can continue to add details. During editing, you can also combine sentences, add transitions, and work on word choice. Remember that several drafts may be necessary before you feel ready to prepare the final version of your essay.

MyWritingLab™   **Exercise 8**   **Practice: Changing the Order of Effects**

Review the order of the effects in the brainstorming list on the previous page, and then look closely at the order of effects in the outline. Why would a writer begin with the positive effect of owning a car (as in the outline) instead of leaving it in the middle of two effects about responsibilities? How does the thesis in the outline differ from the original one?

_____

_____

_____

DRAFTING AND REVISING   EFFECTS ESSAY

Following is a revised draft of the essay on owning a car. As you read it, you'll notice many changes from the outline on pages 301–302.

- An introduction has been added.
- Transitions have been added within and between paragraphs.
- Details have been added.
- A concluding paragraph has been added.

Study the draft carefully and be prepared to respond to the exercises that follow it.

Draft of an Effects Essay

(Note: Thesis, topic sentences, and conclusion are underlined; editing and proofreading are still necessary.)

Ever since I was six years old, I have dreamed of owning my own car. The day I got my driver's license was one of the happiest days of my life. All that was left, I thought, was having a car of my own. That day came, too, and it changed my life. Owning my own car gave me freedom, cost me money, and made me a more careful driver.

The wonderful part of owning a car was the adult freedom it gave me. First of all, I didn't have to beg my father for his truck anymore. Every time I asked him, he seemed reluctant to lend it to me. He was always worried that I would get the interior dirty. Second, I no longer had to get rides from my friends whenever I wanted to go somewhere. I was really tired of begging rides from my buddies, and I am sure they were sick of driving me around. With my own car, I could go to the city whenever I wanted. I could even ride around for fun.

On the more serious side, I had to pay for the car and related expenses. A car costs a lot to maintain. There are oil changes and tune-ups to keep the car in good running condition. Two months after I got my car, I had to buy four new and very expensive tires. Of course, I had monthly payments on my car loan. I also had to pay for car insurance, which, because of my young age, was unbelievably expensive. My insurance cost so much that I had to work overtime to pay it.

Now that I was paying for the car I drove, I became a more careful driver. I became worried about someone hitting the car; I could imagine my beautiful car dented and dinged. These thoughts made me worry about bad drivers and become more nervous on the road. Parking lots made me nervous, too. To avoid the scratches cars can get in parking lots, I parked at the end of the row, away from other cars.

Owning a car gave me adult freedom, but it gave me adult responsibilities and worries, too. Even with the stress of car payments, insurance payments, and car maintenance, I would never give up my car. My fear of dents and scratches can't keep me from the joy of driving whenever and wherever I want. I'm happy to accept the responsibilities that come with being on the road in my own car.

Exercise 9   Practice: Seeing How the Essay Develops   MyWritingLab™

The draft of the essay is structured around a childhood wish for a car, the older phase of wanting to be independent, and the final phase of adult responsibility. Study each body paragraph and underline any words, phrases, or sentences (excluding the topic sentences) that show the stages of growth.

Exercise 10   **Practice: Recognizing the Role of Transitions**

1. Which body paragraph opens with a transition that shows a contrast from the subject of the previous paragraph?

   _____

   _____

2. Which body paragraph opens with a reference to the subject of the previous paragraph?

   _____

   _____

EDITING AND PROOFREADING   **EFFECTS ESSAY**

The final version of the essay about owning a car reflects careful editing and proofreading. When you compare it to the draft on page 303, you will notice the following:

- Some of the word choices have been improved, replacing a vague term like *costs a lot* with the more specific *costs hundreds of dollars*, and avoiding repetition of words like *worry* and *expensive*.
- Details have been added; for instance, in Paragraph 2 there are new details about what makes a car dirty and about how friends feel (*acting like a taxi service*) when they are constantly asked for rides.
- A sentence has been added to Paragraph 4 to support the topic sentence. The focus of the paragraph is on careful driving, and the body of the paragraph gives many examples of the fears of a new-car owner, but it needed one more detail to show the change in the owner's driving.
- A title has been added.

Study the final version carefully and be prepared to respond to the exercise that follows it.

Final Version of an Effects Essay

Owning a Car: Driving into Adulthood

Ever since I was six years old, I have dreamed of owning my own car. The day I got my driver's license was one of the happiest days of my life. All that was left, I thought, was having a car of my own. That day came, too, and it changed my life. Owning my own car gave me freedom, cost me money, and made me a more careful driver.

The wonderful part of owning a car was the adult freedom it gave me. First of all, I didn't have to beg my father for his truck anymore. Every time I asked him, he seemed reluctant to lend it to me. He was always worried that I would dirty the interior with food wrappers and empty soda cans. Second, I no longer had to get rides from my friends whenever I wanted to go somewhere. I was really tired of begging rides from my buddies, and I am sure they were sick of acting like a taxi service. With my own car, I could go to the city whenever I wanted. I could even ride around for fun.

On the more serious side, I had to pay for the car and related expenses. A car costs hundreds of dollars to maintain. There are oil changes and tune-ups to keep the car in good running condition. Two months after I got my car, I had to buy four new and very expensive tires. Of course, I had monthly payments on my car loan. I also had to pay for car insurance, which, because of my young age, was unbelievably high. My insurance cost so much that I had to work overtime to pay the bill.

Now that I was paying for the car I drove, I became a more careful driver. I became worried about someone hitting the car; I could imagine my beautiful car dented and dinged. These thoughts made me fear bad drivers and become more nervous on the road. I began to drive more defensively, and instead of challenging aggressive drivers, I began to avoid them. Parking lots made me nervous, too. To avoid the scratches cars can get in parking lots, I parked at the end of the row, away from other cars.

Owning a car gave me adult freedom, but it gave me adult responsibilities and worries, too. Yet even with the stress of car payments, insurance payments, and car maintenance, I would never give up my car. My fear of dents and scratches can't keep me from the joy of driving whenever and wherever I want. I'm happy to accept the responsibilities that come with being on the road, in my own car.

Exercise 11   Practice: Evaluating Changes in the Final Version   MyWritingLab™

Underline the details added to Paragraph 2. Would you have added these specific details? Defend your answer: _____

Underline the sentence added to Paragraph 4. Do you think it is necessary? Why or why not? _____

_____

Topics for Writing a Cause or Effect Essay

When you write on any of these topics, work through the stages of the writing process in preparing your essay.

1. Think of a time when you had to make an important choice. Then write an essay explaining the reasons for your choice. Your essay can include an explanation of your options as well as the reasons for your choice.   MyWritingLab™

2. Write an essay about the effects one of the following experiences had on you (or someone you know well).   MyWritingLab™

beginning a new job	the first day at college
surviving an accident	the first day in a new country
a sudden change of plans	winning a prize
a random act of kindness	witnessing an act of violence

3. Write an essay on one of the following topics: MyWritingLab™

   Why _____ is the right career for me.

   Why college students may feel lonely _____.

   Why _____ is a great sport to watch.

   Why _____ is a great sport to play.

Why my neighborhood needs better (law enforcement, fire service, roads, public transportation, schools, stores) (pick one).

MyWritingLab™   4. Think of a performer who is currently popular. Write an essay explaining the reasons for that person's popularity.

MyWritingLab™   5. Think of a decision that changed your life. Write about the effects of that choice.

Topics for Critical Thinking and Writing: Cause or Effect Essay

MyWritingLab™   1. Some college students select a major or field of study based on what they believe is popular at the moment. Think about a popular major or field at your school, and write about three key reasons students are attracted to it. You may want to interview career counselors or academic advisers to compile reasons and details behind its popularity. To help you plan your essay, consider whether these reasons are practical, idealistic, or simply driven by unrealistic media images.

MyWritingLab™   2. City and county commissions routinely pass ordinances that are unpopular with certain segments of the population. If you are aware of a local ordinance or county law (e.g., a curfew, a noise ordinance, a zoning regulation, and so forth) that has been unpopular with your peers, write about three reasons for its unpopularity. As an alternative, you can write about three effects (consequences) of the ordinance that were unintended at the time it became law.

ARGUMENT

④ Write an argument essay that takes a stand, uses reason, and considers its audience.

Hints for Writing an Argument Essay

1. **Pick a topic based on your own experience and observation.** Although you may not realize it, you have a wide range of experience because you play many roles: consumer, student, parent, child, husband or wife, driver, pet owner, athlete. These and many other roles may fit you. In each of your roles, you may have noticed or experienced something that can lead to a topic.

2. **Be sure to take a stand in your thesis.** That is, don't merely state a problem, but make a point about how to solve or eliminate it.

not this: The potholes on Johnson Road are terrible.
but this: The Department of Public Works must fix the potholes on Johnson Road immediately.

not this: Skateboarders have nowhere to go in Mason Heights.
but this: Mason Heights needs a skateboard park.

3. **Use the reasons in your argument as a way to focus your body paragraphs.**   If you have three reasons, for instance, you can write three body paragraphs.

4. **Consider your audience's objections.**   Always ask yourself who the audience is for your argument. If you are arguing that your

office needs a new copier, you will probably be writing to your supervisor. If you are arguing for an after-school program at your child's elementary school, you will probably be writing to the school board. Consider why your audience should support your points and how they might object.

There are several ways to handle objections and apply your critical thinking skills. If you can *refute* an objection (that is, you can prove that it isn't valid), you have removed a major obstacle. Sometimes you may have to admit the other side has a valid objection by *conceding* it. Even by conceding, however, you win confidence by showing that you know both sides of the argument and are fair enough to consider another point of view.

Another way to handle an objection is to *turn an objection into an advantage*. Adopting this ploy, you admit the objection is valid but use it to reinforce your own point. If you are arguing for a new copier and your supervisor says it is too expensive, you can agree that it is expensive but that the office is losing time and money by constantly repairing the old copier. Turning an obstacle into an advantage shows that you are informed, open-minded, resourceful, and a *critical thinker*.

Even if you do not openly refer to objections in your argument essay, being aware of possible objections helps you frame your points effectively, with your audience in mind.

CRITICAL THINKING

If you know your argument (or proposal) will be controversial, show that you understand the opposition's views. Your argument will then appear reasonable.

WRITING THE ARGUMENT ESSAY IN STEPS

PREWRITING ARGUMENT ESSAY

Imagine that your instructor has given you this assignment:

> Write a letter to the editor of your local newspaper. Argue for something in your town that needs to be changed.

One way to begin is to brainstorm for some specific issue that you can write about. You can ask questions such as these: Is there a part of town that needs to be cleaned up? Should something be changed at a school? What do I notice on my way to work or school that needs improvement? What could be improved in my neighborhood?

By answering these questions, you may come up with one topic, and then you can list ideas on it.

topic

Cleaning Up Roberts Park

ideas

dirty and overgrown
benches are all cracked and broken

full of trash
could be fixed up
people work nearby
they would use it

You can consider your audience and possible objections:

audience

local people of all ages who read the local paper

possible objections from this audience

would cost money
more important things to spend money on

answering objections

Money would be well spent to beautify the downtown.
City children could play there in the fresh air and in nature; workers could eat
    lunch there.

Once you have a list, you can start grouping the ideas on your list. Some of the objections you wrote down may actually lead you to reasons that support your argument. That is, by answering objections, you may come up with reasons that support your point. Following is a list with a point to argue, three supporting reasons, and some details about cleaning up Roberts Park.

List for an Argument Essay

Topic: Cleaning Up a Park

point:	We should fix up Roberts Park.
reason:	Improving the park would make the downtown area more attractive to shoppers.
details:	Shoppers could stroll in the park or rest from their shopping.
	Friends could meet in the park for a day of shopping and lunch.
reason:	City children could play in the park.
details:	They could get fresh air.
	They could play in a natural setting.
reason:	Workers could eat lunch outdoors.
details:	Several office complexes are nearby.
	Workers would take a break outdoors.

With your reasons and details, you can draft a thesis sentence:

Roberts Park should be cleaned up and improved.

With a thesis sentence, three reasons, and details, you are ready to move on to the planning stage of preparing an argument essay.

PLANNING ARGUMENT ESSAY

Following is an outline for an argument essay on cleaning up a park. Study the outline carefully and be prepared to respond to the exercise that follows it.

Outline for an Argument Essay

paragraph 1 ———————— I. Thesis: Roberts Park should be cleaned up and improved.

paragraph 2, topic sentence ———————— II. Improving the park would make the downtown area more attractive to shoppers.

A. If the city could clean, landscape, and refurnish the park, it would be a natural refuge for shoppers.

B. It is located in the middle of the shopping district.

C. Those who already shop in the city could stroll through the park or rest there after shopping.

details about reason 1: a place for shoppers ———————— D. Soon, shoppers would tell their friends about the attractive, new-looking park.

E. Eventually, friends could agree to meet at the park for a day of shopping and lunch.

F. City shops and department stores would see business improve.

G. Business would be good for restaurants, too.

paragraph 3, topic sentence ———————— III. Workers from nearby offices and stores could eat lunch outdoors.

A. Several office buildings are nearby.

B. During the lunch break, many people, even those who bring their lunch, want to get out of the office or store.

C. Everyone wants to get up and forget the job for a little while.

details about reason 2: a place for workers ———————— D. Some want fresh air.

E. Others want to read a book or magazine while they eat.

F. Others want to get some exercise by walking a little.

G. Others just want to observe nature and people.

H. An improved park could meet all these needs.

paragraph 4, topic sentence ———————— IV. City children could play there.

A. City children live in apartments.

B. They don't have backyards to enjoy.

C. They are reduced to playing in dangerous streets or on narrow sidewalks.

D. Many aren't allowed outside at all.

details about reason 3: a place for children ———————— E. They go from sitting all day at school to sitting at home.

F. In the park, children could interact rather than sit alone inside, watching television and playing video games.

G. They could play on grass, not asphalt.

H. They would not have to play near traffic.

paragraph 5, conclusion ———————— V. Roberts Park used to be the city's landmark, and it could be once again.

The outline combined some of the details from the list with new details devised during the planning process. It focused each body paragraph on one reason to clean up the park. As you write and revise your draft, you can continue to add details and arrange them in the most effective order to strengthen your argument. Later, as you edit, you can also combine sentences, add transitions, and refine word choice.

MyWritingLab™   **Exercise 12**   **Practice: Recognizing Added Details in the Outline of an Argument Essay**

Many new details help to develop the body paragraphs of the outline. Paragraph 3, for example, contains four new items to support the topic sentence. Underline these items.

DRAFTING AND REVISING   **ARGUMENT ESSAY**

Following is a revised draft of the essay on cleaning up a park. As you read it, you'll notice several changes from the outline on page 309.

- An introduction has been added.
- Transitions have been added within and between paragraphs.
- Details have been added.
- A concluding paragraph has been added.

Study the draft carefully and be prepared to respond to the exercises that follow it.

Draft of an Argument Essay

(Note: Thesis, topic sentences, and conclusion are underlined; editing and proofreading are still necessary.)

Roberts Park was once a pretty little park with a fountain, dark wood benches, carefully landscaped paths, and lush trees and flowers. Today, however, the fountain is cracked and dry, the benches are faded and splintered, and the paths are overgrown. Trash fills the flowerbeds. <u>Roberts Park should be cleaned up and improved</u>.

There are several reasons why a better park would make a better city. First, <u>improving the park would make the downtown area more attractive to shoppers</u>. If the city could clean, landscape, and refurnish the park, it would be a natural refuge for shoppers. It is right in the middle of the shopping district, making it convenient for those who already shop in the city to stroll through the park or rest there. Soon, shoppers might tell their friends about the attractive, new-looking park. Eventually, friends could agree to meet at the park for a day of shopping and lunch. City shops and department stores would see an increase in business, and restaurants would benefit, too.

Those who do business in the city would appreciate a renovated park as well. <u>Workers from nearby offices and stores could eat lunch outdoors</u>. Several high-rise office buildings are nearby, full of office workers. During their lunch break, many people, even those who bring their lunch, want to get out of the office or store. Everyone wants to get up and forget the job for a little while. Some want fresh air, and others want to read a book or magazine while they eat. The more ambitious want to get some exercise by walking a little; however, many people just want to observe nature and people. An improved park could meet all these needs.

The most important reason to clean up the park is to help children. <u>City children could play in Roberts Park</u>. City children, who live in apartments, don't have backyards to enjoy. If they go outside, they are reduced to playing in dangerous streets or on narrow sidewalks. Many aren't allowed outside at all. They go from sitting all day at school to sitting at home. In a restored park, children could interact rather than sit alone inside, watching television and playing video games. They could play on grass, not asphalt. Best of all, they would not have to play near traffic.

Today, the words "Roberts Park" describe a rundown, ragged plot of broken benches, weeds, and trash. But the place could be a haven for children, shoppers, and workers. Once the park was green, the fountain shimmered, and the benches shone. <u>Roberts Park</u> used to be <u>the city's landmark, and it</u> could be once <u>again</u>.

Exercise 13   **Practice: Identifying Time Contrasts in the Draft of an Argument Essay**   MyWritingLab™

The introduction to the essay talks about the past of the park (what it "once" was), and its present ("Today" it is in bad shape). The conclusion also refers to time: past, present, and future. Underline the words or phrases in the conclusion that refer to each time.

_____

_____

Exercise 14   **Practice: Recognizing the Importance of Time Sequence Transitions**   MyWritingLab™

Paragraph 2 also organizes its details with time transitions. Underline four time transitions in this paragraph, and consider why time is such an important part of this essay.

_____

_____

EDITING AND PROOFREADING   **ARGUMENT ESSAY**

Following is the final version of the essay on cleaning up a park. When you compare it to the draft on pages 310–311, you will notice some changes:

- Paragraph 1, the introduction, needed a transitional sentence linking the description of the park to the thesis statement.

- In Paragraph 2, the fourth sentence has been revised to eliminate some wordiness.
- Also in Paragraph 2, the words *shop*, *shoppers*, and *shopping* became too repetitive, so one phrase, *these people*, replaced one use of *shoppers*.
- In Paragraph 4, a new sentence has been added.

- Also in Paragraph 4, a transition (*In addition*) has been added.
- A title has been added.

Study the final version carefully and be prepared to respond to the exercise that follows it.

Final Version of an Argument Essay

The Case for Renovating Roberts Park

Roberts Park was once a pretty little park, with a bubbling fountain, dark wood benches, carefully landscaped paths, and lush trees and flowers. Today, however, the fountain is cracked and dry, the benches are faded and splintered, and the paths are overgrown. Trash fills the flowerbeds. It is time to make this place park-like again. Roberts Park should be cleaned up and improved.

There are several reasons why a better park would make a better city. First, improving the park would make the downtown area more attractive to shoppers. If the city could clean, landscape, and refurnish the park, it would be a natural refuge for shoppers. Because it is right in the middle of the shopping district, those who already shop in the city would be likely to stroll through the park or rest there. Soon, these people might tell their friends about the attractive, new-looking park. Eventually, friends could agree to meet at the park for a day of shopping and lunch. City shops and department stores would see an increase in business, and restaurants would benefit, too.

Those who do business in the city would appreciate a renovated park as well. Workers from nearby offices and stores could eat lunch outdoors. Several high-rise office buildings are nearby, full of office workers. During their lunch break, many people, even those who bring their lunch, want to get out of the office or store. Everyone wants to get up and forget the job for a little while. Some want fresh air, and others want to read a book or magazine while they eat. The more ambitious want to get some exercise by walking a little; however, many people just want to observe nature and people. An improved park could meet all these needs.

The most important reason to clean up the park is to help children. City children could play in Roberts Park. City children, who live in apartments, don't have backyards to enjoy. If they go outside, they are reduced to playing in dangerous streets or on narrow sidewalks. Many aren't allowed outside at all. They go from sitting all day at school to sitting at home. In a restored park, children could interact rather than sit alone inside, watching television and playing video games. They would get some much-needed exercise. In addition, they could play on grass, not asphalt. Best of all, they would not have to play near traffic.

Today, the words "Roberts Park" describe a rundown, ragged site full of broken benches, weeds, and trash. But the place could be a haven for children, shoppers, and workers. Once the park was green, the fountain shimmered, and the benches shone. Roberts Park used to be the city's landmark, and it could be once again.

MyWritingLab™ **Exercise 15** **Practice: Spotting Changes in the Final Version of an Argument Essay**

Underline the transition sentence added to the introduction; then, in Paragraph 4, underline the new detail in sentence form and the new transitional phrase.

Topics for Writing an Argument Essay

When you write on any of these topics, work through the stages of the writing process in preparing your essay.

1. Write an essay for readers of your local newspaper, arguing for or against one of the following:

    a. video surveillance cameras that record all activity in high-crime areas

    b. a ban on using a cell phone (or texting) while driving

    c. a leash law for dog owners

    MyWritingLab™

2. As a consumer, you purchase a number of products and services. Think of one product (like toothpaste, a calculator, or a pair of athletic shoes) or a service (like a flight on a plane, a car repair, or a meal in a restaurant) that you feel needs improvement. Write an essay in the form of a letter to the president of the company that produces the product or offers the service. Argue for the improvement you want. Be specific. For example, if you are dissatisfied with a brand of cereal, you might want less deceptive packaging, a lower price, or less sugar in the cereal.

    MyWritingLab™

3. Write to the president of a company whose advertising offends you. The advertising can be television, print, or online advertising. In an essay in the form of a letter, argue for removing that advertising.

    MyWritingLab™

4. Argue for one of the following college issues. Your audience will be the president, vice presidents, and deans at your college. Topics to argue:

    a. open parking (with the exception of handicapped spaces) at your college

    b. a laptop (at a minimal rental fee and with a security deposit) for each registered student

    c. a twenty-four-hour study area with computers available

    d. security escorts for all evening students who ask to be accompanied to their cars

    MyWritingLab™

Topics for Critical Thinking and Writing: Argument Essay

1. Argue for some change in your neighborhood, at your workplace, or on your campus. It must be a change that would not cost any money but would improve the quality of life.

    MyWritingLab™

2. Assume an anonymous donor has just given your local government a grant of $200,000 with the stipulation that the money should be used to pay some of the operating costs of city-sponsored programs that help teenagers. After you have researched the needs, operating expenses, and effectiveness of these programs, make your case for allocating most of the money to your choice of the most deserving program.

    MyWritingLab™

THE MULTIPATTERN ESSAY

Many essays rely on more than one essay pattern to make their point. For example, if you want to *describe* a city landmark, you might want to include a history (*narration*) of the place. If your goal is to convince a reader to take some action such as to get regular dental check-ups, your essay might include

5 Write a multipattern essay that has a clear topic and thesis, stays with the same pattern within a paragraph, and uses transitions effectively.

sections on the health risks of avoiding the dentist and the relatively painless process of regularly scheduled appointments. In that case, your essay could use the patterns of *argument* (convincing a reader), *effects* (discussing what can happen to those who avoid the dentist), and *process* (tracing the steps of a typical check-up).

Hints for Writing a Multipattern Essay

1. Start with a topic, not with a concern about the patterns you use. Most conversation and writing begin with a subject. You may tell your best friend about a party, for instance. When you start the conversation, you may be thinking about the story (*narrative*) of the party. However, you may soon find yourself *describing* an attractive stranger at the gathering. Soon, you may be explaining why (*causes*) you had to leave the party early, without getting to meet the stranger. In writing, as in conversation, the patterns you choose depend on what you want to say.

2. When you write a multipattern essay, do not shift patterns within a paragraph. Telling the story of a party and shifting to a description of a stranger in the same paragraph will be (1) confusing and (2) skimpy on development of either pattern.

If you begin with a developed *story*, you tell the reader who held the party, why it was held, where it took place, when it began, what people said and did at the party, and so forth.

If you intend to make the stranger a key part of the essay, he or she deserves a detailed *description* in another paragraph. So does an explanation of your *reasons* for leaving without meeting the good-looking stranger.

3. Your thesis does not have to include a reference to each pattern you are using. Your thesis is about the point of all your body paragraphs, but it can be short and focused.

> **not this:** After spending several hours dancing, eating, gossiping, and flirting at Kim and Mario's housewarming party, I noticed a guest that made my heart beat faster, but we were destined not to meet.
>
> **but this:** Love and celebration did not come together at a recent party.

4. Be especially careful about transitions between paragraphs. Transitions are always important in clear, smooth writing, but they are particularly important here. Because you are moving from one pattern to another, you need clear transitions that signal these moves.

WRITING THE MULTIPATTERN ESSAY IN STEPS

PREWRITING   **MULTIPATTERN ESSAY ON PINE RIVER**

Imagine that you are asked to write about a financial problem that affects you or people you know. You might begin by listing your first thoughts:

Money is tight
Unemployment in our area
Our town relying on summer tourists
Someone who left town after a foreclosure

You decide that the subject you know best is how much your town relies on summer tourism. To develop and focus the idea, you start listing questions:

> What are summer tourists?
> How do they bring money to our town?
> Why do they visit here?
> Do residents like tourists?
> What do tourists do when they visit?
> What are the attractions in this town?
> Why is it only summer tourism?
> How can the town survive or even grow?
> What does the town need?

CRITICAL THINKING

When writing a multipattern essay, be sure you carefully determine the essay's organization and the most logical order of patterns. Be especially careful not to shift between ideas.

Organizing Your Ideas for a Multipattern Essay

By scanning the questions and answering as many as you can, you may realize that your writing is falling into three essay patterns. Following is a list of three patterns and details (formed by answering the questions). The list could be developed into a multipattern essay.

Grouped Details for a Multipattern Essay

Topic: Pine River

description: summer tourists love to visit
the weather is cool and sunny
area has much to do
town has camping, boating, fishing
small bed and breakfasts, a motel
friendly local restaurants, souvenir and crafts shops

effects: tourist economy is part time
after Labor Day, the town is empty
cold weather and storms discourage camping and boating
the bed and breakfasts struggle
the motel closes until spring
local stores suffer

argument: year-round businesses can save the town
a big-box store to employ people all year
store will bring customers from nearby towns all year
a local factory or plant is important
steady jobs mean better income

Grouping the details can help you shape your thesis. As you study your list, you realize that the town thrives in the summer but suffers in the winter. Tourists help to support the town, but since they are the main source of income, money dries up after Labor Day. You devise a thesis that makes this point and recommends a solution:

Pine River must grow beyond its reliance on tourist money.

Notice that the thesis includes the name of the town. This thesis can be supported three ways: by *describing* the summer prosperity, by writing about the *effects* on the community when tourist season ends, and by *arguing* for a solution to this problem.

> **PLANNING**   **MULTIPATTERN ESSAY ON PINE RIVER**

Following is an outline for a multipattern essay on helping Pine River to grow. Study the outline carefully and be prepared to respond to the exercise that follows it.

Outline for a Multipattern Essay

Topic: Pine River

paragraph 1 —————— I. Thesis: Pine River must grow beyond its reliance on tourist money.

paragraph 2, topic sentence —————— II. Pine River is a beautiful New England town that thrives when summer tourists visit.
  A. People who visit in the summer love the cool, sunny weather.
  B. There is much to do in Pine River.
  C. Boating and fishing attract many visitors to the river.

details: description of the town in summer —————
  D. Many people camp in the nearby hills.
  E. There are small bed-and-breakfast establishments.
  F. The one motel is always full in the summer.
  G. Downtown, friendly local restaurants, crafts shops, and souvenir stores charm people.

paragraph 3, topic sentence —————— III. When summer ends and the tourists leave, Pine River's economy falls apart.
  A. Cold weather, rain, and storms mean the end of boating, fishing, and camping.
  B. Bed and breakfasts lose guests.
  C. The motel owners close their business until summer.

details: effects of the end of tourist season —————
  D. The small downtown area becomes nearly empty.
  E. Without a supply of tourists as customers, some restaurants close until late spring.
  F. Local people are not likely to buy souvenirs or craftwork.

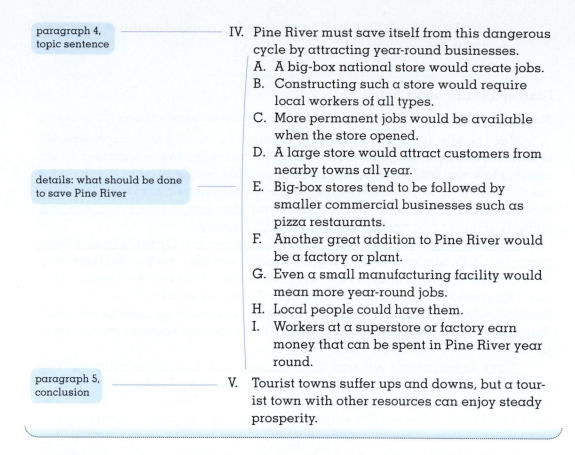

paragraph 4,
topic sentence

IV. Pine River must save itself from this dangerous cycle by attracting year-round businesses.
  A. A big-box national store would create jobs.
  B. Constructing such a store would require local workers of all types.
  C. More permanent jobs would be available when the store opened.
  D. A large store would attract customers from nearby towns all year.

details: what should be done to save Pine River

  E. Big-box stores tend to be followed by smaller commercial businesses such as pizza restaurants.
  F. Another great addition to Pine River would be a factory or plant.
  G. Even a small manufacturing facility would mean more year-round jobs.
  H. Local people could have them.
  I. Workers at a superstore or factory earn money that can be spent in Pine River year round.

paragraph 5,
conclusion

V. Tourist towns suffer ups and downs, but a tourist town with other resources can enjoy steady prosperity.

The outline added many new details gathered during the planning process. The topic sentences indicate the pattern of each body paragraph: Paragraph 2 uses the descriptive words "beautiful little" town; Paragraph 3 begins by discussing effects ("When the summer ends . . . Pine River's economy falls apart"), and Paragraph 4 opens by saying that the town "must save itself" (argument).

Exercise 16 **Practice: Noting the Development of Paragraph 4**   MyWritingLab™

Compare the grouped details in the prewriting stage for Paragraph 4 to the same paragraph and details in outline form. Underline what is new in the outline.

DRAFTING AND REVISING   **MULTIPATTERN ESSAY ON PINE RIVER**

Following is a revised draft of a multipattern essay on Pine River, its summer tourists, and the town's needs. As you read it, you will notice many changes from the outline on pages 316–317.

- An introduction has been added.
- Details have been added.
- The conclusion has been expanded.
- One sentence that was in the passive voice in Section IV of the outline has been revised so that it is now in the active voice (a better and less wordy choice).

Study the draft carefully and be prepared to respond to the exercises that follow it.

Draft of a Multipattern Essay

(Note: Thesis, topic sentences, and conclusion are underlined; editing and proofreading are still necessary.)

Many people like to visit a place that is known for its attractions in one special season. For example, Northerners love to visit Florida in the winter because Florida weather is sunny and warm. At the same time, other people head to Colorado for the snow-covered slopes of the skiing season. In the summer, many tourists go to New England for relaxation and natural beauty. <u>However, if Pine River is to find stability, it must go beyond its reliance on tourist money</u>.

<u>Pine River is a beautiful little New England town that thrives when summer tourists visit</u>. People who visit during the summer months love the cool but sunny weather. There is much to do in Pine River. Boating and fishing attract many to the river. Many people camp in the nearby hills. There are small bed-and-breakfast establishments. The one motel in town is always full in the summer. In the small downtown area, friendly local restaurants, crafts shops, and souvenir stores charm people.

<u>When the summer ends and the tourists leave, Pine River changes</u>. The town falls apart. Cold weather, rain, and storms mean the end of boating, fishing, and camping. Bed and breakfasts lose guests. The motel owners close their business until next summer. The small downtown area becomes nearly empty. Without a supply of tourists as customers, some restaurants close until late spring. Since local people are not likely to buy souvenirs or crafts, many small shops suffer.

<u>Pine River must save itself from this dangerous financial cycle by attracting year-round businesses</u>. For example, bringing a national superstore such as Target or Walmart would create jobs. Constructing such a store would require local workers of all kinds. Staffing the store would mean more year-round jobs, and a large store would attract customers from nearby towns all year. In addition, big-box stores tend to be followed by smaller businesses such as pizza restaurants, home improvement centers, and electronics stores. They, too, employ people year-round. Another great addition to Pine River would be a factory or plant. Even a small manufacturing facility would most likely hire local people. Best of all, workers employed at the new large or small stores could spend money in Pine River all year-round.

Pine River in the summer is a beautiful place for residents and tourists. However, when summer ends, life in Pine River changes. <u>Tourist towns suffer ups and downs, but a tourist town with other resources can enjoy economic prosperity</u>.

MyWritingLab™   **Exercise 17** **Practice: Evaluating the Role of Contrasts in the Introduction**

The introduction contains a number of contrasts (for example, winter and summer). Underline as many of these contrasts as you can and consider why they are important to the subject of the essay.

Exercise 18   **Practice: Recognizing the Changes from Outline to Draft**   MyWritingLab™

Compare Paragraph 4 of the essay in outline and paragraph form. Underline the added specific details such as brand names and types of businesses.

EDITING AND PROOFREADING   **MULTIPATTERN ESSAY ON PINE RIVER**

Following is a final version of the essay on Pine River's summer tourists and the town's needs. As you read it, you will notice some changes:

- A title has been added.

- A sentence has been added to the introduction so that the link between the New England towns and one specific town, Pine River, is clear. (*Many of these tourists come to Pine River.*)

- In Paragraph 2, sentences have been combined.

- Also in Paragraph 2, the word choices have been improved; for example, the reference to shops and restaurants that *charm people* has been revised to *appeal to visitors* because *visitors* is more specific and refers to the town's dependence on tourists. (See end of Paragraph 2.)

- In Paragraph 4, a transition (*more important*) has been added to emphasize a point. (See line 5.).

- Also in Paragraph 4, what became one long sentence loaded with too much information has been divided into two. (See lines 5 and 6.)

- The conclusion has been revised and expanded so that it is more specific in describing how the year-round residents of Pine River can begin the work of transformation.

- A final sentence in the conclusion also links the title to the essay's point.

Study the final version carefully and be prepared to respond to Exercise 19 which follows it.

Final Version of a Multipattern Essay

The Two Pine Rivers

Many people like to visit a place that is known for its attractions in one special season. For example, Northerners love to visit Florida in the winter because Florida weather is sunny and warm. At the same time, other people head to Colorado for the snow-covered slopes of the skiing season. In the summer, many tourists go to New England for relaxation and natural beauty. Many of these tourists come to Pine River. However, if Pine River is to find stability, it must go beyond its reliance on tourist money.

Pine River is a beautiful little New England town that thrives when summer tourists visit. People who visit during the summer months love the cool but sunny weather. There is much to do in Pine River. Boating and fishing attract many to the river. Many people camp in the nearby hills. There are small bed-and-breakfast establishments, and the one motel in town is always full in the summer. In the small downtown area, friendly local restaurants, crafts shops, and souvenir stores appeal to visitors.

(Continued)

When the summer ends and the tourists leave, Pine River changes. The town falls apart. Cold weather, rain, and storms mean the end of boating, fishing, and camping. Bed and breakfasts lose guests. The motel owners close their business until next summer. The small downtown area becomes nearly empty. Without a supply of tourists as customers, some restaurants close until late spring. Since local people are not likely to buy souvenirs or crafts, many small shops suffer.

Year-round residents of Pine River have seen this pattern develop each year. Pine River must save itself from this dangerous financial cycle by attracting year-round businesses. For example, bringing a national superstore such as Target or Walmart would create jobs. Constructing such a store would require local workers of all kinds. More important, staffing the store would mean additional permanent, year-round jobs. Such a large store would attract customers from nearby towns all year. In addition, big-box stores tend to be followed by smaller businesses such as pizza restaurants, home improvement centers, and electronics stores. They, too, employ people year-round. Another great addition to Pine River would be a factory or plant. Even a small manufacturing facility would most likely hire local people. Best of all, workers employed at the new large or small stores could spend money in Pine River all year round.

Pine River in the summer is a beautiful place for residents and tourists. However, when summer ends, life in Pine River changes. The leaders of the community such as the mayor and the members of the Chamber of Commerce must work with every citizen to find the ways and means to attract year-round businesses to Pine River. Tourist towns suffer ups and downs, but a tourist town with other resources can enjoy economic prosperity. Then Pine River could have two images: one as an attractive summer place and the other as a thriving year-round community.

MyWritingLab™   Exercise 19   **Practice: Analyzing the Significance of an Essay's Title**

Explain the meaning of the essay's title. To understand its meaning, reread the essay's conclusion and also consider how the "two Pine Rivers" that currently exist could change if the town's economy is transformed.

_____

_____

_____

ANOTHER EXAMPLE OF A MULTIPATTERN ESSAY

The essay on Pine River is just one example of an essay that relies on more than one pattern. There is no rule about how many patterns to choose or how to organize them. You can decide what kind of paragraphs will work best to support your thesis and what order works best for your topic.

The second multipattern essay is also shown from prewriting through the final version. It relies on narrative and on an analysis of effects to support a thesis.

PREWRITING   **MULTIPATTERN ESSAY ON ONE FAMILY'S FIGHT AGAINST AGORAPHOBIA**

Imagine that you are asked to write about a common psychological problem. You decide to write about _agoraphobia_, a fear of open spaces or of being alone in crowded spaces. Because the illness has affected a member of your family, you know something about its effects. You could begin by freewriting:

Freewriting for a Multipattern Essay on One Family's Fight Against Agoraphobia

I only know it from dealing with my sister. She wouldn't leave the house. Started with not going to crowded places like sports arenas or concerts. Later, Sarah didn't want to visit friends. Even family. We didn't know what to do. She lived in fear of everything. Family members get frustrated. Impatient. Insist on trying to drag her out. Then she's a prisoner. We worried about her. Finally, therapy starts. Kinds of therapy. Therapy and the family.

As you consider the freewriting, you decide that you will use two patterns to develop this essay: narrative and effects. You brainstorm and consider what details will help you develop the essay. With both the details from freewriting and additional details from brainstorming, you devise a possible grouping of the three body paragraphs:

Sarah's fall into fear (narration)

She wouldn't leave the house.
Started with not going to crowded places like sports arenas or concerts.
Later, Sarah didn't want to visit friends, even family.
She lived in fear of everything.
She's a prisoner.

Family panic (effects)

We didn't know what to do.
Family members get frustrated, impatient.
Insist on trying to drag her out.
We worried about her.

Therapy helps (effects)

Finally, therapy starts.
Sarah seeks help.
Kinds of therapy
Therapy and the family.

With a topic for three body paragraphs and some details for each, you can think about a thesis for this multipattern essay. Your thesis does not have to refer to the patterns you will use, but it needs to make some point about Sarah's illness and the family's reaction. Here is a possible thesis statement:

> My sister's battles with agoraphobia required the strength of an entire family.

This thesis will work well with the topics of your three body paragraphs because they will cover *the story* of Sarah's illness, its *effects* on the family, and the *effects* of therapy. With a thesis statement, three topic sentences for the body paragraphs, and a list of details, you are ready to write an outline for your essay.

PLANNING   MULTIPATTERN ESSAY ON ONE FAMILY'S FIGHT AGAINST AGORAPHOBIA

Following is an outline for a multipattern essay on one family and its fight against agoraphobia. Study the outline carefully and be prepared to respond to the exercise that follows it.

Outline for a Multipattern Essay

Topic: A Family's Fight Against Agoraphobia

paragraph 1 —————— I. Thesis: My sister's battle with agoraphobia required the strength of an entire family.

paragraph 2, topic sentence —————— II. Agoraphobia slowly suffocated my sister.

   A. The symptoms started a few months after Sarah's husband left her.

   B. First, she would not go to crowded places such as sports arenas or concerts.

details in narrative form about agoraphobia ——————   C. Then she didn't want to join me or her friends on our regular trips to the mall or other places.

   D. She said the trips made her nervous.

   E. Soon she was asking me to pick up items from the supermarket.

   F. I realized that she was no longer leaving her house, even to buy food.

   G. Later, she began to tremble when the doorbell or phone rang.

paragraph 3, topic sentence —————— III. Sarah's loved ones suffered as well.

   A. Neither I nor my parents could persuade her to leave the house.

   B. Our constant visits did not seem to help her.

   C. My parents and I became fearful.

details about the effects of Sarah's illness on her family ——————   D. We could not help Sarah.

   E. Our fear became frustration, impatience, and anger.

   F. Sarah sensed these emotions.

   G. We realized that she was dreading our visits.

paragraph 4, topic sentence —————— IV. Therapy brought help to all of us.

   A. A compassionate therapist convinced Sarah to seek help.

   B. With the support of her family, Sarah was brave enough to begin regular visits to her therapist.

   C. These visits and appropriate medication eased her fears.

details about the effects of therapy on Sarah and her family ——————   D. Additional group therapy convinced Sarah that she was not alone in her illness.

   E. My parents and I joined a support group for family members.

   F. The group taught us how to help Sarah.

   G. It also taught us how to take care of ourselves.

paragraph 5, conclusion —————— V. For a long time, everyone in my family was afraid, but courage, love, and the right kinds of support brought us out of a world of terror.

Exercise 20 | Practice: Adding Details to an Outline   MyWritingLab™

How is Section IV of the outline different from the "therapy helps" grouping in the earlier list of effects? Does it add more description of the same points or does it add new information? Give examples.

_____

_____

DRAFTING AND REVISING MULTIPATTERN ESSAY ON ONE FAMILY'S FIGHT AGAINST AGORAPHOBIA

Following is a revised draft of a multipattern essay on one family and its fight against agoraphobia. As you read it, you will notice many changes from the outline on page 322:

- An introduction has been added.
- A conclusion has been written.
- Details have been added, including one sentence at the end of Paragraph 2.
- Transitions have been added, especially in Paragraph 4 (_Later_, _meanwhile_, _also_).

Study the draft carefully and be prepared to respond to the exercises that follow it.

Draft of a Multipattern Essay

(Note: Thesis, topic sentences, and conclusion are underlined; editing and proofreading are still necessary.)

In his acclaimed inaugural address at the depth of the Great Depression, President Franklin Delano Roosevelt advised Americans not to let fear consume them, for "the only thing we have to fear is fear itself." This famous quote might well have been describing agoraphobia. It is a fear that grows and grows. I know about this disease because <u>my sister's battles with agoraphobia required the strength of an entire family</u>.

<u>Agoraphobia slowly suffocated my sister</u>. The symptoms started a few months after her husband left her. First, she would not go to crowded places such as sports arenas or concerts. Then she didn't want to join me or her friends on our regular trips to the mall and other places. She said the trips made her nervous. Soon she was asking me to pick up items from the supermarket. I realized she was no longer leaving her house, even to buy food. Later, she began to tremble when the doorbell or phone rang. Her fear of the outside world had made her a prisoner in her own home.

<u>Sarah's loved ones suffered when she did</u>. Even if we coaxed her, neither I nor my parents could persuade her to leave the house. Our constant visits did not seem to help her. Soon my parents and I became fearful. We could not do anything for Sarah. Our fear revealed itself as anger, frustration, and impatience. Sarah sensed these emotions. She began to dread our visits.

<u>Therapy brought help to all of us</u>. A compassionate therapist convinced Sarah to seek help. Accompanied by a family member, Sarah became brave enough to begin regular visits to her therapist. These visits and appropriate medication eased

(Continued)

her fears. Later, additional group therapy convinced Sarah she was not alone. Meanwhile, my parents and I joined a support group for family members of agoraphobics. The group taught us how to encourage and support Sarah. It also taught us how to take care of ourselves.

Agoraphobia caused our whole family to fight a battle against fear. The war is not over, but Sarah and the rest of us are winning. Courage, love, and the right kinds of support brought us out of a world of terror.

MyWritingLab™   **Exercise 21** **Practice: Identifying the Type of Introduction Used in the Essay**

Circle the type of introduction used in this essay: (1) using one or more questions, (2) opening with a contradiction of your main point, or (3) opening with a quotation.

MyWritingLab™   **Exercise 22** **Practice: Recognizing the Frame in the Essay**

To understand how the essay opens and closes with words that refer to being afraid or enduring conflict, underline the synonyms for these words in the introduction and conclusion of the draft.

EDITING AND PROOFREADING **MULTIPATTERN ESSAY ON ONE FAMILY'S FIGHT AGAINST AGORAPHOBIA**

Following is the final version of a multipattern essay on one family's fight against agoraphobia. As you read it, you may notice these changes:

- A title has been added.
- A transitional sentence has been added to the beginning of one paragraph.
- Sentences have been combined in Paragraph 3.

Study the final version carefully and be prepared to respond to the exercise that follows it.

Final Version of a Multipattern Essay

One Family's Fight Against an Enemy Within

In his acclaimed inaugural address at the depth of the Great Depression, President Franklin Delano Roosevelt advised Americans not to let fear consume them, for "the only thing we have to fear is fear itself." This famous quote might well have been describing agoraphobia. It is a fear that grows and grows. I know about this disease because my sister's battles with agoraphobia required the strength of an entire family.

Agoraphobia slowly suffocated my sister. The symptoms started a few months after her husband left her. First, she would not go to crowded places such as sports arenas or concerts. Then she didn't want to join me or her friends on our regular trips to the mall and coffee shop. She said the trips made her nervous. Soon she was asking me to pick up items from the supermarket. At that time, I realized she was no longer leaving her house, even to buy food. Later, she began to tremble when the doorbell or phone rang. Her fear of the outside world had made her a prisoner in her own home.

Sarah's loved ones suffered when she did. Even if we coaxed her, neither I nor my parents could persuade her to leave the house. Our constant visits did not seem to help her. Soon my parents and I became fearful because we could not do anything for Sarah. Our fear revealed itself as anger, frustration, and impatience. Sarah sensed these emotions. She began to dread our visits. When Sarah reacted to our visits with fear, we felt guilty.

Everyone seemed to be falling into despair, but therapy brought help to all of us. A compassionate therapist convinced Sarah to seek help. Accompanied by a family member, Sarah became brave enough to begin regular visits to her therapist. These visits and appropriate medication eased her fears. Later, additional group therapy convinced Sarah she was not alone. Meanwhile, my parents and I joined a support group for family members of agoraphobics. The group taught us how to encourage and support Sarah. It also taught us how to take care of ourselves.

Agoraphobia caused our whole family to fight a battle against fear. The war is not over, but Sarah and the rest of us are winning. Courage, love, and the right kinds of support brought us out of a world of terror.

Exercise 23 **Practice: Recognizing the Revisions in the Final Version**   MyWritingLab™

Underline these revisions in the final version: (1) an additional sentence and (2) a paragraph that begins with an added transitional sentence.

Topics for Writing a Multipattern Essay

> **Note:** When you choose your own topic for writing an essay, you may decide which pattern (or patterns) are most appropriate to express your ideas. The topics below suggest patterns for a *specific* topic and are meant to give you some possibilities for writing a multipattern essay.

1. This topic requires you to write an essay that will be structured around   MyWritingLab™
   two patterns. First, tell the story (narration) of a time when you had to
   make a tough choice. The choice could involve jobs, romantic partners, places to live, or another difficult decision. After you have told
   that story, write about the effects of that choice. (Note: You can write
   two paragraphs of narration and one of effects or vice versa.)

2. Write an essay that is structured around three patterns: process,   MyWritingLab™
   contrast, and causes. First, write about the wrong way to perform a
   task (process); second, contrast the wrong way with the correct
   way; and third, discuss the reasons (causes) why many people
   choose the wrong way to perform the activity.

3. Write an essay that tells the story of an event that changed your life   MyWritingLab™
   (narration) and also explains why this event affected you strongly
   (cause).

4. Write an essay that describes a place in your community where   MyWritingLab™
   people are working together to create more family-friendly places.
   Then write about the effects of this environment on the residents
   of that place. They can be emotional, economic, political, physical,
   health-related, personal, long range, or short range.

Topics for Critical Thinking and Writing: Multipattern Essay

MyWritingLab™

1. Think of three common psychological problems that people in your age group may face. Define each problem and classify it according to its severity, cause, or any other basis that works for you. Once you have completed the classification part of your essay, argue what could be done in your community to help those who suffer from these afflictions.

MyWritingLab™

2. Write an essay about a time you observed or experienced unfair treatment by someone in authority. Relate what happened (narration), why you feel the person in authority acted inappropriately (causes), what resulted from his or her actions (effects), and what should be done to prevent or discourage someone in a similar position from acting so inappropriately (argument).

MyWritingLab™ Visit Chapter 13, "Different Essay Patterns: Part Two," in *MyWritingLab* to test your understanding of the chapter objectives.

Using Research to Strengthen Essays

CHAPTER 14

Jumping In

*Have you ever investigated a possible career? For example, have you looked into the salary range, job duties, or kinds of college courses you would need to take to prepare for a position in a certain field, such as medicine, law, or business? If so, you have already used **research** techniques.*

Learning Objectives

In this chapter, you will learn how to:

1. Search reliable print and electronic sources to strengthen essays.
2. Avoid plagiarism by properly incorporating and acknowledging sources.
3. Cite works in MLA and APA documentation styles.
4. Prepare a final version of an essay with research.

THE ROLES OF RESEARCH

During your college experience, you will no doubt use research techniques in your coursework as well as in your daily life. Even if you have not yet written a formal paper involving research, you probably have already employed various research techniques to solve problems or make crucial decisions.

Most of the writing assignments you have completed thus far have probably been based on your own experiences, observations, or opinions. By writing regularly, you now know the importance of the writing process in producing a polished, final version of an essay. This chapter illustrates how a student writer can strengthen his or her original essay by smoothly incorporating supporting material from outside sources.

Starting with a Basic Outline and Essay

The following outline and short essay about dog-rescue groups are based solely on the writer's own experience and knowledge about dog-rescue operations. You may notice that the outline is in the same format as the outlines you reviewed in Chapter 11, "Writing an Essay."

Outline for an Essay Without Research

I. Dog-rescue organizations perform a humane service by saving homeless dogs and matching responsible adopters with a devoted new family member.

II. Dog-rescue volunteers play several roles.
   A. Some volunteers are "spotters" who look for specific breeds at local shelters.
   B. Experienced rescue volunteers may become coordinators and arrange assistance from various sources.
   C. Volunteers work with national organizations such as Adopt-a-Pet and Petfinder.com, which maintain databases of adoptable dogs from rescue groups throughout the United States and Canada.
   D. Volunteers assist at rescue-dog "Adoption Days" hosted by pet supply chains such as Petco and PetSmart.

III. Rescue groups provide important information and benefits for prospective adopters.
   A. By viewing a rescue group's Web site, potential adopters can read about a dog's age, temperament, adoption fee, and any special medical conditions.
   B. If a potential adopter does not find a suitable dog, he or she can still complete an online application.
   C. On an application, a potential adopter can list his or her preferences for the age, gender, and size of the dog.
   D. Although some dogs are puppies rescued from abusive situations, most are adult dogs already socialized and housebroken.

IV. Careful screening often results in a successful adoption.
   A. Rescue groups routinely conduct home visits to check the living conditions and the neighborhood.
   B. The applicant must have access to veterinary care.
   C. The applicant must agree to return the dog to the rescue organization if he or she can no longer care for the animal.
   D. A foster parent can fully inform the adoptive parent about potential adjustment problems.
   E. Careful attention to such details leads to a winning adoption process.

V. Rescue groups not only provide care for homeless dogs; they also remind us of the joy made possible by compassionate adoption.

An Essay Without Research

The following essay, written from the outline you have just reviewed, contains no research from outside sources; *it is based solely on the writer's own knowledge and experience.*

Draft of an Essay Without Research

The Humane Work of Dog-Rescue Groups

Although the United States is generally regarded as a country that loves and pampers its pets, animal shelters are often filled to capacity with dogs that have been abandoned, abused, or surrendered by their owners. Sadly, some shelters routinely euthanize healthy dogs if no one claims or adopts them after a grace period ranging from just days to a few weeks. Fortunately, however, many shelters work closely with dog-rescue organizations that find loving, temporary homes where foster parents can provide care and, if necessary, rehabilitation. Staffed by dedicated volunteers, rescue groups perform a humane service by saving homeless dogs and enabling responsible adopters to gain a devoted new family member.

From rescuing retired greyhounds to saving mini "mutts," dog-rescue volunteers play several roles. For example, they often serve as "spotters" at local shelters, looking for dogs that can be fostered by individuals who specialize in specific breeds such as boxers and golden retrievers. Experienced volunteers may become coordinators who arrange for assistance from a variety of sources, including local veterinarians, groomers, transporters, and Web site designers. Many rescue groups work closely with national organizations such as Adopt-a-Pet and Petfinder.com, whose Web sites publish comprehensive lists of adoptable rescue dogs throughout the United States and Canada. On weekends, rescue volunteers can be seen helping out during "Adoption Days" sponsored by national chains, including Petco and PetSmart.

Rescue groups provide both crucial information and welcome benefits for potential adopters. When one becomes interested in a specific dog on a rescue group's Web site, he or she can read about the animal's medical needs, age, temperament, and adoption fee. Even if he or she does not spot a suitable dog but remains interested in adopting one from rescue, he or she can fill out an application and list preferences regarding a dog's age, gender, and size. Although rescue groups occasionally receive puppies and young dogs that have been picked up during police raids of abusive puppy mills and backyard breeders, the majority of dogs available for adoption are older ones. Any pet owner who has experienced the aggravation of sleepless nights and numerous housetraining "accidents" can appreciate the benefits of adopting an older, socialized, and housebroken dog.

Although the adoption process may take several weeks or even months to find the best match, careful screening improves the chances for a successful adoption. Rescue groups routinely conduct home visits of prospective dog owners to see if both the living conditions and the neighborhood will be suitable for the dog's size, temperament, and exercise needs. In addition, the applicant must have access to veterinary care and agree to return the dog to the rescue organization if he or she can no longer properly care for it. A foster parent can fully inform the adoptive parent about a dog's potential adjustment problems because the animal's behavior has been observed over a period of weeks—if not months—in a home setting. Careful attention to such details leads to a winning adoption process.

(Continued)

Whichever way a dog comes to a rescue group—by an owner surrender, a good Samaritan, or even by a police raid of an illegal breeding operation—it will have an opportunity to live out the rest of its life free from harm and neglect. Rescue groups not only provide care for homeless dogs; they also remind us of the joy made possible by compassion, commitment, and unconditional love.

> **Note:** Later in this chapter, you will see how the outline for this essay and the essay itself are strengthened by research.

FINDING RESEARCH TO STRENGTHEN ESSAYS

① Search reliable print and electronic sources to strengthen essays.

Locating Material in Your College Library

The Online Catalog Your college library probably has an online catalog system that lists all of the library's books and major holdings. You can search the online catalog by a key word related to your subject, or, if you already have information about authors who deal with your subject, you can search by the author's last name or the title of an author's book. An online catalog can provide you with a list of sources, the call number of each source (the number that will help you find the book on the library shelves), and information regarding the availability of the source.

Popular Periodical Indexes College libraries commonly subscribe to several index services that provide access to complete articles (called "full-text" articles) from periodicals (magazines, journals, and newspapers). Some of the most widely used periodical indexes include *EBSCOhost*, *InfoTrac*, *LexisNexis*, *JSTOR*, and *Reader's Guide to Periodical Literature*.

Always preview articles carefully to see if they contain useful information for your research essay. Scan articles online and print copies of the pages that will be useful for highlighting and note taking later. Also, copy the first and last page of the article, which include information you will need for giving credit to the author and the source of the article.

Internet Search Engines Search engines take a term or phrase and mine all of the data on the Internet to return potential sources of information you can then access for research purposes. Some of the most often used search engines include Google Scholar (*scholar.google.com*), RefSeek (*refseek.com*), and ipl2 (*ipl.org*).

Sometimes, outdated information may remain posted on a Web site indefinitely, so you will need to be cautious about using statistics or expert opinions that are several years old.

Checking for Validity of Sources

The writer of the dog-rescue essay decided to strengthen his paper by adding material from outside sources. The instructor required students to incorporate information from at least one print publication and two valid electronic (online) sources. A short essay is enhanced by adding relevant material from experts.

The student began his Internet search by typing the key phrase "dog rescue organizations" into Google Scholar. This resulted in several hundred potential sources. The student was able to narrow his list to several dozen suitable sources.

Although the Internet is a valuable research tool, students are often tempted to use information from a Web site without checking for accuracy or validity. Students should check the author's credentials, such as educational background, professional experience, and so on. In addition, students should locate any information about the background of the company or individuals responsible for a Web site. For example, if a student is investigating dog-rescue groups, the words of a veterinarian or background information from a nonprofit organization such as the Humane Society of the United States can generally be considered reliable.

Similarly, print sources need to be evaluated just as carefully. For example, a brochure advertising quick or foolproof dog-training programs would not be as reliable as an article from a magazine endorsed by the American Society for the Prevention of Cruelty to Animals (ASPCA).

INCORPORATING AND ACKNOWLEDGING YOUR SOURCES

Gathering and Organizing Sources

Once you have selected the sources best suited for your topic, you will need printouts of any online article for highlighting and note taking. If you are using a book or a magazine in its original form, you will need to photocopy the relevant pages.

2️⃣ Avoid plagiarism by properly incorporating and acknowledging sources.

Your instructor may want to see a preliminary list of your potential sources. There are two great ways to organize your sources. One method is to use 4" × 6" note cards. Another, more popular method is to use a digital tool to store your research. Many of these tools are free and allow you to store digital sources, make notes, and organize. Such tools can be found at *zotero.org, evernote.com,* and *easybib.com. Be sure to follow your instructor's guidelines.*

Taking Notes and Acknowledging Your Sources

When you take notes from one of your sources and use the information in your paper, you must acknowledge the source. This acknowledgment is called **documentation**. When you provide documentation within a research essay, you are using **internal citation**. At the end of your essay, you list all the sources you cited within the paper. This list is called **Works Cited**. The list of works cited is on a separate page and is the last numbered page of the essay.

Using Sources

There are three different ways to incorporate sources into your writing.

1. A quote
2. A summary
3. A paraphrase

A *quote* repeats exactly what the source states. It is common to begin with the author's name, followed by a **signal verb** (also called a **reporting verb**): For example:

> Leigh and Geyer notes that the "safest and most reliable identification is provided by a combination of an ID tag, which is easily visible, and a microchip, which is permanent" (2).

A *summary* includes only the scope or main idea(s) found in the source, and it should be written solely in your own words. Here is an example of a summary statement (no internal citation is necessary):

In One at a Time: A Week in an American Animal Shelter, Leigh and Geyer describe the fate of seventy-five animals who passed through a local shelter in Northern California over a seven-day period.

A *paraphrase* can include main ideas, details, and even examples found in the source. A paraphrase is written in your own words, and it is approximately the same length as the original statement(s) from the source. Sentences or short passages are paraphrased.

> A clearly marked ID tag, along with a permanent microchip, provides an animal with the best and safest means of identification (Leigh and Geyer 2).

Deciding when to quote or paraphrase can sometimes be a difficult decision. It is best to quote when the source has a distinctive way of saying something. While it may be easier to quote, a paraphrase demonstrates your understanding of the source.

Avoiding Plagiarism

Plagiarism occurs when you use a source's words or ideas and fail to give proper credit to the author and/or source of the work. Even if you paraphrase (state someone else's ideas in your own wording), you must give credit to the original source.

Whether you summarize material from an outside source, quote directly from it, or even paraphrase from it, you must acknowledge the source. Failure to do so is a form of academic theft. Penalties for plagiarism are severe, ranging from receiving a failing grade on the plagiarized paper or failing a course, to expulsion. Some departments now use special software programs to check all student papers for plagiarism.

Options for Acknowledging Your Sources

The **Modern Language Association (MLA) system of documentation** is preferred by English instructors. Over the next several pages, you will see how MLA documentation is used for summarizing, paraphrasing, and directly quoting information from sources. *You will also see how sources should be listed on a Works Cited page.*

③ Cite works in MLA documentation style.

MLA Internal ("In-text") Citation When using internal citations, you have several options. If you use a combination of techniques, your paper will read more smoothly. Notice that authors and/or page numbers appear in parentheses, and this form is called **parenthetical documentation**.

A Summary Statement of a Book's Subject or Scope

One at a Time: A Week in an American Animal Shelter describes the fate of seventy-five animals who passed through a local shelter in Northern California over a seven-day period (Leigh and Geyer).

Note: No page numbers or other documentation is necessary for this statement because the work's entire scope is summarized. MLA style now uses italics rather than underlining for all titles of published works and names of in-text Web site domains (e.g., *petfinder.com*).

A Direct Quotation

According to Leigh and Geyer, "The safest and most reliable identification is provided by a combination of an ID tag, which is easily visible, and a microchip, which is permanent" (2).

> **Note:** If you do not introduce the author before you quote from his or her work, you must put the author's name in parentheses at the end of the quoted material. In this case, there are two authors. Both of their names could be placed in parentheses, as follows: (Leigh and Geyer 2). Notice that the period goes *after* the closing parenthesis.

A Paraphrase

A clearly marked ID tag, along with a permanent microchip, provides an animal with the best and safest means of identification (Leigh and Geyer 2).

A Combination of a Direct Quote and a Paraphrase

Leigh and Geyer emphasize that the best means of identification for an animal is "provided by a combination of an ID tag, which is easily visible, and a microchip, which is permanent" (2).

A Source Quoted in Another Author's Work

Kathy Nicklas-Varraso, author of *What to Expect from Breed Rescue*, notes that adopters will "most often get an adult whose chewing phase, housebreaking phase, and general puppy wildness are gone" (qtd. in Mohr).

> **Note:** Nicklas-Varraso is the author being quoted; her comment was found in an online magazine by Mohr. Mohr is the source that the student writer found. Therefore, Mohr is the source cited in parentheses and in the Works Cited list. No page numbers are cited when the article comes from an online magazine.

Signal Verbs and Signal Phrases

Several preceding examples use either **signal verbs** or **signal phrases** (also called **reporting verbs** or **reporting phrases**) to introduce quoted or paraphrased material. Using signal verbs (such as "Leigh and Geyer *emphasize*") and signal phrases (such as "*According to* Leigh and Geyer") enable you to lead smoothly into documented information.

Each signal verb has a unique function, so choose carefully. For example, if you are using the source to persuade, you may use "Smith emphasizes" or "Smith argues." If you are using the source to show disagreement, you may use "Smith disputes" or "Smith refutes."

Documenting Information from a Source with an Unknown Author

If there is no author listed for a source, you can introduce the full title of the work after a signal phrase or place an abbreviation of the title in parentheses at the end of the information cited. For example, you can choose either of the following forms:

> As the article "The Rules of Local Zoning Boards" notes, many counties prohibit businesses from operating out of garages in residential communities (C1).

or

> Many counties prohibit businesses from operating out of garages in residential communities ("Rules" C1).

> **Note:** When your source is a newspaper article, as in the examples above, give the section of the newspaper and the page number, as in C1, which stands for section C, page 1. Article titles are placed within quotation marks; book titles are placed in italics according to MLA style.

MyWritingLab™   **Exercise 1**   **Practice: Paraphrasing from Sources**

Paraphrase each of the short excerpts below and include the appropriate parenthetical documentation. Use a signal phrase in at least one of the excerpts you paraphrase. The first excerpt is done for you and shows two options.

1. "A dog's sense of smell is not only exquisitely sensitive, but it communicates with a brain that can make fine discriminations among scents and learn new ones when they become important." (from *How Dogs Think*, by Stanley Coren, page 63)

   paraphrase (no signal phrase): Dogs have a keen sense of smell that enables the brain to distinguish between scents and remember new ones (Coren 63).

   or

   paraphrase (with a signal phrase): Coren notes that dogs have a very sensitive sense of smell that enables the brain to recognize and remember important scents (63).

2. "The world is full of damaged dogs who desperately need homes. Lots of wonderful people rescue them, and those people deserve our heartfelt appreciation. Patience and hard work can go a long way to rehabilitate dogs damaged in their youth by unstable environments." (from *For the Love of a Dog*, by Patricia O'Connelly, page 87)

paraphrase: _____

_____

_____

_____

3. "The sniffing ritual is designed in part to help dogs establish who has the more forceful personality and deserves extra respect. This is an essential component of all of their introductions as well as the interactions that follow." (from *The Secret Lives of Dogs*, by Jane Murphy, page 64)

paraphrase (Use a combination of paraphrasing and direct quoting in your version.): _____

_____

_____

_____

WORKS CITED ENTRIES: MLA FORMAT

The Works Cited list of sources contains only the works you cited in your paper. This alphabetized list is the last page of your essay and is numbered accordingly. **On the Works Cited page, entries should be double spaced, and the second and subsequent lines of each entry should be indented five spaces. Double-space between each entry. MLA requires that the medium of publication (print, etc.) be listed for all Works Cited entries.**

WORKS CITED ENTRIES: A COMPREHENSIVE LIST (MLA)

Books

Book by One Author

Stevens, Paul Drew. *Real Animal Heroes*. New York: Signet, 1997. Print.

Note: New York is the place of publication, Signet is the publisher, and 1997 is the year of publication. Short forms of the publisher's name should be used, so "Inc.," "Co.," and "Books" can be omitted.

Book by Two Authors

Leigh, Diane, and Marilee Geyer. *One at a Time: A Week in an American Animal Shelter*. Santa Cruz: No Voice Unheard, 2003. Print.

Note: When two or three authors are listed, the name of the first author is listed last name first, and the other author(s) are listed in regular order. If there are more than three authors, the name of the first author is listed last name first and followed by the Latin phrase *et al.*, which means *and others*.

A Short Work in an Anthology

Wong, Edward. "A Long Overdue Apology." *Tales from the Times*. Ed. Lisa Belkin.

New York: St. Martin's Griffin, 2004. 29-34. Print.

> **Note:** An anthology is a book-length collection of short works such as articles, essays, poems, or short stories. It usually has at least one editor who compiles and organizes all of the short works, which are by different authors. When you are citing from an anthology, begin with the author of the short work and its title; then list the name of the anthology and its editor. At the end of the entry, list the page numbers of the short work.

Introduction from a Book

Curtis, Jamie Lee. Foreword. *Second Chances: More Tales of Found Dogs*.

By Elise Lufkin. Guilford: Lyons, 2003. ix-x. Print.

Dictionary or Encyclopedia

"Luxate." *The American Heritage College Dictionary*. 3rd ed. New York:

Houghton, 1993. Print.

> **Note:** *Luxate* is the word you defined by using this dictionary.

Periodicals

Periodicals are newspapers, magazines, and scholarly journals. In Works Cited listings, all months except May, June, and July are abbreviated.

Newspaper Article

Caldwell, Tanya. "Boca Names Its New Dog Park." *South Florida Sun-Sentinel*

10 Aug. 2005: B1+. Print.

> **Note:** B1 refers to the section (B) and page number (1) of the article. The plus sign (+) means that the article was continued on another page.

Newspaper Editorial

"Disaster Aid." Editorial. *South Florida Sun-Sentinel* 9 Aug. 2005: A10. Print.

Note: Newspaper editorials do not list an author.

Magazine Article (From a Monthly or Bimonthly Publication)

Richard, Julie. "The Lost Tigers of China." *Best Friends* Mar. 2005: 27-29. Print.

Magazine Article (From a Weekly Publication)

Boks, Ed. "The Dirty Little Secret in Your Community." *Newsweek* 27 June 2005:

15. Print.

Journal Article

Newkirk, Thomas. "The Dogma of Transformation." *College Composition and*

Communication 56.2 (2004): 251-71. Print.

Note: The number 56 is the volume number, 2 is the issue number, and 2004 is the year of publication.

Electronic Sources

Electronic sources can include professional Web sites, online periodicals, works from subscription services (such as LexisNexis), e-mails, and even CD-ROMs.

When you list a Web site as one of your sources, you should include as many of the following items as you can find on the site:

1. Author or group author's name
2. Title of the site
3. Date of publication or date of latest update
4. The company or organization that sponsors the Web site (if it is different from the group author)
5. Date you accessed the Web site
6. The URL (in angle brackets) if your instructor or department requires it.

Entire Web Site

Humane Society of the United States. 2014. Humane Society of the United States.

Web. 20 Apr. 2014.

> **Note:** In this example, the sponsoring organization, the Humane Society of the United States, is also the group author of the site. 2014 is the date of the Web site's most recent update. The second date is the date of access by the user.

Article or Short Work

Mohr, Lori. "Adopting from a Breed Rescue Group." *Animal Forum*, June 2006. Web.

23 Apr. 2014.

Article from an Online Magazine

Woolf, Norma Bennett. "Getting Involved in Purebred Rescue." *Dog Owner's Guide.*

Canis Major Publications, 18 May 2005. Web. 20 Apr. 2014.

Article from an Online Subscription Service

Foss, Brad. "No Braking for Higher Prices." *South Florida Sun-Sentinel* 11 Aug. 2005:

D1. *NewsBank.* Web. 16 Apr. 2014.

> **Note:** If you use one of your library's online subscription services, you can first follow the same format as a print periodical, but you will need to add the name of the subscription service and the date you accessed the article.

E-mail

Brown, Vernon. "Re: Answers to Your Questions." Message to Jason Roberts.

15 Apr. 2014. E-mail.

Other Sources: Non-Print

Personal Interview

Carter, Michael. Personal interview. 17 Apr. 2014.

Radio or Television Program

"Babies Having Babies." *Live on Five*. Narr. Harry Anderson.

NBC. WPTV, West Palm Beach. 6 Aug. 2004. Television.

Exercise 2 **Listing Works Cited Entries in MLA Format** MyWritingLab™

Arrange the items from the basic sources below in correct MLA format.
Consult either the "Works Cited Entries" starting on page 335 or the "At a
Glance" feature on the next page for proper form and punctuation.

1. **Book**
   City where published: New York
   Publisher: Free Press
   Author: Stanley Coren
   Title: How Dogs Think
   Year published: 2002

   _____

   _____

2. **Magazine Article** (from a monthly publication)
   Article: The Pug Who Came to Dinner
   Author: Gail MacMillan
   Magazine: Bark
   Pages: 67–69
   Month: March
   Year: 2007

   _____

   _____

AT A GLANCE: SEVEN COMMON TYPES OF WORKS CITED ENTRIES (MLA)

Book

Stevens, Paul Drew. *Real Animal Heroes*. New York: Signet, 1997. Print.

author · title · city where published · publisher · date · medium

Magazine Article

Boks, Ed. "The Dirty Little Secret in Your Community." *Newsweek*
27 June 2005: 15. Print.

author · article title · name of magazine · date · page · medium

Newspaper Article

Caldwell, Tanya. "Boca Names Its New Dog Park." *South Florida*
Sun-Sentinel 10 Aug. 2005: B1. Print.

author · article title · name of newpaper · name of newspaper · date · medium · section and page number

Journal Article

Newkirk, Thomas. "The Dogma of Transformation." *College Compo-*
sition and Communication 56.2 (2004): 251-71. Print.

author · article title · name of journal · name of journal · volume and issue number · year · pages · medium

Article from an Online Magazine

Woolf, Norma Bennett. "Getting Involved in Purebred Rescue."
Dog Owner's Guide. Canis Major Publications, 18 May 2005.
Web. 20 Apr. 2014. <http://www.canismajor.com/dog/rescinv.html>.

author · article title · name of magazine · publisher · date published · medium · date of access · URL address

> **Note:** The medium, "Web," is placed before the date of access. Include the URL
> address *only* if requested by your instructor or your department. Page numbers
> are not listed for online articles because different printers will affect the page
> numbering of the printed article. *Exception*: If an article is contained within
> a PDF file, page numbers can be listed because numbers will be consistent
> regardless of the program used.

Article from an Online Database Subscription Service

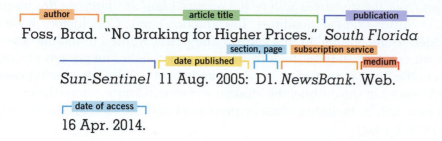

Foss, Brad. "No Braking for Higher Prices." *South Florida Sun-Sentinel* 11 Aug. 2005: D1. *NewsBank*. Web.
16 Apr. 2014.

An Entire Web Site (No Named Author)

Humane Society of the United States. 2007. Humane Society of the United States, Web. 20 Apr. 2014.

> **Note:** The first date is the year listed for the Web site's most recent update. The second date is the date of access by the user. The name of the Web site here is also the sponsoring organization and group author.

④ Prepare a final version of an essay with research.

INCORPORATING RESEARCH INTO YOUR OUTLINE

After you have compiled all of your notes from your sources, you need to determine what information you will use and where it best fits into your essay. The best way to do this is to work with your original outline before you draft a research version of your essay. Here again is the outline for the dog-rescue essay. This version now includes references to sources; *key information from these sources will be the research that strengthens the essay*.

Notice that the headings "Introduction" and "Conclusion" have been added to the outline. In this version, the writer wanted to include some relevant research in both the introductory and concluding paragraphs as well as in the body paragraphs, so he expanded his outline. By placing research references in the outline, the student writer will know where the new information will be included when he prepares the drafts and final version of his research essay.

Note: The references to the added research appear in bold print so that you can compare this outline to the previous one on page 328.

Outline for an Essay with Research

I. Introduction
   A. Six to eight million dogs and cats are placed in shelters each year; three to four million are euthanized. **See Humane Society, source #2.**
   B. Some shelters euthanize animals routinely. **See Leigh and Geyer, source #3.**
   C. Some shelters work with rescue groups.

   Thesis Statement: Dog-rescue organizations perform a humane service by saving homeless dogs and matching responsible adopters with a devoted new family member.

II. Dog-rescue volunteers play several roles.
   A. Some volunteers are "spotters" who look for specific breeds at local shelters.
   B. Experienced rescue volunteers may become coordinators and arrange assistance from various sources. **See Woolfe, source #5.**
   C. Volunteers work with national organizations such as Adopt-a-Pet and Petfinder.com, which maintain databases of adoptable dogs from rescue groups throughout the United States and Canada.
   D. Volunteers assist at rescue-dog "Adoption Days" hosted by pet supply chains such as Petco and PetSmart.

III. Rescue groups provide important information and benefits for prospective adopters.
   A. By viewing a rescue group's Web site, potential adopters can read about a dog's age, temperament, adoption fee, and any special medical conditions.
   B. If a potential adopter does not find a suitable dog, he or she can still complete an online application.
   C. On an application, a potential adopter can list his or her preferences for the age, gender, and size of the dog.

D. Although some dogs are puppies rescued from abusive situations, most are adult dogs already socialized and housebroken. **See Nicklas-Varraso in Mohr, source #4.**

IV. Careful screening often results in a successful adoption.
 A. Rescue groups routinely conduct home visits to check the living conditions and the neighborhood.
 B. The applicant must have access to veterinary care.
 C. The applicant must agree to return the dog to the rescue organization if he or she can no longer care for the animal.
 D. A foster parent can fully inform the adoptive parent about potential adjustment problems.
 E. Careful attention to such details leads to a winning adoption process.

V. Conclusion
 A. Rescue groups provide an opportunity for a dog to live out the rest of its life free from harm and neglect.
 B. We should "embrace non-lethal strategies" to show we are a humane society. **See Bok, source #1.**

Concluding Statement: Rescue groups not only provide care for homeless dogs; they also remind us of the joy made possible by compassionate adoption.

A Draft of an Essay with Research

The following is a rough version of the original essay strengthened with material from outside sources (underlined). The marginal annotations will alert you to (1) places where the information is directly quoted or paraphrased, and (2) places where editing is necessary to achieve a better style.

Draft of an Essay with Research

(Blue marginal notes refer to underlined portions; editing and proofreading are still necessary.)

The Humane Work of Dog-Rescue Groups

statistic and paraphrased statement from online source as part of introduction

direct quotation from the preface of a book with two authors

Although the United States is generally regarded as a country that loves and pampers its pets, animal shelters are often filled to capacity with dogs that have been abandoned, abused, or surrendered by their owners. Each year, six to eight million dogs and cats are placed in shelters, and three to four million of them are euthanized (*Humane Society*). Sadly, some shelters routinely euthanize healthy dogs if no one claims or adopts them after a grace period ranging from just days to a few weeks. These dogs have only "about a fifty percent chance of getting out alive" (Leigh and Geyer viii). Fortunately, however, many shelters work closely with dog-rescue organizations that find loving, temporary homes where foster parents can provide care and, if necessary, rehabilitation. Staffed by dedicated volunteers, rescue groups perform a humane service by saving homeless dogs and enabling responsible adopters to gain a devoted new family member.

(Continued)

From rescuing retired greyhounds to saving mini "mutts," dog-rescue volunteers play several roles. For example, they often serve as "spotters" at local shelters, looking for dogs that can be fostered by individuals who specialize in specific breeds such as boxers and golden retrievers. Experienced volunteers may become coordinators who arrange for assistance from a variety of sources, including local veterinarians, groomers, transporters, and Web site designers. <u>Norma Bennett Woolf writes for the online magazine *Dog Owner's Guide*. Woolf states, "There's always room for more foster homes, fund-raisers, dog spotters, kennels, public relations workers, and trainers."</u> Many rescue groups work closely with national organizations such as Adopt-a-Pet and Petfinder .com, whose Web sites publish comprehensive lists of adoptable rescue dogs throughout the United States and Canada. On weekends, rescue volunteers can be seen helping out during "Adoption Days" sponsored by national chains, including Petco and PetSmart.

direct quotation from an online magazine; sentence combining needed

Rescue groups provide both crucial information and welcome benefits for potential adopters. When one becomes interested in a specific dog on a rescue group's Web site, he or she can read about the animal's medical needs, age, temperament, and adoption fee. Even if he or she does not spot a suitable dog but remains interested in adopting one from rescue, he or she can fill out an application and list preferences regarding a dog's age, gender, and size. Although rescue groups occasionally receive puppies and young dogs that have been picked up during police raids of abusive puppy mills and backyard breeders, the majority of dogs available for adoption are older ones. <u>Kathy Nicklas-Varraso wrote *What to Expect from Breed Rescue*. This writer says, "You'll most often get an adult whose chewing phase, housebreaking phase, and general puppy wildness are gone"</u> (qtd. in Mohr). Any pet owner who has experienced the aggravation of sleepless nights and numerous housetraining "accidents" can appreciate the benefits of adopting an older, socialized, and housebroken dog.

a source quoted in another author's work; needs to blend more smoothly

Although the adoption process may take several weeks or even months to find the best match, careful screening improves the chances for a successful adoption. Rescue groups routinely conduct home visits of prospective dog owners to see if both the living conditions and the neighborhood will be suitable for the dog's size, temperament, and exercise needs. In addition, the applicant must have access to veterinary care and agree to return the dog to the rescue organization if he or she can no longer properly care for it. A foster parent can fully inform the adoptive parent about a dog's potential adjustment problems because the animal's behavior has been observed over a period of weeks—if not months—in a home setting. Nicklas-Varraso states, <u>"Borderline pets are offered for adoption within strict guidelines, such as no other pets or fenced yards only"</u> (qtd. in Mohr). Careful attention to such details leads to a winning adoption process.

direct quote; needs a transition

However a dog finds its way to a rescue group—by an owner surrender, a good Samaritan, or even by a police raid of an illegal breeding operation—it will have an opportunity to live out the rest of its life free from harm and neglect. <u>Ed Bok is director of Animal Care and Control for New York City. He believes that we should "embrace preventive, non-lethal strategies that reveal that at our core we truly are a humane society" (15)</u>. Rescue groups not only follow Bok's advice by providing care for homeless dogs; they also remind us of the joy made possible by compassion, commitment, and unconditional love.

> print source is a magazine; sentence combining needed; put Bok's name in a signal phrase

Note: A Works Cited page will be included in the final version of this essay.

PREPARING THE FINAL VERSION OF AN ESSAY WITH RESEARCH

Making Final Changes and Refinements

The final version of the research essay includes the refinements suggested in the margins of the previous draft. The final essay reflects proper MLA format. Other improvements relate to the style of the essay. Changes include the following:

- The title has been changed to be more descriptive and appealing.

- Information from sources has been more smoothly blended by sentence combining and the use of signal phrases.

- An awkward repetition of *he or she* has been changed to the more specific term *a potential adopter* in the third paragraph.

- The word *humane* has been added in the last paragraph to reinforce the idea of compassionate care for animals.

- To conform to MLA format, the writer has placed his name, his instructor's name, the course title, and the date in the upper left-hand corner of the first page.

- Again following MLA style, the writer has placed his last name and page number in the upper right-hand corner of each page of the essay.

- A Works Cited page, in proper MLA format, is included and appears as the last page of the essay.

Note: Pages in the sample paper are not 8 ½ × 11 standard size. MLA format requires margins of at least one inch but no more than an inch and a half on all sides of the page. The last page of the sample paper (Works Cited page) has been abbreviated for space considerations.

Jason Roberts

Professor Alvarez

English 100

May 7, 2014

Crusading for Canines:

Dog-Rescue Groups and Winning Adoptions

Although the United States is generally regarded as a country that loves and

pampers its pets, animal shelters are often filled to capacity with dogs that have been

abandoned, abused, or surrendered by their owners. Each year, six to eight million

dogs are placed in shelters, and three to four million of them are euthanized (*Humane

Society*). Sadly, some shelters routinely euthanize healthy dogs if no one claims or

adopts them after a grace period ranging from just days to a few weeks. These dogs

have only "about a fifty percent chance of getting out alive" (Leigh and Geyer viii).

Fortunately, however, many shelters work closely with dog-rescue organizations that

find loving, temporary homes where foster parents can provide care and, if necessary,

rehabilitation. Staffed by dedicated volunteers, rescue groups perform a humane

service by saving homeless dogs and enabling responsible adopters to gain a devoted

new family member.

From rescuing retired greyhounds to saving mini "mutts," dog-rescue volunteers

play several roles. For example, they often serve as "spotters" at local shelters, looking

for dogs that can be fostered by individuals who specialize in specific breeds such as

boxers and golden retrievers. Experienced volunteers may become coordinators who

arrange for assistance from a variety of sources, including local veterinarians, groomers, transporters, and Web site designers. As Norma Bennett Woolf suggests in the online magazine *Dog Owner's Guide*, "There's always room for more foster homes, fund-raisers, dog-spotters, kennels, public relations workers, and trainers." Many rescue groups work closely with national organizations such as Adopt-a-Pet and Petfinder, whose Web sites publish comprehensive lists of adoptable rescue dogs throughout the United States and Canada. On weekends, rescue volunteers can be seen helping out during "Adoption Days" sponsored by national chains, including Petco and PetSmart.

Rescue groups provide both crucial information and welcome benefits for potential adopters. When one becomes interested in a specific dog on a rescue group's Web site, he or she can read about the animal's medical needs, age, temperament, and adoption fee. Even if a potential adopter does not spot a suitable dog but remains interested in adopting one from rescue, he or she can fill out an application and list preferences regarding a dog's age, gender, and size. Although rescue groups occasionally receive puppies and young dogs that have been picked up during police raids of abusive puppy mills and backyard breeders, the majority of dogs available for adoption are older ones. Kathy Nicklas-Varraso, author of *What to Expect from Breed Rescue*, notes that adopters will "most often get an adult whose chewing phase, housebreaking phase, and general puppy wildness are gone" (qtd. in Mohr). Any pet owner who has experienced the aggravation of sleepless nights and numerous housetraining "accidents" can appreciate the benefits of adopting an older, socialized, and housebroken dog.

Although the adoption process may take several weeks or even months to find the best match, careful screening improves the chances for a successful adoption. Rescue groups routinely conduct home visits of prospective dog owners to see if both the living conditions and the neighborhood will be suitable for the dog's size, temperament, and exercise needs. In addition, the applicant must have access to veterinary care and agree to return the dog to the rescue organization if he or she can no longer properly care for it. A foster parent can fully inform the adoptive parent about a dog's potential adjustment problems because the animal's behavior has been observed over a period of weeks—if not months—in a home setting. Nicklas-Varraso stresses that the "borderline pets are offered for adoption within strict guidelines, such as no other pets or fenced yards only" (qtd. in Mohr). Careful attention to such details leads to a winning adoption process.

However a dog finds its way to a rescue group—by an owner surrender, a good Samaritan, or even by a police raid of an illegal breeding operation—it will have an opportunity to live out the rest of its life free from harm and neglect. Ed Boks, director of Animal Care and Control for New York City, urges us to "embrace preventive, non-lethal strategies that reveal that at our core, we truly are a humane society" (15). Rescue groups not only provide humane care for homeless dogs; they also remind us of the joy made possible by compassion, commitment, and unconditional love.

Roberts 4

Works Cited

Boks, Ed. "The Dirty Little Secret in Your Community." *Newsweek* 27 June 2005:

15. Print.

Humane Society of the United States. 2007. Humane Society of the United States,

Web. 20 Apr. 2014.

Leigh, Diane, and Marilee Geyer. Preface. *One at a Time: A Week in an American*

Animal Shelter. Santa Cruz: No Voice Unheard, 2003. vii-viii. Print.

Mohr, Lori. "Adopting from a Breed Rescue Group." *Animal Forum*, June 2006.

Web. 14 Apr. 2014.

Woolf, Norma Bennett. "Getting Involved in Purebred Rescue." *Dog Owner's*

Guide. Canis Major Publications, 18 May 2005. Web. 20 Apr. 2014.

More Options for Acknowledging Your Sources: APA Format

In the previous pages, we covered how to use the MLA system of documentation for papers in the humanities. But other major systems of documentation serve other fields of study, and you might be required to use a system other than MLA in some of your classes. The American Psychological Association (APA) system of documentation is the most commonly used format for papers in the social sciences (psychology, anthropology, social work, etc.).

Let's start with how APA documentation writers in the social sciences summarize, paraphrase, and directly quote information from their sources. In addition to understanding how to format these in-text citations using APA style, you will see how those sources are listed in a **References** list (similar to the Works Cited page in the MLA system) that gives the complete documentation for all the sources you cited in your paper.

APA In-Text Citations You'll find that both the APA and MLA documentation systems share a common feature—they both have in-text citations corresponding to a list of sources at the end of the paper. But the format of these in-text citations is not the same in APA format as it is in MLA format.

In APA format, an in-text citation has two main parts—the author or authors of a source and the publication year. For example, for a journal article written by Cornelia Guell and published in December 2012, the main elements to use in your in-text citation are *Guell* and *2012*. (Although you don't need to give the rest of the source information, such as the journal title, within the rest of your paper, you do need to provide it in a References list at the end of your paper.)

Variations on In-Text Citations APA in-text citations always include the author(s) and the year. The way you provide your readers with this information, however, depends on how you construct your sentences. Basically, you should include within parentheses any author or date information that you did not mention in your actual sentence. Here are some examples of APA in-text citations and how they can vary:

Author Name Included in Your Sentence

According to Kottak (2010), cultural notions of what a woman should look like can influence what competitive sport she chooses to pursue.

No Author Name(s) in Your Sentence

Cultural notions of what a woman should look like can influence what competitive sport she chooses to pursue (Kottak, 2010).

> **Note:** Notice that a comma is placed between the author and the year of the work's publication, unlike MLA format, which does not use the comma.

Two or More Sources Cited Within the Same Sentence

According to two similar studies of Brazilian culture (Kottak, 2010; Sanchez, 2014), body image can have far-reaching influences on women's lives.

> **Note:** If you cite more than one work in your sentence, list the sources in alphabetical order and separate them with semicolons.

Two Author Names Included in Your Sentence

Sanchez and Steinman (2014) argue that a desire to imitate the cultural ideal of female beauty causes young women to avoid physical activity, such as strenuous sports, that might develop their muscles in a way that is considered masculine.

Two Author Names Included in Your Parenthetical Citation

Because competitive swimming develops the upper body, parents

consider it too masculine for girls (Sanchez & Steinman, 2014).

Note: Combine two author names with an ampersand.

Three to Five Authors

Bikhchandani, Hirshleifer, and Welch (1992) emphasize that conformity is

a common feature of fads, fashion, and custom.

or

Bikhchandani et al. (1992) observed that individuals often imitate others without

stopping to think about their own experiences.

Note: Name all authors at first mention, and then give just the last name of the
first author, followed by *et al.*, which means "and others." For six or more
authors, give just the last name of the first author, followed by *et al.*

A Source Without an Author

Women in college sports "have yet to reach parity with men," given that only

about one-third of college athletes are women ("Empowering Women," 2014).

Note: Use the first two or three main words of the title. In this case, the title is
of a webpage, so it is in quotation marks.

Exercise 3   **Practice Creating In-Text Citations**   MyWritingLab™

Rewrite each of the following sentences to include the appropriate in-text
citation, using the source information, format, and citation method (paraphrase or direct quote). The first one is done for you.

1. "The good news is if you are in a bossy relationship you aren't
   doomed to a life of heartbreak."
   Author: J. R. Bruns
   Date: 2014
   Format: Author name in sentence.
   Direct quote:

   According to Bruns (2014), "The good news is if you are in a bossy relation-

   ship you aren't doomed to a life of heartbreak."

2. "As quickly as you fall in love, you can fall out of love."
   Author: Susan Pease Gadoua
   Publication date: 2014
   Format: Author name in sentence
   Paraphrase:

   _____

   _____

3. "The affordability of alcohol in the EU continues to be a major facilitator for harmful drinking in many European countries."
   Author: Ann Hope
   Date: 2013
   Format: Author name _not_ in sentence
   Direct quote:

   _____

   _____

4. "What is clear from research evidence is that delaying the onset of young people's drinking is an imperative if adolescents are to be protected from alcohol harm."
   Author: Ann Hope
   Date: 2013
   Format: Author name _not_ in sentence
   Paraphrase:

   _____

   _____

APA Reference List Entries Writers of papers in both MLA and APA documentation styles always include a list, placed at the end of the paper, that contains all the sources cited in the paper. Like the MLA Works Cited page, the APA References list includes the complete publication information for each source. This information helps readers locate your original sources. You will supply readers with the following key components:

- Author(s) full name(s)

- Date published (if none given, write _n.d._ in parentheses, without italics)

- Title of work

- Publication information (such as publisher name and location)

- Page numbers (as a range) for articles

- For electronic sources, such as journal articles on the Internet, include either the URL for the source, or instead, if it is provided, the **DOI** (digital object identifier). A DOI is a unique series of letters and numbers that identifies journal articles or other content and provides a link to their location on the Internet.

Arrangement of Reference List Entries Although the basic components of the MLA Works Cited list and the APA References list are the same, the way you arrange information within an entry is different. Take a look at the following guidelines for organizing your APA References list entries:

- Entries are alphabetical by author last name. (Use initials only for first and middle names).

- If an entry has no author, arrange it alphabetically by the first main word of the title.

- Place the publication year in parentheses after the author names, followed by a period.

- Italicize titles, but capitalize only the first word of the title, the first word of the subtitle, and any proper nouns.

- All entries should be double-spaced.

Now that you know the key parts of an APA reference and some of the ways the entries can be arranged, take a look at the following examples of how you would enter specific types of sources in a References list.

Book

Winzeler, R. L. (2012). *Anthropology and religion: What we know, think, and question* (2nd ed.). Lanham, MD: Altamira Press.

Book by Multiple Authors

Booth, W. C., Colomb, G. G., & Williams, J. M. (1995). *The craft of research.* Chicago, IL: University of Chicago Press.

Book with a Group Author

University of Chicago Press. (2010). *The Chicago manual of style* (16th ed.). Chicago, IL: Author.

Note: The word *Author* in the publishing information part of the entry means that the author is the same as the publisher.

Journal Article, Print, One Author

Banks, J. A. (2006). Improving race relations in schools: From theory and research to practice. *Journal of Social Issues, 62,* 607–614.

Journal Article, Print, Two Authors

McGlynn, E. A., & Brook, R. H. (2001). Keeping quality on the policy agenda.

Health Affairs, 20(3), 82–90.

> **Note:** The number in parentheses after the volume number is the issue number; it is not italicized.

Journal Article, Print, Three to Five Authors

Cadinu, M., Maass, A., Frigerio, S., Impagliazzo, L., & Latinotti, S. (2003).

Stereotype threat: The effect of expectancy on performance. *European*

Journal of Social Psychology, 33, 267–285.

Journal Article, Web Source, DOI

Aronson, R.B., Macintyre, I.G., Lewis, S.A., & Hilbun., N.L. (2005).

Emergent zonation and geographic convergence of coral reefs.

Ecology, 86, 2586-2600. http://dx.doi.org/10.1890/05-0045

Web Source, URL

U.S. Department of Housing and Urban Development. (2005). *Discrimination*

in metropolitan housing markets: National results from phase 1, phase

2, and phase 3 of the Housing Discrimination Study (HDS). Retrieved

from http://www.huduser.org/publications/hsgfin/hds.html

Non-Print Source, Film

Chaiken, J., & Dungan, S. (Producers), & Kornbluth, J. (Director). (2013).

Inequality for All [Documentary]. United States: 72 Productions.

Non-Print Source, Personal Interview (Exception)

No personal communications, such as personal interviews or e-mails, will appear in your References list; instead include these in an in-text citation, in parentheses, with the identifier "personal communication" without quotation marks, and the month, date, and year.

Exercise 4 **Practice Creating Reference List Entries**

Create a References list entry in APA format for each of the following sources. Use the information provided about each source. The first one is done for you.

1. **Authors:** Frederick J. Gravetter and Lori-Ann B. Forzano
   Publication date: 2012
   Book title: *Research Methods for the Behavioral Sciences*, fourth edition
   Publication city and state: Belmont, California
   Publisher name: Wadsworth

   Gravetter, F. J., & Forzano, L.-A. B. (2012). *Research methods for the*
           behavioral sciences (4th ed.). Belmont, CA: Wadsworth.

2. **Authors:** P. Moyer, J. Bolyard, and M. Spikell
   Publication date: June 15, 2012
   Article title: "What Are Virtual Manipulatives?"
   Journal title: *Teaching Children Mathematics*
   Volume number: 8
   Issue number: 6
   Page numbers: 372 through 377

   _____

   _____

3. **Authors:** A. Raj and S. Bertolone
   Publication date: 2010
   Publication title: "Sickle Cell Anemia"
   URL: http://emedicine.medscape.com/article/958614-overview

   _____

   _____

4. **Authors:** Gueorgi Kossinets and Duncan J. Watts
   Publication date: 2009
   Article title: "Origins of Homophily in an Evolving Social Network"
   Journal title: *American Journal of Sociology*
   Volume number: 115
   Page number: 411
   DOI: 10.1086/599247

   _____

   _____

   _____

For your information: A sample research essay in APA format can be found at *mywritinglab.com*.

Jumping In

Your conversations with good friends no doubt cover a wide spectrum of topics. As you voice your opinions, ask questions, and respond to others' comments, you become actively engaged. Similarly, writing-from-reading assignments may require that you engage in active, focused "conversations" with authors. Whenever you summarize key points, question content, or react strongly to a reading selection's premise, you sharpen your critical-thinking skills and become an active learner.

Learning Objectives

In this chapter, you will learn to:

1 Apply prereading strategies to assigned readings.
2 Write an effective summary of a reading.
3 Use critical thinking strategies to evaluate what you are reading.

WHAT IS WRITING FROM READING?

One way to find topics for writing is to draw on your ideas, memories, and observations. Another way is to write from reading you have done. You can *react* to it; you can *agree* or *disagree* with something you have read. In fact, many college assignments or tests ask you to write about an assigned reading: an essay, a chapter in a textbook, an article in a journal. This kind of reading is done in steps:

1. Preread
2. Read
3. Reread with a pen or pencil

After you have completed these steps, you can write from your reading. You can write about what you have read, or you can react to what you have read.

PREREADING

Prereading takes very little time, but it helps you immensely. Some students believe it is a waste of time to scan an assignment; they think they should jump right in and finish the reading quickly. However, spending just a few minutes on preliminaries can save hours later. Most importantly, prereading helps you become a *focused reader*.

If you scan the length of an assignment, you can pace yourself. Also, if you know how long a reading is, you can alert yourself to its plan. A short reading, for example, has to come to its point fairly soon. A longer essay may take time to develop its point and may use more details and examples. Any highlighted material, including subheadings, charts, graphs, boxes, or illustrations, is important enough that the author wants to emphasize it. A list of vocabulary words and their definitions that accompanies a reading selection is worth scanning, too. Looking over that material *before* you read gives you an overview of the important points the reading will contain.

Introductory material or introductory questions will also help you know what to look for as you read. Background on the author or on the subject may hint at ideas that will come up in the reading. Sometimes even the title of the reading will give you the main idea.

You should preread so that you can start reading with as much knowledge about the writer and the subject as you can get. Then, when you read the entire assignment, you will be reading *actively* for more knowledge.

If you want to read with a focus, it helps to ask questions before you read. Form questions by using the information you gained from prereading. For example, if the title of the article is "Manners Matter Online," you may turn the title into a question: "What basic etiquette is required online?" You can jot down such questions, but it's not necessary. Just forming questions and keeping them in the back of your mind helps you read actively and stay focused.

① Apply prereading strategies to assigned readings.

> ### Checklist for Prereading
>
> ✓ How long is this reading?
>
> ✓ Will I be able to read it in one sitting, or will I have to schedule several sessions to finish it?
>
> ✓ Are there any subheadings in the reading? Do they give any hints about the reading?
>
> ✓ Are there any charts? Graphs? Boxed information?
>
> ✓ Are there any photographs or illustrations with captions? Do the photos or captions give me any hints about the reading?

(Continued)

> ✓ Is there any introductory material about the reading or its author? Does the introductory material give me any hints about the reading?
>
> ✓ What is the title of the reading? Does the title hint at the point of the reading?
>
> ✓ Are any parts of the reading underlined, italicized, or emphasized in some other way? Do the emphasized parts hint at the point of the reading?

READING

The first time you read, try to get a sense of the whole piece you are reading. Reading with questions in mind can help you do this. If you find that you are confused by a certain part of the reading selection, go back and reread that part. If you do not know the meaning of a certain word, check the list of vocabulary words if the article includes one. If there is no list or the word is not defined, try to determine the meaning from the way the word is used in the sentence.

If you find that you have to read more slowly than usual, don't worry. People vary their reading speed according to what they read and why they are reading it. If you are reading for entertainment, for example, you can read quickly; if you are reading a chapter in a textbook, you must read more slowly. The more complicated the reading selection, the more carefully you will read it.

REREADING WITH A PEN OR PENCIL

The second reading is the crucial one. At this point, you begin to *think on paper* as you read. In this step, you can make notes or write about what you read. Some students are reluctant to do this, for they are not sure what to note or write. Think of these notes as a way of learning, thinking, reviewing, and reading. Reading with a pen or pencil in your hand keeps you alert. With that pen or pencil, you can do the following:

- Mark the main point (premise or thesis) of the reading.
- Mark other key points.
- Define words you don't know.
- Question parts of the reading that seem unclear to you.
- Evaluate the writer's ideas.
- React to the writer's opinions or examples.
- Add ideas, opinions, and examples of your own.

There is no single system for marking or writing as you read. Some readers like to underline the main idea with two lines and to underline other important ideas with one line. Some students like to put an asterisk (a star) next to important ideas, while others like to circle key words.

Some people like to use the margins to write comments such as "I agree!" or "Not true!" or "That's happened to me!" Sometimes readers put questions in the margins; sometimes they summarize a point in the margin next to its location in the essay. Some people make notes on the white space above the reading and list important points, and others use the space at the end of the reading. Every reader who writes while he or she reads has a personal system; what these systems share is an attitude. If you write as you read, you will concentrate on the reading selection, become familiar with the writer's ideas, and develop ideas of your own.

AN EXAMPLE OF REREADING WITH A PEN OR PENCIL

Following is the article, "Manners Matter Online: Basic Etiquette Applies Even for E-Mail." It has been marked as if a student reader were rereading it after prereading and reading the selection.

Manners Matter Online: Basic Etiquette Applies Even for E-Mail

Amritha Alladi

Alladi wrote this article for the Gainesville Sun *(Florida), and she focuses on why students and other young people seeking employment need to sharpen their e-mail communication skills.*

Words You May Need to Know (Corresponding paragraph numbers are in parentheses.)

jargon (3): language used by a specific group or profession
indecipherable (3): impossible to understand
protocol (5): a formal procedure
hierarchical (5): organized by a person's rank or status
sublimated the role of the gatekeeper (6): eliminated the traditional, more rigid channels of communication
incoherent (6): not logically consistent
psychosocial implications (7): psychological and social effects
demeanor (9): behavior

Before you click "Send," reread the last line of that e-mail, will you?   1

After all, you wouldn't appreciate a message from your boss that read, "Dude, what's up with ur presentation? CU in my office ASAP," so it's best to extend him or her the same courtesy. When it comes to professional e-mails, business etiquette is no Laughing Out Loud matter.   2

Eric Hall, assistant director for employer relations at the University of Florida's Career Resource Center, says he has heard from job recruiters that students are too casual when corresponding with prospective employers and professors. Many young professionals have become accustomed to sending quick messages to friends and peers, and they sometimes forget that abbreviations and jargon may be inappropriate, or at times, even indecipherable. "In this day and age of text messaging, there are occasionally the LOLs," Hall says.   3 *thesis* *example*

Meanwhile, communications professors feel the issue goes beyond e-mail etiquette. Professors at UF's Warrington College of Business say the problem is rooted more in the generation's behavioral trends rather than in technological ones.   4

Jane Douglas, associate professor of management communication, says young people entering the workforce are generally unaware of protocol with regard to addressing people in higher positions. "There is this illusion that   5 *example* communication is horizontal. They don't understand that it's hierarchical." Douglas says that during her twenty-five years of teaching, she has noticed a huge difference in the way students interact with faculty.

6   E-mail communication and the Internet have sublimated the role of the gatekeeper entirely, said Douglas. Last year, her college faced some "very problematic undergrads" <u>who took it upon themselves to address their complaints directly to the dean and provost</u>. "It's just one keystroke from the dean, and usually it's incoherent," she says. "Students seldom proofread or think of the entire impression."

Why is this so awful?

7   Basic etiquette teaches that you avoid the obvious (improprieties)— abbreviations, slang, poor grammar, and informal greetings—no matter who you're sending an e-mail to. Formality is necessary anytime you are communicating with someone for the first time. However, Douglas, who has done extensive research in the psychosocial implications of communication, says she has noted some other major pitfalls that land this budding generation of professionals in hot water with future employers.

improper actions

8   "<u>You see a lot of unprofessional e-mail addresses like tequilagirl@aol</u><u>.com,</u>" Douglas says. "They don't understand that when you're communicating with someone you don't know, you need to be somewhat formal."

example

9   Hall says UF's Career Resource Center tries to teach students appropriate business demeanor through <u>outreach programs</u> that focus on etiquette workshops, business attire, and interviewing tips. Experts at the center also review resumes and cover letters and give the students feedback for employment. Communication at all stages is important because managers are not just assessing your professional communication within the office. "They're also examining how you might work with potential clients," Hall says. "It's in a person's best interest to use formal language at all times. "

no one has time

10   Of course, if you don't know whether your e-mail is appropriate, seek advice. "If you have any professional contacts, especially in the way of networking," Hall says, "they can be a good guiding force."

What the Notes Mean

In the sample above, the underlining indicates sentences or phrases that seem important. The words in the margin, such as "thesis" or "example," can refer to important sections of the reading. Sometimes a word is circled in the selection itself and defined in the margin; for instance, "improprieties" is circled in Paragraph 7 and defined in the margin as "improper actions."

Sometimes, words in the margin are personal reactions. When a university administrator, Eric Hall, notes that his university offers outreach programs for teaching students about business demeanor and interviewing, the reader notes "no one has time" for such programs. The marked-up article is a flexible tool. If you are asked to write a summary of the article, you can use the thesis and the examples you noted as important components of the summary. A comment about students' lack of time for workshops or outreach programs may lead a reader to develop his or her own writing that agrees or disagrees with a point made in the article. Another underlined part, about some undergraduate students who went directly to high-level admin-istrators instead of talking to their professors, could be the basis for writing on a related topic about student–faculty interaction.

The marked-up article is a flexible tool. You can go back and mark it further. Writing as you read involves you in the reading process. It can help you to write about or react to important points in the article. In addition, if you are to be tested on the reading selection or asked to discuss it, you can scan your markings and notations later for a quick review.

A SAMPLE SUMMARY

A summary of a reading tells the important ideas in brief form. It includes (1) the writer's main idea, (2) the ideas used to explain the main idea, and (3) some examples used to explain the ideas. It also refers to the author and the title of the article you are summarizing. Following is a sample summary of "Manners Matter Online: Basic Etiquette Applies Even for E-Mail."

2 Write an effective summary of a reading.

A Summary

"Manners Matter Online: Basic Etiquette Applies Even for E-Mail" by Amritha Alladi warns that college students tend to be "too casual when corresponding with prospective employers and professors." The article refers to concerned professors who believe that technology, which has made e-mail and texting so popular, is partly to blame. When younger people rely on such quick communication, they may forget that abbreviations and jargon can be out of place or confusing. Other professors believe that the cause of this violation of business etiquette is linked to this generation's belief that employee and employer, student and professor are equals. Alladi's research into business etiquette stresses that if today's students can learn correct communications skills, they can improve their relationships with faculty and employers.

Note: When you refer to an author in something that you write, use the author's first and last name the first time you make a reference. For example, you write "Amritha Alladi" the first time you refer to this author. Later in the paragraph, if you want to refer to the same author, use only his or her last name. Thus, a second reference would be to "Alladi," as in the summary, which refers to "Alladi's research."

WRITING A REACTION TO A READING

A summary is one kind of writing you can complete after reading, but there are other kinds. You can react to a reading by agreeing or disagreeing with some idea within the reading or by writing on a topic related to the reading. The effectiveness of your reaction will depend on your careful evaluation of the reading selection.

THE ROLE OF CRITICAL THINKING

When you start forming opinions based on what you observe, hear, read, or discuss, you are applying **critical thinking skills**. Thinking critically as you read involves examining an issue from different sides as well as evaluating the validity, or truthfulness, of the information presented.

3 Use critical thinking strategies to evaluate what you are reading.

Applying the critical thinking process to evaluate what you are reading requires that you ask yourself the following questions:

- What is the writer's main idea or proposal?
- Is the main idea supported by facts? Personal experience? Expert opinion(s)?
- Does the writer reach logical conclusions based on his or her evidence?

Sharpening your critical thinking skills by using this type of questioning as you read can enable you to form reasonable opinions and express them confidently. Reading critically can help you succeed in all of your college classes, and it will be especially beneficial in your future composition courses.

DEVELOPING POINTS OF AGREEMENT OR DISAGREEMENT

One way to use a reading selection to lead you to a topic is to review the reading selection and jot down any statements that provoke a strong reaction in you. You will be looking for statements with which you agree or disagree. If you already marked "Manners Matter Online: Basic Etiquette Applies Even for E-Mail," you might focus your own writing on your disagreement with the point that outreach programs can change students' modes of communication with potential employers. The sample reaction paragraph below acknowledges that students need help in learning how to communicate with potential employers, but the student writer *disagrees* that outreach programs will reach everyone who needs them.

Developing Points of Agreement or Disagreement: A Sample Reaction

One part of "Manners Matter Online: Basic Etiquette Applies Even for E-mail" by Amritha Alladi discusses college students' lack of the skills they need to communicate with employers. It also refers to one university that offers outreach programs that can teach students proper business etiquette, business attire, interviewing tips, and resume writing. Outreach programs are valuable, but I do not agree that they are an effective way to train many students who want to find jobs. Most students will not find time for these sessions because participating in any "outreach" means spending extra time and doing extra work. The realistic way to motivate students is to include lessons on interviewing, conducting job searches, and professional communications in a for-credit course. It could be a one-credit course tailored for different fields of study, or it could be part of a required course in such fields as business, education, science, and so forth. Students would get the information they need, and prospective employers would get the type of employees they need.

WRITING ON A RELATED IDEA

Another type of writing requires critical thinking and writing. Your instructor might ask you to react by writing about some idea connected to your reading. For example, your instructor might ask you to react to "Manners Matter Offline: Basic Etiquette Applies Even for E-Mail" by writing about whether every description of college students in the article is accurate.

Writing on a Related Idea: A Sample

In Amritha Alladi's article, "Manners Matter Online: Basic Etiquette Applies Even for E-Mail," the author refers to one university professor who was concerned when some undergraduate students "took it upon themselves to address their complaints directly to the dean and provost." This action seemed to create a problem because the students did not go first to their professors and other teaching staff. I understand why students should not skip steps in dealing with their problems, but I don't agree that all students who bring their problems directly to a dean or provost are being impatient or unreasonable. Sometimes, student concerns have been ignored so often that undergraduates become frustrated. Unfortunately, some professors do not respond to students' e-mails. When students try to talk to their instructors after class, most faculty are on their way to another class or an appointment. A few faculty do not always keep their office hours. Some part-time faculty do not have offices or are busy teaching at more than one campus. While people in high positions should not have to deal with everyday student concerns, students need to have their voices heard.

Writing from reading can develop your abilities to challenge others' ideas, widen your perspective, and help you build confidence in your critical thinking skills.

Grammar for Writers

INTRODUCTION

Overview

In this section, you'll be working with the basics of grammar that you need to master to be a clear writer. If you are willing to memorize certain rules and work through the activities here, you will be able to apply grammatical rules automatically as you write.

Using "Grammar for Writers"

Since this section of the textbook is divided into self-contained segments, it does not have to be studied in sequence. Your instructor may suggest you review specific rules and examples, or you may be assigned various segments as either a class or group assignment. Various approaches are possible, and thus you can regard this section as a "user-friendly" grammar handbook for quick reference. Mastering the practical parts of grammar will improve your writing, helping you become more sure of yourself and better prepared for future composition courses.

Contents   Page

Quick Question MyWritingLab™

True or False: A subject is only one word.

(After you study this chapter, you will be confident of your answer.)

Learning Objectives

In this chapter, you will learn to:

1. Identify subjects and verbs in sentences.
2. Identify prepositional phrases and correct word order.
3. Use verbs correctly in sentences.

Identifying the crucial parts of a sentence is the first step in many writing decisions: how to punctuate, how to avoid sentence fragments, how to be sure that subjects and verbs "agree" (match). To move forward to these decisions requires a few steps back—to basics.

1. Identify subjects and verbs in sentences.

RECOGNIZING A SENTENCE

Let's start with a few basic definitions. A basic unit of language is a **word**.

> **examples:** *car, student, sun*

A group of related words can be a **phrase**.

> **examples:** *shiny new car; dedicated college student; in the bright sun*

When the group of words contains a subject and a verb, it is called a **clause**. When the word group has a subject and a verb and is a complete thought, it is called a **sentence** or an **independent clause**. When the word group has a subject and a verb but does not represent a complete thought, it is called a **dependent clause**.

If you want to check to see whether you have written a sentence, and not just a group of related words, you first have to check for a subject and a verb. Locating the verbs first can be easier.

RECOGNIZING VERBS

Verbs are words that express some kind of action or being. Verbs about the five senses—sight, touch, smell, taste, sound—are part of the group called **being verbs**. Look at some examples of verbs as they work in sentences:

action verbs:
We *walk* to the store every day.
The children *ran* to the playground.

being verbs:
My mother *is* a good cook.
The family *seems* unhappy.
The soup *smells* delicious.

Exercise 1   **Practice: Recognizing Verbs**

Underline the verbs in each of the following sentences.

  1. A loud cry woke me out of a sound sleep.

  2. This game appears simple.

  3. You are the hardest worker at the restaurant.

  4. Two brave joggers run in the coldest weather.

  5. The soldier saluted his mother.

  6. Instructors give homework.

  7. Vanessa and Chris were my neighbors in Providence.

  8. Emilio sounds thrilled about the new baby.

More on Verbs

The verb in a sentence can be more than one word. First of all, there can be **helping verbs** in front of the main verb, the action or being verb. Helping verbs are often a form of the verb *be (is, am, are, was, were), have (have, has, had)*, or they can be **modals**. Modals include the words *can, could, will, may, might, should,* and *must*.

I *was watching* the Super Bowl. (The helping verb is *was*.)
You *should have called* me. (The helping verbs are *should* and *have*.)
The president *can select* his assistants. (The helping verb is *can*.)
Leroy *will graduate* in May. (The helping verb is *will*.)

Helping verbs can make the verb in a sentence more than one word long. However, there can also be more than one main verb:

Andrew *planned* and *practiced* his speech.
I *stumbled* over the rug, *grabbed* a chair, and *fell* on my face.

Collaborate

Exercise 2 **Collaborate: Writing Sentences with Helping Verbs**

Complete this exercise with a partner or a group. First, ask one person to add at least one helping verb to the verb given. Then work together to write two sentences using the main verb and the helping verb(s). As a final step, appoint one spokesperson for your group to read all your sentences to the class. Notice how many combinations of main verbs and helping verbs you hear.

The first one is done for you.

1. **verb:** named

   verb with helping verb(s): was named

   sentence 1: I was named after my father.

   sentence 2: Washington, D.C., was named after the first president.

2. **verb:** staring

   verb with helping verb(s): _____

   sentence 1: _____

   sentence 2: _____

3. **verb:** forget

   verb with helping verb(s): _____

   sentence 1: _____

   sentence 2: _____

4. **verb:** study

   verb with helping verb(s): _____

   sentence 1: _____

   sentence 2: _____

RECOGNIZING SUBJECTS

After you can recognize verbs, finding the subjects of sentences is easy because subjects and verbs are linked. If the verb is an action verb, for example, the subject will be the word or words that answer the question, "Who or what is doing that action?"

The truck stalled on the highway.

Step 1: Identify the verb: *stalled*

Step 2: Ask, "Who or what stalled?"

Step 3: The answer is the subject: The *truck* stalled on the highway. *Truck* is the subject.

If your verb expresses being, the same steps apply to finding the subject.
Spike was my best friend.

Step 1: Identify the verb: *was*

Step 2: Ask, "Who or what was my best friend?"

Step 3: The answer is the subject: *Spike* was my best friend. *Spike* is the subject.

Just as there can be more than one word to make up a verb, there can be more than one subject.

examples:
David and *Leslie* planned the surprise party.
My *father* and *I* worked in the yard yesterday.

GERUNDS AND INFINITIVES AS SUBJECTS

Words that look like verbs do not always act like verbs, but they are subjects. For example, verbs with *-ing*, a **gerund**, can often be the subject of a sentence.

Texting can be dangerous when you are driving.
Volunteering your time is rewarding.

In both of these examples, verbs (text and volunteer) are subjects.

Infinitives can also be subjects. An infinitive is *to* + verb.

To pay for textbooks is often difficult.
To tolerate rude people takes patience.

In both of these examples, infinitives are subjects. Keep in mind, however, that using infinitives as subjects in your writing can be awkward in style. "Tolerating" as a subject (gerund) is better style than "to tolerate" (infinitive).

Exercise 3   Practice: Recognizing Verbs That Are Subjects

Read each sentence. Decide if the underlined word is a subject or a part of the verb. Write an *S* for subject and a *V* for verb in the space provided.

1. <u>Calling</u> home is important when we are away. _____

2. She is <u>working</u> and <u>going</u> to school. _____

3. <u>To try</u> new things can be scary. _____

4. Our class likes <u>to work</u> in groups. _____

5. Not <u>being</u> allowed to use her calculator upset Emma. _____

6. We need <u>to research</u> animal behavior for this paper. _____

Exercise 4   Practice: Recognizing the Subjects in Sentences

Underline the subjects in the following sentences.

1. Nobody has been taking out the trash lately.

2. Something is happening at our neighbor's house.

3. After my last exam, worry and hope battled in my brain.

4. Sometimes, shopping offers an escape from my troubles.

5. Airports are becoming more crowded with holiday travelers.

6. Confidence can be an asset for a job seeker.

7. On Mondays, Chris, Bill, and I meet for coffee before class.

8. With great joy, Maria handed in her essay.

More About Recognizing Subjects and Verbs

When you look for the subject of a sentence, look for the core word or words; don't include descriptive words around the subject. The idea is to look for the subject, not for the words that describe it.

> The dark blue *dress* looked lovely.
> Dirty *streets* and grimy *houses* destroy a neighborhood.

The subjects are the core words *dress*, *streets*, and *houses*, not the descriptive words *dark blue*, *dirty*, and *grimy*.

❷ Identify prepositional phrases and correct word order.

PREPOSITIONS AND PREPOSITIONAL PHRASES

Prepositions are relatively short words that often signal a kind of position or possession, as shown in the following list:

INFO BOX **Common Prepositions**

about	before	beyond	inside	on	under
above	behind	during	into	onto	up
across	below	except	like	over	upon
after	beneath	for	near	through	with
among	beside	from	of	to	within
around	between	in	off	toward	without
at	by				

A prepositional phrase is made up of a preposition and its object. Here are some prepositional phrases. In each one, the first word is the preposition; the other words are the object of the preposition.

Prepositional Phrases

about the movie	of mice and men
around the corner	off the record
between two lanes	on the mark
during recess	up the wall
near my house	with my sister and brother

There is an old memory trick to help you remember prepositions. Think of a chair. Now, think of a series of words you can put *in front of* the chair:

around the chair	*with* the chair
behind the chair	*to* the chair
between the chairs	*near* the chair
by the chair	*under* the chair
of the chair	*on* the chair
off the chair	*from* the chair

Those words are prepositions.

You need to know about prepositions because they can help you identify the subject of a sentence. There is an important grammar rule about prepositions:

> **Nothing in a prepositional phrase can ever be the subject of the sentence.**

Prepositional phrases describe people, places, or things. They may describe the subject of a sentence, but they never include the subject. Whenever you are looking for the subject of a sentence, begin by putting parentheses around all the prepositional phrases.

> The restaurant (around the corner) makes the best fried chicken (in town).

The prepositional phrases are in parentheses. Since *nothing* in them can be the subject, once you have eliminated the prepositional phrases, you can follow the steps to find the subject of the sentence:

> What is the verb? *makes*
> Who or what makes the best fried chicken? The *restaurant.*
> *Restaurant* is the subject of the sentence.

By marking off the prepositional phrases, you are left with the *core* of the sentence. There is less to look at.

> (Behind the library), the *football field* was filled (with excited fans).
> **subject:** football field

> The *dog* (with the ugliest face) was the winner (of the contest).
> **subject:** *dog*

Exercise 5 **Practice: Recognizing Prepositional Phrases, Subjects, and Verbs**

Put parentheses around every prepositional phrase in the following sentences. Then underline the subject and verb and put an *S* above each subject and a *V* above each verb.

1. Alicia has been wondering about her chances for a job in nursing at a hospital near the military base.

2. An argument between my mother and father affected all the children in the family.

3. Elderly people in our neighborhood are becoming substitute grandparents to many children without older relatives in the area.

4. On the top of the essay, the teacher wrote comments about the student's work.

5. Nothing in the refrigerator except an apple looks edible to me.

6. Before dinner, I can run to the bakery and get some cookies for dessert.

7. The girl with the long dark hair sat near me during the pep rally inside the gym.

8. A couple of raindrops fell on Cody's newly waxed car and left tiny water marks.

Collaborate

Exercise 6 **Collaborate: Writing Sentences with Prepositional Phrases**

Complete this exercise with a partner. First, add one prepositional phrase to the core sentence. Then ask your partner to add a second prepositional phrase to the same sentence. For the next sentence, switch places. Let your partner add the first phrase; you add the second. Keep reversing the process throughout the exercise. When you have completed the exercise, be ready to read the sentences with two prepositional phrases to the class. The first set of prepositional phrases has already been done for you as a sample.

1. core sentence: Rain fell.

   Add one prepositional phrase: _Rain fell on the mountains._

   Add another prepositional phrase: _From a dark sky, rain fell on the mountains._

   _____

2. core sentence: Eddie shouted.

   Add one prepositional phrase: _____

   Add another prepositional phrase: _____

   _____

3. core sentence: A student studied.

   Add one prepositional phrase: _____

   Add another prepositional phrase: _____

   _____

4. core sentence: A cat can be amused.

   Add one prepositional phrase: _____

   Add another prepositional phrase: _____

   _____

WORD ORDER

When we speak, we often use a very simple word order: first comes the subject; then comes the verb. For example, when someone says, "I am going to the store," *I* is the subject that begins the sentence; *am going* is the verb that comes after the subject.

But not all sentences are in such a simple word order. Prepositional phrases, for example, can change the word order:

sample sentence: Among the contestants was an older man.

Step 1: Mark off the prepositional phrase(s) with parentheses: *(Among the contestants) was an older man.* Remember that nothing in a prepositional phrase can be the subject of a sentence.

Step 2: Find the verb: *was*

Step 3: Who or what was? An older *man* was. The subject of the sentence is *man.*

After you change the word order of this sentence, you can see the subject (S) and verb (V) more easily:

    S   V
An older *man was* among the contestants.

Exercise 7   **Practice: Finding Prepositional Phrases, Subjects, and Verbs in Complicated Word Order**

Start by putting parentheses around the prepositional phrases in the following sentences. Then underline the subjects and verbs and put an *S* above each subject and a *V* above each verb.

1. Among my favorite pieces of clothing was an old baseball cap from my high school days.

2. Under my grandmother's bed is a box with old photographs of her and my grandfather in their wild teenage years.

3. Beneath the floorboards lurks a family of the craftiest mice on this continent.

4. Between my house on Daley Road and the corner was a huge old house behind a rusted iron fence.

5. From the back of the classroom came the soft snoring sound of a student in dreamland.

6. Beyond the layers of deception and intrigue was a simple answer to the mystery of the hero's death.

7. Among the most irritating programs on television are a talent show for deluded contestants and a comedy without any jokes.

8. Inside my backpack are class notes from last semester and an old

dictionary.

More on Word Order

The expected word order of subject first, then verb, changes when a sentence starts with *There is/are, There was/were, Here is/are, Here was/were.* In such cases, look for the subject after the verb.

        V   S   S
There *are* a *bakery* and a *pharmacy* down the street.

     V   S
Here *is* the *man* with the answers.

To understand this pattern, try changing the word order:

   S   S   V
A *bakery* and a *pharmacy are* there, down the street.

   S   V
The *man* with the answers *is* here.

You should also note that even if the subject comes after the verb, the verb has to "match" the subject. For instance, if the subject refers to more than one thing, the verb must also refer to more than one thing.

There *are* a *bakery* and a *pharmacy* down the road. (Two things, a bakery and a pharmacy, *are* down the road.)

Word Order in Questions

Questions may have a different word order. The main verb and the helping verb may not be next to each other.

question:	Do you like pizza?
subject:	*you*
verbs:	*do, like*

To understand this concept, think of answering the question. If someone accused you of not liking pizza, you might say, "I *do like* it." You would use two words as verbs.

question:	Will he think about it?
subject:	*he*
verbs:	*will, think*
question:	Is Maria telling the truth?
subject:	*Maria*
verbs:	*is, telling*

> **Exercise 8** **Practice: Recognizing Subjects and Verbs in Complicated Word Order: A Comprehensive Exercise**

Underline the subjects and verbs, putting an *S* above the subjects and a *V* above the verbs.

1. There were one hundred text messages and e-mails on my phone today.

2. Will you drive to Biloxi on Saturday?

3. From the end of the long hall came the sound of laughter.

4. Was there anything in your coat pocket?

5. Have Jimmy and Chris spoken about the boat trip on the Hudson River?

6. Here are the most recent photographs of my nephew.

7. Among the healthy choices in the cafeteria was a small salad

8. Can we think about a reasonable solution to the problem?

Words That Cannot be Verbs

3 Use verbs correctly in sentences.

Sometimes there are words which look like verbs in a sentence, but they are not verbs. Such words include adverbs (words like *always, often, nearly, rarely, never, ever*) that are placed close to the verb but are not verbs. Another word that is placed between a helping verb and a main verb is *not. Not* is not a verb.

When you are looking for verbs in a sentence, be careful to eliminate words like *often* and *not*.

He *will* not *listen* to me. (The verbs are *will listen.*)
Althea *can* always *find* a bargain. (The verbs are *can find.*)

Be careful with contractions.

They *have*n't *raced* in years. (The verbs are *have raced. Not* is not a part of the verb, even in contractions.)
Don't you *come* from Arizona? (The verbs are *do come.*)
Won't he ever *learn*? (The verbs are *will learn. Won't* is a contraction for *will not.*)

Recognizing Main Verbs

If you are checking to see if a word is a main verb, try the *pronoun test.* Combine your word with this simple list of pronouns: *I, you, he, she, it, we, they.* A main verb is a word such as *drive* or *noticed* that can be combined with the words on this list. Now try the pronoun test.

For the word *drive:* I drive, you drive, he drives, she drives, it drives, we drive, they drive
For the word *noticed:* I noticed, you noticed, he noticed, she noticed, it noticed, we noticed, they noticed

But words such as *never* cannot be used alone with the pronouns:

~~I never, you never, he never, she never, it never, we never, they never~~
(Never did what?)

Never is not a verb. *Not* is not a verb either, as the pronoun test indicates:

~~I not, you not, he not, she not, it not, we not, they not~~
(These combinations do not make sense because *not* is not a verb.)

Verb Forms That Cannot be Main Verbs

There are forms of verbs that cannot be main verbs by themselves either. **An -*ing* verb, by itself, cannot be the main verb**, as the pronoun test shows.

For the word *voting*: ~~I voting, you voting, he voting, she voting, we voting, they voting~~

If you see an *-ing* verb by itself, correct the sentence by adding a helping verb.

Scott ~~riding~~ his motorcycle. (*Riding*, by itself, cannot be a main verb.)
correction: Scott *was riding* his motorcycle.

Another verb form, called an infinitive, also cannot be a main verb. An infinitive is the form of the verb that has *to* placed in front of it.

INFO BOX **Some Common Infinitives**

to care	to vote	to repeat
to feel	to play	to stumble
to need	to reject	to view

Try the pronoun test, and you'll see that infinitives cannot be main verbs:

For the infinitive *to vote*: ~~I to vote, you to vote, he to vote, she to vote, we to vote, they to vote~~

So if you see an infinitive being used as a verb, correct the sentence by adding a main verb.

We ~~to vote~~ in the election tomorrow. (There is no verb, just an infinitive.)
correction: We *are going* to vote in the election tomorrow. (Now there is a verb.)

The infinitives and the *-ing* verbs just do not work as main verbs. You must put a verb with them to make a correct sentence.

Exercise 9 **Practice: Correcting Problems with *-ing* or Infinitive Verb Forms**

Most—but not all—of the sentences below are faulty; an *-ing* verb or an infinitive may be taking the place of a main verb. Rewrite the sentences with errors.

1. Behind the heavy purple curtains, a little girl in a nightgown hiding from the noise of the thunderstorm.

   rewritten: _____

   _____

2. After dinner, Mr. Stein wants to sit in front of his big-screen television until bedtime.

   rewritten: _____

   _____

3. The weeds around the stepping-stones creeping between the cracks and over the broken stones.

   rewritten: _____

   _____

4. After hours of negotiation, an escaped convict from Utah to surrender to police in New Mexico.

   rewritten: _____

   _____

5. At a high point in his career, the internationally known tennis star
   quitting for personal reasons.

   rewritten: _____

   _____

6. On weekends, my sisters to ride their bicycles to the park near our
   house.

   rewritten: _____

   _____

7. After the midterm exam, a few of the students in my science class
   were complaining about the grading scale.

   rewritten: _____

   _____

8. Without a second look, I turned my back on my former friend and
   walked calmly to my car.

   rewritten: _____

   _____

Exercise 10   Practice: Finding Subjects and Verbs: A Comprehensive Exercise

Underline the subjects and verbs in these sentences and put an *S* above each
subject and a *V* above each verb.

1. There were a pen, a pencil, and a crumpled piece of paper in
   Sophie's book bag.

2. Melanie could have been waiting for you at the coffee shop.

3. At the front of the classroom is a large box with a stack of papers
   in it.

4. My computer does not offer quick access to the Internet.

5. You have suddenly developed an interest in our handsome neighbor on the third floor.

6. Won't you think about a career in mechanical engineering?

7. Alec is dreaming of making a return visit to Cancun.

8. At the top of my list of worries are the fear of missing an opportu-

   nity and the fear of failure.

Exercise 11 **Practice: Finding Subjects and Verbs: Another Comprehensive Exercise**

Underline the subjects and verbs in these sentences and put an *S* above each subject and a *V* above each verb.

1. Before my speech to the scholarship committee, I thought about my dream of higher education, looked into each person's eyes, and hoped for the best.

2. In any marriage, there will be a period of adjustment for both partners.

3. Here is the old scrapbook with the pictures of you in your Little League uniform.

4. Alicia would never ask for help from her brother.

5. Haven't you always wanted a house near the ocean?

6. With his giant television on the living room wall and his huge collection of films, Todd rarely goes to a movie theater for entertainment.

7. Can't the two of you ever think about anyone except yourselves?

8. In the bright light, the large dog seemed weird and dangerous.

Collaborate

Exercise 12 **Collaborate: Create Your Own Text**

Complete this activity with two partners. Below is a list of rules you've just studied. Each member of the group should write one example of each rule. When your group has completed three examples for each rule, trade your completed exercise with another group, and check their examples while they check yours.

The first rule has been done for you.

Rule 1: The verb in a sentence can express some kind of action.
examples:

a. Wanda sleeps late on the weekends.

b. On Monday I found a wallet in the street.

c. Melted snow covered the sidewalks and steps.

Rule 2: The verb in a sentence can express some state of being or one of the five senses.

examples:

a. _____

b. _____

c. _____

Rule 3: The verb in a sentence can consist of more than one word.
examples:

a. _____

b. _____

c. _____

Rule 4: There can be more than one subject of a sentence.
examples:

a. _____

b. _____

c. _____

Rule 5: If you remove the prepositional phrases, it is easier to identify the subject of a sentence since nothing in a prepositional phrase can be the subject of a sentence. (Write sentences with at least one prepositional phrase and put parentheses around the prepositional phrases.)
examples:

a. _____

b. _____

c. _____

Rule 6: Not all sentences have the simple word order of subject first, then verb. (Give examples of more complicated word order.)

examples:

a. _____

b. _____

c. _____

Rule 7: Words like *not, never, often, always,* and *ever* are not verbs. (Write sentences using those words, but write *V* above the correct verb or verbs.)
examples:

a. _____

b. _____

c. _____

Rule 8: An -*ing* verb form by itself or an infinitive (*to* preceding the verb) cannot be a main verb. (Write sentences with -*ing* verb forms or infinitives, but write *V* above the main verb.)

examples:

a. _____

b. _____

c. _____

Exercise 13 Connect: Recognizing Subjects and Verbs in a Paragraph

Underline the subjects and verbs in this paragraph and put an *S* above each subject and a *V* above each verb.

My father could never have fit into his old U.S. Army uniform without a rigorous program of exercise and diet. In January, he received an invitation to the twenty-fifth reunion of his army buddies. He was eager to attend. However, he wanted to look like the fit, trim soldier of long ago. He had six months for getting fit before the reunion. During those six months, my father joined a local gym and arrived faithfully at 6:00 a.m. on every day of the week. In the evening, he jogged through the neighborhood for two miles. On Saturdays, my father pushed me into walking long distances in the mountains near our house. In addition, he rarely drank beer or ate junk food in front of the television. Salads, broiled chicken, and grilled fish became frequent dinner choices. He stuck to his program for fitness and transformed himself from a typical middle-aged man with too little energy and too much flab into a perfect model of a former fighting man.

Chapter Test The Simple Sentence

Underline the subjects and verbs in these sentences and put an *S* above each subject and a *V* above each verb.

1. The smell of freshly baked bread at the bakery near my apartment is making me hungry.

2. After a dental check-up, Dr. Talbott usually gives me a small bag with a new toothbrush and a small tube of toothpaste.

3. Inside the pancake restaurant are bright yellow booths and posters with photos of every kind of pancake and topping in the world.

4. Didn't you ever dream about living in a big city?

5. The warm wind in my hair and the sun in my eyes were a pleasant change from the sleet and snow at home.

6. Kyla never asked about my background or questioned my motives for leaving town suddenly.

7. Manny's nasty tantrum at dinner could have resulted in hurt feelings among the family members at the table.

8. Behind her carefree attitude and silly behavior is a woman with anxieties about her future.

Beyond the Simple Sentence: Coordination

Learning Objectives

In this chapter, you will learn to:

1 Combine simple sentences using a comma and a coordinating conjunction.

2 Combine simple sentences using a semicolon.

3 Combine simple sentences using a semicolon and a conjunctive adverb.

AVOIDING SIMPLE SENTENCES

A group of words containing a subject and a verb is called a **clause**. When that group is a complete thought, it is called a sentence or an independent clause.

The kind of sentence that is one independent clause is called a **simple sentence**. If you rely too heavily on a sentence pattern of simple sentences, you risk writing paragraphs like this:

> I am a college student. I am also a salesperson in a mall. I am always busy. School is time-consuming. Studying is time-consuming. Working makes me tired. Balancing these activities is hard. I work too many hours. Work is important. It pays for school.

Here is a better version:

> I am a college student and a salesperson at a mall, so I am always busy. School and study are time-consuming, and working makes me tired. Balancing these activities is hard. I work too many hours, but that work is important. It pays for school.

OPTIONS FOR COMBINING SIMPLE SENTENCES

Good writing involves sentence variety; it means mixing a simple sentence with a more complicated one, a short sentence with a long one. Sentence variety is easier to achieve if you can combine related, short sentences into one.

It is true that punctuation involves memorizing a few rules, but once you know them, you will be able to use them automatically and write with more confidence. Following are three options for combining simple sentences and the punctuation rules to follow in each case.

OPTION 1: USING A COMMA WITH A COORDINATING CONJUNCTION

1 Combine simple sentences using a comma and a coordinating conjunction.

You can combine two simple sentences with a comma and a coordinating conjunction. The coordinating conjunctions are *for, and, nor, but, or, yet,* and *so.*

To coordinate means to join equals. When you join two simple sentences with a comma and a coordinating conjunction (CC), each half of the combination remains an independent clause, with its own subject (S) and verb (V).

Here are two simple sentences:

> S   V   S   V
> *He cooked* the dinner.   *She worked* late.

Here are the two simple sentences combined with a comma, and with the word *for,* a coordinating conjunction (CC):

> S   V   , CC S   V
> *He cooked* the dinner, *for she worked* late.

The combined sentences keep the form they had as separate sentences; that is, they are still both independent clauses, with a subject and a verb and with the ability to stand alone.

The word that joins them is the **coordinating conjunction**. It is used to join equals. Look at some more examples. These examples use a variety of coordinating conjunctions to join two simple sentences.

sentences combined with *and*:

> S   V   , CC S   V
> *Jennifer likes* Italian food, *and Mark prefers* Korean dishes.

sentences combined with *nor*:

S   V   V   , CC V S V

I didn't like the book, nor did I like the movie made from the book.
(Notice what happens to the word order when you use *nor*.)

sentences combined with *but*:

S V   , CC S V

I ran to the library, but it was already closed.

S   V   , CC S   V

She can write a letter to Jim, or she can call him.

sentences combined with *yet*:

S V   , CC S   V

Leo tried to please his sister, yet she never seemed appreciative of his efforts.

sentences combined with *so*:

S V   , CC S V

I was the first in line for the concert tickets, so I got the best seats in the stadium.

> **Note:** One easy way to remember the coordinating conjunctions is to call them, as a group, **fanboys** (**f**or, **a**nd, **n**or, **b**ut, **o**r, **y**et, **s**o).

Where Does the Comma Go?

Notice that the comma comes before the coordinating conjunction (*for, and, nor, but, or, yet, so*). It comes before the new idea, the second independent clause. It goes where the first independent clause ends. Try this punctuation check. After you've placed the comma, look at the combined sentences. For example:

> She joined the army, and she traveled overseas.

Then split it into two sentences at the comma:

> She joined the army. And she traveled overseas. (The split makes sense.)

If you put the comma in the wrong place, after the coordinating conjunction, your split sentences would be:

> She joined the army and. She traveled overseas. (The split doesn't make sense.)

This test helps you see whether the comma has been placed correctly—*where the first independent clause ends*. (Notice that you can begin a sentence with *and*. You can also begin a sentence with *but, or, nor, for, yet,* or *so*—as long as you're writing a complete sentence.)

> **Caution:** Do *not* insert a comma every time you use the words *and, but, or, nor, for, yet,* or *so*; put it only when the coordinating conjunction joins independent clauses. Do not put the comma when the coordinating conjunction joins words:
>
> blue and gold   tired but happy   hot or cold
>
> Do not put the comma when the coordinating conjunction joins phrases:
>
> on the chair or under the table
> in the water and by the shore
> with a smile but without an apology

The comma is used when the coordinating conjunction joins two independent clauses. Another way of expressing this same rule is to state that the comma is used when the coordinating conjunction joins two simple sentences.

Placing the Comma by Using Subject–Verb (S–V) Patterns

An independent clause, or simple sentence, follows one of these basic patterns:

> S   V
> He ran.

or

> S   S V
> He and I ran.

or

> S   V   V
> He ran and swam.

or

> S   S V   V
> He and I ran and swam.

Study all four patterns for the simple sentence, and you will notice that you can draw a line separating the subjects on one side and the verbs on the other:

S	V
SS	V
S	VV
SS	VV

So whether the sentence has one subject (or more than one) and one verb (or more than one), in the simple sentence the pattern is subject(s) followed by verb(s)—one simple sentence.

When you combine two simple sentences, the pattern changes:

two simple sentences:

> S   V   S V
> He swam. I ran.

two simple sentences combined:

> S   V   S V
> He swam, but I ran.

In the new pattern, *SVSV*, you cannot draw a line separating all the subjects on one side, and all the verbs on the other. This new pattern, with two simple sentences (or independent clauses) joined into one, is called a **compound sentence**.

Recognizing the *SVSV* pattern will help you place the comma for compound sentences.

Here is another way to remember this rule. If you have this pattern:

> SV | SV

use a comma in front of the coordinating conjunction. Do not use a comma in front of the coordinating conjunction with these patterns:

S	V
SS	V
S	VV
SS	VV

For example, use a comma for this pattern:

   S   V   ,   S V

Jane followed directions, *but I rushed* ahead.

Do not use a comma for this pattern:

   S   V   V

Carol cleans her kitchen every week *but* never *wipes* the top of the refrigerator.

You have just studied one way to combine simple sentences. If you are going to take advantage of this method, you have to memorize the coordinating conjunctions—*for, and, nor, but, or, yet,* and *so*—so that your use of them, with the correct punctuation, will become automatic.

Exercise 1   **Practice: Recognizing Compound Sentences and Adding Commas**

Add commas only where they are needed in the following sentences. Do not add any words.

1. The new technology store offers a wide range of new gadgets so Edward spends most of his paycheck there.

2. Claudia is looking for a two-bedroom apartment in a good neighborhood or a small house with a porch.

3. My mother won't tell me about her trip to the emergency room nor will she explain her decision to take a class in self-defense.

4. Antonio seems worried about something but never confides in me or his sister.

5. My best friend can eat every item in the refrigerator yet he has maintained the same healthy weight for years.

6. The kitchen table is covered in scratches and dents for the family cuts and carves food on it every day.

7. Michelle rides her bicycle to class every day so she saves money on gas for her car.

8. We worked really hard on our presentation but we still didn't do very well.

Exercise 2   **Practice: Recognizing Compound Sentenzces and Adding Commas**

Add commas only where they are needed in the following sentences. Do not add any words.

1. The detective at the scene of the crime was neither thorough nor efficient in investigating the site.

2. This smartphone is beneficial for someone who needs to check e-mail frequently.

3. Next week we can go to the mall or I can come to your house for coffee.

4. Sam is always complaining about his job yet never has the initiative to look for a better position.

5. Mark and Melanie saved money and worked overtime to buy a new home.

6. Most horror movies rely on the same plots yet the films always attract big crowds.

7. You should drink eight glasses of water a day or you will get dehydrated in the summer heat.

8. Someone sprayed paint on my car and I called the police.

Exercise 3 Practice: Combining Sentences Using Coordinating Conjunctions

Combine each pair of sentences using a coordinating conjunction and the appropriate punctuation.

1. Jordan was a wonderful father to his three boys.
   He was not a great husband.

   combined: _____

   _____

2. Kevin made a reservation at the most popular restaurant in town.
   He wanted to please his new girlfriend.

   combined: _____

   _____

3. Many of my friends are sick of the congestion of city life.
   They are looking for jobs in the country.

   combined: _____

   _____

4. He can buy a new car with great style and huge monthly payments.
   He can settle for a used car with less style and much smaller payments.

   combined: _____

   _____

5. Marta works really hard in calculus. Marta doesn't understand calculus.

   combined: _____

6. Ramon Ramirez played football in high school.
   Hector Ramirez attended college on a baseball scholarship.

   combined: _____

   _____

7. My grandfather always wanted to visit his family in Barbados. He never saved enough money for the trip.

   combined: _____

   _____

8. I caught a bad cold at the hockey game last weekend. I couldn't go to work yesterday.

   combined: _____

   _____

❷ Combine simple sentences using a semicolon.

OPTION 2: USING A SEMICOLON BETWEEN TWO SIMPLE SENTENCES

Sometimes you may want to combine two simple sentences (independent clauses) without using a coordinating conjunction. If you want to join two simple sentences that are related in their ideas and you do not use a coordinating conjunction, you can combine them with a semicolon.

two simple sentences:

S   V   S   V
I cooked the turkey. *She made* the stuffing.

two simple sentences combined with a semicolon:

S   V   ; S   V
I cooked the turkey; *she made* the stuffing.

Here's another example of this option in use:

S   V V   ; S   V
Rain can be dangerous; *it makes* the roads slippery.

Notice that when you join two simple sentences with a semicolon, the second sentence begins with a lowercase letter, not a capital letter.

You need to memorize the seven coordinating conjunctions so that you can make a decision about punctuating your combined sentences. Remember these rules:

- If a coordinating conjunction joins the combined sentences, put a comma in front of the coordinating conjunction.

  S   V   ,   S   V
  Tom had a barbecue in his back yard, and the *food was* delicious.

- If there is no coordinating conjunction, put a semicolon in front of the second independent clause.

  S   V   ;   S   V
  Tom had a barbecue in his back yard; the *food was* delicious.

❸ Combine simple sentences using a semicolon and a conjunctive adverb.

OPTION 3: USING A SEMICOLON AND A CONJUNCTIVE ADVERB

Sometimes you may want to join two simple sentences (independent clauses) with a connecting word called a **conjunctive adverb**.

Here is a list of some conjunctive adverbs:

INFO BOX	Common Conjunctive Adverbs		
also	furthermore	likewise	otherwise
anyway	however	meanwhile	similarly
as a result	in addition	moreover	still
besides	in fact	nevertheless	then
certainly	incidentally	next	therefore
consequently	indeed	now	thus
finally	instead	on the other hand	undoubtedly

You can use a conjunctive adverb (CA) to join simple sentences, but when you do, you still need a semicolon in front of the adverb.

two simple sentences:

$\quad$ S $\qquad$ V $\qquad\qquad\qquad\qquad\qquad\qquad$ S V
My *parents checked* my homework every night. *I did* well in math.

two simple sentences joined by a conjunctive adverb and a semicolon:

$\quad$ S $\qquad$ V $\qquad\qquad\qquad\qquad$; CA S V
My *parents checked* my homework every night; *thus I did* well in math.

$\quad$ S $\quad$ V $\qquad\qquad$; $\quad$ CA $\quad$ S $\quad$ V
She gave me good advice; *moreover, she helped* me follow it.

Punctuating After a Conjunctive Adverb

Notice the comma after the conjunctive adverb in the preceding sentence. Here is the generally accepted rule:

> **Put a comma after the conjunctive adverb if the conjunctive adverb is more than one syllable long.**

For example, if the conjunctive adverb is a word such as *consequently, furthermore,* or *moreover*, you use a comma. If the conjunctive adverb is one syllable, you do not have to put a comma after the conjunctive adverb. One-syllable conjunctive adverbs are words such as *then* or *thus*.

> I saw her cruelty to her staff; *then* I lost respect for her.
> We worked on the project all weekend; *consequently,* we finished a week ahead of the deadline.

Exercise 4   **Practice: Combining Simple Sentences with Semicolons and Conjunctive Adverbs**

Some of the following sentences need a semicolon; others need a semicolon and a comma. Do not add, change, or delete any words; just add the correct punctuation.

1. Desmond likes insects in fact he has a pet spider at home.

2. At the end of dinner came an unpleasant surprise it was the bill for our fancy meal.

3. My first year in college is almost over then I'll be a sophomore with a fairly respectable academic record.

4. Professor Mackenzie talks too fast I can't keep up with his explanations of the math problems.

5. Shane never paid me back for the loan of twenty dollars instead he took me to the movies yesterday.

6. She always forgets to do her homework furthermore she rarely does well on her exams.

7. My hectic work schedule prevents me from having any fun on the other hand the extra hours at my job are paying my bills.

8. We must protect our planet we must conserve our natural resources.

Exercise 5 **Practice: Combining Simple Sentences with Semicolons and Conjunctive Adverbs**

Below are pairs of simple sentences. Combine each pair into one sentence. You have two options: (1) use a semicolon or (2) use a semicolon and a conjunctive adverb (with a comma if it is needed). Choose the option that makes the most sense for each sentence.

1. Green fuzz covered the leftover chicken and rice.
   The casserole had been in the refrigerator for two weeks.

   combined: _____

   _____

2. The band on the stage started throwing trinkets to the audience.
   A huge crowd pushed toward the first row of seats.

   combined: _____

   _____

3. Amanda bolted the apartment door.
   Connor frantically called an emergency number.

   combined: _____

   _____

4. She is not sure what she wants to study.
   She went to see an advisor.

   combined: _____

   _____

5. Tyler refused to speak to me yesterday at school.
   He even avoided eye contact.

   combined: _____

   _____

6. The first snow of the year began to fall.
   The white coating transformed the hills and trees into a strange scene.

   combined: _____

   _____

7. Molly has to do well on her next two Introduction to Sociology tests.
   She could fail the course.

   combined: _____

   _____

8. Skip is turning into a fine dog.
   He has learned all the essential skills of obeying commands and
   walking on a leash.

   combined: _____

   _____

Exercise 6   Practice: Combining Simple Sentences Three Ways

Add a comma, a semicolon, or a semicolon and a comma to the following
sentences. Do not add, change, or delete any words; just add the correct
punctuation.

1. It was very quiet no one was talking.

2. You should apologize to Sean moreover you should apologize sincerely and soon.

3. We will get to the electronics store early thus we will be the first
   ones at the grand opening sale.

4. Kelly buys a lottery ticket every week yet she has never won a penny.

5. Andrew regretted his angry words to his wife similarly his wife felt
   guilty about the cruelty of her responses.

6. I ran into your old girlfriend at the mall yesterday incidentally she
   is going to be in your biology class next semester.

7. My five-year-old son spent three hours at the beach now he is a
   tired but happy child with sand in his hair, toes, and ears.

8. She wanted to get the latest smartphone but the store was out of stock.

Exercise 7   Collaborate: Using Three Options to Combine Simple Sentences

Collaborate

Below are pairs of simple sentences. Working with a partner or partners,
combine each pair into one sentence in two different ways. Remember, you
have three options: (1) use a comma and a coordinating conjunction, (2) use
a semicolon, or (3) use a semicolon and a conjunctive adverb (with a comma
if it is needed). Pick the options that make the most sense for these sentences. The first one has been done for you.

1. Crystal ran out of money for her electric bill.
   I lent her enough to pay it.

   combinations:

   a. Crystal ran out of money for her electric bill, so I lent her enough to pay it.

   _____

   b. Crystal ran out of money for her electric bill; therefore, I lent her enough

   to pay it.

2. The museum is holding an exhibition.
   We want to go to it.

   combinations:

   a. _____

   _____

   b. _____

   _____

3. Luis can be an irritating person.
   He deserves a little sympathy at this sad time.

   combinations:

   a. _____

   _____

   b. _____

   _____

4. Uncle Scott could have gotten stuck in traffic.
   Uncle Scott could have taken a wrong turn off the highway.

   combinations:

   a. _____

   _____

   b. _____

   _____

5. My father never paid me a compliment.
   My father never spent much time with me.

   combinations:

   a. _____

   _____

   b. _____

   _____

6. We expected a delicious meal at the stylish and expensive
   restaurant.
   We got food poisoning.

   combinations:

   a. _____

   _____

   b. _____

   _____

7. Allison will take me to school tomorrow.
She owes me a favor.

combinations:

a. _____

_____

b. _____

_____

8. Nelson Pinder was offered a great job in Boston.
He decided to move there.

combinations:

a. _____

_____

b. _____

_____

Exercise 8   **Connect: Editing a Paragraph for Errors in Coordination**

Connect

Edit the following paragraph for errors in coordination. You do not need to add or change words. Just add, delete, or change punctuation. There are seven errors in the paragraph.

Maintaining a healthy weight is a challenge for Demetrius. He struggles with the temptations of junk food and his mother's ideas about nutrition. Demetrius has a busy schedule at school and at work consequently, he eats most of his meals on the run. He tries to focus on choosing healthy items but the choices are difficult. A salad at a salad bar can be loaded with fat in the choice of toppings such as croutons, meat, cheese, and thick, creamy, or even oily salad dressings. The special sauces on fatty burgers are a double temptation; even a serving of frozen yogurt, can be filled with sugar and fat. Demetrius's goal of eating healthy foods is challenged at home for his mother believes in large helpings of comfort food. Fried chicken, vegetables in creamy sauces, and homemade biscuits tempt him, moreover, his mother has strong feelings about food. To her, feeding people is part of her mission in life; so she pushes huge helpings of food on everyone at her table. In the fight against flab, Demetrius is trying hard but his battle is a tough one.

MyWritingLab™   **Chapter Test** Beyond the Simple Sentence: Coordination

Add a comma, a semicolon, or a semicolon and a comma to the following sentences. Do not add, change, or delete any words; just add the correct punctuation.

1. At the end of the meeting, the president of the club stormed out of the room then the club members looked at each other and smiled.

2. LaShonda has never seen snow nor has she experienced the beauty of spring in a northern climate.

3. Archie is a good-natured person still he won't listen to his cousin's constant criticism.

4. I should have taken a class in yoga years ago now I am enjoying my Yoga for Beginners sessions.

5. The new student experienced culture shock for the classroom culture was new.

6. Rain began to pound the roof next the palm trees bent against the fierce winds.

7. I don't like wearing a heavy coat instead I wear layers of sweaters.

8. The destructive effects of global warming have been prevalent for years yet too many countries ignored the early warning signs.

MyWritingLab™ Visit Chapter 17, "Beyond the Simple Sentence: Coordination," in *MyWritingLab* to test your understanding of the chapter objectives.

Avoiding Run-on Sentences and Comma Splices

Learning Objectives

In this chapter, you will learn to:

1 Recognize and correct run-on sentences.

2 Recognize and correct comma splices.

RUN-ON SENTENCES

1 Recognize and correct run-on sentences.

Run-on sentences are independent clauses that have not been joined correctly. This error is also called a **fused sentence**.

> **run-on sentence error:**
> Carol cleans her kitchen every week she shines every pot and pan.
> **run-on sentence error corrected:**
> Carol cleans her kitchen every week; she shines every pot and pan.
>
> **run-on sentence error:**
> I studied for the test all weekend I am well prepared for it.
> **run-on sentence error corrected:**
> I studied for the test all weekend, so I am well prepared for it.

run-on sentence error:
People crowded into the stadium they scrambled for seats.
run-on sentence error corrected:
People crowded into the stadium. They scrambled for seats.

Exercise 1   **Practice: Identifying Run-on Sentences**

Read each sentence. If the sentence is correct, write OK. If the sentence is a run-on, write an X.

1. _____ We worked on the project all day we went out at night.

2. _____ The college cafeteria is open all day on Saturdays, but it isn't open on Sundays.

3. _____ Driving and texting is very dangerous Bill does it all the time.

4. _____ People lined up to see the new sci-fi movie it sold out quickly.

5. _____ My advisor works in the advising center during the day, and she teaches English in the evening.

6. _____ Working and studying isn't easy for Becky she has no free time to socialize with her friends.

7. _____ The science lab courses fill up quickly, and many students are unable to get the schedule they want.

8. _____ The painting was stolen the police haven't found the thieves.

STEPS FOR CORRECTING RUN-ON SENTENCES

When you edit your writing, you can correct run-on sentences by following these steps:

> **Step 1:** Check for two independent clauses.

> **Step 2:** Check that the clauses are separated by either a coordinating conjunction and a comma or by a semicolon.

Follow the steps in checking this sentence:

> The meeting was a waste of time the club members argued about silly issues.

> **Step 1:** Check for two independent clauses. You can do this by checking for the subject–verb, subject–verb pattern that indicates two independent clauses:

>   S   V   S   V
> The *meeting was* a waste of time the club *members argued* about silly issues.

The pattern indicates that you have two independent clauses.

> **Step 2:** Check that the clauses are separated by either a coordinating conjunction (*for, and, nor, but, or, yet, so*) and a comma or by a semicolon.

There is no punctuation between the independent clauses, so you have a run-on sentence. You can correct it three ways:

> **run-on sentence corrected with a coordinating conjunction and a comma:**
> The meeting was a waste of time, *for* the club members argued about silly issues.

> **run-on sentence corrected with a semicolon:**
> The meeting was a waste of time; the club members argued about silly issues.

> **run-on sentence corrected with a period and a capital letter:**
> The meeting was a waste of time. The club members argued about silly issues.

Follow the steps once more as you check this sentence:

> Working and studying isn't easy for Becky she has no free time to hang out with her friends.

> **Step 1:** Check for two independent clauses. Do this by checking the subject–verb, subject–verb pattern:

> S   V   S V
> Working and studying *isn't* easy for *Becky she has* no time to hang out with her friends.

> **Step 2:** Check that the clauses are separated by either a coordinating conjunction (*for, and, nor, but, or, yet, so*) and a comma or by a semicolon.

There is no punctuation between the independent clauses, so you have a run-on sentence. You can correct the run-on sentence three ways:

> **run-on sentence corrected with a period and a capital letter:**
> Working and studying isn't easy for Becky. She has no time to hang out with her friends.

> **run-on sentence corrected with a coordinating conjunction and a comma:**
> Working and studying isn't easy for Becky, *so* she has no time to hang out with her friends.

> **run-on sentence corrected with a semicolon:**
> Working and studying isn't easy for Becky; she has no time to hang out with her friends.

Using the steps to check for run-on sentences can also help you avoid unnecessary punctuation. Consider this sentence:

> The manager gave me my schedule for next week and told me about a special sales promotion.

> **Step 1:** Check for two independent clauses. Do this by checking the subject–verb, subject–verb pattern.

> S V   V
> The *manager gave* me my schedule for next week and *told* me about a special sales promotion.

The pattern is SVV, not SVSV. The sentence is not a run-on sentence. It does not need any additional punctuation.

Following the steps in correcting run-on sentences can help you avoid a major grammar error.

Exercise 2 Practice: Correcting Run-on (Fused) Sentences

Some of the sentences below are correctly punctuated. Some are run-on (fused) sentences; that is, they are two simple sentences run together without any punctuation. If the sentence is correctly punctuated, write *OK* in the space provided. If it is a run-on sentence, put an *X* in the space provided and correct the sentence above the lines.

1. _____ I can drive you to the clinic now or on Friday after my last class.

2. _____ Tamara won't like the movie she isn't interested in martial arts action films.

3. _____ A heavy rain came after lunch everyone raced for cover.

4. _____ I had two cups of coffee after dinner now I can't get to sleep.

5. _____ A smile on your face encourages strangers to let go of their natural defensiveness and relax.

6. _____ Shopping online can be easy; it can also be addictive.

7. _____ The kitten grabs my hand with her front paws she puts her tiny teeth into my fingers.

8. _____ Driving on the highway and maneuvering in city traffic require different skills.

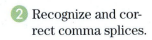 Recognize and correct comma splices.

COMMA SPLICES

A comma splice is an error that occurs when you punctuate with a comma but should use a semicolon instead. If you are joining two independent clauses without a coordinating conjunction (*for, and, nor, but, or, yet, so*) you must use a semicolon. A comma is not enough.

comma splice error:
The crowd pushed forward, people began to panic.

comma splice error corrected:
The crowd pushed forward; people began to panic.

comma splice error:
I forgot my glasses, thus I couldn't read the small print in the contract.

comma splice error corrected:
I forgot my glasses; thus I couldn't read the small print in the contract.

CORRECTING COMMA SPLICES

When you edit your writing, you can correct comma splices by following these steps:

Step 1: Check for two independent clauses.

Step 2: Check that the clauses are separated by a coordinating conjunction (*for, and, nor, but, or, yet, so*). If they are, then a comma in front of the coordinating conjunction is sufficient. If they are not separated by a coordinating conjunction, you have a comma splice. Correct it by changing the comma to a semicolon.

Follow the steps to check for a comma splice in this sentence:

I dropped the glass, it shattered on the tile floor.

Step 1: Check for two independent clauses. You can do this by checking for the subject–verb, subject–verb pattern that indicates two independent clauses.

S   V   S   V
I dropped the glass, *it shattered* on the tile floor.

The pattern indicates that you have two independent clauses.

Step 2: Check that the clauses are separated by a coordinating conjunction.

There is no coordinating conjunction. To correct the comma splice error, you must use a semicolon instead of a comma.

comma splice error corrected:
I dropped the glass; it shattered on the tile floor.

Be careful not to mistake a short word such as *then* or *thus* for a coordinating conjunction. Only the seven coordinating conjunctions (*for, and, nor, but, or, yet, so*) with a comma in front of them can join independent clauses.

comma splice error:
Yuiko did her homework, then she checked her e-mail.

comma splice error corrected:
Yuiko did her homework; then she checked her e-mail.

Then is not a coordinating conjunction; it is a conjunctive adverb. When it joins two independent clauses, it needs a semicolon in front of it.

Also remember that conjunctive adverbs that are two or more syllables long (like *consequently, however, therefore*) need a comma after them as well as a semicolon in front of them when they join independent clauses:

Harry has been researching plane fares to New York; consequently, he knows how to spot a cheap flight.

(For a list of some common conjunctive adverbs, see Chapter 17, p. 389.)

Sometimes writers see commas before and after a conjunctive adverb and think the commas are sufficient. Check this sentence for a comma splice by following the steps:

Jonathan loves his job, however, it pays very little.

Step 1: Check for two independent clauses by checking for the subject–verb, subject–verb pattern.

    S   V   S   V

Jonathan loves his job, however, *it pays* very little.

The pattern indicates that you have two independent clauses.

Step 2: Check for a coordinating conjunction.

There is no coordinating conjunction. *However* is a conjunctive adverb, not a coordinating conjunction. Because there is no coordinating conjunction, you need a semicolon between the two independent clauses.

comma splice error corrected:
Jonathan loves his job; however, it pays very little.

Exercise 3 **Practice: Identifying Independent Clauses and Coordination**

Read each sentence below. Underline each independent clause(s) and circle the coordination.

1. Michele works in a hospital; she loves helping others.

2. Biology and chemistry aren't easy courses for Justin , yet he must take both of them.

3. Living in a new country isn't easy; therefore, it takes time to adjust.

4. Writing essays is a big part of this class, so it's important we do well on them.

5. Some people think big cities are exciting; however, others find them too congested.

6. I have a great app on my smartphone; it organizes all of my passwords.

7. Zachary takes only three courses a semester; therefore, he will take longer to graduate.

8. In the United States, students take general education courses first; on the other hand, in China, students only take courses in their major.

Exercise 4 **Practice: Correcting Comma Splices**

Some of the sentences below are correctly punctuated. Some contain comma splices. If the sentence is correctly punctuated, write *OK* in the space provided. If it contains a comma splice, put an *X* in the space provided and correct the sentence above the lines. To correct a sentence, do not add any words, just correct the punctuation.

1. _____ Eric changed the channel he couldn't watch any more celebrity gossip.

2. _____ Melinda and Tony were born in Taiwan and came to America as children, therefore, they speak two languages fluently.

3. _____ The bookstore was out of books, so I had to order mine online.

4. _____ Our math instructor should have reviewed the new material before the test, anyway, he should have hinted about the kinds of questions on the test.

5. _____ My dog loves to run in an open field, and I often take her to a huge dog park near the university.

6. _____ Most of my friends dress casually for work, a few wear uniforms.

7. _____ A pencil is an inexpensive writing instrument, but I hate the faded look of penciled words on paper.

8. _____ I tried to study the material meanwhile, my brother was yelling in the other room.

Collaborate

Exercise 5 Collaborate: Completing Sentences

With a partner or group, write the first part of each of the following incomplete sentences. Make your addition an independent clause. Be sure to punctuate your completed sentences correctly. The first one is done for you.

1. _The driver ignored the railroad warning signals,_____ and his car was hit by the train.

2. _____ then I ran out of money.

3. _____ incidentally, you also told several lies about me to my friends.

4. _____ he was arrested for driving under the influence of alcohol.

5. _____ otherwise, I won't be able to get a good job.

6. _____ but I didn't recognize the number.

7. _____ or someone will get hurt.

8. _____ now my friend has to testify in court.

9. _____ and I have a big test on Friday.

10. _____ besides, you can always change your mind.

Connect

Exercise 6 Connect: Editing a Paragraph for Run-on Sentences and Comma Splices

Edit the following paragraph for run-on sentences and comma splices. There are six errors.

My girlfriend's car was stolen outside of her apartment we were both

shocked. The apartment is in a safe neighborhood and many young people live in the area. Most of the residents are college students or people at the beginning of their careers. My girlfriend is usually careful about safety, however, one evening she was careless and left her car doors unlocked. On the next morning, she could not find her car in the parking lot. For half an hour she searched every section of the parking lot and the nearby parking areas. After her desperate search, she called the police and reported the crime. Two days later, the officers called with some news. Her car had been found in a wooded area near the local airport the auto had dented fenders and two smashed windows. First, my girlfriend was horrified by the damage, then she realized her good luck in getting her car back. In the future, she will be more vigilant about securing her car and keeping it safe from car thieves. One careless mistake had cost her money and misery so she doesn't want to make the same error again.

MyWritingLab™   **Chapter Test** **Avoiding Run-on Sentences and Comma Splices**

Some of the sentences below are correctly punctuated. Some are run-on sentences, and some contain comma splices. If a sentence is correctly punctuated, write *OK* in the space provided. If it is a run-on sentence or contains a comma splice, put an *X* in the space provided and correct the sentence above the lines. To correct a sentence, add the necessary punctuation. Do not add any words.

1. _____ Kristen loves to visit historical sites thus she has been to Philadelphia, Washington, D.C., and Charleston this year.

2. _____ Leon is nearsighted, as a result, he likes a seat near the front of the movie theater.

3. _____ The first quarter of the game was full of action but did not please the fans of the visiting team.

4. _____ Eddie was nosy, he bombarded me with personal questions.

5. _____ You're a good athlete, so you will enjoy the challenges of this game.

6. _____ I am spending the night at my sister's apartment, otherwise, I would go out with you tonight.

7. _____ Our new puppy raced around the back yard for hours today; now he's sleeping.

8. _____ My smartphone was stolen, thus I am in a panic about keeping up with the news from my family and friends.

MyWritingLab™ Visit Chapter 18, "Avoiding Run-on Sentences and Comma Splices," in *MyWritingLab* to test your understanding of the chapter objectives.

Beyond the Simple Sentence: Subordination

CHAPTER 19

Quick Question MyWritingLab™

Which sentence(s) is/are correct?

A. After I moved to Albuquerque, I felt content.

B. I felt content after I moved to Albuquerque.

(After you study this chapter, you will be confident of your answer.)

Learning Objectives

In this chapter, you will learn to:

1 Use a dependent clause to begin a sentence.

2 Use a dependent clause to end a sentence.

3 Generate and punctuate sentences correctly.

MORE ON COMBINING SIMPLE SENTENCES

Before you go any further, look back. Review the following:

- A clause has a subject and a verb.
- An independent clause is a simple sentence; it is a group of words, with a subject and a verb, that makes sense by itself.

There is another kind of clause called a **dependent clause**. It has a subject and a verb, but it does not express a complete thought. It cannot stand alone. That is, it *depends* on the rest of the sentence to give it meaning. You can use a dependent clause as another option for combining simple sentences.

> **Note:** Options 1–3 for sentence combining are explained in Chapter 17 on coordination.

1 Use a dependent clause to begin a sentence.

OPTION 4: USING A DEPENDENT CLAUSE TO BEGIN A SENTENCE

Often, you can combine simple sentences by changing an independent clause from one sentence into a dependent clause and placing it at the beginning of the new sentence.

two simple sentences:

S V   S   V
I was late for work. My *car had* a flat tire.

changing one simple sentence into a beginning dependent clause:

                          S   V   S V
Because my *car had* a flat tire, *I was* late for work.

2 Use a dependent clause to end a sentence.

OPTION 5: USING A DEPENDENT CLAUSE TO END A SENTENCE

You can also combine simple sentences by changing an independent clause from one sentence into a dependent clause and placing it at the end of the new sentence:

S   V   S   V
I was late for work because my *car had* a flat tire.

Notice how one simple sentence can be changed into a dependent clause in two ways:

two simple sentences:

        S   V   S   V
The *teacher explained* the lesson. *I took* notes.

changing one simple sentence into a dependent clause:

        S   V   S V
The *teacher explained* the lesson while *I took* notes.

or

        S   V   S V
While the *teacher explained* the lesson, *I took* notes.

Using Subordinating Conjunctions

Changing an independent clause to a dependent one is called **subordinating**. How do you do it? You add a subordinating word, called a **subordinating conjunction**, to an independent clause, making it dependent—less "important," or subordinate—in the new sentence.

Keep in mind that the subordinate clause is still a clause; it has a subject and a verb, but it does not make sense by itself. For example, let's start with an independent clause:

> S   V
> Caroline studies.

Somebody (Caroline) does something (studies). The statement makes sense by itself. But if you add a subordinating conjunction to the independent clause, the clause becomes dependent and unfinished, like this:

> *When* Caroline studies. (When she studies, what happens?)
> *Unless* Caroline studies. (Unless she studies, what will happen?)
> *If* Caroline studies. (If Caroline studies, what will happen?)

Now, each dependent clause needs an independent clause to finish the idea:

> dependent clause   independent clause
> When Caroline studies, she gets good grades.

> dependent clause   independent clause
> Unless Caroline studies, she forgets key ideas.

> dependent clause   independent clause
> If Caroline studies, she will pass the course.

There are many subordinating conjunctions. When you put any of these words in front of an independent clause, you make that clause dependent. Here is a list of some subordinating conjunctions:

> **3** Generate and punctuate sentences correctly.

INFO BOX **Subordinating Conjunctions**

after	before	so that	whenever
although	even though	though	where
as	if	unless	whereas
as if	in order that	until	whether
because	since	when	while

If you pick the right subordinating conjunction, you can effectively combine simple sentences (independent clauses) into a more sophisticated sentence pattern. Such combining helps you add sentence variety to your writing and helps to explain relationships between ideas.

simple sentences:

> S   V   V   S   V
> *Leo could* not *read* music. His *performance was* exciting.

new combination:

> dependent clause   independent clause
> Although Leo could not read music, his performance was exciting.

simple sentences:

S V   S V
I forgot to do the English assignment. *I was* busy working and preparing for an algebra test.

new combination:

independent clause   dependent clause
I forgot to do the English assignment because I was busy working and preparing for an algebra test.

| Exercise 1 | Practice: Identifying Subordinating Conjunctions |

Read each sentence. Circle the subordinating conjunction.

1. The movie had already started when we arrived.

2. Because her favorite actor is Chris Hemsworth, she has seen all of his movies.

3. Unless we run into traffic, we will be at your house at 8:00 p.m.

4. Puri was studying literature before she moved to the United States.

5. Living in a new city can be difficult if you don't know anyone.

6. Whenever he plays games online, his mother gets angry.

7. The bookstore is really crowded since it's the first week of classes.

8. Although the weather is getting better, it still doesn't feel like summer.

| Exercise 2 | Practice: Choosing the Right Subordinating Conjunction |

Read each sentence and then add the appropriate subordinating conjunction. Use the Info Box on page 405.

1. Ben was working on his research paper _____ his friends stopped by.

2. _____ I finished the assignment, I reviewed for the test.

3. They went to the movies _____ they had a lot of work to complete.

4. _____ John visits, he brings some fresh vegetables from his garden.

5. _____ I have to work all weekend, I must complete all of my class work.

6. Mary will be late for class _____ she left her house late.

7. _____ Bill took algebra in high school, he still doesn't completely understand it.

8. We plan to have the picnic outside _____ or not it is warm.

Punctuating Complex Sentences

A sentence that has one independent clause and one (or more) dependent clause(s) is called a **complex sentence**. Complex sentences are very easy to punctuate. See if you can figure out the rule for punctuating by yourself. Look at the following examples. All are punctuated correctly.

> **dependent clause**   **independent clause**
> Whenever the baby smiles, his mother is delighted.

> **independent clause**   **dependent clause**
> His mother is delighted whenever the baby smiles.

> **dependent clause**   **independent clause**
> While you were away, I saved your mail for you.

> **independent clause**   **dependent clause**
> I saved your mail for you while you were away.

In the examples above, look at the sentences that have a comma. Look at the ones that do not have a comma. Both kinds of sentences are punctuated correctly. Do you see the rule?

> **If the dependent clause comes at the beginning of the sentence, put a comma after the dependent clause. If the dependent clause comes at the end of the sentence, do not put a comma in front of the dependent clause.**

> Although we played well, we lost the game.
> We lost the game although we played well.

> Until he called, I had no date for the dance.
> I had no date for the dance until he called.

Exercise 3 **Practice: Punctuating Complex Sentences**

All the sentences below are complex sentences; that is, they have one independent and one (or more) dependent clause(s). Add a comma to each sentence that needs one.

1. Until I can afford a new car I have to keep paying for repairs on my old one.

2. Give me a call if you want me to drive you to school tomorrow.

3. After my parents stopped arguing about my bad behavior I fell into a restless and troubled sleep.

4. I couldn't fall asleep after I watched the scary movie.

5. Kristin never buys much when she and I spend time at the mall on the weekends.

6. Because my supervisor insists on punctuality I come to work early every morning.

7. My brother won't come to dinner unless I make his favorite banana cake.

8. The children became obsessed with the snapchat while the babysitter was texting her friends.

Exercise 4   Practice: Punctuating Complex Sentences

All the sentences below are complex sentences; that is, they have one independent clause and one or more dependent clauses. Add a comma to each sentence that needs a comma, and circle the subject of the independent clause.

1. Gina struggled to hold on to her purse as the crowd around her began pushing forward.

2. The dining room was the biggest room in the house so that the large family could sit comfortably for weekly dinners, birthdays, and holiday celebrations.

3. Whether Al joins the U.S. Army or goes to flight school he will need the support of his friends.

4. Alicia wouldn't accept a gift from her father because he hasn't been a part of her life for years.

5. While you were wasting your time playing video games I finished my book report for sociology class.

6. Since we had missed the first part of the movie we couldn't understand the plot.

7. When an aggressive driver follows my car too closely I want to scream.

8. I will pass chemistry even if I have to go to tutoring every day.

Here are all five options for combining sentences:

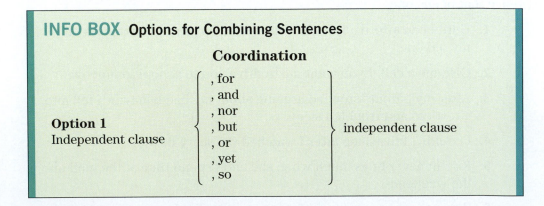

INFO BOX Options for Combining Sentences

Coordination

| Option 1
Independent clause | , for
, and
, nor
, but
, or
, yet
, so | independent clause |

Option 2
Independent clause

;
; also,
; anyway,
; as a result,
; besides,
; certainly,
; consequently,
; finally,
; furthermore,
; however,
; in addition,
; in fact,
; incidentally,
; indeed,
; instead,
; likewise,
; meanwhile,
; moreover,
; nevertheless,
; next
; now
; on the other hand,
; otherwise,
; similarly,
; still
; then
; therefore,
; thus
; undoubtedly,

independent clause

Option 3
Independent clause

independent clause

Subordination

Option 4
Dependent clause
(Put a comma at the end of the dependent clause.)

After
Although
As
As if
Because
Before
Even though
If
In order that
Since
So that
Though
Unless
Until
When
Whenever
Where
Whereas
Whether
While

independent clause

(Continued)

	after although as as if because before even though if in order that since so that though unless until when whenever where whereas whether while	
Option 5 Independent clause		dependent clause

Note: In Option 4, words are capitalized because the dependent clause will *begin* your complete sentence.

Exercise 5   Practice: Using the Five Options for Combining Sentences

Add the necessary commas and/or semicolons to the following sentences. Some are correct as they are.

1. After the rain stopped the plants in the garden looked fresh and new.

2. One of the puppies in the exercise pen began to bark at the visitor then all the puppies joined in the barking.

3. When the table I bought online arrived it was shattered into pieces.

4. Caleb has a hot temper even though he seems easygoing and calm.

5. Whenever the phone rings in the middle of the night I expect bad news.

6. Unless Samantha gets a good night's sleep she is irritable the next day.

7. Give me your answer I need to know it now.

8. My wild curly hair grows fast consequently I spend a significant part of my paycheck on haircuts.

Exercise 6   Practice: Using the Five Options for Combining Sentences

Add the necessary commas and/or semicolons to the following sentences. Some are correct as they are.

1. My brother turned my parents' wedding anniversary into something special he made a video out of their old, forgotten home movies.

2. Because I can't stand the smell of smoke on a person's clothing I rarely socialize with smokers.

3. My house is not the cleanest house in town but it is warm and comfortable.

4. My sister doesn't spend money on the latest toys for her children instead she takes them to the park, to the zoo, or to the library for new adventures.

5. Some parking lots were designed many years ago and the parking spaces in them are too small for many of today's large cars.

6. I always feel guilty when I gossip about a friend.

7. Although Raymond drives a tow truck at work his own car is a tiny Volkswagen.

8. The pot of spaghetti boiled over while I was distracted by my phone conversation with Eli.

Exercise 7 **Collaborate: Combining Sentences**

Collaborate

Do this exercise with a partner or a group. Below are pairs of sentences. Combine each pair of sentences into one clear, smooth sentence in two different ways. You can add words as well as punctuation. The first pair of sentences is done for you.

1. We always go to Country Ice Cream for a treat.
   The store has the best hot fudge sundaes in the world.

   combination 1: We always go to Country Ice Cream for a treat because the store has the best hot fudge sundaes in the world.

   combination 2: We always go to Country Ice Cream for a treat; the store has the best hot fudge sundaes in the world.

2. My cousin wouldn't drive me to the gym.
   I had to take the bus.

   combination 1: _____

   _____

   combination 2: _____

   _____

3. The snowstorm kept everyone inside.
   People were starting to feel restless.

   combination 1: _____

   _____

   combination 2: _____

   _____

4. A sleazy towing company removed my car from a no-parking zone.
   The company demanded a large cash payment.

   combination 1: _____

   _____

   combination 2: _____

   _____

5. Charlie wouldn't listen to Tommy's explanation for the delay.
   He wouldn't accept Tommy's apology.

   combination 1: _____

   _____

   combination 2: _____

   _____

6. I always wake Mark up in the morning.
   He sleeps through the sound of the alarm clock.

   combination 1: _____

   _____

   combination 2: _____

   _____

7. My dog has never caught a squirrel.
   She begins each day with the dream of catching one.

   combination 1: _____

   _____

   combination 2: _____

   _____

8. Bill wanted a career in music.
   He became a physician's assistant.

   combination 1: _____

   _____

   combination 2: _____

   _____

Collaborate

Exercise 8   **Collaborate: Create Your Own Text on Combining Sentences**

Below is a list of rules for coordinating and subordinating sentences. Working with a group, write two examples for each rule.

Option 1: You can join two simple sentences (two independent clauses) into a compound sentence with a coordinating conjunction and a comma in front of it. (The coordinating conjunctions are *for, and, nor, but, or, yet, so.*)

example 1: _____

_____

example 2: _____

_____

Option 2: You can combine two simple sentences (two independent clauses) into a compound sentence with a semicolon between independent clauses.

example 1: _____

_____

example 2: _____

_____

Option 3: You can combine two simple sentences (two independent clauses) into a compound sentence with a semicolon and a conjunctive adverb between independent clauses. (Some conjunctive adverbs are *also, anyway, as a result, besides, certainly, consequently, finally, furthermore, however, in addition, in fact, incidentally, instead, likewise, meanwhile, moreover, nevertheless, next, now, on the other hand, otherwise, similarly, still, then, therefore, thus,* and *undoubtedly.*)

example 1: _____

_____

example 2: _____

_____

Option 4: You can combine two simple sentences (two independent clauses) into a complex sentence by making one clause dependent. The dependent clause starts with a subordinating conjunction. Then, if the dependent clause begins the sentence, the clause ends with a comma. (Some common subordinating conjunctions are *after, although, as, as if, because, before, even though, if, in order that, since, so that, though, unless, until, when, whenever, where, whereas, whether,* and *while.*)

example 1: _____

_____

example 2: _____

_____

Option 5: You can combine two simple sentences (two independent clauses) into a complex sentence by making one clause dependent. Then, if the dependent clause comes after the independent clause, no comma is needed.

example 1: _____

_____

example 2: _____

_____

Exercise 9 **Connect: Editing a Paragraph for Errors in Coordination and Subordination**

Connect

Edit the following paragraph for errors in coordination and subordination. You do not have to add words to the paragraph; just add, delete, or change punctuation. There are ten errors.

My mother always dreamed about being a nurse finally, her dream will come true. When she was a young woman she wanted an education, so that she could enter the medical field. Poverty and other family struggles prevented her from finishing high school and she went to work at sixteen. My mother married at twenty, and had three children before she was twenty-four. She raised them, while she continued working at various low-paying jobs. After my father died she worked

for fifty hours a week and put every penny into a college fund. The college fund

began to grow but all of the money in it was spent on her children's education.

When her children were grown up and educated my mother remembered her lost

dream of an education. A guidance counselor told my mother about earning a

G.E.D. My mother studied hard, moreover, she often studied with the help of her

college-educated children. She was proud of earning her high school diploma then

she tackled college. Years of part-time enrollment and constant study passed, and

today she is close to her longtime dream. At sixty-two, my mother will graduate

from the nursing program at Roosevelt College.

MyWritingLab™ **Chapter Test** **Coordination and Subordination**

Some of the following sentences need commas and/or semicolons. Write *OK* next to the correct sentences; write *X* next to the incorrect sentences and correct them above the lines.

1. _____ I began to feel ill after I ate a seafood dinner at the Oyster House restaurant and had a piece of homemade key lime pie for dessert.

2. _____ On the plane, his complaining started at take-off and continued until landing finally the other passengers got some relief from the loud and constant whining.

3. _____ I packed my boxes of shoes and clothes in the trunk of my car and then stuffed every space inside the old Kia with pillows, blankets, and sporting goods.

4. _____ Trevor was always helpful and polite to the customers at the garden store for he was afraid of offending someone and losing his job in a time of high unemployment.

5. _____ My grandparents have lived in the same house for thirty years thus they haven't dealt with the ups and downs of the current real estate market.

6. _____ We can save enough money for a summer trip to Yellowstone if you will sacrifice your annual fishing trip with your cousin.

7. _____ Kira loves dance music yet rarely goes to any of the dance clubs in either of the nearby cities.

8. _____ As the water level in the basement began to rise and threaten the first floor of the house my brother frantically called the number of an emergency plumbing service.

MyWritingLab™ Visit Chapter 19, "Beyond the Simple Sentence: Subordination," in *MyWritingLab* to test your understanding of the chapter objectives.

Avoiding Sentence Fragments

CHAPTER 20

Quick Question MyWritingLab™

True or False: These are both sentences:

A. *While he was sitting in class.*
B. *Without a word, Michael fainted.*

(After you study this chapter, you will be confident of your answer.)

Learning Objectives

In this chapter, you will learn to:

1. Recognize and correct sentence fragments by checking for subject and verb.
2. Recognize and correct sentence fragments by making sure the group of words makes a complete statement.

AVOIDING SENTENCE FRAGMENTS

A **sentence fragment** is a group of words that looks like a sentence and is punctuated like a sentence, but it is *not* a sentence. Writing a sentence fragment is a major grammatical error because it reveals that the writer is not sure what comprises a sentence.

The following groups of words are all fragments:

Because customers are often in a hurry and have little time to look for bargains.
My job being very stressful and fast-paced.
For example, the introduction of salads into fast-food restaurants.

There are two easy steps that can help you check your writing for sentence fragments:

> **INFO BOX** Two Steps in Recognizing Sentence Fragments
>
> **Step 1:** Check each group of words punctuated like a sentence, looking for a subject and a verb.
>
> **Step 2:** If you find a subject and a verb, check that the group of words makes a complete statement.

1 Recognize and correct sentence fragments by checking for subject and verb.

RECOGNIZING FRAGMENTS: STEP 1

Check for a subject and a verb. Some groups of words that look like sentences may actually have a subject but no verb, or they may have a verb but no subject, or they may have no subject *or* verb.

> The puppy in the pet store window. (*Puppy* could be the subject of a sentence, but there is no verb.)
> Doesn't matter to me one way or the other. (There is a verb, *Does matter*, but there is no subject.)
> In the back of my mind. (There are two prepositional phrases, *In the back* and *of my mind*, but there are no subject and verb.)

Remember that an *-ing* verb by itself cannot be the main verb in a sentence. Therefore groups of words like the ones below may look like sentences, but they lack a verb and are really fragments:

> Your sister having all the skills required of a good salesperson.
> The two top tennis players struggling with exhaustion and the stress of a highly competitive tournament.
> Jack being the only one in the room with a piece of paper.

An infinitive (*to* plus a verb) cannot be a main verb in a sentence, either. The following groups of words are also fragments:

> The manager of the store to attend the meeting of regional managers next month in Philadelphia.
> The purpose to explain the fine points of the game to new players.

Groups of words beginning with words like *also, especially, except, for example, in addition,* and *such as* need subjects and verbs, too. Without subjects and verbs, these groups can be fragments, like the ones below:

> Also a good place to grow up.
> Especially the youngest member of the family.
> For example, a person without a high school diploma.

Exercise 1 **Practice: Identifying Subjects and Verbs**

Read each sentence. Underline the subject of each sentence and circle the verb. Be sure to circle the complete verb form.

1. The manager closed the store early due to the storm.

2. Anna and Parker were studying in the library Friday afternoon.

3. Playing soccer is his favorite activity.

4. I only need one more course to graduate.

5. Trying to work full time and attend classes isn't easy.

6. Unlike other classes, English requires extensive writing assignments.

7. Shopping and eating makes up her usual Saturday.

8. Anonymous bloggers often post hurtful comments.

> **Exercise 2**   **Practice: Checking Groups of Words for Subjects and Verbs**

Some of the following groups of words have subjects and verbs; these are sentences. Some are missing subjects, verbs, or both; these are fragments. Put an *S* by each sentence and an *F* by each fragment.

1. _____ Would consider changing the admission fee for the boxing match to be held on Friday night.

2. _____ No one at the house is answering the phone.

3. _____ My brother Jerome driving me to the Denver airport and my best friend meeting me at O'Hare Airport in Chicago.

4. _____ Two dogs with their noses sticking out of the car window and their ears flapping in the wind.

5. _____ Thai food may be too spicy for my mother.

6. _____ Should have asked me about spending our savings on an entertainment unit.

7. _____ Except one required course in sociology or psychology.

8. _____ When my smartphone vibrates.

RECOGNIZING FRAGMENTS: STEP 2

If a group of words has both a subject and a verb, check that it makes a complete statement. Many groups of words that have both a subject and a verb do not make sense by themselves. They are **dependent clauses**. How can you tell if a clause is dependent? After you have checked each group of words for a subject and a verb, check to see if it begins with one of the subordinating conjunctions that start dependent clauses. (Some common subordinating words are *after, although, as, as if, because, before, even though, if, in order that, since, so that, though, unless, until, when, whenever, where, whereas, whether, while.*)

A clause that begins with a subordinating conjunction is a dependent clause. When you punctuate a dependent clause as if it were a sentence, you have a kind of fragment called a **dependent clause fragment**.

> After I woke up this morning.
> Because he liked football better than soccer.
> Unless it stops raining by lunchtime.

It is important to remember both steps in checking for fragments:

Step 1: Check for a subject and a verb.

Step 2: If you find a subject and a verb, check that the group of words makes a complete statement.

2 Recognize and correct sentence fragments by making sure the group of words makes a complete statement.

Exercise 3 **Practice: Checking for Dependent-Clause Fragments**

Some of the following groups of words are sentences. Some are dependent clauses punctuated like sentences, which are sentence fragments. Put an *S* by each sentence and an *F* by each fragment.

1. _____ After the interview at the bank was over.

2. _____ Without a word, Ben took the check.

3. _____ Even though the computer lab closes at 6:00 p.m. on Fridays.

4. _____ Near the administration building is a patio with stone tables and benches.

5. _____ Then my computer shut down.

6. _____ Because no one told me about the nosy neighbors next door.

7. _____ Until Carl and Eddie can get some free time to work on restoring the car.

8. _____ Before Jose can choose his classes for the fall term.

Exercise 4 **Practice: Using Two Steps to Recognize Sentence Fragments**

Some of the following are complete sentences; some are fragments. To recognize the fragments, check each group of words by using the two-step process:

Step 1: Check for a subject and a verb.
Step 2: If you find a subject and verb, check that the group of words makes a complete statement.

Then put an *S* by each sentence and an *F* by each fragment.

1. _____ If my little boy can take swimming lessons at the community center.

2. _____ Regret was obvious in his tone of voice.

3. _____ One of my neighbors starting a project to send packages of goodies to American troops in foreign countries.

4. _____ Without my help, my five-year-old tied her own shoes.

5. _____ Around the front door was a string of holiday lights.

6. _____ Without a sign of regret for his actions.

7. _____ Whenever she plays that song on her iPod.

8. _____ As Gloria and Brian studied the brochure on travel in India.

Exercise 5 **Practice: Identifying Fragments in a Paragraph**

Read George's text message to his friend Barbara. There are five fragments. Circle the fragments.

Got your message. I can't finish by Friday. How is Monday? Kim and Jonathan will be back then, so I should be able to get it done by then. What about the party? Still on Saturday? Need to know so I can get a babysitter. I will text you later to confirm. Bringing chips.

CORRECTING FRAGMENTS

You can correct fragments easily if you follow the two steps for identifying them.

Step 1: Check for a subject and a verb. If a group of words is a fragment because it lacks a subject or a verb, or both, *add what is missing*.

> **fragment:** My father being a very strong person. (This fragment lacks a main verb.)
> **corrected:** My father *is* a very strong person. (The verb *is* replaces *being*, which is not a main verb.)

> **fragment:** Need to know, so I can get a babysitter. (This fragment lacks a subject.)
> **corrected:** I need to know, so I can get a babysitter. (A subject, *I*, is added.)

> **fragment:** Especially on dark winter days. (This fragment has neither a subject nor a verb.)
> **corrected:** *I love* a bonfire, especially on dark winter days. (A subject, *I*, and a verb, *love*, are added.)

Step 2: If you find a subject and a verb, check that the group of words makes a complete statement. To correct the fragment, you can turn a dependent clause into an independent one by removing the subordinating conjunction, *or* you can add an independent clause to the dependent one to create a sentence.

> **fragment:** When the rain beat against the windows. (The statement does not make sense by itself. The subordinating conjunction *when* leads the reader to ask, "What happened when the rain beat against the windows?" The subordinating conjunction makes this a dependent clause, not a sentence.)
> **corrected:** The rain beat against the windows. (Removing the subordinating conjunction makes this an independent clause, a sentence.)
> **corrected:** When the rain beat against the windows, *I reconsidered my plans for the picnic.* (Adding an independent clause turns this into a sentence.)

Sometimes you can correct a fragment by linking it to the sentence before it or after it.

> **fragment (underlined):** I have always enjoyed outdoor concerts. <u>Like the ones at Pioneer Park</u>.
> **corrected:** I have always enjoyed outdoor concerts *like the ones at Pioneer Park.*

fragment (underlined): <u>Even if she apologizes for that nasty remark</u>. I will never trust her again.

corrected: *Even if she apologizes for that nasty remark,* I will never trust her again.

You have several choices for correcting fragments: you can add words, phrases, or clauses; you can also remove words or combine independent and dependent clauses. You can transform fragments into simple sentences or create compound or complex sentences. To punctuate your new sentences, remember the rules for combining sentences.

Exercise 6 Practice: Correcting Fragments

Correct each sentence fragment below in the most appropriate way.

1. I spent two hours waiting at the airport. Until Jessica's flight finally arrived.

    corrected: _____

    _____

2. To earn the money for my little brother's series of operations. My father took a second job.

    corrected: _____

    _____

3. Colin searched for candles and matches. After the electricity went off.

    corrected: _____

    _____

4. Because a severe drought has struck our area. We are not allowed to water our lawns.

    corrected: _____

    _____

5. Then took a sharp left turn across oncoming traffic and nearly caused a serious accident.

    corrected: _____

    _____

6. One reason for the sharp downturn in the economy being the sharp increase in the price of gasoline.

    corrected: _____

    _____

7. Mosquitoes had bitten every exposed area of David's skin. Especially his neck and feet.

    corrected: _____

    _____

8. Choosing a difficult topic for her speech. Shawna researched her subject for hours.

   corrected: _____

   _____

Exercise 7   **Collaborate: Correcting Fragments Two Ways**

Working with a partner or group, correct each fragment below in two ways. The first one is done for you.

1. Whenever I am waiting for an important phone call.

   corrected: _____

   _____

   corrected: _____

   _____

2. Except for three days of blizzard conditions.

   corrected: _____

   _____

   corrected: _____

   _____

3. While the hostage negotiators waited.

   corrected: _____

   _____

   corrected: _____

   _____

4. You will damage your suede jacket. If you wear it in wet weather.

   corrected: _____

   _____

   corrected: _____

   _____

5. On the other side of town, where Tyler lives.

   corrected: _____

   _____

   corrected: _____

   _____

6. Although no one at the college knew him well.

    corrected: _____

    _____

    corrected: _____

    _____

7. After the returning soldier had hugged his mother and kissed his girlfriend. He noticed the television cameras pointed at him.

    corrected: _____

    _____

    corrected: _____

    _____

8. The defense attorney delivering a strong case for acquittal.

    corrected: _____

    _____

    corrected: _____

    _____

Connect

Exercise 8 **Connect: Editing a Paragraph for Sentence Fragments**

Correct the sentence fragments in the following paragraph. There are seven fragments.

There is nothing in the world. Like sleeping under a soft, warm quilt. My grandmother had an old quilt on her guest room bed. I was always thrilled to sleep under that puffy covering. When I was a child. In fact, I always hoped for cold weather during my visits to her house. Then I could enjoy the nighttime comfort of the quilt. In addition, adult enjoyment of a good night's sleep under a quilt. My first purchase for my apartment was a big, warm quilt. To be used not only for my bed but also for napping on the sofa. With my own quilt covering me, a soothing, warm cocoon. I can reenter my childhood place. Everyone needing a quilt. Days of racing to work, sitting on hard plastic chairs, standing behind a counter, staring at a screen, or performing back-breaking labor difficult to endure. Sleeping under a quilt is a little reward for such days.

Chapter Test Avoiding Sentence Fragments

Some of the following are complete sentences; some are sentence fragments. Put an *S* by each sentence and an *F* by each fragment.

1. _____ A total stranger to assume the job now vacant as a result of the resignation of my supervisor.

2. _____ Unless someone can drive my mother to her doctor's appointment on Tuesday afternoon.

3. _____ The fumes in the basement giving Dylan a terrible headache during his two hours of work on the heating system.

4. _____ On the top shelf of the bookcase sits an old leather catcher's mitt from my father's high school days.

5. _____ While a group of happy children threw snowballs at each other.

6. _____ The reason for my lack of enthusiasm about the wedding being my distrust of the groom's intentions.

7. _____ Unlike the birthday celebrations in my family, Jordan's birthday party was an elaborate and highly planned gathering.

8. _____ Then a man in a cat mask appeared at the window of the fraternity house.

Using Parallelism in Sentences

Learning Objectives

In this chapter, you will learn to:

1 Recognize parallel structure in a sentence.

2 Use parallel structure to revise awkwardly worded sentences.

1 Recognize parallel structure in a sentence.

WHAT IS PARALLELISM?

Parallelism means balance in a sentence. To create sentences with parallelism, remember this rule:

Similar points should get a similar structure.

Often, you will include two or three (or more) related ideas, examples, or details in one sentence. If you express these ideas in a parallel structure, they will be clearer, smoother, and more convincing.

Here are some pairs of sentences with and without parallelism:

not parallel: Of all the sports I've played, I prefer tennis, handball, and playing golf.

parallel: Of all the sports I've played, I prefer *tennis, handball, and golf.* (Three words are parallel.)

not parallel: The professor said she needed to do all her work, on time, and study for the final exam.

parallel: The professor said she needed to *do all her work, get it in on time,* and *study for the final exam.* (Three verb phrases are parallel.)

not parallel: He is a good choice for manager because he works hard, he keeps calm, and well liked.

parallel: He is a good choice for manager because *he works hard, he keeps calm, and he is well liked.* (Three clauses are parallel.)

From these examples you can see that parallelism involves matching the structures of parts of your sentence. There are two steps that can help you check your writing for parallelism.

INFO BOX Two Steps in Checking a Sentence for Parallel Structure

Step 1: Look for the list in the sentence.

Step 2: Put the parts of the list into a similar structure. (You may have to change or add something to get a parallel structure.)

ACHIEVING PARALLELISM

Let's correct the parallelism of the following sentence:

sample sentence: The student government association met to decide on student activities, creating a budget, and for the purpose of reviewing the by-laws.

To correct this sentence, we'll follow the steps.

Step 1: Look for the list. The student government association met to do three things. Here's the list:

1. to decide on student activities
2. creating a budget
3. for the purpose of reviewing the by-laws.

Step 2: Put the parts of the list into a similar structure:

1. *to decide* on student activities
2. *to create* a budget
3. *to review* the by-laws.

Now revise to get a parallel sentence.

parallel: The student government association met *to decide* on student activities, *to create* a budget, and *to review* the by-laws.

② Use parallel structure to revise awkwardly worded sentences.

If you follow Steps 1 and 2, you can also write the sentence like this:

parallel: The student government association met to *decide on* student activities, *create* a budget, and *review* the by-laws.

But you cannot write a sentence like this:

not parallel: The student government association met *to decide* on student activities, *create* a budget, and *to review* the by-laws.

Think of the list again. You can have:
The student government association met

1. to decide ⎱
2. to create ⎰ parallel
3. to review

Or you can have:
The student government association met to

1. decide ⎱
2. create ⎰ parallel
3. review

But your list cannot be:
The student government association met to

1. decide ⎱
2. create ⎰ not parallel
3. to review

In other words, use the *to* once (if it fits every part of the list), or use it with every part of the list.

> **Caution:** Sometimes making ideas parallel means adding something to a sentence because all the parts of the list cannot match exactly.

sample sentence: In his pocket the little boy had a ruler, rubber band, baseball card, and apple.

Step 1: Look for the list. In his pocket the little boy had a
1. ruler
2. rubber band
3. baseball card
4. apple

Because they are all nouns, they will each need an article. The *a* goes with *a ruler, a rubber band, a baseball card*, and *a apple*. But *a* isn't the right word to put in front of *apple*. Words beginning with vowels (*a, e, i, o, u*) need *an* in front of them: *an apple*. So to make the sentence parallel, you have to change something in the sentence.

Step 2: Put the parts of the list into a parallel structure.

parallel: In his pocket the little boy had *a ruler, a rubber band, a baseball card*, and *an apple*.

Here's another example:

sample sentence: She was amused and interested in the silly plot of the movie.

Step 1: Look for the list. She was

1. amused
2. interested in the silly plot of the movie.

Check the sense of that sentence by looking at each part of the list and how it works in the sentence: "She was *interested in* the silly plot of the movie." That part of the list seems clear. But "She was *amused* the silly plot of the movie"? Or "She was *amused in* the silly plot of the movie"? Neither sentence is right. People are not *amused in*.

Step 2: The sentence needs a word added to make the structure parallel.

parallel: She was *amused by* and *interested in* the silly plot of the movie.

When you follow the two steps to check for parallelism, you can write clear sentences and improve your style.

Exercise 1 **Practice: Revising Sentences for Parallelism**

Some of the following sentences need to be revised so that they have parallel structures. Revise the ones that need parallelism.

1. Billy would rather help people in need than staring at a computer screen all day.

   revised: _____

   _____

2. The wedding reception was the fanciest I have ever attended, also the most expensive, and the biggest of all.

   revised: _____

   _____

3. At my old school, wearing last year's styles was like when you wear a sign that says "loser."

   revised: _____

   _____

4. The car's price, size, and the condition it was in made it a good buy for a college student.

   revised: _____

   _____

5. After we studied for the test, we spent the rest of the afternoon watching TV, eat popcorn, and we chatted online.

   revised: _____

   _____

6. Cleaning out closets, having to throw away junk, and packing endless boxes are all part of moving out of your home.

   revised: _____

   _____

7. Put the money in the kitchen drawer or on the dresser.

   revised: _____

   _____

8. Every time I run into Katie, she talks so long that I wind up looking at my watch, making restless motions, and interrupt her before
   I can get away.

   revised: _____

   _____

Collaborate

Exercise 2   **Collaborate: Writing Sentences with Parallelism**

Complete this exercise with a partner or a group. First, brainstorm a draft
list; then revise the list for parallelism. Finally, complete the sentence in
parallel structure. You may want to assign one step (brainstorming a draft
list, revising it, etc.) to each group member, then switch steps on the next
sentence. The first one is done for you.

1. Three habits I'd like to break are

   draft list   **revised list**

   a. worrying too much _____   a. worry too much _____

   b. talking on the phone for hours   b. talking on the phone for hours

   c. lose my temper _____   c. losing my temper _____

   sentence: Three habits I'd like to break are worrying too much, talking on the

   phone for hours, and losing my temper. _____

2. Three ways to stay healthy are

   draft list   **revised list**

   a. _____   a. _____

   b. _____   b. _____

   c. _____   c. _____

   sentence: _____

   _____

3. Two reasons why people choose not to marry are

   draft list   **revised list**

   a. _____   a. _____

   b. _____   b. _____

   sentence: _____

   _____

4. Three gifts that money cannot buy are

draft list   **revised list**

a. _____   a. _____

b. _____   b. _____

c. _____   c. _____

sentence: _____

_____

5. Saving money is important because (add three reasons)

draft list   **revised list**

a. _____   a. _____

b. _____   b. _____

c. _____   c. _____

sentence: _____

_____

6. Starting a new job can be stressful because (add three reasons)

draft list   **revised list**

a. _____   a. _____

b. _____   b. _____

c. _____   c. _____

sentence: _____

_____

7. When I finish college, I want to (add two goals)

draft list   **revised list**

a. _____   a. _____

b. _____   b. _____

sentence: _____

_____

8. Two things a smartphone can do are (add two things)

draft list   **revised list**

a. _____   a. _____

b. _____   b. _____

sentence: _____

_____

| Exercise 3 | **Practice: Combining Sentences and Creating a Parallel Structure** |

Combine each cluster of sentences below into one clear, smooth sentence that includes parallel structure. The first one is done for you.

1. Before you buy a used car, you should research what similar models are selling for.
   It would be a good idea to have a mechanic examine the car.
   Also, how much mileage it has racked up is a consideration.

   combination: _Before you buy a used car, you should compare prices of_

   similar models, get a mechanic to examine the car, and think carefully about

   the mileage.

2. The qualifications for the job include some sales experience.
   Applicants also have to have good telephone skills.
   Another requirement is being trained in computers.

   combination: _____

   _____

   _____

3. Jake was the funniest friend I ever had.
   He was more generous than any other friend I ever had.
   His loyalty was the best, too.

   combination: _____

   _____

   _____

4. Hundreds of students waited in line to register for their classes.
   They also were paying their tuition fees.
   Their other goal was to see an advisor.

   combination: _____

   _____

   _____

5. My aunt started as a night security guard at Crescent Rehabilitation Center.
   Then she was promoted to head of the night security shift.
   Eventually she worked her way up to head of security for the center.

   combination: _____

   _____

   _____

6. Shopping malls sell goods.
   Contests are often held at shopping malls.
   Early morning exercise for mall-walkers is offered.
   Special events such as celebrity appearances are another sponsored feature at malls.

combination: _____

_____

_____

7. He was tall.
   His skin was dark.
   He looked muscular.
   He dressed fashionably.
   He was the new dean of students.

   combination: _____

   _____

   _____

8. When I need advice, I go to Sean, who is a sensible person.
   Sean has insight.
   Perceptiveness is another one of his strengths.

   combination: _____

   _____

   _____

Exercise 4   **Connect: Editing a Paragraph for Errors in Parallelism**

Correct any errors in parallelism in the following paragraph. There are five errors.

Most people get angry when they lose an argument or losing a game. For

instance, my mother is usually a calm and polite individual. However, when she

has a difference of opinion with me about my social life, she becomes a wild

woman. Her eyes give off a fiery glint, her mouth stiffening into a pout, and her

jaw juts out with rage if I make an intelligent observation. She does not like a chal-

lenge to her beliefs and opinions even if the challenge is polite. Similarly, my best

friend becomes very upset when he loses one of our neighborhood soccer games.

These games are supposed to be informal get-togethers where everyone can get a

little exercise, release some stress, and to enjoy each other's company. However,

to my friend, these competitions are tests. Whenever he plays in a silly little soc-

cer game, he reacts as if he were in the World Cup and becoming an aggressive

fool. To him, losing means slinking away in disgrace, misery, and with fury. I

would love to advise my mother and my friend that their anger does not win an

argument nor change the outcome of a game.

MyWritingLab™ **Chapter Test** Using Parallelism in Sentences

Some of the following sentences have errors in parallelism; some are correct. Write *OK* next to the correct sentences; write *X* by the sentences with errors in parallelism.

1. _____ The honors ceremony will celebrate the academic achievements of many scholars, the success of various sports teams, the ability of individual athletes, and award recognition of the many student clubs.

2. _____ Alonzo is a dear friend, a neighbor who is kind, a hardworking police officer, and a committed volunteer.

3. _____ The specialist in tropical diseases was puzzled by and afraid of the new form of malaria.

4. _____ My backpack has a chemistry book, a notebook to take notes, pencil, and energy bar for when I get hungry.

5. _____ Visiting my grandmother makes me nervous because she asks me personal questions, offers me strange food, and bores with long and pointless stories.

6. _____ If you get to the movie theater and I am not there yet, you can stand in the ticket line, buy the tickets, and waiting for me at the entrance.

7. _____ A whining worker can irritate the other employees, the boss, create a negative atmosphere, and take all the energy out of the room.

8. _____ I tried the front door, checked every window, and explored the entrance to the basement, but I could not find a way into the house.

MyWritingLab™ Visit Chapter 21, "Using Parallelism in Sentences," in *MyWritingLab* to test your understanding of the chapter objectives.

Using Adjectives and Adverbs

Learning Objectives

In this chapter, you will learn to:

1 Identify adjectives.

2 Identify adverbs.

3 Use adjectives and adverbs correctly in your writing.

1 Identify adjectives.

WHAT ARE ADJECTIVES?

Adjectives describe nouns (persons, places, or things) or pronouns (words that substitute for nouns).

> **adjectives:**
>
> She stood in a *dark* corner. (*Dark* describes the noun *corner.*)
> I need a *little* help. (*Little* describes the noun *help.*)
> She looked *happy*. (*Happy* describes the pronoun *she.*)

An adjective usually comes before the word it describes.

> He gave me a *beautiful* ring. (*Beautiful* describes *ring.*)
> A *small* flash drive stores millions of files. *(Small* describes *flash drive.)*

Sometimes an adjective comes after a **being verb**, a verb that tells what something is. Being verbs are words like *is, are, was, am,* and *has been.* Words such as *feels, looks, seems, smells, sounds,* and *tastes* are part of the group called being verbs.

> He seems *unhappy*. (*Unhappy* describes *he* and follows the being
>   verb *seems.*)
> Alan was *confident*. (*Confident* describes *Alan* and follows the being
>   verb *was.*)

Exercise 1 **Practice: Recognizing Adjectives**

Circle the adjective in each of the following sentences, and then underline the noun or pronoun it describes.

1. Larry got caught in a heavy rainstorm.

2. Mr. and Mrs. Salazar were kind neighbors.

3. A small mouse skittered across the floor.

4. The dean of students shares a large office with the assistant dean of students.

5. The enormous snake was curled inside a box.

6. The cough medicine smelled horrible.

7. I want your honest opinion of my performance.

8. TechCom sells innovative devices.

ADJECTIVES: MULTIPLE ADJECTIVE WORD ORDER

We often use more than one adjective to describe someone or something. For example:

> This is a **classic old American** classroom.
> Where are my **red Italian leather** shoes?
> **Large modern glass** buildings are common in this city.

When we use more than one adjective, we need to follow adjective word order. Adjective word order is based on category. Look at the categories:

1. Opinion or evaluation (*beautiful, horrible, classic*)
2. Size/shape/condition (*small, triangular, broken*)

3. Age (*new, old*)
4. Color (*red, multicolored*)
5. Origin (*Italian, American*)
6. Material (*glass, leather*)

Note: Commas are only placed between adjectives that are from the same category. Example: I live in a beautiful, friendly neighborhood. (Both *beautiful* and *friendly* are opinions or evaluations.)

---

incorrect: I have a large, black TV (The adjectives are from different categories, so no commas are needed.)
correct: I have a large black TV.

Exercise 2   Practice: Identifying and Correcting Adjective Word Order

Some of the following sentences have errors with adjective word order while others are correct. Put an X next to the incorrect sentences and then correct them.

1. _____ Ms. Taylor prefers modern busy cities over peaceful small towns.

2. _____ A new exciting British band will play in the park next week.

3. _____ A slimy green disgusting liquid was leaking from the pipes.

4. _____ Her favorite possession is her white lightweight useful reader.

5. _____ I decided to wear my old floppy red hat.

6. _____ Audra is an energetic, smart, and loyal employee.

7. _____ The homeowners wanted to redesign their circular huge concrete driveway.

8. _____ Isabel decided to sell her red new racing skates.

ADJECTIVES: COMPARATIVE AND SUPERLATIVE FORMS

The **comparative** form of an adjective compares two persons or things. The **superlative** form compares three or more persons or things.

comparative: Your car is *cleaner* than mine.
superlative: Your car is the *cleanest* one in the parking lot.

comparative: Hamburger is *cheaper* than steak.
superlative: Hamburger is the *cheapest* meat on the menu.

comparative: Lisa is *friendlier* than her sister.
superlative: Lisa is the *friendliest* of the three sisters.

For most adjectives of one syllable, add -*er* to form the comparative, and add -*est* to form the superlative:

The weather is *colder* than it was yesterday, but Friday was the *coldest* day of the year.
Orange juice is *sweeter* than grapefruit juice, but the *sweetest* juice is grape juice.

For adjectives that have two syllables and end in -*y*, drop the *y* and add -*ier* for the comparative form, or -*iest* for the superlative form.

She is *happier* today than she was yesterday, but she still isn't the *happiest* in class.

This chapter is *easier* than the last chapter, but the first chapter was the *easiest*.

For adjectives with two or more syllables, use *more* to form the comparative, and *most* to form the superlative:

I thought algebra was *more difficult* than composition; however, physics was the *most difficult* course I ever took.

My brother is *more outgoing* than my sister, but my father is the *most outgoing* member of the family.

The three forms of adjectives usually look like this:

Adjective	**Comparative** (two)	**Superlative** (three or more)
sweet	sweeter	sweetest
fast	faster	fastest
short	shorter	shortest

Or they may look like this:

Adjective	**Comparative**	**Superlative**
busy	busier	busiest
friendly	friendlier	friendliest
nasty	nastier	nastiest
easy	easier	easiest
pretty	prettier	prettiest

They may even look like this:

Adjective	**Comparative** (two)	**Superlative** (three or more)
confused	more confused	most confused
specific	more specific	most specific
dangerous	more dangerous	most dangerous

However, there are some *irregular* forms of adjectives:

Adjective	**Comparative** (two)	**Superlative** (three or more)
good	better	best
bad	worse	worst
little	less	least
many, much	more	most

Exercise 3   Practice: Selecting the Correct Adjective Form

Write the correct form of the adjective in each of the following sentences.

1. Milk chocolate tastes _____ (good) than dark chocolate.

2. After my surgery, I had to make _____ (many) calls to my insurance company; in fact, I called the insurance company _____ (many) often than I called my boyfriend.

3. Nick's communications class requires _____ (little) public speaking than my communications class does.

4. Which of the four games would be the _____ (many) suitable for a four-year-old boy?

5. My brother did a _____ (good) job painting my bathroom, but he would have done a _____ (good) job if he had been painting his own bathroom.

6. My sister is learning to cook and has been trying out her creations on me; of the three dishes I've eaten, the broiled swordfish was the _____ (bad).

7. I love both my brothers, but Oscar is _____ (much) loveable than Malcolm.

8. *Pirates of the Caribbean*, *Spiderman*, and *Shrek* all produced sequels; I think *Spiderman* offers the _____ (good) of the sequels.

Exercise 4   **Collaborate: Writing Sentences with Adjectives**

Collaborate

Working with a partner or group, write a sentence that correctly uses each of the following adjectives. Be prepared to share your answers with another group or with the class.

1. oldest   _____

2. more useful   _____

3. richest   _____

4. least   _____

5. most foolish _____

6. stronger   _____

7. easier   _____

8. more alert   _____

WHAT ARE ADVERBS?

2 Identify adverbs.

Adverbs describe verbs, adjectives, or other adverbs.

> **adverbs:**
> As she spoke, Steve listened *thoughtfully*. (*Thoughtfully* describes the verb *listened*.)
> I said I was *really* sorry for my error. (*Really* describes the adjective *sorry*.)
> The cook worked *very* quickly. (*Very* describes the adverb *quickly*.)

Adverbs answer questions such as "How?" "How much?" "How often?" "When?" "Why?" and "Where?"

Exercise 5 Practice: Recognizing Adverbs

Circle the adverbs in the following sentences.

1. The dog across the street is usually quiet, but he barks uncontrollably at cats.

2. Sometimes, Sarah Sanchez can be very irritable.

3. The burglar moved swiftly and silently through the house.

4. Ethan was extremely proud of his lovingly rebuilt motorcycle.

5. The teacher could not clearly understand the student's paper.

6. Mr. Li regularly complains about the noise from the construction crew.

7. My English professor is genuinely interested in my stories about my childhood in Nigeria.

8. David Dowd's beautifully designed furniture won first prize at a decorator's showcase.

Collaborate

Exercise 6 Collaborate: Writing Sentences with Adverbs

Working with a partner or group, write a sentence that correctly uses each of the following adverbs. Be prepared to share your answers with another group or with the class.

1. rarely _____

2. completely _____

3. never _____

4. sadly _____

5. slowly _____

6. often _____

7. viciously _____

8. truly _____

3 Use adjectives and adverbs correctly in your writing.

HINTS ABOUT ADJECTIVES AND ADVERBS

Do not use an adjective when you need an adverb. Some writers make the mistake of using an adjective when they need an adverb.

not this: Talk to me ~~honest~~.
but this: Talk to me *honestly*.

not this: You can say it ~~simple~~.
but this: You can say it *simply*.

Exercise 7 Practice: Changing Adjectives to Adverbs

In each pair of sentences, change the underlined adjective in the first sentence to an adverb in the second sentence. The first one is done for you.

1. **a.** She is a <u>graceful</u> dancer.

   b. She dances ___*gracefully*___.

2. **a.** Gloria gave an <u>impatient</u> response.

   b. Gloria responded _____.

3. **a.** Mrs. Goldstein was a <u>recent</u> visitor to Concord.

   b. Mrs. Goldstein _____ visited Concord.

4. **a.** As she drove to the emergency room, Abigail was <u>nervous</u>.

   b. Abigail _____ drove to the emergency room.

5. **a.** After the contestant conquered his stage fright, his singing was <u>magnificent.</u>

   b. After the contestant conquered his stage fright, he sang _____.

6. **a.** The team's second try for the title had <u>significant</u> differences from its first attempt.

   b. The team's second try for the title was _____ different from its first attempt.

7. **a.** When the student government president made a decision, she was <u>calm</u>.

   b. The student government president _____ made a decision.

8. **a.** Cristina made a <u>steady</u> advance to the finish line.

   b. Cristina _____ advanced to the finish line.

Do Not Confuse *Good* and *Well*, or *Bad* and *Badly*

Remember that *good* is an adjective; it describes nouns. *Well* is an adverb; it describes verbs. (The only time *well* can be used as an adjective is when it means "healthy": *I feel well today.*

> **not this:** You ran that race ~~good~~.
> **but this:** You ran that race *well*.

> **not this:** I cook eggs ~~good~~.
> **but this:** I cook eggs *well*.

Bad is an adjective; it describes nouns. It also follows being verbs such as *is, are, was, am, has been.* Words such as *feels, looks, seems, smells, sounds,* and *tastes* are part of the group called being verbs. *Badly* is an adverb; it describes action verbs.

> **not this:** He feels ~~badly~~ about his mistake.
> **but this:** He feels *bad* about his mistake. (*Feels* is a being verb; it is described by the adjective *bad*.)

> **not this:** He dances ~~bad~~.
> **but this:** He dances *badly*. (*Dances* is an action verb; it is described by the adverb *badly*.)

| Exercise 8 | Practice: Using *Good* and *Well, Bad* and *Badly* |

Write the appropriate word in the following sentences.

1. Arthur sold his car to his sister Kathleen, who wanted it _____ (bad, badly).

2. Teresa skipped her math class yesterday because she didn't feel _____ (good, well).

3. A day after I had my computer repaired, it worked _____ (good, well), but a week later, it started working _____ (bad, badly) again.

4. Wen dropped his tablet, and the screen is _____ cracked. (bad, badly)

5. When Pete concentrates on his game, he does _____ (good, well) at regional golf tournaments.

6. My sister has never been a _____ (good, well) liar, but my brother has a gift for lying _____ (good, well).

7. No one wanted to buy the house because it was _____ (bad, badly) decorated.

8. How _____ (good, well) do you think the movie will be?

Not More + *-er* or Most + *-est*

Be careful. Never write both an *-er* ending and *more*, or an *-est* ending and *most*.

not this: I want to work with someone ~~more smarter~~.
but this: I want to work with someone *smarter*.

not this: Alan is the ~~most richest~~ man in town.
but this: Alan is the *richest* man in town.

Use *Than*, not *Then*, in Comparisons

When you compare things, use *than*. *Then* means "at a later time."

not this: You are taller ~~then~~ I am.
but this: You are taller *than* I am.

not this: I'd like a car that is faster ~~then~~ my old one.
but this: I'd like a car that is faster *than* my old one.

When Do I Need a Comma Between Adjectives?

Sometimes you use more than one adjective to describe a noun.

I visited a cold, dark cave.
The cat had pale blue eyes.

If you look at the preceding examples, one uses a comma between the adjectives *cold* and *dark*, but the other does not have a comma between the adjectives *pale* and *blue*. Both sentences are correctly punctuated. To decide whether you need a comma, try one of these tests:

Test 1: Try to put *and* between the adjectives. If the sentence still makes sense, put a comma between the adjectives.

> **check for comma:** I visited a cold, dark cave. (Do you need the comma? Add *and* between the adjectives.)
> **add *and*:** I visited a cold *and* dark cave. (Does the sentence still make sense? Yes. You need the comma.)
> **correct sentence:** I visited a cold, dark cave.

> **check for comma:** The cat had pale, blue eyes. (Do you need the comma? Add *and* between the adjectives.)
> **add *and*:** The cat had pale *and* blue eyes. (Does the sentence still make sense? No. You do not need the comma.)
> **correct sentence:** The cat had pale blue eyes.

Test 2: Try to reverse the order of the adjectives. If the sentence still makes sense, put a comma between the adjectives.

> **check for comma:** I visited a cold, dark cave. (Do you need the comma? Reverse the order of the adjectives.)
> **reverse order:** I visited a dark, cold cave. (Does the sentence still make sense? Yes. You need the comma.)
> **correct sentence:** I visited a cold, dark cave.

> **check for comma:** The cat had pale, blue eyes. (Do you need the comma? Reverse the order of the adjectives.)
> **reverse order:** The cat had blue pale eyes. (Does the sentence still make sense? No. You don't need a comma.)
> **correct sentence:** The cat had pale blue eyes.

You can use Test 1 or Test 2 to determine whether you need a comma between adjectives.

Exercise 9 **Connect: Editing for Errors in Adjectives and Adverbs**

Connect

Edit the following paragraph, correcting all the errors in the use of adjectives and adverbs. Write your corrections above the errors. There are six errors.

When you see my new haircut, I want you to be honestly with me. Don't try to cover up the truth with tactful remarks or badly disguised lies. The haircut cost me more money then a week's groceries, so it should be more better than any other haircut I've ever had. In addition, I don't want to fool myself about my appearance. I need to know very quick whether I should cover my head with a cap for a few weeks. Of all the good friends in my life, you are my better friend, so I am relying on your judgment. Go ahead; breathe deep, and give me your opinion.

MyWritingLab™ **Chapter Test** Using Adjectives and Adverbs

Some of the following sentences have errors in the use of adjectives and adverbs. Some are correct. Write *OK* next to the correct sentences; write *X* by each incorrect sentence.

1. _____ I have had three different phone plans; the first one looked like a bargain, but it turned out to be the worst deal.

2. _____ The tutor from the student learning center was more kinder to me than any of my math instructors in high school.

3. _____ She feels bad that she can't attend the wedding next month.

4. _____ When Maya left the hospital, she looked healthy, but she wasn't feeling well.

5. _____ On his trip to Savannah, Trevor saw three old friends; one had become a real successful cartoonist.

6. _____ My sister wants to meet a young, dark, and handsome man with a good job.

7. _____ After I gave her the giant teddy bear, my daughter gave me a great big kiss.

8. _____ Driving to Providence seems to be a more better idea than spending a great deal of money on plane tickets.

Correcting Problems with Modifiers

CHAPTER 23

Quick Question MyWritingLab™

Which sentence(s) is/are correct?

A. *Melted by the heat of the sun, my nephew could not eat the chocolate bar.*

B. *My nephew could not eat the chocolate bar melted by the heat of the sun.*

(After you study this chapter, you will be confident of your answer.)

Learning Objectives

In this chapter, you will learn to:

1. Identify modifiers within sentences.
2. Recognize and correct misplaced modifiers.
3. Recognize and correct dangling modifiers.

WHAT ARE MODIFIERS?

1. Identify modifiers within sentences.

Modifiers are words, phrases, or clauses that describe (modify) something in a sentence. All the italicized words, phrases, and clauses below are modifiers.

the *blue* van (word)
the van *in the garage* (phrase)
the van *that she bought* (clause)

foreign tourists (word)
tourists *coming to Florida* (phrase)
tourists *who visit the state* (clause)

Sometimes modifiers limit another word. They make another word (or words) more specific.

> the girl *in the corner* (tells exactly which girl)
> *fifty* acres (tells exactly how many acres)
> the movie *that I liked best* (tells which movie)
> He *never* calls. (tells how often)

Exercise 1   Practice: Recognizing Modifiers

In each of the following sentences, underline the modifiers (words, phrases, or clauses) that describe the italicized word or phrase.

1. A chocolate *sundae* with sprinkles on top makes my nephew smile with pleasure.

2. Walking confidently down the red carpet, *the celebrity* waved to his fans.

3. Ava searched through the debris for family *photographs* lost in the flood.

4. Smiling at me from the back row of the classroom, *my sister* applauded my speech.

5. Daniela carries her textbooks, notebooks, and tablet in an old green backpack.

6. *The passengers* waiting at the terminal for hours began to complain loudly.

7. *The woman* selected for the top job once worked at a local bank.

8. The website with online tutorials was created by a famous professor.

CORRECTING MISPLACED MODIFIER PROBLEMS

2 Recognize and correct misplaced modifiers.

Modifiers can make your writing more specific. Used effectively and correctly, modifiers give the reader a clear, exact picture of what you want to say, and they help you to say it precisely. However, modifiers have to be used correctly. The most common type of modifier error is called a **misplaced modifier**. As you edit your sentences, you can check for misplaced modifiers by following these three steps:

INFO BOX   Three Steps to Check for Misplaced Modifiers in Your Sentences

Step 1: Find the modifier.

Step 2: Ask, "Does the modifier have something to modify?"

Step 3: Ask, "Is the modifier in the right place, as close as possible to the word, phrase, or clause it modifies?"

If you answer no in either Step 2 or Step 3, you need to revise your sentence. Let's use the steps in the following example.

sample sentence: I saw a girl driving a Mazda wearing a bikini.

Step 1: Find the modifier. The modifiers are *driving a Mazda, wearing a bikini.*

Step 2: Ask, "Does the modifier have something to modify?" The answer is yes. The girl is driving a Mazda. The girl is wearing a bikini. Both modifiers go with *a girl*.

Step 3: Ask, "Is the modifier in the right place?" The answer is yes and no. One modifier is in the right place:

I saw a *girl driving a Mazda*

The other modifier is *not* in the right place

a *Mazda wearing a bikini*

The Mazda is not wearing a bikini.

> **revised:** I saw a girl *wearing a bikini* and *driving a Mazda.*

Let's work through the steps once more:

> **sample sentence:** Scampering through the forest, the hunters saw two rabbits.

Step 1: Find the modifier. The modifiers are *scampering through the forest,* and *two.*

Step 2: Ask, "Does the modifier have something to modify?" The answer is yes. There are *two rabbits.* The *rabbits* are *scampering through the forest.*

Step 3: Ask, "Is the modifier in the right place?" The answer is yes and no. The word *two* is in the right place:

two rabbits

But *scampering through the forest* is in the wrong place:

Scampering through the forest, the hunters

The hunters are not scampering through the forest—the rabbits are.

> **revised:** The hunters saw two rabbits *scampering through the forest.*

Caution: Be sure to put words such as *almost, even, exactly, hardly, just, merely, nearly, only, scarcely,* and *simply* as close as possible to what they modify. If you put them in the wrong place, you may write a confusing sentence.

> **sample sentence:** Etienne only wants to grow carrots and zucchini. (The modifier that creates confusion here is *only.* Does Etienne have only one goal in life—to grow carrots and zucchini? Or are these the only vegetables he wants to grow? To create a clearer sentence, move the modifier.)
>
> **revised:** Etienne wants to grow *only* carrots and zucchini.

The examples you have just reviewed involve **misplaced modifiers**, words that describe something but are not where they should be in the sentence. Here is the rule to remember:

> **Put a modifier as close as possible to the word, phrase, or clause it modifies.**

| Exercise 2 | Practice: Correcting Sentences with Misplaced Modifiers |

Some of the following sentences contain misplaced modifiers. Revise any sentence that has a misplaced modifier by putting the modifier as close as possible to whatever it modifies.

1. Hanging from the ceiling, I noticed a giant spider.

   revised: _____

   _____

2. The village is well known for its giant garbage dump where I was born.

   revised: _____

   _____

3. Emma lent her handbook to a friendly classmate that she bought at the bookstore.

   revised: _____

   _____

4. Callie and Jeremy were surprised by the sudden appearance of two deer driving in the national forest.

   revised: _____

   _____

5. Painted a pale green, the old house looked new again.

   revised: _____

   _____

6. Dipped in chocolate, my aunt enjoyed the large, plump strawberries.

   revised: _____

   _____

7. Standing in line at the ticket counter, the children grew restless and bored.

   revised: _____

   _____

8. Right from the oven, Annie served the cinnamon cookies.

   revised: _____

   _____

③ Recognize and correct dangling modifiers.

CORRECTING DANGLING MODIFIERS

The three steps for correcting modifier problems can help you recognize another kind of error. Let's use the steps to check the following sentence.

sample sentence: Strolling through the tropical paradise, many colorful birds could be seen.

Step 1: Find the modifier. The modifiers are *Strolling through the tropical paradise*, and *many colorful*.

Step 2: Ask, "Does the modifier have something to modify?" The answer is yes and no. The words *many* and *colorful* modify birds. But who or what is *strolling through the tropical paradise*? There is no person mentioned in this sentence. The birds are not strolling.

This kind of error is called a **dangling modifier**. It is a modifier that does not have anything to modify; it just dangles in the sentence. To correct this kind of error, you cannot just move the modifier:

still incorrect: Many colorful birds could be seen strolling through the tropical paradise. (There is still no person strolling.)

The way to correct this kind of error is to add something to the sentence. If you gave the modifier something to modify, you might come up with several different revised sentences:

revised sentences: *As I strolled through the tropical paradise, I saw* many colorful birds.

or

Many colorful birds could be seen *when we were strolling through the tropical paradise.*

or

While the tourists strolled through the tropical paradise, they saw many colorful birds.

Try the process for correcting dangling modifiers once more:

sample sentence: Ascending in the glass elevator, the hotel lobby glittered in the light.

Step 1: Find the modifier. The modifiers are *Ascending in the glass elevator*, and *hotel*.

Step 2: Ask, "Does the modifier have anything to modify?" The answer is yes and no. The word *hotel* modifies lobby, but *ascending in the glass elevator* doesn't modify anything. Who is ascending in the elevator? There is nobody mentioned in the sentence.

To revise this sentence, put somebody or something in it for the modifier to describe:

As the guests ascended in the glass elevator, the hotel lobby glittered in the light.

or

Ascending in the glass elevator, she saw the hotel lobby glitter in the light.

Remember that you cannot correct a dangling modifier just by moving the modifier. You have to give the modifier something to modify; you have to add something to the sentence.

Exercise 3 Practice: Correcting Sentences with Dangling Modifiers

Some of the following sentences use modifiers correctly; some sentences have dangling modifiers. Revise the sentences with dangling modifiers. To revise, you will have to add words and change words.

1. When accelerating to make a green light, an accident can occur.

   revised: _____

   _____

2. While volunteering at an animal shelter on the weekends, Christopher met a beautiful woman.

   revised: _____

   _____

3. To find a house in a lower price range, looking farther from the city is necessary.

   revised: _____

   _____

4. Having trained as a paramedic in the army, Jose's skills would help him to find a job in civilian life.

   revised: _____

   _____

5. Unprepared for a hot day, people began shedding their coats and sweaters.

   revised: _____

   _____

6. Reading another of his school's requests for donations, disgust began to fill Taylor's head.

   revised: _____

   _____

7. With hard work and a positive attitude, many of the setbacks and disappointments of a new job can be handled.

   revised: _____

   _____

8. At the age of five, my brother was born, and I had some difficulty being the older brother.

   revised: _____

   _____

REVIEWING THE STEPS AND THE SOLUTIONS

It is important to recognize problems with modifiers and to correct these problems. Modifier problems can result in confusing or even silly sentences.

When you confuse or unintentionally amuse your reader, you are not making your point.

Remember to check for modifier problems in three steps and to correct each kind of problem appropriately:

> **INFO BOX** **A Summary of Modifier Problems**
>
> **Checking for Modifier Problems**
>
> **Step 1:** Find the modifier.
>
> **Step 2:** Ask, "Does the modifier have something to modify?"
>
> **Step 3:** Ask, "Is the modifier in the right place?"
>
> **Correcting Modifier Problems**
>
> If the modifier is in the wrong place (a **misplaced modifier**), put it as close as possible to the word, phrase, or clause it modifies.
>
> If the modifier has nothing to modify (a dangling modifier), add or change words so that it has something to modify.

Collaborate

Exercise 4   **Collaborate: Revising Sentences with Modifier Problems**

All of the following sentences have modifier problems. Working with a partner or group, write a new, correct sentence for each incorrect one. You may move words, add words, change words, or remove words. The first one is done for you.

1. Written in stone, the archaeologist could not understand the ancient message.

   revised: _The archaeologist could not understand the ancient message_

   written in stone.

2. Looking for a compatible mate, friends and family members may know several potential partners.

   revised: _____

   _____

3. Proudly carrying a large diploma, Belinda saw her friend emerge from the college auditorium.

   revised: _____

   _____

4. Exhausted after a long day at work, Tina only watched half an hour of television before she fell asleep.

   revised: _____

   _____

5. An angry man stormed into the police station covered in mud.

   revised: _____

   _____

6. Before buying a new home, the needs of all the family members should be considered.

    revised: _____

    _____

7. To restore the downtown plaza to its place as the center of the community, the support of all the citizens is necessary.

    revised: _____

    _____

8. Covered in fudge icing, I couldn't stop eating the brownies.

    revised: _____

    _____

Connect

Exercise 5   **Connect: Editing a Paragraph for Modifier Problems**

Correct any errors in the use of modifiers in the following paragraph. There are seven errors. Write your corrections above the line.

When two roommates and I moved into our first home, we were lucky to have my uncle checking the premises for safety hazards. First, my roommates and I would nearly have missed all the problems in the electrical system. My uncle found fire hazards in the wiring. I brought another danger into the house. Wanting to save on heating costs, an old space heater from a garage sale was brought into our new home. On its first use, the condition of the heater would have been a fire hazard. Heat became an issue in the kitchen, too. Without a fire extinguisher, there was danger in the kitchen. A pantry near the kitchen filled with stacks of old newspapers could ignite, and we would not see the fire until it spread past the pantry. My uncle also noticed cracked many windows that created security problems. Finally, my uncle explored our yard and installed bright lights at the front door. We were grateful for his careful inspection, although we had only wanted a quick survey of our home.

Chapter Test **Correcting Problems with Modifiers**

MyWritingLab™

Some of the sentences below have problems with modifiers; some are correct. Write *OK* next to the correct sentences; write *X* by each sentence containing a modifier error.

1. _____ Stuck in an endless line of traffic and late for work, nothing seemed to be going well for me on Wednesday morning.

2. _____ At the age of nineteen, a beautiful baby entered my mother's life.

3. _____ In order to make money in a small business, patience and a realistic attitude about profit and loss are necessary.

4. _____ Racing through the airport, I nearly made the last flight to Puerto Rico but arrived at the gate as the doors of the plane closed.

5. _____ When cleaning the interior of a car, a portable vacuum cleaner, a brush, and a few soft cloths can be helpful.

6. _____ Caught in a lie, Sean and Mason tried talking fast as a way to cover their dishonesty.

7. _____ Whipped by strong winds, the beach cabana did not seem a safe place for us to to take shelter in a tropical storm.

8. _____ Josue got to know several kind and friendly classmates while taking the subway to school.

MyWritingLab™ Visit Chapter 23, "Correcting Problems with Modifiers," in *MyWritingLab* to test your understanding of the chapter objectives.

CHAPTER 24

Using Verbs Correctly: Standard Verb Forms, Irregular Verbs, Consistency, and Voice

Quick Question MyWritingLab™

Which sentence(s) is/are correct?

A. *My friend and I shared a cab ride, but I pay the entire fare.*

B. *My friend and I shared a cab ride, but I paid the entire fare.*

(After you study this chapter, you will be confident of your answer.)

Learning Objectives

In this chapter, you will learn to:

1. Identify verbs.
2. Recognize errors in verb tense or consistency.
3. Distinguish between passive and active voice.

1. Identify verbs.

THE ROLE OF VERBS

Verbs are words that show some kind of action or being. The following verbs show action or being:

> He *runs* to the park.
> Melanie *is* my best friend.
> The library *opens* at 8:00 a.m.

Verbs also tell about time.

> He *will run* to the park. (The time is future.)
> Melanie *was* my best friend. (The time is past.)
> The library *opens* at 8:00 a.m. (The time is present.)

The time of a verb is called its *tense*. You can say a verb is in the *present tense*, *future tense*, or many other tenses.

Using verbs correctly involves knowing which form of the verb to use, choosing the right verb tense, and being consistent in verb tense.

THE PRESENT TENSE

Look at the standard verb forms for the present tense of the word *listen*:

> **verb:** listen

I listen	we listen
you listen	you listen
he, she, it listens	they listen

2 Recognize errors in verb tense or consistency.

Take a closer look at the verb forms. Only one form is different:

> he, she, it *listens*

This is the only form that ends in *s* in the present tense.

INFO BOX

In the present tense, use an *-s* or *-es* ending on the verb only when the subject is *he*, *she*, or *it*, or the equivalent, such as a proper name or a singular noun.

Take another look at the present tense.

> *I attend* every lecture.
> *You care* about the truth.
> *He visits* his grandfather regularly.
> *She drives* a new car.
> The new *album sounds* great.
> *We follow* that team.
> *You work* well when you both compromise.
> *They buy* the store brand of cereal.

Exercise 1 **Practice: Picking the Correct Verb in the Present Tense**

Underline the subject and circle the correct verb form in parentheses in each of the following sentences.

1. In the spring, my allergies (make, makes) me miserable.

2. This class (get, gets) more difficult every day.

3. My cousins in Puerto Rico (turn, turns) my visits into special occasions.

4. With a smile, my daughter's kindergarten teacher (welcome, welcomes) each child to class.

5. The construction workers across the street never (arrive, arrives) before 8:00 a.m.

6. Around the corner (stand, stands) an old house and a new apartment building.

7. Arriving quickly and without warning, thunderstorms (strike, strikes) the area on summer afternoons.

8. Our English class (require, requires) more writing than my math class.

Exercise 2   **Practice: Correcting the Form of the Verb in the Present Tense**

Read Eric's e-mail to his friend. You may spot several slang expressions, but just correct the verb tense errors. There are ten mistakes involving present-tense verbs.

Hey Tyler

I hope you are well. Things here is busy as usual. My weeks are filled with school and work. Every day I wakes up at 6:00 a.m. I take a shower, gets dressed, and grab a quick bite to eat before school. I catch a ride with my friend Judy. Judy and I has class together at 8:00 a.m. Sometimes Judy trys to talk me into stopping for a cup of coffee before school, but I don't like to because we be late to school. Once we get to school, we goes to English class. English class is pretty good. Our professor, Ms. Hubbard, is cool. She push us real hard to learn. After English, I have Algebra and History. They are okay. Judy go to work after English, so I usually take the bus home. At home I prepare a quick meal. After, I go to work. My job is really boring, but the people are nice. My coworker John and I laughs a lot. Sometimes after work we grab a bite to eat.

Well, look at the time! I have to go. Say hi to everyone.

Eric

THE PAST TENSE

The past tense of most verbs is formed by adding *-d* or *-ed* to the verb.

verb: listen

I listened	we listened
you listened	you listened
he, she, it listened	they listened

Add *-ed* to *listen* to form the past tense. For some other verbs, you may add *-d*.

> The sun *faded* from the sky.
> He *shouted* the answer.
> She *crumpled* the paper into a ball.

Exercise 3   **Practice: Writing the Correct Verb Forms in the Past Tense**

Write the correct past tense form of each verb in parentheses in each sentence, and underline the noun or proper noun that represents the subject of the verb.

1. You _____ (ignore) the slow leak in the basement for months.

2. Last night, Ira _____ (play) cards for two hours.

3. In sixth grade, I _____ (earn) an award for perfect attendance.

4. For many years, my father _____ (talk) about coming to America.

5. The class _____ (visit) the writing center together last Monday.

6. On Friday, someone _____ (call) me in the middle of the night.

7. After the movie, my friends _____ (invite) me to a Chinese restaurant.

8. After getting lost on the highway, we finally _____ (discover) the correct exit to the Miami airport.

THE FOUR MAIN FORMS OF A VERB: PRESENT, PAST, PRESENT PARTICIPLE, AND PAST PARTICIPLE

When you are deciding which form of a verb to use, you will probably rely on one of four forms: the present tense, the past tense, the present participle, and the past participle. Most of the time, you will use one of these forms or add a helping verb to it. As an example, look at the four main forms of the verb *listen*.

Present	**Past**	**Present Participle**	**Past Participle**
listen	listened	listening	listened

You use the four verb forms—present, past, present participle, past participle—alone or with helping verbs, to express time (tense). Forms of regular verbs like *listen* are very easy to remember. Use the present form for the present tense:

> We *listen* to the news on the radio.

The past form expresses past tense:

> I *listened* to language tapes for three hours yesterday.

The present participle, or *-ing* form, is used with helping verbs to express an action in progress or an action that was in progress at a specific time:

> He *was listening* to me.
> I *am listening* to you.
> You *should have been listening* more carefully.

The past participle is the form used with the helping verbs *have, has,* or *had* to express actions that began in the past and have continued to now, show a connection to the past, or were completed at an unspecified time in the past:

> I *have listened* for hours.
> She *has listened* to the tape.
> We *had listened* to the tape before we bought it.

Of course, you can add helping verbs (or modals) to the present tense:

present tense:
We *listen* to the news on the car radio.

add helping verbs:
We *will* listen to the news on the car radio.
We *should* listen to the news on the car radio.
We *can* listen to the news on the car radio.

When a verb is regular, the past form is created by adding *-d* or *-ed* to the present form. The present participle is formed by adding *-ing* to the present form, and the past participle form is the same as the past form.

IRREGULAR VERBS

Irregular verbs do not follow the same rules for creating verb forms that regular verbs do. Three verbs that we use all the time—*be, have, do*—are irregular verbs. You need to study them closely. Look at the present tense forms for all three:

verb: be	**verb:** have	**verb:** do
I am	I have	I do
you are	you have	you do
he, she, it is	he, she, it has	he, she, it does
we are	we have	we do
you are	you have	you do
they are	they have	they do

> **Caution:** Be careful when you add *not* to *does*. If you are writing a contraction of *does not*, be sure you write *doesn't*, not *don't*.

not this: ~~The light don't work.~~
but this: The light doesn't work.

> **Exercise 4   Practice: Choosing the Correct Form of *Be, Have,* or *Do* in the Present Tense**

Circle the correct form of the verb in parentheses in each sentence.

1. If you (has, have) a free afternoon, you can spend some time with Karen and her children.

2. These directions (be, are) very clear.

3. The blue paint (has, have) the right tint of green to match your turquoise chairs.

4. Alicia won't come to the party because she (doesn't, don't) care about her old friends.

5. Dogs can be wonderful pets, but they (has, have) to be treated humanely.

6. Before I socialize with a stranger, I (do, does) a little investigating into his or her background.

7. Although she is very busy, she (do, does) take her time with her assignments.

8. Caroline (has, have) dreams of moving to Massachusetts.

The Past Tense of *Be, Have, Do*

Irregular past forms can be confusing because they often do not follow the same pattern as present forms. Take a look at the forms below:

verb: be	**verb:** have	**verb:** do
I was	I had	I did
you were	you had	you did
he, she, it was	he, she, it had	he, she, it did
we were	we had	we did
you were	you had	you did
they were	they had	they did

Exercise 5   **Practice: Choosing the Correct Form of *Be, Have*, or *Do* in the Past Tense**

Circle the correct verb form in parentheses in each sentence below and underline the subject of each sentence.

1. Years ago, my family (have, had) pizza for dinner once a week.

2. I do not feel guilty about ignoring Todd's calls because he (done, did) nothing but argue with me for two days.

3. Yesterday, Shakira (had, have) to pay for a new smartphone.

4. After our senior year, Jamie Perez and I (was, were) best friends for a while.

5. Last Wednesday, several members of the local crime watch group (had, have) a meeting with residents in the Birch Glen area.

6. When I saw the grade on my psychology test, I (was, were) too surprised to say anything.

7. My sister bought the plants for a garden, but my brother-in-law (done, did) the planting, watering, clipping, and fertilizing.

8. The new library and student center (was, were) once vacant buildings.

More Irregular Verb Forms

Be, have, and *do* are not the only verbs with irregular forms. There are many such verbs, and everybody who writes uses some form of an irregular verb. When you write and are not certain if you are using the correct form of a verb, review the list of irregular verbs on the next page.

For each irregular verb listed below, the *present*, the *past*, and the *past participle* forms are given. The present participle isn't included because it is always formed by adding *-ing* to the present form.

Irregular Verb Forms

Present	Past	Past Participle
(Today I *arise*.)	(Yesterday I *arose*.)	(I have/had *arisen*.)
arise	arose	arisen
awake	awoke, awaked	awoken, awaked
bear	bore	born, borne
beat	beat	beaten
become	became	become
begin	began	begun
bend	bent	bent
bite	bit	bitten
bleed	bled	bled
blow	blew	blown
break	broke	broken
bring	brought	brought
build	built	built
burst	burst	burst
buy	bought	bought
catch	caught	caught
choose	chose	chosen
cling	clung	clung
come	came	come
cost	cost	cost
creep	crept	crept
cut	cut	cut
deal	dealt	dealt
draw	drew	drawn
dream	dreamed, dreamt	dreamed, dreamt
drink	drank	drunk
drive	drove	driven
eat	ate	eaten
fall	fell	fallen
feed	fed	fed
feel	felt	felt
fight	fought	fought
find	found	found
fling	flung	flung
fly	flew	flown
freeze	froze	frozen
get	got	got, gotten
give	gave	given
go	went	gone
grow	grew	grown
hear	heard	heard
hide	hid	hidden
hit	hit	hit
hold	held	held
hurt	hurt	hurt

Present	Past	Past Participle
keep	kept	kept
know	knew	known
lay (means to put)	laid	laid
lead	led	led
leave	left	left
lend	lent	lent
let	let	let
lie (means to recline)	lay	lain
light	lit, lighted	lit, lighted
lose	lost	lost
make	made	made
mean	meant	meant
meet	met	met
pay	paid	paid
ride	rode	ridden
ring	rang	rung
rise	rose	risen
run	ran	run
say	said	said
see	saw	seen
sell	sold	sold
send	sent	sent
sew	sewed	sewn, sewed
shake	shook	shaken
shine	shone, shined	shone, shined
shrink	shrank	shrunk
shut	shut	shut
sing	sang	sung
sit	sat	sat
sleep	slept	slept
slide	slid	slid
sling	slung	slung
speak	spoke	spoken
spend	spent	spent
stand	stood	stood
steal	stole	stolen
stick	stuck	stuck
sting	stung	stung
stink	stank, stunk	stunk
string	strung	strung
swear	swore	sworn
swim	swam	swum
teach	taught	taught
tear	tore	torn
tell	told	told
think	thought	thought
throw	threw	thrown
wake	woke, waked	woken, waked
wear	wore	worn
win	won	won
write	wrote	written

Exercise 6 **Practice: Choosing the Correct Form of Irregular Verbs**

Write the correct form of the verb in parentheses in each sentence below.
Be sure to check the list of irregular verbs.

1. You have never _____ (swim) in a pool like this one.

2. She wore a necklace of glass beads _____ (string) on a silver chain.

3. Once Leila picked a major, she _____ (feel) more focused and motivated in college.

4. Marie Elena has _____ (swear) to lose weight so that she can fit into her favorite jeans.

5. I _____ (lend) my pencil and calculator to her yesterday.

6. My mother _____ (wear) the same old coat for years.

7. The police found a warehouse full of electronic goods that the thieves had _____ (steal).

8. We are all very tired. His car alarm has _____ (ring) every morning.

Collaborate

Exercise 7 **Collaborate: Writing Sentences with Correct Verb Forms**

With a partner or a group, write two sentences that correctly use each of the following verb forms. In writing these sentences, you may add helping verbs to the verb forms, but do not change the verb form itself. The first one is done for you.

1. sent

   a. He sent her a dozen roses on Valentine's Day.

   b. I have sent him all the information he needs.

2. lie (means to recline)

   a. _____

   b. _____

   _____

3. shrank

   a. _____

   b. _____

4. meant

   a. _____

   b. _____

5. paid

   a. _____

   b. _____

6. lain

a. _____

b. _____

7. shined

a. _____

b. _____

8. seen

a. _____

b. _____

Connect

Exercise 8   **Connect: Editing a Paragraph for Correct Verb Forms**

Correct the errors in verb forms in the following paragraph. There are six errors.

My father should stop nagging me about my future. I has been in college for only a few weeks, and since my first day of class, he has been a nuisance. Last spring, he were thrilled when I received a grant and some other financial aid, and he burst with pride when I registered for my first semester. However, lately he has chose to lay a million questions on me whenever he sees me. For instance, he constantly asks me about my choice of a college major. Since I have not yet decided, I try to explain to him that at this time I do not need to select a major. He never lets me gets to the second part of my explanation when I patiently tell him that my current courses are useful and required for any major. Instead, he interrupts me and recites a list of possible careers for me. The list include everything from brain surgeon to accountant. I have grown to ignore his lists and simply remain silent. However, his constant quizzing has begun to wear me down. I know he means well, but his pressure don't help me to succeed in college.

Section Test   **Using Verbs Correctly**

Some of the sentences below use verbs correctly; others do not. Put an *X* by each sentence with an error in using verbs correctly.

1. _____   We swum in the pool until sunset, when the water became too cold.

2. _____   My mother sewed like a professional but never teached me how to do anything as simple as threading a needle.

3. _____ She hasn't spoken to her lab partner since he blew up their science project.

4. _____ Yesterday morning I lay on the couch so I could rest my eyes until my headache medicine began to work.

5. _____ Chelsea will do well in her new position at the bank as long as she don't become impatient with rude customers.

6. _____ A social worker visited my uncle when he was in the hospital, but she done nothing about arranging home healthcare for him.

7. _____ Daniel and Lucy have chose to have a small wedding and have found a perfect place for the ceremony.

8. _____ During our class project, our group grew closer together.

Remember that your choice of verb form indicates the time (tense) of your statements. Be careful not to shift from one tense to another unless you have a reason to change the time.

CONSISTENT VERB TENSES

Tenses represent a time frame. It is important to keep the same time frame (unless you are making comparisons between two time frames). This is called **consistency of verb tense**.

incorrect shifts in tense:
The waitress *ran* to the kitchen with the order in her hand, *raced* back with glasses of water for her customers, and *smiles* calmly. He *grins* at me from the ticket booth and *closed* the ticket window.

You can correct these errors by putting all the verbs in the same tense.

consistent present tense:
The waitress *runs* to the kitchen with the order in her hand, *races* back with glasses of water for her customers, and *smiles* calmly. He *grins* at me from the ticket booth and *closes* the ticket window.

consistent past tense:
The waitress *ran* to the kitchen with the order in her hand, *raced* back with glasses of water for her customers, and *smiled* calmly. He *grinned* at me from the ticket booth and *closed* the ticket window.

Whether you correct the errors by changing all the verbs to the present tense or by changing them to the past tense, you are making the tenses consistent. Consistency of tense is important in the events you are describing because it helps the reader understand what happened and when it happened.

Exercise 9 **Practice: Correcting Sentences That Are Inconsistent in Tense**

In each sentence following, one verb is inconsistent in tense. Cross it out and write the verb in the correct tense above the space.

1. My brother asked me to dinner, picked a fancy restaurant, and then leaves me with the entire bill.

2. Tanisha takes evening classes because they don't interfere with her work schedule, require attendance only once a week, attracted serious students, and offer a highly concentrated version of the course content.

3. As soon as Rick saved enough money, he packed up his car, drove across the country, and gets a job near a ski resort.

4. Because a new version of a popular phone was about to be introduced, people line up outside the local phone store and camped out overnight.

5. After Charlyce received her exam score, she slammed her book on the table and storms out of the classroom.

6. Yesterday, my boss didn't show up at the office; at the same time, major problems occur in the phone system, and no one knew how to handle the emergency.

7. Sometimes Matthew is good-natured and open, but occasionally he worries about minor problems, lost his temper, and hurts his closest friends.

8. At the courthouse, the police department made plans for the highly publicized trial; it increased the number of security guards, made room for members of the media to file reports, and blocks many entrances to the building.

Exercise 10 Connect: Editing a Paragraph for Consistency of Tenses

Connect

Read the following paragraph. Then cross out any verbs that are inconsistent in tense and write the corrections above. There are six errors.

My best friend Ryan tried college years ago but gave up after one wasted semester. He had no real purpose in going to college. He was a recent high school graduate and starts college because all his friends were going. Ryan has no idea of the demands of higher education. He took advantage of the freedom of college, skipped classes, avoids completing assignments, and relied on taking makeup

tests instead of keeping up with the class. Ryan never thinks about the outcome.

He just floated through the semester until he starts drowning. Unfortunately, he

fails all his courses and dropped out of college. He swore that college was not

right for him, but he was sad and a little defensive.

> **Exercise 11** **Collaborate: Writing a Paragraph with Consistent Verb Tenses**

The following paragraph has many inconsistencies in verb tenses; it shifts
between past and present tenses. Working with a group, write two versions
of the paragraph: *write it once in the present tense, then a second time in
the past tense*. Divide your activity; half the group can write it in one tense
while the other half can write it in the other tense.

After both rewrites are complete, read the new paragraphs aloud to
both parts of the team as a final check.

> My best friend took me for a ride in the country and tells me some bad
> news. He says that in two weeks he was moving to another state. This news is
> very sudden and shocks me to my core. My friend is more than a friend; he was
> a brother, a partner in pranks, a teammate in games, and a keeper of secrets.
> After he told me, we walk in the woods together. We find it hard to say much
> because we each knew what the other is feeling. After what seems like hours,
> he stops walking and faces me. He says the move wasn't what he wanted, but
> he added that his family needs him. I see sadness in his eyes, and I knew he
> saw the sorrow in mine.

Paragraph Revised for Consistent Tenses:

_____

_____

_____

_____

_____

_____

_____

_____

_____

_____

_____

_____

_____

_____

THE PRESENT PERFECT TENSE

When you are choosing the right verb tense, you should know about two verb tenses, the present perfect and the past perfect, that can make your meaning clear.

The **present perfect tense** is made up of the past participle form of the verb plus *have* or *has* as a helping verb. Use this tense to show an action that started in the past but is still going on in the present, or to state an action that was completed at an unspecified time in the past.

> **past tense:** My father *drove* a truck for five months. (He doesn't drive a truck anymore, but he did drive one in the past.)
>
> **present perfect tense:** My father *has driven* a truck for five months. (He started driving a truck five months ago; he is still driving a truck.)
>
> **past tense:** For years, I *studied* ballet. (I don't study ballet now; I used to.)
>
> **present perfect tense:** For years, I *have studied* ballet. (I still study ballet.)
>
> **past tense:** I *went* to Miami Beach last year for spring break. (I am not in Miami now.)
>
> **present perfect tense:** I *have been* to Miami. I *loved* it! (I am not there now, but you don't know when I was there.)

Remember, use the present perfect tense to show that an action started in the past and is still going on.

Exercise 12 Practice: Distinguishing Between the Past Tense and the Present Perfect Tense

Circle the correct verb in parentheses in each sentence below. Be sure to look carefully at the meaning of the sentences.

1. Janet (sent, has sent) me a text message every morning for months now.

2. After heavy rain hit the area, the brakes on my car (felt, have felt) less efficient.

3. We (studied, have studied) the differences between the past and the present perfect for three days now.

4. Martina has a lot of life experience; she (traveled, has traveled) to eight different countries.

5. One of the instructors in the business department at the college (was, has been) a well-known banker but now teaches classes in finance.

6. My four-year-old son (was, has been) clinging to my leg for five minutes and is still begging me for ice cream.

7. Yesterday I finally confronted my roommate and (demanded, have demanded) an explanation for the unpaid light bill.

8. The academic advising office (moved, has moved) to the Student Center.

THE PAST PERFECT TENSE

The **past perfect tense** is made up of the past participle form of the verb and *had* as a helping verb. You can use the past perfect tense to show more than one event in the past—that is, when two or more things happened in the past but at different times.

> **past tense:** He *washed* the dishes.
> **past perfect tense:** He *had washed* the dishes by the time I came home. (He washed the dishes *before* I came home. Both actions happened in the past, but one happened earlier than the other.)

> **past tense:** Susan *waited* for an hour.
> **past perfect tense:** Susan *had waited* for an hour when she gave up on him. (Waiting came first; giving up came second. Both actions are in the past.)

The past perfect tense is especially useful because you write most of your essays in the past tense, and you often need to get further back into the past. Remember, to form the past perfect tense, use *had* with the past participle of the verb.

Exercise 13 Practice: Distinguishing Between the Past Tense and the Past Perfect Tense

Circle the correct verb in parentheses in each sentence below. Be sure to look carefully at the meaning of the sentences.

1. Most of the audience (guessed, had guessed) the ending to the mystery before the movie was half finished.

2. Melissa was not sure whether Jerry (tried, had tried) to call her earlier that morning.

3. On Mother's Day, my daughter (surprised, had surprised) me with a necklace she had made at her preschool arts and crafts class.

4. By the time Nelson remembered the soup, it (boiled, had boiled) over on the stove.

5. As Brianna brushed her hair, she (studied, had studied) her face in the mirror.

6. Jacob looked at the exam questions and wondered if he (read, had read) the right chapters in his textbook.

7. The defense attorney examined the transcripts of the trial that (took, had taken) place two years earlier.

8. On Sunday morning, I took part in a charity walk-a-thon because my sister (was, had been) nagging me about it for weeks.

Exercise 14 Practice: Using the Past Perfect

Complete each sentence with what happened before the first action.

1. Before I wrote my essay, _____

2. When the power went out, _____

3. Before I completed the homework assignment, _____

4. By the time the professor arrived, _____

5. Before Apple products were very popular, _____

6. By the time the movie was over, _____

7. Before they finished the game, _____

8. Before Bill and Emma went to the library, _____

9. By the time all the students go to class, _____

10. When I got to work, _____

PASSIVE AND ACTIVE VOICE

3 Distinguish between passive and active voice.

Verbs not only have tenses, but they also have voices. When the subject in the sentence is doing something, the verb is in the **active voice**. When something is done to the subject—when it receives the action of the verb—the verb is in the **passive voice**.

> **active voice:**
> I painted the house. (*I*, the subject, did it.)
> The people on the corner made a donation to the emergency fund.
>   (The *people*, the subject, did it.)
>
> **passive voice:**
> The house was painted by me. (The *house*, the subject, didn't do anything. It received the action—it was painted.)
> A donation to the emergency fund was made by the people on the corner. (The *donation*, the subject, didn't do anything. It received the action—it was given.)

Notice what happens when you use the passive voice instead of the active:

> **active voice:**
> I painted the house.
>
> **passive voice:**
> The house was painted by me.

The sentence in the passive voice is two words longer than the one in the active voice. Yet the sentence that uses the passive voice does not say anything different, and it does not say it more clearly than the one in the active voice.

Using the passive voice can make your sentences wordy, it can slow them down, and it can make them boring. The passive voice can also confuse readers. When the subject of the sentence is not doing anything, readers may have to look carefully to see who or what *is* doing something. Look at this sentence, for example:

> A decision to fire you was reached.

Who decided to fire you? In this sentence, it is hard to find the answer to that question.

Of course, there will be times when you have to use the passive voice. For example, you may have to use it when you do not know who did something, as in these sentences:

> Our house was broken into last night.
> A leather jacket was left behind in the classroom.

But in general, you should avoid using the passive voice and rewrite sentences so they are in the active voice.

> **Exercise 15** **Practice: Rewriting Sentences, Changing the Passive Voice to the Active Voice**

In the following sentences, change the passive voice to the active voice. If the original sentence does not tell you who or what performed the action, add words that tell who or what did it. An example is done for you.

example: Sandy Adams was appointed chief negotiator last night.

rewritten: *The union leaders appointed Sandy Adams chief negotiator last*

night.

1. A twenty-two-year-old man from Idaho has been arrested and charged with the kidnapping of Kelly Romano.

   rewritten: _____

   _____

2. Questions are being asked about the missing funds at the health center.

   rewritten: _____

   _____

3. The true story of his mother's death was never told to Arthur.

   rewritten: _____

   _____

4. Several paintings were donated to the museum by a wealthy woman.

   rewritten: _____

   _____

5. Once a month, the kindergarten class is entertained by a professional storyteller.

   rewritten: _____

   _____

6. Just before takeoff, an airline safety demonstration was conducted by a flight attendant.

   rewritten: _____

   _____

7. Due to the rising costs of energy, a slight increase in your cable bill has been instituted.

   rewritten: _____

   _____

8. Finally, the ringing phone was answered by the man behind the counter.

rewritten: _____

_____

Avoiding Unnecessary Shifts in Voice

Just as you should be consistent in the tense of verbs, you should be consistent in the voice of verbs. Do not shift from active voice to passive voice, or vice versa, without some good reason to do so.

>   **active**   **passive**
> **shift:** *I designed* the decorations for the dance; *they were put up* by Chuck.

>   **active**   **active**
> **rewritten:** *I designed* the decorations for the dance; *Chuck put* them *up*.

>   **passive**   **active**
> **shift:** Many *problems were discussed* by the council members, but *they found* no easy answers.

>   **active**   **active**
> **rewritten:** The council *members discussed* many problems, but *they found* no easy answers.

Being consistent in voice can help you to write clearly and smoothly.

Exercise 16   **Practice: Rewriting Sentences to Correct Shifts in Voice**

Rewrite the sentences below so that all the verbs are in the active voice. You may change the wording to make the sentences clear, smooth, and consistent in voice.

1. I enjoyed the party until red wine was spilled all over my silk shirt.

rewritten: _____

_____

2. If a window was broken by my son, I never knew about the incident.

rewritten: _____

_____

3. Esther screamed with rage when she was called a liar.

rewritten: _____

_____

4. My uncle used to be a pilot; airplanes and airports are loved by him.

rewritten: _____

_____

5. Today a humble fisherman was honored by the city council; the fisherman had risked his life to save a drowning woman.

    rewritten: _____

    _____

6. The local roads were packed by frustrated drivers when flash floods closed two major highways.

    rewritten: _____

    _____

7. Because Paul is my old friend, he can be trusted by me.

    rewritten: _____

    _____

8. The schedule of summer classes is being posted online today; the college will also distribute paper copies of the schedule throughout the campus.

    rewritten: _____

    _____

A Few Tips About Verbs

There are a few errors that people tend to make with verbs. If you are aware of these errors, you'll be on the lookout for them as you edit your writing.

Used to: Be careful when you write that someone *used to* do, say, or feel something. It is incorrect to write *use to.*

> **not this:** Janine ~~use to~~ visit her mother every week.
> They ~~use to~~ like Thai food.
> **but this:** Janine *used to* visit her mother every week.
> They *used to* like Thai food.

Could Have, Should Have, Would Have: Using *of* instead of *have* is another error with verbs.

> **not this:** I ~~could of~~ done better on the test.
> **but this:** I *could have* done better on the test.

> **not this:** He ~~should of~~ been paying attention.
> **but this:** He *should have* been paying attention.

> **not this:** The girls ~~would of~~ liked to visit Washington.
> **but this:** The girls *would have* liked to visit Washington.

Would Have/Had: If you are writing about something that might have been possible, but that did not happen, use *had* as the helping verb.

> **not this:** If I ~~would have~~ taken a foreign language in high school, I wouldn't have to take one now.
> **but this:** If I *had* taken a foreign language in high school, I wouldn't have to take one now.

> **not this:** I wish they ~~would have~~ won the game.
> **but this:** I wish they *had* won the game.

not this: If she ~~would have~~ been smart, she would have called a plumber.

but this: If she *had* been smart, she would have called a plumber.

Collaborate

Exercise 17 **Collaborate: Writing Sentences with the Correct Verb Forms**

Do this exercise with a partner or a group. Follow the directions to write or complete each sentence below.

1. Complete this sentence and add a verb in the correct tense: My instructor explained the process before

_____

_____

2. Write a sentence that is more than eight words long and that uses the words *would have been happier* in the middle of the sentence.

_____

_____

3. Write a sentence that uses the past tense form of these words: *act* and *lose*.

_____

_____

4. Write a sentence in the passive voice.

_____

_____

5. Write a sentence in the active voice.

_____

_____

6. Write a sentence that uses *would have* and *had*.

_____

_____

7. Write a sentence that is more than six words long and that uses the words *had decided* and *before*.

_____

_____

8. Write a sentence of more than six words that uses the words *used to*.

_____

_____

Connect

Exercise 18   Connect: Editing a Paragraph for Errors in Verbs: Consistency, Tense, and Voice

Edit the following paragraph for errors in verb consistency, tense, or voice. There are six errors.

My great aunt Emma Paluska has a pretty glass bowl that is a piece of family history. The bowl comes from Poland. Only one factory near Warsaw made this type of bowl, and during World War II, the Nazis bombed the factory. The bowl has been in the family for years. If my Aunt Emma's mother would not have brought the bowl to America in 1937, it could of been destroyed by the bombing near the Paluska home. Generations of Paluskas have cherished this bowl. I remember the bowl from the big Saturday night dinners of years ago. We use to eat the contents of the bowl, fruits and nuts, for dessert. Today the bowl is displayed by my great aunt on special occasions. She fills it with glittery pine cones in the winter; in spring, flowers are put in the bowl. I hope that one day, the bowl will be passed on to me by my great aunt.

Section Test **Verbs: Consistency and Voice**

Some of the sentences below are correct; others have errors in verb consistency, correct tense, and voice. Put an *X* next to the sentences with errors.

1. _____   If I had checked the oil in my car, I would have been spared hundreds of dollars in car repairs and the misery of begging rides from family members.

2. _____   Hope for a better life came to the peasants of France and Spain when a treaty between the warring nations was signed.

3. _____   After the noise of the trucks at the dump site stopped, the workers can hear the thunder approaching from the western part of the woods.

4. _____   Amanda worked at the preschool for two years; then she left for a position at Memorial Hospital where she had enjoyed her interactions with the physical therapy patients.

5. _____   My sister had been nagging me about my hair until I finally agreed to get it cut before her wedding.

6. _____   Two of my cats ate a special treat of leftover turkey but had refused a small portion of sweet potatoes.

7. _____   I had finished my homework after I had spent two hours procrastinating and playing games on my computer.

8. _____   My vacation in South Carolina was terrible; for three days, I have done nothing but sweat and swat buzzing mosquitoes away from every part of my body.

Chapter Test **Using Verbs Correctly: Standard Verb Forms, Irregular**   MyWritingLab™
Verbs, Consistency, and Voice

Some of the sentences below use verbs correctly; other have errors in standard verb forms, irregular verbs, consistency, and voice. Write *OK* next to the correct sentences; write *X* by each incorrect sentence.

1. _____ My grandparents are wonderful; every weekend, they takes me out to dinner at my favorite diner.

2. _____ The air conditioner in my bedroom is working, but it do make a strange noise every time I turn it on.

3. _____ Nathan is my oldest friend; therefore, he should be introduced by me at the sports banquet.

4. _____ If I had known about the surprise party, I would have dressed better and washed my hair.

5. _____ For five months, Marcy has worked as a receptionist at a dentist's office; unfortunately, the dentist plans to close his office next month.

6. _____ Olivia stared at her reflection in the mirror and wondered whether she had chosen the right haircut.

7. _____ By the time Caleb was in his early twenties, his tendency to borrow money and never repay it had caused his brother and sister to avoid Caleb's desperate calls and woeful stories.

8. _____ I will ask my sister-in-law to take care of my dog over the weekend; she have done this chore for me before.

CHAPTER **25**

Making Subjects and Verbs Agree

Quick Question MyWritingLab™

Which sentence(s) is/are correct?

A. *Everybody in the office needs a raise.*

B. *Either the manager or the owners need to find the money.*

(After you study this chapter, you will feel confident of your answer.)

Learning Objectives

In this chapter, you will learn to:

1. Identify correct subject–verb agreement.
2. Recognize prepositional phrases.
3. Identify compound subjects, indefinite pronouns, and collective nouns.

474

SUBJECTS AND VERBS: SINGULAR VS. PLURAL

Subjects and verbs have to agree in number. That means a singular subject must be matched to a singular verb form; a plural subject must be matched to a plural verb form.

singular subject, singular verb:
My *sister walks* to work every morning.

plural subject, plural verb:
Mary, David, and *Sam believe* in ghosts.

singular subject, singular verb:
Linguistics is the study of languages.

plural subject, plural verb:
The committee *members are* in the meeting room.

① Identify correct subject–verb agreement.

Caution: Remember that a regular verb has an *-s* ending in only one singular form in the present tense—the form that goes with *he, she, it,* or their equivalents:

He *makes* me feel confident.
She *appreciates* intelligent conversation.
It *seems* like a good buy.
Bo *runs* every day.
That girl *swims* well.
The machine *breaks* down too often.

Exercise 1   **Practice: Subject–Verb Agreement: Selecting the Correct Verb Form**

Circle the correct form of the verb in each sentence.

1. My nephew (is, are) a natural athlete with a great future.

2. The camera sometimes (give, gives) a false impression of the size of a room.

3. My classmates, John and Eric, rarely (go, goes) to the tutoring center.

4. That watch (cost, costs) more than you can afford.

5. By 10:00 p.m., the bar (smell, smells) like spilled beer.

6. People in the middle of a crisis may become startled when a phone (ring, rings).

7. Reviewing the same chapter as last week (seem, seems) redundant.

8. Constantly blaming others (appear, appears) to be John's way of avoiding responsibility.

Connect

| Exercise 2 | **Connect: Correcting Errors in Subject–Verb Agreement in a Paragraph** |

There are errors in subject–verb agreement in the paragraph below. If a verb does not agree with its subject, change the verb form. Cross out the incorrect verb form and write the correct one above. There are seven agreement errors in agreement in the paragraph.

Malcolm always bring a present when he visits his mother. He does not have much money but manage to find an appropriate gift every time. Sometimes he arrives with a bunch of flowers or some fresh fruit from a nearby fruit stand. His mother love his thoughtfulness; it make her feel valued. Occasionally, she scolds him for spending money on her. In addition, when he arrives with a small box of chocolates, she say, "Malcolm, you are tempting me to get fat." However, he know his mother too well to believe her complaints. She actually looks forward to his small surprises. Besides, he, too, like to eat a little of the fruit or chocolate.

PRONOUNS AS SUBJECTS

Pronouns can be used as subjects. Pronouns are words that take the place of nouns. When pronouns are used as subjects, they must agree in number with verbs.

Here is a list of the subject pronouns and the regular verb forms that agree with them, in the present tense:

> **INFO BOX**   **Subjective Pronouns and a Present Tense Verb**
>
> | pronoun | verb | |
> |---------|------|--|
> | I | listen | |
> | you | listen | all singular forms |
> | he, she, it | listens | |
> | we | listen | |
> | you | listen | all plural forms |
> | they | listen | |

In all the sentences below, the pronoun used as the subject of the sentence agrees in number with the verb:

singular pronoun, singular verb:
I make the best omelet in town.

singular pronoun, singular verb:
You read very well.

singular pronoun, singular verb:
She performs like a trained athlete.

plural pronoun, plural verb:
We need a new refrigerator.

plural pronoun, plural verb:
They understand the situation.

SPECIAL PROBLEMS WITH AGREEMENT

Agreement seems fairly simple: If a subject is singular, you use a singular verb form, and if a subject is plural, you use a plural verb form. However, there are special problems with agreement that will come up in your writing. Sometimes, it is hard to find the subject of a sentence; at other times, it is hard to determine if a subject is singular or plural.

Finding the Subject

When you are checking for subject–verb agreement, you can find the real subject of the sentence by first eliminating the prepositional phrases. To find the real subject, put parentheses around the prepositional phrases. Then it is easy to find the subject because nothing in a prepositional phrase is the subject of a sentence.

2 Recognize prepositional phrases.

prepositional phrases in parentheses:

S   V
One (of my oldest friends) *is* a social worker.

S   V
A *student* (from one)(of the nearby school districts) *is* the winner.

S   V
The *store* (across the street) (from my house) *is* open all night.

S   V
Jim, (with all his silly jokes), *is* a nice person.

> **Note:** Words and phrases such as *along with, as well as, except, in addition to, including, plus,* and *together with* introduce prepositional phrases. The words that follow them are part of the prepositional phrase and cannot be part of the subject.

S   V   V
My *sister*, (along with her husband), *is planning* a trip to Bolivia.

S   V
Tom's *house*, (as well as his apartment), *is* part of a family inheritance.

| Exercise 3 | **Practice: Finding the Real Subject by Recognizing Prepositional Phrases** |

Put parentheses around all the prepositional phrases in the sentences below. Put an *S* above each subject and a *V* above each verb.

1. Jealousy, in addition to lack of trust, threatens the stability

   of a marriage.

2. Cristina, plus her mother-in-law, is visiting Venezuela over the summer.

3. Without much thought, the student asked the instructor a question about the test.

4. In the early morning, a tall man with a Great Dane jogs through the park.

5. The truth behind the actors' brawl at the nightclub is a simple story of too much alcohol.

6. Yogurt, as well as low-fat cheese, is a good source of calcium in any diet.

7. My best friend from high school arrived a day early for the reunion.

8. Two of my classes during the day are canceled today for weather.

Exercise 4 **Practice: Selecting the Correct Verb Form by Identifying Prepositional Phrases**

Put parentheses around all the prepositional phrases in the sentences below. Then circle the verb that agrees with the subject.

1. A motel with clean rooms, a small pool, and free breakfast (is, are) at the exit to Masonville.

2. Mr. Kelly's patience, in addition to his years of experience, (explain, explains) his popularity with students.

3. Gossiping about friends (is, are) a clear sign of a deficiency in loyalty.

4. One of the most handsome men in town (is, are) my best friend, Tyler.

5. Under suspicion of murder, the young man, together with his fiancée, (was, were) the subject of a police search.

6. The house with the blue shutters (has, have) been sold to a family from Missouri.

7. Tennis players at summer tournaments often (compete, competes)

in dangerously hot weather.

8. One of the judges on the daytime television shows (go, goes) into

a fit of anger during every episode.

Changed Word Order

You are probably used to looking for the subject of a sentence in front of the verb, but not all sentences follow this pattern. Questions, sentences beginning with words like *here* or *there*, and other sentences change the word order. So you have to look carefully to check for subject–verb agreement.

>   V   S
> Where *are* my *friends?*
>
>   V S V
> When *is he going* to work?
>
>   V   S
> Behind the Adams Student Center *is* a *memorial* for fallen soldiers.
>
>   V   S
> There *are potholes* in the road.
>
>   V   S
> There *is* a *reason* for his impatience.

Exercise 5 Practice: Making Subjects and Verbs Agree in Sentences with Changed Word Order

In each of the sentences below, underline the subject; then circle the correct verb in parentheses.

1. Besides Scott's bad temper, there (is, are) his cruel and violent tendencies.

2. Across the courtyard in the Student Center (is, are) an area with concrete benches and tables.

3. Beneath the layers of dirt and grime (was, were) a beautiful marble bathtub in pale beige stone.

4. About an hour after dark, there (was, were) an ambulance with flashing lights and a police car in front of the house across the street.

5. Stuck in the small space between the refrigerator and the cabinet (was, were) the lost Super Bowl tickets.

6. On the walls of the waiting room at the dentist's office (was, were) a large collection of posters about dental hygiene.

7. Inside the flea market (is, are) an endless row of stalls with all kinds of merchandise from tee-shirts to ten-foot artificial plants.

8. After a few awkward moments, there (was, were) smiles and laughter among the guests at the singles-only party.

3 Identify compound subjects, indefinite pronouns, and collective nouns.

COMPOUND SUBJECTS

A **compound subject** is two or more subjects joined by *and, or,* or *nor.*

When subjects are joined by *and,* they are usually plural.

      S   S   V
Jermaine and *Lisa are* bargain hunters.

      S   S   V
My *tablet* and *smartphone need* updating.

      S   S   V
A *bakery* and a *pharmacy are* down the street.

Caution: Be careful to check for a compound subject when the word order changes.

        V   S   S
There *are* a *bakery* and a *pharmacy* down the street. (Two things, a *bakery* and a *pharmacy, are* down the street.)

       V   S   S
Here *are* a *picture* of your father and a *copy* of his birth certificate. (A *picture* and a *copy,* two things, *are* here.)

When subjects are joined by *or, either . . . or, neither . . . nor, not only . . . but also,* the verb form agrees with the subject closer to the verb.

                         singular S   plural S, plural V
Not only the restaurant *manager* but also the *waiters were* pleased with the new policy.

                   plural S   singular S, singular V
Not only the *waiters* but also the restaurant *manager was* pleased with the new policy.

               plural S   singular S, singular V
Either the *instructors* or the *director makes* the tutoring schedule.

               singular S   plural S, plural V
Either the *director* or the *instructors make* the tutoring schedule.

              plural S   singular S, singular V
Neither the *tenants* nor the *landlord cares* about the parking situation.

              singular S   plural S, plural V
Neither the *landlord* nor the *tenants care* about the parking situation.

Exercise 6 **Practice: Making Subjects and Verbs Agree: Compound Subjects**

Circle the correct form of the verb in parentheses in each sentence below.

1. Either the woman in the upstairs apartment or the men across the street (is, are) leaving garbage in the street.

2. Not only the fried chicken but also the vegetables (taste, tastes) homemade.

3. Neither the slipcovers on the sofa nor the huge pillow on the chair (hide, hides) the decrepit condition of the furniture.

4. Here (is, are) the baby's formula and his blanket.

5. There (was, were) a problem with the oil in my car and with a strange grinding sound in the engine.

6. After dinner, either my mother or my brother (clear, clears) the table while I do the dishes.

7. Anger and bitterness never (solve, solves) a problem.

8. Neither the textbook nor the handout (helps, help) me understand this new concept.

INDEFINITE PRONOUNS

Certain pronouns that come from a group called **indefinite pronouns** always take a singular verb:

INFO BOX Indefinite Pronouns

one	nobody	nothing	each
anyone	anybody	anything	either
someone	somebody	something	neither
everyone	everybody	everything	

If you want to write clearly and correctly, you must memorize these words and remember that they always take a singular verb. Using your common sense is not enough because some of these words seem plural; for example, *everybody* seems to mean more than one person, but in grammatically correct English, it takes a singular verb. Here are some examples of the pronouns used with singular verbs:

singular S   singular V
Everyone in town *is talking* about the scandal.

singular S   singular V
Each of the boys *is* talented.

singular S   singular V
One of their biggest concerns *is* crime in the streets.

singular S   singular V
Neither of the cats *is* mine.

Hint: You can memorize the indefinite pronouns as the *-one*, *-thing*, and *-body* words (every*one*, every*thing*, every*body*, and so forth) plus *each*, *either*, and *neither*.

Exercise 7 Practice: Making Subjects and Verbs Agree: Using Indefinite Pronouns

Circle the correct verb in parentheses in each sentence below.

1. (Was/Were) anybody from school at the club on Friday night?

2. Either of the cell phones (cost, costs) too much for my budget.

3. (Is/Are) someone taking photographs during the ceremony?

4. Each of my classes (has, have) an attendance requirement.

5. Neither of the boys (has, have) ever given me any trouble.

6. Beyond the college parking lot there (is, are) a tennis court and a soccer field.

7. After the party, (was, were) anyone talking to Michelle?

8. Everyone in my night classes (seem, seems) much smarter than I am.

COLLECTIVE NOUNS

Collective nouns refer to more than one person or thing:

team	company	council	majority
class	corporation	government	minority
committee	family	group	faculty
audience	jury	crowd	army

Most of the time, collective nouns take a singular verb.

singular S   **singular V**

The *committee is sponsoring* a fundraiser.

singular S **singular V**

The *audience was* impatient.

singular S, singular V

The *faculty has reached* a decision.

The singular verb is used because the group is sponsoring, or getting impatient, or reaching a decision, *as one unit.*

Collective nouns take a plural verb only when the members of the group are acting individually, not as a unit:

The sophomore *class are fighting* among themselves. (The phrase *among themselves* shows that the class is not acting as one unit.)

Exercise 8 **Practice: Making Subjects and Verbs Agree: Using Collective Nouns**

Circle the correct verb in parentheses in each sentence below.

1. The Green Corporation (give, gives) all its full-time employees ten vacation days.

2. The family from Nevada (is, are) looking for a house to rent for at least one year.

3. Some members of the jury (was, were) falling asleep in the late afternoon sessions.

4. My son's kindergarten class (sing, sings) songs at the start of each day.

5. The Merrill College Student Council (was, were) determined to raise the issue of student fees.

6. The most popular team in baseball history (is/are) deeply divided on the issue of steroid use.

7. Although rain delayed the outdoor concert, the crowd at the park (was, were) patient and cheerful.

8. The committee (raise, raises) money for those less fortunate through its annual bake sale.

MAKING SUBJECTS AND VERBS AGREE: THE BOTTOM LINE

As you have probably realized, making subjects and verbs agree is not as simple as it first appears. But if you can remember the basic ideas in this section, you will be able to apply them automatically as you edit your own writing. Below is a quick reference of subject–verb agreement principles:

> **INFO BOX** Making Subjects and Verbs Agree: A Summary
>
> 1. Subjects and verbs should agree in number: singular subjects get singular verb forms; plural subjects get plural verb forms.
> 2. When pronouns are used as subjects, they must agree in number with verbs.
> 3. Nothing in a prepositional phrase can be the subject of the sentence.
> 4. Questions, sentences beginning with *here* or *there*, and other sentences can change word order, making subjects harder to find.
> 5. Compound subjects joined by *and* are usually plural.
> 6. When subjects are joined by *or, either . . . or, neither . . . nor,* or *not only . . . but also,* the verb form agrees with the subject closest to the verb.
> 7. Certain indefinite pronouns always take singular verbs. (See Info Box on p. 481.)
> 8. Collective nouns usually take singular verbs.

Exercise 9 Practice: A Comprehensive Exercise on Subject–Verb Agreement

Circle the correct verb form in parentheses in each sentence below.

1. Yesterday, there (was, were) a dining room table and four chairs on sale at Furniture Warehouse.

2. Around the back of the restaurant (is, are) a huge dumpster and a recycling bin.

3. Neither the child nor his parents (use, uses) the front porch very often because the house is on a busy street.

4. Before the semester begins, everyone (has, have) to register for classes.

5. When (was, were) your brothers planning to visit?

6. Everything in Jackie's room (seem, seems) dusty and grimy.

7. Either of my sisters (is, are) capable of handling a family emergency.

8. Axel George, as well as Mina Patel, (work, works) in the computer lab.

Collaborate

Exercise 10   Collaborate: Writing Sentences with Subject–Verb Agreement

With a partner or a group, turn each of the following phrases into a sentence—twice. That is, write two sentences for each phrase. Use a verb that fits, and put the verb in the present tense. Be sure that the verb agrees with the subject.

1. A large bag of rocks _____

   _____

   A large bag of rocks _____

   _____

2. Either the library or the student center _____

   _____

   Either the library or the student center _____

   _____

3. The company _____

   _____

   The company _____

   _____

4. Mickey and Minnie _____

   _____

   Mickey and Minnie _____

   _____

5. Everything on the menu _____

   _____

   Everything on the menu _____

   _____

6. Someone on the Safe City Council _____

   _____

   Someone on the Safe City Council _____

   _____

7. Not only my friends but also my brother _____

   _____

   Not only my friends but also my brother _____

   _____

8. Anybody from this state _____

_____

Anybody from this state _____

_____

| Exercise 11 | Collaborate: Create Your Own Text on Subject–Verb Agreement |

Collaborate

Working with a partner or a group, create your own grammar handbook. Below is a list of rules on subject–verb agreement. Write one sentence that is an example of each rule. The first one is done for you.

Rule 1: Subjects and verbs should agree in number: singular subjects get singular verb forms; plural subjects get plural verb forms.

example: _____

_____

Rule 2: When pronouns are used as subjects, they must agree in number with verbs.

example: _____

_____

Rule 3: Nothing in a prepositional phrase can be the subject of the sentence.

example: _____

_____

Rule 4: Questions, sentences beginning with *here* or *there*, and other sentences can change word order, making subjects harder to find.

example: _____

_____

Rule 5: When subjects are joined by *and*, they are usually plural.

example: _____

_____

Rule 6: When subjects are joined by *or, either . . . or, neither . . . nor,* or *not only . . . but also,* the verb form agrees with the subject closest to the verb.

example: _____

_____

Rule 7: Indefinite pronouns always take singular verbs.

example: _____

_____

Rule 8: Collective nouns usually take singular verbs.

example: _____

_____

Connect

| **Exercise 12** | **Connect: Editing a Paragraph for Errors in Subject–Verb Agreement** |

Edit the following paragraph by correcting any verbs that do not agree with their subjects. Write your corrections above the lines. There are seven errors.

There is either thoughtlessness or cruelty in hurting someone's feelings. Spite, jealousy, and anger often prompt a person to lash out at another. Such behavior is deliberate and open. Children, who are less skilled in handling their emotions than adults are, can be cruel to another child. There is times when one four-year-old may call another "stupid" or "disgusting" while both children plays a game on the street. The speaker is simply venting his or her rage and soon forgets, but the victim shamed in front of other children may not forget. Adult cruelty are more sophisticated. This cruelty can be the critical remark a boss make to an employee or the constant sarcasm of a wife speaking to her husband. Habitual cruelty often turns into thoughtless cruelty. When one person constantly belittles another, the victim suffer with every repetition of the meanness, but the attacker feels very little. Another kind of thoughtless cruelty is the assignment of a nickname. A man often cringes for years because some childhood "buddies" was too eager to call him "Moose" or "Skinny," and the nickname stuck. Although adults may try to laugh about their nicknames, neither the intentionally cruel names or a thoughtlessly assigned name is a person's choice. In all stages of life, people need to show a little kindness and restraint. Not only the child on the playground but also adults in all their interactions deserves some of that kindness.

Chapter Test Making Subjects and Verbs Agree   MyWritingLab™

Some of the sentences below are correct; others have errors in making subjects and verbs agree. Write *OK* next to the correct sentences; write *X* next to the incorrect ones.

1. _____ After the Safety Committee approves the new street signs, the signs will be placed in the school zones at the two elementary schools and the middle school.

2. _____ Everybody on the three highest floors of the skyscraper gets a wonderful view of Central Park.

3. _____ There is a certain taste and a special texture in the cornbread from Ed's Barbecue Hut in Asheville, North Carolina.

4. _____ Neither a long day at work nor a long ride to our home in the suburbs keeps my father from maintaining a positive attitude.

5. _____ Something about seeing my son in a school play make me want to smile and cry at the same time.

6. _____ At the end of the dirt road in the dilapidated part of town was an old barn and a broken-down gate to the nearby pasture.

7. _____ Your concern about the price of car insurance make me worry about your ability to handle the costs of driving and maintaining your own car.

8. _____ What is the real causes of this massive forest fire?

CHAPTER 26

Using Pronouns Correctly: Agreement and Reference

CHAPTER 22

Quick Question MyWritingLab™

Is the following sentence correct?
Yes /No

The class decided to have its next project meeting outside.

(After you study this chapter, you will be confident of your answer.)

Learning Objectives

In this chapter, you will learn to:

1 Identify pronouns and make their antecedents agree.

2 Identify collective nouns.

3 Correct errors in pronoun agreement and reference.

1 Identify pronouns and make their antecedents agree.

NOUNS AND PRONOUNS

Nouns are the names of persons, places, or things.

> *Jack* is a good friend. (*Jack* is the name of a person.)
> The band is from *Orlando*. (*Orlando* is the name of a place.)
> We understood the *lecture*. (*Lecture* is the name of a thing.)

Pronouns are words that substitute for nouns. A pronoun's **antecedent** is the word or words it replaces.

> antecedent   pronoun
> *Jack* is a good friend; *he* is very loyal.

antecedent   **pronoun**
I hated *the movie* because *it* was too violent.

antecedent   **pronoun**
Playing tennis was fun, but *it* started to take up too much of my time.

antecedent   **pronoun**
Micah and Jessie are sure *they* understood the assignment.

antecedent   **pronoun**
Sharon gave away *her* old clothes.

antecedent   **pronoun**
The course's weekly assignments are posted on *its* Web site.

| Exercise 1 | Practice: Identifying the Antecedents of Pronouns |

Underline the word or words that are the antecedent of the italicized pronoun in each of the following sentences.

1. A short walk is healthy for workers because *it* takes them away from the workplace and relieves stress.

2. Your brother called me yesterday; *he* seemed a little depressed.

3. Camille looked at two used cars this afternoon; *they* were overpriced and unattractive.

4. Some students love this class, but I hate *it*.

5. The baby can't go outside without *his* down jacket.

6. The television show lost *its* special charm a few episodes ago.

7. Luis, do *you* need a ride to work?

8. The parrots have finally ended *their* conversation.

AGREEMENT OF A PRONOUN AND ITS ANTECEDENT

A pronoun must agree in number with its antecedent. If the antecedent is singular; the pronoun must be singular. If the antecedent is plural, then the pronoun must be plural.

singular antecedent   **singular pronoun**
Susan tried to arrive on time, but *she* got caught in traffic.

plural antecedent   **plural pronoun**
Susan and Ray tried to arrive on time, but *they* got caught in traffic.

plural antecedent   **plural pronoun**
The visitors tried to arrive on time, but *they* got caught in traffic.

There are some special problems with agreement of pronouns, and these problems will come up in your writing. If you become familiar with the explanations, examples, and exercises that follow, you will be ready to handle the special problems.

INDEFINITE PRONOUNS

As you know, certain indefinite pronouns always take a singular verb. Whenever one of these indefinite pronouns acts as an antecedent in a sentence, the pronoun that replaces it must also be singular. However, several indefinite pronouns always take a plural verb. If any of them acts as an antecedent, the replacement pronoun must be plural. Interestingly, some indefinite pronouns can be considered singular or plural depending on the sentence's meaning. The lists in the Info Box can serve as a quick reference guide and help you complete the exercises in this chapter on pronoun–antecedent agreement.

INFO BOX **Common Indefinite Pronouns**

Indefinite Pronouns (Singular)		Indefinite Pronouns (Plural)	Indefinite Pronouns (Singular or Plural)
another	neither	both	all
anybody	no one	few	any
anyone	nothing	many	more
anything	one	others	most
each	other	several	none
either	someone		some
everyone	something		

(For a complete list of indefinite pronouns, see page 481.)

---

singular antecedent   singular possessive pronoun
Everyone in the sorority donated *her* time to the project.

plural antecedent   plural possessive pronoun
Several new students forgot to bring *their* IDs to registration.

Avoiding Gender Bias

Consider this sentence:

Everybody in the math class brought _____ own calculator.

How do you choose the correct pronoun to fill in the blank? If everybody in the class is male, you can write:

Everybody in the math class brought *his* own calculator.

Or if everybody in the class is female, you can write:

Everybody in the math class brought *her* own calculator.

Or if the class has students of both genders, you can write:

Everybody in the math class brought *his or her* own calculator.

In the past, most writers used the pronoun *his* to refer to both men and women. Today, many writers try to use *his or her* to avoid gender bias. If you find using *his or her* is getting awkward or repetitive, you can rewrite the sentence and make the antecedent plural:

correct: *The students* in the math class brought *their* own calculators.

But you cannot shift from singular to plural:

incorrect: ~~Everybody in the math class brought their own calculators~~.

Exercise 2   **Practice: Making Pronouns and Antecedents Agree**

Write the appropriate pronoun in the blank in each of the following sentences. Look carefully for the antecedent before you choose the pronoun.

1. During the men's semifinals, one of the tennis players seemed to lose _____ confidence as the match went into its final minutes.

2. Everyone in the Women's Sculptors Association hopes to exhibit _____ best work at the Richardson Museum.

3. When the first snow falls, Chet and Nelson strap _____ skis on the car and head for the mountains.

4. Some of the players were upset about _____ new field assignments.

5. Most of the food from the catering truck was missing, but all of the guests enjoyed _____ time at the party anyway.

6. Once I visited the tiny set of a popular television comedy, everything about the show lost _____ glamour.

7. Yesterday, someone left _____ car keys in the restaurant.

8. Either of the singer's former husbands could have sold _____ personal stories about her to the media.

COLLECTIVE NOUNS

Collective nouns refer to more than one person or thing:

2 Identify collective nouns.

team	faculty	council
class	corporation	government
committee	family	group
audience	jury	crowd

Most of the time, collective nouns take a singular pronoun.

collective noun   **singular pronoun**
The *team* that was ahead in the playoffs lost *its* home game.

collective noun   **singular pronoun**
The *corporation* changed *its* policy on parental leave.

Collective nouns are usually singular because the group is losing a game or changing a policy as one, as a unit. Collective nouns take a plural pronoun only when the members of the group are acting individually, not as a unit.

The *class* picked up *their* class rings this morning. (The members of the class pick up their rings individually.)

Exercise 3   **Practice: Making Pronouns and Antecedents Agree: Collective Nouns**

Circle the correct pronoun in each of the following sentences and underline the corresponding noun.

1. The commissioners at the Sprucedale City Council gave (its, their) approval to the construction of a new teen center.

2. A gang of my brother's army buddies met for (its, their) annual picnic at Still Waters Park.

3. Before the semester ended, the committee gave (its, their) recommendations to the academic dean.

4. A family from China opened (its, their) second furniture company in Baton Rouge.

5. After the club meets, one of (its, their) members always suggests adjourning to a nearby restaurant.

6. Marilyn no longer orders movies from Film Net because of (its, their) poor delivery record.

7. Several of the drawing and design classes held (its, their) last class meeting outdoors because of the beautiful spring weather.

8. The team meets in (its, their) locker room before every game.

Collaborate

Exercise 4   **Collaborate: Writing Sentences with Pronoun–Antecedent Agreement**

With a partner or a group, write a sentence for each pair of words below, using each pair as a pronoun and its antecedent. The first pair is done for you.

1. parents . . . their

   sentence: _Parents who work outside the home have to plan their time_
   carefully.

2. family . . . its

   sentence: _____

   _____

3. anybody . . . his or her

   sentence: _____

   _____

4. drivers . . . they

   sentence: _____

   _____

5. security . . . it

   sentence: _____

   _____

6. either . . . her

sentence: _____

_____

7. everybody . . . his or her

sentence: _____

_____

8. North America . . . it

sentence: _____

_____

| Exercise 5 | Connect: Editing a Paragraph for Errors in Pronoun– Antecedent Agreement |

Connect

Read the following paragraph carefully, looking for errors in agreement of pronouns and their antecedents. Cross out each pronoun that does not agree with its antecedent and write the correct pronoun above it. Six pronouns need correcting.

My job at the reception desk at Millennium General Hospital can be challenging. My work is stressful when the hospital is busy. During visiting hours, I have to be helpful, cheerful, and alert because many people are in the hospital for the first time and don't know the layout of the place. They get anxious when they are faced with too many signs and hallways. In addition, each visitor is worrying about their loved one, sick and alone in a hospital bed. When the hospital is busy, time goes quickly for me. When visiting hours are over and nobody is with their family, time drags on. For example, in the quiet hours of the holidays, when patients want to be back in his or her homes, the staff works extra hard to cheer up patients and visitors. Fortunately, special events brighten up the atmosphere. Sometimes everyone in a local club visits the wards and does their best to entertain the staff, patients, and visitors in the hospital. At other times, the Steely Corporation, which owns Millennium General, brings a little brightness to their patients and staff. It lights up the corridors with bright lights, plays holiday music, and even brings clowns to the lounges. On Independence Day, the corporation has been known to celebrate by offering a small fireworks display on their front lawn.

③ Correct errors in pronoun agreement and reference.

PRONOUNS AND THEIR ANTECEDENTS: BEING CLEAR

Remember that pronouns are words that replace or refer to other words, and the words that are replaced or referred to are antecedents.

Make sure that a pronoun has one clear antecedent. Your writing will be vague and confusing if a pronoun appears to refer to more than one antecedent or if it doesn't have any specific antecedent to refer to. In grammar, such confusing language is called a problem with **pronoun reference**.

When a pronoun refers to more than one thing, the sentence becomes confusing or silly. The following are examples of unclear reference:

> Jim told Leonard his bike had been stolen. (Whose bike was stolen? Jim's? Leonard's?)

> She put the cake on the table, took off her apron, pulled up a chair, and began to eat it. (What did she eat? The cake? The table? Her apron? The chair?)

If there is no one clear antecedent, you must rewrite the sentence to make the reference clear. Sometimes the rewritten sentence may seem repetitive, but a little repetition is better than a lot of confusion.

> **unclear:** Jim told Leonard his bike had been stolen.
> **clear:** Jim told Leonard Jim's bike had been stolen.
> **clear:** Jim told Leonard, "My bike has been stolen."
> **clear:** Jim told Leonard that Leonard's bike had been stolen.
> **clear:** Jim told Leonard, "Your bike has been stolen."

> **unclear:** She put the cake on the table, took off her apron, pulled up a chair, and began to eat it.
> **clear:** She put the cake on the table, took off her apron, pulled up a chair, and began to eat the cake.

Sometimes the problem is a little more tricky. Can you spot what's wrong with this sentence?

> **unclear:** Bill decided to take a part-time job, which worried his parents. (What worried Bill's parents? His decision to work part time? Or the job itself?)

Be very careful with the pronoun *which*. If there is any chance that using *which* will confuse the reader, rewrite the sentence and get rid of *which*.

> **clear:** Bill's parents were worried about the kind of part-time job he chose.
> **clear:** Bill's decision to work part time worried his parents.

Sometimes, a pronoun has nothing to refer to; it has no antecedent.

> **no antecedent:** When Bill got to the train station, they said the train was going to be late. (Who said the train was going to be late? The ticket agents? Strangers Bill met on the tracks?)

> **no antecedent:** Maria has always loved medicine and has decided that's what she wants to be. (What does "that" refer to? The only word it could refer to is "medicine," but Maria certainly doesn't want to be a medicine. She doesn't want to be an aspirin or a cough drop.)

If a pronoun lacks an antecedent, add an antecedent or get rid of the pronoun.

add an antecedent: When Bill got to the train station and asked the ticket agents about the schedule, they said the train was going to be late. ("They" refers to the ticket agents.)

drop the pronoun: Maria has always loved medicine and has decided she wants to be a physician.

> **Note:** To check for clear reference of pronouns, underline any pronoun that may not be clear. Then try to draw a line from that pronoun to its antecedent. Are there two or more possible antecedents? Is there no antecedent? In either case, you will need to revise for clarity.

Exercise 6 **Practice: Rewriting Sentences for Clear Reference of Pronouns**

Rewrite the following sentences so that the pronouns have clear references. You may add, take out, or change words.

1. Leonard took his mother to a violent movie, which was stupid.

2. Years ago, they believed that black cats were a sign of bad luck.

3. The heavy bowl fell on the tile floor, and it cracked.

4. Laura told her best friend Celia that she worried too much.

5. I'm glad I didn't go to Emerson High School because they're all snobs and phonies.

6. My brother has always been fascinated by space flight, and that's what he dreams of being.

7. Most of the conflicts between teenagers and their parents occur because they always think age makes people wiser.

8. Searching in his grandparents' attic, Tyler found some old love letters, which shocked him.

Exercise 7 **Connect: Editing a Paragraph for Errors in Pronoun Agreement and Reference**

Connect

Correct any errors in pronoun agreement or reference in the following paragraph. There are six errors. Write your corrections above the line.

Anyone with a strong will and enough motivation can change their attitude from negative to positive. I am living proof of this statement. Each day I used to focus on what could go wrong, which made me constantly anxious. I was also terribly self-conscious. Every time I entered a room or spoke in public, I was extremely nervous. I imagined everyone looking at me with their attention focused on my flaw. Each member of my family tried their best to brighten my moods and boost my confidence, but their efforts couldn't help. Fortunately, I signed up for a class in psychology and it led me to an important discovery. About halfway through the term, the assigned readings and class lectures helped me to realize that I was suffering from depression. I decided to do something about it. I began to see a counselor, and I am now learning to think of myself and my future in a new way. I am ready to focus on hope, not fear.

MyWritingLab™ **Chapter Test** **Using Pronouns Correctly: Agreement and Reference**

Some of the sentences below are correct; others have errors in pronoun agreement or reference. Write *OK* next to the correct sentences; write *X* next to the incorrect ones.

1. _____ When Brendan came home, Colton announced that his dog had chewed up a leather sandal.

2. _____ I want to go to the University of Springfield because their business school has an excellent reputation for placing recent graduates in good jobs.

3. _____ Everyone in my old neighborhood wanted to sell their home before major road construction started nearby.

4. _____ Graham had always had a dream of musical stardom, which made him special.

5. _____ We desperately wanted the local football team to win, but it was no match for the opponents from out of town.

6. _____ After the argument, either of my sisters could have offered their apologies, but the feud continued for months.

7. _____ Marcia didn't understand her mathematics textbook; she feels frustrated when she reads them.

8. _____ After dinner, somebody took the leftover cookies from the kitchen counter and put them in his or her pocket.

MyWritingLab™ Visit Chapter 26, "Using Pronouns Correctly: Agreement and Reference," in *MyWritingLab* to test your understanding of the chapter objectives.

Using Pronouns Correctly: Consistency and Case

CHAPTER 27

Quick Question MyWritingLab™

Which sentence(s) is/are correct?

A. My brother is more aggressive than I.

B. You have to keep this story a secret between you and me.

(After you study this chapter, you will be confident of your answer.)

Learning Objectives

In this chapter, you will learn to:

1 Recognize first-, second-, and third-person points of view.

2 Identify and choose the correct pronoun case.

3 Correct errors in pronoun case.

POINTS OF VIEW AND PRONOUN CONSISTENCY

1 Recognize first-, second-, and third-person points of view.

When you write, you write from a point of view, and each point of view gets its own form. If you write from the first-person point of view, your pronouns are in the *I* (singular) or *we* (plural) forms. If you write from the second-person point of view, your pronouns are in the *you* form, whether they are singular or plural. If you write from the third-person point of view, your pronouns are in the *he*, *she*, or *it* (singular) or *they* (plural) forms.

Different kinds of writing may require different points of view. When you are writing a set of directions, for example, you may use the second-person (*you*) point of view. An essay about your childhood may use the first-person (*I*) point of view.

Whatever point of view you use, be consistent in using pronouns. That is, do not shift the form of your pronouns without some good reason.

not consistent: Every time *I* go to that mall, the parking lot is so crowded *you* have to drive around for hours, looking for a parking space.

consistent: Every time *I* go to that mall, the parking lot is so crowded *I* have to drive around for hours, looking for a parking space.

| Exercise 1 | **Practice: Consistency in Pronouns** |

Correct any inconsistency in point of view in the sentences below. Cross out the incorrect pronoun and write the correct one above it.

1. Studying for long stretches doesn't work well for me; you become too tired to concentrate.

2. After the arriving airline passengers stare at the empty revolving luggage carousel for ten or twenty minutes, a long stream of luggage rolls slowly before you.

3. My favorite kind of class is one that makes you motivated to read more about a subject.

4. Drivers on the interstate highways need to be careful about entering the road; you have to be sure to gather enough speed to merge into traffic.

5. Hallie and I like to shop at the Dollar Bargain Bin because you can always find cheap cosmetics or jewelry there.

6. Sometimes I don't return Joe's calls, for once I start talking to him, he keeps you on the phone for hours.

7. My boyfriend and I like camping near Lake Lion, but you have to be prepared for hordes of mosquitoes in the summer.

8. Whenever I take the time to eat breakfast, I realize how a decent breakfast can give you the energy to face a long day.

Exercise 2 **Practice: Correcting Sentences with Consistency Problems**

Rewrite the following sentences, correcting any pronoun consistency errors. To make the corrections, you may have to change, add, or eliminate words.

1. Unless a teenager is strong enough to resist peer pressure and smart enough to recognize true friends, you will not have an easy trip to adulthood.

   rewrite: _____

   _____

2. Pierre becomes aware of his mother's sadness whenever she tells you about her childhood in Haiti.

   rewrite: _____

   _____

3. Students registering for next semester must bring your ID and signed advisement form.

   rewrite: _____

   _____

4. Laura and I cannot trust her cousin Miranda; if you tell her a secret, she reveals it to the whole neighborhood.

   rewrite: _____

   _____

5. Students who have never used the college library should not be nervous because, after their library tour, you will discover that everything is easy to find.

   rewrite: _____

   _____

6. Yolanda loves beginning a new semester; she likes seeing her old instructors, bumping into your old classmates, and meeting her new instructors.

   rewrite: _____

   _____

7. To me, Mrs. Carmichael is a strict teacher; you can give her a million excuses, but she will never let me out of class early.

   rewrite: _____

   _____

8. I can't let Cade go outside by himself anymore; since he learned to open the gate, you can't trust him to stay in the yard.

   rewrite: _____

   _____

2 Identify and choose the correct pronoun case.

CHOOSING THE CASE OF PRONOUNS

Pronouns have forms that show number and person, and they also have forms that show **case**.

Singular Pronouns	Subjective Case	Objective Case	Possessive Case
1st person	I	me	my
2nd person	you	you	your
3rd person	he, she, it	him, her, it	his, her, its
	who, whoever	whom, whomever	whose

Plural Pronouns			
1st person	we	us	our
2nd person	you	you	your
3rd person	they	them	their
	who, whoever	whom, whomever	whose

The rules for choosing the case of pronouns are simple:

1. When a pronoun is used as a subject, use the subjective case.
2. When a pronoun is used as the object of a verb or the object of a preposition, use the objective case.
3. When a pronoun is used to show ownership, use the possessive case.

pronouns used as subjects:
He studies his sociology notes every day.
Bill painted the walls, and *we* polished the floors.
Who is making that noise?

pronouns used as objects:
Sarah called *him* yesterday.
He gave his old computer science textbook to me.
With *whom* did you argue?

pronouns used to show possession:
I am worried about *my* grade in Spanish.
The nightclub has lost *its* popularity.
I wonder *whose* tablet this is.

Pronoun Case in a Related Group of Words

You need to be careful in choosing case when the pronoun is part of a related group of words. If the pronoun is part of a related group of words, isolate the pronoun. Next, try out the pronoun choices. Then decide which pronoun is correct and write the correct sentence. For example, which of these sentences is correct?

Aunt Sophie planned a big dinner for Tom and *I*.

or

Aunt Sophie planned a big dinner for Tom and *me*.

Step 1: Isolate the pronoun. Eliminate the related words *Tom and*.

Step 2: Try each case:

> Aunt Sophie planned a big dinner for *I*.

> or

> Aunt Sophie planned a big dinner for *me*.

Step 3: The correct sentence is

> Aunt Sophie planned a big dinner for Tom and me.

The pronoun acts as an object, so it takes the objective case.

Try working through the steps once more to be sure that you understand this principle. Which of the following sentences is correct?

> Last week, *me* and my friend studied in the library until midnight.

> or

> Last week, *I* and my friend studied in the library until midnight.

Step 1: Isolate the pronoun. Eliminate the related words *and my friend*.

Step 2: Try each case:

> Last week, *me* studied in the library until midnight.

> or

> Last week, *I* studied in the library until midnight.

Step 3: The correct sentence is

> Last week, I and my friend studied in the library until midnight.

The pronoun acts as a subject, so it takes the subjective case.

> **Note:** You can also write it this way for better style:
> *Last week, my friend and I studied in the library until midnight.*

COMMON ERRORS WITH CASE OF PRONOUNS

❸ Correct errors in pronoun case.

Be careful to avoid these common errors:

1. *Between* is a preposition, so the pronouns that follow it are objects of the preposition: between *us*, between *them*, between *you and me*. It is never correct to write *between you and I*.

   not this: ~~The plans for the surprise party must be kept a secret between you and I~~.
   but this: The plans for the surprise party must be kept a secret between you and me.

2. Never use *myself* as a replacement for *I* or *me*.

   not this: ~~My father and myself want to thank you for this honor~~.
   but this: My father and I want to thank you for this honor.

   not this: ~~She thought the prize should be awarded to Arthur and myself~~.
   but this: She thought the prize should be awarded to Arthur and me.

3. The possessive pronoun *its* has no apostrophe.

not this: ~~The car held it's value~~.
but this: The car held its value.

not this: ~~The baby bird had fallen from it's nest~~.
but this: The baby bird had fallen from its nest.

4. Pronouns that complete comparisons can be in the subjective, objective, or possessive case.

subjective: Christa speaks better than *I*.
objective: The storm hurt Manny more than *her*.
possessive: My car is as fast as *his*.

Note: To decide on the correct pronoun, add the words that complete the comparison and say them aloud:

Christa speaks better than I *speak*.
The storm hurt Manny more than *the storm hurt* her.
My car is as fast as his *car*.

5. *Who* and *whoever* are in the subjective case. *Whom* and *whomever* are in the objective case.

subjective: *Who* came to the house?
subjective: *Whoever* wants the books can take them.
objective: *Whom* did Larry bring to the house?
objective: You can bring *whomever* you like to the house.

Note: If you have trouble choosing between *who* and *whom*, or *whoever* and *whomever*, substitute *he* for *who* and *whoever*, and *him* for *whom* and *whomever* to check the correctness of your choice.

Check this sentence:

Who made the cake?

Is it correct? Change the sentence, substituting *he* in one version, and *him* in another version.

He made the cake.
Him made the cake.

If *he* is correct, then *who* is correct.
Check another sentence:

With *whom* are you arguing?

Is it correct? Change the sentence, substituting *he* in one version, and *him* in another version. To make your choice simpler, write the sentence as a statement, not a question:

You are arguing with *he*.
You are arguing with *him*.

If *him* is correct, then *whom* is correct.

Exercise 3   **Practice: Choosing the Correct Pronoun Case**

Circle the correct pronoun in parentheses in each of the following sentences.

1. (She, Her) and Mr. Bergman were married in Austin many years ago.

2. The mentoring program created a partnership between a senior and (me, myself).

3. Moving to Montana was the right decision for Josh and (I, me) because it offered a new beginning in a new place.

4. Captain Stacy Matella is a highly admired leader, but Captain Harry Hutchins has just as many good qualities as (she, her).

5. Our long-awaited trip to the big city ended in disappointment for my parents and (I, me).

6. You and Tony both majored in business, but your skills in closing a deal are different from (him, his).

7. The advising center posted (its, it's) hours for summer advising.

8. Sometimes I become impatient with Joe and (she, her); they procrastinate about making even the smallest choices.

Exercise 4   **Collaborate: Write Your Own Text on Pronoun Case**

Collaborate

With a partner or with a group, write two sentences that could be used as examples for each of the following rules. The first one is done for you.

Rule 1: When a pronoun is used as a subject, use the subjective case.

examples: *He complained about the noise in the street.*

Tired and hungry, they stopped for lunch.

Rule 2: When a pronoun is used as the object of a verb or the object of a preposition, use the objective case.

examples: _____

_____

Rule 3: When a pronoun is used to show ownership, use the possessive case.

examples: _____

_____

Rule 4: When a pronoun is part of a related group of words, isolate the pronoun to choose the case. (For your examples, write two sentences in which the pronoun is part of a related group of words.)

examples: _____

_____

Connect

Exercise 5   **Connect: Editing a Paragraph for Errors in Pronoun Consistency and Case**

In the following paragraph, correct any errors in pronoun consistency and case. There are seven errors. Write your corrections above the line.

I am very grateful for this award from the Community Cares Club. Many people encouraged, supported, and even changed me in my work with local homeless children. One is my mother, whom introduced me to the organization several years ago. At that time, I thought of my mother's work in the club as worthy but depressing. I never realized how mistaken I was until you actually met the children. Because of my mother's involvement in the club, I had a chance to learn about the spirit, courage, and strength of disadvantaged boys and girls. Interacting with these children created a bond between them and I. I gave them the stability of regular attention, academic support, and physical activity. Around them, I became a more positive person. They were a good influence on I. Them and me were a good combination. Therefore I have to thank the Community Cares Club. They brought me and the children together.

MyWritingLab™   **Chapter Test** **Using Pronouns Correctly: Consistency and Case**

Some of the sentences below are correct; others have errors in pronoun consistency or case. Write *OK* next to the correct sentences; write *X* next to the incorrect ones.

1. _____ Who did you gossip about after I left the party?
2. _____ Sometimes I get angry at Claudia and he; they take advantage of my generosity.
3. _____ It was difficult for my parents and I to leave our house in the suburbs and move to a small apartment in a decrepit part of the city.
4. _____ Whoever gets to the restaurant first needs to find a table for six.
5. _____ I am a little upset with my brother; he always gets better grades in English than me.
6. _____ How to use the file-sharing site is unclear to everyone except me and Alexia.
7. _____ After the blizzard, Kate and myself were grateful for the emergency vehicles that rescued us from the huge drifts of snow around the cabin.
8. _____ Whom do you expect at the farewell party for your supervisor?

MyWritingLab™ Visit Chapter 27, "Using Pronouns Correctly: Consistency and Case," in *MyWritingLab* to test your understanding of the chapter objectives.

Punctuation

Quick Question MyWritingLab™

Which sentence(s) is/are correct?

A. *Brew and Chew, a popular coffee shop near campus, is offering a discount to students.*

B. *Brew and Chew a popular coffee shop near campus is offering a discount to students.*

(After you study this chapter, you will feel confident of your answer.)

Learning Objectives

In this chapter, you will learn to:

1. Use the period and question mark correctly.
2. Identify the four main ways to use a comma in a sentence.
3. Use the comma correctly with quotations, dates and addresses, and numbers.
4. Use the semicolon and colon correctly within a sentence.
5. Use the apostrophe correctly in contractions and to show possession.
6. Use the exclamation mark, dash, parentheses, and hyphen correctly.
7. Use quotations and capital letters correctly.
8. Use numbers and abbreviations correctly.

THE PERIOD

Periods are used two ways:

1. **Use a period to mark the end of a sentence that makes a statement or gives a command**.

   We invited him to dinner at our house.
   When Richard spoke, no one paid attention.

1 Use the period and question mark correctly.

Don't be late for class.
Leave your paper on your desk.

2. **Use a period after abbreviations**.

Mr. Ryan
James Wing, Sr.
10:00 p.m.

Note: If a sentence ends with a period marking an abbreviation, do not add a second period.

Exercise 1 **Practice: Using Periods**

Add periods where they are needed in each of the following sentences.

1. Oscar bought about fifteen lbs of special food for his sick terrier

2. When the elementary school children went on field trips, they were nervous around people like Mr Carlson, the principal

3. Isaac wants to get a BS degree in Biology, and his friend, Dr Hamilton, told him to prepare by taking many science classes in high school

4. Tell Ms Marko or Mr Scanlon about the parking problems in the gymnasium parking lot.

5. Last night I studied for my psychology test until 1:00 am but had to be alert to take the test at 8:00 am

6. Nicholas Anderson, Sr, is a better businessman than his son

7. Someday, I want to be known as Cecilia Knowles, RN, so I am going to college to study nursing.

8. You can buy textbooks tablets notebooks and pens at the college bookstore

THE QUESTION MARK

Use a question mark after a direct question, a tag question, or a request.

Isn't she adorable?
We have homework tonight, don't we?
Could you lend me a sheet of paper?

If a question is not a direct question, it does not get a question mark.

They asked if I thought their grandchild was adorable.
She questioned whether I had car insurance.

Exercise 2 **Practice: Punctuating with Periods and Question Marks**

Add any missing periods and question marks to each sentence below.

1. Are the people upstairs moving out of their apartment

2. Have you ever thought about getting a BA in graphic design

3. Two of my friends have been asking me about my plans for semester break

4. She didn't explain that clearly, did she

5. I'm not certain that the meeting will take place as scheduled

6. Don't you think 6:00 am is a little early to start driving to Tallahassee

7. Would you tell Prof Thomas that I may be late

8. I wonder why you never call me on Saturdays

Exercise 3 Connect: Editing a Paragraph for Errors in Periods and Question Marks

In the following paragraph, correct errors in punctuating with periods and question marks. The errors may involve missing or incorrect punctuation. There are eight errors.

Last Tuesday, a simple errand started me wondering if I had lost my mind?

First, I visited my allergy doctor for a routine check of my sinuses and bronchial

tubes. Then I went to my local pharmacy to refill a prescription for an antihista-

mine. This is a regular prescription for me; I have been taking the medicine since

I developed seasonal allergies several years ago. After I received the bag with the

vial of pills in it, I ran several more errands. I returned to my house at about

6:30 pm. for dinner and a good night's sleep. The next morning, I opened the plastic

container with my allergy pills inside. Suddenly I noticed a problem with the pills.

The pills were large and blue. My allergy pills are always small and pink. I didn't

know what to do. First, I asked myself whether I had paid enough attention to Dr

Kasabian during my visit a day earlier? Had he changed my medication. Or had

the pharmacist given me the wrong pills? What would happen if I took one of the

new pills? I needed my allergy medicine, and I was slipping into a state of panic.

After obsessing for a few more minutes, I decided not to take an allergy pill until

I called the pharmacist. My heart beat wildly as I waited to be connected to the

pharmacy department at the drug store. The woman who answered the phone was

Ms Patel, and she seemed very calm. I wondered how she could be so calm when

my life might be at stake? Soon, I learned the real story. My prescription medicine

was now being manufactured by a new company. The company was producing the same pill in the same dose, but the pill was now large and blue. I began to feel

calm, and my voice lost its hysterical tone I swallowed my pill, smiled, and vowed

never again to create a crisis out of nothing.

Section Test **Punctuation: The Period and the Question Mark**

Some of the sentences below are correct; others have errors in the use of periods and question marks. Put an X next to the sentences with errors.

1. _____ After I got to know Dr Stefanovic, I trusted her with my medical care.

2. _____ Parker was not sure whether the computer lab was open on Saturdays.

3. _____ The officer could have asked Kate Gomez about the time of the break-in.

4. _____ Now that Eddie has finished medical school, he has become Edward Obara, M D

5. _____ This book must weigh three lbs more than my laptop.

6. _____ Will Abraham ever finish restoring his old Ford Mustang?

7. _____ My roommate woke me up at 6:00 am yesterday so that we could study for our botany test.

8. _____ Could you let me see your notes from yesterday?

THE COMMA

2 Identify the four main ways to use a comma in a sentence.

There are four main ways to use a comma, as well as other, less important ways. *Memorize the four main ways.* If you can learn and understand these four rules, you will be more confident and correct in your punctuation. That is, you will use a comma only when you have a reason to do so; you will not be scattering commas in your sentences simply because you think a comma might fit, as many writers do.

The four main ways to use a comma are as a lister, a linker, an introducer, or an inserter (use two commas).

Use a Comma as a Lister

Commas support items in a series. These items can be words, phrases, or clauses.

comma between words in a list: She has enrolled in literature, history, and art classes this semester.

comma between phrases in a list: I looked for my ring under the coffee table, between the sofa cushions, and behind the chairs.

comma between clauses in a list: Last week he graduated from college, he found the woman of his dreams, and he won the lottery.

Note: In a list, the comma before *and* is optional, but many writers use it.

Exercise 4   **Practice: Using a Comma as a Lister**

Add commas only where they are needed in the following sentences. Do not add any other punctuation or change existing punctuation.

1. Meat fish cheese beans and dairy products are sources of protein.

2. Nicole can do the laundry Mike can vacuum the house and I can clean the kitchen.

3. The thief caught with the money was silent snarling and slippery.

4. Bargain prices for DVD players satellite radios and flat-screen televisions drew shoppers to the electronics store.

5. I will wash dry and fold your dirty clothes when you take them off the floor and put them in the laundry basket.

6. My aunt knew she was spending too much time and money on television shopping channels when boxes of glittering jewelry expensive makeup and household gadgets started piling up in her house.

7. Eric is self-centered he lacks any sense of responsibility and he lies to his friends.

8. Working full time going to school part time and managing a household keep Jenna quite busy.

Use a Comma as a Linker

A comma and a coordinating conjunction link two independent clauses. The coordinating conjunctions are *for, and, nor, but, or, yet, so*. The comma goes in front of the coordinating conjunction:

> I have to get to work on time, or I'll get into trouble with my boss.
> My mother gave me a beautiful card, and she wrote a note on it.

Exercise 5   **Practice: Using a Comma as a Linker**

Add commas only where they are needed in the following sentences. Some sentences do not need commas. Do not change words or add any other punctuation.

1. Dr. Pinsky used to clean my teeth and he would give me a new toothbrush afterward.

2. My daughter can spend the weekend with her father or she can stay at her grandmother's house.

3. A day with my best friend lets me escape from my worries and act like a child again.

4. Marsha wouldn't take her professor's advice nor would she listen to her academic advisor.

5. Sophie must be sick for she has missed every class this week.

6. George had planned a perfect holiday party but something went wrong.

7. Jerry has tried several diets and exercise plans yet can't seem to lose weight.

8. My dancing and photography classes are enjoyable but I know that jobs are scarce in those fields.

Use a Comma as an Introducer

Put a comma after introductory words, phrases, or clauses in a sentence.

a comma after an introductory word:
Yes, I agree with you on that issue.
Generally, students prefer electronic textbooks, or e-books.

a comma after an introductory phrase:
In the long run, you'll be better off without him.
Before the anniversary party, my father bought my mother a necklace.

a comma after an introductory clause:
If you call home, your parents will be pleased.
When my smartphone buzzes, I am always in the shower.

> **Exercise 6**   Practice: Using a Comma as an Introducer

Add commas only where they are needed in the following sentences. Some sentences do not need commas. Do not change words or add any other punctuation.

1. In the back of the dark room stood a man from my past.
2. Unless the weather improves we won't be able to hunt tomorrow.
3. Absolutely I can help you with that assignment.
4. Courtney do you have an extra pencil or pen?
5. On my little brother's birthday I took him to a water park.
6. While the professor explained the problem I took careful notes.
7. Behind the curtains are two children playing hide-and-seek.
8. After a few days Luisa got used to the noisy city streets.

Use a Comma as an Inserter

When words or phrases that are *not* necessary are inserted into a sentence, put a comma on *both* sides of the inserted material:

The game, unfortunately, was rained out.
My test score, believe it or not, was the highest in the class.
Potato chips, my favorite snack food, are better-tasting when they're fresh.
James, caught in the middle of the argument, tried to keep the peace.

Using commas as inserters requires that you decide what is essential to the meaning of the sentence and what is nonessential. Here is a good rule to remember:

If you do not need material in a sentence, put commas around the material. If you need material in a sentence, do not put commas around the material.

For example, consider this sentence:

The girl who called me was selling magazine subscriptions.

Do you need the words "who called me" to understand the meaning of the sentence? To answer that question, write the sentence without those words:

> The girl was selling magazine subscriptions.

Reading the shorter sentence, you might ask, "Which girl?" The words *who called me* are essential to the sentence. Therefore you do not put commas around them.

> **correct:** The girl who called me was selling magazine
> subscriptions.

Remember that the proper name of a person, place, or thing is always sufficient to identify it. Therefore any information that follows a proper name is inserted material; it gets commas on both sides.

> Carlton Furniture, which is nearby, has the best prices on futons and
> sofa beds.
> Sam Harris, the man who won the marathon, lives on my block.

Note: Sometimes the material that is needed in a sentence is called **essential** (or **restrictive**), and the material that is not needed is called **nonessential** (or **nonrestrictive**).

Exercise 7   **Practice: Using Commas as Inserters**

Add commas only where they are needed in the following sentences. Some sentences do not need commas.

1. A house full of toys will not always make a troubled child happy.
2. My best friend his eyes red and swollen mourned the loss of his cousin.
3. Mr. Murdock could of course decide to raise the rent.
4. Drivers who take the shortcut to the airport can save at least ten minutes and avoid the congestion at the toll plaza.
5. Our neighbor an enthusiastic gardener has transformed his yard into a small park.
6. *The Polar Express* which both children and adults enjoy was created with an experimental animation process.
7. The little girl at the end of the line has dropped the ice cream out of her cone.
8. Ultimate Books the bookstore in the Midland Mall has the biggest collection of fantasy books and magazines.

Remember the four main ways to use a comma—as a lister, a linker, an introducer, and an inserter—and you'll solve many of your problems with punctuation.

Exercise 8 **Practice: Punctuating with Commas: The Four Main Ways**

Add commas only where they are needed in the following sentences. Do not add any other punctuation, and do not change any existing punctuation. Some sentences do not need commas.

1. As Philip turned the key in the front door he heard a strange noise coming from the second floor.

2. The giant shrimp the best item on the buffet table disappeared in about five minutes.

3. Anyone who loves art will want to visit the new exhibit at the Student Center.

4. I had to work overtime at the hospital of course and couldn't go to the lake with Martin.

5. A house with a fireplace seems more appealing to me than a house with a pool.

6. Well you can do whatever you want and I'll just stay home and watch television.

7. Because we bought an old house we spent a year painting the exterior refinishing the wooden floors repairing the plumbing and remodeling the kitchen.

8. Shelley would you like a mango cake from the Cuban bakery for your birthday?

③ Use the comma correctly with quotations, dates and addresses, numbers, tags, and interjections.

Other Ways to Use a Comma

There are other places to use a comma. Reviewing these uses will help you feel more confident as a writer.

1. Use commas with quotations. Use a comma to set off a direct quotation from the rest of the sentence.

> My father told me, "Money doesn't grow on trees."

> "Let's split the bill," Raymond said.

Note that the comma that introduces the quotation goes before the quotation marks. But once the quotation has begun, commas or periods go inside the quotation marks.

2. Use commas with dates and addresses. Use commas between the items in dates and addresses.

> August 5, 1992, is Chip's date of birth.

> We lived at 133 Emerson Road, Lake Park, Pennsylvania, before we moved to Florida.

Notice the comma after the year in the date, and the comma after the state in the address. These commas are needed when you write a date or address within a sentence.

3. Use commas in numbers. Use commas in numbers of one thousand or larger.

> The price of equipment was $1,293.

4. Use commas with tags. Place the commas after the statement and before the question.

> You aren't going to the cafe now, are you?

> Professor Jones is giving us the test on Monday, isn't she?

5. Use commas with yes, no, and other interjections.

> Yes, I am coming to the park.

> Oh, did I forget to do the assignment for today?

Exercise 9 Practice: Punctuation: Other Ways to Use a Comma

Add commas wherever they are needed in the following sentences. Do not add any other punctuation, and do not change any existing punctuation.

1. "There isn't any milk in the refrigerator" my little boy complained.

2. On January 1 2002 Suzanne and Colin moved into a small house in Clifton New Jersey.

3. Be sure that anything you do you do for the right reasons.

4. She wasn't in class yesterday was she?

5. "I have lived at 535 Orchid Place Denver Colorado for more than six years" Alex told me.

6. Kevin graduated from high school on June 15 2007 and soon started work as a landscaper in Mobile Alabama.

7. Melissa stood in front of the clothes in her closet and muttered "I have got to clean out this mess."

8. No I cannot tell Dr. James that you will not attend his help session.

Exercise 10 Practice: Punctuating with Commas: A Comprehensive Exercise

Add commas only where they are needed in the following sentences. Do not add any other punctuation, and do not change any existing punctuation. Some of the sentences do not need commas.

1. The spoiled little boy refused to eat any of his chicken nuggets nor would he touch his French fries.

2. My old sneakers are in bad shape yet they are more comfortable than any other shoes I own.

3. Cough syrup in tasty flavors should be kept out of children's reach because they might drink the syrup for its taste.

4. Digital Literacy II the hardest class to get into has another section added for next semester.

5. People who enter the theater after a movie has started should stay in one place until their eyes adjust to the darkness.

6. Tim can meet me at the coffee shop or call me when he gets home.

7. Running as fast as he could the officer shouted "Get out of the building!"

8. Dr. Levin the famous psychiatrist has written a book about depression and teenagers.

Connect

Exercise 11 Connect: Editing a Paragraph for Errors in Commas

In the following paragraph, correct any errors related to punctuating with commas. The errors may involve missing or incorrect use of commas. There are nineteen errors.

My grandparents live in an old but very sturdy home. Whoever built it built it well. They bought it in 1970 for $35450 and it was a bargain even in those days. The house has survived several blizzards and my grandfather has never had to make major repairs for heating problems or burst pipes. When a huge hurricane hit the area the house suffered only minor roof damage. The home a two-story wooden house is strong solid, and stable. Part of the story of the house is of course a story of luck. Cable Road where the house sits on several acres of land is full of old houses. Many, have survived bad times and bad weather but most have been hit by a falling tree or flooded by melting snow. My grandparents have watched their neighbors pump the water out of basements cut tree limbs away from the roof or tape broken windows on the storm side of a house. My grandfather and grandmother have helped the other residents of Cable Road deal with the effects of time and weather. On the other hand the neighbors have never had to come to my grandparents' rescue. "We're just grateful for our home" my grandfather says and I envy his good luck.

Section Test Punctuation: The Comma

Some of the sentences below are correct; others have errors in punctuating with commas. Put an *X* next to the sentences with errors.

1. _____ Christina Roberts, my best friend since high school was born in Fort Lauderdale, during a powerful hurricane.

2. _____ The damage to the empty house was senseless, and whoever did it, did it out of pure meanness.

3. _____ No I don't want your old computer, printer, or digital camera.

4. _____ English hasn't borrowed words from many languages, but many languages have borrowed words from English.

5. _____ Super Foods, which is open twenty-four hours a day, is the best place for last-minute grocery shopping.

6. _____ "No one will criticize you for telling the truth," my brother told me.

7. _____ Ella, her face beaming with happiness, graduated from college on May 22, 2007 with a degree in physical therapy.

8. _____ Getting my truck repaired cost me $1214, but it was cheaper than making enormous car payments on a new truck.

THE SEMICOLON

There are two ways to use semicolons:

4 Use the semicolon and colon correctly within a sentence.

1. **Use a semicolon to join two independent clauses:**

   Michael loved his old Camaro; he worked on it every weekend.
   The situation was hopeless; I couldn't do anything.

   > **Note:** If the independent clauses are joined by a conjunctive adverb, you will still need a semicolon. You will also need a comma after any conjunctive adverb that is more than one syllable long.

   conjunctive adverb

   He was fluent in Spanish; *consequently*, he was the perfect companion for our trip to Venezuela.

   conjunctive adverb

   I called the hotline for twenty minutes; *then* I called another number.

   > **For your information:** A list of common conjunctive adverbs is in Chapter 17 on page 389.

   Independent clauses joined by coordinating conjunctions (the words *for, and, nor, but, or, yet, so*) do not need semicolons. Use a comma in front of the coordinating conjunction:

   coordinating conjunction

   Michael loved his old Camaro, *and* he worked on it every weekend.

   coordinating conjunction

   He was fluent in Spanish, *so* he was the perfect companion for our trip to Venezuela.

2. **Use semicolons to separate the items on a list that contains commas.** Adding semicolons will make the list easier to read:

   The contestants came from Rochester, New York; Pittsburgh, Pennsylvania; Trenton, New Jersey; and Boston, Massachusetts. (The semicolons show that Rochester is a city in the state of New York, Pittsburgh is a city in the state of Pennsylvania, and so forth.)

   The new officers of the club will be Althea Bethell, president; Francois Riviere, vice-president; Ricardo Perez, secretary; and Lou Phillips, treasurer. (The semicolons link the person, Althea Bethell, with the office, president, and so forth.)

Exercise 12 **Practice: Punctuating with Semicolons**

Add any missing semicolons to the following sentences. In some sentences, you may have to change commas to semicolons.

1. The noise of construction workers outside the building grew louder meanwhile, I was trying to conduct a serious conversation on the telephone.

2. Two years ago, I was terrified of water now I love to jump into the deep end of the pool.

3. The campus tour allowed us to see classes in action in addition, we were able to speak to a few professors.

4. Stacey is smart, attractive, and outgoing, yet she longs to be more like her younger sister.

5. Mario, my father, Mark, my older brother, Michael, my younger brother, and Michelle, my sister, all have first names that begin with *M*.

6. The research paper is due Tuesday the final exam is on Wednesday.

7. Sarah will call the cable company or stop by its office for an explanation of the latest bill.

8. I have to pack my suitcase tonight otherwise, I might forget something in the morning rush to the airport.

THE COLON

A colon is used at the end of a complete statement. It introduces a list or an explanation:

> **colon introduces a list:** When I went grocery shopping, I picked up a few things: milk, eggs, and coffee.

> **colon introduces an explanation:** The room was a mess: dirty clothes were piled on the chairs, wet towels were thrown on the floor, and an empty pizza box was tossed in the closet.

Remember that the colon comes after a complete statement. What comes after the colon explains or describes what came before the colon. Look once more at the two examples, and you'll see the point.

> When I went grocery shopping, I picked up a few things: milk, eggs, and coffee. (The words after the colon—*milk, eggs, and coffee*—explain what few things I picked up.)

> The room was a mess: dirty clothes were piled on the chairs, wet towels were thrown on the floor, and an empty pizza box was tossed in the closet. (In this sentence, all the words after the colon describe what the mess was like.)

Some people use a colon every time they put a list in a sentence, but this is not a good rule to follow. Instead, remember that a colon, even one that introduces a list, must come after a complete statement.

> **not this:** ~~When I go to the beach, I always bring: suntan lotion, a big towel, and a cooler with iced tea.~~

> **but this:** When I go to the beach, I always bring my supplies: suntan lotion, a big towel, and a cooler with iced tea.

A colon may also introduce long quotations.

> On December 8, 1941, the day after the Japanese attacked Pearl
> Harbor, President Franklin Delano Roosevelt summed up the
> situation: "Hostilities exist. There is no blinking at the fact that our
> people, our territory, and our interests are in grave danger." *(Note
> that what comes after the colon explains what came before it.)*

Exercise 13   **Practice: Punctuating with Colons**

Add colons where they are needed in the following sentences. Some sentences do not need a colon.

1. When you go to the cabin for the weekend, be sure to fill your car with groceries, extra blankets, insect repellent, books, binoculars, and fishing gear.

2. My brother did a superb job of cleaning the bathroom a shining bathtub, a spotless sink, a gleaming toilet, and even a floor free of footprints.

3. Since I had twenty dollars left over at the end of the week, I bought some small surprises for my husband a can of cashews, a bottle of wine, and his favorite magazine.

4. Until we cleaned out the garage, we had a collection of tools, ladders, empty boxes, lawn chairs, broken appliances, and rags crowded into the space.

5. Be sure to bring the following to the next class a dictionary, five sheets of paper and a blue-ink pen.

6. Our neighborhood has several Fourth of July traditions flags flying in people's yards, a parade of small children on their bikes or in strollers, and a community barbecue on a dead-end street.

7. If you want to contribute to the food drive for victims of the storm, you can bring canned food, bread and rolls, bottled water, and paper plates and towels.

8. My grandmother believes that there are two kinds of children the ones who behave and the ones who don't.

Exercise 14   **Practice: Using Semicolons and Colons**

Add semicolons and colons where they are needed in the following sentences. You might have to change a comma to a semicolon.

1. I will never go to a sushi restaurant the thought of eating raw fish makes me nauseous.

2. You need floor mats for your car, and be sure to look for the usual auto supplies motor oil, car wax, and windshield wiper fluid.

3. All the students passed the exam, they had worked hard on this unit.

4. If you go to the drug store, get me some toothpaste, hair gel, and aspirin.

5. Arthur seems like a trustworthy employee, on the other hand, I don't know that much about him.

6. There has been a shake-up in the managerial staff of Tompkins Motors, so the new leaders are Karen Killian, manager, Pierre LaValle, assistant manager, Ron Jessup, service manager, and Lorena Robles, business manager.

7. After my father got a job with a hotel, he took classes in accounting, customer relations, restaurant management, and business law.

8. We take notes on our tablets however, our professor makes us send them to her.

Connect

Exercise 15 **Connect: Editing a Paragraph for Errors in Semicolons and Colons**

In the following paragraph, correct any errors related to punctuating with semicolons or colons. The errors may involve missing or incorrect use of semicolons or colons. There are nine errors.

On one subzero day in Minnesota, my friend and I dreamed of a tropical vacation, but we did not exactly find our dream. We started by listing all the warm places we craved Miami; Florida; Cancun; Mexico; Honolulu; Hawaii; and Kingston; Jamaica. Of course, we soon discovered that the price of traveling to and staying at any of these four places was well beyond our means. We were ready to give up our dreams, then we thought of another way to enjoy fun in the sun without spending thousands of dollars. My sister and her husband had recently returned from a bargain cruise in the Bahamas. The reasonable price included the following round-trip airfare to the port of departure, accommodations in a double cabin, all meals, and all entertainment. Our ship would stop at two ports and also spend a day at a private island where we could swim, snorkel, and soak up the sun. This trip sounded like a perfect way for us to spend our spring break. Of course, nothing is perfect, and we soon experienced many small and large snags. Just as we flew into the city where we would board the ship, a rare winter rain storm hit the tropics. As we left the port of departure, we stood on deck and held giant umbrellas over our heads. The storm followed us to the ports we visited it also hit the private island. Dancing the limbo on a rain-swept patio is not exciting even when the steel drums play. Snorkeling in the rain is not much fun even when the setting is a private island. By the time we returned to Minnesota, we had learned one hard lesson; pack more than sunscreen and swimsuits when you prepare for any cruise.

Section Test Punctuation: The Semicolon and the Colon

Some of the following sentences are correct; others have semicolon or colon errors. Put an *X* next to the incorrect sentences.

1. _____ Drawn by the famous country singer's last concert, people came from all over the southern states: Gainesville, Florida; Savannah, Georgia; Huntsville, Alabama; and Jackson, Mississippi.

2. _____ Don't try to convince me; I'm not going anywhere with you.

3. _____ Amanda forgot to pack her medication; so we had to turn around and drive fifty miles back to her house.

4. _____ Chris will eat just about any cookie in the world: stale cookies, cookie crumbs, half-eaten cookies, even cookies that have fallen on the floor.

5. _____ My cousin got stuck in traffic: then his car overheated.

6. _____ If you go to the islands, be sure to enjoy the natural beauty: the turquoise water, the powdery white beaches, and the amazing undersea creatures.

7. _____ The college debate team won tournaments in Jacksonville, Florida, Athens, Georgia, and Charleston, South Carolina.

8. _____ Charlie won't talk to me about his worries; nor will he share them with his mother.

THE APOSTROPHE

Use the apostrophe in the following ways:

1. Use an apostrophe in contractions to show that letters have been omitted.

do not	= don't
I will	= I'll
is not	= isn't
she would	= she'd
will not	= won't

Also use the apostrophe to show that numbers have been omitted:

the summer of 1998 = the summer of '98

⑤ Use the apostrophe correctly in contractions and to show possession.

Exercise 16 Practice: Using Apostrophes in Contractions

Add apostrophes where they are necessary in each sentence below.

1. Dr. Fanelli is a great veterinarian; shell tell you whats wrong with your potbellied pig.

2. My grandfather never stops talking about the blizzard of 84 and how he didnt think hed live through it.

3. The trip wasnt what Id expected, but Ill never forget it.

4. Hows your new baby doing?

5. Terry wont tell you that theres a problem with the financing for the car.

6. Henry and Lori couldnt make the trip this week; theyll come next month when theyve got more time.

7. If youre sick, youd better stay home from work today.

8. Its wonderful to see dolphins in their natural habitat.

2. Use an apostrophe to show possession. If a word does not end in s, show ownership by adding an apostrophe and s.

the ring belongs to Jill	= Jill's ring
the wallet belongs to somebody	= somebody's wallet
the books arc owned by my father	= my father's books

If two people jointly own something, put the *'s* on the name of the second person listed.

Ann and Mike own a house = Ann and Mike's house

If a word already ends in *s* and you want to show ownership, just add an apostrophe.

the ring belongs to Frances	= Frances' ring
two boys own a dog	= the boys' dog
the house belongs to Ms. Jones	= Ms. Jones' house

Caution: Be careful with apostrophes. These words, the possessive pronouns, do not take apostrophes: *his, hers, theirs, ours, yours, its.*

---

not this: ~~The pencils were their's.~~
but this: The pencils were theirs.

not this: ~~The steak lost it's flavor.~~
but this: The steak lost its flavor.

Exercise 17 **Practice: Using Apostrophes to Show Possession**

Add apostrophes where they are needed in the following sentences. Some sentences do not need apostrophes.

1. Mrs. Noriko promised to improve the companys marketing division and expand its overseas office.

2. I went to Charles and Agnes wedding yesterday, and I thought their wedding cake tasted better than yours.

3. I have been looking for a new smartphone case because my cases design has worn off.

4. Catherine and Anthony are creative people, and the credit for renovating the pediatric wing of the hospital is all theirs.

5. I hope that, when I mentioned the changes at the womens club, I did not hurt anyones feelings.

6. Be careful with Saras tablet; she just bought it.

7. I miss San Diegos weather, but I love Bostons college life and its sense of history.

8. My sister Allisons musical ability is all hers; no one else in the family can sing, play an instrument, or read music.

3. Use the apostrophe for special uses of time, and to create a plural of numbers mentioned as numbers, letters mentioned as letters, and words that normally do not have plurals.

> **special uses of time:** It will take a week's work.
> **numbers mentioned as numbers:** Take out the 5's.
> **letters mentioned as letters:** Cross your *t*'s.
> **words that normally do not have plurals:** I want no more *maybe*'s.

Caution: Do not add an apostrophe to a simple plural.

> **not this:** ~~He lost three suitcase's.~~
> **but this:** He lost three suitcases.

Exercise 18 Practice: Special Uses of Apostrophes

Add apostrophes where they are needed in the following sentences. Some sentences do not need apostrophes. Do not change or add any words.

1. I have *B*s on all my science quizzes, so I feel confident about the test.

2. Alice is going to New Zealand for three weeks; she will stay with relatives who live there.

3. Jennifer deserves a days pay for all the time she spent on cleaning up your office.

4. The winner of the lottery won an amount of money with six *0*s at the end, so it has to be at least one million dollars.

5. It will be several months before I can save up enough vacation days for a trip to Wyoming.

6. My mother writes very fancy capital *A*s because she used to study calligraphy.

7. The down payment on my new house is less than a years worth of rent on my old one.

8. Dont forget your "*excuse me*s" and "*please*s" when you visit Aunt Claudia.

Exercise 19 Practice: Using Apostrophes: A Comprehensive Exercise

Circle the correct form in parentheses in each sentence below.

1. Could the white rabbit in our yard be (someones, someone's) pet?

2. (Theres, There's) nothing wrong with your computer.

3. A new (mens, men's) store just opened in the Palms Plaza.

4. The advisor handed back the registration cards to English II, but they were (ours, our's).

5. I fell in love for the first time in the spring of (99, '99).

6. Tell me if you like (Laura's and Kim's, Laura and Kim's) new roommate.

7. Lamont's answers to my requests are too full of (*nos*, *no's*).

8. Staying out late began to lose (its, it's) appeal for me when I became a father.

Connect

Exercise 20 **Connect: Editing a Paragraph for Errors in Apostrophes**

In the following paragraph, correct any errors related to punctuating with apostrophes. The errors may involve missing or incorrect use of apostrophes. There are eleven errors.

Watching the Super Bowl in Aunt Kathleen's and Uncle Manny's basement lounge is almost as good as being in the stadium. First of all, the room is huge, and its filled with sports memorabilia, comfortable chairs, and a giant television screen. A big refrigerator is packed with food and beverages that are all our's. This basement is soundproof, so the crowd in front of the screen can cheer or cry loudly. Everyone can look at this years most outrageous commercials and wait for the surprise's of the halftime show. Enjoying the Super Bowl while we sit in my aunt and uncles basement has become a tradition for me, my cousin Anthony, my parent's, and my fathers' best friend, Patrick. Also, new faces appear at the party each year. After some games, it takes me a weeks worth of family calls to identify newcomers such as the woman sitting with my cousin or the old man who kissed my aunt. I know that I would love to sit in the seat's at the Super Bowl, but I also love game day with my aunt and uncle. That special Sunday has it's own pleasures.

Section Test **Punctuation: The Apostrophe**

Some of the sentences below are correct; others have errors in using punctuation. Put an *X* by each sentence with an error.

1. _____ Morris is sure to say his "*thank yous*" when he visits his grandfather's house.

2. _____ I'm not sure if Mark and Maria left behind the serving bowls, but I know the platters are theirs.

3. _____ The stray kitten has to be somebodys pet, so we'll post the kitten's photo throughout the neighborhood and keep the little cat safe until it's owner shows up.

4. _____ Although the two data-sharing sites look similiar, the site's are completely different.

5. _____ We'll go to Rita's and Carlos' party after we've had dinner.

6. _____ Tammy got a months salary as a bonus after she'd broken the company's record for sales.

7. _____ I'd like to see a few more *0*'s at the end of my income tax refund check.

8. _____ There's no one under the bed; the monster is a product of Charles imagination.

THE EXCLAMATION MARK

6 Use the exclamation mark, dash, parentheses, and hyphen correctly.

The exclamation mark is used at the end of sentences that express strong emotion:

> **appropriate:** You've won the lottery!
> **inappropriate:** We had a great time! (*Great* already implies excitement.)

Be careful not to overuse the exclamation mark. If your choice of words is descriptive, you should not have to rely on the exclamation point for emphasis. Use it sparingly, for it is easy to rely on exclamations instead of using better vocabulary.

THE DASH

Use a dash to interrupt a sentence. Dashes are used for emphasis, to further explain or define something, or to make a dramatic shift.

> I picked up the crystal bowl carefully, cradled it in my arms, walked softly—and tripped, sending the bowl flying.

Two dashes set off dramatic words that interrupt a sentence.

> Ramon took the life preserver—our only one—and tossed it far out to sea.

> Everyone at the university—faculty, students, and administration— was in shock when the power went out.

Because dashes are somewhat dramatic, use them sparingly.

PARENTHESES

Use parentheses to enclose extra material and afterthoughts.

> I was sure that Ridgefield (the town I'd just visited) was not the place for me.
> Her name (which I have just remembered) was Celestine.

> **Note:** Commas in pairs, dashes in pairs, and parentheses are all used as inserters. They set off material that interrupts the flow of the sentence. The least dramatic and smoothest way to insert material is to use commas.

THE HYPHEN

Use a hyphen to join two or more descriptive words that act as a single-word adjective or **phrasal adjective**.

> Bill was a smooth-talking charmer.
> The stadium had state-of-the-art scoreboards.

Also, use a hyphen in the written form of compound numbers from twenty-one to ninety-nine.

Exercise 21 **Practice: Punctuating with Exclamation Marks, Dashes, Parentheses, and Hyphens**

Add any exclamation marks, dashes, parentheses, and hyphens that are needed in the sentences below.

1. Larry took the airline ticket my last chance at freedom and threw it into the incinerator.

2. There's someone hiding in the closet

3. Lenny Montalbano the boy who used to live next door grew up to start his own medical research company.

4. Mr. Okada is a caring, competent, and good natured supervisor.

5. Mr. Thompson is known for his eccentric ways; one day he came to work in a handsome blue blazer, striped silk tie, gray flannel slacks and bright orange sneakers.

6. Get off the train tracks

7. The salesperson said the radio was a top of the line product.

8. Amanda was a trend setting dresser; she always looked fantastic.

7 Use quotations and capital letters correctly.

QUOTATION MARKS

Use quotation marks for direct quotes, for the titles of short works, and for other special uses.

1. Put quotation marks around direct quotes, a speaker or writer's exact words:

> My mother told me, "There are plenty of fish in the sea."
> "I'm never going there again," said Irene.
> "I'd like to buy you dinner," Peter said, "but I'm out of cash."
> My best friend warned me, "Stay away from that guy. He will break your heart."

Look carefully at the preceding examples. Notice that a comma is used to introduce a direct quotation, and that at the end of the quotation, the comma or period goes inside the quotation marks:

> My mother told me, "There are plenty of fish in the sea."

Notice how direct quotes of more than one sentence are punctuated. If the quote is written in one unit, quotation marks go before the first quoted word and after the last quoted word:

> My best friend warned me, "Stay away from that guy. He will break your heart."

But if the quote is not written as one unit, the punctuation changes:

> "Stay away from that guy," my best friend warned me. "He will break your heart."

Caution: Do *not* put quotation marks around indirect quotations.

> **indirect quotation:** He asked if he could come with us.
> **direct quotation:** He asked, "Can I come with you?"

> **indirect quotation:** She said that she wanted more time.
> **direct quotation:** "I want more time," she said.

2. Put quotation marks around the titles of short works. If you are writing the title of a short work like a short story, an essay, a newspaper or magazine article, a poem, or a song, put quotation marks around the title:

> In middle school, we read Robert Frost's poem "The Road Not Taken."
> My little sister has learned to sing "Itsby Bitsy Spider."

If you are **handwriting** the title of a longer work like a book, movie, magazine, play, television show, or CD, underline the title:

> Last night I saw an old movie, <u>The Godfather</u>.
> I read an article called "Campus Changes" in <u>Newsweek</u>.

In typed papers and printed publications such as books or magazines, titles of long works are italicized:

> Last night I saw an old movie, *The Godfather*.
> I read an article called "Campus Changes" in *Newsweek*.

3. There are other, special uses of quotation marks. You use quotation marks around words mentioned as words in a sentence.

> When you said "never," did you mean it?
> People from the Midwest pronounce "water" differently than I do.

If you are using a quotation within a quotation, use single quotation marks.

> My brother complained, "Every time we get in trouble, Mom has to say 'I told you so.' "
> Kyle said, "Linda has a way of saying 'Excuse me' that is really very rude."

CAPITAL LETTERS

There are ten main situations in which you capitalize:

1. Capitalize the first word of every sentence:

> Yesterday we saw our first soccer game.

2. Capitalize the first word in a direct quotation if the word begins a sentence:

> My aunt said, "This is a gift for your birthday."
> "Have some birthday cake," my aunt said, "and have some more ice cream." (Notice that the second section of this quote does not begin with a capital letter because it does not begin a sentence.)

3. Capitalize the names of persons:

> Nancy Perez and Frank Murray came to see me at the store.
> I asked Mother to feed my cat.

Do not capitalize words like *mother*, *father*, or *aunt* if you put a possessive in front of them.

> I asked my mother to feed my cat.

4. Capitalize the titles of persons:

> I spoke with Dr. Wilson.
> He has to see Dean Johnston.

Do not capitalize when the title is not connected to a name:

> I spoke with that doctor.
> He has to see the dean.

5. Always capitalize countries, cities, languages, nationalities, religions, races, months, days of the week, documents, organizations, holidays, and historical events or periods:

> In high school, we never studied the Vietnam War.
> The Polish-American Club will hold a picnic on Labor Day.

Use small letters for the seasons:

> I love fall because I love to watch the leaves change color.

6. Capitalize the names of particular places:

> We used to hold our annual meetings at Northside Auditorium in Springfield, Iowa, but this year we are meeting at Riverview Theater in Langton, Missouri.

Use small letters if a particular place is not given:

> We are looking for an auditorium we can rent for our meeting.

7. Use capital letters for geographic locations:

> Jim was determined to find a good job in the West.

But use small letters for geographic directions:

> To get to my house, you have to drive west on the turnpike.

8. Capitalize the names of specific products:

> I always drink Diet Pepsi for breakfast.

But use small letters for a kind of product:

> I always drink a diet cola for breakfast.

9. Capitalize the names of specific school courses (and do not abbreviate the course):

> I have to take Child Psychology next term (*not* "Child Psych").

But use small letters for a general academic subject:

> My advisor told me to take a psychology course.

10. Capitalize the first and last words in the titles of long or short works, and capitalize all other significant words in the titles:

> I've always wanted to read *The Old Man and the Sea.*
> Whenever we go to see the team play, my uncle sings "Take Me Out to the Ballgame."

> **Note:** Remember that the titles of long works, like books, are italicized (unless these titles are handwritten; then they are underlined). The titles of short works, like songs, are placed within quotation marks.

Exercise 22 | **Practice: Using Quotation Marks, Underlining, and Capital Letters**

Add any missing quotation marks, underlining, and capital letters to the sentences below. You can assume that all these sentences are in printed form.

1. When I was growing up, uncle Richard was my favorite relative, but I later discovered my uncle had a dangerous temper.

2. When Melanie signed up for her winter term at college, she registered for classes in social science, writing, and music.

3. I can't stand it, my girlfriend said, when you say maybe instead of giving me a definite answer.

4. I finally found a good preschool for my son; it's the Madison school for early childhood education, and dr. Howard of Miller university is the director.

5. One night, my brother Jason was watching a television show called Dirty Jobs; I watched it for a minute and said, Ugh! Turn off that disgusting program."

6. David is looking for a job in the midwest because he wants to be near his parents, who live north of Chicago.

7. Whenever Mimi says the word love, she means the word infatuation.

8. There is nothing funnier than listening to my grandfather sing Marvin Gaye's old song, heard It Through the Grapevine.

8 Use numbers and abbreviations correctly.

NUMBERS

Spell out numbers that take one or two words:

Alice mailed two hundred brochures.
I spent ninety dollars on car repairs.

Use the numbers themselves if it takes more than two words to spell them out.

We looked through 243 old photographs.
The sticker price was $10,397.99.

Also use numbers to write dates, times, addresses, and parts of a book.

We live at 24 Cambridge Street.
They were married on April 3, 1993.
Chapter 3 had difficult maps to read, especially the one on page 181.

ABBREVIATIONS

Although you should spell out most words rather than abbreviate them, you may abbreviate *Mr.*, *Mrs.*, *Ms.*, *Jr.*, *Sr.*, and *Dr.* when they are used with a proper name. You should abbreviate references to time and to organizations widely known by initials.

The moderator asked Ms. Steinem to comment.
The bus left at 5:00 p.m., and the trip took two hours.
He works for the FBI.

You should spell out the names of places, months, days of the week, courses of study, and words referring to parts of a book:

not this: ~~I missed the last class, so I never got the notes for Chap. 3~~.
but this: I missed the last class, so I never got the notes for Chapter 3.

not this: ~~He lives on Chestnut Street in Boston, Mass~~.
but this: He lives on Chestnut Street in Boston, Massachusetts.

not this: ~~Pete missed his psych. test~~.
but this: Pete missed his psychology test.

Exercise 23 Practice: Using Numbers and Abbreviations

Correct any errors in the use of numbers or abbreviations in the following sentences. Some sentences may not need corrections.

1. Ellen came into our soc. class last Mon., carrying her research paper, which looked about three in. thick.

2. Mr. and Mrs. Chang sent one hundred fifty five invitations to their daughter's wedding in Minneapolis, Minn.

3. My parents' apartment on Sunset Ave. had 4 rooms.

4. Matthew left Fla. on Mar. third, 2014, to begin a job with the Abraham and Braun Co. in N. Dakota.

5. My phys. ed. teacher starts class promptly at 8:30 a.m. every Fri.

6. It took me two hrs. to finish Chap. 3 of my sociology textbook.

7. Gregory charges twenty-five dollars an hour to help people with their computer problems.

8. Charles Woods, Jr., was an executive with the NFL for ten years before he took a job with ABC Sports.

Note: Exercises incorporating concepts from all punctuation sections follow the section test.

Section Test Other Punctuation

Some of the sentences below are correct; others have errors in using quotation marks, capital letters, numbers, and abbreviations. Put an *X* next to the sentences.

1. _____ My mother warned, "Before you do anything impulsive, think about your future".

2. _____ Carlotta spent one thousand and eighty dollars on new curtains for her house even though she owes her brother hundreds of dollars for fixing her roof.

3. _____ At my aunt's wedding reception, my sister sang "I Will Always love You" as the bride and groom danced.

4. _____ Dr. Gillespie is teaching an online course in Intro. to Psychology in the summer term.

5. _____ In our elementary school library, there was a framed copy of the Declaration of Independence on the wall.

6. _____ Mike always says "eventually" when I ask him when he will graduate.

7. _____ "Give me a few minutes," Father said, "and I'll take you to the park."

8. _____ I used to walk down the fashionable streets in Chicago, Ill., and stare at the the expensive cars and luxury stores.

Practice: A Comprehensive Exercise on Punctuation

Add any missing punctuation to the following sentences. Also, correct any errors in capitalization and in the use of numbers or abbreviations. Assume that all the sentences are in printed or typed form.

1. We had a second rate meal at Frank and Maries house of Ribs last Sat. night we can't recommend the place to you.

2. I'm looking for a book called the rule of four my friend recommended it.

3. The five year old boy began to pour chocolate syrup on the kitchen floor meanwhile the babysitter dozed on the living room couch.

4. Lance took 2 spanish courses at National H.S. so he does not have to take a foreign language class at Centenary college.

5. The star athlete wanted to know if she could miss a days practice.

6. The star athlete asked Can I miss a days practice

7. I love a whole new world, the song from the movie Aladdin.

8. Now that we live in Buffalo N.Y. I need some warm clothes sweaters, gloves, hats, and a coat with a heavy lining.

Connect

Connect: Editing a Paragraph for Errors in Punctuation

In the following paragraph, correct any errors related to punctuation or mechanics. The errors may involve missing or incorrect punctuation, capitalization, use of numbers, or abbreviations. There are twenty-one errors.

When I agreed to do some work at a dirty old house I was not prepared, for the consequences. The house had belonged to my Mothers second cousin. When he died, he left it to my mother. She persuaded me and my brother to clean the house for her. After it was cleaned, she planned to sell the property. As my brother Sam and I approached the decrepit house we noticed that a dark, blue sky covered us. Beneath the brooding sky, the roof of the house had lost many of it's shingles. The rickety gate creaked ominously when we entered the yard. I reached the front entrance, and grabbed the rusty doorknob. Almost immediately, a hairy spider crawled across my hand. The atmosphere did not improve when we entered the house. Spider webs, and dust covered each room, then a horrible smell repelled us as we moved toward the basement stairs. The stairs to the basement were creaky. Some were missing. My brother stumbled and had to grab my hand, after he put his foot into an open space where a stair should have been. Soon we saw more horror. At least 100 rats were crawling around the dark basement spaces. Racing back to the smelly safety of the upper floor's, I wondered, "What else was waiting for us in this miserable place?" We decided not to explore any more of this crazy place. Our short time in the house had made us feel like ready made victims in a movie like *Dawn Of The Dead*.

Chapter Test Punctuation

MyWritingLab™

Some of the sentences below are punctuated correctly; others have errors. Write *OK* next to the correct sentences; write *X* next to the incorrect sentences.

1. _____ I wonder if you would like me to bake a cake for your birthday.

2. _____ Andrew tried to fit in with his brother's friends, but never felt at ease around them.

3. _____ At the back of the house was a large patio surrounded by palm trees.

4. _____ Burgers and More, the most popular restaurant near campus, is closing its doors.

5. _____ Lisa warned her sister, "Stay away from people who love to gossip."

6. _____ Lightning struck the old school; fortunately no one was hurt.

7. _____ I would never drive a long distance without: my phone, water, and snacks.

8. _____ The credit for Jan and Jimmy's success in business is all theirs.

Quick Question MyWritingLab™

Does the following sentence contain a spelling error? Yes/No

A week in the mountains appealled to me because I could find relief from the city's heat.

(After you study this chapter, you will be confident of your answer.)

Learning Objectives

In this chapter, you will learn to:

1. Know the difference between vowels and consonants.
2. Apply basic spelling rules to determine correct word endings.
3. Recognize when a one- or two-word spelling applies to certain terms.

No one is a perfect speller, but there are ways to become a better speller. If you can learn a few spelling rules, you can answer many of your spelling questions.

VOWELS AND CONSONANTS

1 Know the difference between vowels and consonants.

To understand the spelling rules, you need to know the difference between vowels and consonants. **Vowels** are the letters *a, e, i, o, u,* and sometimes *y.* **Consonants** are all the other letters.

The letter *y* is a vowel when it has a vowel sound.
    silly (The *y* sounds like *ee,* a vowel sound.)
    cry (The *y* sounds like *i,* a vowel sound.)

The letter *y* is a consonant when it has a consonant sound.
>   yellow (The *y* has a consonant sound.)
>   yesterday (The *y* has a consonant sound.)

SPELLING RULE 1: DOUBLING A FINAL CONSONANT

When you add an ending, double the final consonant of a word if all three of the following are true:

1. The word is one syllable, or the accent is on the last syllable.
2. The word ends in a single consonant preceded by a single vowel.
3. The ending you are adding starts with a vowel.

> begin + ing = beginning
> shop   + er   = shopper
> stir   + ed   = stirred
> occur + ed   = occurred
> fat   + est = fattest
> pin   + ing = pinning

2 Apply basic spelling rules to determine correct word endings.

Exercise 1 Practice: Doubling a Final Consonant

Add *-ed* to the following words by applying the rules for double consonants.

1. stammer _____
2. swat _____
3. trick _____
4. order _____
5. admit _____
6. drip _____
7. stop _____
8. excel _____

SPELLING RULE 2: DROPPING THE FINAL *e*

Drop the final *e* before you add an ending that starts with a vowel.

> observe + ing   = observing
> excite   + able = excitable
> fame   + ous   = famous
> create   + ive   = creative

Keep the final *e* before an ending that starts with a consonant.

> love   + ly   = lovely
> hope   + ful   = hopeful
> excite + ment = excitement
> life   + less = lifeless

Exercise 2 Practice: Dropping the Final *e*

Combine the following words and endings by following the rule for dropping the final *e*.

1. imagine + able _____
2. care   + less _____

3. arrange + ment _____

4. resource + ful _____

5. behave + ing _____

6. expense + ive _____

7. intense + ly _____

8. refuse + ing _____

SPELLING RULE 3: CHANGING THE FINAL *y* TO *i*

When a word ends in a consonant plus *y*, change the *y* to *i* when you add an ending:

try	+ es	=	tries
silly	+ er	=	sillier
rely	+ ance	=	reliance
tardy	+ ness	=	tardiness

> **Note:** When you add -*ing* to words ending in *y*, always keep the *y*.

cry	+ ing	=	crying
rely	+ ing	=	relying

Exercise 3   Practice: Changing the Final *y* to *i*

Combine the following words and endings by applying the rule for changing the final *y* to *i*.

1. happy + er _____

2. apply + ing _____

3. penny + less _____

4. marry + ed _____

5. deny + es _____

6. ally + ance _____

7. comply + ant _____

8. ready + ness _____

SPELLING RULE 4: ADDING -*s* OR -*es*

Add -*es* instead of -*s* to a word if the word ends in *ch*, *sh*, *ss*, *x*, or *z*. The -*es* adds an extra syllable to the word.

box	+ es	=	boxes
witch	+ es	=	witches
class	+ es	=	classes
clash	+ es	=	clashes

Exercise 4   **Practice: Adding -s or –es**

Apply the rule for adding -s or -es to the following words.

1. polish   _____   5. fix   _____

2. defeat   _____   6. pass   _____

3. march   _____   7. back   _____

4. stock   _____   8. tax   _____

SPELLING RULE 5: USING *ie* OR *ei*

Use *i* before *e*, except after *c*, or when the sound is like *a*, as in *neighbor* and *weigh*.

i before *e*:

relief   convenience   friend   piece

e before *i*:

conceive   sleigh   weight   receive

Exercise 5   **Practice: Using *ie* or *ei***

Add *ie* or *ei* to the following words by applying the rule for using *ie* or *ei*.

1. dec _ _ t   5. perc _ _ ve

2. fr _ _ ght   6. ch _ _ f

3. conc _ _ t   7. n _ _ ce

4. bel _ _ f   8. f _ _ ld

Exercise 6   **Practice: Spelling Rules: A Comprehensive Exercise**

Combine the following words and endings by applying the spelling rules.

1. blur   +   ed   _____

2. carry   +   ed   _____

3. fizz   +   s or es   _____

4. tidy   +   er   _____

5. perch   +   s or es   _____

6. harass   +   s or es   _____

7. plan   +   ed   _____

8. ready   +   ness   _____

9. ply   +   able   _____

10. concur   +   ed   _____

Connect

Exercise 7   **Connect: Editing a Paragraph for Spelling**

Correct the spelling errors in the following paragraph. Write your corrections above each error. There are ten errors.

Buying store-brand products, which are usually cheaper than national-brand products, is a good way to save money. I used to think that buying national brands of items such as cereal or peanut butter meant getting food of better quality. However, I have stoped beleiving in that distinction. For example, how much difference can there be in two boxs of raisin bran from different companys? In addition, I have learned that many of the store brands are produced in the same mills or factorys as the national brands. It is quite possible that Kellogg's raisin bran and Publix raisin bran were made with the same bran, sugar, raisins, and other ingredients and were made in the same place. The only difference between a can of peachs sold by a national brand and one sold by a store brand may be the price. The national brand usually costs more because nationally known companies have to pay more for their expensive national advertising campaigns. Recently, I have tryed to be a smarter shoper, and I have concentrated on buying store brands of such items as bottled water, English muffinns, ice cream, and peanuts. In most cases, I cannot tell the difference between the national and the store brands. Now, when I visit my nieghborhood supermarket, I am a little smarter than I used to be.

DO YOU SPELL IT AS ONE WORD OR TWO?

3 Recognize when a one- or two-word spelling applies to certain terms.

Sometimes you can be confused about certain words. You are not sure whether to combine them to make one word or to spell them as two words. The lists below show some commonly confused words.

Words That Should Not Be Combined

a lot	each other	high school	every time
even though	good night	all right	no one
living room	dining room	in front	

Words That Should Be Combined

another	newspapers	bathroom
bedroom	playroom	good-bye, goodbye, or good-by
bookkeeper	roommate	cannot
schoolteacher	downstairs	southeast, northwest, etc.
grandmother	throughout	nearby
worthwhile	nevertheless	yourself, himself, myself, etc.

Words Whose Spelling Depends on Their Meaning

one word: *Already* means "before."
He offered to do the dishes, but I had *already* done them.
two words: *All ready* means "ready."
My dog was *all ready* to play Frisbee.

one word: *Altogether* means "entirely."
That movie was *altogether* too confusing.
two words: *All together* means "in a group."
My sisters were *all together* in the kitchen.

one word: *Always* means "every time."
My grandfather is *always* right about baseball statistics.
two words: *All ways* means "every path" or "every aspect."
We tried *all ways* to get to the beach house.
He is a gentleman in *all ways*.

one word: *Anymore* means "any longer."
I do not want to exercise *anymore*.
two words: *Any more* means "additional."
Are there *any more* pickles?

one word: *Anyone* means "any person at all."
Is *anyone* home?
two words: *Any one* means "one person or thing in a special group."
I'll take *any one* of the chairs on sale.

one word: *Apart* means "separate."
Liam stood *apart* from his friends.
two words: *A part* is "a piece or section."
I read *a part* of the chapter.

one word: *Everyday* means "ordinary."
Tim was wearing his *everyday* clothes.
two words: *Every day* means "each day."
Sam jogs *every day*.

one word: *Everyone* means "all the people."
Everyone has bad days.
two words: *Every one* means "all the people or things in a specific group."
My father asked *every one* of the neighbors for a donation to the Red Cross.

Exercise 8   **Practice: Do You Spell It as One Word or Two?**

Circle the correct word in parentheses in each sentence below.

1. Jason apologized to me yesterday; he said he wanted to make everything (all right, allright) between us.

2. Terry would be happy to own (any one, anyone) of the beautiful houses being built on Pinewood Avenue.

3. If you have (all ready, already) seen the new Jamie Foxx movie, let's go see the one with Jennifer Lopez and Matt Damon.

4. Robin is thinking of moving back to the (North East, Northeast); she misses her friends in Vermont.

5. Being snowed in at the airport was an (all together, altogether) horrible experience.

6. My father sold insurance, and my mother was a (school teacher, schoolteacher) in an elementary school.

7. (Every time, Everytime) I hear that song, I think of Luis.

8. My math professor says he doesn't want to hear (any more, anymore) complaints about the homework.

Connect

Exercise 9　**Connect: Do You Spell It as One Word or Two? Correcting Errors in a Paragraph**

The following paragraph contains errors in word combinations. Correct the errors in the space above each line. There are ten errors.

My friends all ways want to go to a club on Saturday nights, but I am not willing to go with them any more. Like many women, I want to meet people, but I don't think I want to meet men in a bar. Everytime I go to a bar, I meet two kinds of men: drunk men or arrogant men. Of course, most of my girlfriends and I drink too much at a bar or a club, too. Perhaps we also appear to be arrogant. I have begun to think that, a part from putting men and women under the same roof, bars don't do much to help people get to know eachother. Loud music, crowded spaces, and role-playing don't help anyone make a new friend. Worth while relationships are likely to begin in a more natural environment such as a classroom, snack bar, gym, workplace, or place of worship. I can not put myself in the same situation of dressing up, trying to look cool, and scanning the crowd for any one who might become a friend. The night all ways ends in a headache, a disappointment, or a mistake. I am saying goodby to my Saturday night routine and looking for something healthier.

A LIST OF COMMONLY MISSPELLED WORDS

Following is a list of words you use often in your writing. Study this list and use it as a reference.

1. absence
2. absent
3. accept
4. achieve
5. ache
6. acquire
7. across
8. actually
9. advertise
10. again
11. a lot
12. all right

13. almost
14. always
15. amateur
16. American
17. answer
18. anxious
19. apparent
20. appetite
21. apology
22. appreciate
23. argue
24. argument
25. asked
26. athlete
27. attempt
28. August
29. aunt
30. author
31. automobile
32. autumn
33. avenue
34. awful
35. awkward
36. balance
37. basically
38. because
39. becoming
40. beginning
41. behavior
42. belief
43. believe
44. benefit
45. bicycle
46. bought
47. breakfast
48. breathe
49. brilliant
50. brother
51. brought
52. bruise
53. build
54. bulletin
55. bureau
56. buried
57. business
58. busy
59. calendar
60. cannot
61. career
62. careful
63. catch
64. category

65. caught
66. cemetery
67. cereal
68. certain
69. chair
70. cheat
71. chief
72. chicken
73. children
74. cigarette
75. citizen
76. city
77. college
78. color
79. comfortable
80. committee
81. competition
82. conscience
83. convenient
84. conversation
85. copy
86. cough
87. cousin
88. criticism
89. criticize
90. crowded
91. daily
92. daughter
93. deceive
94. decide
95. definite
96. dentist
97. dependent
98. deposit
99. describe
100. desperate
101. development
102. different
103. dilemma
104. dining
105. direction
106. disappearance
107. disappoint
108. discipline
109. disease
110. divide
111. doctor
112. doesn't
113. don't
114. doubt
115. during
116. dying

117. early
118. earth
119. eighth
120. eligible
121. embarrass
122. encouragement
123. enough
124. environment
125. especially
126. etc.
127. every
128. exact
129. exaggeration
130. excellent
131. except
132. exercise
133. excite
134. existence
135. expect
136. experience
137. explanation
138. factory
139. familiar
140. family
141. fascinating
142. February
143. finally
144. forehead
145. foreign
146. forty
147. fourteen
148. friend
149. fundamental
150. general
151. generally
152. goes
153. going
154. government
155. grammar
156. grateful
157. grocery
158. guarantee
159. guard
160. guess
161. guidance
162. guide
163. half
164. happiness
165. handkerchief
166. heavy
167. height
168. heroes

(Continued)

169. holiday
170. hospital
171. humorous
172. identity
173. illegal
174. imaginary
175. immediately
176. important
177. independent
178. integration
179. intelligent
180. interest
181. interfere
182. interpretation
183. interrupt
184. irrelevant
185. irritable
186. iron
187. island
188. January
189. jewelry*
190. judgment
191. kindergarten
192. kitchen
193. knowledge
194. laboratory
195. language
196. laugh
197. leisure
198. length
199. library
200. loneliness
201. listen
202. lying
203. maintain
204. maintenance
205. marriage
206. mathematics
207. meant
208. measure
209. medicine
210. million
211. miniature
212. minute
213. muscle
214. mysterious
215. naturally
216. necessary
217. neighbor
218. nervous
219. nickel

220. niece
221. ninety
222. ninth
223. occasion
224. o'clock
225. often
226. omission
227. once
228. operate
229. opinion
230. optimist
231. original
232. parallel
233. particular
234. peculiar
235. perform
236. perhaps
237. permanent
238. persevere
239. personnel
240. persuade
241. physically
242. pleasant
243. possess
244. possible
245. potato
246. practical
247. prefer
248. prejudice
249. prescription
250. presence
251. president
252. privilege
253. probably
254. professor
255. psychology
256. punctuation
257. pursue
258. quart
259. really
260. receipt
261. receive
262. recognize
263. recommend
264. reference
265. religious
266. reluctantly
267. remember
268. resource
269. restaurant
270. ridiculous

271. right
272. rhythm
273. sandwich
274. Saturday
275. scene
276. schedule
277. scissors
278. secretary
279. seize
280. several
281. severely
282. significant
283. similar
284. since
285. sincerely
286. soldier
287. sophomore
288. strength
289. studying
290. success
291. surely
292. surprise
293. taught
294. temperature
295. theater
296. thorough
297. thousand
298. tied
299. tomorrow
300. tongue
301. tragedy
302. trouble
303. truly
304. twelfth
305. unfortunately
306. unknown
307. until
308. unusual
309. using
310. variety
311. vegetable
312. Wednesday
313. weird
314. which
315. writing
316. written
317. yesterday

judgement is an alternate
spelling

MyWritingLab™ Visit Chapter 29, "Spelling," in *MyWritingLab* to test
your understanding of the chapter objectives.

Words That Sound Alike/ Look Alike

CHAPTER 30

Quick Question MyWritingLab™

Which sentence uses advise *correctly?*

A. *The academic office advises students on courses to take to complete their course of study.*

B. *The academic office has counselors who give advise on what courses to take.*

(After you study this chapter, you will be confident of your answer.)

Learning Objectives

In this chapter, you will learn to:

1. Distinguish between sound-alike and look-alike words.
2. Use sound-alike and look-alike words correctly in writing.

WORDS THAT SOUND ALIKE/LOOK ALIKE

Words that sound alike or look alike (often called **homonyms**) can be confusing. Here is a list of some of the confusing words. Study this list, and make a note of any words that give you trouble.

a/an/and *A* is used before a word beginning with a consonant or consonant sound:

> Jason bought *a* car.

An is used before a word beginning with a vowel or vowel sound:

> Nancy took *an* apple to work.

1. Distinguish between sound-alike and look-alike words.

And joins words or ideas:

> Psychology 101 *and* English Literature are my favorite courses.
> Fresh vegetables taste delicious, *and* they are nutritious.

accept/except *Accept* means "to receive":

> I *accept* your apology.

Except means "excluding":

> I'll give you all my books *except* my dictionary.

addition/edition An *addition* is something that is added:

> My father built an *addition* to our house in the form of a porch.

An *edition* is an issue of a newspaper or one of a series of printings of a book:

> I checked the latest *edition* of the *Daily News* to see if my advertisement is in it.

advice/advise *Advice* is an opinion offered as a guide; it is what you give someone:

> Betty asked for my *advice* about which classes she should take next semester.

Advise is what you do when you give an opinion offered as a guide:

> I couldn't *advise* Betty about the courses.

affect/effect *Affect* means "to influence something":

> Getting a bad grade will *affect* my chances for a scholarship.

Effect means "a result" or "to cause something to happen":

> Your kindness had a great *effect* on me.
> The committee struggled to *effect* a compromise.

allowed/aloud *Allowed* means "permitted":

> I'm not *allowed* to skateboard on those steps.

Aloud means "out loud":

> The teacher read the story *aloud*.

all ready/already *All ready* means "ready":

> The dog was *all ready* to go for a walk.

Already means "before":

> David had *already* made the salad.

altar/alter An *altar* is a table or place in a church:

> They were married in front of the *altar*.

Alter means "to change":

> My plane was delayed, so I had to *alter* my plans for the evening.

angel/angle An *angel* is a heavenly being:

> That night, I felt an *angel* guiding me.

An *angle* is the space within two lines:

> The road turned at a sharp *angle*.

are/our *Are* is a verb, the plural of *is:*

> We *are* friends of the mayor.

Our means "belonging to us":

> We have *our* writing workshop in the Pate Building today.

beside/besides *Beside* means "next to":

> He sat *beside* me at the concert.

Besides means "in addition":

> I would never lie to you; *besides*, I have no reason to lie.

brake/break *Brake* means "to stop" or "a device for stopping":

> That truck *brakes* at railroad crossings.
> When he saw the animal on the road, he hit the *brakes*.

Break means "to come apart," or "to make something come apart":

> The eggs are likely to *break*.
> I can *break* the seal on that package.

breath/breathe *Breath* is the air you take in, and it rhymes with *death:*

> I was running so fast, I lost my *breath*.

Breathe means "to take in air":

> He found it hard to *breathe* in high altitudes.

buy/by *Buy* means "to purchase something":

> Sylvia wants to *buy* a new laptop.

By means "near," "by means of," or "before":

> He sat *by* his sister.
> I learn *by* taking good notes in class.
> *By* ten o'clock, Nick was tired.

capital/capitol *Capital* means "city" or "wealth":

> Albany is the *capital* of New York.
> Jack invested his *capital* in real estate.

A *capitol* is a building where a legislature meets:

> The city has a famous *capitol* building.

cereal/serial *Cereal* is a breakfast food or type of grain:

> My favorite *cereal* is Cheerios.

Serial means "in a series":

> Look for the *serial* number on the appliance.

choose/chose *Choose* means "to select." It rhymes with *snooze:*

> Today I am going to *choose* a new sofa.

Chose is the past tense of *choose:*

> Yesterday I *chose* a new rug.

close/clothes/cloths *Close* means "near" or "intimate." It can also mean "to end or shut something":

> We live *close* to the train station.
> James and Margie are *close* friends.
> Noreen wants to *close* her eyes for ten minutes.

Clothes are wearing apparel:

Eduardo has new *clothes*.

Cloths are pieces of fabric:

I clean the silver with damp *cloths* and a special polish.

coarse/course *Coarse* means "rough" or "crude":

The top of the table had a *coarse* texture.
His language was *coarse*.

A *course* is a direction or path. It is also a subject in school:

The hurricane took a northern *course*.
In my freshman year, I took a *course* in drama.

complement/compliment Complement means "complete" or "make better":

The colors in that room *complement* the style of the furniture.

A *compliment* is praise:

Trevor gave me a *compliment* about my cooking.

conscience/conscious Your *conscience* is your inner, moral guide:

His *conscience* bothered him when he told a lie.

Conscious means "aware" or "awake":

The accident victim was not fully conscious.

council/counsel A *council* is a group of people:

The Student Government *Council* meets this afternoon.

Counsel means "advice" or "to give advice":

I need your *counsel* about my investments.
My father always *counsels* me about my career.

decent/descent *Decent* means "suitable" or "proper":

I hope Mike gets a *decent* job.

Descent means "going down, falling, or sinking":

The plane began its *descent* to the airport.

desert/dessert A *desert* is dry land. To *desert* means "to abandon":

To survive a trip across the *desert*, people need water.
He will never *desert* a friend.

Dessert is the sweet food we eat at the end of a meal.

I want ice cream for *dessert*.

do/due *Do* means "perform":

I have to stop complaining; I *do* it constantly.

Due means "owing" or "because of":

The rent is *due* tomorrow.
The game was canceled *due* to rain.

does/dose *Does* is a form of *do:*

My father *does* the laundry.

A *dose* is a quantity of medicine.

> Whenever I had a cold, my mother gave me a *dose* of cough syrup.

fair/fare *Fair* means "unbiased." It can also mean "promising" or "good":

> I received a *fair* grade for my project.
> Jose has a *fair* chance of winning the title.

A *fare* is the amount of money a passenger must pay.

> I couldn't afford the plane *fare* to Miami.

farther/further *Farther* means "a greater physical distance":

> His house is a few blocks *farther* down the street.

Further means "greater" or "additional." Use it when you are not describing a physical distance:

> My second French class gave me *further* training in French conversation.

flour/flower *Flour* is ground-up grain, an ingredient used in cooking:

> I use whole-wheat *flour* in my muffins.

A *flower* is a blossom:

> She wore a *flower* in her hair.

forth/fourth *Forth* means "forward":

> The pendulum on the clock swung back and *forth.*

Fourth means "number four in a sequence":

> I was *fourth* in line for tickets.

hear/here *Hear* means "to receive sounds in the ear":

> I can *hear* the music.

Here is a place:

> We can have the meeting *here.*

heard/herd *Heard* is the past tense of *hear:*

> I *heard* you talk in your sleep last night.

A *herd* is a group of animals:

> The farmer has a fine *herd* of cows.

hole/whole A *hole* is an empty place or opening:

> I see a *hole* in the wall.

Whole means "complete" or "entire":

> Silvio gave me the *whole* steak.

isle/aisle An *isle* is an island:

> We visited the *isle* of Capri.

An *aisle* is a passageway between sections of seats:

> The flight attendant came down the *aisle* and offered us coffee.

its/it's *Its* means "belonging to it":

> The car lost *its* rear bumper.

It's is a shortened form of *it is* or *it has*:

> *It's* a beautiful day.
> *It's* been a pleasure to meet you.

knew/new *Knew* is the past tense of *know*:

> I *knew* Teresa in high school.

New means "fresh, recent, not old":

> I want some *new* shoes.

know/no Know means "to understand":

> They *know* how to play soccer.

No is a negative:

> Carla has *no* fear of heights.

Exercise 1   Practice: Words That Sound Alike/Look Alike

Circle the correct words in parentheses in each sentence below.

1. I need to look (farther, further) into the circumstances of the crime before I can (advice, advise) you about possible suspects.

2. The rich investment banker collects first (additions, editions) of famous books; he has an expert tell him which ones to (buy, by).

3. Edward must have no (conscience, conscious), for he was willing to (desert, dessert) his children in order to satisfy his own desires.

4. Whenever Kim (complements, compliments) me, I (hear, here) a hint of insincerity in her voice.

5. Eric needs a (does, dose) of reality before he makes plans to walk to the (altar, alter) with Sabrina.

6. I spent a (hole, whole) lot of money on dresses and other (close, clothes, cloths) last month, and now payment is (do, due).

7. When I had to speak in front of the town (council, counsel), I was so nervous I could hardly (breath, breathe).

8. In (are, our) Algebra course, the professor reviewed how to find the correct (angel, angle) of different shapes.

Collaborate

Exercise 2   Collaborate: Words That Sound Alike/Look Alike

Working with a partner or group, write one sentence for each word below.

1. a. its   _____
   b. it's   _____

2. a. coarse   _____
   b. course   _____

3. a. fair   _____
   b. fare

4. **a.** forth _____

    b. fourth _____

5. **a.** capital _____

    b. capitol _____

6. **a.** accept _____

    b. except _____

7. **a.** brake _____

    b. break _____

8. **a.** affect _____

    b. effect _____

| Exercise 3 | Connect: Editing a Paragraph for Words That Sound Alike/ Look Alike |

Connect

The following paragraph has errors in words that sound alike/look alike. Correct each error in the space above it. There are ten errors.

Driving an old truck presented several challenges for me recently. I usually ride my bike to school and sometimes drive my girlfriend's car. However, one afternoon she called me and asked for help. She was stranded on a country road about ten miles from home. Her car had broken down, and she needed me to pick her up. I couldn't leave her desperate and desserted, waiting alone for a tow truck. Since I had no car, I borrowed my friend's old truck. I had never driven a truck before; beside, I was nervous about driving on strange roads. Nevertheless, I set fourth bravely. As soon as I started the engine, I was conscience of weird sounds. They seemed to be coming from the engine. A few minutes later, I hit a whole in the road. I imagined the worst consequences. Maybe I had broken something important under the truck. Perhaps I had lost the ability to steer. Nervously, I drove further down the rough road. My next challenge was a steep decent down a hill. At that moment, I feared a loss of break power, but fortunately, I made it safely down the hill. Several miles later, I saw my girlfriend and her car at the side of a wooded area. After a long wait, we managed to get her car towed and to return safely to town. The series of mishaps involved in driving that truck led me to make a promise to myself: I will never drive that truck again. I would rather pay bus or even taxi fair, hitchhike, or even stay home. I will do anything accept get behind the wheel of that decrepit vehicle.

2 Use sound-alike and look-alike words correctly in writing.

MORE WORDS THAT SOUND ALIKE/LOOK ALIKE

lead/led When *lead* rhymes with *need*, it means "to give directions, to take charge." If *lead* rhymes with *bed*, it is a metal:

> The tutor will *lead* our study group this afternoon.
> Your bookbag is as heavy as *lead*.

Led is the past form of *lead* when it means "to give directions, to take charge":

> The cheerleaders *led* the parade last year.

lessen/lesson *Lessen* means make less or reduce:

> I took an aspirin to *lessen* the pain of my headache.

A *lesson* is something to be learned or studied:

> I had my first guitar *lesson* yesterday.

loan/lone A *loan* is something you give on the condition that it be returned:

> When I was broke, I got a *loan* of fifty dollars from my aunt.

Lone means "solitary, alone":

> A *lone* shopper stood in the checkout line.

loose/lose *Loose* means "not tight":

> In the summer, *loose* clothing keeps me cool.

To *lose* something means "to be unable to keep it":

> I'm afraid I will *lose* my car keys.

medal/meddle/metal A *medal* is a badge of honor or a coinlike piece of bronze, silver, or similar substance used to commemorate an event.

> Mandy won a *medal* for swimming at the regional competition.
> At the Revolutionary War museum, visitors could buy souvenir *medals* depicting famous battles.

To *meddle* means to interfere when the interference is not justified.

> Ben didn't think his mother should *meddle* in his romantic attachments.

Metal is an element such as gold or silver that often has a particular luster.

> Her bracelet was a thick cuff of a beaten *metal*.

moral/morale *Moral* means "upright, honorable, connected to ethical standards":

> I have a *moral* obligation to care for my children.

Morale is confidence or spirit:

> After the game, the team's *morale* was low.

pain/pane *Pain* means "suffering":

> I had very little *pain* after the surgery.

A *pane* is a piece of glass:

> The girl's wild throw broke a window *pane*.

pair/pear A *pair* is a set of two:

> Mark has a *pair* of antique swords.

A *pear* is a fruit:

> In the autumn, I like a *pear* for a snack.

passed/past *Passed* means "went by." It can also mean "handed to," or received a successful score:

> The happy days *passed* too quickly.
> Janice *passed* me the mustard.
> It's amazing, but the whole class *passed* the test.

Past means "the time that has gone by":

> Let's leave the *past* behind us.

patience/patients *Patience* is calm endurance:

> When I am caught in a traffic jam, I should have more *patience*.

Patients are people under medical care:

> There are too many *patients* in the doctor's waiting room.

peace/piece *Peace* is calmness:

> Looking at the ocean brings me a sense of *peace*.

A *piece* is a part of something:

> Norman took a *piece* of coconut cake.

personal/personnel *Personal* means "connected to a person." It can also mean "intimate":

> Whether to lease or own a car is a *personal* choice.
> That information is too *personal* to share.

Personnel are the staff in an office:

> The Digby Electronics Company is developing a new health plan for
>   its *personnel*.

plain/ plane *Plain* means "simple, clear, or ordinary." It can also mean "flat land":

> The restaurant serves *plain* but tasty food.
> Her house was in the center of a windy *plain*.

A *plane* is an aircraft:

> We took a small *plane* to the island.

pray/prey A person who *prays* is speaking to a spiritual being:

> Every night, my mother *prayed* for my safe return from the war.

Prey is a victim, whether it is an animal killed for food or a person. It can also mean to make another person into a victim:

> Small animals such as rabbits are often the *prey* of larger ones.
> The robber *preyed* on those who walked alone at night.

presence/presents Your *presence* is your attendance, your being somewhere:

> We request your *presence* at our wedding.

Presents are gifts:

> My daughter got too many birthday *presents*.

principal/principle *Principal* means "most important." It also means "the head of a school":

> My *principal* reason for returning to school is to prepare for a better job.
> The *principal* of Crestview Elementary School is popular with students.

A *principle* is a guiding rule:

> Betraying a friend is against my *principles*.

quiet/quit/quite *Quiet* means "without noise":

> The library has many *quiet* corners.

Quit means "stop":

> Will you *quit* complaining?

Quite means "truly" or "exactly":

> Victor's speech was *quite* convincing.

rain/reign/rein *Rain* is wet weather:

> We have had a week of *rain*.

To *reign* is to rule; *reign* is royal rule:

> King Arthur's *reign* in Camelot is the subject of many poems.

A *rein* is a leather strap in an animal's harness:

> When Charlie got on the horse, he held the *reins* very tight.

residence/residents A *residence* is a place to live.

> For years, my *residence* was a garage apartment with no kitchen.

Residents are the people who live in a certain place.

> *Residents* of the Florida Keys are used to the uncertainty of hurricane season.

right/rite/write *Right* is a direction (the opposite of left). It can also mean "correct":

> To get to the gas station, turn *right* at the corner.
> On my sociology test, I got nineteen out of twenty questions *right*.

A *rite* is a ceremony:

> I am interested in the funeral *rites* of other cultures.

To *write* is to set down in words:

> Brian has to *write* a book report.

sight/site/cite A *sight* is something you can see:

> The truck stop was a welcome *sight*.

A *site* is a location:

> The city is building a courthouse on the *site* of my old school.

Cite means "to quote an authority." It can also mean "to give an example":

> In her term paper, Christina wanted to *cite* several computer experts.
>
> When my father lectured me on speeding, he *cited* the story of my best friend's car accident.

soar/sore To *soar* is to fly upward. It can also mean to rise higher.

> We watched the eagle *soar* from its perch in the tree.
>
> Sam sang at the audition and *soared* above the competition.

Sore means "painful."

> After I spent the afternoon raking leaves, I had a *sore* back.

sole/soul A *sole* is the bottom of a foot or shoe:

> My left boot needs a new *sole*.

A *soul* is the spiritual part of a person:

> Some people say meditation is good for the *soul*.

stair/stare A *stair* is a step:

> The toddler carefully climbed each *stair*.

A *stare* is a long, fixed look:

> I wish that woman wouldn't *stare* at me.

stake/steak A *stake* is a stick driven into the ground:

> The gardener put *stakes* around the tomato plants.

A *steak* is a piece of meat or fish:

> I like my *steak* cooked medium rare.

stationary/stationery *Stationary* means "standing still":

> As the speaker presented his speech, he remained *stationary*.

Stationery is writing paper:

> For my birthday, my uncle gave me some *stationery* with my name printed on it.

steal/steel To *steal* means "to take someone else's property without permission or right":

> Last night, someone tried to *steal* my car.

Steel is a form of iron:

> The door is made of *steel*.

than/then *Than* is used to compare things:

> Composition I is much easier *than* Composition II.

Then means "at that time":

> I studied Spanish I in high school; *then* I took Spanish II my first year of college.

their/there/they're *Their* means "belonging to them":

> My grandparents donated *their* old television to a women's shelter.

There means "at that place." It can also be used as an introductory word:

Sit *there*, next to Simone.
There is a reason for his happiness.

They're is a contraction of *they are:*

Jaime and Sandra are visiting; *they're* my cousins.

thorough/through/threw *Thorough* means "complete":

I did a *thorough* cleaning of my closet.

Through means "from one side to the other." It can also mean "finished":

We drove *through* Greenview on our way to Lake Western.
I'm *through* with my studies.

Threw is the past tense of *throw:*

I *threw* the ball to him.

to/too/two *To* means "in a direction toward." It is also a word that can go in front of a verb:

I am driving *to* Miami.
Selena loves *to* write poems.

Too means "also." It also means "very":

Anita played great golf; Adam did well, *too.*
It is *too* kind of you to visit.

Two is the number:

Mr. Almeida owns *two* clothing stores.

vain/vane/vein *Vain* means "conceited." It also means "unsuccessful":

Victor is *vain* about his dark, curly hair.
The doctor made a *vain* attempt to revive the patient.

A *vane* is a device that moves to indicate the direction of the wind:

There was an old weather *vane* on the barn roof.

A *vein* is a blood vessel:

I could see the *veins* in his hands.

waist/waste The *waist* is the middle part of the body:

He had a leather belt around his *waist.*

Waste means "to use carelessly." It also means "thrown away because it is useless":

I can't *waste* my time watching trashy television shows.
That manufacturing plant has many *waste* products.

wait/weight *Wait* means "to hold yourself ready for something":

I can't *wait* until my check arrives.

Weight means "heaviness":

He tested the *weight* of the bat.

weather/whether *Weather* refers to conditions outside.

If the *weather* is warm, I'll go swimming.

Whether means "if":

>   *Whether* you help me or not, I'll paint the hallway.

were/we're/where *Were* is the past form of *are:*

>   Only last year, we *were* scared freshmen.

We're is the contraction of *we are:*

>   Today *we're* confident sophomores.

Where refers to a place:

>   Show me *where* you used to play basketball.

whined/wind/wined *Whined* means "complained":

>   Polly *whined* about the weather because the rain kept her indoors.

Wind (if it rhymes with *find*) means "to coil or wrap something" or "to turn a key":

>   *Wind* that extension cord, or you'll trip on it.

Wind (if it rhymes with *sinned*) is air in motion:

>   The *wind* blew my cap off.

If someone *wined* you, he or she treated you to some wine:

>   My brother *wined* and dined his boss.

who's/whose *Who's* is a contraction of *who is* or *who has:*

>   *Who's* driving?
>   *Who's* been leaving the door unlocked?

Whose means "belonging to whom":

>   I wonder *whose* dog this is.

woman/women *Woman* means "one adult female person":

>   A *woman* in the supermarket gave me her extra coupons.

Women means "more than one woman":

>   Three *women* from Missouri joined the management team.

wood/would *Wood* is a hard substance made from trees:

>   I have a table made of a polished *wood*.

Would is the past form of *will:*

>   Albert said he *would* think about the offer.

your/you're *Your* means "belonging to you":

>   I think you dropped *your* wallet.

You're is the short form of *you are:*

>   *You're* not telling the truth.

Exercise 4 **Practice: More Words That Sound Alike/Look Alike**

Circle the correct words in each sentence below.

1. During the (rain, reign) of King George III of England, the American colonies lost (patience, patients) with the king's restrictive laws and fought for (their, there, they're) freedom.

2. (Moral, Morale) at the fraternity has declined since the group was criticized for its reckless initiation (rights, rites, writes).

3. The poor and trusting are often the (pray/prey) of con artists who offer get-rich-quick schemes such as fake overseas lotteries and worthless (medal/meddle/metal) disguised as gold.

4. It was (quiet, quit, quite) noisy in the library today until the librarian asked the three elderly men to (quiet, quit, quite) laughing and chatting at the computers.

5. We thought we were lost at first, but eventually Diane's directions (lead, led) us to a large red barn with a (weather, whether)(vain, vane, vein).

6. The (whined, wind, wined) swept the rain against the car with such force that we hardly knew (were, we're, where) we (were, we're, where) going.

7. I want to know (who's, whose) responsible for making that (woman, women) wait for an hour and (than, then) giving her the wrong prescription.

8. If (your, you're) looking for a (loan, lone) to start your business, you will have to (site, cite) other, similar projects that have been successful.

Collaborate

Exercise 5 **Collaborate: More Words That Sound Alike/Look Alike**

Working with a partner or group, write one sentence for each of the words below.

1. a. loose _____

   b. lose _____

2. a. stationary _____

   b. stationery _____

3. a. residence _____

   b. residents _____

4. a. passed _____

   b. past _____

5. a. plain _____

   b. plane _____

6. a. thorough _____

   b. through _____

   c. threw _____

7. a. sole _____

   b. soul _____

8. a. stake _____

   b. steak _____

Exercise 6   **Connect: Editing a Paragraph for Errors in More Words That Sound Alike/Look Alike**   Connect

The following paragraph has errors in words that sound alike or look alike. Correct each error in the space above it. There are sixteen errors.

Silvio hated his job. He didn't know how he would make it threw another day at work. Yet he was afraid to loose his job because times were tough. Moral at the party and costume store was low. Months of misery had past. Silvio didn't know if he could endure many more days of dissatisfaction. The principle problem was the assistant manager. He had no idea how to deal with personal and had no patients. Most of the staff worked in quite despair, but Silvio's days past in a silent, growing anger. Then the horrible rain of the assistant manager ended. He resigned when the owner of the store discovered a discrepancy between the sales records and the bank deposits. Soon the assistant manager was identified as the one who had been steeling money. Rumors spread. Supposedly, the assistant manager had pleaded in vane for another chance. As the news of the assistant manager's departure spread, Silvio and the other employees we're relieved. Surely a new boss wood have to be better then there old one, they felt. At last, Silvio was able to let go of his anger.

Exercise 7   **Practice: Words That Sound Alike/Look Alike: A Comprehensive Exercise**

Circle the correct words in parentheses in each sentence below.

1. As the officer began to (advice, advise) Lucy of her (rights, rites, writes), Lucy remained (stationary, stationery).

2. Mrs. Kowalski is such a good (sole, soul) that I sometimes feel she is an (angel, angle) (hear, here) on earth.

3. (Its, It's) a sad day when a science fiction movie loses (its, it's) power to entertain me, but this movie is a (waist, waste) of my time.

4. The color in the foreground of that painting (complements, compliments) the colors in the background, and it (wood, would) look attractive in my apartment, (to, too, two).

5. I was not (conscience, conscious) of Anita's bad temper until she jerked hard on her horse's (rains, reigns, reins) and (than, then) kicked the poor animal.

6. It was so cold that I could see my (breath, breathe) on the window (pane, pain) and (knew, new) that winter had arrived.

7. Sam was not willing to (accept, except) his brother's (council, counsel) about applying for financial aid.

8. (Your, You're) behavior in court can (affect, effect) the outcome of the trial, no matter how (fair, fare) the jury tries to be.

9. As I walked down the (isle, aisle) with my bride, I suddenly realized that we were about to go (forth, fourth) into a (knew, new) life.

10. My doctor is encouraging his (patience, patients) to try a (does, dose) of an over-the-counter cold medicine instead of overusing antibiotics.

11. My brother's class is taking a trip to Tallahassee, the (capital, capitol) of Florida, as part of a (coarse, course) in political science.

12. I hope that the loss of his home will have no (farther, further) (affect, effect) on the (all ready, already) unhappy child.

13. Larry doesn't follow fashion trends; when he needs (close, clothes, cloths), he buys (plain, plane) old jeans and flannel shirts from discount stores.

14. My first goal is to find a (decent, descent) apartment; (then, than) I want to meet someone (who's, whose) (principals, principles) are the same as mine.

15. I (wander, wonder) if I should go to the (personal, personnel) department of Satellite Services and apply for a job; I've (heard, herd) that (moral, morale) is high among the staff.

Connect

| **Exercise 8** | **Connect: Editing a Paragraph for Errors in Words That Sound Alike/Look Alike: A Comprehensive Exercise** |

The following paragraph has errors in words that sound alike or look alike. Correct each error in the space above it. There are eleven errors.

A family tradition in are house was celebrated every Sunday when we enjoyed homemade pancakes. Although many advertisements show woman cooking, a man made our Sunday breakfast. I wood stand beside my father as he stirred the batter and carefully poured spoonfuls into a buttered pan. I learned to weight for him to flip each pancake at the rite time. A pancake cannot be too soft or too solid when it is flipped, he said. My father new the right way to make them: he showed patients. Whether he made plane or blueberry pancakes, he made delicious ones. My memories of this ritual came to me recently when I was far from home. I was in the U.S. Army, and I woke to the sight of the sun rising in the dessert. Suddenly I thought of my father's pancakes. I wanted to be in the family kitchen, watching my father make breakfast. Someday I will enjoy the quite pleasure and piece of such a day.

MyWritingLab™ Visit Chapter 30, "Words That Sound Alike/Look Alike," in *MyWritingLab* to test your understanding of the chapter objectives.

Word Choice

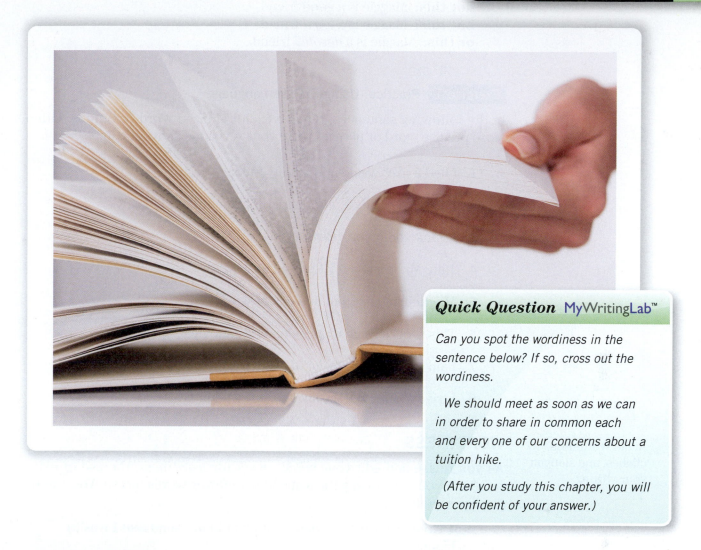

Learning Objectives

In this chapter, you will learn to:

1 Write precisely.

2 Avoid wordiness, clichés, and slang in your writing.

PRECISE LANGUAGE

1 Write precisely.

One way to improve your writing is to pay close attention to your choice of words. As you revise and edit, be careful to use precise language and avoid wordiness, clichés, and slang.

Try to be as specific as you can in explaining or describing. Replace vague, general words or phrases with more precise language.

not this: Yesterday, our English instructor assigned ~~a lot of~~ reading.
but this: Yesterday, our English instructor assigned *twenty-five pages* of reading.

not this: He gave me a ~~nice~~ smile.
but this: He gave me a *friendly* smile.
or this: He gave me a *reassuring* smile.
or this: He gave me a *welcoming* smile.

not this: Maggie is a ~~good~~ friend.
but this: Maggie is a *loyal* friend.
or this: Maggie is a *devoted* friend.

> **Exercise 1** **Practice: Using Precise Language**

In the following sentences, replace each italicized word or phrase with a more precise word or phrase. Write your revisions above the lines.

1. I had a *nice* weekend with my folks.

2. You need to buy *a lot* of paper for the printer.

3. I think about you *often*.

4. Take Mr. Benson for English; he's *nice*.

5. Mitchell had another *bad* day at work.

6. This time, let's go to an *interesting* movie.

7. I am going to need *a lot* of pasta for the party.

8. I tried to practice my speech, but it sounds *stupid*.

WORDINESS

② Avoid wordiness, clichés, and slang in your writing.

As you revise and edit your work, check for *wordiness:* the use of extra words. If you can convey the same idea in fewer words, do so. You can be precise *and* direct.

not this: After the accident, I thought ~~in my mind that~~ I was to blame.
but this: After the accident, *I thought* I was to blame.

not this: ~~In my opinion~~, I think children should exercise daily.
but this: *I think* children should exercise daily.

not this: Jorge bought a CD for ~~the price of~~ $10.95.
but this: Jorge bought a CD *for* $10.95.

Here is a list of some wordy expressions and possible substitutes:

Wordy Expressions	Possible Substitutes
alternative choices	alternatives, choices
asset group	assets
at a later date and time	later
at a future date	later
at that time	then
at the present moment	now, presently
at the present time	now, presently
at this point in time	now, today
attach together	attach
basic essentials	essentials
blend together	blend

Wordy Expressions	**Possible Substitutes**
bring together	unite
by means of	by
by the fact that	because
change out (or swap out)	replace
combine together	combine
consider the fact that	consider
continue on	continue
day in and day out	daily
deep down inside he believed	he believed
due to the fact that	because
each and every one	each one
end result	result
for all intents and purposes	realistically
for the reason that	because
gather together	gather
have a need for	need
have a realization of	realize
I felt inside	I felt
I personally feel	I feel
I thought in my head	I thought
in the field of art (music, etc.)	in art (music, etc.)
in the near future	soon
in this day and age	today
in this modern world	today
in my mind, I think	I think
in my opinion, I think	I think
in order to	to
in today's society	today
join together	join
maximum amount	maximum
mix together	mix
of a remarkable kind	remarkable
on a daily basis	daily
on and on	endlessly
on a regular basis	regularly
past experience	experience
point in time	time
reached a decision	decided
really and truly	really
reason why	reason
refer back	refer
reflect back	reflect
repeat again	repeat
separate out	separate
shadow of a doubt	doubt
share in common	share
short in stature	short
small in size	small
skills set	skills
start off	start
switch out	replace

(*Continued*)

Wordy Expressions	Possible Substitutes
the reason being	because
the shape is a circle	circular
things of that nature	similar traits/objects
top priority	priority
true facts	facts
two different kinds	two kinds
unite together	unite
until and unless	until, unless
very unique	unique

Exercise 2 **Practice: Revising for Wordiness**

Revise the following sentences, eliminating the wordiness. Write your revisions in the space above the lines.

1. At this point in time, I personally feel that smartphones are the best technological devices.

2. I cannot approve a promotion for Walter Ford because in my opinion I think that his skills set would not be adequate in the new position.

3. By means of researching the alternatives, our committee has reached a decision to continue the office's contract with the Info-Fix computer maintenance company due to the fact that Info-Fix offers us the maximum amount of service at a reasonable price.

4. In this day and age, consumers are willing to spend their money on some computer products of a remarkable kind.

5. I thought to myself that I had better start studying on a regular basis if I really and truly wanted to finish college.

6. Todd asked me to repeat my refusal again because deep down inside he believed that I would never say "no" to him.

7. Christina is small in size and short in stature, yet she has a powerful personality and a very unique ability to motivate others.

8. Past experience has taught me that in today's society we can blend together two different kinds of music and create a popular and profitable sound.

CLICHÉS

Clichés are worn-out expressions. Once they were a new way of making a point, but now they are old and tired. You should avoid them in your writing.

not this: I know that Monica will always ~~be there for me~~.
but this: I know that Monica will always support me.

not this: Alan experienced the ~~trials and tribulations~~ of late registration.
but this: Alan experienced the difficulties of late registration.

Following are some common clichés. If you spot clichés in your writing, replace them with more direct or thoughtful statements of your own.

Some Common Clichés

acting like there's no tomorrow
all in all
all the time in the world
at the end of the day
avoid like the plague
beat around the bush
between a rock and a hard place
break the ice
break new ground
breathtaking
by the same token
can't hold a candle to
climb the ladder of success
cold as ice
cry my eyes out
cutting edge
dead as a doornail
dead tired
down in the dumps
down on his luck
a drop in the bucket
few and far between
first and foremost
free as a bird
give it your best shot
go the distance
go the extra mile
good as gold
grass is always greener
hard as a rock
he (she) is always there for me
hit the ground running
hit the nail on the head
hot under the collar
hustle and bustle

in the blink of an eye
in the final analysis
information superhighway
I wouldn't be where I am today
it is what it is
kick the bucket
let bygones be bygones
light as a feather
live and let live
live life to the fullest
make ends meet
on the same page
on top of the world
one day at a time
over the hill
pure as the driven snow
quick as a wink
ready on day one
rock solid
shoulder to cry on
sick as a dog
smooth as silk
state of the art
the ball's in your court
the sky's the limit
through thick and thin
trials and tribulations
tried and true
up at the crack of dawn
when all is said and done
worked and slaved
worked like a dog

Collaborate

Exercise 3 **Collaborate: Revising Clichés**

The following sentences contain clichés (italicized). Working with a partner or a group, rewrite the sentences, replacing the clichés with more direct or thoughtful words or phrases. Write in the space above the lines.

1. When I lost my best friend, I was ready to *cry my eyes out*.

2. An accident can change a person's life *in the blink of an eye*.

3. *I wouldn't be where I am today* without Professor Miyori's inspiring classes.

4. Since I lost my weekend job at the hospital, I am struggling to *make ends meet*.

5. Hank has a *tried and true* method of repairing leaky windows.

6. When I take my dog for a walk, she acts like she is *on top of the world*.

7. On the first day of registration, I woke up *at the crack of dawn*.

8. Tanika has been *down in the dumps* ever since she had an argument with her sister.

Exercise 4 **Practice: Identifying Clichés**

Underline all the clichés in the following paragraph. There are nine clichés.

Since first grade, you and I have been best friends. Our disagreements have been few and far between. Thinking about our shared history, our talents, and our goals, I have come to an important conclusion. If we can maintain our friendship through thick and thin, then the sky's the limit if we want to start a small business together. However, we have to be on the same page about our goals and financial arrangements. Once we have learned to go the distance in the early days of building our business, we will break new ground in our cutting-edge technology lab. It may be a challenge to climb the ladder of success as quickly as we would like. However, in the final analysis, our achievements will be great if we can become just as loyal business partners as we are friends.

Exercise 5	Connect: Editing for Imprecise Language, Wordiness, and Clichés

Connect

Edit the following paragraph for imprecise language and clichés. Cross out wordiness and write your revisions above the lines. There are nine places that need editing.

A few years ago, my boyfriend Jimmy had a hard time finding work by the fact that he never finished high school and had no clear goals. At this point in time, he is studying for his GED and at a future date wants to study law enforcement at a community college. Without a shadow of a doubt he has changed dramatically from the teenager with no direction and no self-esteem. After a long struggle with dead-end jobs and family conflicts, Jimmy has reached a decision to look forward with determination and things. Now he needs to work on his skills set and stay patient and focused through the trials and tribulations of testing, training, and preparing for a career. When I look at the hardships he has already survived, I really and truly believe in Jimmy's future.

SLANG

Slang is an informal vocabulary frequently used during conversations among friends. It is also used by fiction writers when they try to create realistic dialogue. Slang expressions and their meanings can change frequently. "Cool" and "hot" can both mean "popular," while "bad" as a slang term can mean "good." Today, "guys" as slang refers to males and females. Slang expressions change often, and because they can easily be misunderstood, you should avoid them in formal writing assignments that require precise word choice.

The following list may contain slang that you use in everyday conversation, but you may also notice several expressions that are now considered outdated. See how many you recognize from your own daily conversations.

Slang	Standard English
a slam dunk	a certainty
All bets are off.	The future is uncertain.
awesome	terrific
back in the day	in the past (or when I was younger)
been there for me	supported me
bent out of shape	upset
big time	major
blowback	harsh reaction
bounce (verb)	leave
Bring it on.	Challenge me.
bummed	disappointed
call him/her out	criticize (or shame him/her)
chill (or chill out)	relax (or calm down)

(Continued)

Slang	Standard English
creeps me out	makes me uneasy
Don't do me like that.	Don't treat me that way.
don't have a clue	have no idea
Don't mess with me.	Don't bother me.
Dial it back.	Be less intense.
ditch (verb)	throw away
Do you know what I'm saying?	Do you understand?
Don't go there.	Don't talk about it.
Feel me?	Do you understand?
For real?	Really?
for sure	certainly
from the get go	from the beginning
get his/her act together	become more organized or focused
get his/her groove on	regain momentum or confidence
get (or wrap) my head around	understand (or imagine)
Get real.	Be realistic.
gets me down	upsets me, saddens me
give it up for; give a shout out	applaud for; recognize
Give me a break.	Be more lenient with me.
got game	has excellent skills
He bailed on us.	He quit on us.
he/she goes	he/she says
he's all about	he's very interested in
Here's the thing (or here's the deal).	Here's what's important.
Hold up.	Wait.
I freaked.	I became upset.
I got your back.	I'll protect you.
I'm down with that.	I agree with that; I accept that.
I'm into	I'm interested in
I'm not buying it.	I don't believe it.
I'm with you.	I agree with you.
It's all good.	Everything is fine.
It's on you.	It's your fault.
stoked	excited
keeping it real	being realistic
Lighten up.	Be less serious.
mess up	make a mistake
mix it up	fight (or use a variety of tactics)
my bad	my mistake
my ride	my car
No worries. (after "Thank you.")	don't worry; you're welcome.
not feelin' it	don't like it
party (verb)	socialize (or celebrate)
pushback	resistance
seal (or close) the deal	reach an agreement (or win)
set of wheels	automobile
Show me some love.	Be considerate (or kind) to me.
That's how we roll.	That's what we do.
That's on you.	That's your fault.
That's sick.	That's the best. (or That's terrific.)
That's what I'm talkin' about.	That's what I like.
They got served.	They were soundly defeated/insulted.

Slang	**Standard English**
They're tight.	They are close friends.
This is huge.	This is very important.
totaled	destroyed
tripping	acting strangely (or irrationally)
True story?	Is it true?
true that	definitely
wasted	inebriated
What's the deal?	Why (or How) did that happen?
What's up with that?	What does that mean?

Exercise 6 **Collaborate: Identifying Slang**

Collaborate

Working with a partner or group, write your own examples of slang that you and your friends use today. After each example of slang, write its meaning in standard English.

1. **slang:** _____

    standard English: _____

2. **slang:** _____

    standard English: _____

3. **slang:** _____

    standard English: _____

4. **slang:** _____

    standard English: _____

5. **slang:** _____

    standard English: _____

Exercise 7 **Collaborate: Revising Slang**

Collaborate

Working with a partner or group, revise each sentence to eliminate slang. For smoother style, you can change the word order as well as wording that is not slang.

1. My brother was really bummed about ditching on me; I told him to show me a little love next time.

    _____

    _____

    _____

2. Driving down a dark, deserted road creeps me out at times, but my sister can't even lighten up enough to drive anywhere.

    _____

    _____

    _____

3. Kesha hopes to win a lead role in our civic center's production of *Rent*, but she knows that all bets are off if professional actors are allowed to audition.

_____

_____

_____

4. Back in the day, my father was all about being the starting quarter-back for his high school, and he often brags that he's still got game.

_____

_____

_____

5. In my speech at the academic awards ceremony, I gave a shout out to my parents because they had always been there for me. Their support was huge for me.

_____

_____

_____

6. Whenever Jenna drinks too much, she starts tripping and shouting at strangers, "Bring it on!"

_____

_____

_____

7. My little brother and I are tight, so I told him that he should get real about living on his own since he works only part time and barely has enough money for the security deposit on a small apartment.

_____

_____

_____

8. Sometimes it gets me down when my parents argue, but I know that's just how they roll and they'll always have each other's back.

_____

_____

_____

Connect

Exercise 8 **Connect: Editing for Imprecise Language, Wordiness, Clichés, and Slang**

Edit the following paragraph for imprecise language, wordiness, clichés, and slang. Cross out problem areas and write any necessary revisions above the lines. There are thirteen places that need editing.

Nina and I stopped seeing each other because she didn't know how to

dial it back, and I couldn't find a way to get her to chill. We never seemed to be on the same page in our emotional responses. She expressed a lot of anger and anxiety if I did things with other people. I began to feel funny about having a girlfriend who acted as if we were married. At the present moment she is not speaking to me, and I feel relieved of stress and guilt. Nina and I are two different kinds of people, and I am not crying my eyes out about the situation. I only hope that Nina can learn to lighten up. I personally feel that she is a nice person who needs to change out her emotional dramas with a little self-confidence.

Sentence Variety

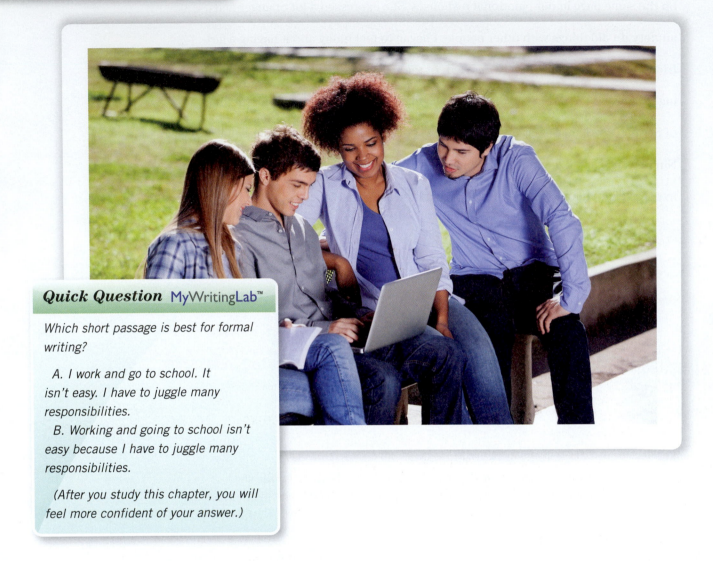

Learning Objectives

In this chapter, you will learn to:

1 Recognize a variety of sentence patterns.

2 Incorporate a mix of long and short sentences into your writing.

1 Recognize a variety of sentence patterns.

BALANCING LONG AND SHORT SENTENCES

One way to improve your writing is to work on **sentence variety**, the use of different lengths and kinds of sentences. You can become skilled in sentence variety by (1) revising your writing for a balance of short and long sentences and for a mix of sentence types, and (2) being aware of the kinds of sentences you can use.

There are no grammar errors in the following paragraph, but it needs revision for sentence variety.

> I have a routine for getting ready for classes. First, I turn on the coffee pot. I start the shower. I turn on some music. I jump in the shower. I get out of the shower. I have a cup of coffee. Then I review my class notes. Afterward, I usually text my friend. She takes me to school.

The paragraph is filled with short sentences. Read it aloud, and you will notice the choppy, boring style of the writing. Compare it to the following revised paragraph, which contains a variety of short and long sentences:

> I have a routine for getting ready for classes. First, I turn on the coffee pot and start the shower. Next, I turn on some music as I jump in the shower. When I get out of the shower, I have a cup of coffee while I review my class notes. Afterward, I usually text my friend who takes me to school.

The revised paragraph balances short and long sentences. Read it aloud, and you will notice the way the varied lengths create a more flowing, interesting style.

Some writers rely too heavily on short sentences; others use too many long sentences. The following paragraph contains too many long sentences.

> Randall wanted to make new friends because his old friends had become a bad influence. Randall loved his old friends, especially Michael, but they had begun to be involved in some dangerous activities, and Randall didn't want to be part of these crimes because Randall wanted to apply to the police academy, and he knew that having a record would destroy his chances of admission. Consequently, Randall was honest with Michael, and Randall told him that Randall couldn't risk his future by mixing with people who liked to joyride in stolen cars or steal from neighborhood stores. Soon Randall's friends stopped asking him out, and for a while Randall felt lonely and isolated, but eventually, Randall formed some new friendships, and he was happy to be part of a new group and happy it was one that didn't break the law.

Read the previous paragraph aloud, and you will notice that the sentences are so long and complicated that part of their meaning is lost. Piling on one long sentence after another can make a paragraph boring and difficult to follow. Compare the previous paragraph to the following revised version.

> Randall wanted to make new friends because his old friends had become a bad influence. Randall loved his old friends, especially Michael. However, they had begun to be involved in some dangerous activities, and Randall didn't want to be a part of these crimes. He wanted to apply to the Police Academy and knew that having a record would destroy his chances of admission. Consequently, Randall spoke honestly to Michael. Randall explained that he couldn't risk his future by mixing with people who liked to joyride in stolen cars or steal from neighborhood stores. Soon Randall's friends stopped asking him out, and for a while, Randall felt lonely and isolated. Eventually, Randall formed some new friendships and was happy to be part of a new, law-abiding group.

Read the revised paragraph aloud, and you will notice the combination of long and short sentences makes the paragraph clearer and smoother. Careful revision helps you achieve such a mix.

| Exercise 1 | **Connect: Revising Short Sentences** |

Connect

The following paragraph is composed entirely of short sentences. Rewrite it so that it contains a mix of short and long sentences. Write your revisions above the lines.

My great aunt leads an active life for a woman of seventy-five. She works at a drug store. She has worked there for thirty years. She works five days a week. Every Friday night she meets her friends. They drink coffee and play cards. They also gossip about their neighbors. Each weekend, she sings in a choir. Afterwards, the members of the choir go out for brunch. My great aunt also keeps up with the latest fashions. She is well known for her style. It is clearly expressed in her elaborate hats. She is a young woman of seventy five. I'd like to be like her someday.

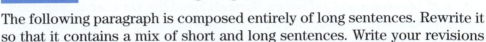

Connect

Exercise 2 **Connect: Revising Long Sentences**

The following paragraph is composed entirely of long sentences. Rewrite it so that it contains a mix of short and long sentences. Write your revisions above the lines.

Yesterday I heard a conversation that hurt me deeply. I am still upset about it because I cannot figure out why people would be so unkind about me when they hardly know me or have any right to assess me so negatively. It all began at work as I was about to enter the break room and I heard two people I considered to be my friends talking. All I heard was my name, and then someone laughed as if I were a joke of some kind, and by this point I decided to stay outside the door and listen. Soon I heard one of my so-called friends say, "Jerome? He's not invited." I decided to walk away from the room so the two wouldn't notice me outside and since I couldn't walk in without them wondering what I might have heard. I have spent hours trying to understand why they laughed at me and, even worse, why I'm being left out of some party or other event. I know I'm being silly, and I tell myself I heard only part of a conversation that could be interpreted in a different way, but I still feel that hearing others discuss me was a terrible experience.

2 Incorporate a mix of long and short sentences into your writing.

USING DIFFERENT WAYS TO BEGIN SENTENCES

Most of the time, writers begin sentences with the subject. However, if you change the word order, you can break the monotony of using the same pattern over and over.

Begin with an Adverb

One way to change the word order is to begin with an adverb, a word that describes verbs, adjectives, or other adverbs. (For more on adverbs, see Chapter 22.) You can move adverbs from the middle to the beginning of the sentence as long as the meaning is clear.

> **adverb in middle:** Ricky opened the package *carefully* and checked the contents.
>
> **adverb at beginning:** *Carefully*, Ricky opened the package and checked the contents.
>
> **adverb in middle:** The policewoman *calmly* issued a ticket to the aggressive driver.
>
> **adverb at beginning:** *Calmly*, the policewoman issued a ticket to the aggressive driver.

| Exercise 3 | **Practice: Writing Sentences That Begin with an Adverb**

In the following sentences, move the adverb to the beginning of the sentence.

1. Isabel smiled slyly at the unsuspecting new team member.

2. Emilio searched frantically for his lost tablet.

3. My sister responded angrily when I told her I dropped her smartphone.

4. Ernie stroked the horse rhythmically to calm it.

5. My mother frequently spends her Saturdays at garage sales.

6. Amber walked carefully between the shelves filled with antiques.

7. The evil scientist in the film laughed cruelly at his victim.

8. Andrew thoughtlessly revealed his sister's infatuation with his new friend.

Begin with a Prepositional Phrase

A prepositional phrase contains a preposition and its object. (For more on prepositions, see Chapter 16.) You can change the usual word order of a sentence by moving a prepositional phrase from the end of a sentence to the beginning. You can do this as long as the meaning of the sentence remains clear.

> **prepositional phrase at the end:** A gleaming silver convertible suddenly passed me *in the left lane*.
>
> **prepositional phrase at the beginning:** *In the left lane*, a gleaming silver convertible suddenly passed me.
>
> **prepositional phrase at the end:** She completed the cross-fitness class *with fierce intensity*.
>
> **prepositional phrase at the beginning:** *With fierce intensity*, she completed the cross-fitness class.

> **Note:** Usually, you should put a comma after a prepositional phrase that begins a sentence. However, you do not need a comma if the prepositional phrase is short.

Exercise 4   **Practice: Writing Sentences That Begin with a Prepositional Phrase**

Rewrite the following sentences, moving a prepositional phrase to the beginning of the sentence. Write your revisions above the lines.

1. Oscar was in bed with the flu during most of spring break.

2. The white van with a dented rear panel remained abandoned in the alley.

3. Daniel felt most lonely on the weekends.

4. You can get homemade lemon cake at the Superior Bakery.

5. Ardeese can't write a letter or an essay without her dictionary.

6. I'll do the laundry before I go to work.

7. The heroic soldier received letters and gifts from hundreds of strangers.

8. An old letter was concealed inside a dusty leather book.

Collaborate

Exercise 5   **Collaborate: Creating Sentences That Begin with Prepositional Phrases**

Working with a partner or group, write sentences that begin with the following prepositional phrases.

1. In a year _____

2. On long weekends _____

3. After the accident _____

4. For amusement _____

5. Under too much pressure _____

6. Between us _____

7. Near my house _____

8. With no regret _____

USING DIFFERENT WAYS TO JOIN IDEAS

Another way to create sentence variety is to try different methods of combining ideas. Among these methods are (1) using an -*ing* modifier, (2) using an -*ed* modifier, (3) using an appositive, and (4) using a *who, which,* or *that* clause.

Use an *-ing* Modifier

You can avoid short, choppy sentences by using an *-ing* modifier. This way, one of the short sentences becomes a phrase. (For more on modifiers, see Chapter 23.)

> **two short sentences:** Sarah was talking on her cell phone. She drove into a tree.
>
> **combined with an *-ing* modifier:** Talking on her cell phone, Sarah drove into a tree.

Note: If the modifier begins the sentence, be sure that the next word is the one the modifier describes.

> **two short sentences:** Mr. Martinez loves to read travel books. He plans his next vacation.
>
> **combined with an *-ing* modifier:** Mr. Martinez loves to read travel books, *planning his next vacation.*

Exercise 6 Practice: Using *-ing* Modifiers

Following are pairs of sentences. Combine each pair by using an *-ing* modifier.

1. Carlos was texting his friend. He sat in the back of the room.
   combined: _____

   _____

2. The earrings gleamed in the velvet box. They invited me to try them on.
   combined: _____

   _____

3. Tonya wiped her little boy's tears. She struggled to comfort the child.
   combined: _____

   _____

4. The sound of my neighbor's television blasted through my apartment walls. It irritated me all weekend.
   combined: _____

   _____

5. One of my friends hoped to get good tips. She took a job at a popular restaurant.
   combined: _____

   _____

6. Aggressive drivers tailgate at high speeds. They risk their own and others' lives.
   combined: _____

   _____

7. My mother worried about my first job away from home. She called me three times a day.
   combined: _____

   _____

8. Philip Delgado needed a favor. He showed up at my house last night.
   combined: _____

   _____

Use an -ed Modifier

You can also avoid short, choppy sentences by using an -ed modifier. This way, one of the short sentences becomes a phrase. (For more on modifiers, see Chapter 23.)

> **two short sentences:** The text was filled with equations and problems. It was difficult.
>
> **combined with an -ed modifier:** *Filled with equations and problems*, the text was difficult.

Note: If the modifier begins the sentence, be sure that the next word is the one the modifier describes.

> **two short sentences:** Sam gave me a jewelry box. It was painted with silver and blue flowers.
>
> **combined with an -ed modifier:** Sam gave me a jewelry box *painted with silver and blue flowers.*

Exercise 7 **Practice: Using -ed Modifiers**

Following are pairs of sentences. Combine each pair, using an -ed modifier.

1. The chicken was stuffed with herb dressing. The chicken was delicious.
   combined: _____

   _____

2. Armand's boat was a total loss. Armand's boat was wrecked in a fierce storm.
   combined: _____

   _____

3. Alan followed every rule. Alan was motivated by fear of his supervisor.
   combined: _____

   _____

4. I lost a beautiful bracelet. The bracelet was studded with coral beads.
   combined: _____

   _____

5. My new belt had a large silver buckle. The buckle was engraved with an elaborate design.
   combined: _____

   _____

6. Sergeant Thomas Levy was named "Officer of the Year". He risked his life to save a woman drowning in a canal.
   combined: _____

   _____

7. The old house was designed for a large family. It was converted into three spacious apartments.
   combined: _____

   _____

8. Patrick is inspired by his famous mother. He is studying to become a child psychologist.
   combined: _____

   _____

Exercise 8   **Collaborate: Completing Sentences with *-ing* or *-ed* Modifiers**   Collaborate

Working with a partner or group, complete each sentence below.

1. Stranded in the airport _____

   _____

2. Looking for trouble _____

   _____

3. Taking the wrong turn _____

   _____

4. Suspected of cheating _____

   _____

5. Deprived of sleep _____

   _____

6. Smiling at me _____

   _____

7. Trapped in the cave _____

   _____

8. Dropping the ball _____

   _____

Use an Appositive

Another way to combine short, choppy sentences is to use an appositive. An **appositive** is a phrase that renames or describes a noun. Appositives can go in the beginning, middle, or end of a sentence. Use commas to set off the appositive.

> **two short sentences:** Chocolate milk contains calcium and vitamins. It is a favorite of children.
> **combined with an appositive:** Chocolate milk, *a favorite of children*, contains calcium and vitamins.

> **two short sentences:** Jollof is a famous dish from Nigeria. It is also very spicy.
> **combined with an appositive:** Jollof, *a famous dish from Nigeria*, is very spicy.

> **two short sentences:** I am looking forward to Thanksgiving. It is my favorite holiday.
> **combined with an appositive:** I am looking forward to Thanksgiving, *my favorite holiday*.

Exercise 9 Practice: Using Appositives

Following are pairs of sentences. Combine each pair by using an appositive.

1. Inez is an accountant. She is helping me with my taxes.
    combined: _____

    _____

2. Island Theaters is an old movie house. It is being sold to a restaurant chain.
    combined: _____

    _____

3. You should buy your new smartphone from Phones 'R Us. It is the cheapest store in the area.
    combined: _____

    _____

4. My new boyfriend took me to dinner at Sunflower. It is the fanciest restaurant in the city.
    combined: _____

    _____

5. Kima is a warm-hearted person. She adopted a shelter cat last week.
    combined: _____

    _____

6. Arrogance and impatience are my brother's worst qualities. They show up whenever he is under stress.
    combined: _____

    _____

7. Yesterday, I heard the buzz of a mosquito. It is a sure sign of summer.
combined: _____

_____

8. Dr. Harjo dresses like a college student. He is a world-renowned scientist.
combined: _____

_____

Use a *Who*, *Which*, or *That* Clause

Clauses beginning with *who*, *which*, or *that* can combine short sentences.

> **two short sentences:** Jacob is my favorite cousin. He won the golf tournament.
> **combined with a *who* clause:** Jacob, *who is my favorite cousin,* won the golf tournament.

> **two short sentences:** Good running shoes can be expensive. They make running easier.
> **combined with a *which* clause:** Good running shoes, *which can be expensive,* make running easier.

> **two short sentences:** The cinnamon buns were delicious. I tasted them.
> **combined with a *that* clause:** The cinnamon buns *that I tasted* were delicious.

Punctuating *who*, *which*, or *that* clauses requires some thought. Decide whether the information in the clause is *essential* or *nonessential*. If the information is essential, do not put commas around it:

> **essential clause:** Students *who like history* will love the movie. (Without the clause *who like history*, the sentence would not have the same meaning. Therefore the clause is essential and is not set off by commas.)

> **nonessential clause:** Mel, *who has been singing for years,* deserves to win. (The clause *who has been singing for years* is not essential to the meaning of the sentence. Therefore, it is set off by commas.)

If you have to choose between *which* and *that*, *which* usually begins a nonessential clause, and *that* usually begins an essential clause.

> **essential clause:** The car *that he was driving* is expensive.
> **nonessential clause:** The car, *which I've had for years,* needs a new muffler.

> **Note:** Essential and nonessential clauses are also referred to as **restrictive** and **nonrestrictive** clauses.

Exercise 10 **Practice: Using *Who*, *Which*, or *That* Clauses**

Following are pairs of sentences. Combine each pair by using a *who*, *which*, or *that* clause.

1. Sharon told me a secret. The secret shocked me.
   combined: _____

   _____

2. Belgian chocolate is available in the United States. Some consider it the best chocolate in the world.
   combined: _____

   _____

3. Clara works with a young man. The young man teaches yoga in the evenings.
   combined: _____

   _____

4. Tyler Nelson is married to my sister. He used to play baseball on a minor league team.
   combined: _____

   _____

5. People love their pets. They will spend a great deal of money to keep their animals healthy and happy.
   combined: _____

   _____

6. Pocket scooters are popular with children. The scooters can be dangerous on public roads.
   combined: _____

   _____

7. Joanna bought a new coffeemaker. The coffeemaker brews one cup of coffee at a time.
   combined: _____

   _____

8. Selena wants to go back to Albuquerque. Albuquerque is her favorite vacation spot.
   combined: _____

   _____

Connect

Exercise 11 **Connect: Revising for Sentence Variety: A Comprehensive Exercise**

Rewrite the following paragraph, combining each pair of underlined sentences using one of the following: an *-ing* modifier, an *-ed* modifier, an appositive, or a *who*, *which*, or *that* clause. Write your revisions in the spaces above the lines.

Jealousy is like a poison. <u>My last girlfriend was a beautiful woman. She swore she had not a drop of jealous blood</u>. At first, she was understanding and tolerant of the time I spent without her. Then I noticed a slight change. <u>She would check my eyes carefully. She tried to detect any lies about my social activities</u>. This subtle surveillance made me somewhat uneasy. <u>Antonio was my best friend. He advised me to break off the relationship</u>. Antonio said I would soon see my girlfriend become more possessive. <u>I was blinded by my infatuation. I hoped that my girlfriend would change</u>. She did, but the change made me jealous. She left me when she found someone she liked better.

Appendix: Readings for Writers

READINGS FOR WRITERS: THE WRITING PROCESS

Getting Carded

David Migoya

"Getting carded" usually means getting checked for identification at bars, restaurants, or clubs, but Denver Post *writer David Migoya uses it to mean getting one's first credit card, a milestone for many college students. He warns that the card, a symbol of maturity, has its dangers.*

Words You May Need to Know (Corresponding paragraph numbers are in parentheses.)

bombard (1): attack
entice (1): draw on by exciting hope or desire
"maxed out" (3): slang for "used to the maximum amount allowed"
rescinded (4): taken back
droves (5): herds
savvy (6): knowledgeable
jalopy (6): an old car that is falling apart

travesty (6): grotesque imitation (in this case, of graduating with a bright future)
cavalier (7): free and easy
pitfalls (8): hidden dangers
vulnerable (8): liable to be hurt
ultimately (9): eventually
perks (10): slang for "perquisites" (extra payments or rewards)

They remember their first love, their first car, and, if financial institutions have it right, their first credit card. Because the result could be a commitment that outlasts the first two, banks bombard college students with credit offers designed to entice them to sign up and start charging. And the unsuspecting will be lured by methods ranging from free tee shirts and university-logo coffee mugs to inconceivably low interest rates and high spending limits. "Every year, there's a fresh pack of prospects called freshmen," said Kim McGrigg of Consumer Credit Counseling Services in Denver. "College students are the largest identifiable segment of new customers." 1

It didn't take long for the credit-card offers to land at Jeffrey Kaczmarek's feet. "It seemed like they showed up the moment I moved into the dorm," said Kaczmarek, an Iowa State University graduate. "Most of the problems I created have been behind me for only two years." The thirty-three-year-old computer programmer recalls a freshman year filled with important purchases—"pizza, beer, cigarettes, and other really useful things for college," he said with sarcastic tone—all of them on a $500-limit credit card, his first. 2

3   With one card "maxed out," Kaczmarek said, getting a second card was easy. "It was a chain reaction," the Denver resident said. "And when all was said and done, I was into it for $4,500." Not only did the debt follow him, but the creditors did, too. "When you're in school and the creditors are calling all the time, it's stress you don't need," he said. "I turned off my phone; I screened calls; it was a terrible way to live."

4   The time after college wasn't any better because a poor credit history affected interest rates Kaczmarek was offered on car loans. He said he even suspects a job offer was rescinded because of it. "As a freshman, I had no way to pay the $500 card," he said, "but it looked soooo good."

5   As colleges and universities begin the new school year, the credit offers come in droves. More than fifty-eight percent of college students said they saw credit-card marketers on campus for two or more days at the beginning of a semester, and seventy-eight percent of all students say they have a card, according to the U.S. Public Interest Research Group. "There's significant data supporting the theory that if you can be the first card in their wallet, they'll remain loyal," said John Ulzheimer, president of education services at Credit.com. "Some issuers mail over a billion pieces a year."

6   The savvy student will use the new card to build credit responsibly so that it later comes in handy to rent an apartment, get a car loan, obtain a mortgage, or even land a job. Used improperly, though, a credit card can cause more heartache to a student than a breakup and cost a lot more than a tune-up. In the end, some students learn it's easier to part ways with a jalopy than with the bad credit they got from buying it. "That low credit score is the grade they never thought about or wanted to earn," Ulzheimer said. "The students spend their time working on an impressive GPA, and they get a degree in one hand and a bad credit score in the other. It's a sad travesty."

7   The worst problems occur not from overspending or maxing out credit limits—which typically are kept low to start—but from fees associated with late payments or interest rates. Put simply, a student who consistently pays only the monthly minimum is likely to hit financial ruin quickly. In fact, the number of eighteen-to-twenty-four-year-olds who filed for bankruptcy has ballooned by ninety-six percent in the past decade, according to the Richmond Credit Abuse Resistance Education Program. "The biggest issue is in the attitude toward using the card, and it's usually very cavalier," McGrigg of Consumer Credit Counseling said. "It's a tool of convenience, not an extension of your income."

8   Problems come from a lack of understanding about how credit cards work and the everlasting pitfalls of abuse. Some students just aren't ready for them, said Judy McKenna, a Fort Collins-based financial planner. "It's a particularly vulnerable population that may not come from much money, or it's a group of the temporarily poor," McKenna said. "The pulls to use the cards can be very strong." The average college student has a credit-card balance

of $552, according to the Credit Research Center at Georgetown University. Yet forty-five percent of students say they're in serious debt with balances averaging $3,000, Jumpstart Coalition reports.

Despite the possible long-term association, why do credit card issuers   9
pursue students if they pose such a financial risk? The answer, according to experts, is Mom and Dad. "Ultimately, the cards get paid by parents who swoop in and save them," said Susan Black, director of financial planning at eMoney Advisor. Said Ulzheimer, "It's actually a safer bet to sign up a student than what common sense tells you."

The experts offer several approaches to avoiding problems. The easiest,   10
McKenna said, is simply to avoid problems, at least until a student gets a full-time job. "Living on a checkbook or cash is smarter," she said. If a student must have a card, he or she should shop around for the best offer, including a competitive interest rate, low or no annual fee, a payment grace period, and user perks such as bonus points or cash back. Sometimes, the perks can pay for a student's trip home or a spring break destination. "Credit isn't for you if you're not serious enough about your financial future to take the time and research which card is best," McGrigg said.

Alternatives to credit cards and good ways to build a student's credit his-   11
tory include secured cards—those that require a deposit equaling the credit limit—and charge cards, which require full payment for all purchases each month. Prepaid cards, known as "stored-value cards," are popular because they limit spending. They are accepted like a credit card but are more like a gift certificate. The owner buys an amount on the card and spends it down, either by purchases or cash advances. "They're easy to control and can't be abused," Ulzheimer said.

Reading Comprehension

MyWritingLab™

1. What is the thesis (main point) of this essay? Does the author's description of former student Jeffrey Kaczmarek in Paragraphs 2 through 4 help support it? Which example(s) most effectively support the thesis?

2. In Paragraphs 10 and 11, Migoya offers the reader some alternatives to credit-card reliance in college. Which suggestion do you feel would be most effective for preventing you and/or your college friends from accumulating too much debt?

Discussion Prompts/Writing Options

MyWritingLab™

If you write on any of the following topics, work through the stages of the writing process in preparing your assignment.

1. "Getting Carded" discusses the dangers that shadow a student getting his or her first credit card. Write a summary of the article. Describe the short-term and long-term dangers, and explain how a student bombarded with credit card offers can avoid "maxing out" or can find a better alternative to a credit card.

2. Discuss or write about three items (small or large) that many people purchase with a credit card but that should be bought only with cash or a check. Explain why these items should not be purchased on credit.

3. Although college students must cope with the dangers and temptations of credit cards, students also enjoy the advantages of owning at least one credit card. Working with a partner or group, brainstorm some examples of these advantages. When you have at least five examples, share your list with the class or work individually on writing about these advantages.

MyWritingLab™ ## Topics for Critical Thinking and Writing

If you write on any of the following topics, work through the stages of the writing process in preparing your assignment.

1. If you were the parent of a college student, would you advise him or her to get a credit card? Why or why not?

2. Why do so many college students fall into debt? What financial pressures make the college years a difficult time?

3. As you read "Getting Carded," did you notice some of the phrases that revealed the attitudes of some financial experts? For example, Judy McKenna, a Fort Collins–based financial planner, called first-year college students "a particularly vulnerable population that may not come from much money," or "a group of the temporarily poor." Do you believe these are valid descriptions? Another expert, Susan Black, director of financial planning at eMoney Advisor, said that credit card issuers pursue student business even when the companies expect many students to fall into debt because "the cards get paid by parents who swoop in and save them." In your experience, do parents save their college-aged children from credit card debt? Are these experts creating an accurate picture of the freshman student population?

READINGS FOR WRITERS: ILLUSTRATION

The Heroism of Day-to-Day Dads

Susan Straight

Susan Straight is an American author. She has written several books and was a 2001 National Book Award finalist for her novel, Highwire Moon. *She cofounded the Master of Fine Arts in Creative Writing and Writing for the Performing Arts program at the University of California, Riverside, where she serves as Distinguished Professor of Creative Writing.*

Words You May Need to Know (Corresponding paragraph numbers are in parentheses.)

trinkets (2): small inexpensive items
forlornly (10): sadly, miserably

orchestrated (17): arranged, organized
pact (19): a deal, agreement, or contract between people

1   Marvin Sanders has a tree house in his back yard, made by two boys who are not his sons but who come and stay with him often. They come to visit their sister, who is his daughter, and to be a family again. Sanders is a long-distance truck driver, and at least once a month after returning from a thousand-mile run, he gets back on the freeway with his daughter to drive another two hours so she can see her brothers. He meets up with two other men, all of them working and fathering full time, all of them traveling extra miles to keep four children together.

2   These men are hardly "deadbeat dads." We hear those words all the time in this decade of divorced fathers who never support or see their children, and who never find the rime for even their required weekend visitation. "Disneyland Dad." We hear that phrase, too, describing a divorced father who doesn't do the everyday things for his kids, who only buys them fancy trinkets and takes them to amusement parks to fulfill his role as a playmate.

3   But what about three fathers who not only have full custody of their children, who do all the daily chores of preparing lunches and helping with homework, but who also travel hundreds of miles every year to make sure the four siblings get a chance to see each other? Three men, all married to the same woman in years past, who laugh and joke and even spend the night in each other's houses so that their kids can hang out together, the way brothers and sisters should? Three men and four children at Knott's Berry Farm amusement park? Not Disneyland Dads, but dads who might go to Disneyland this year if they can arrange it, and to Mexico and San Francisco—or maybe just to the local playground.

4   Marvin Sanders, DeWitt Cheateam, and Eric Gaines are everyday heroes to me for their unfailing generosity to their children. I have known Eric since our high school days in Riverside, California. When he married a woman with three children, our kids went to the same day care. Eric soon had a son from

that marriage. We both ended up driving dark-green minivans, and we got teased for hauling around loads of children and smiling about it.

5   Then Eric's marriage broke up, and after a few months, the children's circumstances became increasingly difficult. All four children were taken from their mother by child protective services, and the three fathers were abruptly told that they had full custody. Eric's young son came to live with him in January of 1997.

6   Marvin Sanders, 40, was called on his cell phone, informed that if he didn't pick up his daughter, Amanda, then 13, she would be placed in foster care. Sanders said, "I'm in Needles, California, right now, headed to Philadelphia!" He made emergency phone calls to find a place for Amanda, and drove all that night and the next day to return and start making a life with her in Fullerton, California, where he has a comfortable home with his fiancée.

7   DeWitt Cheateam, 39, a correctional officer in El Centro, California, 150 miles from Riverside, came to pick up his two sons, DeWitt Jr., then 9, and Matthew, then 7. They settled into a routine of early-morning rising, school buses, and no more double shifts for DeWitt, who turned down extra hours, saying, "I've got two boys getting home from school in half an hour. I have to be there."

8   Eric Gaines, 37, a roofer, moved back in with his parents so he wouldn't have to take his son, Aaron, then 2, to day care at 5:00 a.m., when he has to leave for work. But while trying to create a normal life for Aaron—going with his son to the mall or drugstore after work, buying Pez dispensers his son loves to collect—he realized that Aaron thought the green van seemed empty without his sister and brothers.

9   Before they became full-time dads, all the fathers had visited their children often. Amanda had just spent a month in Detroit with Marvin, getting to know all his relatives, and DeWitt saw his sons frequently in Riverside when they were living there with their mother. He would spend a weekend taking them to a local park. Eric had taken care of Aaron for days at a time after his divorce. So the children seemed to adjust well to their new lives with their fathers—but one thing bothered them: They missed each other terribly.

10   When all four children lived with Eric and their mother, they were inseparable, he said. And now, Aaron kept asking forlornly, "Where do the boys live? Where?"

11   Eric said, "I felt relieved that all the kids were in a better situation, but they wanted to see each other real bad. I'd driven out a few times to pick up Amanda, and she stayed with us. But Aaron wanted to go all the way to El Centro. So I called Marvin and DeWitt, and we started putting together these trips."

12   DeWitt said, "It was kind of unusual, getting all the kids together and we dads not even knowing each other that well." DeWitt is a native of New York City, Marvin was born in Detroit, and Eric is a lifelong Riverside resident. They had seen each other many times, of course, but how many times do men, all divorced from the same woman, spend an entire weekend laughing together?

Eric and Marvin made the three-hour drive to the desert city of El Centro, near the Mexican border, for Labor Day weekend. The kids played in the house, visited a nearby construction site, and watched TV. When Eric told me about the weekend, I had to laugh, picturing the three fathers playing endless hands of cards and eating pizza. But didn't they talk about their ex-wife? How could they not bring up their common bond? Eric laughed, too, saying they'd each received a recent letter from her, and they discussed it for about five minutes. Then they talked about the kids, work, the world, and the kids again.   13

They are the day-to-day dads. DeWitt says, "I have so much respect for mothers now—with the laundry, the bruises, the sickness, and the colds. I get up at 3:30 a.m. to make their lunches, get their breakfasts ready and lay out their school clothes. Then I do my own stuff, and the day starts. When we spend the night at Marvin's place, we discuss all the different things he has to deal with by raising a girl."   14

Marvin stopped doing the cross-country trucking jobs, traveling mostly to San Francisco, Sacramento, Las Vegas, or Phoenix so he could work 24 hours and then be home for 24. "Amanda has a lot of homework," Marvin says, chuckling. "But she had a lot of responsibilities before," he says, "like feeding the boys and taking care of the house. I think she just saw what needed to be done back then. Amanda has a lot of maternal instincts, and when she came to live with me, there weren't any kids around to mother. So I would do whatever it took—letting Aaron stay here for a weekend, driving them to El Centro or taking DeWitt Jr. and Matthew with us for a truck run."   15

That was a highlight of the summer, when Marvin took the three older kids with him in his truck. "I've got the sleeper, the double bunk, refrigerator, and TV," Marvin chuckles. "It's really funny—the boys washed the windows, and one day when we were in San Leandro, they got out and helped me unload all these cans of crushed pineapple at an ice-cream store. They were great."   16

I saw the kids at Aaron's third birthday, here in Riverside. Eric had rented a jumping cage, hired a clown, and orchestrated a daylong affair. My two older daughters remembered Matthew and DeWitt, but they didn't have a chance to talk to them much because Aaron was following his big brothers around as though they were minor gods, as big brothers often are. He touched them constantly, ran around and then came back as if to make sure they were still there, to make sure they hadn't disappeared.   17

Siblings who are separated must always feel like people missing a limb—the phantom limb phenomenon, in which an arm or leg is missing but still aches. Kids sent to different foster homes are miserable. But these four children have remarkable fathers. Marvin says, "One thing that really got to me was people saying, 'Oh, they shouldn't be separated. Can't their grandmother keep them all?' But the fact remains that they have fathers who collectively care about all of them."   18

"We made a pact," DeWitt says, "to keep them seeing each other. If there's a birthday or holiday, we barbecue somewhere. We take them to   19 their grandmother's house in Riverside once a month, and another weekend I'll drive the four hours to Marvin's and spend the night. It's worth it to see them all together."

20   Eric took the four kids to a dinosaur-themed ecological park in Riverside one weekend. And last January, a year after the three dads got the kids, they all met at Knott's Berry Farm. DeWitt organized the outing. "For Law Enforcement Day, all the kids were free admissions, so I said, 'Let's do it!' It was good to see them all running around the park. It means something to keep them all together. They need to know they haven't been taken away from each other."

21   When I spoke with all three fathers, each mentioned something different coming up. Eric knows a roller-skating rink in Riverside, and DeWitt can't wait to take the kids to an amusement park and fishing place right across the Mexican border. They will probably get together for a week this summer.

22   Every day, Marvin can look into his backyard and see the huge pepper tree with the tree house that Matthew and DeWitt made with Amanda last summer. "It has a wooden floor, and they got a front seat from this old MG I had. They made rope pulleys to lift stuff up to each other. They're still working on it. Amanda came up with the idea, but the boys loved it so much, every time they come over, they find wood and keep adding on to it." Marvin paused, then said, "I know the other kids aren't mine, but I treat them like mine—they're kids, and they all need love."

MyWritingLab™ ## Reading Comprehension

1. Paragraph 1 of this essay describes a complex set of relationships between three men, two boys, and a girl who are all related. Reread the paragraph; then create a chart or web that identifies the relationships between these group members based only on the information given in the first paragraph. Write a one-sentence "caption" describing your visual aid.

2. In Paragraph 2, Straight gives a definition of *deadbeat dad*, explaining that the three men discussed in her essay are *not* examples of deadbeat dads. Thinking about what you have read in this essay, create a word or phrase (other than *day-to-day dads*, which Straight uses) that describes the kind of father that these men represent, and then write a brief definition of your descriptive term. List three to five examples from the essay to illustrate your definition.

MyWritingLab™ ## Discussion Prompts/Writing Options

If you write on any of the following topics, work through the stages of the writing process in preparing your assignment.

1. Interview a classmate about a time he or she was separated from a sibling for an extended period. Did they miss each other more than they expected? Did they even miss arguing? Why? Based on your notes (and perhaps your own experiences), write a paragraph that describes the special bond between brothers and sisters.

2. Straight believes that the fathers in the article are heroes "for their unfailing generosity to their children." Do you agree or disagree? Defend your viewpoint by evaluating (or judging) specific "sacrifices" by the fathers in the article to illustrate your position.

3. Families can come in many forms. A common term for the extended family that Straight describes in this essay is *blended family*, defined as a family that includes children from a previous relationship or marriage. If you are a member of a blended family, describe your environment. Whether you share your perspective with the class or write a short essay, illustrate your key points by providing specific details about the advantages or disadvantages of being raised in a blended family.

Topics for Critical Thinking and Writing

MyWritingLab™

If you write on any of the following topics, work through the stages of the writing process in preparing your assignment.

1. Consider the differences between (1) the unusual arrangement, involving frequent travel and much planning, described by Straight in this essay and (2) a more traditional arrangement worked out by parents or the family law courts after parents separate or divorce. Write a paragraph or essay illustrating which type of arrangement is better for the well-being of all concerned. Be sure to use specific examples to support your choice.

2. In her essay, Straight provides many examples of the daily activities the three fathers accomplish in order to provide a good life for their children, from laying out school clothes to planning special outings that often involve driving long distances. Straight provides direct quotes from the dads who talk about the arrangements they make and why they believe they are doing what's best for the siblings. For example, in Paragraph 19, DeWitt concludes, "'It's worth it to see them all together.'" However, the essay does not provide direct quotes from any of the children, understandably so, as they were too young to speak for themselves. Write an illustration essay from the first-person point of view (using "I") of one of the children. Tell what you imagine that child would say about the family's unusual arrangement and whether he or she feels that it is worth it. Be sure to give numerous examples, either taken from the essay or imagined, to support the child's perspective.

READINGS FOR WRITERS: DESCRIPTION

Memories of New York City Snow

Oscar Hijuelos

Oscar Hijuelos (1951–2013) was born in New York to Cuban immigrant parents. He was the author of notable fiction and memoirs, including the novel The Mambo Kings Play Songs of Love *(1989), for which he became the first Hispanic to win a Pulitzer Prize for fiction in 1990. The novel was made into a movie in 1992 and a musical in 2005. In addition to being a prolific writer, Hijuelos taught English at both Hofstra University and Duke University.*

Words You May Need to Know (Corresponding paragraph numbers are in parentheses.)

begloved (1): formal term for "gloved"

recede (1): fade into the background

trestles (2): the supporting frameworks for elevated trains

tenement (2): a substandard urban apartment building

girded (2): encircled as if with a belt or band

stint (3): a period of time spent at a particular activity

toque (3): a brimless hat

nostalgia (4): sentimental remembrance

connotation (4): implied additional meaning

inaccessible (4): unreachable, distant

divinity (4): God, or the quality of being godlike

1   For immigrants of my parents' generation, who had first come to New York City from the much warmer climate of Cuba in the mid-1940s, the very existence of snow was a source of fascination. A black-and-white photograph that I have always loved, circa 1948, its surface cracked like that of a thawing ice-covered pond, features my father, Pascual, and my godfather, Horacio, fresh up from Oriente Province, posing in a snow-covered meadow in Central Park. Decked out in long coats, scarves, and black-brimmed hats, they are holding, in their begloved hands, a huge chunk of hardened snow. Trees and their straggly witch's hair branches, glimmering with ice and frost, recede into the distance behind them. They stand on a field of whiteness, the two men seemingly afloat in midair, as if they were being held aloft by the magical substance itself.

2   That they bothered to have this photograph taken—I suppose to send back to family in Cuba—has always been a source of enchantment for me. That something so common to winters in New York would strike them as an object of exotic admiration has always spoken volumes about the newness—and innocence—of their immigrants' experience. How thrilling it all must have seemed to them, for their New York was so very different from the small town surrounded by farms in eastern Cuba that they hailed from. Their New York was a fanciful and bustling city of endless sidewalks and unimaginably high buildings; of great bridges and twisting outdoor elevated train trestles; of walkup tenement houses with mysteriously dark basements, and

subways that burrowed through an underworld of girded tunnels; of dance-halls, burlesque houses, and palatial department stores with their complement of Christmastime Salvation Army Santa Clauses on every street corner. Delightful and perilous, their New York was a city of incredibly loud noises, of police and air raid sirens and factory whistles and subway rumble; a city where people sometimes shushed you for speaking Spanish in a public place, or could be unforgiving if you did not speak English well or seemed to be of a different ethnic background. (My father was once nearly hit by a garbage can that had been thrown off the rooftop of a building as he was walking along La Salle Street in upper Manhattan.)

Even so, New York represented the future. The city meant jobs and   3
money. Newly arrived, an aunt of mine went to work for Pan Am; another aunt, as a Macy's saleslady. My own mother, speaking nary a word of English, did a stint in the garment district as a seamstress. During the war some family friends, like my godfather, were eventually drafted, while others ended up as factory laborers. Landing a job at the Biltmore Men's Bar, my father joined the hotel and restaurant workers' union, paid his first weekly dues, and came home one day with a brand new white chef's toque in hand. Just about everybody found work, often for low pay and ridiculously long hours. And while the men of that generation worked a lot of overtime, or a second job, they always had their day or two off. Dressed to the hilt, they'd leave their uptown neighborhoods and make an excursion to another part of the city—perhaps to one of the grand movie palaces of Times Square or to beautiful Central Park, as my father and godfather, and their ladies, had once done, in the aftermath of a snowfall.

Snow, such as it can only fall in New York City, was not just about the   4
cold and wintry differences that mark the weather of the north. It was about a purity that would descend upon the grayness of its streets like a heaven of silence, the city's complexity and bustle abruptly subdued. But as beautiful as it could be, it was also something that provoked nostalgia; I am certain that my father would miss Cuba on some bitterly cold days. I remember that whenever we were out on a walk and it began to snow, my father would stop and look up at the sky, with wonderment—what he was seeing I don't know. Perhaps that's why to this day my own associations with a New York City snowfall have a mystical connotation, as if the presence of snow really meant that some kind of inaccessible divinity had settled his breath upon us.

Reading Comprehension

MyWritingLab™

1. In Paragraph 1, the author describes an old photograph picturing his father and his godfather standing in the snow in New York's Central Park. After reading the essay, describe the significance of this family photo to the author.

2. Reread the final sentence of this essay. What do you think Hijuelos means by "inaccessible divinity" in connection with snowfall?

Discussion Prompts/Writing Options

If you write on any of the following topics, work through the stages of the writing process in preparing your assignment.

1. Did you grow up in a region where snowfall was common, or was it rare or nonexistent for you? Describe a real or imagined experience you had with snow as a child or an adult, and include as many sensory details as possible that convey what the experience was like for you (e.g., Exciting? Disappointing? Frightening? Magical? etc.).

2. The author uses many sensory details in his descriptive essay (such as "glimmering" in Paragraph 1). List them, and write a few sentences about how the sensory details Hijuelos uses contribute to the dominant impression communicated in this essay. Be sure to state what you think that dominant impression is.

3. Reread Paragraphs 2 and 3, in which Hijuelos describes New York City through the eyes of his immigrant father. List some of the author's words and phrases that capture this impression of the city. In a separate column, list some words and phrases that describe the author's impression of New York City snow. Find and discuss similarities and differences between the two lists.

Topics for Critical Thinking and Writing

If you write on any of the following topics, work through the stages of the writing process in preparing your assignment.

1. Find an old photograph showing one or both of your parents when they were young adults, or find an image in a book or online depicting a previous generation. Write a paragraph describing this image, drawing from your prior knowledge about those times. Since your paragraph should be focused on a dominant impression you provide for the reader, try to incorporate sensory details to support that impression.

2. Recall a time when you were new to a city or town. Write a first-person, present tense description of this locale as though you have just arrived. As a newcomer, what is your dominant impression of the place? (e.g., Does it seem familiar? Inviting? Mysterious?) Do you feel comfortable or apprehensive in this new environment? Use sensory details to support your dominant impression and convey your emotions.

READINGS FOR WRITERS: NARRATION

Field of Dreams: From Farm Work to Medical Work

Alfredo Quiñones-Hinojosa

Alfredo Quiñones-Hinojosa grew up outside Mexicali, Mexico, and entered the United States at age nineteen. He received a scholarship to the University of California, Berkeley, and completed an honors thesis in neuroscience. Subsequently, he gained admission to Harvard Medical School and graduated with honors in 1999. "Dr. Q," as he calls himself, is internationally known for his work as a neurosurgeon at Johns Hopkins Hospital in Baltimore, Maryland.

Words You May Need to Know (Corresponding paragraph numbers are in parentheses.)

commencement (1): beginning, graduation ceremony
novel (3): new
migrant (4): moving from place to place

terra firma **(9):** solid ground
primed (14): prepared
inculcated (16): installed, implanted

My father used to tell me when I was a little kid that "aunque no tengas buena punteria, si le tiras al cielo, a lo mejor le pegas a una estrella" (even if you do not have good aim, if you shoot at the sky, you may hit a star). Well, I am not known for my baseball abilities, so Pedro Martinez does not have to worry about his job. I am better known for my perseverance. I am thankful and honored to have the opportunity to give this commencement speech. Please, let me echo what was told to me by many of my friends and classmates graduating today from Harvard Dental and Medical School. It was the support of our loved ones and mentors, our determination, discipline, and dreams that have taken us here today. 1

"Con trabajo, deterrminación, y apoyo, puedes llegar a ser el arquitecto de tu propio destino" (With hard work, determination, and support, you can become the architect of your own destiny), my family constantly told me. Growing up in Mexicali, Mexico, I developed self-confidence and a sense of independence at an early age. In order to help my parents financially, as the oldest child, I was simultaneously attending elementary school and pumping gas in my parents' small gas station at the age of five. Helping to shoulder the financial burdens we carried developed my determination and inner strength while I was quite young—qualities for which I continue to be thankful today. 2

The idea that our dreams are within our reach is not novel. I am no different from any of my classmates graduating today. We are all here with incredible and interesting stories. The only difference, perhaps, is that I am in front of you willing to share my own. 3

My story in the United States began one night in January 1987. As an eager, ambitious young Mexican, I crossed the border illegally, landed in the 4 fields of California, and became a migrant farm worker. I packed the little I had, and with $65 in my pocket, decided to explore "El Norte." I migrated to the United States to fulfill a dream: the dream that many people, like myself, have of escaping poverty and one day returning "triumphant" to our countries.

5   The reality was a stark contrast. I spent long days in the fields picking fruits and vegetables, sleeping under leaky camper shells, my hands bloodied from pulling weeds, eating anything I could. My only comfort was that I had a good tan and I was in top shape.

6   One day in the fields, while I was talking with a coworker, I told him that I wanted to learn English and go to school. He laughed and said, "This is your fate; you will spend the rest of your life working in the fields." Those words were painful to hear. I realized that without English language skills, without an education, and without support, this predicted fate of being a migrant farm worker for the rest of my life seemed very likely.

7   I wish I could tell you what inspired me to leave the fields of the San Joaquin Valley that day. What possessed me to move without a job, the ability to speak English, and knowledge of what was going to happen next? I do not know, but I did it. I think that my dream, although it was fogged by uncertainty, was more powerful than the fear of the unknown. It was one of those decisions that changed my life entirely since, miraculously, four years later, I ended up at the University of California at Berkeley.

8   This experience has always reminded me of what Henrik Ibsen once said: "Rob a man of his life-illusion, and you rob him also of his happiness."

The Importance of Mentoring

9   After the fields, I began to work in a rail car repair company in Stockton, California. I first cleaned railroad cars. Then I was a welder, a painter, and a high-pressure valve specialist, and within sixteen months, a supervisor. On April 14, 1989, an event took place that made me reevaluate my direction and my life. I fell into a tank carrying liquified petroleum gas—I almost died! I woke up in the hospital and saw a person dressed all in white; I felt assured to know that a doctor was taking care of me. I had a feeling of being on *terra firma*. This brush with death gave me the strength to continue pursuing my dreams with a rejuvenated force.

10   I constantly daydreamed. I have learned that if our minds can conceive a dream and our hearts can feel it, it will be much easier to achieve that dream. At night, I attended community college. I started out taking English as a Second Language courses. Less than three years of hard work later, I was a member of the track and field team and captain of the debate team. As a member of the track team, I found that a race does not end once you reach the finish line; rather, every time you reach the end, a new race begins. During my speech

class, a mentor who believed in me made me the captain of the debate team. I began to appreciate that the ability to work as part of a team is vital to succeed.

Everything went well in community college; my life in academia was beginning to take off. My mentors helped me to get to my next stop, the University of California–Berkeley. I met more important role models and mentors. I learned from them that "knowledge is better learned by action than by contemplation." I also learned that it takes much more than intelligence to succeed; it also takes discipline, dedication, determination, and a dream. Without knowing it, I was being prepared for medical school. When one of my mentors told me that I should apply to Harvard, I thought that he was a very nice man but clearly *living la vida loca* (or a little insane in the brain).

11

After my acceptance to Harvard Medical School, I hesitated to attend. I was not sure it was the institution where a poor student who grew up in a small rural community in Mexico, like I did, would thrive. My mentors at Berkeley insisted that I travel to Boston and visit Harvard. During that visit, I met two distinguished professors, Drs. Edward A. Kravitz and David D. Potter. From them and other important mentors at Harvard, I have learned to see academic medicine as an opportunity to understand and treat human diseases better, but more, as an opportunity to provide leadership and support to future physicians-scientists in order to serve our communities the best possible way. These outstanding professors embody the words of Plutarch: "The mind is not a vessel to be filled but a fire to be ignited."

12

Like many others here today, I realized long ago the great extent to which I have depended on the help received from my mentors in pursuing my dreams of being a physician-scientist. Henry Brooke Adams once said that "A teacher affects eternity; he can never tell where his influence stops." I, like many of us, hope that I can begin to have the same impact as a mentor to future medical students and graduate students—to change their lives for the better.

13

Our Dreams Have No Barriers, No Borders, and No Limits

It is no secret that minority communities have the highest dropout and lowest educational achievement rates in the country. The "pipeline" to higher education and especially in professional programs is not fully "primed" for minority students. Although members of minority groups make up about 18 percent of the U.S. population, in 1994, they accounted for only 3.7 percent of the M.D. faculty at the nation's medical schools.[*]

14

---

[*]According to the 2010 U.S. Census, about 36 percent of the U.S. population belonged to a racial or ethnic minority group. In 2010, minority representation in medical school faculty members was 8 percent.

Recent investigations found that Black and Hispanic physicians are much more likely to serve minority communities and to include minorities and poor people among their patients. Minority physicians are twice as likely to work in locations designated as health workforce shortage areas by the federal government. Minority patients are more than four times as likely as Whites to receive their regular care from a minority physician. I have been very fortunate in my involvement in education to meet outstanding minority role models— the quality of the role models is high, but the numbers are low.

15   Drs. Willam Bowen and Derek Bok, in their book, *The Shape of the River*, point out that a "healthy society in the 21st century will be one in which the most challenging, rewarding career possibilities are perceived to be, and truly are, open to all races and ethnic groups." The effort to recruit underrepresented minority students in selective institutions has come under "heavy fire." Changes in admissions policies in places such as California and Texas have occurred recently. The astounding effects that a "race-neutral admissions policy" has had in decreasing the number of Blacks, Hispanics, and Native Americans being admitted to institutions in these states indicate that the time is "ripe" for re-evaluating how race-sensitive admissions policies have been applied and what their consequences have been during the past thirty years.

16   Recently, while having dinner with some of my friends, we spoke about Harvard's contributions and commitment to making our institution a leader in science, in community service, and in recruitment of underrepresented students. We felt privileged and honored to be part of this family that has demonstrated dedication, discipline, love, and passion for everything it has done. Many of us have constantly commented that we hope one day as future physicians we can all embody the value that this institution and its dedicated faculty has inculcated in us—the value of being a role model, a mentor, an outstanding physician, a colleague, and a friend.

17   Like many other illegal immigrants, I arrived able only to contemplate what my dreams might be. Now, due to the support I have from my family; my wife, Anna; and our dear daughter, Gabriella; the support of my friends and mentors; and the backing of vital organizations such as our institution, I feel that I can contribute greatly to our community as a physician-scientist.

18   Today, we graduate from this fine institution, happy, ready to take on the world, perhaps also slightly nervous about starting residency. Let us not forget that thanks to our loved ones and our mentors, and the determination we all carry, we have been able to fulfill our dreams.

19   I now can welcome and accept my fate of "working in the fields" for the rest of my life—but in the "field of academic neurosurgery."

Reading Comprehension

My**Writing**Lab™

1. Referring to Paragraph 1, identify the author's specific audience and thesis for this commencement address.

2. Quiñones-Hinojosa writes, in Paragraph 2, "With hard work, determination, and support, you can become the architect of your own destiny." List several examples from the reading that support this claim.

Discussion Prompts/Writing Options

My**Writing**Lab™

If you write on any of the following topics, work through the stages of the writing process in preparing your assignment.

1. Discuss or write a short essay about a time when you achieved a goal that was important to your future success. Did you reach your goal through hard work, a determined attitude, support from others, or some combination of these? Incorporate some dialogue in your narrative, include specific details, and be sure your sequence of events is easy to follow.

2. In Paragraph 15, the author elaborates on the notion that a "healthy society in the 21st century will be one in which the most challenging, rewarding career possibilities are perceived to be, and truly are, open to all races and ethnic groups." Do you agree? Why or why not? Provide reasons and specific examples to support your view.

3. In Paragraph 6, the author describes a time when a coworker discouraged him from pursuing his dream of learning English and going to school. Discuss a time when you refused to be discouraged by someone who told you that a goal of yours was dialogue, or write a short narrative about this time that includes dialogue.

Topics for Critical Thinking and Writing

My**Writing**Lab™

If you write on any of the following topics, work through the stages of the writing process in preparing your assignment.

1. Quiñones-Hinojosa emphasizes the positive impact that mentoring can have on young people's lives. Have you ever acted as someone's mentor or been mentored yourself? Based on your own experiences or observations, write a short essay on the benefits of being mentored or serving as a mentor.

2. Imagine that you have agreed to deliver a motivating speech to high school seniors about overcoming one's fears about adjusting to college life. Plan to incorporate some specifics about the challenges you faced when you started college and how you dealt with them successfully. Brainstorming about financial, social, and time-management pressures, as well as how you learned to cope with them, can help you generate ideas for your speech.

READINGS FOR WRITERS: PROCESS

Five Steps for Handling a Workplace Bully

Chrissy Scivicque

Author Chrissy Scivicque, based in Colorado, is a certified career coach, professional speaker, and trainer as well as the CEO of a company dedicated to professional development and career advancement. She blogs at EatYourCareer.com, so named because Scivicque wants to help people "create a nourishing professional life." The following article was published as an "On Careers" column at usnews.com, where Scivicque's writing frequently appears.

Words You May Need to Know (Corresponding paragraph numbers are in parentheses.)

cliques (1): exclusive groups
passive-aggressive (1): expressing negative feelings in a passive way, such as stubbornness or procrastination
sabotage (6): deliberate destruction or action to obstruct

tit-for-tat (10): equivalent retaliation
ally (11): friend
bait (11): tempt, lure
ramification (14): complicating result
unchecked (15): unrestrained

1   Sometimes, the workplace can feel a lot like high school: full of cliques, gossip, and passive-aggressive behavior. Bullying has been a hot topic as of late and sadly, adults are not immune to it. Bullies certainly exist in the workplace, though they aren't quite as obvious as they were in grade school. They don't go around throwing people into trash cans and stealing lunch money. But their torment can be just as destructive.

2   Whether the bully is criticizing you, conveniently "forgetting" to include you in important conversations, stealing credit for your work, or talking badly about you to others his goal is always the same: to tear you down, typically in an effort to build himself up. *(Please note: The male pronoun is used here for ease of reading. Bullies can, indeed, be female too.)*

3   As much as your children would like to believe you have all the answers, should you find yourself bullied in the workplace, you may feel as lost as a third grader regarding what to do. Here are a few tried-and-true recommendations:

4   **Evaluate the situation**. First, look at the situation objectively. What's really happening here? Is this person nasty to everyone, or is it just you? Are you, possibly, giving this person too much power? Maybe this bully just has a bad attitude and it has nothing to do with you. Is there any chance you're being overly sensitive, taking his or her words or actions to heart when they should be simply ignored?

5   This isn't intended to place the blame on the victim, but remember that the workplace is a professional environment, which means it won't always

feel warm and fuzzy. You don't have to be friends with everyone. There are bound to be some people you just don't get along with, and that's OK.

Bullies, on the other hand, engage in persistently aggressive and/or unreasonable behavior against a person. That means you're singled out and the person is being more than just annoying or rude. Various definitions of workplace bullying use the words *systematic, hostile, threatening, abusive, humiliating, intimidating,* and *sabotage.* In short, bullies are intentionally trying to harm you and your ability to do your work.   6

So take a step back and look at what's going on. If the person is simply unpleasant and difficult to work with, you're probably not the only one who sees it, and you're certainly not alone. Practice patience and don't let their bad attitude affect you. If your situation does indeed rise to the level of bullying, keep reading.   7

Stand up for yourself. Don't be an easy target. If you shrink away and allow the behavior to continue without consequence, there's nothing to stop your bully from continuing on. Remember that people treat you the way you teach them to treat you (as Oprah has said about a thousand times). You give people instructions regarding what's acceptable behavior and what's not.   8

The trick is to remain polite and professional while still setting your limits firmly. Don't let the bully get under your skin—that's what he wants. Practice your response so you're prepared the next time something happens and you can respond swiftly without getting emotional. Keep it simple and straightforward, for example. "I don't think your tone is appropriate."   9

Don't get in a verbal tit-for-tat with your bully, but look him in the eye, stay calm, and be strong. Set your limits clearly and consistently, and your bully will eventually learn he can't get away with it.   10

Document your situation. Get in the habit of noting what happens with this person and when. Keep a detailed log regarding your interactions—what he says and does, as well as what you say and do. Documentation will be your biggest ally should things take a turn for the worse in the future. And, of course, remember to always act in a way that you can be proud of. Don't let the bully push your buttons and bait you into an emotional reaction.   11

Get superiors involved. Unfortunately, there may only be so much you can do on your own in this situation. Bullies can be stubborn and irrational. Often, when it's gotten to this point, there's no use trying to simply sit down and hash it out with the person. You need to call in the cavalry.   12

Again, be sure you have your documentation in order and that you've objectively looked at the situation. Then, take the issue to your Human Resources department for help. Describe what is happening in detail and explain how the situation is impacting your ability to do your work. It's important to stress that you want to find a productive, comfortable way of addressing the situation.   13

14   In most environments, HR is your best bet for action. If you choose to go to a trusted supervisor instead, he or she may not want to get involved. HR, however, is specifically designed to handle these kinds of complaints. That doesn't mean it will always be addressed as quickly or effectively as you'd like, but they typically have more experience and a greater interest in resolving the issue, as they understand the potential legal ramification if the situation escalates.

15   **Move on**. Bullying left unchecked can harm your mental, physical, and emotional health. If you've done your best to manage the situation and you've sought assistance from HR but still no improvements have occurred, it's time to consider moving on. No, you're not letting the bully "win." You're simply taking care of yourself. You won't prove a point or teach anyone a lesson by staying in a dangerous situation. Everyone deserves a safe, comfortable work environment. If your current employer is not able to provide that to you, take your skills elsewhere.

MyWritingLab™ ## Reading Comprehension

1. Before listing the steps in the process of how to handle workplace bullying, Scivicque defines the term by comparing it to schoolyard bullying. List some of the characteristics of workplace bullying from Paragraph 1. State in a sentence or two how workplace bullying is similar to, or different from, bullying in high school and elementary school.

2. At the end of her article, Scivicque stresses that "Bullying left unchecked can harm your mental, physical, and emotional health" and suggests that "moving on" may be the best decision. How does she justify this option, and do you agree with her?

MyWritingLab™ ## Discussion Prompts/Writing Options

If you write on any of the following topics, work through the stages of the writing process in preparing your assignment.

1. Do you think any of Scivicque's steps for dealing with a workplace bully would be particularly difficult to initiate at your own workplace? Include at least three specific reasons in your answer. If you select this topic as a writing assignment, use emphatic order (least to most important) for the sequence of your reasons and supporting details.

2. Have you ever been bullied at work, school, or somewhere else? If you successfully resolved the problem, write a paragraph or short essay about the steps you took to end the bullying.

MyWritingLab™ ## Topics for Critical Thinking and Writing

If you write on any of the following topics, work through the stages of the writing process in preparing your assignment.

1. What motivates a workplace bully? Is it insecurity about oneself, a need to defend one's territory against perceived trespassers, a lack

of empathy for others, a symptom of corporate culture, boredom, or something else? Do some Internet research, interview others, and put yourself in the mindset of a bully. Based on your reading and informal interviews, what do you believe is the primary motivation behind such selfish and destructive behavior? In a short essay, describe this motivation and provide specific examples of how severe or widespread workplace bullying has become. End your paper by making a recommendation, prediction, or warning related to workplace bullying.

2. An outdated workplace policy can have negative consequences. If you are aware of such a policy, imagine that you have been given the responsibility to develop a new one that must be more relevant and practical for employees. You are expected to gather as much employee input as possible during the process. Write a letter that will be distributed to all employees that explains why a new policy is needed, what kind of feedback you are seeking from them, and when the new policy should be implemented. Then describe the specific steps you are taking to ensure maximum employee participation in the planning, drafting, and refining phases of the policy's development. End your essay by re-emphasizing the need for a new policy and its benefits for all employees.

READINGS FOR WRITERS: COMPARISON AND CONTRAST

A New Game Plan

Lisa Bennett

High school football coach Bill Miller says he "was a jerk" during the years he was an All-American football player and college coach. He insulted opponents, treated women badly, and drank heavily. Now he's a different man, "teaching players to be accountable on and off the field."

Words You May Need to Know (Corresponding paragraph numbers are in parentheses.)

strides (1): walks with long steps
adorned (2): decorated
convert (2): a person who has been persuaded to change his or her beliefs
taunting (3): insulting, provoking
belittling (3): treating as if others have little value
accountable (4): responsible
mandatory (5): required

pre-empt (5): prevent
CEOs (6): chief executive officers, usually a title given to people who head large businesses
ushered (6): led
anticipated (7): prevented
monitoring (8): observing, checking
sexist (8): biased in favor of a particular gender
progressive (12): improving

1   At Brattleboro Union High School, in the southeastern corner of Vermont, football coach Bill Miller sips a Pepsi from an oversized plastic cup as he strides about his office, rarely pausing to sit during a two-hour conversation. Miller is a former All-American football player and Gettysburg College coach. Young people are drawn to him like fans to a rock star. They stop in his office to talk about a game, a relationship, a drug problem, or anything that concerns them.

2   When they're not stopping in, as on this cold November morning, Miller stands outside his office and watches them walk by on the way to class: "Did you get a part in the play this semester?" he asks a student at his locker. "Wow, new hairstyle—looks great!" he calls to a girl as she turns the corner, her head newly adorned in braids. "What are you going to do about college?" he asks another. His voice is loud, his posture confident, his dress impeccable. Miller is a man with a mission—a convert, as it were, to the idea that school sports should be about something more than just winning.

3   "In the old days, I was a jerk," he says, referring to his years as a player and college coach. Miller recalls taunting opponents on the field, belittling women off the field, and drinking heavily between games. This, he explains, was what he thought it meant to be a "cool" athlete. But time made Miller see things differently. By his mid-thirties, he recognized not only that his behavior was insulting and beside the point of academic competition, but that it got in the way of his being a good player and coach.

He took the coaching job at Brattleboro eight years ago, armed with a new philosophy: "There's more to football than just playing. Players have to be accountable for their mistakes, on and off the field. And they have to know that everything doesn't revolve around them."   4

At the beginning of every season, Miller calls a mandatory meeting for players and their parents in which he announces his rules of the game. He asks parents to be present, he says, because he wants their support. He also wants to pre-empt complaints if one of their sons or daughters is suspended from a game because of a violation of the rules. In some cases, he also wants parents present because whatever they teach their children at home, when it comes to football, he wants them to know, "It's my way or the highway."   5

Among Miller's rules: Any player who puts down a teammate, taunts an opponent, argues with an official, or scores a touchdown and does anything but hand the ball to an official *will be pulled from the game*. Further, any player who gets into a fight will be pulled from that game, plus the next two. Even parents who engage in disruptive taunting as spectators at a game will be asked to leave. "We've even had CEOs in this town ushered out of a game for their behavior—and after a warning!" says Brattleboro soccer coach and health teacher Steve Holmes.   6

But not everything in football can be anticipated by a rule, as Miller discovered six years ago when his juniors and seniors taped some sophomore players' legs together and taped another to the locker room bench. In the spirit of the movie "Scared Straight," he took the offending students on a field trip to the county courthouse, introduced them to the district attorney, and required them to observe a full day of court proceedings. Miller recalls their reaction to sentence after sentence that the judge handed down: "It was a shell-shocker. They kept saying, 'You can go to *jail* for that?'"   7

To be sure, Miller takes a broad view of coaching, monitoring his players' behavior off the field as well as on it. If they drive too fast out of the parking lot, he makes them run laps after practice. If they are caught drunk, he requires them to sit out the next two games. If he hears his male players making sexist put-downs—especially to their girlfriends—he confronts both players and girlfriends.   8

"Athletes get away with that because everybody thinks that's the way they're supposed to be," he says. "But I ask the girl, 'Why do you allow him to talk that way to you? Don't you want him to respect you? Walk away. Tell him you won't put up with it anymore until he cleans up his act.'"   9

Recently, Miller required a number of his worst offenders to view a one-woman play and discussion about a teenage victim of dating violence. "You want to talk about eyes opening?" he says. "They got the message because, deep-down, they know it's wrong."   10

Jason Houle, an eighteen-year-old senior who has been on the team for three years, believes that Miller's message is something most athletes   11 want to hear. "It makes me feel respected," he says, "to think that somebody cares about what others think about us. I don't want to be thought of as a bad person."

12   For all his progressive efforts, Miller is the first to admit that old habits die hard. "I'm spoiled," he says. "I lose my temper sometimes and yell and swear and get caught up in the moment. And when I first came here, I was called into the office for my language more than the kids. But," he adds, "I've gotten better."

MyWritingLab™ ## Reading Comprehension

1. What are some examples of Bill Miller's former behavior that "got in the way of his being a good player and coach" (Paragraph 3)?

2. Why did student athlete Jason Houle respond positively to Miller's message (Paragraph 11)? Do you agree with his statements? Why or why not?

MyWritingLab™ ## Discussion Prompts/Writing Options

If you write on any of the following topics, work through the stages of the writing process in preparing your assignment.

1. In his mid-thirties, Miller changed from an arrogant bully to an empathetic mentor. Have you or has someone you know experienced a change of attitude as dramatic as Miller's? Was the change for better or worse, and what caused it?

2. Lisa Bennett refers to "the idea that school sports should be about something more than just winning." What can happen to high school or college athletes, coaches, and programs when winning becomes everything? As you formulate an answer, support your point(s) with specific examples from your own school experiences or observations.

MyWritingLab™ ## Topics for Critical Thinking and Writing

If you write on any of the following topics, work through the stages of the writing process in preparing your assignment.

1. Is there a better solution to holding high school athletes accountable for their own behavior than the "tough love" disciplinary tactics Miller uses? In a paragraph or short essay, explain how you would handle unacceptable behavior by athletes—drunkenness, sexism, violence—if you were the coach at Brattleboro Union High School. Explain why your method would be more effective than Coach Miller's approach.

2. At the beginning of every football season, Coach Miller calls a mandatory meeting of players and their parents "to announce his rules of the game." What is his motivation for holding this meeting? Do you think his strategy could be effective at other schools? Write a short essay describing at least three realistic ways teachers and parents could work together to enrich academic programs or provide support for students who need more structure or discipline in their lives.

READINGS FOR WRITERS: CLASSIFICATION

Three Disciplines for Children

John Holt

John Holt (1923–1985) was an influential educator who supported homeschooling and unschooling (a philosophy that rejects mandatory school attendance as a primary means for learning), as well as youth rights. His many books include How Children Learn *(1967),* Escape from Childhood *(1974), and* Instead of Education *(1976).*

Words You May Need to Know (Corresponding paragraph numbers are in parentheses.)

discipline (1): training to develop a skill

impersonal (2): without personal or human connection

impartial (2): fair, unbiased

indifferent (2): not prejudiced

wheedled (2): persuaded, coaxed

courteous (3): polite

yield (5): give into, submit

impotent (5): powerless

A child, in growing up, may meet and learn from three different kinds of disciplines. The first and most important is what we might call the Discipline of Nature or of Reality. When he is trying to do something real, if he does the wrong thing or doesn't do the right one, he doesn't get the results he wants. If he doesn't pile one block right on top of another, or tries to build on a slanting surface, his tower falls down. If he hits the wrong key, he hears the wrong note. If he doesn't hit the nail squarely on the head, it bends, and he has to pull it out and start with another. If he doesn't measure properly what he is trying to build, it won't open, close, fit, stand up, fly, float, whistle, or do whatever he wants it to do. If he closes his eyes when he swings, he won't hit the ball. A child meets this kind of discipline every time he tries to *do* something, which is why it is so important in school to give children more chances to do things instead of just reading or listening to someone talk (or pretending to).   1

This discipline is a great teacher. The learner never has to wait long for his answer; it usually comes quickly, often instantly. Also it is clear, and very often points to the needed correction; from what happened, he can not only see what he did was wrong, but also why, and what he needs to do instead. Finally, and most important, the giver of the answer, call it Nature, is impersonal, impartial, and indifferent. She does not give opinions or make judgments; she cannot be wheedled, bullied, or fooled; she does not get angry or disappointed; she does not praise or blame; she does not remember past failures or hold grudges. With her, one always gets a fresh start; this time is the one that counts.   2

The next discipline we might call the Discipline of Culture, of Society, of What People Really Do. Man is a social, cultural animal. Children sense around them this culture, this network of agreements, customs, habits, and rules binding the adults together. They want to understand it and be a   3 part of it. They watch very carefully what people around them are doing and want to do the same. They want to do right unless they become convinced they can't do right. Thus children rarely misbehave seriously in church but sit as quietly as they can. The example of all those grown-ups is contagious. Some mysterious ritual is going on, and children, who like rituals, want to be part of it. In the same way, the little children I see at concerts or operas, though they may fidget a little or perhaps take a nap now and then, rarely make any disturbance. With all those grownups sitting there, neither moving or talking, it is the most natural thing in the world to imitate them. Children who live among adults who are habitually courteous to each other, and to them, will soon learn to be courteous. Children who live surrounded by people who speak a certain way will speak that way, however much we may try to tell them that speaking that way is bad or wrong.

4   The third discipline is the one that most people mean when they speak of discipline—the Discipline of Superior Force, of sergeant to private, of "You do what I tell you, or I'll make you wish you had." There is bound to be some of this in a child's life. Living as we do surrounded by things that can hurt children, or that children can hurt, we cannot avoid it. We can't afford to let a small child find out from experience the danger of playing in a busy street, or of fooling with the pots on top of a stove, or of eating up the pills in the medicine cabinet. So, along with other precautions, we say to him, "Don't play in the street, or touch things on the stove, or go into the medicine cabinet, or I'll punish you." Between him and the danger too great for him to imagine, we put a lesser danger but one he can imagine and maybe therefore want to avoid. He can have no idea of what it would be like to be hit by a car, but he can imagine being shouted at, or spanked, or sent to his room. He avoids these substitutes for the greater danger until he can understand it and avoid it for its own sake.

5   However, we ought to use this discipline only when it is necessary to protect the life, health, safety, or well-being of people or other living creatures, or to prevent destruction of things that people care about. We ought not to assume too long, as we usually do, that a child cannot understand the real nature of the danger from which we want to protect him. The sooner he avoids the danger, not to escape our punishment but as a matter of good sense, the better. He can learn that faster than we think. In Mexico, for example, where people drive their cars with a good deal of spirit, I saw many children no older than five or four walking unattended on the streets. They understood about cars; they knew what to do. A child whose life is full of the threat and fear of punishment is locked into babyhood. There is no way for him to grow up, to learn to take responsibility for his life and acts. Most important of all, we should not assume that having to yield to the threat of our superior force is good for the child's character. It is never good for anyone's character. To bow to superior force makes us feel impotent and cowardly for not having had the strength or courage to resist. Worse, it makes us resentful and vengeful.

We can hardly wait to make someone pay for our humiliation, yield to us as we were once made to yield. No, if we cannot always avoid using the Discipline of Superior Force, we should at least use it as seldom as we can.

Reading Comprehension

MyWritingLab™

1. According to the essay, what are the three different kinds of disciplines that children learn from? List them and give an example of each.

2. In Paragraph 5, Holt writes, "However, we ought to use this discipline only when it is necessary to protect the life, health, safety, or well-being of people or other living creatures, or to prevent destruction of things that people care about." Which discipline is he referring to, and why do you think he says this? Give examples from the reading.

Discussion Prompts/Writing Options

MyWritingLab™

If you write on any of the following topics, work through the stages of the writing process in preparing your assignment.

1. Reflect on a time in your life when you learned something valuable outside of a school setting. Write a paragraph that makes a point about a valuable lesson.

2. Respond to Holt's statement in Paragraph 1 that "it is so important in school to give children more chances to do things instead of just reading or listening to someone talk." Do you agree or disagree with this view? Support your answer with specific reasons and examples based on your own experience in classes that used multiple activities to promote learning.

Topics for Critical Thinking and Writing

MyWritingLab™

If you write on any of the following topics, work through the stages of the writing process in preparing your assignment.

1. As an educator, Holt has written extensively about homeschooling. Research the topic of homeschooling, and then develop a persuasive essay taking a stand for or against it. Back up your point of view with evidence, such as statistics, facts, and personal experience. Conclude with a call for action directed at your target audience.

2. Evaluate the author's statement in Paragraph 5: "To bow to superior force makes us feel impotent and cowardly for not having had the strength or courage to resist. Worse, it makes us resentful and vengeful. We can hardly wait to make someone pay for our humiliation, yield to us as we were once made to yield." Do you agree? Based on your observations and experience, devise a thesis statement related to this analysis, and then develop an essay that follows the principles of classification.

READINGS FOR WRITERS: DEFINITION

Spontaneous Happiness

Andrew Weil

Andrew Weil is an American medical doctor and naturopath (a form of alternative medicine incorporating numerous "natural" treatments) who writes about health issues, including alternative therapies and herbal remedies. He is the director of the Arizona Center for Integrative Medicine at the University of Arizona. In the following excerpt from his book, Spontaneous Happiness, *Weil explores different cultures' perspectives on the term "happiness" and questions the "perpetual happiness expected and demanded in our society."*

Words You May Need to Know (Corresponding paragraph numbers are in parentheses.)

norm (1): usual situation
counterproductive (2): not helpful
solstice (2): one of the two times during the year when the sun is farthest from the equator

discordance (2): being in a state of disagreement with someone or something
sustain (4): provide what is needed for someone or something

1 Are we more or less happy than people in other parts of the world? That is not an easy question to answer, in part because different cultures define *happiness* in different ways, and translations of the word might not convey the same meaning. A number of scholarly articles on this subject have appeared in the *Journal of Happiness Studies.* One, from 2004, notes that in Europe and North America, where independence of the self is a cultural norm, happiness is often construed as a positive attribute of the self, to be pursued through personal striving and achievement. In East Asia, on the other hand, happiness is dependent on positive social relationships of which the self is a part; in those cultures, pursuing personal happiness often damages social relationships by creating envy in others, and there is less desire for it. Other scholarly articles report significant differences from country to country in rates of reported happiness, with North Americans at the top, but it is far from clear whether we are actually happier than Germans or Greeks or whether we are just more likely to say we are. (One interesting note is that while the meaning of *happiness* in English has not changed, the adjective *happy* has weakened, so that many people now use it interchangeably with *okay* or *all right*, as in statements like "I'm happy with the new schedule.")

2 Our cultural insistence on being happy is most obviously counterproductive during the annual holiday season. Throughout most of recorded history, people in the Northern Hemisphere regarded the days around the winter solstice as a time of danger, with the source of light and warmth at its lowest, weakest point in the sky, the months of harshest weather about

to come, and a time of short days and long nights, when only the wise could discern the return of the light. The natural cultural response was to gather indoors and huddle in front of fires, feasting together, telling stories, and drawing strength from social bonds. Our culture today, in contrast, tells us that the holiday season is the most wonderful time of the year, when we should all be constantly happy. Bombarded with this message, over and over, at top volume, on all channels so that we cannot escape it, we have developed impossible expectations. The discordance between our expectations of happiness and the emotional realities of the holidays is a major reason for the high incidence of depression at this time of year.

One word that describes a more realistic emotional goal is *lagom*,   3
a Swedish term that does not have an exact English equivalent; it means something like "just right" or "exactly enough." It has been called the most Swedish of Swedish words, and it permeates the entire culture: architecture, politics, economics, and every aspect of daily life.

Contentment, serenity, comfort, balance, and resilience together con-   4
stitute a *lagom* version of positive emotionality and a sane alternative to the perpetual happiness expected and demanded in our society. It should be more than enough to sustain us, and it will not burn us out or condemn us to alternating cycles of bliss and despair.

Reading Comprehension

MyWritingLab™

1. In your own words, summarize Weil's explanation for the high incidence of depression in people living in the Northern Hemisphere during the holiday season (Paragraph 2).

2. In Paragraphs 3 and 4, Weil states that the Swedish word *lagom* does not have an exact English equivalent. Write a brief, one sentence definition of *lagom* based on Weil's discussion. (Try to follow the "term/category/distinguishing characteristics" format for defining a term as explained in Chapter 8.)

Discussion Prompts/Writing Options

MyWritingLab™

If you write on any of the following topics, work through the stages of the writing process in preparing your assignment.

1. Have you ever experienced unhappiness in a situation where others expected you to be happy? Did you admit your unhappiness to yourself? To others? Why or why not?

2. Choose one of the adjectives from Paragraph 4 (*contentment, serenity, comfort, balance, resilience*) that Weil uses to describe "a sane alternative to the perpetual happiness expected and demanded in our society." In a paragraph or short essay, define the adjective you selected and then illustrate how a person you know reflects the characteristics often associated with this term.

MyWritingLab™ ## Topics for Critical Thinking and Writing

If you write on any of the following topics, work through the stages of the writing process in preparing your assignment.

1. Weil explains the differences between the North American definition of happiness and the Swedish concept of *lagom*. In a paragraph or short essay, explain which attitude you think better equips people to live a satisfying life. You may need to provide a personal definition of "satisfying" for your reader.

2. Do you think that people who adopt the *lagom* or "exactly enough" attitude can experience true happiness? In a short essay, write about the advantages or disadvantages of settling for contentment over happiness and balance over "alternating cycles of bliss or despair." You may need to provide personal definitions and/or examples of contentment, happiness, bliss, and despair so your reader will understand your perspective.

READINGS FOR WRITERS: CAUSE AND EFFECT

Say Something

Lucie Prinz

Lucie Prinz writes about some adults' fear of teenagers and explains the effects of that fear. She uses two incidents, both of which take place on a subway, to ask why these adults are reluctant to interact with "the ordinary, harmless children we all come in contact with every day."

Words You May Need to Know (Corresponding paragraph numbers are in parentheses.)

engrossed (2): giving all their attention to

disdain (2): scorn

imperative (3): obligation

distended (4): swollen

testosterone (5): a male hormone

ebullient (7): very excited

collective (7): combined

rambunctious (9): noisy and unrestrained

recoil (10): spring back

flourish (10): thrive

1   was sitting on a subway a few weeks ago when I looked up and saw a baby, just a little less than a year old, swinging from the overhead bar. She was flanked by two young teenage girls who thought this was a great way to entertain their little sister. As the train began to move, I could visualize the baby flying across the car. Without really thinking, I said to the girls, "Hey, that's not a good idea. That baby is going to get hurt. You better sit down with her on the seat." The kids gave me one of those "Who do you think you are?" looks they reserve for meddling adults, but they took the baby off the bar and sat down.

2   I was suddenly struck by the silence in the subway car. The normal hum of conversation had vanished. My fellow passengers, who had witnessed my encounter with the kids, were now engrossed in their newspapers and books or staring at something fascinating on the subway-tunnel wall. The car was not very crowded, and everyone had seen that endangered baby just as I had, but they had chosen not to get involved. Although most of them now avoided eye contact with me, a few treated me to the kind of disdain reserved for troublemakers. Could it be that my fellow passengers didn't care about that baby? Or were they just afraid to interfere?

3   We've all heard the old African saying, "It takes a whole village to raise a child." Americans have adopted it, and I understand why. It expresses some things that we can all easily accept: family values, shared responsibility, community spirit. But do we really believe in it as a guiding principle? When we repeat it, are we pledging ourselves to carry out its imperative? I don't think so.

4   Americans are known for generosity. We're ready to rescue the suffering children of the world. We send food to Ethiopia after our television screens show us little kids with huge eyes and distended bellies. We help the victims of floods, and we fund agencies to take care of refugees and abandoned children. We are the nation that invented the poster child and the telethon.

These nameless suffering children touch our hearts—but they do not touch our lives.

5   The same adults who are profoundly moved by the plight of children they will never know seem to be willing to ignore the children they encounter every day, even if it is obvious that these children are in trouble or that they need a little guidance. I've watched adults actually move away from children they see approaching. I'm not talking about hostile, swaggering gangs of teenage boys—although even some of them are just exhibiting the high that comes with that first surge of testosterone. I'm talking about the ordinary, harmless children we all come in contact with every day on the streets of our cities, towns, and yes, villages.

6   I'm keeping score, counting the number of times I find myself the only person in a crowd who dares to interact with a child she doesn't know.

7   A few days after the swinging-baby incident, I was waiting on a crowded subway platform when someone pushed me from behind. I turned to see three teenage girls, giggling, ebullient, and so eager to get on the train just pulling into the station that they were shoving. Again I reacted without thinking. "Stop pushing—we'll all get on," I said. After a few murmured remarks along the lines of "Get lost, lady," they stopped. So did the conversation around me. Eyes swiveled away. I felt a collective intake of breath. Disapproval hung in the air, but mainly I sensed fear.

8   Seconds later the train doors opened, and we all stepped in. The woman who dropped into the seat next to me said, "Wow, that was a brave thing to do." When I suggested that it was no such thing, she said, "Well, you can't be too careful these days." That's just it, I thought. You *can* be too careful.

9   In both these encounters, I treated harmless children as if they were indeed harmless. They may have been foolish, thoughtless, rambunctious, rude, or annoying. But the only one in any danger was that baby swinging on the bar.

10   I live in a big city. I know that there are violent armed children, hopeless and desperate kids out there. There is no way that I can attack the serious urban problems we all hear about on the evening news. But I am convinced that I can contribute to the larger solutions by refusing to recoil from kids just because they are acting like kids. A lost child who encounters fear instead of concern is twice lost. By responding to these children, we may begin to build a village where they will flourish and adults can live without fear.

My**Writing**Lab™ **Reading Comprehension**

1. Describe how the other adults reacted when Prinz asked the girls to sit down and hold onto the baby. Why do you think the adults reacted the way they did? Whom do you think acted properly: Prinz for speaking up or the other adults for remaining silent? Explain.

2. In Paragraph 8, Prinz emphasizes that "You can be too careful." What do you think the author means by that statement, and how,

specifically, is the statement related to Prinz's experience on the subway? Do you agree with Prinz? Justify your answers by using specific examples from your own observations and experiences.

Discussion Prompts/Writing Options

MyWritingLab™

If you write on any of the following topics, work through the stages of the writing process in preparing your assignment.

1. Prinz wrote this article in 1996. What do you think might happen today if adults in public places followed her advice about dealing with "kids acting like kids" in public places? Are there appropriate times for adults to intervene and other times when adult guidance can be misinterpreted?

2. If an adult in your neighborhood cautioned or scolded two or more teens at a bus stop, in a store, or on the street, what could be the result? Would the reaction be different if only one teen were present?

3. What public behavior would make you intervene? Careless or cruel behavior involving a pet? A child? How would you become involved? Would you call a police officer or take action yourself?

Topics for Critical Thinking and Writing

MyWritingLab™

If you write on any of the following topics, work through the stages of the writing process in preparing your assignment.

1. Some people believe that bad behavior in public places has increased among all age groups. For example, brawls in sports arenas (on the court, field, or among the crowd) have multiplied, people have been crushed in the stampede to enter stores at after-holiday sales, and some airline passengers have refused to remain seated until the plane has come to a complete stop even though the safety of others is jeopardized. Do you believe that we have lost our sense of civility? If so, what has caused this change? If you believe that public behavior is more civil than it used to be, give examples of the improvement.

2. What does Prinz mean when she says that "A lost child who encounters fear is twice lost"? Who is afraid? Who is lost, and how is the child lost twice?

READINGS FOR WRITERS: ARGUMENT

It's Time for the Federal Government to Legalize Internet Gambling

Matt Rousu

Matthew Rousu is an associate professor of economics at Susquehanna University in Pennsylvania. An expert on experimental auction design and implementation, he applies his expertise to the study of problems in economics and public health and has published more than thirty-five scholarly articles.

Words You May Need to Know (Corresponding paragraph numbers are in parentheses.)

state of limbo (2): state of uncertainty or state of being kept waiting

proclivity (2): tendency, inclination

intrastate (3): within one state

1 While Americans love to wager money, our country has an interesting relationship with legalized gambling. Although it's legal in Las Vegas, Atlantic City, many Indian reservations, and other places in the United States, gambling is illegal elsewhere. Further, the legality of online gambling sites has also been questioned.

2 Many people who enjoy wagering a few dollars over a game of poker, blackjack, or other game, however, do not have the access or ability to get to a casino. Others, perhaps, have a bit of time to unwind in the evening, and wish to play but don't have the time to visit a casino. For these Americans, gambling on the Internet could be a great option. Unfortunately, online gambling is in a state of limbo right now. In April 2011, the Federal government effectively shut down the three biggest Internet poker sites. They've also taken action against other online gambling sites in the past. There are still websites where Americans can gamble online, but they're not as trusted, especially given the government's proclivity for shutting down online gambling websites.

3 More recently, however, the Federal government has decided that individual states can license Internet gambling sites and that these sites would be viewed as legal under Federal laws. Nevada now has intrastate online gambling available (i.e., Nevadans can play other Nevadans), and New Jersey also legalized online gambling, but the online sites aren't up yet. This is good news.

4 There are several key reasons why Internet gambling should be completely legalized. The first is that, contrary to online gaming opponents, legal and regulated online gambling can better catch problem gamblers than other systems.

With the current system, those with gambling problems who play online are playing on sites that aren't regulated by authorities in any manner. If they don't play online and play in a casino, they could lose thousands of dollars in relative anonymity. The current system makes it more likely that a problem gambler could "slip through the cracks." If legalized and regulated, additional safeguards could be put into place to help those with gambling problems.

Second, online gambling will also be good for the economy. Up until the recent state legalization efforts, almost all online gambling sites are based overseas. If legalized, we would expect many of the existing online gambling sites to move some of their operations to the United States, while other sites would be newly created here. The jobs created would range from computer programmers to customer service jobs. Given our high unemployment rates, we shouldn't be turning down this opportunity. Another benefit is that with online gambling sites that are located in this country they would have to pay U.S. and state corporate income taxes.   **5**

The main reason online poker should be legalized is that individuals should have the freedom to gamble in the privacy of their own homes. The case to prevent consenting adults from engaging in a game of chance, simply because it is over the Internet, is the ultimate in nanny-state behavior. In the United States, we often claim we are the land of the free. Legalizing online gambling would give our politicians an opportunity to once again help make our country "the land of the free."   **6**

Reading Comprehension   MyWritingLab™

1. Starting with Paragraph 4, Rousu gives three main reasons why online gambling should be legalized. Restate each reason in a sentence or two. Which reason do you find the most convincing? Why?

2. According to Rousu, how would online gambling be good for the U.S. economy?

Discussion Prompts/Writing Options   MyWritingLab™

If you write on any of the following topics, work through the stages of the writing process in preparing your assignment.

1. If you know someone who enjoys gambling and views it merely as recreation (perhaps over the Internet or in a casino), how would he or she defend being engaged in this activity? Do you share the same view? Explain.

2. In Paragraph 6, Rousu uses the term "nanny-state behavior." What do you think he means by this term? Give examples.

3. In Paragraph 4, Rousu attempts to address the concern of online gambling's opponents who believe that problem gamblers would

be harmed if Internet gambling were legalized. What is his argument? Summarize it, and then state in a sentence or two whether or not you agree with it.

MyWritingLab™ ## Topics for Critical Thinking and Writing

If you write on any of the following topics, work through the stages of the writing process in preparing your assignment.

1. Write an argument based on another type of non-drug- or alcohol-related addiction, such as being addicted to shopping, overeating, or obtaining repeated plastic surgeries. What action should be taken regarding this addiction? Provide specific reasons and examples to support your view.

2. Research "Prohibition," an era in history which has some similarities to the U.S. restrictions on Internet gambling. Next, argue for or against Prohibition as if you were a concerned citizen during that time.

READINGS FOR WRITERS: THE ESSAY

Black Men and Public Space

Brent Staples

Journalist Brent Staples writes for the New York Times *and currently serves on the newspaper's editorial board. He is the author of the award-winning memoir,* Parallel Time: Growing Up in Black and White *(1995), and his essays have appeared in numerous periodicals. His widely acclaimed "Black Men and Public Space," first published by* Harper's Magazine *in 1985, is as relevant today as it was thirty years ago.*

Words You May Need to Know (Corresponding paragraph numbers are in parentheses.)

affluent (1): wealthy
impoverished (1): poor
discreet (1): capable of keeping a secret
uninflammatory (1): not intended to provoke danger
billowing (1): rising up; swelling out
unwieldy (2): difficult to manage or handle
quarry (2): prey; one that is pursued or hunted
wayfarers (2): travelers on foot
tyranny (2): government that rules by absolute (complete) power
errant (2): improper; straying from acceptable standards
taut (4): tight (as in space is *taut* between buildings)
warrenlike (5): confusing, maze-like passageways

bandolier (5): shoulder belt that holds catridges
solace (5): source of comfort
entity (5): a distinct, self-contained unit
in retrospect (6): thinking about the past
bravado (7): boldness intended to impress
fearsomeness (8): causing fear, awe, or respect
perilous (8): dangerous
ad hoc (8): formed for a specific or immediate purpose
labyrinthine (8): like a maze
wide berth (11): a comfortable or safe distance
skittish (11): nervous
congenial (11): friendly
constitutionals (12): brief walks

My first victim was a woman—white, well-dressed, probably in her early twenties. I came upon her late one evening on a deserted street in Hyde Park, a relatively affluent neighborhood in an otherwise mean, impoverished section of Chicago. As I swung onto the avenue behind her, there seemed to be a discreet, uninflammatory distance between us. Not so. She cast back a worried glance. To her, the youngish black man—a broad 6 feet 2 inches with a beard and billowing hair, both hands shoved into the pockets of a bulky military jacket—seemed menacingly close. After a few more quick glimpses, she picked up her pace and was soon running in earnest. Within seconds she disappeared into a cross street.   1

That was more than a decade ago. I was 22 years old, a graduate student newly arrived at the University of Chicago. It was in the echo of that terrified woman's footfalls that I first began to know the unwieldy inheritance I'd come into—the ability to alter public space in ugly ways. It was clear that she thought   2 herself the quarry of a mugger, a rapist, or worse. Suffering a bout of insomnia, however, I was stalking sleep, not defenseless wayfarers. As a softy who is scarcely able to take a knife to a raw chicken—let alone hold one to a person's throat—I was surprised, embarrassed, and dismayed all at once. Her flight made me feel like an accomplice in tyranny. It also made it clear that I was indistinguishable from the muggers who occasionally seeped into the area from the surrounding ghetto. That first encounter, and those that followed, signified that a vast, unnerving gulf lay between nighttime pedestrians—particularly women—and me. And I soon gathered that being perceived as dangerous is a hazard in itself. I only needed to turn a corner into a dicey situation, or crowd some frightened, armed person in a foyer somewhere, or make an errant move after being pulled over by a policeman. Where fear and weapons meet—and they often do in urban America—there is always the possibility of death.

3   In that first year, my first away from my hometown, I was to become thoroughly familiar with the language of fear. At dark, shadowy intersections, I could cross in front of a car stopped at a traffic light and elicit the *thunk, thunk, thunk, thunk* of the driver—black, white, male, or female—hammering down the door locks. On less traveled streets after dark, I grew accustomed to but never comfortable with people crossing to the other side of the street rather than pass me. Then there were the standard unpleasantries with policemen, doormen, bouncers, cabdrivers, and others whose business it is to screen out troublesome individuals *before* there is any nastiness.

4   I moved to New York nearly two years ago and I have remained an avid night walker. In central Manhattan, the near-constant crowd cover minimizes tense one-on-one street encounters. Elsewhere—in SoHo, for example, where sidewalks are narrow and tightly spaced buildings shut out the sky—things can get very taut indeed.

5   After dark, on the warrenlike streets of Brooklyn where I live, I often see women who fear the worst from me. They seem to have set their faces on neutral, and with their purse straps strung across their chests bandolier-style, they forge ahead as though bracing themselves against being tackled. I understand, of course, that the danger they perceive is not a hallucination. Women are particularly vulnerable to street violence, and young black males are drastically overrepresented among the perpetrators of that violence. Yet these truths are no solace against the kind of alienation that comes of being ever the suspect, a fearsome entity with whom pedestrians avoid making eye contact.

6   It is not altogether clear to me how I reached the ripe old age of 22 without being conscious of the lethality nighttime pedestrians attributed to me. Perhaps it was because in Chester, Pennsylvania, the small, angry industrial town where I came of age in the 1960s. I was scarcely noticeable against a backdrop of gang warfare, street knifings, and murders. I grew up one of the good boys, had perhaps a half-dozen fistfights. In retrospect, my shyness of combat has clear sources.

As a boy, I saw countless tough guys locked away; I have since buried several, too. They were babies, really—a teenage cousin, a brother of 22, a childhood friend in his mid-twenties—all gone down in episodes of bravado played out in the streets. I came to doubt the virtues of intimidation early on. I chose, perhaps unconsciously, to remain a shadow—timid, but a survivor.   7

The fearsomeness mistakenly attributed to me in public places often has a perilous flavor. The most frightening of these confusions occurred in the late 1970s and early 1980s, when I worked as a journalist in Chicago. One day, rushing into the office of a magazine I was writing for with a deadline story in hand, I was mistaken for a burglar. The office manager called security and, with an ad hoc posse, pursued me through the labyrinthine halls, nearly to my editor's door. I had no way of proving who I was. I could only move briskly toward the company of someone who knew me.   8

Another time I was on assignment for a local paper and killing time before an interview. I entered a jewelry store on the city's affluent Near North Side. The proprietor excused herself and returned with an enormous red Doberman pinscher straining at the end of a leash. She stood, the dog extended toward me, silent to my questions, her eyes bulging nearly out of her head. I took a cursory look around, nodded, and bade her good night.   9

Relatively speaking, however, I never fared as badly as another black male journalist. He went to nearby Waukegan, Illinois, a couple of summers ago to work on a story about a murderer who was born there. Mistaking the reporter for the killer, police officers hauled him from his car at gunpoint and but for his press credentials would probably have tried to book him. Such episodes are not uncommon. Black men trade tales like this all the time.   10

Over the years, I learned to smother the rage I felt at so often being taken for a criminal. Not to do so would surely have led to madness. I now take precautions to make myself less threatening. I move about with care, particularly late in the evening. I give a wide berth to nervous people on subway platforms during the wee hours, particularly when I have exchanged business clothes for jeans. If I happen to be entering a building behind some people who appear skittish, I may walk by, letting them clear the lobby before I return, so as not to seem to be following them. I have been calm and extremely congenial on those rare occasions when I've been pulled over by the police.   11

And on late-evening constitutionals I employ what has proved to be an excellent tension-reducing measure: I whistle melodies from Beethoven and Vivaldi and the more popular classical composers. Even steely New Yorkers hunching toward nighttime destinations seem to relax, and occasionally they even join in the tune. Virtually everybody seems to sense that a mugger wouldn't be warbling bright, sunny selections from Vivaldi's *Four Seasons*. It is my equivalent of the cowbell that hikers wear when they know they are in bear country.   12

Reading Comprehension

1. In Paragraph 2, Staples says that he "soon gathered that being perceived as dangerous is a hazard in itself." Reread the paragraph and explain what he means.

2. Staples writes, in Paragraph 5, about "the kind of alienation that comes of being ever the suspect, against being set apart, a fearsome entity with whom pedestrians avoid making eye contact." What does that statement mean? Paraphrase it so that your version clearly reflects the meaning of "alienation" as Staples intended.

Discussion Prompts/Writing Options

If you write on any of the following topics, work through the stages of the writing process in preparing your assignment.

1. Staples writes about being mistakenly perceived as a threat to others based solely on his appearance. Have you ever been judged, negatively or positively, based on your appearance alone? How did you feel? Compare your experience to the judgments made about Staples' appearance.

2. At the beginning of his essay, Staples assumes that his appearance ("a broad 6 feet 2 inches with a beard and billowing hair, both hands shoved into the pockets of a military jacket") seemed "menacingly close" to a young white woman walking ahead of him. She glanced back a few times and then "picked up her pace . . . soon running in earnest." Staples' race and appearance apparently threatened the woman.

   Brainstorm about harmful stereotypes that are still perpetuated through certain movies, television shows, and music videos. Make a list of these stereotypes and decide if each one is largely related to age, appearance, gender, race, nationality (or region), religion, or a combination of these classifications. Choose the three most common or hurtful stereotypes, and then provide specific, recent examples of how and to what extent the media reinforces them.

Topics for Critical Thinking and Writing

If you write on any of the following topics, work through the stages of the writing process in preparing your assignment.

1. In Paragraph 12, the author discusses the self-protective behavior he began to adopt in order to seem less threatening, from changing the way he walks and talks around others to whistling classical music. Brainstorm examples of members of minority groups altering their behavior in order to fit in or seem less threatening. Does this type of behavior demean them or make them less powerful in society? Is it necessary or justified? Devise a thesis statement that takes a stand for or against such behavior; then develop an essay that includes at least three reasons for your position. Arrange your reasons and supporting details in a logical and effective sequence to maintain your readers' interest.

2. In Paragraph 5, Staples describes the fearful, defensive posture of frightened women after dark who fear being mugged. Write a descriptive paragraph or short essay about a similar defensive posture you have seen people exhibit in tense situations. Use sensory details to describe this posture and the behavior of people who adopt it.

READINGS FOR WRITERS: THE ESSAY

Roaring Waves of Fire

Christi Lester

Christi Lester won second place in the 2012 Pearson Education Writing Rewards Contest, a national competition for college students enrolled in basic composition classes. Lester wrote "Roaring Waves of Fire" when she was enrolled in Developmental English at Palm Beach State College (Palm Beach Gardens Campus) in Florida. The essay is about an experience that changed her life.

Words You May Need to Know (Corresponding paragraph numbers are in parentheses.)

drought (1): period of dry weather
veld (1): grassland
traumatic (1): psychologically painful
frantically (2): desperately or wildly
massive (2): huge
drenching (2): soaking, flooding
dreaded (4): feared

tractor (5): high-powered, low-speed vehicle, often used for pulling farm machinery
soot (5): black dust given off by fire
pessimism (6): tendency to expect the worst
motto (6): rule to live by
strive (6): try, struggle

Many would think that living on a calm, peaceful farm would be perfect aside from the occasional dry season. However, with dry seasons come droughts, and with droughts come fires. We call these fires veld fires in South Africa. I had never experienced anything quite so scary until I moved to my grandparents' beautiful farm outside a small town called Bronkhorstspruit. Until that day, August 3, farm life had been absolutely serene. This traumatic day changed everything.   1

"Look at the strange yellow light," yelled Megan as we walked down the winding dirt road. "It's getting bigger as we walk." We continued down the path and soon arrived at our grandparents' house. Granny was frantically filling up massive buckets of water and drenching as much of the ground around her beautiful brick house as she could. It seemed very strange for a second, but it suddenly struck us. That light that reminded us so much of the beautiful sun, that we so often took for granted, was actually an unwanted, raging fire. It was moving faster than any human could ever run, and it would soon overtake us if we did not take action.   2

Megan, one of my four cousins living on the same farm, quickly made her way to her house, as did I. As soon as I got home, I found my mother doing just what my grandmother had been doing. The only difference between the two was that my mother looked a lot more panicked. The fire was now nearing us way too fast and would reach our little brick house first. I joined her in making sure that all areas of the garden were drenched. We hoped that the water would keep the fire from coming too close to our house.   3

4   Before I knew it, I was pouring one last bucket of water out onto the dry grass. Glancing over my shoulder as I ran inside, I noticed that the fire was about seven feet away from me. As soon as I got inside, I locked the door (as anyone trying to escape something would do) but then realized that doing so was useless. Fire could destroy wood; it could destroy *me*. Next, my mother, sister, and I started running a bath in case we needed to escape the flames. If the fire were to reach into our house with its merciless flames, a bath full of water would be our only hope for staying alive. We were taking sensible steps to protect ourselves, but at the same time, they generated many awful images of what would happen in the next few minutes. I pictured everything belonging to me slowly crackling and then melting away completely—total destruction. I envisioned my two adorable cats and my bulldog trying to escape. I tried to call my friends to say my last goodbyes but felt sick to my stomach when I found I had no signal on my phone. Everything seemed hopeless.

5   Minutes later, as the fire reached my bedroom window, I was on my knees, praying, when my grandfather and Uncle Alan appeared on a big red tractor. On it was a tank of water that we hoped would save our house and our lives. For a time, it seemed that we were helplessly watching them frantically spray the fire. Just when it seemed that the flames would overtake my grandfather and uncle, their hard work began to pay off. It seemed that my prayers had been heard in that moment. They were finally gaining control of the fire; they were winning the battle. Soon, the fire was all out except for a few little flames that were too small to spread. Calm was in the air. Although we were surrounded by black soot, and our lungs were filled with smoke, we were safe.

6   The evidence of the fire remained for months. Everything was completely black; still we saw only the beautiful blue sky that reminded us how beautiful life can be. I realized that for years, I had been too pessimistic about life. My outlook changed on the day I was surrounded by roaring flames of fire. I finally appreciated the beauty of life; I live by the motto that one should always focus on the positive. I will admit that on some days, I find it difficult not to submit to negativity; I strive to think positively. After the fire, I was alive. To this day, that is enough for me.

MyWritingLab™   ## Reading Comprehension

1. What actions did the women take to prevent the house from burning down? In your own words, describe Lester's emotions during this ordeal.

2. At the end of Paragraph 4, Lester states, "Everything seemed hopeless." Summarize the sequence of events that occurred next that
restored her hope.

Discussion Prompts/Writing Options

MyWritingLab™

If you write on any of the following topics, work through the stages of the
writing process in preparing your assignment.

1. Lester states that before her home was saved from burning, she had
often felt pessimistic about life and maintained a negative attitude
(Paragraph 6). But after the family was able to save their home, Lester says that she tries hard to stay positive. Can chance events per-
manently change a person's outlook on life? If not, what else needs
to happen? Support your ideas with specific examples from your
observations and experience.

2. Consider the behavior of Lester and her family as they joined forces
to fight the fire. What positive traits did they exhibit? Write a paragraph or develop an essay about the strength of character exhibited
by a friend or someone in your family during an emergency. Be sure
your sequence of events is easy to follow and that you incorporate
sensory details to capture the interest of your readers or listeners if
you are asked to share your experience with the class.

Topics for Critical Thinking and Writing

MyWritingLab™

If you write on any of the following topics, work through the stages of the
writing process in preparing your assignment.

1. Imagine how you would handle yourself in a life-threatening situation similar to the Lester family. Compare or contrast your potential behavior with theirs.

2. Write a narrative essay about an event that gave you a more positive outlook on life. Incorporate specific reasons for your new
perspective and include specific details about how your life has
changed. Conclude your essay by imagining how your story might
help others.

Text Credits

Page 359: Amritha Alladi, "Manners Matter Online: Basic Etiquette Applies Even for E-Mail" in *Gainesville Sun* (FL), © June 2, 2008. Reprinted with permission.

Page 581: "Getting Carded at College" By David Migoya. Denver Post, August 23, 2007. http://www.denverpost.com/headlines/ci_6692541. Copyright 2007. Used by permission.

Page 585: Straight, Susan: "The Heroism of Day-to-Day Dads" by Susan Straight. First published in FAMILY CIRCLE Magazine. Reprinted by permission of the Richard Parks Agency.

Page 590: Oscar Hijuelos, "Memories of New York City Snow" from METROPOLIS FOUND: NEW YORK IS BOOK COUNTRY 25TH ANNIVERSARY COLLECTION (New York: New York Is Book Country, 2003). Copyright 2003. by Oscar Hijuelos. Reprinted with permission of The Jennifer Lyons Literary Agency, LLC for the estate of the author.

Page 593: Alfredo Quinones-Hinojosa, "Field of Dreams: From Farm Work to Medical Work" in *The Hispanic Outlook in Higher Education Magazine.* 10.6:25, December 3, 1999. © 1999. Reprinted with permission.

Page 598: Chrissy Scivicque, "Five Steps for Handling a Workplace Bully" in *U.S News and World Report*, June 24, 2013. © 2013. Reprinted with permission.

Page 602: "A New Game Plan" by Lisa Bennett from Teaching Tolerance, Number 14, Fall 1998. Copyright 1998. Used with permission of Teaching Tolerance, a project of the Southern Poverty Law Center.

Page 605: "Three Kinds of Discipline" from FREEDOM AND BEYOND (1995) by John Holt. Reprinted with permission from HoltGWS LLC.

Page 608: From Spontaneous Happiness by Andrew Weil, M.D. pp 22-24. Copyright 2010 by Andrew Weil, M.D. By permission of Little, Brown, and Company. All rights reserved.

Page 611: Lucie Prinz, "Say Something" in *The Atlantic Monthly*, © October 1996. Reprinted with permission.

Page 614: "It's Time for the Federal Government to Legalize Internet Gambling" by Matt Rousu from Forbes, June 25, 2013 © 2013 Forbes. All rights reserved. Used by permission and protected by the Copyright Laws of the United States. The printing, copying, redistribution, or retransmission of this Content without express written permission is prohibited. http://www.forbes.com/sites/realspin/2013/06/25/its-time-for-the-federal-government-to-legalize-internet-gambling/

Page 617: Brent Staples, "Black Men and Public Space" in *Harper's Magazine*, December 1986. © 1986. Reprinted with permission of the author.

Page 621: Christi Lester, Pearson Writing Rewards student essay winner, 2012.

Photo Credits

INDEX

> **Note:** Reading selections are listed under "Readings for Writers." Each selection contains vocabulary definitions, comprehension questions, discussion prompts, writing options, and topics for critical thinking and writing.

A

a, 541–42
abbreviations, 506, 528–29
accept, 542
action verbs, 367, 368
active voice, 467–69
addition, 542
addresses
  commas with, 512
  numbers to write, 528
adjectives, 434–42
  comparative, 435–37
  definition of, 434
  hints about, 438–41
    confusing *good* and *well*, or *bad* and *badly*, 439
    mistake of using an adjective instead of adverb, 438
    not more + –*er* or most + –*est*, 440
    use *than*, not *then*, in comparisons, 440
    using commas between, 440–41
  superlative, 435–37
  word order in, 434–35
adverbs, 437–42
  to begin sentences, 571
  conjunctive (*See* conjunctive adverbs)
  definition of, 437
  hints about, 438–41
    confusing *good* and *well*, or *bad* and *badly*, 439
    mistake of using an adjective instead of adverb, 438
    not more + –*er* or most + –*est*, 440
    use *than*, not *then*, in comparisons, 440
  as words that cannot be verbs, 375
advice, 542
advise, 542
affect, 542
agreement
  of pronoun and antecedent, 489
  subject and verb, 474–87
aisle, 545
allowed, 542
all ready, 542
aloud, 542
already, 542
altar, 542
alter, 542

American Psychological Association (APA), 349–55
  in-text citations, 349–52
  reference list entries, 352–55
an, 541–42
and, 383, 384, 386, 480, 508, 509, 541–42
angel, 542
angle, 542
announcements made into topic sentences, 17–18
antecedent
  agreement of pronoun and, 489
  clear, 494–95
  definition of, 488–89
APA. *See* American Psychological Association (APA)
apostrophe, 519–23
appositive, 576–77
are, 543
argument essay, 306–13
  audience in, 306–7
  body in, 306
  drafting, 310–11
  editing, 311–12
  final version of, 311–12
  outline for, 308–10
  planning, 308–10
  prewriting, 307–8
  proofreading, 311–12
  Readings for Writers
    "It's Time for the Federal Government to Legalize Internet Gambling" (Rousu), 614–16
  revising, 310–11
  thesis in, 306
  topics for
    critical thinking, 307
    picking, 306
    writing, 312–13
  transitions for, 310, 311
  writing
    hints for, 306–7, 313
    topics for, 312–13
argument paragraph, 201–19
  audience in, 202–3
  brainstorming for, 205
  definition of, 201
  drafting, 211–14
  editing, 214–17
  final version of, 214–17
  ideas for, grouping, 205–7

lines of detail
  (walk-through assignment), 217
  outline for, 207–10
  planning, 207–10
  prewriting, 205–7
  problems or issues in, explaining, 211
  proofreading, 214–17
  reasons in
    checking, 211
    order of, 208–10
  revising, 211–14
  specificity in, 203
  topics for
    critical thinking, 205, 219
    picking, 202
    writing, 218–19
  transitions for, 211–14
  writing
    hints for, 202–4
    topics for, 218–19
audience, 3
  for argument essay, 306–7
  for argument paragraph, 202–3

B

bad, 439
badly, 439
be, 456–57
being verbs, 367, 369
beside, 543
besides, 543
between, 501
-*body*, 481
body of essay, 237–38
  argument essay, 306
  cause and effect essay, 300
  definition essay, 293
  definition of, 220
  developing, 237–38
  length of, 237
book parts, 528
books, MLA format for citing, 335–36
brainstorming
  for argument paragraph, 205
  for cause and effect essay, 301
  for classification paragraph, 147–48
  definition of, 6
  for descriptive paragraph, 59
  for details, 8–9, 10
  for prewriting, 3–4
  questions for, 6–7